The Econometric Modelling of Financial Time Series

Terence Mills' best-selling graduate textbook provides detailed coverage of the latest research techniques and findings relating to the empirical analysis of financial markets. In its previous editions it has become required reading for many graduate courses on the econometrics of financial modelling.

This third edition, co-authored with Raphael Markellos, contains a wealth of new material reflecting the developments of the last decade. Particular attention is paid to the wide range of non-linear models that are used to analyse financial data observed at high frequencies and to the long memory characteristics found in financial time series. The central material on unit root processes and the modelling of trends and structural breaks has been substantially expanded into a chapter of its own. There is also an extended discussion of the treatment of volatility, accompanied by a new chapter on non-linearity and its testing.

Terence C. Mills is Professor of Applied Statistics and Econometrics at Loughborough University. He is the co-editor of the *Palgrave Handbook of Econometrics* and has over 170 publications.

Raphael N. Markellos is Senior Lecturer in Quantitative Finance at Athens University of Economics and Business, and Visiting Research Fellow at the Centre for International Financial and Economic Research (CIFER), Loughborough University.

The Econometric Modelling of Financial Time Series

Third edition

Terence C. Mills

Professor of Applied Statistics and Econometrics
Department of Economics
Loughborough University

Raphael N. Markellos

Senior Lecturer in Quantitative Finance
Department of Management Science and Technology
Athens University of Economics and Business

CAMBRIDGE
UNIVERSITY PRESS

CAMBRIDGE UNIVERSITY PRESS
Cambridge, New York, Melbourne, Madrid, Cape Town, Singapore, São Paulo, Delhi

Cambridge University Press
The Edinburgh Building, Cambridge CB2 8RU, UK

Published in the United States of America by Cambridge University Press, New York

www.cambridge.org
Information on this title: www.cambridge.org/9780521710091

First published 1995
Second edition 1999
Third edition 2008

Printed in the United Kingdom at the University Press, Cambridge

A catalogue record for this publication is available from the British Library

Library of Congress Cataloging in Publication Data

Mills, Terence C.
    The econometric modelling of financial time series / Terence C. Mills, Raphael N. Markellos. – 3rd edn.
       p.   cm.
    Includes bibliographical references and index.
    ISBN 978-0-521-88381-8 (hbk.: alk. paper) – ISBN 978-0-521-71009-1 (pbk.: alk. paper)
    1. Finance – Econometric models. 2. Time-series analysis.
    3. Stochastic processes. I. Markellos, Raphael N. II. Title.

    HG174.M55 2008
    332.01′5195 – dc22
2007048450

ISBN 978-0-521-88381-8 hardback
ISBN 978-0-521-71009-1 paperback

Contents

v

Figures

Tables

Preface to the third edition

In the nine years since the manuscript for the second edition of *The Econometric Modelling of Financial Time Series* was completed there have continued to be many advances in time series econometrics, some of which have been in direct response to features found in the data coming from financial markets, while others have found ready application in financial fields. Incorporating these developments was too much for a single author, particularly one whose interests have diverged from financial econometrics quite significantly in the intervening years! Raphael Markellos has thus become joint author, and his interests and expertise in finance now permeate throughout this new edition, which has had to be lengthened somewhat to accommodate many new developments in the area.

Chapters 1 and 2 remain essentially the same as in the second edition, although examples have been updated. The material on unit roots and associated techniques has continued to expand, so much so that it now has an entire chapter, 3, devoted to it. The remaining material on univariate linear stochastic models now comprises chapter 4, with much more on fractionally differenced processes being included in response to developments in recent years. Evidence of non-linearity in financial time series has continued to accumulate, and stochastic variance models and the many extensions of the ARCH process continue to be very popular, along with the related area of modelling volatility. This material now forms chapter 5, with further non-linear models and tests of non-linearity providing the material for chapter 6. Chapter 7 now contains the material on modelling return distributions and transformations of returns. Much of the material of chapters 8, 9 and 10 (previously chapters 6, 7 and 8) remains as before, but with expanded sections on, for example, non-linear generalisations of cointegration.

1 Introduction

The aim of this book is to provide the researcher in financial markets with the techniques necessary to undertake the empirical analysis of financial time series. To accomplish this aim we introduce and develop both univariate modelling techniques and multivariate methods, including those regression techniques for time series that seem to be particularly relevant to the finance area.

Why do we concentrate exclusively on time series techniques when, for example, cross-sectional modelling plays an important role in empirical investigations of the capital asset pricing model (CAPM; see, as an early and influential example, Fama and MacBeth, 1973)? Moreover, why do we not address the many issues involved in modelling financial time series in continuous time and the spectral domain, although these approaches have become very popular, for example, in the context of derivative asset pricing? Our answer is that, apart from the usual considerations of personal expertise and interest plus constraints on manuscript length, it is because time series analysis, in both its theoretical and empirical aspects, has been for many years an integral part of the study of financial markets.

The first attempts to study the behaviour of financial time series were undertaken by financial professionals and journalists rather than by academics. Indeed, this seems to have become a long-standing tradition, as, even today, much empirical research and development still originates from the financial industry itself. This can be explained by the practical nature of the problems, the need for specialised data and the potential gains from such analysis. The earliest and best-known example of published research on financial time series is by the legendary Charles Dow, as expressed in his editorials in the *Wall Street Times* between 1900 and 1902. These writings formed the basis of 'Dow theory' and influenced what later became known as technical analysis and chartism. Although Dow did not collect and publish his editorials separately, this was done posthumously by his follower Samuel Nelson (Nelson, 1902). Dow's original ideas were later interpreted and further extended by Hamilton (1922) and Rhea (1932). These ideas enjoyed some recognition amongst academics at the time: for example, Hamilton was elected a fellow of the Royal Statistical Society. As characteristically treated by Malkiel (2003), however, technical analysis and chartist approaches became anathema to academics, despite their widespread popularity amongst financial professionals. Although Dow and his followers discussed many of the ideas we encounter in modern finance and time series analysis, including stationarity, market efficiency, correlation between asset returns and indices, diversification and unpredictability, they made no serious effort to adopt formal statistical methods. Most of the empirical analysis involved the painstaking interpretation of detailed charts of sectoral stock price averages, thus forming the celebrated Dow-Jones indices. It was argued that these indices discount all necessary information and provide the best predictor of future events. A fundamental idea, very relevant to the theory of cycles by Stanley Jevons and the 'Harvard A-B-C curve' methodology of trend decomposition by Warren Persons, was that market price variations consisted of three primary movements: daily, medium-term and long-term (see Samuelson, 1987). Although criticism of Dow theory and technical analysis has been a favourite pastime of academics for many years, evidence regarding its merit remains controversial (see, for example, Brown, Goetzmann and Kumar, 1998).

The earliest empirical research using formal statistical methods can be traced back to the papers by Working (1934), Cowles (1933, 1944) and Cowles and Jones (1937). Working focused attention on a previously noted characteristic of commodity and stock prices: namely, that they resemble cumulations of purely random changes. Alfred Cowles 3rd, a quantitatively trained financial analyst and founder of the Econometric Society and the Cowles Foundation, investigated the ability of market analysts and financial services to predict future price changes, finding that there was little evidence that they could. Cowles and Jones reported evidence of positive correlation between successive price changes, but, as Cowles (1960) was later to remark, this was probably due to their taking monthly averages of daily or weekly prices before computing changes: a 'spurious correlation' phenomenon, analysed by Working (1960).

The predictability of price changes has since become a major theme of financial research but, surprisingly, little more was published until Kendall's (1953) study, in which he found that the weekly changes in a wide variety of financial prices could not be predicted either from past changes in the series or from past changes in other price series. This seems to have been the first explicit reporting of this oft-quoted property of financial prices, although further impetus to research on price predictability was provided only by the publication of the papers by Roberts (1959) and Osborne (1959). The former presents a largely heuristic argument as to why successive price changes should be independent, while the latter develops the proposition that it is not absolute price changes but the logarithmic price changes that are independent of each other. With the auxiliary assumption that the changes themselves are normally distributed, this implies that prices are generated as Brownian motion.

The stimulation provided by these papers was such that numerous articles appeared over the next few years investigating the hypothesis that price changes (or logarithmic price changes) are independent, a hypothesis that came to be termed the 'random walk' model, in recognition of the similarity of the evolution of a price series to the random stagger of a drunk. Indeed, the term 'random walk' is believed to have first been used in an exchange of correspondence appearing in *Nature* in 1905 (see Pearson and Rayleigh, 1905), which was concerned with the optimal search strategy for finding a drunk who had been left in the middle of a field at the dead of night! The solution is to start exactly where the drunk had been placed, as that point is an unbiased estimate of the drunk's future position since he will presumably stagger along in an unpredictable and random fashion.

The most natural way to state formally the random walk model is as

$$P_t = P_{t-1} + a_t \tag{1.1}$$

where P_t is the price observed at the beginning of time t and a_t is an error term which has zero mean and whose values are independent of each other. The price change, $\Delta P_t = P_t - P_{t-1}$, is thus simply a_t and hence is independent of past price changes. Note that, by successive backward substitution in (1.1), we can write the current price as the cumulation of all past errors, i.e.

$$P_t = \sum_{i=1}^{t} a_i$$

so that the random walk model implies that prices are indeed generated by Working's 'cumulation of purely random changes'. Osborne's model of Brownian motion implies that equation (1.1) holds for the logarithms of P_t and, further, that a_t is drawn from a zero mean normal distribution having constant variance.

Most of the early papers in this area are contained in the collection of Cootner (1964), while Granger and Morgenstern (1970) provide a detailed development and empirical examination of the random walk model and various of its refinements. Amazingly, much of this work had been anticipated by the French mathematician Louis Bachelier (1900; English translation in Cootner, 1964) in a remarkable PhD thesis in which he developed an elaborate mathematical theory of speculative prices, which he then tested on the pricing of French government bonds, finding that such prices were consistent with the random walk model. What made the thesis even more remarkable was that it also developed many of the mathematical properties of Brownian motion that had been thought to have first been derived some years later in the physical sciences, particularly by Einstein! Yet, as Mandelbrot (1989) remarks, Bachelier had great difficulty in even getting himself a university appointment, let alone getting his theories disseminated throughout the academic community! The importance and influence of Bachelier's path-breaking work is discussed in Sullivan and Weithers (1991) and Dimand (1993).

It should be emphasised that the random walk model is only a hypothesis about how financial prices move. One way in which it can be tested is by examining the autocorrelation properties of price changes: see, for example, Fama (1965). A more general perspective is to view (1.1) as a particular model within the class of autoregressive integrated moving average (ARIMA) models popularised by Box and Jenkins (1976). Chapter 2 thus develops the theory of such models within the general context of (univariate) linear stochastic processes. An important aspect of specifying ARIMA models is to be able to determine correctly the order of integration of the series being analysed and, associated with this, the appropriate way of modelling trends and structural breaks. To do this formally requires the application of unit root tests and a vast range of related procedures. Tests for unit roots and alternative trend specifications are the focus of chapter 3.

We should avoid giving the impression that the only financial time series of interest are stock prices. There are financial markets other than those for stocks, most notably for bonds and foreign currency, but there also exist the various futures, commodity and derivative markets, all of which provide interesting and important series to analyse. For certain of these, it is by no means implausible that models other than the random walk may be appropriate, or, indeed, models from a class other than the ARIMA. Chapter 4 therefore discusses various topics in the general analysis of linear stochastic models: for example, methods of decomposing an observed series into two or more unobserved components and of determining the extent of the 'memory' of a series, by which is meant the behaviour of the series at low frequencies or, equivalently, in the very long run. A variety of examples taken from the financial literature are provided throughout these chapters.

The random walk model has been the workhorse of empirical finance for many years, mainly because of its simplicity and mathematical tractability. Its prominent role was also supported by theoretical models that obtained unpredictability as a direct implication of market efficiency, or, more broadly speaking, of the condition whereby market prices fully, correctly and instantaneously reflect all the available information. An evolving discussion of this research can be found in a series of papers by Fama (1970, 1991, 1998), while Timmermann and Granger (2004) address market efficiency from a forecasting perspective. As LeRoy (1989) discusses, it was later shown that the random walk behaviour of financial prices is neither a sufficient nor a necessary condition for rationally determined financial prices. Moreover, the assumption in (1.1) that price changes are independent was found to be too restrictive to be generated within a reasonably broad class of optimising models. A model that is appropriate, however, can be derived for stock prices in the following way (similar models can be derived for other sorts of financial prices, although the justification is sometimes different: see LeRoy, 1982). The return on a stock from t to $t+1$ is defined as the sum of the dividend yield and the capital gain – i.e. as

$$r_{t+1} = \frac{P_{t+1} + D_t - P_t}{P_t} \tag{1.2}$$

where D_t is the dividend paid during period t. Let us suppose that the expected return is constant, $E_t(r_{t+1}) = r$, where $E_t(\ )$ is the expectation conditional on information available at t: r_t is then said to be a *fair game*. Taking expectations at t of both sides of (1.2) and rearranging yields

$$P_t = (1 + r)^{-1} E_t(P_{t+1} + D_t) \tag{1.3}$$

which says that the stock price at the beginning of period t equals the sum of the expected future price and dividend, discounted back at the rate r. Now assume that there is a mutual fund that holds the stock in question and that it reinvests dividends in future share purchases. Suppose that it holds h_t shares at the beginning of period t, so that the value of the fund is $x_t = h_t P_t$. The assumption that the fund ploughs back its dividend income implies that h_{t+1} satisfies

$$h_{t+1} P_{t+1} = h_t(P_{t+1} + D_t)$$
Thus

$$E_t(x_{t+1}) = E_t(h_{t+1} P_{t+1}) = h_t E_t(P_{t+1} + D_t) = (1 + r)h_t P_t = (1 + r)x_t$$

i.e. x_t is a *martingale* (if, as is common, $r > 0$, we have $E_t(x_{t+1}) \geq x_t$, so that x_t is a *submartingale*; LeRoy (1989, pp. 1593–4) offers an example, however, in which r could be negative, in which case x_t will be a *supermartingale*). LeRoy (1989) emphasises that price itself, without dividends added in, is not generally a martingale, since from (1.3) we have

$$r = E_t(D_t)/P_t + E_t(P_{t+1})/P_t - 1$$

so that only if the expected dividend/price ratio (or dividend yield) is constant, say $E_t(D_t)/P_t = d$, can we write P_t as the submartingale (assuming $r > d$)

$$E_t(P_{t+1}) = (1 + r - d)P_t$$

The assumption that a stochastic process – y_t, say – follows a random walk is more restrictive than the requirement that y_t follows a martingale. The martingale rules out any dependence of the conditional expectation of Δy_{t+1} on the information available at t, whereas the random walk rules out not only this but also dependence involving the higher conditional moments of Δy_{t+1}. The importance of this distinction is thus evident: financial series are known to go through protracted quiet periods and also protracted periods of turbulence. This type of behaviour could be modelled by a process in which successive conditional variances of Δy_{t+1} (but *not* successive levels) are positively autocorrelated. Such a specification would be consistent with a martingale, but not with the more restrictive random walk.

Martingale processes are discussed in chapter 5, and lead naturally on to non-linear stochastic processes that are capable of modelling higher conditional moments, such as the autoregressive conditionally heteroskedastic (ARCH) model introduced by Engle (1982) and stochastic variance models. Related to these models is the whole question of how to model volatility itself, which is of fundamental concern to financial modellers and is therefore also analysed in this chapter. Of course, once we entertain the possibility of non-linear generating processes a vast range of possible processes become available, and those that have found, at least potential, use in modelling financial time series are developed in chapter 6. These include bilinear models, Markov switching processes, smooth transitions and chaotic models. The chapter also includes a discussion of computer intensive techniques such as non-parametric modelling and artificial neural networks. An important aspect of nonlinear modelling is to be able to test for nonlinear behaviour, and testing procedures thus provide a key section of this chapter.

The focus of chapter 7 is on the unconditional distributions of asset returns. The most noticeable future of such distributions is their leptokurtic property: they have fat tails and high peakedness compared to a normal distribution. Although ARCH processes can model such features, much attention in the finance literature since Mandelbrot's (1963a, 1963b) path-breaking papers has concentrated on the possibility that returns are generated by a stable process, which has the property of having an infinite variance. Recent developments in statistical analysis have allowed a much deeper investigation of the tail shapes of empirical distributions, and methods of estimating tail shape indices are introduced and applied to a variety of returns series. The chapter then looks at the implications of fat-tailed distributions for testing the covariance stationarity assumption of time series analysis, data analytic methods of modelling skewness and kurtosis, and the impact of analysing transformations of returns rather than the returns themselves.

The remaining three chapters focus on multivariate techniques of time series analysis, including regression methods. Chapter 8 concentrates on analysing the relationships between a set of *stationary* – or, more precisely, *non-integrated* – financial time series and considers such topics as general dynamic regression, robust estimation, generalised methods of moments, multivariate regression, ARCH-in-mean and multivariate ARCH models, vector autoregressions, Granger causality, variance decompositions and impulse response analysis. These topics are illustrated with a variety of examples drawn from the finance literature: using forward exchange rates as optimal predictors of future spot rates; modelling the volatility of stock returns and the risk premium in the foreign exchange market; testing the CAPM; and investigating the interaction of the equity and gilt markets in the United Kingdom.

Chapter 9 concentrates on the modelling of *integrated* financial time series, beginning with a discussion of the spurious regression problem, introducing cointegrated processes and demonstrating how to test for cointegration, and then moving on to consider how such processes can be estimated. Vector error correction models are analysed in detail, along with associated issues in causality testing and impulse response analysis, alternative approaches to testing for the presence of a long-run relationship, and the analysis of both common cycles and trends. The techniques introduced in this chapter are illustrated with extended examples analysing the market model and the interactions of the UK financial markets.

Finally, chapter 10 considers modelling issues explicit to finance. Samuelson (1965, 1973) and Mandelbrot (1966) have analysed the implications of equation (1.3), that the stock price at the beginning of time t

equals the discounted sum of the next period's expected future price and dividend, to show that this stock price equals the expected discounted, or present, value of *all* future dividends – i.e. that

$$P_t = \sum_{i=0}^{\infty} (1 + r)^{-(i+1)} E_t(D_{t+i}) \qquad (1.4)$$

which is obtained by recursively solving (1.3) forwards and assuming that $(1 + r)^{-n} E_t(P_{t+n})$ converges to zero as $n \to \infty$. Present value models of the type (1.4) are analysed comprehensively in chapter 10, with the theme of whether stock markets are excessively volatile, perhaps containing speculative bubbles, being used extensively throughout the discussion and in a succession of examples, although the testing of the expectations hypothesis of the term structure of interest rates is also used as an example of the general present value framework. The chapter also discusses recent research on non-linear generalisations of cointegration and how structural breaks may be dealt with in cointegrating relationships.

Having emphasised earlier in this chapter that the book is exclusively about modelling financial time series, we should state at this juncture what the book is not about. It is certainly not a text on financial market theory, and any such theory is discussed only when it is necessary as a motivation for a particular technique or example. There are numerous texts on the theory of finance, and the reader is referred to these for the requisite financial theory: two notable texts that contain both theory and empirical techniques are Campbell, Lo and MacKinlay (1997) and Cuthbertson (1996). Neither is it a textbook on econometrics. We assume that the reader already has a working knowledge of probability, statistics and econometric theory, in particular least squares estimation. Nevertheless, it is also non-rigorous, being at a level roughly similar to Mills (1990), in which references to the formal treatment of the theory of time series are provided.

When the data used in the examples throughout the book have already been published, references are given. Previous unpublished data are defined in the data appendix, which contains details on how they may be accessed. All standard regression computations were carried out using *EVIEWS 5.0* (EViews, 2003), but use was also made of *STAMP 5.0* (Koopman *et al.*, 2006), *TSM 4.18* (Davidson, 2006a) and occasionally other econometric packages. 'Non-standard' computations were made using algorithms written by the authors in *GAUSS* and *MatLab*.

2 Univariate linear stochastic models: basic concepts

Chapter 1 has emphasised the standard representation of a financial time series as that of a (univariate) linear stochastic process, specifically as being a member of the class of ARIMA models popularised by Box and Jenkins (1976). This chapter provides the basic theory of such models within the general framework of the analysis of linear stochastic processes. As already stated in chapter 1, our treatment is purposely non-rigorous. For detailed theoretical treatments, but which do not, however, focus on the analysis of financial series, see, for example, Brockwell and Davis (1996), Hamilton (1994), Fuller (1996) or Taniguchi and Kakizawa (2000).

2.1 Stochastic processes, ergodicity and stationarity

2.1.1 Stochastic processes, realisations and ergodicity

When we wish to analyse a financial time series using formal statistical methods, it is useful to regard the observed series, $(x_1, x_2, \ldots, x_T)$, as a particular *realisation* of a stochastic process. This realisation is often denoted $\{x_t\}_1^T$, while, in general, the stochastic process itself will be the family of random variables $\{X_t\}_{-\infty}^{\infty}$ defined on an appropriate probability space. For our purposes it will usually be sufficient to restrict the index set $T = (-\infty, \infty)$ of the parent stochastic process to be the same as that of the realisation, i.e. $T = (1, T)$, and also to use x_t to denote both the stochastic process and the realisation when there is no possibility of confusion.

With these conventions, the stochastic process can be described by a T-dimensional probability distribution, so that the relationship between a realisation and a stochastic process is analogous to that between the sample and population in classical statistics. Specifying the complete form of the probability distribution will generally be too ambitious a task, and we usually content ourselves with concentrating attention on the first and second moments: the T means

$$E(x_1), E(x_2), \ldots, E(x_T)$$

T variances

$$V(x_1), V(x_2), \ldots, V(x_T)$$

and $T(T-1)/2$ covariances

$$Cov(x_i, x_j), \quad i < j$$

If we could assume joint normality of the distribution, this set of expectations would then completely characterise the properties of the stochastic process. As we shall see, however, such an assumption is unlikely to be appropriate for many financial series. If normality cannot be assumed but the process is taken to be *linear*, in the sense that the current value of the process is generated by a linear combination of previous values of the process itself and current and past values of any other related processes, then, again, this set of expectations would capture its major properties. In either case, however, it will be impossible to infer all the values of the first and second moments from just one realisation of the process, since there are only T observations but $T + T(T+1)/2$ unknown parameters. Hence, further simplifying assumptions must be made to reduce the number of unknown parameters to more manageable proportions.

We should emphasise that the procedure of using a single realisation to infer the unknown parameters of a joint probability distribution is valid only if the process is *ergodic*, which essentially means that the sample moments for finite stretches of the realisation approach their population counterparts as the length of the realisation becomes infinite. For more on ergodicity, see, for example, Granger and Newbold (1986, chap. 1) or Hamilton (1994, chap. 3.2) and, since it is difficult to test for ergodicity using just (part of) a single realisation, it will be assumed from now on that all time series have this property. Domowitz and El-Gamal (2001) have provided a set of sufficient assumptions under which a single time series trajectory will contain enough information to construct a consistent non-parametric test of ergodicity.

2.1.2 Stationarity

One important simplifying assumption is that of *stationarity*, which requires the process to be in a particular state of 'statistical equilibrium' (Box and

Jenkins, 1976, p. 26). A stochastic process is said to be *strictly stationary* if its properties are unaffected by a change of time origin. In other words, the joint probability distribution at *any* set of times $t_1, t_2, \ldots t_m$ must be the same as the joint probability distribution at times $t_1 + k, t_2 + k, \ldots, t_m + k$, where k is an arbitrary shift in time. For $m = 1$, this implies that the marginal probability distributions do not depend on time, which in turn implies that, so long as $E|x_t|^2 < \infty$, both the mean and variance of x_t must be constant – i.e.

$$E(x_1) = E(x_2) = \cdots = E(x_T) = E(x_t) = \mu$$

and

$$V(x_1) = V(x_2) = \cdots = V(x_T) = V(x_t) = \sigma_x^2$$

If $m = 2$, strict stationarity implies that all bivariate distributions do not depend on t: thus all covariances are functions only of the time shift (or lag) k – i.e. for all k

$$Cov(x_1, x_{1+k}) = Cov(x_2, x_{2+k}) = \cdots = Cov(x_{T-k}, x_T) = Cov(x_t, x_{t-k})$$

Hence, we may define the *autocovariances* and *autocorrelations* as

$$\gamma_k = Cov(x_t, x_{t-k}) = E[(x_t - \mu)(x_{t-k} - \mu)]$$

and

$$\rho_k = \frac{Cov(x_t, x_{t-k})}{[V(x_t) \cdot V(x_{t-k})]^{\frac{1}{2}}} = \frac{\gamma_k}{\gamma_0}$$

respectively, both of which depend only on the lag k. Since these conditions apply just to the first- and second-order moments of the process, this is known as *second-order* or *weak stationarity* (and sometimes *covariance stationarity* or *stationarity in the wide sense*). While strict stationarity (with finite second moments) thus implies weak stationarity, the converse does not hold, for it is possible for a process to be weakly stationary but *not* strictly stationary; this would be the case if higher moments, such as $E(x_t^3)$, were functions of time. If, however, joint normality could be assumed, so that the distribution was entirely characterised by the first two moments, weak stationarity does indeed imply strict stationarity. More complicated relationships between these concepts of stationarity hold for some types of non-linear processes (as is discussed in chapter 4).

The autocorrelations considered as a function of k are referred to as the *autocorrelation function* (ACF). Note that, since

$$\gamma_k = Cov(x_t, x_{t-k}) = Cov(x_{t-k}, x_t) = Cov(x_t, x_{t+k}) = \gamma_{-k}$$

it follows that $\rho_k = \rho_{-k}$, and so only the positive half of the ACF is usually given. The ACF plays a major role in modelling dependencies among observations, since it characterises, along with the process mean $\mu = E(x_t)$ and variance $\sigma_x^2 = \gamma_0 = V(x_t)$, the stationary stochastic process describing the evolution of x_t. It therefore indicates, by measuring the extent to which one value of the process is correlated with previous values, the length and strength of the 'memory' of the process.

2.2 Stochastic difference equations

A fundamental theorem in time series analysis, known as *Wold's decomposition* (Wold, 1938: see Hamilton, 1994, chap. 4.8), states that every weakly stationary, purely non-deterministic stochastic process $(x_t - \mu)$ can be written as a linear combination (or linear *filter*) of a sequence of uncorrelated random variables. By 'purely non-deterministic' we mean that any linearly deterministic components have been subtracted from $(x_t - \mu)$. Such a component is one that can be perfectly predicted from past values of itself, and examples commonly found are a (constant) mean, as is implied by writing the process as $(x_t - \mu)$, periodic sequences, and polynomial or exponential sequences in t. A formal discussion of this theorem, well beyond the scope of this book, may be found in, for example, Brockwell and Davis (1996, chap. 5.7), but Wold's decomposition underlies all the theoretical models of time series that are subsequently to be introduced.

This linear filter representation is given by

$$x_t - \mu = a_t + \psi_1 a_{t-1} + \psi_2 a_{t-2} + \cdots = \sum_{j=0}^{\infty} \psi_j a_{t-j}, \quad \psi_0 = 1 \qquad (2.1)$$

The $\{a_t : t = 0, \pm 1, \pm 2, \ldots\}$ are a sequence of uncorrelated random variables, often known as *innovations*, drawn from a fixed distribution with

$$E(a_t) = 0, \quad V(a_t) = E(a_t^2) = \sigma^2 < \infty$$

and

$$Cov(a_t, a_{t-k}) = E(a_t a_{t-k}) = 0, \quad \text{for all } k \neq 0$$

We will refer to such a sequence as a *white-noise* process, often denoting it as $a_t \sim WN(0, \sigma^2)$. The coefficients (possibly infinite in number) in the linear filter are known as ψ-*weights*.

We can easily show that the model (2.1) leads to autocorrelation in x_t. From this equation it follows that

$$E(x_t) = \mu$$

$$\begin{aligned}
\gamma_0 = V(x_t) &= E(x_t - \mu)^2 \\
&= E(a_t + \psi_1 a_{t-1} + \psi_2 a_{t-2} + \cdots)^2 \\
&= E(a_t^2) + \psi_1^2 E(a_{t-1}^2) + \psi_2^2 E(a_{t-2}^2) + \cdots \\
&= \sigma^2 + \psi_1^2 \sigma^2 + \psi_2^2 \sigma^2 + \cdots \\
&= \sigma^2 \sum_{j=0}^{\infty} \psi_j^2
\end{aligned}$$

by using the result that $E(a_{t-i} a_{t-j}) = 0$ for $i \neq j$. Now

$$\begin{aligned}
\gamma_k &= E(x_t - \mu)(x_{t-k} - \mu) \\
&= E(a_t + \psi_1 a_{t-1} + \cdots + \psi_k a_{t-k} + \cdots)(a_{t-k} + \psi_1 a_{t-k-1} + \cdots) \\
&= \sigma^2(1 \cdot \psi_k + \psi_1 \psi_{k+1} + \psi_2 \psi_{k+2} + \cdots) \\
&= \sigma^2 \sum_{j=0}^{\infty} \psi_j \psi_{j+k}
\end{aligned}$$

and this implies

$$\rho_k = \frac{\sum_{j=0}^{\infty} \psi_j \psi_{j+k}}{\sum_{j=0}^{\infty} \psi_j^2}$$

If the number of ψ-weights in (2.1) is infinite, we have to assume that the weights are absolutely summable, i.e. that $\sum_{j=0}^{\infty} |\psi_j| < \infty$, in which case the linear filter representation is said to *converge*. This condition can be shown to be equivalent to assuming that x_t is stationary, and guarantees that all moments exist and are independent of time, in particular that the variance of x_t, γ_0, is finite.

Wold's theorem is fundamental, in that it allows us to represent any arbitrary linear process as a stochastic difference equation with infinite lags. In practical terms this representation may not seem very useful, since it requires the estimation of an infinite number of ψ-weights in (2.1). As will be shown in subsequent sections, however, this infinite-order stochastic difference equation can be represented exactly or approximately by a parsimonious ratio of finite-order stochastic difference equation models.

2.3 ARMA processes

2.3.1 Autoregressive processes

Although equation (2.1) may appear complicated, many realistic models result from particular choices of the ψ-weights. Taking $\mu = 0$ without loss of generality, choosing $\psi_j = \phi^j$ allows (2.1) to be written

$$
\begin{aligned}
x_t &= a_t + \phi a_{t-1} + \phi^2 a_{t-2} + \cdots \\
&= a_t + \phi(a_{t-1} + \phi a_{t-2} + \cdots) \\
&= \phi x_{t-1} + a_t
\end{aligned}
$$

or

$$
x_t - \phi x_{t-1} = a_t \tag{2.2}
$$

This is known as a *first-order autoregressive* process, often given the acronym AR(1). The *backshift* (or *lag*) *operator*, B, is now introduced for notational convenience. This shifts time one step back, so that

$$
Bx_t \equiv x_{t-1}
$$

and, in general,

$$
B^m x_t = x_{t-m}
$$

noting that $B^m \mu \equiv \mu$. The lag operator allows (possibly infinite) distributed lags to be written in a very concise way. For example, by using this notation the AR(1) model can be written as

$$
(1 - \phi B)x_t = a_t
$$

so that

$$
\begin{aligned}
x_t &= (1 - \phi B)^{-1} a_t = \left(1 + \phi B + \phi^2 B^2 + \cdots\right) a_t \\
&= a_t + \phi a_{t-1} + \phi^2 a_{t-2} + \cdots
\end{aligned} \tag{2.3}
$$

This linear filter representation will converge as long as $|\phi| < 1$, which is therefore the stationarity condition.

We can now deduce the ACF of an AR(1) process. Multiplying both sides of (2.2) by $x_{t-k}, k>0$, and taking expectations yields

$$\gamma_k - \phi\gamma_{k-1} = E(a_t x_{t-k}) \qquad (2.4)$$

From (2.3), $a_t x_{t-k} = \sum_{i=0}^{\infty} \phi^i a_t a_{t-k-i}$. As a_t is white noise, any term in $a_t a_{t-k-i}$ has zero expectation if $k+i>0$. Thus, (2.4) simplifies to

$$\gamma_k = \phi\gamma_{k-1}, \quad \text{for all } k>0$$

and, consequently, $\gamma_k = \phi^k\gamma_0$. An AR(1) process therefore has an ACF given by $\rho_k = \phi^k$. Thus, if $\phi>0$, the ACF decays exponentially to zero, while, if $\phi>0$, the ACF decays in an oscillatory pattern, both decays being slow if ϕ is close to the non-stationary boundaries of $+1$ and -1.

The ACFs for two AR(1) processes with (a) $\phi=0.5$, and (b) $\phi=-0.5$, are shown in figure 2.1, along with generated data from the processes with a_t assumed to be normally and independently distributed with $\sigma^2=25$, denoted $a_t \sim NID(0,25)$, and with starting value $x_0=0$. With $\phi>0$ (c), adjacent values are positively correlated and the generated series has a tendency to exhibit 'low-frequency' trends. With $\phi<0$ (d), however, adjacent values have a negative correlation and the generated series displays violent, rapid oscillations.

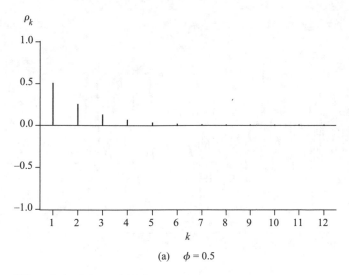

(a) $\phi = 0.5$

Figure 2.1 ACFs and simulations of AR(1) processes

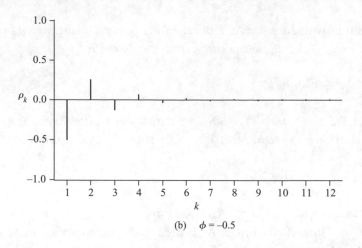

(b) $\phi = -0.5$

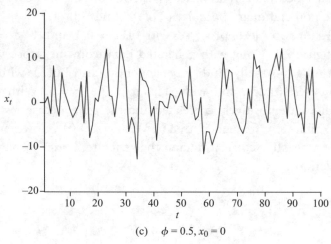

(c) $\phi = 0.5,\ x_0 = 0$

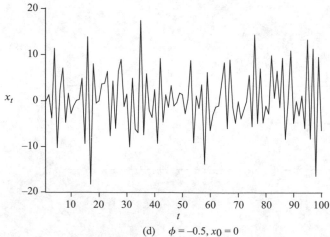

(d) $\phi = -0.5,\ x_0 = 0$

Figure 2.1   (continued)

2.3.2 Moving average processes

Now consider the model obtained by choosing $\psi_1 = -\theta$ and $\psi_j = 0, j \geq 2$, in (2.1):

$$x_t = a_t - \theta a_{t-1}$$

or

$$x_t = (1 - \theta B)a_t \tag{2.5}$$

This is known as the *first-order moving average*, or MA(1), process and it follows immediately that

$$\gamma_0 = \sigma^2 (1 + \theta^2), \quad \gamma_1 = -\sigma^2 \theta, \quad \gamma_k = 0 \quad \text{for } k > 1$$

and hence its ACF is described by

$$\rho_1 = \frac{-\theta}{1 + \theta^2}, \quad \rho_k = 0, \quad k > 1$$

Thus, although observations one period apart are correlated, observations more than one period apart are not, so that the 'memory' of the process is just one period: this 'jump' to zero autocorrelation at $k = 2$ may be contrasted with the smooth, exponential decay of the ACF of an AR(1) process.

The expression for ρ_1 can be written as the quadratic equation $\theta^2 \rho_1 + \theta + \rho_1 = 0$. Since θ must be real, it follows that $-\frac{1}{2} < \rho_1 < \frac{1}{2}$. Both θ and $1/\theta$ will satisfy this equation, however, and thus two MA(1) processes can always be found that correspond to the same ACF. Since any moving average model consists of a finite number of ψ-weights, all MA models are stationary. In order to obtain a converging autoregressive representation, however, the restriction $|\theta| < 1$ must be imposed. This restriction is known as the *invertibility* condition, and implies that the process can be written in terms of an infinite autoregressive representation

$$x_t = \pi_1 x_{t-1} + \pi_2 x_{t-2} + \cdots + a_t$$

where the π-*weights* converge – i.e. $\sum_{j=1}^{\infty} |\pi_j| < \infty$. In fact, the MA(1) model can be written as

$$(1 - \theta B)^{-1} x_t = a_t$$

and expanding $(1 - \theta B)^{-1}$ yields

$$\left(1 + \theta B + \theta^2 B^2 + \cdots\right) x_t = a_t$$

The weights $\pi_j = -\theta^J$ will converge if $|\theta| < 1$, i.e. if the model is invertible. This implies the reasonable assumption that the effect of past observations decreases with age.

Figure 2.2 presents plots of generated data from two MA(1) processes with (a) $\theta = 0.8$ and (b) $\theta = -0.8$, in each case with $a_t \sim NID(0,25)$. On comparison of these plots with those of the AR(1) processes in figure 2.1, it is seen that realisations from the two types of processes are often quite similar, suggesting that it may, on occasions, be difficult to distinguish between the two.

2.3.3 General AR and MA processes

Extensions to the AR(1) and MA(1) models are immediate. The general autoregressive model of order p, AR(p), can be written as

$$x_t - \phi_1 x_{t-1} - \phi_2 x_{t-2} - \cdots - \phi_p x_{t-p} = a_t$$

or

$$\left(1 - \phi_1 B - \phi_2 B^2 - \cdots - \phi_p B^p\right)x_t = \phi(B)x_t = a_t$$

The linear filter representation $x_t = \psi(B)a_t$ can be obtained by equating coefficients in $\phi(B)\psi(B) = 1$ (see Mills, 1990, chap. 5, for examples of how to do this). The stationarity conditions required for convergence of the ψ-weights are that the roots of the characteristic equation

$$\phi(B) = (1 - g_1 B)(1 - g_2 B) \cdots (1 - g_p B) = 0$$

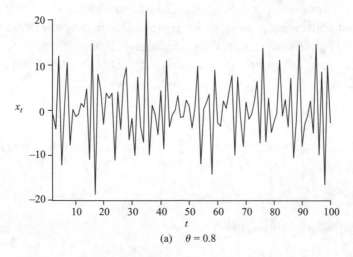

(a) $\theta = 0.8$

Figure 2.2   Simulations of MA(1) processes

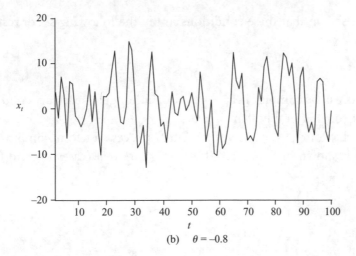

(b) $\theta = -0.8$

Figure 2.2   (continued)

are such that $|g_i| < 1$ for $i = 1, 2, \ldots, p$, an equivalent phrase being that the roots g_i^{-1} all lie outside the unit circle. The behaviour of the ACF is determined by the difference equation

$$\phi(B)\rho_k = 0, \quad k > 0 \tag{2.6}$$

which has the solution

$$\rho_k = A_1 g_1^k + A_2 g_2^k + \cdots + A_p g_p^k$$

Since $|g_i| < 1$, the ACF is thus described by a mixture of damped exponentials (for real roots) and damped sine waves (for complex roots). As an example, consider the AR(2) process

$$\left(1 - \phi_1 B - \phi_2 B^2\right) x_t - a_t$$

with characteristic equation

$$\phi(B) = (1 - g_1 B)(1 - g_2 B) = 0$$

The roots g_1 and g_2 are given by

$$g_1, g_2 = \frac{1}{2}\left(\phi_1 \pm \left(\phi_1^2 + 4\phi_2\right)^{1/2}\right)$$

and can both be real, or they can be a pair of complex numbers. For stationarity, it is required that the roots be such that $|g_1| < 1$ and $|g_2| < 1$, and it can be shown that these conditions imply the following set of restrictions on ϕ_1 and ϕ_2:

$$\phi_1 + \phi_2 < 1, \quad -\phi_1 + \phi_2 < 1, \quad -1 < \phi_2 < 1$$

The roots will be complex if $\phi_1^2 + 4\phi_2 < 0$, although a necessary condition for complex roots is simply that $\phi_2 < 0$.

The behaviour of the ACF of an AR(2) process for four combinations of (ϕ_1, ϕ_2) is shown in figure 2.3. If g_1 and g_2 are real (cases (a) and (b)), the

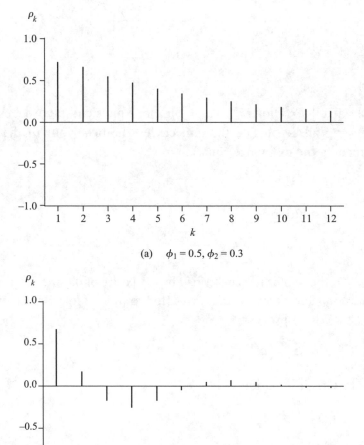

(a) $\phi_1 = 0.5, \phi_2 = 0.3$

(b) $\phi_1 = 1, \phi_2 = -0.5$

Figure 2.3   ACFs of various AR(2) processes

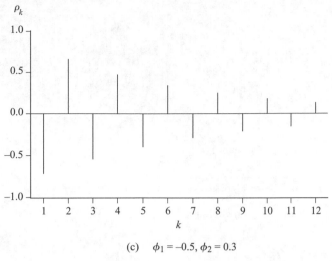

(c) $\phi_1 = -0.5,\ \phi_2 = 0.3$

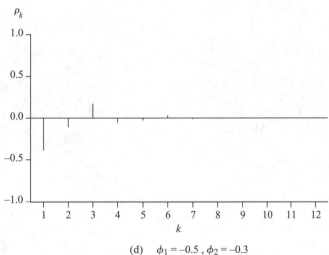

(d) $\phi_1 = -0.5,\ \phi_2 = -0.3$

Figure 2.3   (continued)

ACF is a mixture of two damped exponentials. Depending on their sign, the autocorrelations can also damp out in an oscillatory manner. If the roots are complex (cases (c) and (d)), the ACF follows a damped sine wave. Figure 2.4 shows plots of generated time series from these four AR(2) processes, in each case with $a_t \sim NID(0, 25)$. Depending on the signs of the real roots, the series may be either smooth or jagged, while complex roots tend to induce 'pseudo-periodic' behaviour.

Since all AR processes have ACFs that 'damp out', it is sometimes difficult to distinguish between processes of different orders. To aid with such

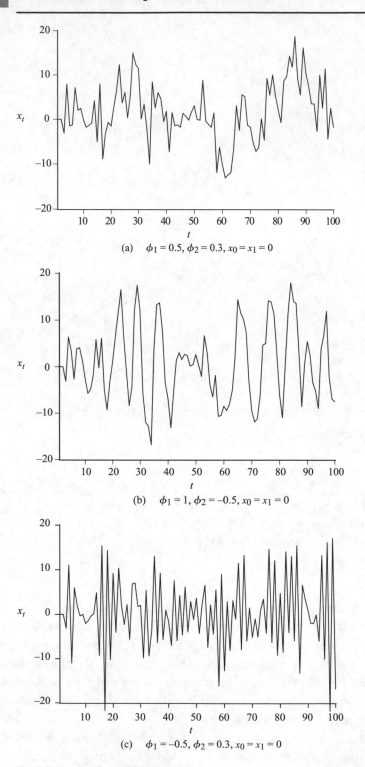

(a) $\phi_1 = 0.5, \phi_2 = 0.3, x_0 = x_1 = 0$

(b) $\phi_1 = 1, \phi_2 = -0.5, x_0 = x_1 = 0$

(c) $\phi_1 = -0.5, \phi_2 = 0.3, x_0 = x_1 = 0$

Figure 2.4   Simulations of various AR(2) processes

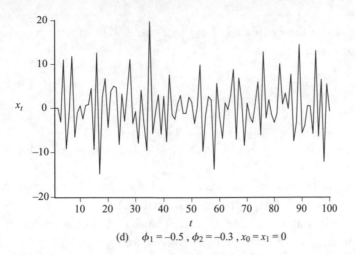

(d) $\phi_1 = -0.5$, $\phi_2 = -0.3$, $x_0 = x_1 = 0$

Figure 2.4   (continued)

discrimination, we may use the *partial autocorrelation function* (PACF). In general, the correlation between two random variables is often due to both variables being correlated with a third. In the present context, a large portion of the correlation between x_t and x_{t-k} may be due to the correlation this pair have with the intervening lags $x_{t-1}, x_{t-2}, \ldots, x_{t-k+1}$. To adjust for this correlation, the *partial autocorrelations* may be calculated.

The kth partial autocorrelation is the coefficient ϕ_{kk} in the AR(k) process

$$x_t = \phi_{k1}x_{t-1} + \phi_{k2}x_{t-2} + \cdots + \phi_{kk}x_{t-k} + a_t \tag{2.7}$$

and measures the additional correlation between x_t and x_{t-k} after adjustments have been made for the intervening lags.

In general, ϕ_{kk} can be obtained from the *Yule–Walker* equations that correspond to (2.7). These are given by the set of equations (2.6) with $p = k$ and $\phi_i = \phi_{ii}$, and solving for the last coefficient ϕ_{kk} using Cramer's rule leads to

$$
\phi_{kk} = \frac{\begin{vmatrix} 1 & \rho_1 & \cdots & \rho_{k-2} & \rho_1 \\ \rho_1 & 1 & \cdots & \rho_{k-3} & \rho_2 \\ \cdot & \cdot & \cdots & \cdot & \cdot \\ \cdot & \cdot & \cdots & \cdot & \cdot \\ \rho_{k-1} & \rho_{k-2} & \cdots & \rho_1 & \rho_k \end{vmatrix}}{\begin{vmatrix} 1 & \rho_1 & \cdots & \rho_{k-2} & \rho_{k-1} \\ \rho_1 & 1 & \cdots & \rho_{k-3} & \rho_{k-2} \\ \cdot & \cdot & \cdots & \cdot & \cdot \\ \cdot & \cdot & \cdots & \cdot & \cdot \\ \rho_{k-1} & \rho_{k-2} & \cdots & \rho_1 & 1 \end{vmatrix}}
$$

It follows from the definition of ϕ_{kk} that the PACFs of AR processes are of a particular form:

$$\text{AR}(1): \phi_{11} = \rho_1 = \phi, \qquad\qquad\qquad\qquad\qquad \phi_{kk} = 0 \qquad \text{for } k{>}1$$

$$\text{AR}(2): \phi_{11} = \rho_1, \qquad \phi_{22} = \frac{\rho_2 - \rho_1^2}{1 - \rho_1^2}, \qquad\qquad \phi_{kk} = 0 \qquad \text{for } k{>}2$$

$$\text{AR}(3): \phi_{11} \neq 0, \qquad \phi_{22} \neq 0, \ldots, \phi_{pp} \neq 0, \quad \phi_{kk} = 0 \qquad \text{for } k{>}p$$

Thus, the partial autocorrelations for lags larger than the order of the process are zero. Hence, an AR(p) process is described by

(i)   an ACF that is infinite in extent and is a combination of damped exponentials and damped sine waves, and

(ii) a PACF that is zero for lags larger than p.

The general moving average of order q, MA(q), can be written as

$$x_t = a_t - \theta_1 a_{t-1} - \cdots - \theta_q a_{t-q}$$

or

$$x_t = \left(1 - \theta_1 B - \cdots - \theta_q B^q\right) a_t = \theta(B) a_t$$

The ACF can be shown to be

$$\rho_k = \frac{-\theta_k + \theta_1 \theta_{k+1} + \cdots + \theta_{q-k}\theta_q}{1 + \theta_1^2 + \cdots + \theta_q^2}, \quad k = 1, 2, \ldots, q, \quad \rho_k = 0, \quad k{>}q$$

The ACF of an MA(q) process therefore cuts off after lag q; the memory of the process extends q periods, observations more than q periods apart being uncorrelated.

The weights in the AR(∞) representation $\pi(B)x_t = a_t$ are given by $\pi(B) = \theta^{-1}(B)$ and can be obtained by equating coefficients of B^j in $\pi(B)\theta(B) = 1$. For invertibility, the roots of

$$\left(1 - \theta_1 B - \cdots - \theta_q B^q\right) = \left(1 - h_1 B\right) \cdots \left(1 - h_q B\right) = 0$$

must satisfy $|h_i|{<}1$ for $i = 1, 2, \ldots, q$.

Figure 2.5 presents generated series from two MA(2) processes, again using $a_t \sim NID(0, 25)$. The series tend to be fairly jagged, similar to AR(2) processes with real roots of opposite signs, and, of course, such MA processes are unable to capture periodic-type behaviour.

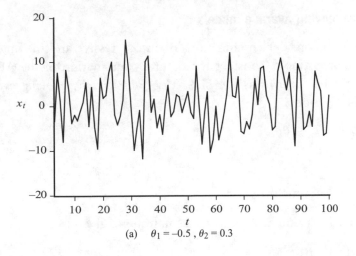

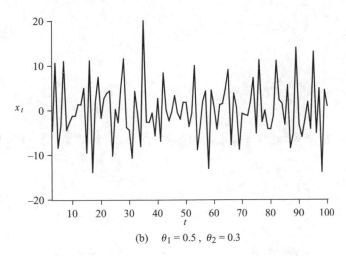

Figure 2.5   Simulations of MA(2) processes

The PACF of an MA(q) process can be shown to be infinite in extent (i.e. it tails off). Explicit expressions for the PACFs of MA processes are complicated but, in general, are dominated by combinations of exponential decays (for the real roots in $\theta(B)$) and/or damped sine waves (for the complex roots). Their patterns are thus very similar to the ACFs of AR processes. Indeed, an important duality between AR and MA processes exists: while the ACF of an AR(p) process is infinite in extent, the PACF cuts off after lag p. The ACF of an MA(q) process, on the other hand, cuts off after lag q, while the PACF is infinite in extent.

2.3.4 Autoregressive moving average models

We may also consider combinations of autoregressive and moving average models. For example, consider the natural combination of the AR(1) and MA(1) models, known as the *first-order autoregressive moving average*, or ARMA(1,1), model:

$$x_t - \phi x_{t-1} = a_t - \theta a_{t-1}$$

or

$$(1 - \phi B)x_t = (1 - \theta B)a_t. \tag{2.8}$$

The ψ-weights in the MA(∞) representation are given by

$$\psi(B) = \frac{(1 - \theta B)}{(1 - \phi B)}$$

i.e.

$$x_t = \psi(B)a_t = \left(\sum_{i=0}^{\infty} \phi^i B^i \right)(1 - \theta B)a_t = a_t + (\phi - \theta) \sum_{i=1}^{\infty} \phi^{i-1} a_{t-i} \tag{2.9}$$

Likewise, the π-weights in the MA(∞) representation are given by

$$\pi(B) = \frac{(1 - \phi B)}{(1 - \theta B)}$$

i.e.

$$\pi(B)x_t = \left(\sum_{i=0}^{\infty} \theta^i B^i \right)(1 - \phi B)x_t = a_t$$

or

$$x_t = (\phi - \theta) \sum_{i=1}^{\infty} \theta^{i-1} x_{t-i} + a_t$$

The ARMA(1,1) model thus leads to both moving average and auto-regressive representations having an infinite number of weights. The ψ-weights converge for $|\phi|<1$ (the stationarity condition) and the π-weights converge for $|\theta|<1$ (the invertibility condition). The stationarity condition for the ARMA(1,1) model is thus the same as that of an MA(1) model.

From equation (2.9) it is clear that any product $x_{t-k}a_{t-j}$ has zero expectation if $k > j$. Thus, multiplying both sides of (2.8) by x_{t-k} and taking expectations yields

$$\gamma_k = \phi\gamma_{k-1}, \quad \text{for } k>1$$

whilst for $k=0$ and $k=1$ we obtain, respectively,

$$\gamma_0 - \phi\gamma_1 = \sigma^2 - \theta(\phi - \theta)\sigma^2$$

and

$$\gamma_1 - \phi\gamma_0 = -\theta\sigma^2$$

Eliminating σ^2 from these two equations allows the ACF of the ARMA(1,1) process to be given by

$$\rho_1 = \frac{(1 - \phi\theta)(\phi - \theta)}{1 + \theta^2 - 2\phi\theta}$$

and

$$\rho_k = \phi\rho_{k-1}, \quad \text{for } k>1$$

The ACF of an ARMA(1,1) process is therefore similar to that of an AR(1) process, in that the autocorrelations decay exponentially at a rate ϕ. Unlike the AR(1), however, this decay starts from ρ_1 rather than from $\rho_0 = 1$. Moreover, $\rho_1 \neq \phi$ and, since for typical financial series both ϕ and θ will be positive with $\phi > \theta$, ρ_1 can be much less than ϕ if $\phi - \theta$ is small.

More general ARMA processes are obtained by combining AR(p) and MA(q) processes:

$$x_t - \phi_1 x_{t-1} - \cdots - \phi_p x_{t-p} = a_t - \theta_1 a_{t-1} - \cdots - \theta_q a_{t-q}$$

or

$$\left(1 - \phi_1 B - \cdots - \phi_p B^p\right) x_t = \left(1 - \theta_1 B - \cdots - \theta_q B^q\right) a_t \qquad (2.10)$$

i.e.

$$\phi(B)x_t = \theta(B)a_t$$

The resultant ARMA(p,q) process has the stationarity and invertibility conditions associated with the constituent AR(p) and MA(q) processes, respectively. Its ACF will eventually follow the same pattern as that of an

AR(p) process after $q-p+1$ initial values $\rho_0, \rho_1, \ldots, \rho_{q-p}$ (if $q-p<0$ there will be no initial values), while its PACF eventually (for $k>p-q$) behaves like that of an MA(q) process.

Throughout this development, we have assumed that the mean of the process, μ, is zero. Non-zero means are easily accommodated by replacing x_t with $x_t - \mu$ in (2.10), so that in the general case of an ARMA(p,q) process we have

$$\phi(B)(x_t - \mu) = \theta(B)a_t$$

Noting that $\phi(B)\mu = \left(1 - \phi_1 - \cdots - \phi_p\right)\mu = \phi(1)\mu$, the model can equivalently be written as

$$\phi(B)x_t = \theta_0 + \theta(B)a_t$$

where $\theta_0 = \phi(1)\mu$ is a constant or intercept.

2.4 Linear stochastic processes

In this development of ARMA models, we have assumed that the innovations $\{a_t\}$ are uncorrelated and drawn from a fixed distribution with finite variance, and hence the sequence has been termed white noise – i.e. $a_t \sim WN(0,\sigma^2)$. If these innovations are also *independent* (in which case we denote them as being *iid*), then the sequence is termed *strict* white noise, denoted $a \sim SWN(0,\sigma^2)$. A stationary process $\{x_t\}$ generated as a linear filter of strict white noise is said to be a linear process. It is possible, however, for a linear filter of a white noise process to result in a non-linear stationary process. The distinctions between white and strict white noise and between linear and non-linear stationary processes are extremely important when modelling financial time series, and, as was alluded to in section 2.1.2, will be discussed in more detail in chapter 5.

2.5 ARMA model building

2.5.1 Sample autocorrelation and partial autocorrelation functions

An essential first step in fitting ARMA models to observed time series is to obtain estimates of the generally unknown parameters, μ, σ_x^2 and the ρ_k. With our stationarity and (implicit) ergodicity assumptions, μ and σ_x^2 can be estimated by the sample mean and sample variance, respectively, of the realisation $\{x_t\}_1^T$:

$$\bar{x} = T^{-1} \sum_{t=1}^{T} x_t$$

$$s^2 = T^{-1} \sum_{t=1}^{T} (x_t - \bar{x})^2$$

An estimate of ρ_k is then given by the lag k *sample autocorrelation*

$$r_k = \frac{\sum_{t=k+1}^{T} (x_t - \bar{x})(x_{t-k} - \bar{x})}{Ts^2}, \qquad k = 1, 2, \ldots$$

the set of r_ks defining the *sample autocorrelation function* (SACF).

For independent observations drawn from a fixed distribution with finite variance ($\rho_k = 0$, for all $k \neq 0$), the variance of r_k is approximately given by T^{-1} (see, for example, Box and Jenkins, 1976, chap. 2). If, moreover, T is large, $\sqrt{T} r_k$ will be approximately standard normal, i.e. $\sqrt{T} r_k \overset{a}{\sim} N(0, 1)$, so that an absolute value of r_k in excess of $2T^{-1/2}$ may be regarded as 'significantly' different from zero. More generally, if $\rho_k = 0$ for $k > q$, the variance of r_k, for $k > q$, is

$$V(r_k) = T^{-1}\left(1 + 2\rho_1^2 + \cdots + 2\rho_q^2\right)$$

Thus, by successively increasing the value of q and replacing the ρ_ks by their sample estimates, the variances of the sequence $r_1, r_2, \ldots r_k$ can be estimated as T^{-1}, $T^{-1}\left(1 + 2r_1^2\right), \ldots, T^{-1}\left(1 + 2r_1^2 + \cdots + 2r_{k-1}^2\right)$, and, of course, these will be larger, for $k > 1$, than those calculated using the simple formula $t - 1$.

The *sample partial autocorrelation function* (SPACF) is usually calculated by fitting autoregressive models of increasing order: the estimate of the last coefficient in each model is the sample partial autocorrelation, $\hat{\phi}_{kk}$. If the data follow an AR(p) process, then for lags greater than p the variance of $\hat{\phi}_{kk}$ is approximately T^{-1}, so that $\sqrt{T}\hat{\phi}_{kk} \overset{a}{\sim} N(0, 1)$.

2.5.2 Model-building procedures

Given the r_k and $\hat{\phi}_{kk}$, with their respective standard errors, the approach to ARMA model building proposed by Box and Jenkins (1976) is essentially to

Table 2.1 ACF of real S&P 500 returns and accompanying statistics

k	r_k	$s.e.(r_k)$	$Q(k)$
1	0.089	0.086	1.08 [0.30]
2	− 0.146	0.086	4.03 [0.13]
3	0.063	0.088	4.59 [0.20]
4	− 0.074	0.089	5.37 [0.25]
5	− 0.121	0.089	7.45 [0.19]
6	0.043	0.090	7.72 [0.26]
7	0.122	0.090	9.86 [0.20]
8	− 0.064	0.091	10.46 [0.23]
9	− 0.022	0.092	10.53 [0.31]
10	0.067	0.092	11.19 [0.34]
11	− 0.015	0.093	11.23 [0.42]
12	− 0.112	0.093	13.10 [0.36]

Note: Figures in [..] give $P(\chi_k^2 > Q(k))$.

match the behaviour of the SACF and SPACF of a particular time series with that of various theoretical ACFs and PACFs, picking the best match (or set of matches), estimating the unknown model parameters (the ϕ_is, θ_is and σ^2) and checking the residuals from the fitted models for any possible misspecifications.

Another popular method is to select a set of models based on prior considerations of maximum possible settings of p and q, estimate each possible model and select that model which minimises a chosen selection criterion based on goodness of fit considerations. Details of these model-building procedures, and their various modifications, may be found in many texts, such as Mills (1990, chap. 8), and hence will not be discussed in detail; rather, they will be illustrated by way of a sequence of examples.

Example 2.1 Are the returns on the S&P 500 a fair game?

An important and often analysed financial series is the real return on the annual Standard and Poor's (S&P) 500 stock index for the United States. Annual observations from 1872 to 2006 are plotted in figure 2.6 and its SACF up to $k = 12$ is given in table 2.1. It is seen that the series appears to be stationary around a constant mean, estimated to be 3.59 per cent. This is confirmed by the SACF, and a comparison of each of the r_k with their corresponding standard errors, computed using equation (2.10), shows that none is individually significantly different from zero, thus suggesting that the series is, in fact, white noise.

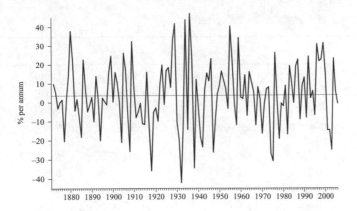

Figure 2.6   Real S&P returns (annual 1872–2006)

We can construct a 'portmanteau' statistic based on the complete set of r_ks. On the hypothesis that $x_t \sim SWN(\mu, \sigma^2)$, Box and Pierce (1970) show that the statistic

$$Q^*(k) = T \sum_{i=1}^{k} r_i^2$$

is asymptotically distributed as χ^2 with k degrees of freedom – i.e. $Q^*(k) \overset{a}{\sim} \chi_k^2$. Unfortunately, simulations have shown that, even for quite large samples, the true significance levels of $Q^*(k)$ could be much smaller than those given by this asymptotic theory, so that the probability of incorrectly rejecting the null hypothesis will be smaller than any chosen significance level. Ljung and Box (1978) argue that a better approximation is obtained when the modified statistic

$$Q(k) = T(T+2) \sum_{i=1}^{k} (T-i)^{-1} r_i^2 \overset{a}{\sim} \chi_k^2$$

is used. $Q(k)$ statistics, with accompanying marginal significance levels of rejecting the null, are also reported in table 2.1 for $k = 1, \ldots, 12$, and they confirm that there is no evidence against the null hypothesis that returns are white noise. Real returns on the S&P 500 would therefore appear to be consistent with the fair game model in which the expected return is constant, being 3.59 per cent per annum.

Example 2.2 Modelling the UK interest rate spread

As we shall see in chapter 10, the 'spread', the difference between long-term and short-term interest rates, is an important variable in testing the

Table 2.2 SACF and SPACF of the UK spread

k	r_k	$s.e.(r_k)$	$\hat{\phi}_{kk}$	$s.e.\ (\hat{\phi}_{kk})$
1	0.969	0.039	0.969	0.039
2	0.927	0.066	-0.200	0.039
3	0.886	0.084	0.020	0.039
4	0.847	0.097	0.007	0.039
5	0.806	0.108	-0.059	0.039
6	0.763	0.116	-0.052	0.039
7	0.721	0.124	-0.003	0.039
8	0.680	0.130	-0.012	0.039
9	0.643	0.135	0.049	0.039
10	0.612	0.140	0.045	0.039
11	0.584	0.144	0.006	0.039
12	0.557	0.147	-0.013	0.039

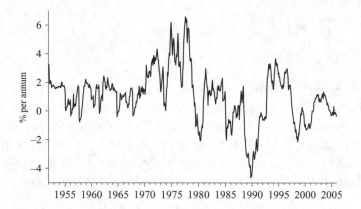

Figure 2.7   UK interest rate spread (monthly March 1952–December 2005)

expectations hypothesis of the term structure of interest rates. Figure 2.7 shows the spread between twenty-year UK gilts and ninety-one-day Treasury bills using monthly observations for the period 1952 to 2005 ($T = 648$), while table 2.2 reports the SACF and SPACF up to $k = 12$, with accompanying standard errors. (The spread may be derived from the interest rate series $R20$ and RS given in the data appendix).

The spread is seen to be considerably smoother than one would expect if it was a realisation from a white noise process, and this is confirmed by the SACF, all of whose values are positive and significant (the accompanying portmanteau statistic is $Q(12) = 4557$!). The SPACF has both $\hat{\phi}_{11}$ and $\hat{\phi}_{22}$

significant, thus identifying an AR(2) process. Fitting such a model to the series by ordinary least squares (OLS) regression yields

$$x_t = \underset{(0.019)}{0.032} + \underset{(0.039)}{1.180}\, x_{t-1} - \underset{(0.038)}{0.216}\, x_{t-2} + \hat{a}_t, \quad \hat{\sigma} = 0.419$$

Figures in parentheses are standard errors and the intercept implies a fitted mean of $\hat{\mu} = \hat{\theta}_0 \big/ \left(1 - \hat{\phi}_1 - \hat{\phi}_2\right) = 0.906$, with standard error 0.469. Since $\hat{\phi}_1 + \hat{\phi}_2 = 0.965, -\hat{\phi}_1 + \hat{\phi}_2 = -1.396$ and $\hat{\phi}_2 = -0.216$, the stationarity conditions associated with an AR(2) process are satisfied, but, although $\hat{\phi}_2$ is negative, $\hat{\phi}_1^2 + 4\hat{\phi}_2 = 0.528$, so that the roots are real, being $\hat{g}_1 = 0.95$ and $\hat{g}_2 = 0.23$. The closeness of $\hat{g}_1$ to unity will be discussed further later in the chapter.

Having fitted an AR(2) process, it is now necessary to check whether such a model is adequate. As a 'diagnostic check', we may examine the properties of the residuals $\hat{a}_t$. Since these are estimates of a_t, they should mimic its behaviour – i.e. they should behave as white noise. The portmanteau statistics Q^* and Q can be used for this purpose, although the degrees of freedom attached to them must be amended: if an ARMA(p,q) process is fitted, they are reduced to $k - p - q$. With $k = 12$, our residuals yield the value $Q(12) = 7.98$, which is now asymptotically distributed as χ_{10}^2 and hence gives no evidence of model inadequacy.

An alternative approach to assessing model adequacy is to overfit. For example, we might consider fitting an AR(3) process or, perhaps, an ARMA (2,1) to the series. These yield the following pair of models (methods of estimating MA processes are discussed in, for example, Hamilton, 1994, chap. 5; we use here conditional least squares)

$$x_t = \underset{(0.019)}{0.032} + \underset{(0.039)}{1.183}\, x_{t-1} - \underset{(0.060)}{0.222}\, x_{t-2} + \underset{(0.039)}{0.004}\, x_{t-3} + \hat{a}_t, \quad \hat{\sigma} = 0.417$$

$$x_t = \underset{(0.021)}{0.034} + \underset{(0.178)}{1.091}\, x_{t-1} - \underset{(0.174)}{0.129}\, x_{t-2} + \hat{a}_t + \underset{(0.179)}{0.092}\, \hat{a}_{t-1}, \quad \hat{\sigma} = 0.419$$

In both models, the additional parameter is insignificant, thus confirming the adequacy of our original choice of an AR(2) process.

Other methods of testing model adequacy are available. In particular, we may construct formal tests based on the Lagrange multiplier (LM) principle: see Godfrey (1979), with Mills (1990, chap. 8.8) providing textbook discussion.

Table 2.3 SACF and SPACF of FTA All Share nominal returns

k	r_k	$s.e.(r_k)$	$\hat{\phi}_{kk}$	$s.e.(\hat{\phi}_{kk})$
1	0.105	0.045	0.105	0.045
2	−0.101	0.046	−0.113	0.045
3	0.061	0.046	0.087	0.045
4	0.025	0.047	−0.004	0.045
5	−0.091	0.048	−0.080	0.045
6	−0.009	0.048	0.010	0.045
7	0.024	0.048	0.003	0.045
8	−0.039	0.048	−0.032	0.045
9	0.093	0.048	0.112	0.045
10	0.005	0.049	−0.040	0.045
11	−0.037	0.049	−0.006	0.045
12	0.012	0.049	0.006	0.045

Example 2.3 Modelling returns on the FTA All Share index

The broadest-based stock index in the United Kingdom is the *Financial Times-Actuaries (FTA) All Share.* Table 2.3 reports the SACF and SPACF (up to $k = 12$) of its nominal return calculated using equation (1.2) from monthly observations from 1965 to 2005 ($T = 491$). The portmanteau statistic is $Q(12) = 23.0$, which is significant at the 0.03 level, and both r_k and $\hat{\phi}_{kk}$ at lags $k = 1$ and 2 are greater than two standard errors in size. This suggests that the series is best modelled by some ARMA process of reasonably low order, although a number of models could be consistent with the behaviour shown by the SACF and SPACF.

In such circumstances, there are a variety of selection criteria that may be used to choose an appropriate model, of which perhaps the most popular is Akaike's (1974) information criterion (AIC), defined as

$$AIC(p, q) = \ln \hat{\sigma}^2 + 2(p + q)T^{-1}$$

although a criterion that has better theoretical properties is Schwarz's (1978)

$$BIC(p, q) = \ln \hat{\sigma}^2 + (p + q)T^{-1} \ln T$$

A number of other criteria have been proposed, but all are structured in terms of the estimated error variance $\hat{\sigma}^2$ plus a penalty adjustment involving the number of estimated parameters, and it is in the extent of this penalty that the criteria differ. For more discussion about these, and other, selection criteria, see Tremayne (2006).

The criteria are used in the following way. Upper bounds, say p_{max} and q_{max}, are set for the orders of $\phi(B)$ and $\theta(B)$, and, with $\bar{p} = \{0, 1, \ldots, p_{max}\}$ and $\bar{q} = \{0, 1, \ldots, q_{max}\}$, orders p_1 and q_1 are selected such that, for example,

$$AIC(p_1, q_1) = \min AIC(p, q), \quad p \in \bar{p}, \quad q \in \bar{q}$$

with parallel strategies obviously being employed in conjunction with BIC or any other criterion. One possible difficulty with the application of this strategy is that no specific guidelines on how to determine $\bar{p}$ and $\bar{q}$ seem to be available, although they are tacitly assumed to be sufficiently large for the range of models to contain the 'true' model, which we may denote as having orders (p_0, q_0) and which, of course, will not necessarily be the same as (p_1, q_1), the orders chosen by the criterion under consideration.

Given these alternative criteria, are there reasons for preferring one to another? If the true orders (p_0, q_0) are contained in the set (p, q), $p \in \bar{p}$, $q \in \bar{q}$, then – for all criteria – $p_1 \geq p_0$ and $q_1 \geq q_0$, almost surely, as $T \to \infty$. BIC is *strongly consistent*, however, in that it determines the true model asymptotically, whereas for AIC an overparameterised model will emerge no matter how long the available realisation. Of course, such properties are not necessarily guaranteed in finite samples, as we find below.

Given the behaviour of the SACF and SPACF of our returns series, we set $\bar{p} = \bar{q} = 2$, and table 2.4 shows the resulting AIC and BIC values. AIC selects the orders $(2,2)$ – i.e. an ARMA $(2,2)$ process – while the orders $(0,1)$ and $(0,2)$ have identical (to four decimal places) BIC values, so that an MA(2) process is chosen (these models are shown in bold italics in table 2.4). The two estimated models are

$$x_t = \underset{(0.74)}{1.81} - \underset{(0.119)}{0.959}\, x_{t-1} - \underset{(0.096)}{0.738}\, x_{t-2}$$
$$+ a_t + \underset{(0.120)}{1.083}\, a_{t-1} + \underset{(0.103)}{0.742}\, a_{t-2}, \quad \hat{\sigma} = 5.96$$

and

$$x_t = \underset{(0.28)}{1.21} + a_t + \underset{(0.045)}{0.130}\, a_{t-1} - \underset{(0.045)}{0.107}\, a_{t-2}, \quad \hat{\sigma} = 5.99$$

Although these models appear quite different, they are, in fact, similar in several respects. The estimate of the mean return implied by the ARMA(2,2) model is 1.21 per cent, the same as that obtained directly from the MA(2)

Table 2.4 Model selection criteria for nominal returns

	q	0	1	2
	p			
AIC	0	6.442	6.432	6.423
	1	6.437	6.427	6.429
	2	6.430	6.429	6.417
BIC	0	6.451	6.4488	6.4488
	1	6.454	6.453	6.463
	2	6.456	6.464	6.460

model, while the sum of the weights of the respective AR(∞) representations are 0.98 and 0.96, respectively. The short-run dynamics are quite similar as well. For the ARMA(2,2) model the initial weights are $\pi_1 = -0.124$, $\pi_2 = 0.130$, $\pi_3 = -0.049$ and $\pi_4 = -0.044$, while for the MA(2) they are $\pi_1 = -0.130$, $\pi_2 = 0.124$, $\pi_3 = -0.030$ and $\pi_4 = -0.017$. Both models provide acceptable fits to the returns series: the MA(2) has a $Q(6)$ value of 5.2, with a marginal significance level of 0.27, while the ARMA(2,2) model has a $Q(6)$ value of 2.0, with a marginal significance level of 0.36.

Thus, although theoretically the BIC has advantages over the AIC, it would seem that the latter selects the model that is preferable on more general grounds, given that the AIC-selected model nests the BIC-selected model by including the two significant autoregressive terms. Nonetheless, we should observe that, for both criteria, there are other models that yield criterion values close to that of the model selected. Using this idea of being 'close to', Poskitt and Tremayne (1987) introduce the concept of a *model portfolio*. Models are compared to the selected (p_1, q_1) process by way of the statistic, using AIC for illustration,

$$\Re = \exp\left[-\tfrac{1}{2}T\{AIC(p_1, q_1) - AIC(p, q)\}\right]$$

Although $\Re$ has no physical meaning, its value may be used to 'grade the decisiveness of the evidence' against a particular model. Poskitt and Tremayne (1987) suggest that a value of $\Re$ less than $\sqrt{10}$ may be thought of as being a close competitor to (p_1, q_1), with the set of closely competing models being taken as the model portfolio.

Using this concept, with $\sqrt{10}$ taken as an approximate upper bound, the AIC portfolio contains only the (2,2) model, while the BIC portfolio contains the (0,0), (0,1), (0,2) and (1,1) models (the model portfolios are shown in italics in table 2.4: using $\sqrt{10}$ as an upper bound requires a maximum difference in values of 0.004 here).

All these models have similar fits and, although it is difficult to compare them using the estimated AR and MA polynomials, their 'closeness' can be seen by looking at the roots of the characteristic equations associated with the $\phi(B)$ and $\theta(B)$ polynomials. The estimated models can be written as

$(0,0)$ $\qquad x_t = 1.21 + a_t$

$(0,1)$ $\qquad x_t = 1.21 + (1 + 0.14B)a_t$

$(0,2)$ $\qquad x_t = 1.21 + (1 + 0.13B - 0.11B^2)a_t$

$\qquad\qquad = 1.21 + (1 + 0.40B)(1 - 0.27B)a_t$

$(1,1)$ $\qquad x_t = 1.21 + \dfrac{(1 + 0.60B)}{(1 + 0.46B)}a_t = 1.21 + (1 + 0.60B)(1 + 0.46B)^{-1}a_t$

$\qquad\qquad = 1.21 + (1 + 0.60B)(1 - 0.46B + 0.46^2B^2 - 0.46^3B^3 + \cdots)a_t$

$\qquad\qquad \approx 1.21 + (1 + 0.14B - 0.07B^2)a_t$

$(2,2)$ $\qquad x_t = 1.21 + \dfrac{(1 + 1.083B + 0.742B^2)}{(1 + 0.959B + 0.738B^2)}a_t$

$\qquad\qquad = 1.21 + \dfrac{(1 + (0.54 + 0.67i)B)(1 + (0.54 - 0.67i)B)}{(1 + (0.48 + 0.71i)B)(1 + (0.48 - 0.71i)B)}a_t$

Focusing first on the BIC model portfolio, the $(0,1)$ and $(0,0)$ models are obtained from the $(0,2)$ model by successively restricting the small moving average coefficients to zero, while the $(1,1)$ model is seen to be closely approximated by the $(0,2)$. The AIC-selected $(2,2)$ model looks very different from the other models, but differences can be deceiving. The autoregressive and moving average roots have moduli that are almost identical, 0.859 and 0.861, so that cancellation, or partial cancellation, of these 'common factors' can lead to each of the other models.

2.6 Non-stationary processes and ARIMA models

The class of ARMA models developed in the previous sections of this chapter relies on the assumption that the underlying process is weakly stationary, thus implying that the mean, variance and autocovariances of the process are invariant under time translations. As we have seen, this restricts the mean and variance to be constant and requires the autocovariances to depend only on the time lag. Many financial time series are certainly not stationary, however, and, in particular, have a tendency to exhibit time-changing means and/or variances.

2.6.1 Non-stationarity in variance

We begin by assuming that a time series can be decomposed into a *non-stochastic* mean level and a random error component

$$x_t = \mu_t + \varepsilon_t \tag{2.11}$$

and we suppose that the variance of the errors, ε_t, is functionally related to the mean level μ_t by

$$V(x_t) = V(\varepsilon_t) = h^2(\mu_t)\sigma_x^2$$

where $h(\cdot)$ is some known function. Our objective is to find a transformation of the data, $g(x_t)$, that will stabilise the variance – i.e. the variance of the transformed variable $g(x_t)$ should be constant. Expanding $g(x_t)$ as a first-order Taylor series around μ_t yields

$$g(x_t) \cong g(\mu_t) + (x_t - \mu_t)g'(\mu_t)$$

where $g'(\mu_t)$ is the first derivative of $g(x_t)$ evaluated at μ_t. The variance of $g(\mu_t)$ can then be approximated as

$$\begin{aligned} V[g(x_t)] &\cong V[g(\mu_t) + (x_t - \mu_t)g'(x_t)] \\ &= [g'(\mu_t)]^2 V(x_t) \\ &= [g'(\mu_t)]^2 h^2(\mu_t)\sigma_x^2 \end{aligned}$$

Thus, in order to stabilise the variance, we have to choose the transformation $g(\cdot)$ such that

$$g'(x_t) = \frac{1}{h(\mu_t)}$$

For example, if the standard deviation of x_t is proportional to its level, $h(\mu_t) = \mu_t$ and the variance-stabilising transformation $g(\mu_t)$ has then to satisfy $g'(\mu_t) = \mu_t^{-1}$. This implies that $g(\mu_t) = \log(\mu_t)$, and thus (natural) logarithms of x_t should be used to stabilise the variance. If the variance of x_t is proportional to its level, $h(\mu_t) = \mu_t^{1/2}$, so that $g'(\mu_t) = \mu_t^{-1/2}$. Thus, since $g(\mu_t) = 2\mu_t^{1/2}$, the square root transformation $x_t^{1/2}$ will stabilise the variance. These two examples are special cases of the Box and Cox (1964) class of power transformations

$$g(x_t) = \frac{x_t^\lambda - 1}{\lambda}$$

where we note that $\lim_{\lambda \to 0} \left[(x_t^\lambda - 1)/\lambda \right] = \log(x_t)$. While the use of logarithms is a popular transformation for financial time series, it is rare for a constant variance to be completely induced by this transformation alone. Chapter 5 considers various models in which time-varying variances are explicitly modelled.

2.6.2 Non-stationarity in mean

A non-constant mean level in equation (2.11) can be modelled in a variety of ways. One possibility is that the mean evolves as a polynomial of order d in time. This will arise if x_t can be decomposed into a trend component, given by the polynomial, and a stochastic, stationary, but possibly autocorrelated, zero mean error component. This is always possible given Cramer's (1961) extension of Wold's decomposition theorem to non-stationary processes. Thus, we may have

$$x_t = \mu_t + \varepsilon_t = \sum_{j=0}^{d} \beta_j t^j + \psi(B) a_t \tag{2.12}$$

Since

$$E(\varepsilon_t) = \psi(B) E(a_t) = 0$$

we have

$$E(x_t) = E(\mu_t) = \sum_{j=0}^{d} \beta_j t^j$$

and, as the β_j coefficients remain constant through time, such a trend in the mean is said to be *deterministic*. Trends of this type can be removed by a simple transformation. Consider the linear trend obtained by setting $d = 1$, where, for simplicity, the error component is assumed to be a white-noise sequence

$$x_t = \beta_0 + \beta_1 t + a_t \tag{2.13}$$

Lagging (2.13) one period and subtracting this from (2.13) yields

$$x_t - x_{t-1} = \beta_1 + a_t - a_{t-1} \tag{2.14}$$

The result is a difference equation following an ARMA$(1,1)$ process in which, since $\phi = \theta = 1$, both autoregressive and moving average roots are unity and the model is neither stationary nor invertible. If we consider the *first differences* of $x_t - w_t$, say – then

$$w_t = x_t - x_{t-1} = (1 - B)x_t = \Delta x_t$$

where $\Delta = 1 - B$ is known as the *first difference operator*. Equation (2.14) can then be written as

$$w_t = \Delta x_t = \beta_1 + \Delta a_t$$

and w_t is thus generated by a stationary (since $E(w_t) = \beta_1$ is a constant), but not invertible, MA(1) process.

In general, if the trend polynomial is of order d, and ε_t is characterised by the ARMA process $\phi(B)\varepsilon_t = \theta(B)a_t$, then

$$\Delta^d x_t = (1 - B)^d x_t$$

(obtained by differencing x_t d times) will follow the process

$$\Delta^d x_t = \theta_0 + \frac{\Delta^d \theta(B)}{\phi(B)} a_t$$

where $\theta_0 = d! \beta_d$. Thus, the MA part of the process generating $\Delta^d x_t$ will contain the factor Δ^d and will therefore have d roots of unity. Note also that the variance of x_t will be the same as the variance of ε_t, which will be constant for all t. Figure 2.8 shows plots of generated data for both linear and quadratic trend models. Because the variance of the error component, here assumed to be white noise and distributed as $NID(0,9)$, is constant and independent of the level, the variability of the two series are bounded about their expected values, and the trend components are clearly observed in the plots.

An alternative way of generating a non-stationary mean level is to consider ARMA models whose autoregressive parameters do not satisfy stationarity conditions. For example, consider the AR(1) process

$$x_t = \phi x_{t-1} + a_t \tag{2.15}$$

where $\phi > 1$. If the process is assumed to have started at time $t = 0$, the difference equation (2.15) has the solution

$$x_t = x_0 \phi^t + \sum_{i=0}^{t} \phi^i a_{t-i} \tag{2.16}$$

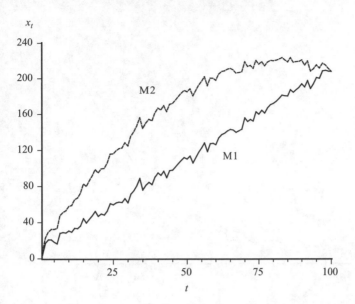

Figure 2.8   Linear and quadratic trends

The 'complementary function' $x_0\phi^t$ can be regarded as the *conditional expectation* of x_t at time $t=0$ (Box and Jenkins, 1976, chap. 4), and is an increasing function of t. The conditional expectation of x_t at times $t = 1, 2, \ldots, t - 2, t - 1$ depends on the random shocks $a_0, a_1, \ldots, a_{t-3}, a_{t-2}$, and hence, since this conditional expectation may be regarded as the trend of x_t, the trend changes *stochastically*.

The variance of x_t is given by

$$V(x_t) = \sigma^2 \frac{\phi^{2(t+1)} - 1}{\phi^2 \ 1}$$

which is an increasing function of time and becomes infinite as $t \to \infty$. In general, x_t will have a trend in both mean and variance, and such processes are said to be *explosive*. A plot of generated data from the process (2.15) with $\phi = 1.05$ and $a_t \sim NID(0,9)$, and having starting value $x_0 = 10$, is shown in figure 2.9. We see that, after a short 'induction period', the series essentially follows an exponential curve, with the generating a_ts playing almost no further part. The same behaviour would be observed if additional autoregressive and moving average terms were added to the model, as long as the stationarity conditions are violated.

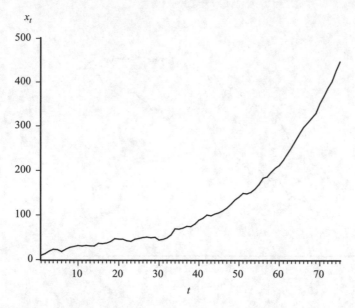

Figure 2.9 Explosive AR(1) model

As we can see from (2.16), the solution of (2.15) is explosive if $\phi > 1$ but stationary if $\phi < 1$. The case $\phi = 1$ provides a process that is neatly balanced between the two. If x_t is generated by the model

$$x_t = x_{t-1} + a_t \tag{2.17}$$

then x_t is said to follow a *random walk*. If we allow a constant, θ_0, to be included, so that

$$x_t = x_{t-1} + \theta_0 + a_t \tag{2.18}$$

then x_t will follow a *random walk with drift*. If the process starts at $t = 0$, then

$$x_t = x_0 + t\theta_0 + \sum_{i=0}^{t} a_{t-i}$$

so that

$$\mu_t = E(x_t) = x_0 + t\theta_0$$

$$\gamma_{0,t} = V(x_t) = t\sigma^2$$

and

$$\gamma_{k,t} = Cov(x_t, x_{t-k}) = (t - k)\sigma^2, \quad k \geq 0$$

Thus, the correlation between x_t and x_{t-k} is given by

$$\rho_{k,t} = \frac{t-k}{\sqrt{t(t-k)}} = \sqrt{\frac{t-k}{t}}$$

If t is large compared to k, all $\rho_{k,t}$ will be approximately unity. The sequence of x_t values will therefore be very smooth, but will also be non-stationary, since both its mean and variance will increase with t. Figure 2.10 shows generated plots of the random walks (2.17) and (2.18) with $x_0 = 10$ and $a_t \sim NID(0,9)$. In part (a) of the figure the drift parameter, θ_0, is set to zero, while in part (b) we have set $\theta_0 = 2$. The two plots differ considerably, but neither show any affinity whatsoever with the initial value x_0; indeed, the expected length of time for a random walk to pass again through an arbitrary value is infinite.

The random walk is an example of a class of non-stationary processes known as *integrated processes*. Equation (2.18) can be written as

$$\Delta x_t = \theta_0 + a_t$$

and so first differencing x_t leads to a stationary model, in this case the white-noise process a_t. Generally, a series may need first differencing d times to

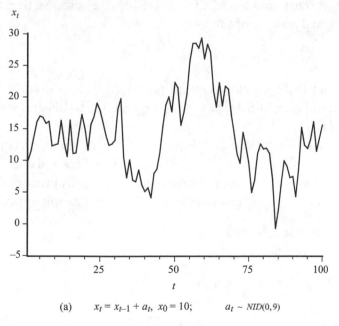

(a) $x_t = x_{t-1} + a_t, \; x_0 = 10; \qquad a_t \sim NID(0,9)$

Figure 2.10 Random walks

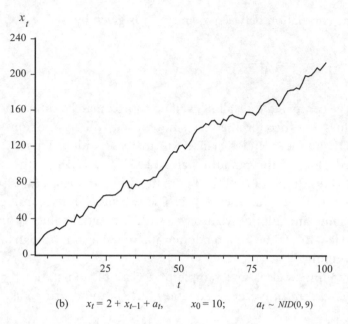

(b) $x_t = 2 + x_{t-1} + a_t,$ $x_0 = 10;$ $a_t \sim NID(0, 9)$

Figure 2.10 (continued)

attain stationarity, and the series so obtained may itself be autocorrelated. If this autocorrelation is modelled by an ARMA(p,q) process, then the model for the original series is of the form

$$\phi(B)\Delta^d x_t = \theta_0 + \theta(B)a_t \tag{2.19}$$

which is said to be an *autoregressive integrated moving average* process of orders p, d and q, or ARIMA(p, d, q), and x_t is said to be integrated of order d, denoted $I(d)$.

It will usually be the case that the order of integration, d, or, equivalently, the degree of differencing, will be zero, one or, very occasionally, two. Again, it will be the case that the autocorrelations of an ARIMA process will be near one for all non-large k. For example, consider the (stationary) ARMA$(1,1)$ process

$$x_t - \phi x_{t-1} = a_t - \theta a_{t-1}$$

whose ACF has been shown to be

$$\rho_1 = \frac{(1 - \phi\theta)(\phi - \theta)}{1 + \theta^2 - 2\phi\theta} \ , \quad \rho_k = \phi\rho_{k-1}, \quad \text{for } k > 1$$

As $\phi \to 1$, the ARIMA$(0,1,1)$ process

$$\Delta x_t = a_t - \theta a_{t-1}$$

results, and all the ρ_k tend to unity.

A number of points concerning the ARIMA class of models are of importance. Consider again (2.19), with $\theta_0 = 0$ for simplicity:

$$\phi(B)\Delta^d x_t = \theta(B)a_t \qquad (2.20)$$

This process can equivalently be defined by the two equations

$$\phi(B)w_t = \theta(B)a_t \qquad (2.21)$$

and

$$w_t = \Delta^d x_t \qquad (2.22)$$

so that, as we have noted above, the model corresponds to assuming that $\Delta^d x_t$ can be represented by a stationary and invertible ARMA process. Alternatively, for $d \geq 1$, (2.22) can be inverted to give

$$x_t = S^d w_t \qquad (2.23)$$

where S is the infinite summation, or *integral*, operator defined by

$$S = \left(1 + B + B^2 + \cdots\right) = (1 - B)^{-1} = \Delta^{-1}$$

Equation (2.23) implies that the process (2.20) can be obtained by summing, or 'integrating', the stationary process d times: hence the term 'integrated process'.

Box and Jenkins (1976, chap. 4) refer to this type of non-stationary behaviour as *homogeneous non-stationarity*, and it is important to discuss why this form of non-stationarity is felt to be useful in describing the behaviour of many financial time series. Consider again the first-order autoregressive process (2.12). A basic characteristic of the AR(1) model is that, for both $|\phi| < 1$ and $|\phi| > 1$, the local behaviour of a series generated from the model is heavily dependent upon the level of x_t. For many financial series, local behaviour appears to be roughly independent of level, and this is what we mean by homogenous non-stationarity.

If we want to use ARMA models for which the behaviour of the process is indeed independent of its level, then the autoregressive operator $\phi(B)$ must be chosen so that

$$\phi(B)(x_t + c) = \phi(B)x_t$$

where c is any constant. Thus,

$$\phi(B)c = 0$$

implying that $\phi(1) = 0$, so that $\phi(B)$ must be able to be factorised as

$$\phi(B) = \phi_1(B)(1 - B) = \phi_1(B)\Delta$$

in which case the class of processes that need to be considered will be of the form

$$\phi_1(B)w_t = \theta(B)a_t$$

where $w_t = \Delta x_t$. Since the requirement of homogenous non-stationarity precludes w_t increasing explosively, either $\phi_1(B)$ is a stationary operator or $\phi_1(B) = \phi_2(B)(1 - B)$, so that $\phi_2(B)w_t^* = \theta(B)a_t$, where $w_t^* = \Delta^2 x_t$. Since this argument can be used recursively, it follows that, for time series that are homogenously non-stationary, the autoregressive operator must be of the form $\phi(B)\Delta^d$, where $\phi(B)$ is a stationary autoregressive operator. Figure 2.11

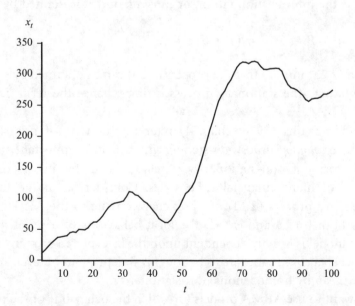

Figure 2.11 'Second difference' model

plots generated data from the model $\Delta^2 x_t = a_t$, where $a_t \sim NID(0,9)$ and $x_0 = x_1 = 10$, and such a series is seen to display random movements in both level and slope.

We see from figures 2.10(a) and 2.11 that ARIMA models without the constant θ_0 in (2.19) are capable of representing series that have *stochastic* trends, which typically will consist of random changes in both the level and slope of the series. As seen from figure 2.10(b) and equation (2.18), however, the inclusion of a non-zero drift parameter introduces a deterministic trend into the generated series, since $\mu_t = E(x_t) = \beta_0 + \theta_0 t$ if we set $\beta_0 = x_0$. In general, if a constant is included in the model for dth differences, then a deterministic polynomial trend of degree d is automatically allowed for. Equivalently, if θ_0 is allowed to be non-zero, then

$$E(w_t) = E\left(\Delta^d x_t\right) = \mu_w = \theta_0 / \left(1 - \phi_1 - \phi_2 - \cdots - \phi_p\right)$$

is non-zero, so that an alternative way of expressing (2.19) is as

$$\phi(B)\tilde{w}_t = \theta(B)a_t$$

where $\tilde{w}_t = w_t - \mu_w$. Figure 2.12 plots generated data for $\Delta^2 x_t = 2 + a_t$, where again $a_t \sim NID(0,9)$ and $x_0 = x_1 = 10$. The inclusion of the deterministic quadratic trend has a dramatic effect on the evolution of the series, with the non-stationary 'noise' being completely swamped after a few periods.

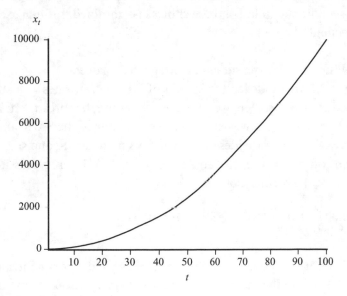

Figure 2.12 'Second difference with drift' model

Model (2.19) therefore allows both stochastic and deterministic trends to be modelled. When $\theta_0 = 0$ a stochastic trend is incorporated, while if $\theta_0 \neq 0$ the model may be interpreted as representing a deterministic trend (a polynomial in time of order d) buried in non-stationary noise, which will typically be autocorrelated. The models presented earlier in this section could be described as deterministic trends buried in *stationary* noise, since they can be written as

$$\phi(B)\Delta^d x_t = \phi(1)\beta_d d! + \Delta^d \theta(B) a_t$$

the stationary nature of the noise in the level of x_t being manifested in d roots of the moving average operator being unity. Further discussion of the relationships between stochastic and deterministic trends is contained in chapter 3.

2.7 ARIMA modelling

Once the order of differencing d has been established then, since $w_t = \Delta^d x_t$ is by definition stationary, the ARMA techniques discussed in section 2.5.2 may be applied to the suitably differenced series. Establishing the correct order of differencing is by no means straightforward, however, and is discussed in detail in chapter 3. We content ourselves here with a sequence of examples illustrating the modelling of ARIMA processes when d has already been chosen; the suitability of these choices is examined through examples in the subsequent chapter.

Example 2.4 Modelling the UK spread as an integrated process

In example 2.2 we modelled the spread of UK interest rates as a stationary, indeed AR(2), process. Here we consider modelling the spread assuming that it is an $I(1)$ process – i.e. we examine the behaviour of the SACF and SPACF of $w_t = \Delta x_t$. Table 2.5 provides these estimates up to $k = 12$ and suggests that, as both cut off at $k = 1$, either an AR(1) or an MA(1) process is identified. Estimation of the former obtains

$$w_t = -\underset{(0.0167)}{0.0045} + \underset{(0.039)}{0.199}\, w_{t-1} + \hat{a}_t, \quad \hat{\sigma} = 0.424$$

The residuals are effectively white noise, as they yield a portmanteau statistic of $Q(12) = 9.9$, and the mean of w_t is seen to be insignificantly different from zero. The spread can thus be modelled as an ARIMA(1,1,0) process without

Table 2.5 SACF and SPACF of the first difference of the UK spread

k	r_k	$s.e.(r_k)$	$\hat{\phi}_{kk}$	$s.e.\ \hat{\phi}_{kk}$
1	0.198	0.039	0.198	0.039
2	0.015	0.041	-0.025	0.039
3	-0.036	0.041	-0.036	0.039
4	0.022	0.041	0.039	0.039
5	0.037	0.041	0.026	0.039
6	-0.005	0.041	-0.020	0.039
7	-0.022	0.041	-0.016	0.039
8	-0.081	0.041	-0.074	0.039
9	-0.087	0.041	-0.062	0.039
10	-0.049	0.042	-0.016	0.039
11	-0.009	0.042	0.000	0.039
12	0.018	0.042	0.020	0.039

drift. In fact, fitting an ARIMA$(0,1,1)$ process obtained almost identical estimates, with θ estimated to be -0.196 and $\hat{\sigma} = 0.423$.

Example 2.5 Modelling the dollar/sterling exchange rate

Figure 2.13 plots daily observations of both the level and first differences of the dollar/sterling exchange rate from January 1993 to December 2005, a total of 3391 observations. The levels exhibit the wandering movement of a driftless random walk: the SACF has $r_1 = 0.997$, $r_{10} = 0.971$, $r_{20} = 0.946$, $r_{50} = 0.867$ and $r_{100} = 0.752$ and thus displays the slow, almost linear, decline typical of an $I(1)$ process (this is discussed further in chapter 3). The differences are stationary about zero and appear to show no discernible pattern. They are very close to being a white-noise process, the only significant sample autocorrelations in the first twenty lags being $r_3 = -0.035$, $r_{11} = -0.044$ and $r_{15} = -0.047$, the standard error here being 0.017.

Example 2.6 Modelling the FTA All Share index

Figure 2.14 plots monthly observations from January 1965 to December 2005 of the FTA All Share index and, as expected, shows the series to exhibit a prominent upward, but not linear, trend, with pronounced and persistent fluctuations about it, which increase in variability as the level of the series increases. This behaviour thus suggests a logarithmic transformation to be appropriate. The so transformed observations are also shown in figure 2.14; taking logarithms does indeed both linearise the trend and stabilise the variance.

(a)   Levels

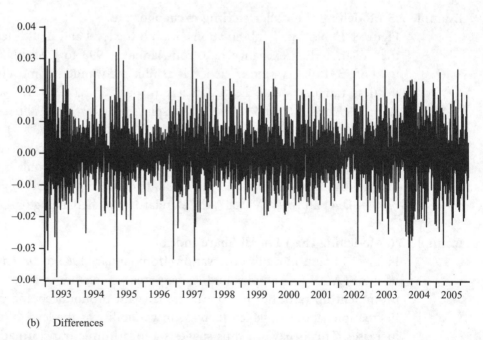

(b)   Differences

Figure 2.13 Dollar/sterling exchange rate (daily January 1993–December 2005)

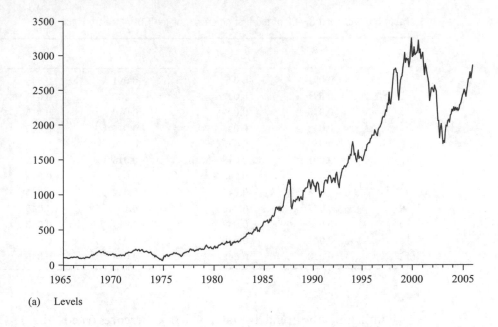

(a)   Levels

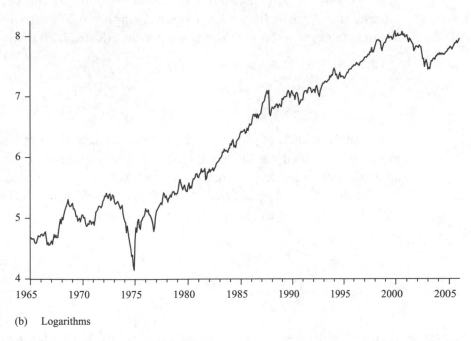

(b)   Logarithms

Figure 2.14 FTA All Share index (monthly 1965–2005)

Table 2.6 SACF and SPACF of the first difference of the FTA All Share index

k	r_k	$s.e.(r_k)$	$\hat{\phi}_{kk}$	$s.e.(\hat{\phi}_{kk})$
1	0.091	0.045	0.091	0.045
2	−0.091	0.047	−0.100	0.045
3	0.050	0.047	0.070	0.045
4	0.036	0.047	0.015	0.045
5	−0.080	0.047	−0.076	0.045
6	−0.001	0.048	−0.018	0.045
7	0.021	0.048	0.001	0.045
8	−0.038	0.048	−0.032	0.045
9	0.087	0.048	0.103	0.045
10	0.018	0.048	−0.019	0.045
11	−0.042	0.048	−0.021	0.045
12	0.010	0.048	0.014	0.045

Eliminating the trend by taking first differences yields the SACF and SPACF shown in table 2.6. Although several low-order r_k and $\hat{\phi}_{kk}$ are significant, they show no discernible pattern. Using a similar procedure to that outlined in example 2.3 obtained the following ARMA$(2, 2)$ process:

$$\Delta x_t = \underset{(0.74)}{1.81} - \underset{(0.124)}{0.953}\,\Delta x_{t-1} - \underset{(0.100)}{0.756}\,\Delta x_{t-2}$$

$$+ \hat{a}_t + \underset{(0.125)}{1.062}\,\hat{a}_{t-1} + \underset{(0.107)}{0.760}\,\hat{a}_{t-2}, \quad \hat{\sigma} = 5.75$$

The implied estimate of μ is 0.67, which, since Δx_t can be interpreted as the monthly growth of the index, implies an annual mean growth rate of approximately 8 per cent. Here x_t is defined as $100\log(P_t)$, where P_t is the level of the index. Thus, $\Delta x_t = 100\log(P_t/P_{t-1})$, which can be compared with the nominal return on the index analysed in example 2.3,

$$r_t = \frac{P_t + D_t - P_{t-1}}{P_{t-1}} \approx \log\left(\frac{P_t + D_t}{P_{t-1}}\right) = \log\left(\frac{P_t}{P_{t-1}}\right)$$

$$+ \log\left(1 + \frac{D_t}{P_t}\right) \approx \Delta x_t + \frac{D_t}{P_t}$$

i.e. the nominal return is equal to the growth of the index plus the dividend yield (the sample medians of the three series are 1.5 per cent, 1.1 per cent and 0.4 per cent per month, respectively). The dividend yield appears to be best modelled as an ARMA$(1, 3)$ process. Granger and Morris (1976) prove that if two independent series y_1 and y_2 are ARMA (p_i, q_i), $i = 1, 2$, processes then their sum is an ARMA (p, q) process, where

$$p \leq p_1 + p_2$$

and

$$q \leq \max(p_1 + q_2, q_1 + p_2)$$

The assumption of independence can be weakened to allow for contemporaneous correlation between the innovations of y_1 and y_2, which is the case for Δx and D/P, so that r_t should be generated by an ARMA process with orders $p \leq 4$ and $q \leq 6$, which is consistent with what was found in example 2.3.

2.8 Seasonal ARIMA modelling

Seasonalities have an important role to play in the analysis of financial time series, with applications ranging from the calendar anomalies literature to the intraday regularities observed at the micro-level of high-frequency data. ARIMA models offer a general framework for explicitly incorporating seasonal effects via seasonal differencing and multiplicative seasonal terms. This framework includes traditional seasonal adjustment models, such as the widely employed X-11 procedure, as special cases. For an extensive treatment of modelling seasonal time series, see, for example, Mills (1990, chap. 10). Here the application of seasonal ARIMA modelling is demonstrated through two examples.

Example 2.7 Seasonal differencing of intradaily absolute returns

High-frequency time series have been used extensively in recent years for uncovering intradaily regularities. Figure 2.15 shows the autocorrelation function of a series of absolute returns for the General Index of the Athens Stock Exchange (GIASE). The data, analysed in Markellos, Mills and Siriopoulos (2003), consists of 12,117 observations sampled at sixty-second intervals over the period 1 June to 10 September 1998, a total of seventy-three days. Absolute returns are important, since they can be used as a proxy for volatility and risk (see, for example, Granger and Ding, 1995). The autocorrelation function of GIASE absolute returns follows a strikingly regular U-shape pattern, implying a frequency of 166 observations (one day). Variations in the peak size of the U-shapes suggest the possibility of additional

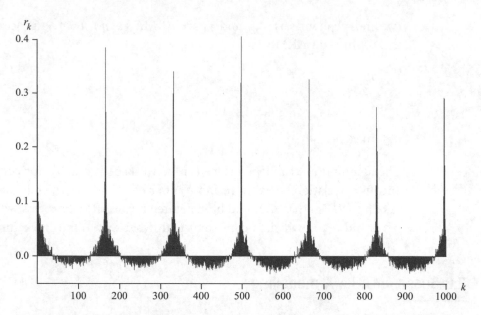

Figure 2.15 Autocorrelation function of the absolute returns of the GIASE (intradaily, 1 June–10 September 1998)

day-of-the-week effects. Similar patterns have been reported for several other markets, and a number of approaches have been proposed for deseasonalising intraday volatility, including seasonal multipliers, time-invariant polynomial approximations of market activity and smooth harmonic and polynomial function approximations. As shown in Figure 2.16, most of the seasonality in volatility is removed if we take 166-lag or one-day differences.

Example 2.8 Seasonal ARIMA modelling of spot energy price returns

Energy series are notorious for their strong seasonal components. Figure 2.17 shows average one-day-ahead spot electricity prices and logarithmic returns from the Nord Pool Exchange. The data cover the period 22 March 2002 to 3 December 2004 ($T = 988$) and are expressed in €/MWh. The plot of prices indicates random walk behaviour with abrupt and violent changes and spikes. Returns appear stationary, at least with respect to the first moment. The SACF and SPACF, shown in table 2.7, display weekly seasonality, with large positive autocorrelations appearing at the seasonal lags ($7k, k \geq 1$). Although seasonally differenced models can be incorporated into the ARIMA framework, the identification of models of this form can lead to a large number of parameters having to be fitted and may result in a model being difficult to interpret. Box and Jenkins (1976, chap. 9) recommend the estimation of the more restricted multiplicative ARIMA model,

Table 2.7 SACF and SPACF of Nord Pool spot electricity price returns

k	r_k	$s.e.(r_k)$	$\hat{\phi}_{kk}$	$s.e.(\hat{\phi}_{kk})$	$Q(k)$
1	−0.049	0.032	−0.049	0.032	2.34
2	−0.180	0.032	−0.183	0.032	34.46
3	−0.082	0.033	−0.105	0.032	41.14
4	−0.084	0.033	−0.136	0.032	48.12
5	−0.167	0.033	−0.235	0.032	75.94
6	0.031	0.034	−0.071	0.032	76.89
7	0.432	0.034	0.361	0.032	262.99
8	0.079	0.039	0.138	0.032	269.18
9	−0.213	0.040	−0.107	0.032	314.58
10	−0.077	0.041	−0.047	0.032	320.57
11	−0.039	0.041	−0.005	0.032	322.11
12	−0.174	0.041	−0.107	0.032	352.45
13	0.020	0.042	−0.055	0.032	352.85
14	0.376	0.042	0.166	0.032	494.55

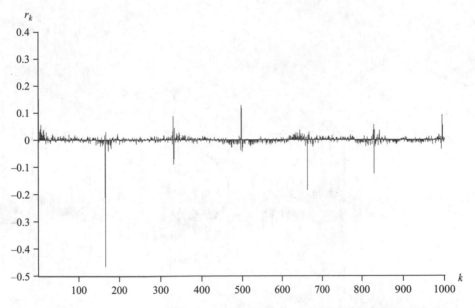

Figure 2.16 Autocorrelation function of the seasonally differenced absolute returns of the GIASE (intradaily, 1 June–10 September 1998)

which includes *seasonal autoregressive* (SAR) and *seasonal moving average* (SMA) terms. The purpose of these models is to allow the formation of products of lag polynomials. For example, estimating a MA(2) model for returns yields

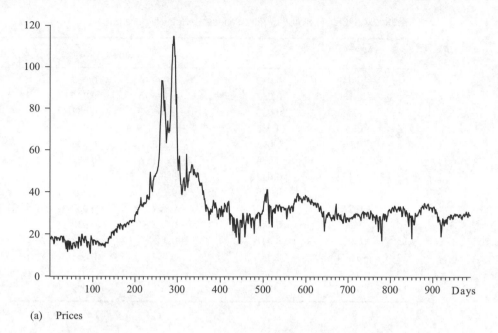

(a)   Prices

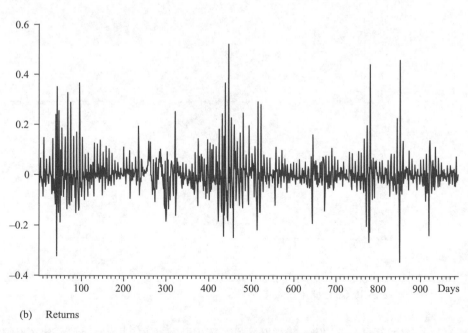

(b)   Returns

Figure 2.17 Nord Pool spot electricity prices and returns (daily averages, 22 March 2002–3 December 2004)

$$\Delta x_t = \left(1 - 0.129B - 0.248B^2\right)\hat{a}_t$$

Including a multiplicative seasonal MA(7) term produces

$$\Delta x_t = \left(1 - 0.156B - 0.166B^2\right)\left(1 + 0.305B^7\right)a_t$$
$$= \left(1 - 0.156B - 0.166B^2 + 0.305B^7 - 0.047B^8 - 0.051B^9\right)a_t$$

The estimated model is an MA(9) process with non-linear restrictions on the coefficients. The best fit to the series was given by

$$\left(1 - \underset{(0.006)}{0.982}\,B^7\right)\Delta x_t = \left(1 - \underset{(0.032)}{0.110}\,B - \underset{(0.031)}{0.090}\,B^2\right)\left(1 - \underset{(0.018)}{0.889}\,B^7\right)a_t$$

which is referred to as a multiplicative ARIMA $(0,1,2)(1,0,1)_7$ process.

2.9 Forecasting using ARIMA models

Given a realisation $\{x_t\}_{1-d}^{T}$ from a general ARIMA (p,d,q) process

$$\phi(B)\Delta^d x_t = \theta_0 + \theta(B)a_t$$

it is often the case that we wish to forecast a future value x_{T+h}. If we let

$$\alpha(B) = \phi(B)\Delta^d = \left(1 - \alpha_1 B - \alpha_2 B^2 - \cdots - \alpha_{p+d}B^{p+d}\right)$$

then a *minimum mean square error* (MMSE) forecast, denoted $f_{T,h}$, made at time T, is given by the conditional expectation

$$f_{T,\,h} = E\big(\alpha_1 x_{T+h-1} + \alpha_2 x_{T+h-2} + \cdots + \alpha_{p+d}x_{T+h-p-d} + \theta_0$$
$$+ a_{T+h} - \theta_1 a_{T+h-1} - \cdots - \theta_q a_{T+h-q}\big|x_T, x_{T-1}, \ldots\big)$$

Now

$$E\big(x_{T+j} \mid x_T, x_{T-1}, \ldots\big) = \begin{cases} x_{T+j}, & j \le 0 \\ f_{T,j}, & j > 0 \end{cases}$$

and

$$E\big(a_{T+j}\big|x_T, x_{T-1}, \ldots\big) = \begin{cases} a_{T+j}, & j \le 0 \\ 0, & j > 0 \end{cases}$$

so that, to evaluate $f_{T,h}$, all we need to do is (i) replace past expectations ($j \leq 0$) by known values, x_{T+j} and a_{T+j}, and (ii) replace future expectations ($j > 0$) by forecast values, $f_{T,j}$ and zero.

Three examples will illustrate the procedure. Consider first the AR(2) model $(1 - \phi_1 B - \phi_2 B^2)x_t = \theta_0 + a_t$, so that $\alpha(B) = (1 - \phi_1 B - \phi_2 B^2)$. Here

$$x_{T+h} = \phi_1 x_{T+h-1} + \phi_2 x_{T+h-2} + \theta_0 + a_{T+h}$$

and hence, for $h = 1$, we have

$$f_{T,1} = \phi_1 x_T + \phi_2 x_{T-1} + \theta_0$$

for $h = 2$

$$f_{T,2} = \phi_1 f_{T,1} + \phi_2 x_T + \theta_0$$

and for $h > 2$

$$f_{T,h} = \phi_1 f_{T,h-1} + \phi_2 f_{T,h-2} + \theta_0$$

An alternative expression for $f_{T,h}$ can be obtained by noting that

$$f_{T,h} = (\phi_1 + \phi_2)f_{T,h-1} - \phi_2(f_{T,h-1} - f_{T,h-2}) + \theta_0$$

from which, by repeated substitution, we obtain

$$f_{T,h} = (\phi_1 + \phi_2)^h x_T$$
$$- \phi_2 \sum_{j=0}^{h-1} (\phi_1 + \phi_2)^j (f_{T,h-1-j} - f_{T,h-2-j}) + \theta_0 \sum_{j=0}^{h-1} (\phi_1 + \phi_2)^j$$

where, by convention, we take $f_{T,0} = x_T$ and $f_{T,-1} = x_{T-1}$. Thus, for stationary processes ($\phi_1 + \phi_2 < 1, |\phi_2| < 1$), as $h \to \infty$,

$$f_{T,h} = \frac{\theta_0}{1 - \phi_1 - \phi_2} = E(x_t) = \mu$$

so that for large lead times the best forecast of a future observation is eventually the mean of the process.

Next consider the ARIMA(0,1,1) model $\Delta x_t = (1 - \theta B)a_t$. Here $\alpha(B) = (1 - B)$ and so

$$x_{T+h} = x_{T+h-1} + a_{T+h} - \theta a_{T+h-1}$$

For $h=1$ we have

$$f_{T,1} = x_T - \theta a_T$$

for $h=2$

$$f_{T,2} = f_{T,1} = x_T - \theta a_T$$

and, in general,

$$f_{T,h} = f_{T,h-1}, \quad h > 1$$

Thus, for all lead times, the forecasts from origin T will follow a straight line parallel to the time axis and passing through $f_{T,1}$. Note that, since

$$f_{T,h} = x_T - \theta a_T$$

and

$$a_T = (1 - B)(1 - \theta B)^{-1} x_T$$

the h-step ahead forecast can be written as

$$\begin{aligned} f_{T,h} &= (1 - \theta)(1 - \theta B)^{-1} x_T \\ &= (1 - \theta)\left(x_T + \theta x_{T-1} + \theta^2 x_{T-2} + \cdots\right) \end{aligned}$$

i.e. the forecast for all future values of x is an exponentially weighted moving average of current and past values.

Finally, consider the ARIMA(0,2,2) model $\Delta^2 x_t = (1 - \theta_1 B - \theta_2 B^2) a_t$, with $\alpha(B) = (1 - B)^2 = (1 - 2B + B^2)$

$$x_{T+h} = 2x_{T+h-1} - x_{T+h-2} + a_{T+h} - \theta_1 a_{T+h-1} - \theta_2 a_{T+h-2}$$

For $h=1$ we have

$$f_{T,1} = 2x_T - x_{T-1} - \theta_1 a_T - \theta_2 a_{T-1}$$

for $h=2$

$$f_{T,2} = 2f_{T,1} - x_T - \theta_2 a_T$$

for $h=3$

$$f_{T,3} = 2f_{T,2} - f_{T,1}$$

and thus, for $h \geq 3$

$$f_{T, h} = 2f_{T, h-1} - f_{T, h-2}$$

Hence, for all lead times, the forecasts from origin T will follow a straight line passing through the forecasts $f_{T,1}$ and $f_{T,2}$.

The h-step ahead forecast error for origin T is

$$e_{T, h} = x_{T+h} - f_{T, h} = a_{T+h} + \psi_1 a_{T+h-1} + \cdots + \psi_{h-1} a_{T+1}$$

where $\psi_1, \ldots \psi_{h-1}$ are the first $h-1$ ψ-weights in $\psi(B) = (B)\theta(B)$. The variance of this forecast error is then

$$V(e_{T, h}) = \sigma^2 (1 + \psi_1^2 + \psi_2^2 + \cdots + \psi_{h-1}^2) \tag{2.24}$$

The forecast error is therefore a linear combination of the unobservable future shocks entering the system after time T and, in particular, the one-step ahead forecast error is

$$e_{T, 1} = x_{T, 1} - f_{T, 1} = a_{T+1}$$

Thus, for an MMSE forecast, the one-step ahead forecast errors must be uncorrelated. h-step ahead forecasts made at different origins will not be uncorrelated, however, and neither will be forecasts for different lead times made at the same origin (see, for example, Box and Jenkins, 1976, appendix A5.1).

For the AR(2) example given above, we have $\psi_1 = \phi_1, \psi_2 = \phi_1^2 + \phi_2$ and, for $j > 2$, $\psi_j = \phi_1 \psi_{j-1} + \phi_2 \psi_{j-2}$. Since we are assuming stationarity, these ψ-weights converge absolutely. As absolute convergence $\left(\sum_{j=1}^{h} |\psi_j| < \infty \right)$ implies $\sum_{j=1}^{h} \psi_j^2 < \infty$, known as square-summability (Hamilton, 1994, chap. 3), $V(e_{T,h})$ converges to a finite value, which is the variance of the process about the ultimate forecast μ.

For the ARIMA(0,1,1) model, $\psi_j = 1 - \theta, j = 1, 2, \ldots$. Thus we have

$$V(e_{T, h}) = \sigma^2 (1 + (h - 1)(1 - \theta)^2)$$

which increases with h. Similarly, the ARIMA(0,2,2) model has ψ-weights given by $\psi_j = 1 + \theta_2 + j(1 - \theta_1 - \theta_2), j = 1, 2, \ldots$, and an h-step ahead forecast error variance of

$$V(e_{T,h}) = \sigma^2 \left(1 + (h-1)(1+\theta_2)^2 + \frac{1}{6}h(h-1)(2h-1)(1-\theta_1-\theta_2)^2 \right.$$
$$\left. + h(h-1)(1+\theta_2)(1-\theta_1-\theta_2) \right)$$

which again increases with h.

The examples in this section thus show how the degree of differencing, or order of integration, determines not only how successive forecasts are related to each other but also the behaviour of the associated error variances.

Example 2.9 ARIMA forecasting of financial time series

Here we examine the properties of ARIMA forecasts for some of the series analysed in the examples of this chapter.

Example 2.2 fitted an AR(2) model to the UK interest rate spread, yielding parameter estimates $\hat{\phi}_1 = 1.180, \hat{\phi}_2 = -0.216, \hat{\theta}_0 = 0.032$ and $\hat{\sigma} = 0.419$. With the last two observations being $x_{T-1} = -0.21$ and $x_T = -0.34$, forecasts are obtained as

$$f_{T,1} = 1.180x_T - 0.216x_{T-1} + 0.032 = -0.324$$
$$f_{T,2} = 1.180f_{T,1} - 0.216x_T + 0.032 = -0.277$$
$$f_{T,3} = 1.180f_{T,2} - 0.216f_{T,1} + 0.032 = -0.225$$

and so on. As h increases, the forecasts eventually tend to 0.963, the sample mean of the spread, although the large autoregressive root makes this convergence to the sample mean rather slow. The ψ-weights are given by

$$\psi_1 = \phi_1 = 1.180$$
$$\psi_2 = \phi_1^2 + \phi_2 = 1.176$$
$$\psi_3 = \phi_1^3 + 2\phi_1\phi_2 = 1.133$$
$$\psi_4 = \phi_1^4 + 3\phi_1^2\phi_2 + \phi_2^2 = 1.083$$

and, hence,

$$\psi_h = 1.180\psi_{h-1} - 0.216\psi_{h-2}$$

The forecast error variances are

$$V(e_{T,1}) = 0.419^2 = 0.176$$
$$V(e_{T,2}) = 0.419^2(1 + 1.180^2) = 0.421$$
$$V(e_{T,3}) = 0.419^2(1 + 1.180^2 + 1.176^2) = 0.664$$
$$V(e_{T,4}) = 0.419^2(1 + 1.180^2 + 1.176^2 + 1.133^2) = 0.890$$

the forecast error variances eventually converging to the sample variance of the spread, 4.09.

If, however, we use the ARIMA$(0,1,1)$ process of example 2.4 to model the spread, with $\hat{\theta} = 0.196$ and $\hat{\sigma} = 0.423$ (and setting the drift to zero), then our forecasts are (using the final residual $\hat{a}_T = -0.10$)

$$f_{T,1} = -0.34 - 0.196(-0.10) = -0.320$$

and, for $h > 1$,

$$f_{T,h} = f_{T,1} = -0.320$$

so that there is no tendency for the forecasts to converge to the sample mean or, indeed, to any other value. Furthermore, the forecast error variances are given by

$$V(e_{T,h}) = 0.423^2(1 + 0.646(h - 1)) = 0.179 + 0.116(h - 1)$$

which, of course, increase with h rather than tending to a constant. This example thus illustrates, within the forecasting context, the radically different properties of ARMA models that have, on the one hand, a unit autoregressive root and, on the other, a root that is large but less than unity.

The dollar/sterling exchange rate was found, in example 2.4, effectively to be a driftless random walk, which therefore implies, given an end-of-sample exchange rate of 1.719, that all future forecasts of the rate are that particular value, although the precision of the forecasts produced by the accompanying forecast error variance diminishes as the forecasting horizon increases: with σ estimated to be 0.008, we have $V(e_{T,h}) = 0.00006h$.

In example 2.6 we modelled the logarithms of the FTA All Share index as an ARIMA$(2,1,2)$ process. Since

$$\phi(B) = 1 + 0.953B + 0.756B^2$$

we have

$$\alpha(B) = 1 - 0.047B - 0.197B^2 - 0.756B^3$$

so that forecasts can be computed recursively by

$$f_{T,1} = 0.047x_T + 0.197x_{T-1} + 0.756x_{T-2} + 1.81 + 1.062a_T + 0.760a_{T-1}$$
$$f_{T,2} = 0.047f_{T,1} + 0.197x_T + 0.756x_{T-1} + 1.81 + 0.760a_T$$
$$f_{T,3} = 0.047f_{T,2} + 0.197f_{T,1} + 0.756x_T + 1.81$$
$$f_{T,4} = 0.047f_{T,3} + 0.197f_{T,2} + 0.756f_{T,1} + 1.81$$

and, for $h \geq 5$,

$$f_{T,h} = 0.047 f_{T,h-1} + 0.197 f_{T,h-2} + 0.756 f_{T,h-3} + 1.81$$

By computing the coefficients in the polynomial $\psi(B) = \alpha^{-1}(B)\,\theta(B)$ as

$$\psi(B) = 1 + 1.109B + 1.009B^2 + 1.022B^3 + 1.084B^4 + \cdots \qquad (2.25)$$

and using the estimate $\hat{\sigma} = 0.0575$, forecast error variances can then be computed using the formula (2.24); since the series is $I(1)$, these variances increase with h.

Additional interpretation of the nature of these forecasts is provided by the *eventual forecast function*, which is obtained by solving the difference equation implicit in the ARIMA(2,1,2) representation of x_t at time $T+h$ (see, for example, Mills, 1990, chap. 7.3, for a general development, and McKenzie, 1988, for further discussion):

$$x_{T+h} - 0.047 x_{T+h-1} - 0.197 x_{T+h-2} - 0.756 x_{T+h-3}$$
$$= 1.81 + a_{T+h} + 1.062 a_{T+h-1} + 0.760 a_{T+h-2}$$

At origin T, this difference equation has the solution

$$x_{T+h} = \sum_{i=1}^{3} b_i^{(T)} f_i(h) + 0.640 \sum_{j=T+1}^{T+h} \psi_{T+h-j} + \sum_{j=T+1}^{T+h} \psi_{T+h-j} a_j$$

where the ψs are as in (2.25) and the functions $f_1(h), \ldots, f_3(h)$ depend upon the roots of the polynomial $\alpha(B)$, which are unity and the pair of complex roots $-0.48 \pm 0.71i$. Hence, the solution can be written as

$$x_{T+h} = b_0 + b_1^{(T)} + b_2^{(T)}(-0.48 + 0.71i)^h + b_3^{(T)}(-0.48 - 0.71i)^h$$

where

$$b_0 = 0.640 \sum_{j=T+1}^{T+h} \psi_{T+h-j} + \sum_{j=T+1}^{T+h} \psi_{T+h-j} a_j$$

For a given origin T, the coefficients $b_j^{(T)}$, $j = 1, \ldots, 3$, are constants applying to all lead times h, but they change from one origin to the next, adapting themselves to the observed values of x_t. They can be obtained by solving a set of recursive equations containing the $f_i(h)$s, ψ_h and a_T.

Since the ψ_hs increase with h, b_0 imparts a deterministic drift into x_{T+h}, so that $b_0 + b_1^{(T)}$ gives the forecasted 'trend' of the series. Around this trend is a damped sine wave provided by the pair of complex roots, its damping factor, frequency and phase being functions of the process parameters (Box and Jenkins, 1976, pp. 58–63). These complex roots provide a damped cyclical AR(2) component with a damping factor of 0.87 and an average period of approximately three months.

3 Univariate linear stochastic models: testing for unit roots and alternative trend specifications

One of the earliest problems that faced time series analysts was the modelling of long-term persistence, or trends, in the observed data. A major motivation for studying the trend properties of time series was the belief that long-term components should be removed in order to uncover any remaining short-term regularities. Until the 1980s the dominant view was that these properties could be well described by the deterministic functions of a time index. This approach was pioneered by Jevons in the mid-nineteenth century and was popularised fifty years later by Persons with the celebrated 'Harvard A-B-C curve' methodology of stock market prediction (see Samuelson, 1987, and Morgan, 1990). At present, the dominant paradigm in economic and financial time series modelling builds upon the random walk model, first introduced into finance by Bachelier (1900), where, as we have seen in chapter 2, stochastic trends arise from the accumulation of random changes.

These two approaches constitute the main apparatus for the analysis of non-stationary time series – i.e. of time series that, broadly speaking, wander without bound and origin and do not have well-defined or finite unconditional moments. The first approach deals with *trend stationary processes*, a class of non-autonomous processes, which can be made stationary by removing a deterministic trend in the form of a polynomial in time. The second approach deals with random walks, which are produced from the accumulation (or integration in continuous time) of white-noise random variables. Random walks belong to the more general class of *unit root* or *integrated processes* that arise from the integration of stochastic variables. Unit root processes, symbolised as $I(d)$, where d denotes the order of integration, can be transformed to stationarity by taking d successive differences; they are therefore also known as *difference stationary processes*. 'Mixed' trend/difference stationary processes can be obtained by imposing deterministic time trends (drifts) on random walks. Knowing whether the non-stationarity in financial data is due to a time trend or a unit root is very important for choosing the appropriate transformation and statistical framework (for a comparison of the two processes, see Hamilton, 1994, chap. 15). In general, if there is no strong presumption in favour of trend stationarity then the random walk should be chosen, since it is likely to cause far fewer econometric problems (see Mills, 1990, chap. 11).

A considerable amount of research on random walks in finance, especially in option pricing theory, is undertaken in continuous-time using the framework of stochastic differential equations and stochastic calculus. The continuous-time counterparts of random walks are called Brownian motions or Wiener processes, which belong to the family of diffusions. Drifting random walks are called generalised Brownian motions/Wiener processes. An important generalisation is the class of Itô processes, where the expected drift and variance of a generalised Wiener process change as a function of the underlying stochastic variable and time. An important result of Itô, known as Itô's lemma, allows us to calculate explicitly the stochastic differential equation that governs arbitrary non-linear functions of an Itô process and time (see, for example, Rogers, 1997).

Although some early studies had provided informal evidence in support of the random walk model for economic and financial time series, such as Working (1934) for stock and commodity prices and Slutsky (1937) for business cycles it was not until Kendall's (1953) investigation that formal statistical evidence was provided to suggest that changes in financial prices were unpredictable on the basis of past information. Much subsequent research has been devoted to empirical investigations of issues related to random walks and predictability. It has been widely reported that returns on financial prices are essentially linearly unpredictable on the basis of historical information, which is consistent with an early version of the efficient market hypothesis in finance (e.g. see Cootner, 1964). The random walk has gained its present popularity on the basis of theoretical rather than empirical arguments, however. More specifically, it was demonstrated that random walks were the empirical consequence of many important theoretical models from the rational expectations family (e.g. with respect to financial market efficiency, hysteresis models of unemployment, the permanent consumption hypothesis, etc.). A considerable amount of research has since been devoted to exploring the validity and consequences of random walks in finance under rational expectations and market efficiency: for example, futures and stock prices (Samuelson, 1965, 1973), dividends and earnings (Kleidon, 1986a), spot and forward exchange rates (Meese and Singleton, 1982) and interest rates (Campbell and Shiller, 1987). This research has also concentrated on examining the validity of the stationarity assumptions made by rational expectations models when solving for the expected future values of fundamental variables. A very important reason for the popularity of the random walk model, especially in finance, was the fact that, unlike the trend stationary process, it was consistent with the intuition that uncertainty increases the further we look into the future – i.e. that risk increases with the investment horizon.

The random walk debate placed many doubts upon empirical and theoretical work based on business cycle theories that distinguished between cyclical components and the determinants of the trend rate of growth. It was also demonstrated that 'pure' random walk behaviour was neither a necessary nor a sufficient condition for rationally determined financial prices (e.g. LeRoy, 1973; Lucas, 1978) and that theoretical models not based on random walks may be better approximations than the standard rational expectations hypothesis (e.g. the noise trading model of Frankel and Froot, 1988). Nevertheless, the majority of theoretical models in the past thirty years, especially in finance, have been based on some variation of the random walk, rather than on a trend stationary model.

Notwithstanding this theoretical preference, the focus of this chapter is on developing a set of techniques for determining the order of integration of a time series. Throughout this development, we emphasise the importance of the chosen alternative hypothesis to the null of a unit root, in particular whether the alternative is that of a constant mean, a linear trend, a segmented trend or a non-linear trend. The importance of these models to finance is demonstrated through a sequence of examples.

3.1 Determining the order of integration of a time series

As shown in the previous chapter, the order of integration, d, is a crucial determinant of the properties that a time series exhibits. If we restrict ourselves to the most common values of zero and one for d, so that x_t is either $I(0)$ or $I(1)$, then it is useful to bring together the properties of such processes.

If x_t is $I(0)$, which we will denote $x_t \sim I(0)$ even though such a notation has been used previously to denote the distributional characteristics of a series, then, assuming for convenience that it has zero mean,

(i)   the variance of x_t is finite and does not depend on t;

(ii) the innovation a_t has only a temporary effect on the value of x_t;

(iii) the expected length of times between crossings of $x = 0$ is finite – i.e. x_t fluctuates around its mean of zero; and

(iv) the autocorrelations, ρ_k, decrease steadily in magnitude for large enough k, so that their sum is finite.

If $x_t \sim I(1)$ with $x_0 = 0$, then

(i)   the variance of x_t goes to infinity as t goes to infinity;

(ii) an innovation a_t has a permanent effect on the value of x_t because x_t is the sum of all previous innovations: see, e.g., equation (2.16);

(iii) the expected time between crossings of $x = 0$ is infinite; and

(iv) the autocorrelations $\rho_k \to 1$ for all k as t goes to infinity.

The fact that a time series is non-stationary is often self-evident from a plot of the series. Determining the actual form of non-stationarity, however, is not so easy from just a visual inspection, and an examination of the SACFs for various differences may be required.

To see why this may be so, recall that a stationary AR(p) process requires that all roots g_i in

$$\phi(B) = (1 - g_1 B)(1 - g_2 B) \ldots (1 - g_p B)$$

are such that $|g_i| < 1$. Now suppose that one of them – g_1, say – approaches one, i.e. $g_1 = 1 - \delta$, where δ is a small positive number. Recalling the solution to the difference equation (2.6), the autocorrelations will then be dominated by $A_1 g_1^k$, since

$$\rho_k = A_1 g_1^k + A_2 g_2^k + \cdots + A_p g_p^k \cong A_1 g_1^k$$

as all other terms will go to zero more rapidly. Furthermore, as g_1 is close to one, the exponential decay $A_1 g_1^k$ will be slow and almost linear, since

$$A_1 g_1^k = A_1 (1 - \delta)^k = A_1 \left(1 - \delta k + \delta^2 k^2 - \cdots\right) \cong A_1 (1 - \delta k)$$

Hence, the failure of the SACF to die down quickly is therefore an indication of non-stationarity, its behaviour tending to be that of a slow, linear decline. If the original series x_t is found to be non-stationary, the first difference Δx_t is then analysed. If Δx_t is still non-stationary, the next difference $\Delta^2 x_t$ is analysed, the procedure being repeated until a stationary difference is found, although it is seldom the case in practice that d exceeds two.

Sole reliance on the SACF can sometimes lead to problems of *over-differencing*. Although further differences of a stationary series will themselves be stationary, overdifferencing can lead to serious difficulties. Consider the stationary MA(1) process $x_t = (1 - \theta B)a_t$. The first difference of this is

$$
\begin{aligned}
\Delta x_t &= (1 - B)(1 - \theta B)a_t \\
&= (1 - (1 + \theta)B + \theta B^2)a_t \\
&= (1 - \theta_1 B - \theta_2 B^2)a_t
\end{aligned}
$$

We now have a more complicated model containing two parameters rather than one, and, moreover, one of the roots of the $\theta(B)$ polynomial is unity since $\theta_1 + \theta_2 = 1$. The model is therefore not invertible, so that the AR(∞) representation does not exist, and attempts to estimate this model will almost inevitably run into difficulties.

Note also that the variance of x_t is given by

$$
V(x) = \gamma_0(x) = (1 + \theta^2)\sigma^2
$$

whereas the variance of $w_t = \Delta x_t$ is given by

$$
\begin{aligned}
V(w) = \gamma_0(w) &= (1 + (1 + \theta)^2 + \theta^2)\sigma^2 \\
&= 2(1 + \theta + \theta^2)\sigma^2
\end{aligned}
$$

Hence,

$$
V(w) - V(x) = (1 + \theta)^2\sigma^2 > 0
$$

thus showing that the variance of the overdifferenced process will be larger than that of the original MA(1) process. The behaviour of the sample variances associated with different values of d can provide a useful means of deciding the appropriate level of differencing: the sample variances will decrease until a stationary sequence has been found, but will tend to increase on overdifferencing. This will not always be the case, however, and a comparison of sample variances for successive differences of a series is best employed as a useful auxiliary method for determining the appropriate value of d.

3.2 Testing for a unit root

3.2.1 An introduction to unit root tests

Given the importance of choosing the correct order of differencing, it is clear that we require a formal testing procedure to determine d. To introduce the issues involved in developing such a procedure, we begin by considering the simplest case, that of the zero-mean AR(1) process with normal innovations:

$$x_t = \phi x_{t-1} + a_t, \quad t = 1, 2, \ldots, T \tag{3.1}$$

where $a_t \sim NID(0, \sigma^2)$ and $x_0 = 0$. The OLS estimate of ϕ is given by

$$\hat{\phi}_T = \frac{\sum_{t=1}^{T} x_{t-1} x_t}{\sum_{t=1}^{T} x_{t-1}^2}$$

and, from the algebra of OLS, we have

$$(\hat{\phi}_T - \phi) = \frac{\sum_{t=1}^{T} x_{t-1} a_t}{\sum_{t=1}^{T} x_{t-1}^2}$$

If the true value of ϕ is less than one in absolute value, then, from Hamilton (1994, p. 216),

$$\sqrt{T}(\hat{\phi}_T - \phi) \overset{a}{\sim} N\left(0, \sigma^2 E\left(x_{t-1}^2\right)^{-1}\right)$$

Since

$$E\left(x_{t-1}^2\right) = E\left(\sum_{i=0}^{\infty} \phi^i a_{t-i}\right)^2 = \sigma^2 \sum_{i=0}^{\infty} \phi^{2i} = \sigma^2 / \left(1 - \phi^2\right)$$

it follows that

$$\sqrt{T}(\hat{\phi}_T - \phi) \overset{a}{\sim} N\left(0, \left(1 - \phi^2\right)\right)$$

from which hypothesis tests concerning ϕ may be constructed.

When $\phi = 1$ there is an immediate problem with this result, however, for it seems to imply that $\sqrt{T}(\hat{\phi}_T - \phi)$ has a zero variance, which is not very helpful for hypothesis testing! To obtain a non-degenerate asymptotic distribution for $\hat{\phi}_T$ when $\phi = 1$, we need to scale $(\hat{\phi}_T - 1)$ by T rather than $\sqrt{T}$. To see why this is so, we need to investigate the distributional properties of the two sums making up the ratio

$$(\hat{\phi}_T - 1) = \frac{\sum_{t=1}^{T} x_{t-1} a_t}{\sum_{t=1}^{T} x_{t-1}^2}$$

When $\phi = 1$, (3.1) is the random walk

$$x_t = \sum_{s=1}^{t} a_s$$

from which it follows that $x_t \sim N(0, \sigma^2 t)$. Note also that

$$x_t^2 = (x_{t-1} + a_t)^2 = x_{t-1}^2 + 2x_{t-1}a_t + a_t^2$$

implying that

$$x_{t-1}a_t = (1/2)\left(x_t^2 - x_{t-1}^2 - a_t^2\right)$$

Thus, the numerator of the ratio can be written as

$$\sum_{t=1}^{T} x_{t-1}a_t = (1/2)\left(x_T^2 - x_0^2\right) - (1/2)\sum_{t=1}^{T} a_t^2$$

Recalling that $x_0 = 0$, we then have

$$\left(\frac{1}{\sigma^2 T}\right)\sum_{t=1}^{T} x_{t-1}a_t = \left(\frac{1}{2}\right)\left(\frac{x_T}{\sigma\sqrt{T}}\right)^2 - \left(\frac{1}{2\sigma^2}\right)\left(\frac{1}{T}\right)\sum_{t=1}^{T} a_t^2$$

$x_T/(\sigma\sqrt{T})$ is $N(0,1)$, so its square is χ_1^2, and $T^{-1}\sum_{t=1}^{T} a_t^2$ converges in probability to σ^2. Thus,

$$T^{-1}\sum_{t=1}^{T} x_{t-1}a_t \overset{a}{\sim} (1/2)\sigma^2(X - 1)$$

where $X \sim \chi_1^2$.

Since $E(x_t^2) = \sigma^2 t$, it follows that the expectation of the denominator of the ratio is

$$E\left[\sum_{t=1}^{T} x_{t-1}^2\right] = \sigma^2 \sum_{t=1}^{T} (t - 1) = \sigma^2(T - 1)T/2$$

which has to be scaled by T^{-2} in order to converge to a finite value:

$$E\left[T^{-2}\sum_{t=1}^{T} x_{t-1}^2\right] = (\sigma^2/2)(1 - 1/T) \rightarrow \sigma^2/2$$

as $T \rightarrow \infty$. Hence,

$$T(\hat{\phi}_T - 1) = \frac{T^{-1}\sum_{t=1}^{T} x_{t-1}a_t}{T^{-2}\sum_{t=1}^{T} x_{t-1}^2} \tag{3.2}$$

has an asymptotic distribution that is a ratio of a (scaled) χ_1^2 variable to a non-standard distribution. But what is this distribution? To answer this question, let us consider the limiting distribution of the standardised variable

$x_t/\sigma\sqrt{T}$. For this, it is convenient to map the increasing interval from 0 to T into the fixed interval $[0,1]$ so that results will be invariant to the actual value of T. We thus define the random *step function* $R_T(r)$ as follows. Denote $[rT]$ as the integer part of rT, where $r \in [0,1]$, and define

$$R_T(r) = x_{[rT]}(r)/\sigma\sqrt{T} = x_{t-1}/\sigma\sqrt{T}$$

In effect, the interval $[0,1]$ is divided into $T+1$ parts at $r = 0, 1/T, 2/T, \ldots, 1$ and $R_T(r)$ is constant at values of r but with jumps at successive integers. As $T \to \infty$, $R_T(r)$ becomes increasingly 'dense' on $[0,1]$. In the limit, $R_T(r)$ *weakly converges* to *standard Brownian motion* (or the *Weiner process*), $W(r)$, denoted

$$R_T(r) \Rightarrow W(r) \sim N(0,r)$$

Hamilton (1994, chap. 17), Banerjee *et al.* (1993), and Davidson (2006b) provide detailed treatments of this result, which is known as *Donsker's theorem* but often referred to as the *functional central limit theorem*. Three implications of the theorem are

$$W(1) \sim N(0,1)$$
$$\sigma.W(r) \sim N(0,\sigma^2 r)$$
$$[W(r)]^2/r \sim \chi_1^2$$

A further implication is that, if $f(\cdot)$ is a continuous functional on $[0,1]$, then, through the *continuous mapping theorem*,

$$f(R_T(r)) \Rightarrow f(W(r))$$

We are now in a position to derive the asymptotic distribution of the denominator of (3.2) (see Phillips, 1987a, theorem 3.1):

$$T^{-2}\sum_{t=1}^{T} x_{t-1}^2 = (\sigma^2 T^{-1})\sum_{t=1}^{T}\left(\frac{x_{t-1}}{\sigma\sqrt{T}}\right)^2 = \sigma^2\sum_{t=1}^{T} T^{-1}\left(R_T\left(\frac{t-1}{T}\right)\right)^2$$

$$= \sigma^2\sum_{t=1}^{T}\int_{(t-1)/T}^{t/T} [R_T(r)]^2 dr = \sigma^2\int_0^1 [R_T(r)]^2 dr$$

$$\Rightarrow \sigma^2\int_0^1 [W(r)]^2 dr$$

Note also that, because $[W(1)]^2$ is distributed as χ_1^2, the numerator of (3.2) can be written as

$$T^{-1}\sum_{t=1}^{T} x_{t-1}a_t \Rightarrow (1/2)\sigma^2\big([W(1)]^2-1\big)$$

Hence,

$$T(\hat{\phi}_T - 1) \Rightarrow \frac{(1/2)\big([W(1)]^2-1\big)}{\int_0^1 [W(r)]^2 \mathrm{d}r} \tag{3.3}$$

The denominator of (3.3) must be positive. Since $[W(1)]^2$ is χ_1^2 and the probability that a χ_1^2 variable is less than unity is 0.68, the probability that $T(\hat{\phi}_T - 1)$ is negative approaches 0.68 as T becomes large. Thus, in two-thirds of samples generated by a random walk, the estimate $\hat{\phi}_T$ will be less than unity. Furthermore, when $[W(1)]^2$ is large so will be the denominator of (3.3), implying that the limiting distribution of $T(\hat{\phi}_T - 1)$ will be skewed to the left, with negative values twice as likely as positive values. Note that, from Phillips (1987a),

$$(1/2)\big([W(1)]^2-1\big) = \int_0^1 W(r)\mathrm{d}W(r)$$

so an equivalent expression is

$$T(\hat{\phi}_T - 1) \Rightarrow \frac{\int_0^1 W(r)\mathrm{d}W(r)}{\int_0^1 [W(r)]^2 \mathrm{d}r}$$

A conventional way of testing the null hypothesis $\phi = 1$ is to construct the t-statistic

$$t_\phi = \frac{(\hat{\phi}_T - 1)}{\hat{\sigma}_{\hat{\phi}_T}} = \frac{(\hat{\phi}_T - 1)}{\big(s_T^2 \big/ \sum_{t=1}^{T} x_{t-1}^2\big)^{1/2}} \tag{3.4}$$

where

$$\hat{\sigma}_{\hat{\phi}_T} = \big(s_T^2 \big/ \sum_{t=1}^{T} x_{t-1}^2\big)^{1/2}$$

is the usual OLS standard error for $\hat{\phi}_T$ and s_T^2 is the OLS estimate of σ^2:

$$s_T^2 = \sum_{t=1}^{T} \big(x_t - \hat{\phi}_T x_{t-1}\big)^2 \big/ (T-1)$$

The distribution of t_ϕ does not have a limiting normal distribution when $\phi = 1$. To find the appropriate limiting distribution, rewrite (3.4) as

$$\tau = (T/s_T)(\hat{\phi}_T - 1)\left(T^{-2}\sum_{t=1}^{T} x_{t-1}^2\right)^{1/2}$$

where, following Fuller (1996), we denote the statistic as τ to distinguish it from the conventional t-statistic. Substituting from (3.2) yields

$$\tau = \frac{T^{-1}\sum_{t=1}^{T} x_{t-1}a_t}{s_T\left(T^{-2}\sum_{t=1}^{T} x_{t-1}^2\right)^{1/2}}$$

Since s_T^2 is a consistent estimator of σ^2, it then follows from our previous results that

$$\tau \Rightarrow \frac{(1/2)\sigma^2([W(1)]^2-1)}{\sigma\left(\sigma^2 \int_0^1 [W(r)]^2 dr\right)^{1/2}} = \frac{(1/2)([W(1)]^2-1)}{\left(\int_0^1 [W(r)]^2 dr\right)^{1/2}} = \frac{\int_0^1 W(r)dW(r)}{\left(\int_0^1 [W(r)]^2 dr\right)^{1/2}} \quad (3.5)$$

An alternative test of the null hypothesis results from the fact that $\hat{\phi}_T$ is a *superconsistent* estimate of $\phi = 1$. Dividing (3.2) by $\sqrt{T}$ yields

$$\sqrt{T}(\hat{\phi}_T - 1) = \frac{T^{-3/2}\sum_{t=1}^{T} x_{t-1}a_t}{T^{-2}\sum_{t=1}^{T} x_{t-1}^2}$$

The numerator converges to $(1/2)T^{-1/2}\sigma^2(X - 1)$. Since X, being χ_1^2, has a variance of two, the variance of this numerator is of order T^{-1}, so that the numerator converges in probability to zero. Hence,

$$\sqrt{T}(\hat{\phi}_T - 1) \xrightarrow{p} 0$$

where $\xrightarrow{p}$ denotes convergence in probability (for a formal definition, see Hamilton, 1994, chap. 7.1). This result allows $T(\hat{\phi}_T - 1)$, which has the limiting distribution given by (3.3), to be used on its own as a test statistic without needing to calculate its standard error. These tests, particularly τ, are known as *Dickey–Fuller* (DF) *tests*, after the original analyses in Fuller (1976) and Dickey and Fuller (1979).

To make hypothesis testing operational, the limiting distributions (3.3) and (3.5) have to be tabulated, and critical values computed. This is typically done by Monte Carlo simulation (see Hendry, 1995, chap. 3.6, for a discussion of Monte Carlo techniques). To tabulate the limiting distribution (3.3), for example, a_t could be simulated by drawing T pseudo-random $N(0,1)$ variates and calculating

$$\frac{T\sum_{t=1}^{T}\left(\sum_{s=0}^{t-1} a_s\right)a_t}{\sum_{t=1}^{T}\left(\sum_{s=0}^{t-1} a_s\right)^2}$$

Repeating this calculation n times and compiling the results into an empirical probability distribution will yield a close approximation to the limiting distribution. Simulated limiting distributions of $T(\hat{\phi}_T - 1)$ and τ are shown in figures 3.1 and 3.2, using $\sigma^2 = 1$, $T = 1000$ and $n = 25,000$. These distributions are computed as smoothed functions of the histogram constructed from the simulated series using a normal kernel. Silverman (1986) provides an excellent reference to this technique, which is available in several econometric software packages. The parameter that controls the amount of smoothing that is carried out was chosen to show the limiting distributions to be as smooth as possible whilst retaining their distinctive shapes relative to the standard normal.

Figure 3.1 shows clearly the skewed limiting distribution of $T(\hat{\phi}_T - 1)$. Critical values are available from many sources (see, for example, Hamilton,

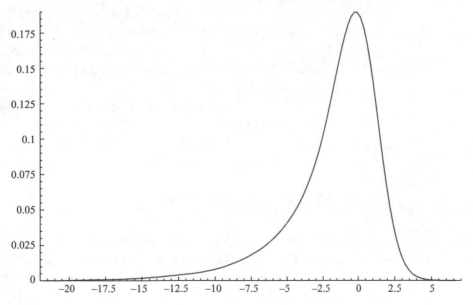

Figure 3.1   Simulated limiting distribution of $T(\hat{\phi}_T - 1)$

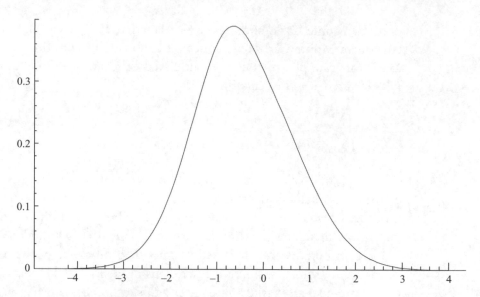

Figure 3.2   Simulated limiting distribution of τ

1994, table B.5 case 1, and Banerjee *et al.*, 1993, table 4.1a, as well as the original source: Fuller, 1976, p. 371). For example, for T as large as it is in these simulations, the 5 per cent, 2.5 per cent and 1 per cent critical values are -8.1, -10.5 and -13.8, respectively. Figure 3.2 shows that the limiting distribution of τ is approximately standard normal but shifted to the left by roughly 0.3: the large T 5 per cent, 2.5 per cent and 1 per cent critical values for τ are -1.95, -2.23 and -2.58, rather than the $N(0,1)$ critical values of -1.65, -1.96 and -2.33.

More extensive critical values than those given in standard tables are available in most econometric packages. These are obtained using the *response surfaces* computed by MacKinnon (1991). For example, 1 per cent critical values of τ for a given sample size T can be calculated from

$$\tau_{.01}(T) = -2.5658 - 1.960T^{-1} - 10.04T^{-2}$$

and response surfaces for 5 per cent and 10 per cent critical values are reported in MacKinnon (1991, table 1) and repeated in Banerjee *et al.* (1993, table 7.2). Much more extensive simulations carried out in MacKinnon (1996) also allow p-values (i.e. marginal significance levels) to be calculated for a wide range of sample sizes.

3.2.2 Extensions to the Dickey–Fuller test

The case discussed in the previous section has the merit of being simple but is not particularly realistic, for it implies that the alternative to a driftless random walk is a stationary AR(1) process about a *zero* mean. A more sensible alternative would be for the AR(1) process to fluctuate about a non-zero mean – i.e. that we have the model

$$x_t = \theta_0 + \phi x_{t-1} + a_t, \quad t = 1, 2, \ldots, T \tag{3.6}$$

in which the unit root null is parameterised as $\theta_0 = 0$, $\phi = 1$. The presence of an intercept in (3.6) alters the distribution of the test statistics: rather than (3.3) and (3.5), we have (see, for example, Hamilton, 1994, chap. 17.4)

$$T(\hat{\phi}_T - 1) \Rightarrow \frac{(1/2)\left([W(1)]^2 - 1\right) - W(1) \cdot \int_0^1 W(r)\mathrm{d}r}{\int_0^1 [W(r)]^2 \mathrm{d}r - \left(\int_0^1 W(r)\mathrm{d}r\right)^2} \tag{3.7}$$

and

$$\tau_\mu \Rightarrow \frac{(1/2)\left([W(1)]^2 - 1\right) - W(1) \cdot \int_0^1 W(r)\mathrm{d}r}{\left\{\int_0^1 [W(r)]^2 \mathrm{d}r - \left(\int_0^1 W(r)\mathrm{d}r\right)^2\right\}^{1/2}}$$

This statistic is denoted τ_μ to emphasise that a non-zero mean is allowed for in the regression (3.6). Figure 3.3 presents the simulated distribution of

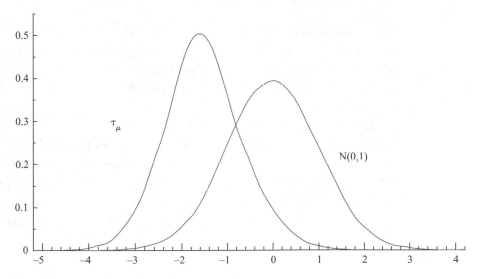

Figure 3.3   Simulated limiting distribution of τ_μ

τ_μ, using the same settings of σ^2, T and n as before, and with a standard normal superimposed for comparison. With the non-zero mean, the distribution under the unit root null deviates further from a standard normal than when the mean is zero (compare with figure 3.2). The large T 5 per cent, 2.5 per cent and 1 per cent critical values are now -2.86, -3.12 and -3.43, and again critical values for other sample sizes can be obtained from response surfaces, e.g.

$$\tau_{\mu,.01}(T) = -3.4335 - 5.999T^{-1} - 29.25T^{-2}$$

These statistics actually concentrate on testing the null hypothesis $\phi = 1$, *conditional upon* the maintained assumption that $\theta_0 = 0$. It might seem more natural to test the joint hypothesis $\theta_0 = 0$, $\phi = 1$, which can be done by constructing, for example, a conventional Wald test. Under this null the model is the driftless random walk, so that $\sum_{t=1}^{T} \Delta x_t^2$ can be regarded as the *restricted residual sum of squares*, which should be compared to the *unrestricted residual sum of squares*

$$\sum_{t=1}^{T} \hat{a}_t^2 = \sum_{t=1}^{T} \left(x_t - \hat{\theta}_0 - \hat{\phi} x_{t-1} \right)^2$$

by constructing the statistic

$$\Phi = \frac{\left(\sum_{t=1}^{T} \Delta x_t^2 - \sum_{t=1}^{T} \hat{a}_t^2 \right) / 2}{\sum_{t=1}^{T} \hat{a}_t^2 \Big/ (T-2)}$$

Rather than being distributed as $F(2, T-2)$, however, the limiting distribution of Φ is tabulated in Dickey and Fuller (1981) (again, also in Hamilton, 1994, table B.7 case 2, and Banerjee *et al.*, 1993, table 4.5(a)). For example, for large T, 5 per cent and 1 per cent critical values of Φ are 4.59 and 6.43, rather than 2.99 and 4.60.

All the simulated distributions have been computed using normal innovations. If the innovations are not normal but have finite variance, the distributions are valid as long as T is large, which will typically be the case with financial applications (the infinite variance case is considered briefly in section 7 of this chapter). A more important generalisation is to allow the innovations to be serially correlated. Suppose that x_t is generated by the AR(p) process

$$\left(1 - \phi_1 B - \phi_2 B^2 - \cdots - \phi_p B^p \right) x_t = \theta_0 + a_t$$

or

$$x_t = \theta_0 + \sum_{i=1}^{p} \phi_i x_{t-i} + a_t \qquad (3.8)$$

A more convenient representation is obtained by defining

$$\phi = \sum_{i=1}^{p} \phi_i$$

$$\delta_i = -\sum_{j=i+1}^{p-1} \phi_j, \quad i = 1, 2, \ldots, p-1$$

so that (3.8) can be written, with $k = p - 1$,

$$x_t = \theta_0 + \phi x_{t-1} + \sum_{i=1}^{k} \delta_i \Delta x_{t-i} + a_t \qquad (3.9)$$

The null of one unit root is thus $\phi = \sum_{i=1}^{p} \phi_i = 1$. OLS provides consistent estimates of (3.8), and a test of $\phi = 1$ can be constructed as

$$\tau_\mu = \frac{\hat{\phi}_T - 1}{se(\hat{\phi}_T)}$$

where $se(\hat{\phi}_T)$ is the OLS standard error attached to the estimate $\hat{\phi}_T$. This statistic is also denoted τ_μ because it has the *same* limiting distribution as the statistic obtained from the AR(1) model (3.6), although it is often referred to as the *augmented Dickey–Fuller* (ADF) test (Dickey and Fuller, 1979; see Hamilton, 1994, chap. 17.7, for a detailed derivation). Similarly, the Wald Φ test has an identical distribution to that obtained in the AR(1) case. On the other hand, it is $T(\hat{\phi}_T - 1)/(1 - \delta_1 - \cdots - \delta_k)$ that is distributed as in (3.7).

The above analysis has implicitly assumed that the AR order p is known, so that we are certain that x_t is generated by a pth-order autoregression. If the generating process is an ARMA(p, q), then Said and Dickey (1985) show that the τ_μ statistic obtained from estimating the model

$$x_t = \theta_0 + \phi x_{t-1} + \sum_{i=1}^{k} \delta_i \Delta x_{t-i} + u_t - \sum_{j=1}^{q} \theta_j u_{t-j}$$

has the same limiting distribution as that calculated from (3.9). The problem here, of course, is that p and q are assumed known, and this is unlikely to be the case in practice. When p and q are unknown, Said and Dickey (1984) show that, under the null hypothesis of a unit root, the test statistic obtained from (3.8) can still be used if k, the number of lags of Δx_t introduced as regressors, increases with the sample size at a controlled rate of $T^{1/3}$. With typical financial data, which do not contain pronounced seasonal variation, the results of Schwert (1987) and Diebold and Nerlove (1990) suggest that setting k at $[T^{0.25}]$ should work well in practice, where $[\cdot]$ again denotes the operation of taking the integer part of the argument. This adjustment is necessary because, as the sample size increases, the effects of the correlation structure of the residuals on the shape of the distribution of τ_μ become more precise. Any choice of k will involve questions of test size and power and of trade-offs between the two, however, and we return to this issue in section 4.

3.2.3 Non-parametric tests for a unit root

An alternative approach to dealing with autocorrelation in a_t, and which also allows for heterogeneity of variance, has been proposed by Phillips (1987a, 1987b; see also Phillips and Perron, 1988). Rather than including extra lags of Δx_t to ensure that the errors in (3.8) are white noise, the idea here is to modify the statistics after estimation of the simple model – (3.6), say – in order to take into account the effects of autocorrelated errors and to enable the same limiting distributions, and hence critical values, to apply.

Consider again the model

$$x_t = \theta_0 + \phi x_{t-1} + a_t, \quad t = 1, 2, \ldots, T \tag{3.10}$$

but we now place the following set of conditions on the stochastic process $\{a_t\}_1^\infty$:

$$E(a_t) = 0 \quad \text{for all } t \tag{3.11a}$$

$$\sup_t E(|a_t|^\beta) < \infty \quad \text{for some } \beta > 2 \tag{3.11b}$$

$$\sigma_S^2 = \lim_{T \to \infty} E(T^{-1} S_T^2) \text{ exists and is positive, where } S_T = \sum_{t=1}^{T} a_t \tag{3.11c}$$

Condition (3.11b) is sufficient to ensure the existence of the variance and at least one higher-order moment of a_t. Normality entails that all moments of finite order exist, and, as we shall see in later chapters, the existence of fourth moments is often required when dealing with financial time series. $E\left(|a_t|^\beta\right)$

is not assumed to be constant, however, so that heterogeneity is allowed. Condition (3.11c) is needed to ensure non-degenerate limiting distributions, while (3.11a) is the conventional one of ensuring that all conditional means are constant, namely zero. A fourth condition is necessary, which requires that

a_t is *strong mixing*, with mixing numbers α_m that satisfy $\sum_{m=1}^{\infty} \alpha_m^{1-2/\beta} < \infty$

$$(3.11d)$$

Strong mixing is related to ergodicity, which was introduced briefly in chapter 2, and implies ergodicity if a_t is stationary, which it need not be. The mixing numbers a_m measure the strength and extent of temporal dependence within the sequence a_t, and condition (3.11d) ensures that dependence declines as the length of memory, represented by m, increases. Strong mixing allows a considerable degree of serial dependence in a_t, but there is a trade-off between the extent of such dependence and the presence of heterogeneity (i.e. the probability of outliers), as is seen by the fact that the same coefficient β is present in both conditions (3.11b) and (3.11d). The overall set of conditions (3.11), which are described in detail in Phillips (1987a), may be characterised by the statement that a_t is *weakly dependent*.

If a_t is stationary in (3.10), then

$$\sigma_S^2 = E(a_1^2) + 2\sum_{j=2}^{\infty} E(a_1 a_j)$$

For example, if a_t is the MA(1) process $a_t = \varepsilon_t - \theta\varepsilon_{t-1}$, where

$$E(\varepsilon_t^2) = \sigma_\varepsilon^2$$

then

$$\sigma_S^2 = \sigma_\varepsilon^2(1 + \theta^2) - 2\sigma_\varepsilon^2\theta = \sigma_\varepsilon^2(1 - \theta)^2$$

Only if a_t is white noise will σ_S^2 equal σ^2, the variance of a_t. In the MA(1) case $\sigma^2 = \sigma_\varepsilon^2(1 + \theta^2)$; in general it can be defined as

$$\sigma^2 = \lim_{T\to\infty} T^{-1} \sum_{t=1}^{T} E(a_t^2)$$

It is this inequality that necessitates the 'non-parametric' corrections to the DF statistics proposed by Phillips. For example, rather than $T(\hat{\phi}_T - 1)$, an asymptotically valid test is

$$Z(\phi) = T(\hat{\phi}_T - 1) - (1/2)(\hat{\sigma}_{S\ell}^2 - \hat{\sigma}^2)\left[T^{-2}\sum_{t=2}^T (x_{t-1} - \bar{x}_{-1})^2\right]^{-1}$$

Here $\bar{x}_{-1} = (T-1)^{-1}\sum_{t=1}^{T-1} x_t$, while $\hat{\sigma}_{S\ell}^2$ and $\hat{\sigma}^2$ are consistent estimates of the variances σ_S^2 and σ^2, respectively. The latter is simply given by

$$\hat{\sigma}^2 = T^{-1}\sum_{t=1}^T \hat{a}_t^2$$

where the $\hat{a}_t$ are the residuals from estimating (3.10). The former is typically calculated as

$$\hat{\sigma}_{S\ell}^2 = T^{-1}\sum_{t=1}^T \hat{a}_t^2 + 2T^{-1}\sum_{j=1}^\ell \omega_j(\ell)\sum_{t=j+1}^T \hat{a}_t\hat{a}_{t-j} \qquad (3.12)$$

The window or kernel function $\omega_j(\ell)$ is typically assumed to satisfy the conditions in Andrews (1991), which ensure that the estimate is positive, with the added restriction that $\omega_j(\ell) = 0$ for $j > \ell$, so that ℓ acts as a truncation lag. A popular choice is the triangular set of lag weights $\omega_j(\ell) = \ell - j/(\ell+1)$ (Newey and West, 1987), but other choices are available and, indeed, there are many other estimators of σ_S^2 (see, for example, Andrews, 1991, and Phillips, 2005a).

Alternatively, τ_μ can be adjusted to become

$$Z(\tau_\mu) = \tau_\mu(\hat{\sigma}/\hat{\sigma}_{S\ell}) - (1/2)(\hat{\sigma}_{S\ell}^2 - \hat{\sigma}^2)\left[\hat{\sigma}_{S\ell}^2 T^{-2}\sum_{t=2}^T (x_{t-1} - \bar{x}_{-1})^2\right]^{-1/2}$$

Under the unit root null, these statistics have the same limiting distributions as $T(\hat{\phi}_T - 1)$ and τ_μ, respectively, and hence the same sets of critical values may be used. When x_t has a zero mean the adjusted statistics are the same as $Z(\phi)$ and $Z(\tau_\mu)$, but with $\bar{x}_{-1}$ removed; these have the same limiting distributions as the zero-mean DF statistics.

For these non-parametric statistics to become operational, the lag truncation parameter ℓ has to be set. Phillips (1987a) shows that ℓ has to increase with T, but at a rate slower than $T^{0.25}$. This does not, however, tell us how to set ℓ in practice, and no simple rule has emerged from the Monte Carlo investigations of Phillips and Perron (1988), Schwert (1987), Kim and Schmidt (1990) and Ng and Perron (1995, 2001). We use the $[T^{0.25}]$ rule in the examples that follow.

As has been discussed earlier, the presence of a unit root is often a theoretical implication of models that postulate the rational use of information available to economic agents, and thus unit roots occur in many theoretical financial models. For example, variables such as futures contracts, stock prices, dividends and earnings, spot and exchange rates, and interest rates should all contain unit roots under rational expectations. Unit root tests are thus extremely important in the analysis of financial time series.

Example 3.1 Unit root tests on financial time series

Examples 2.2 and 2.4 examined two models for the UK interest rate spread, a stationary AR(2) process and an $I(1)$ process without drift, while example 2.9 compared and contrasted the two models. We are now in a position to discriminate between the two through an application of a unit root test. The fitted AR(2) model

$$x_t = \underset{(0.019)}{0.032} + \underset{(0.039)}{1.180}\, x_{t-1} - \underset{(0.039)}{0.216}\, x_{t-2} + a_t$$

can be equivalently estimated as

$$x_t = \underset{(0.019)}{0.032} + \underset{(0.009)}{0.965}\, x_{t-1} - \underset{(0.039)}{0.216}\, \Delta x_{t-1} + a_t$$

so that, with $T = 646$, $T(\hat{\phi}_T - 1)/(1 - \hat{\delta}_1) = 646(0.965 - 1)/(1 + 0.216) = -18.6$, which is significant at the 2.5 per cent level. Alternatively, $\tau_\mu = (0.965 - 1)/0.009 = -3.89$, which is significant at the 1 per cent level, this critical value being -3.44, as obtained from the MacKinnon response surface. Note that the τ_μ statistic can be obtained directly as the t-ratio on x_{t-1} from rewriting the model again as

$$\Delta x_t = \underset{(0.019)}{0.032} - \underset{(0.009)}{0.035}\, x_{t-1} - \underset{(0.039)}{0.216}\, \Delta x_{t-1} + a_t$$

Regressions such as these are often referred to as *Dickey–Fuller regressions*. The non-parametric τ_μ statistic, computed with $\ell = 6$, is $Z(\tau_\mu) = -3.69$, and thus confirms the rejection of a unit root at the 1 per cent significance level, while the joint test of $\theta_0 = 0$, $\phi = 1$, yields a statistic of $\Phi = 7.39$, which is significant at the 2.5 per cent level. We can therefore conclude that the appropriate model for the spread is a stationary AR(2) process. We should also note that the estimate of the innovation standard deviation σ under the unit root null is 0.423, higher than its estimate under the AR(2) model (0.419), both of which are reported in example 2.7. This is in accordance with our earlier discussion of overdifferencing.

A similar approach to testing for a unit root in the dollar/sterling exchange rate, the presence of which was assumed in example 2.5, leads to the estimated equation

$$\Delta x_t = \underset{(0.0019)}{0.0036} - \underset{(0.00115)}{0.00220}\, x_{t-1}$$

Here, with $T = 3391$, we have $T(\hat{\phi}_T - 1) = -7.5$, $\tau_\mu = -1.91$, $\Phi = 1.91$ and, for $\ell = 8$, $Z(\tau_\mu) = -1.91$. All are clearly insignificant, thus confirming that the appropriate model is indeed a random walk.

Figure 3.4 plots the dividend yield (D/P) of the UK All Share index for the period January 1965 to December 2005. Recall that in example 2.6 we stated that it appeared to be generated by an ARMA(1,3) process. Although the series does not contain a trend, its wandering pattern could be a consequence of its being generated by an $I(1)$ process, and hence a unit root test may be performed. Since we are by no means certain that the ARMA orders are correct, it would seem appropriate to compute an ADF test with the lag augmentation order k chosen using the $[T^{0.25}]$ rule. Since $T = 491$, this sets $k = 4$, from which we obtain $\tau_\mu = -3.30$, which is significant at the 2.5 per cent level. The non-parametric version confirms this, for, with $\ell = 5$, $Z(\tau_\mu) = -3.19$, which again is significant at the 2.5 per cent level. The joint test statistic is $\Phi = 5.49$, also significant at the 2.5 per cent level.

Figure 3.4   FTA All Share index dividend yield (monthly 1965–2005)

Although ϕ is estimated to be 0.959, its standard error, 0.012, is sufficiently small for us to reject the null of a unit root in favour of the alternative that the dividend yield is stationary, a finding that will be shown in chapter 10 to be consistent with the implications of one of the most fundamental models in finance: that of the present value relationship linking real stock prices and dividends.

3.3 Trend stationarity versus difference stationarity

In the unit root testing strategy outlined above, the implicit null hypothesis is that the series is generated as a driftless random walk with, possibly, a serially correlated error. In the terminology of Nelson and Plosser (1982), x_t is said to be *difference stationary* (DS)

$$\Delta x_t = \varepsilon_t \tag{3.13}$$

where $\varepsilon_t = \theta(B)a_t$, while the alternative is that x_t is *stationary* in levels. While the null of a driftless random walk is appropriate for many financial time series, such as interest rates and exchange rates, other series often do contain a drift, so that the relevant null becomes

$$\Delta x_t = \theta + \varepsilon_t \tag{3.14}$$

In this case, a plausible alternative is that x_t is generated by a linear trend buried in stationary noise (see chapter 2, section 6) – i.e. it is *trend stationary* (TS)

$$x_t = \beta_0 + \beta_1 t + \varepsilon_t \tag{3.15}$$

Perron (1988, theorem 1) shows that neither the τ_μ statistic obtained from (3.8) nor its non-parametric counterpart, $Z(\tau_\mu)$, are capable of distinguishing a stationary process around a linear trend (model (3.15)) from a process with a unit root and drift (model (3.14)). Indeed, rejection of a null hypothesis of a unit root is unlikely if the series is stationary around a linear trend, and becomes impossible as the sample size increases.

A test of (3.14) against (3.15) is, however, straightforward to carry out by using an extension of the testing methodology discussed above. If the parametric testing procedure is used, then (3.9) is extended by the inclusion of the time trend t as an additional regressor,

$$x_t = \beta_0 + \beta_1 t + \phi x_{t-1} + \sum_{i=1}^{k} \delta_i \Delta x_{t-i} + a_t \tag{3.16}$$

and the statistic

$$\tau_\tau = \frac{\hat{\phi}_T - 1}{se(\hat{\phi}_T)}$$

is constructed. This '*t*-statistic' is denoted τ_τ to distinguish it from τ_μ because it has a different limiting distribution, this time given by

$$\tau_\tau = \frac{(1/2)([W(1)]^2 - 1) - W(1)\int_0^1 W(r)dr + A}{\left\{\int_0^1 [W(r)]^2 dr - \left(\int_0^1 W(r)dr\right)^2 + B\right\}^{1/2}}$$

where

$$A = 12\left[\int_0^1 rW(r)dr - (1/2)\int_0^1 W(r)dr\right] \times \left[\int_0^1 W(r)dr - (1/2)W(1)\right]$$

and

$$B = 12\left[\int_0^1 W(r)dr \int_0^1 rW(r)dr - \left(\int_0^1 rW(r)dr\right)^2\right] - 3\left(\int_0^1 W(r)dr\right)^2$$

It is perhaps more informative to observe the simulated limiting distribution shown in figure 3.5, once again computed with $\sigma^2 = 1$, $T = 1000$ and

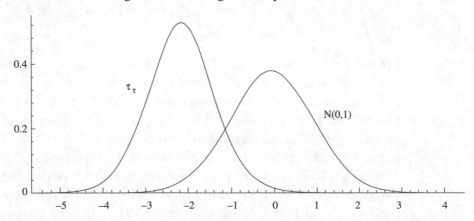

Figure 3.5   Simulated limiting distribution of τ_τ

$n = 25{,}000$, and here with drift $\theta = 1$. The large T 5 per cent, 2.5 per cent and 1 per cent critical values are now -3.41, -3.66 and -3.96, and, again, critical values for other sample sizes can be obtained from the MacKinnon response surfaces – e.g.

$$\tau_{\tau,.01}(T) = -3.9638 - 8.353T^{-1} - 47.44T^{-2}$$

If the non-parametric approach is employed, then a time trend may be added to (3.10) and the analogous adjusted t-ratio can again be compared to the τ_τ distribution. The adjustment in this case is

$$Z(\tau_\tau) = \tau_\tau(\hat{\sigma}^2/\hat{\sigma}^2_{S\ell}) - (1/2)(\hat{\sigma}^2_{S\ell} - \hat{\sigma}^2)T^3\left[4\hat{\sigma}_{S\ell}(3D_x)^{1/2}\right]^{-1}$$

where

$$D_x = \left(T^2(T^2 - 1)/12\right)\sum x^2_{t-1} - T\left(\sum tx^2_{t-1}\right)^2$$
$$+ T(T+1)\sum tx_{t-1}\sum x_{t-1} - (T(T+1)(2T+1)/6)\left(\sum x_{t-1}\right)^2$$

is the determinant of the regressor moment matrix of the time trend augmented regression (3.10).

Strictly, the unit root null requires not only that $\phi = 1$ in (3.16) but also that $\beta_1 = 0$, because, if $\beta_1 \neq 0$, x_t will contain a *quadratic* trend. This is easily seen if we set $p = 1$ for simplicity, for then (3.16) can also be written as

$$x_t = \beta_0\sum_{j=1}^{t}\phi^{t-j} + \beta_1\sum_{j=1}^{t}j\phi^{t-j} + \sum_{j=1}^{t}a_j\phi^{t-j}$$

Under the null $\phi = 1$, this becomes

$$x_t = \beta_0 t + \beta_1\sum_{j=1}^{t}j + \sum_{j=1}^{t}a_j = \beta_0 t + \beta_1 t(t+1)/2 + S_t$$

A quadratic trend might be thought unlikely, because, if, for example, x_t is in logarithms, a non-zero β_1 under the null would imply an ever-increasing (or decreasing) rate of change Δx_t. Nevertheless, a parametric joint test of $\phi = 1$ and $\beta_1 = 0$ is given by the conventional Wald test, comparing the residual sum of squares from the regression of (3.16) with the residual sum of squares from the 'restricted' regression of Δx_t on an intercept and k lags of Δx_t. Rather than having an F-distribution, the statistic has a non-standard distribution whose critical values are given, for example, in Hamilton (1994, table B.7 case 4) or Banerjee *et al.* (1993, table 4.5(c)). A non-parametric version of this test is given in Perron (1988).

It is always possible, of course, that β_1 could be non-zero. If this were the case, the quadratic trend in x_t would dominate the $I(1)$ component S_t so that the variance of x_t, when appropriately normalised, converges to a constant: from Dolado, Jenkinson and Sosvilla-Rivero (1990), $T^{-5} \sum x_t^2 \Rightarrow \beta_1^2/20$. As Banerjee *et al.* (1993, chap. 6.2.1) show, this implies that τ_τ, for example, is asymptotically normal rather than converging to a non-standard distribution. Similarly, if $\beta_1 = 0$ but $\beta_0 \neq 0$ in (3.15), $T^{-3} \sum x_t^2 \Rightarrow \beta_0^2/3$ and τ_μ is asymptotically normal.

To circumvent such complications, Dolado, Jenkinson and Sosvilla-Rivero (1990) propose the following strategy for testing for unit roots in the presence of possible trends. Equation (3.16) is first estimated and τ_τ used to test the null hypothesis that $\phi = 1$. If the null is rejected, there is no need to go further and the testing procedure stops. If the null is not rejected, we test for the significance of β_1 under the null – i.e. we estimate

$$\Delta x_t = \beta_0 + \beta_1 t + \sum_{i=1}^{k} \delta_i \Delta x_{t-i} + a_t$$

and test whether β_1 is zero or not using conventional testing procedures. If β_1 is significant, we compare τ_τ with the standard normal and make our inference on the null accordingly. If, on the other hand, β_1 is not significant, we estimate (3.16) without the trend ($\beta_1 = 0$),

$$x_t = \beta_0 + \phi x_{t-1} + \sum_{i=1}^{k} \delta_i \Delta x_{t-i} + a_t$$

and test the unit root null of $\phi = 1$ using τ_μ. If the null is rejected, the testing procedure is again terminated. If it is not rejected, we test for the significance of the constant β_0 under the null using the regression

$$\Delta x_t = \beta_0 + \sum_{i=1}^{k} \delta_i \Delta x_{t-i} + a_t$$

If β_0 is insignificant, we conclude that x_t contains a unit root, while, if $\beta_0 \neq 0$, we compare τ_μ with the standard normal, again making our inference accordingly.

This procedure is, of course, based on the *asymptotic* normality of τ_τ and τ_μ in the presence of a trend or drift in the relevant unit root null. An interesting question is: what happens in small samples? Both Hylleberg and Mizon (1989) and Schmidt (1990) present evidence that, when the drift parameter β_0 is small compared to σ^2, the small sample distribution of τ_μ is very much closer to the Dickey–Fuller distribution than to the standard normal. Schmidt (1990) and Banerjee *et al.* (1993) present tabulations of the τ_μ distribution for various values of the 'standardised drift' β_0/σ; it is only when this ratio exceeds 0.5 that the critical values are closer to the normal then to the DF distribution. We should, therefore, be careful when applying the asymptotic normality result in the testing strategy outlined above.

3.4 Other approaches to testing for unit roots

Many alternative unit root tests have been developed since the initial tests outlined above, and surveys may be found in, for example, Park (1990), Stock (1994), Maddala and Kim (1998) and Phillips and Xiao (1998). A recurring theme is the low power and severe size distortion inherent in many tests (see, for example, Haldrup and Jansson, 2006). For example, the non-parametric $Z(\phi)$ and $Z(\tau_\mu)$ tests suffer severe size distortions when there are moving average errors with a large negative root and, although the parametric counterparts are more accurate in this respect, the problem is not negligible even here (see Phillips and Perron, 1988, Schwert, 1989, and Perron and Ng, 1996). Moreover, many tests have low power when the largest autoregressive root is close to but nevertheless less than unity (DeJong *et al.*, 1992).

A related issue when dealing with financial time series is that, unlike many hypothesis testing situations, the power of tests of the unit root hypothesis against stationary alternatives depends less on the number of observations per se and more on the *span* of the data. For a given number of observations, the power is largest when the span is longest. Conversely, for a given span, additional observations obtained using data sampled more frequently lead only to a marginal increase in power, the increase becoming negligible as the sampling interval is decreased: see Shiller and Perron (1985), Perron (1991) and Pierse and Snell (1995). Hence, a data set containing fewer annual observations over a long time period will lead to unit root tests having higher power than those computed from a data set containing more observations over a shorter time period. This is of some consequence when analysing financial time series, which often have a large number of observations obtained by sampling at very fine intervals over a fairly short time span.

We thus focus here on recent tests that explicitly concentrate on improving power and reducing size distortion. Elliott, Rothenberg and Stock

(1996; see also Stock, 1991, 1994) appeal to local-to-unity asymptotic approximation theory, where the stationary alternative to a unit root is expressed as $\phi = 1 + c/T$, to propose the DF-GLS (generalised least squares) test, in which the data are detrended prior to running a Dickey–Fuller regression such as (3.9) or (3.16). The test is computed in two steps. If we let $z_t(0) = 1$ and $z_t(1) = (1,t)$, then the first step involves obtaining estimates of $\beta(0) = \beta_0$ or $\beta(1) = (\beta_0, \beta_1)$ by regressing the quasi-differences

$$x_t^d(\bar{\phi}) = [x_1, x_2 - \bar{\phi}x_1, \ldots, x_T - \bar{\phi}x_{T-1}]^\top$$

where $^\top$ denotes the vector/matrix transpose operator, on

$$z_t^d(\bar{\phi}, k) = [z_1(k), z_2(k) - \bar{\phi}z_1(k), \ldots, z_T(k) - \bar{\phi}z_{T-1}(k)]^\top$$

where $k = 0,1$ and $\bar{\phi} = 1 + \bar{c}/T$. Denoting the resulting estimator $\bar{\beta}(k)$, the 'locally detrended' series

$$\bar{x}_t(\bar{\phi}, k) = x_t - z_t(k)\bar{\beta}^\top(k)$$

is then computed. For the second step, the regression (3.16) is then run using $\bar{x}_t(\bar{\phi}, k)$ but without an intercept or time trend. Elliott, Rothenberg and Stock (1996) suggest choosing $\bar{c} = -13.5$ if $k = 1$ and provide critical values for the t-statistic on $\bar{x}_{t-1}$. If no trend is to be included ($k = 0$) then $\bar{c} = -7.5$ and the t-statistic has the τ distribution.

Elliott, Rothenberg and Stock also propose a *point optimal* unit root test – i.e. the most powerful test of a unit root against a simple point alternative. If we define the sum of squared residuals from the first step regression as $S(\bar{\phi})$, then the point optimal test of the null $\phi = 1$ against the alternative that $\phi = \bar{\phi}$ is then defined as

$$P_\tau = (S(\bar{\phi}) - S(1))/\hat{\sigma}_{S\ell}^2$$

where $\hat{\sigma}_{S\ell}^2$ is the estimator of σ_S^2 shown in (3.12). Critical values of P_τ are provided by Elliott, Rothenberg and Stock, with the null of a unit root being rejected if the calculated value of the test statistic is too small.

Ng and Perron (2001) construct four tests that are based upon the GLS detrended data x_t^d. It is useful to define the term

$$\kappa = T^{-2} \sum_{t=2}^{T} \left(x_{t-1}(\bar{\phi}, k) \right)^2$$

whereupon the test statistics are defined as

$$MZ^d(\phi) = \left(T^{-1}\left(x_T(\bar{\phi}, k)\right) - \hat{\sigma}_{Sl}^2\right)/(2\kappa)$$

$$MSB^d = \left(\kappa/\hat{\sigma}_{S\ell}^2\right)^{\frac{1}{2}}$$

$$MZ_t^d = MZ^d(\phi) \times MSB^d$$

and

$$MP_T^d(k) = \bar{c}^2\kappa - \bar{c}T^{-1}\left(x_T(\bar{\phi}, k)\right)^2 + kT^{-1}\left(x_T(\bar{\phi}, k)\right)^2/\hat{\sigma}_{S\ell}^2 \qquad k = 0, 1$$

The genesis of $MZ^d(\phi)$ and MZ_t^d are as modified versions of the non-parametric $Z(\phi)$ and $Z(\tau_\mu)$ tests. Perron and Ng (1996) define the 'M-tests' to incorporate the feature that a series converges in distribution with different rates of normalisation under the null and alternative hypotheses. For example, the M-modified $Z(\phi)$ test is

$$MZ(\phi) = Z(\phi) + (T/2)\left(\hat{\phi} - 1\right)^2$$

$MZ^d(\phi)$ is then defined using the GLS detrended data, with the $MP_t^d(k)$ statistics being similarly modified versions of the point optimal P_τ test. The MSB^d statistic is a modified version of Bhargava's (1986) R_1 statistic, and critical values for all these statistics are tabulated as table 1 of Ng and Perron (2001). On the stationary alternative, MSB^d tends to zero, so that the unit root null is rejected when the statistic is below the critical value.

All the non-parametric statistics have been defined using $\hat{\sigma}_{S\ell}^2$, given by (3.12), which may be interpreted as an estimator of the residual spectral density at frequency zero. An alternative estimator is given by

$$\hat{\sigma}_{S,AR}^2 = \hat{\sigma}_a^2/(1 - \hat{\delta}_1 - \cdots - \hat{\delta}_k)$$

where $\hat{\sigma}_a^2$ is a consistent estimate of the residual error variance from, say, the Dickey–Fuller regression (3.16) and the $\hat{\delta}_i$ are the estimated lag coefficients. This is often referred to as the autoregressive estimate of σ_S^2.

A related development is the set of confidence intervals for the largest autoregressive root provided by Stock (1991). Stock assumes that $\phi = 1 + c/T$ and then uses the local-to-unity asymptotic distribution theory to construct asymptotic confidence intervals for ϕ based on computed τ_μ and τ_τ statistics. Since the distributions of these statistics are non-normal and the dependence on c is not a simple location shift, such confidence intervals cannot be constructed using a simple rule such as '±2 standard errors'. The intervals are highly non-linear, exhibiting a sharp 'bend' for c just above zero (see Stock, 1991, figs. 3.1, 3.2): for positive values of the test statistics the intervals are tight, for large negative values they are wide.

Stock provides tables from which confidence intervals for ϕ can be calculated given a value of τ_μ or τ_τ and the sample size T. As an illustration of such a calculation, recall that the τ_μ statistic for the UK interest rate spread was reported in example 3.1 to be -3.89. From part A of table A.1 in Stock (1991), such a value corresponds to an approximate 95 per cent confidence interval for c of $(-42.47, -10.70)$. Since the statistic was computed from a sample size of $T = 646$, this corresponds to an interval for ϕ of $(1 - 42.47/646, 1 - 10.70/646)$ – i.e. $0.934 \leq \phi \leq 0.983$. Since $\hat{\phi} = 0.965$, this shows the complicated nature of the relationship between $\hat{\phi}$ and the confidence interval constructed by 'inverting' the τ statistic; the point estimate is not, and generally will not be, at the centre of the interval. Nevertheless, unity is excluded from the interval, thus confirming our choice of a stationary process for modelling this series.

Throughout this development of unit root testing procedures, the null hypothesis has been that of a unit root, with a stationary hypothesis (either trend or level stationarity) as the alternative. How might we go about testing the null of stationarity against a unit root alternative? This has been considered by Kwiatkowski *et al.* (1992) and Leybourne and McCabe (1994, 1999), and, in a related fashion, by Tanaka (1990) and Saikkonen and Luukkonen (1993). Consider again the ARIMA$(0,1,1)$ process

$$\Delta x_t = \theta_0 + a_t - \theta a_{t-1} \tag{3.17}$$

As was pointed out in chapter 2, a TS process is obtained if $\theta = 1$, so that this restriction parameterises the trend stationary null, with the unit root alternative being that $\theta < 1$. Equivalently, the null of $\theta = 1$ may be regarded as a case of overdifferencing.

The statistic that has been proposed to test this null when the a_t are strict white noise and normal, often referred to as the KPSS test (after Kwiatkowski, Phillips, Schmidt and Shin), is

$$\eta_\tau = T^{-2} \sum\nolimits_{t=1}^{T} \hat{S}_t^2 / \hat{\sigma}_e^2$$

Here

$$\hat{S}_t = \sum\nolimits_{i=1}^{t} e_i, \quad e_t = x_t - \hat{\beta}_0 - \hat{\beta}_1 t$$

and

$$\hat{\sigma}_e^2 = T^{-1} \sum_{t=1}^{T} e_t^2$$

Kwiatkowski *et al.* (1992) show that the limiting distribution of η_τ is

$$\eta_\tau \Rightarrow \int_0^1 V_2(r)^2 dr$$

where $V_2(r)$ is a demeaned and detrended Brownian motion process, also known as a second-level Brownian bridge, given by

$$V_2(r) = W(r) - \left(3r^2 - 2r\right)W(1) + \left(6r^2 - 6r\right)\int_0^1 W(s)ds$$

On the null of $\theta = 1$, $\eta_\tau = 0$, while, under the alternative, $\eta_\tau > 0$ (Kwiatkowski *et al.*, 1992, show that the test is consistent: a test is consistent if the probability of rejecting a false null goes to one as $T \to \infty$). Upper tail critical values of η_τ are reported in table 1 of Kwiatkowski *et al.*: the 5 per cent critical value is 0.146, while the 1 per cent value is 0.216.

If there is no trend in x_t under the null then the residuals are defined as $e_t = x_t - \bar{x}$. The level stationarity test statistic is then denoted as η_μ, whose limiting distribution is

$$\eta_\mu \Rightarrow \int_0^1 V(r)^2 dr$$

Here $V(r) = W(r) - rW(1)$ is a demeaned Brownian motion process, a Brownian bridge. Upper tail critical values of η_μ are also reported in table 1 of Kwiatkowski *et al.*: 5 per cent and 1 per cent critical values are 0.463 and 0.739, respectively.

Of course, restricting α_t to be strict white noise will typically be inappropriate, but extensions are readily available if we assume the weak dependence conditions (3.11) and replace $\hat{\sigma}_e^2$ by an estimator, say of the form of (3.12):

$$\hat{\sigma}_{e\ell}^2 - T^{-1} \sum_{t=1}^{T} \hat{e}_t^2 + 2T^{-1} \sum_{j=1}^{\ell} \omega_j(\ell) \sum_{t=j+1}^{T} \hat{e}_t \hat{e}_{t-j}$$

These statistics, which we denote $\eta_\mu(\ell)$ and $\eta_\tau(\ell)$, have the same limiting distributions as η_μ and η_τ. Leybourne and McCabe's (1994, 1999) variant of this test corrects for any serial correlation by considering an ARIMA$(p,1,1)$ process rather than (3.17).

The model (3.17) can also be used to illustrate the important concept of *observational equivalence*. Assuming $\theta_0 = 0$ for simplicity, the model can be written as

$$x_t = a_t + (1 - \theta)S_{t-1}$$

For large t, x_t will be dominated by the unit root component $(1 - \theta)S_{t-1}$. If θ is close to one, however, then in a finite sample x_t will behave essentially like the white-noise process a_t. In such circumstances, unit root tests will almost always reject the unit root null, even though it is true! As Cochrane (1991) points out, in general any TS process can be approximated arbitrarily well by a unit root process, and vice versa, in the sense that the ACFs of the two processes will be arbitrarily close.

While attempting to discriminate between the two classes of processes in such circumstances might well be regarded as impossible, distinguishing between the two can yield important advantages. Campbell and Perron (1991) argue that near-stationary integrated processes (θ close to one) seem to be better forecast using stationary models ($\theta = 1$), while near-integrated stationary models, such as

$$x_t = \phi x_{t-1} + a_t - \theta a_{t-1}$$

with ϕ close to, but less than, one, are better forecast using integrated models. It may also be better to use integrated asymptotic theory to approximate finite sample distributions for near-integrated stationary models, and stationary asymptotic theory for near-stationary integrated models.

We should emphasise that all these testing procedures rely on classical methods of statistical inference. An alternative Bayesian methodology has also developed from the work of Sims (1988), Sims and Uhlig (1991), DeJong and Whiteman (1991a, 1991b) and Koop (1992). Special issues of the *Journal of Applied Econometrics* (1991, volume 6, number 4), *Econometric Theory* (1994, volume 10, number 4/5) and the *Journal of Econometrics* (1995, volume 69, number 1) are devoted to Bayesian developments in unit root testing, but it seems fair to say that, perhaps because of both the technical and computational complexity of the Bayesian methodology, the classical approach remains the most convenient for the applied practitioner to adopt.

Example 3.2 Are UK equity prices trend or difference stationary?

In example 2.6 we modelled the logarithms of the UK FTA All Share index as an ARIMA(2, 1, 2) process on noting that it had a pronounced tendency to drift upwards, albeit with some major 'wanderings' about trend. We may thus investigate whether this DS representation is appropriate or whether a TS model would be preferable. Let us first test the null hypothesis that the series contains a unit root against the alternative that it is generated as stationary deviations about a linear trend.

Following the testing strategy outlined in section 3.1.5 requires estimating the following regressions (with absolute t-ratios now shown in parentheses):

(i) $\quad \Delta x_t = \underset{(2.47)}{0.073} + \underset{(2.21)}{0.00016}\, t - \underset{(2.31)}{0.0210}\, x_{t-1} + \sum_{i=1}^{3} \hat{\delta}_i \Delta x_{t-i} + \hat{a}_t$

(ii) $\quad \Delta x_t = \underset{(0.90)}{0.0072} - \underset{(0.12)}{0.000002}\, t + \sum_{i=1}^{3} \hat{\delta}_i \Delta x_{t-i} + \hat{a}_t$

(iii) $\quad \Delta x_t = \underset{(1.10)}{0.0161} - \underset{(0.69)}{0.00156}\, x_{t-1} + \sum_{i=1}^{3} \hat{\delta}_i \Delta x_{t-i} + \hat{a}_t$

(iv) $\quad \Delta x_t = \underset{(2.35)}{0.0063} + \sum_{i=1}^{3} \hat{\delta}_i \Delta x_{t-i} + \hat{a}_t$

From regression (i) a τ_τ test cannot reject the DS null, while β_1 is found to be insignificant under this null from regression (ii). This necessitates estimating regression (iii), from which a τ_μ test still cannot reject the null. Estimating equation (iv) shows that β_0 is non-zero under the null, so that τ_μ strictly should be tested against a standard normal. Since $\tau_\mu = -0.69$, however, this does not alter our conclusion that a unit root in x_t cannot be rejected. Note that the implied estimate of ϕ from regression (i) is 0.979, and, with $T = 488$, the associated 95 per cent confidence interval, calculated using part B of table A.1 of Stock (1991), is $0.999 \le \phi \le 1.011$.

The DF-GLS test statistic, computed using three lags, is -2.13, which is again insignificant, the 10 per cent critical value being -2.57. The Elliott, Rothenberg and Stock (1996) point optimal test is $P_\tau = 9.61$, which is insignificant as the 10 per cent critical value is 6.89. The Ng and Perron (2001) tests produce the following statistics: $MZ^d(\phi) = -9.52$, $MSB^d = 0.228$, $MZ_t^d = -2.17$ and $MP_T^d(1) = 9.64$, all of which are insignificant as the 10 per cent critical values are -14.2, 0.185, -2.62 and 6.67, respectively. In each of these, $\hat{\sigma}_{S\ell}^2$ was used as the estimate of the zero-frequency spectral density with $\ell = 3$. Varying the setting of ℓ and the weight function $\omega_j(\ell)$ did not alter these inferences and nor did using the alternative estimator $\hat{\sigma}^2_{S,AR}$.

If we assume the null of trend stationarity, we find $\eta_\tau(17) = 0.248$, which, as the 1 per cent critical value is 0.216, represents a clear rejection and thus confirms that equity prices do follow an $I(1)$ process with drift, so that the model estimated in example 2.6 is indeed the appropriate one.

3.5 Testing for more than one unit root

The above development of unit root tests has been predicated on the assumption that x_t contains *at most* one unit root – i.e. that it is at most $I(1)$. If the null hypothesis of a unit root is not rejected, then it may be necessary to test whether the series contains a second unit root – i.e. whether it is $I(2)$ and thus needs differencing twice to induce stationarity. Unfortunately, the 'standard' testing procedure on non-rejection of a unit root in the levels x_t, that of testing whether the differences Δx_t contain a unit root, is not justified theoretically, as DF-type tests are based on the assumption of at most one unit root. If the true number of unit roots is greater than one, the empirical size of such tests is greater than the nominal size, so the probability of finding any, let alone all, unit roots is reduced.

Dickey and Pantula (1987) propose a sequence of tests that does have a theoretical justification when we assume that x_t may contain more than one unit root. For example, suppose we assume that x_t contains a maximum of two unit roots. To test the null hypothesis of two unit roots against the alternative of one, we compare the t-ratio on β_2 from the regression

$$\Delta^2 x_t = \beta_0 + \beta_2 \Delta x_{t-1} + a_t$$

with the τ_μ critical values. If the null is rejected, we may then test the hypothesis of exactly one unit root against the alternative of none by comparing with τ_μ the t-ratio on β_1 from

$$\Delta^2 x_t = \beta_0 + \beta_1 x_{t-1} + \beta_2 \Delta x_{t-1} + a_t$$

Example 3.3 Do UK interest rates contain two unit roots?

Figure 3.6 shows plots of the UK short and long interest rates from which the spread, analysed in example 3.1, was calculated. To test for the presence of at most two unit roots we first estimate, under the null hypothesis of exactly

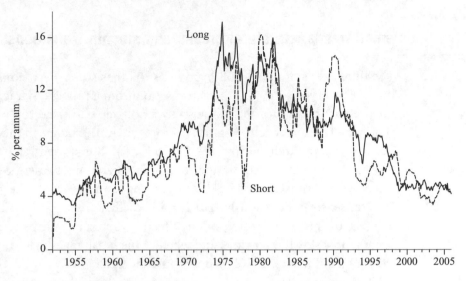

Figure 3.6   UK interest rates (monthly 1952–2005)

two unit roots, the regressions

$$\Delta^2 RS_t = \underset{(0.019)}{0.004} - \underset{(0.038)}{0.712}\,\Delta RS_{t-1}$$

and

$$\Delta^2 R20_t = \underset{(0.012)}{0.0002} - \underset{(0.038)}{0.721}\,\Delta R20_{t-1}$$

where RS_t and $R20_t$ are the short and long rates, respectively, and standard errors are shown in parentheses. The τ_μ statistics are computed to be -18.74 and -18.97, respectively, thus conclusively rejecting the hypothesis of two unit roots in both series. On estimating the regressions

$$\Delta^2 RS_t = \underset{(0.043)}{0.112} - \underset{(0.005)}{0.015}\,RS_{t-1} - \underset{(0.038)}{0.706}\,\Delta RS_{t-1}$$

and

$$\Delta^2 R20_t = \underset{(0.032)}{0.047} - \underset{(0.004)}{0.006}\,R20_{t-1} - \underset{(0.038)}{0.718}\,\Delta R20_{t-1}$$

however, we find that the τ_μ statistics from the estimates of β_1 are -2.76 and -1.59, thus providing no evidence against the hypothesis that both series contain a single unit root.

3.6 Segmented trends, structural breaks and smooth transitions

The difference stationary null hypothesis that has so far been considered is that the observed series $\{x_t\}_0^T$ is a realisation from a process characterised by the presence of a unit root and possibly a non-zero drift. Perron (1989) has generalised the approach so as to allow for a one-time change in the structure occurring at a known time T_B ($1 < T_B < T$). Subsequently, the testing procedure was extended to the situation where the break point T_B is unknown and must be chosen prior to testing for a unit root – i.e. the break is determined endogenously. Further issues that must be considered are whether the break in structure is assumed to occur instantly or whether it occurs more slowly over time, and whether the break takes place under both the null and the alternative or under just the latter.

The approach that we take here follows that of Vogelsang and Perron (1998), who may be consulted for references to the earlier literature on testing for unit roots when the break is endogenous. The case when the break is assumed to occur instantly is known as the *additive outlier* (AO) model, and three alternatives are considered: model (A), which allows a shift in the intercept of the trend function (the 'crash' model); model (B), which allows both a shift in intercept and slope (the 'crash/changing growth' model); and model (C), which allows a 'smooth' shift in the slope by requiring the end points of the two segments of the broken trend to be joined. The models are parameterised as follows, where T_B^c now denotes the 'correct' break date.

Null hypotheses
Model (A): $x_t = \beta + x_{t-1} + \theta DTB_t^c + e_t^*$
Model (B): $x_t = \beta + x_{t-1} + \theta DTB_t^c + \gamma DU_t^* + e_t^*$
Model (C): $x_t = \beta + x_{t-1} + \gamma DU_t^c + e_t^*$

Alternative hypotheses
Model (A): $x_t = \mu + \beta t + \theta DU_t^c + e_t$
Model (B): $x_t = \mu + \beta t + \theta DU_t^c + \gamma DT_t^c + e_t$
Model (C): $x_t = \mu + \beta t + \gamma DT_t^c + e_t$

The errors e_t and e_t^* can be assumed to be stationary processes, say $e_t = \psi(B) a_t$ and $e_t^* = \psi^*(B) a_t$, where $\psi^*(B) = (1 - B)\psi(B)$. The dummy variables are defined as

$$DTB_t^c = 1 \quad \text{if } t = T_B^c + 1, \qquad 0 \text{ otherwise}$$
$$DU_t^c = 1 \quad \text{if } t > T_B^c, \qquad 0 \text{ otherwise}$$
$$DT_t^c = t - T_B^c \quad \text{if } t > T_B^c, \qquad 0 \text{ otherwise}$$

Note that the dummy variables are linked through $DTB_t^c = \Delta DU_t^c = \Delta^2 DT_t^c$. Model (A) characterises the 'crash' in the null hypothesis by a dummy variable that takes the value one at the time of the break, so that the level of x changes by θ at $T_B^c + 1$. Under the alternative of a trend stationary system, model (A) allows for a one-time change in the intercept of the trend function, the magnitude of this change being θ. Model (B), the 'changing growth' model, specifies under the null that the drift parameter changes from β to $\beta + \theta + \gamma$ at time $T_B^c + 1$ and then to $\beta + \gamma$ afterwards. Under the alternative, the intercept changes by θ and the slope changes by γ at $T_B^c + 1$. Model (C) allows both segments of the trend under the alternative to be equal at T_B^c.

Perron (1989) shows that standard tests of the unit root hypothesis are not consistent against trend stationary alternatives where the trend function contains a shift in the slope. Although such tests are consistent against a shift in the intercept of the trend function (if the change is fixed as T increases), their power is likely to be substantially reduced due to the fact that the limiting value of the estimate of the largest autoregressive root is inflated above its true value. (Leybourne, Mills and Newbold, 1998, investigate a converse phenomenon: standard tests can spuriously reject the unit root null if the break occurs early in the series.)

Testing for a unit root in the AO framework consists of a four-step procedure. The first step calculates the 'detrended' series $\tilde{x}_t^j$, whose form depends on which model is being considered. Thus, we let $\tilde{x}_t^j$, $j = A, B, C$, be the residuals from a regression of x_t on:

(1) $j = A$: a constant, a time trend, and DU_t;
(2) $j = B$: a constant, a time trend, DU_t and DT_t; and
(3) $j = C$: a constant, a time trend and DT_t.

Note the change in notation: DU_t and DT_t are defined analogously to DU_t^c and DT_t^c, but for *any* break date T_B.

In the second step, the unit root hypothesis is tested using the t-statistic $\phi = 1$ in the regressions

$$\tilde{x}_t^j = \sum_{i=0}^{k} \omega_i DTB_{t-i} + \phi \tilde{x}_{t-1}^j + \sum_{i=1}^{k} c_i \Delta \tilde{x}_{t-i}^j + u_t \quad j = A, B \qquad (3.17)$$

and

$$\tilde{x}_t^C = \phi \tilde{x}_{t-1}^C + \sum_{i=1}^{k} c_i \Delta \tilde{x}_{t-i}^C + u_t$$

where DTB_t is defined analogously to DTB_t^c. The $k+1$ dummies $DTB_t, \ldots, DTB_{t-k}$ are included in (3.17) to ensure that the limiting distributions of the t-statistics on ϕ are invariant to the correlation structure of the errors, although they are not needed in model C as in this case the distribution of the t-statistic is asymptotically invariant to the correlation structure.

The third step is to compute the set of t-statistics for all possible breaks and to select the date for which the statistic is minimised. Thus, if the set of t-statistics are denoted as $t(j, AO, T_B)$, then we define $\hat{T}_B$ as the break date for which

$$t\left(j, AO, \hat{T}_B\right) = \inf_{t \in \mathrm{T}} t(j, AO, T_B) \qquad \mathrm{T} = [1, T]$$

This choice of $\hat{T}_B$ thus corresponds to choosing the break date that is most likely to reject the unit root hypothesis. Other possibilities are available for choosing $\hat{T}_B$, however. For example, it might be selected as the value that maximises the significance of one or both of the break parameters θ and γ: Vogelsang and Perron (1998) discuss some of these alternatives. The fourth step is then to compare $t\left(j, AO, \hat{T}_B\right)$ with its critical value taken from the appropriate limiting distribution.

One drawback of these models is that they imply that the change in the trend function occurs instantaneously. Perron (1989) generalises the models by assuming that x_t responds to a shock in the trend function in the same way that it reacts to any other shock: this is known as the *innovational outlier* (IO) model. This assumption can be captured using the following specifications.

Null hypotheses

Model (A): $x_t = \beta + x_{t-1} + \psi^*(B)\left(\theta DTB_t^c + a_t\right)$

Model (B): $x_t = \beta + x_{t-1} + \psi^*(B)\left(\theta DTB_t^c + \gamma DU_t^* + a_t\right)$

Model (C): $x_t = \beta + x_{t-1} + \psi^*(B)\left(\gamma DU_t^c + a_t\right)$

Alternative hypotheses

Model (A): $x_t = \mu + \beta t + \psi(B)\left(\theta DU_t^c + a_t\right)$

Model (B): $x_t = \mu + \beta t + \psi(B)\left(\theta DU_t^c + \gamma DT_t^c + a_t\right)$

Model (C): $x_t = \mu + \beta t + \psi(B)\left(\gamma DT_t^c + a_t\right)$

Thus, the immediate impact of a shift in slope for model (C), say, is γ, while the long-run impact is either $\psi^*(1)\gamma$ or $\psi(1)\gamma$. Model (B) can be tested by estimating the regression

$$x_t = \mu + \beta t + dDTB_t + \theta DU_t + \gamma DT_t + \phi x_{t-1} + \sum_{i=1}^{k} \delta_i \Delta x_{t-i} + e_t$$

(3.18)

Under the null hypothesis of a unit root, $\phi = 1$ and $\theta = \beta = \gamma = 0$, whereas, under the alternative of a 'segmented trend stationary' process, $\phi < 1$ and θ, β, $\gamma \neq 0$. The null hypothesis can again be tested using the t-statistic for $\phi = 1$ from (3.18); the set of such statistics for all possible breaks can be denoted $t(j, \text{IO}, T_B)$ and an analogous procedure to that discussed for the AO model may then be followed. For model (A), the same regression is estimated but with $\gamma = 0$, i.e. without DT_t; for model (C), DTB_t and DU_t are deleted $(d = \theta = 0)$. The case where there is no trend in the model is considered in Perron (1990).

The asymptotic distributions of $t(j, \text{AO}, \hat{T}_B)$ and $t(j, \text{IO}, \hat{T}_B)$ depend on whether or not a break occurs under the null of a unit root – i.e. on whether $\theta = \gamma = 0$ under the null. When no break has occurred, so that we do have $\theta = \gamma = 0$, the asymptotic distributions are identical for both $j = A$, B, and critical values are given in Vogelsang and Perron (1998, tables 1, 2). These tables also give finite sample critical values for alternative ways of selecting the lag order k. For $j = C$ the asymptotic distributions differ, and critical values are given in Perron and Vogelsang (1993).

When a break does occur under the null, in particular when γ is non-zero, so that there is a break in the drift, several difficulties can arise. Vogelsang and Perron (1998) show that, in this case, the sizes of the above testing procedures approach one as the sample size T grows, so that for very large samples spurious rejections of the null become almost certain. This is not mitigated by using other approaches to select the break date. Harvey, Leybourne and Newbold (2001), however, propose a modification that looks to have good size and power properties in the IO case. This is to select $\hat{T}_B$ as one plus the date selected by maximising the absolute values of the t-statistics on θ in the sequence of regressions of (3.18), with critical values of the resulting test of $\phi = 1$ being given in their table 2.

More recent work has concentrated on extending these techniques to situations of multiple structural beaks (Bai, 1997; Bai and Perron, 1998) and of general, and possibly non-stationary, serial correlation in the errors (Perron, 1997; Vogelsang, 1997); for a detailed survey, see Perron (2006).

There is also a parallel literature developing on incorporating endogenously determined breaks into the stationarity test discussed in section 3.4; see, for example, Busetti and Harvey (2001, 2003) and Harvey and Mills (2003, 2004).

Rather than including lags of Δx_t, as in (3.18), to relax the instantaneous impact of the break, an alternative is to allow the trend to change gradually and smoothly between the two regimes. One possibility is to use a *logistic smooth transition regression* (LSTR) model. Leybourne, Newbold and Vougas (1998) propose the following three LSTR models to replace the segmented trend alternative hypotheses introduced above:

Model (A): $x_t = \mu_1 + \mu_2 S_t(\gamma, m) + e_t$

Model (B): $x_t = \mu_1 + \beta_1 t + \mu_2 S_t(\gamma, m) + e_t$

Model (C): $x_t = \mu_1 + \beta_1 t + \mu_2 S_t(\gamma, m) + \beta_2 t S_t(\gamma, m) + e_t$

where $S_t(\gamma, m)$ is the logistic smooth transition function

$$S_t(\gamma, m) = (1 + \exp(-\gamma(t - mT)))^{-1}$$

which controls the transition between regimes.

The parameter m determines the timing of the transition midpoint since, for $\gamma > 0$, $S_{-\infty}(\gamma, m) = 0$, $S_{+\infty}(\gamma, m) = 1$ and $S_{mT}(\gamma, m) = 0.5$. The speed of transition is determined by the parameter γ. If γ is small then $S_t(\gamma, m)$ takes a long time to traverse the interval (0,1) and, in the limiting case when $\gamma = 0$, $S_t(\gamma, m) = 0.5$ for all t. For large values of γ, $S_t(\gamma, m)$ traverses the interval (0,1) very rapidly, and as γ approaches $+\infty$ it changes from zero to one instantaneously at time mT. Thus, in model A, x_t is stationary around a mean that changes from an initial value of μ_1 to a final value of $\mu_1 + \mu_2$. Model B is similar, with the intercept changing from μ_1 to $\mu_1 + \mu_2$, but allows for a fixed slope. In model C, in addition to the change in intercept from μ_1 to $\mu_1 + \mu_2$, the slope also changes, with the same speed of transition, from β_1 to $\beta_1 + \beta_2$. If we allow $\gamma < 0$ then the initial and final model states are reversed, but the interpretation of the parameters remains the same.

The smooth transition $S_t(\gamma, m)$ does impose certain restrictions, in that the transition path is monotonic and symmetric around the midpoint. More flexible specifications, which allow for non-monotonic and asymmetric transition paths, could be obtained by including a higher-order time polynomial in the exponential term of $S_t(\gamma, m)$. The constraints that the transitions in intercept and slope occur only once, simultaneously and at the same speed could also be relaxed, although at some cost to interpretation and ease of estimation. For example, Sollis, Leybourne and Newbold (1999) introduce asymmetry into the transition function, while Harvey and Mills (2002) consider double smooth transition functions.

Leybourne, Newbold and Vougas (1998) investigate the question of distinguishing between LSTR models and models containing unit roots, analogous to the analysis developed above with segmented trends. Their proposal is simple: estimate the models by non-linear least squares (NLS) (i.e. detrend x_t), obtain the residuals, and compute an ADF test using these residuals. Once again, standard DF percentiles are invalid, and Leybourne, Newbold and Vougas provide the necessary critical values, which depend upon which LSTR model is fitted. If the null hypothesis is an $I(1)$ process without drift then all three models are possible alternatives, while if the null is an $I(1)$ with drift only models B and C can be realistic alternatives.

Example 3.4 Unit roots and structural breaks in US stock prices

Figure 3.7 plots the logarithms of the nominal annual (January average) S&P stock index for the period 1871 to 2006. A conventional unit root test obtained the value of $\tau_\tau = -1.48$, which, since $\tau_{\tau,0.10} = -3.15$, provides no evidence to reject the null hypothesis that stock prices are DS in favour of the alternative that they are TS.

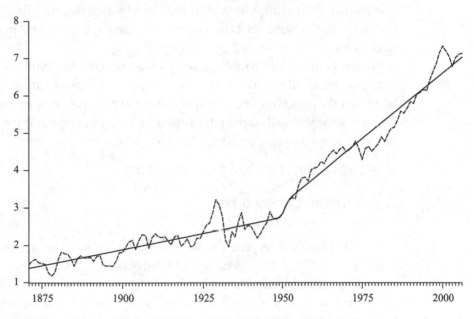

Figure 3.7   Logarithms of the nominal S&P 500 index (1871–2006) with a smooth transition trend superimposed

Following Perron (1989), however, we first consider the possibility of both a change in level and, thereafter, a changed trend rate of growth of the series after a break at an unknown point in time. We thus consider first the AO model (B) with $k=2$, the value selected for the conventional unit root test reported above. This led to an estimated break point of $T_B = 1928$, consistent with the Great Crash of 1929 producing a downward level shift with, perhaps, a subsequent increased trend rate of growth. The t-statistic for testing $\phi = 1$ at this break, however, was -4.52, which is not significant at the 5 per cent level using table 2 of Vogelsang and Perron (1998).

Alternatively, using the IO version yields a break point of 1930 but, again, a t-statistic (of -2.45) that is insignificant. It would therefore appear that the stock price series, although an $I(1)$ process, undergoes a break in level and drift after the Great Crash. Allowing for such a break under the null, in the fashion of Harvey, Leybourne and Newbold (2001), selects $T_B = 1931$ but still provides no evidence against a unit root. Indeed, the fitted model under the null is

$$\Delta x_t = \underset{(0.016)}{0.068}\, DU_t - \underset{(0.162)}{0.284}\, DTB_t - \underset{(0.160)}{0.688}\, DTB_{t-1} + e_t$$

$$e_t = -\underset{(0.088)}{0.183}\, e_{t-2} + a_t, \quad \hat{\sigma}_a = 0.1619$$

The level of x_t thus drops by 0.28 in 1932 and by a further 0.69 in 1933, while the drift in the series is zero before 1931 and 6.9 per cent per annum afterwards.

While the unit root hypothesis cannot be rejected in favour of a crash/ changing trend alternative, it is nevertheless worth investigating the possibility that the trend function could be modelled as a smooth transition. Since it seems sensible to allow for a transition in both intercept and trend, LSTR model C was estimated by NLS, yielding

$$x_t = \underset{(0.061)}{1.388} + \underset{(0.0014)}{0.0171}\, t - \underset{(0.268)}{3.633}\, S_t(1.679, 0.585)$$

$$+ \underset{(0.0027)}{0.0530}\, t S_t(1.679, 0.585) + u_t$$

This model can be interpreted as implying that the intercept decreased from 1.388 to -2.249, while trend growth increased from 1.71 per cent per annum to 7.01 per cent. The midpoint of the smooth transition is estimated to be 1951, and, as $\hat{\gamma} = 1.679$, the speed of the transition is fairly quick. As can be seen from the smooth transition trend also shown in figure 3.7, the transition takes about six years to complete. A unit root test computed using the residuals from this model yielded a value of -4.51. From table 1 of Leybourne, Newbold and Vougas (1998), this is close to being significant at the 10 per cent level, and the residuals are well fitted by the AR(2) process

$$u_t = \underset{(0.085)}{0.935}\, u_{t-1} - \underset{(0.085)}{0.187}\, u_{t-2} + e_t, \quad \hat{\sigma}_e = 0.1613$$

which has roots of 0.65 and 0.29 and a standard error only a little larger than that obtained from the unit root model. This finding that stock prices can reasonably be modelled as the sum of a deterministic trend and a stationary innovation is, as Perron (1989, p. 1384) remarks, 'particularly striking given the vast amount of theoretical and empirical studies supporting the random walk hypothesis in this situation'.

3.7 Stochastic unit root processes

Granger and Swanson (1997), McCabe and Tremayne (1995) and Leybourne, McCabe and Tremayne (1996) investigate an extension of the $I(1)$ model to the case where the process has a *stochastic* unit root (STUR). A simple example is the *random coefficient* AR(1) process

$$x_t = \phi_t x_{t-1} + a_t \tag{3.20}$$

$$\phi_t = 1 + \delta_t$$

where a_t and δ_t are independent zero-mean strict white-noise processes with variances σ_a^2 and σ_δ^2. If $\sigma_\delta^2 = 0$ then, clearly, $\phi_t = 1$ for all t, whereas, if $\sigma_\delta^2 > 0$, ϕ_t has a mean of unity and x_t hence has a stochastic unit root. Why should such models be of interest here? Suppose that x_t is the price of a financial asset, which then has a time t expected return of

$$E(r_t) = \frac{E(x_t) - x_{t-1}}{x_{t-1}}$$

if any dividend payments are ignored for simplicity. Rearranging yields

$$E(x_t) = (1 + E(r_t))x_{t-1}$$

Setting $a_t = x_t - E(x_t)$ and defining $\delta_t = E(r_t)$ thus yields the STUR(1) model (3.20). The assumption that a_t is white noise – i.e. returns are white noise – thus implies that the price *levels* have a stochastic unit root.

The STUR model can be extended in various ways, apart from considering higher-order processes with possible trends. Granger and Swanson (1997) consider (3.20) but with

$$\phi_t = \exp(\alpha_t)$$

where α_t is a zero-mean stationary stochastic process. Since we can write

$$\phi_t = (x_t/x_{t-1})(1 - a_t/x_t)$$

we have

$$\alpha_t = \Delta\log(x_t) + \log(1 - a_t/x_t) \approx \Delta\log(x_t) - a_t/x_t$$

again showing that, while $\log(x_t)$ has an exact unit root, x_t has a stochastic unit root. Leybourne, McCabe and Mills (1996) allow δ_t to be an AR(1) process that may itself contain a unit root, so the transition between stationary ($\phi_t < 1$) and explosive ($\phi_t > 1$) regimes does not necessarily occur randomly but is allowed to evolve in a more gradual fashion.

Granger and Swanson (1997) show that standard DF tests usually have little power to distinguish a STUR model from a standard unit root process, but Leybourne, McCabe and Tremayne (1996) and Leybourne, McCabe and Mills (1996) provide alternative tests that perform much better.

These papers also discuss maximum likelihood (ML) estimation and forecasting of STUR models and provide some evidence in favour of such models over standard unit root models for both the levels and logarithms of a variety of stock market indices and interest rates. For example, Leybourne, McCabe and Mills (1996) find that the following STUR model fits the daily levels of the London Stock Exchange FTSE 350 index over the period 1 January 1986 to 28 November 1994:

$$\Delta x_t = \beta + \phi_1 \Delta x_{t-1} + \phi_4 \Delta x_{t-4} + \delta_t(x_{t-1} - \beta(t - 1) - \phi_1 x_{t-2} - \phi_4 x_{t-5}) + a_t$$

$$\delta_t = \delta_{t-1} + \eta_t$$

Here the level of the index, x_t, follows a (restricted) STUR(4) process with drift in which the stochastic unit root is itself a random walk. The root $\phi_t = 1 + \delta_t$ fluctuates in a narrow band around 0.96, and hence is stationary. This model is found to produce a 7 per cent reduction in error variance over the competing ARIMA(4,1,0) model and some evidence of a better forecasting performance.

The list of non-stationary processes described in this chapter is by no means exhaustive. Rather than allowing a one-time change or smooth transition in the trend parameters, a more general approach is provided by structural time series models that allow the parameters of the time trend to vary continuously, such as in a random walk fashion; these models are discussed in chapter 4. Granger, Inoue and Morin (1997) have proposed a general class of non-linearly drifting random walks, called non-linear stochastic trend processes. These are based on the so-called 'growth processes' and have increments that are equal to a positive function of the lagged series plus an innovation whose variance depends on the lagged series. The deterministic trends in these series are smooth parametric (e.g. sub-linear, sub-exponential, exponential or super-exponential) or non-parametric (e.g. kernel) functions of time. Another extension is the family of seasonal unit root processes (Hylleberg et al., 1990), which allow for deterministic or drifting seasonal variation. Both stochastic and seasonal unit roots are in the style of structural models in that they are based on time-varying parameters.

Example 3.5 Unit roots in the Japanese equity premium

An interesting issue concerning unit roots in the capital asset pricing model is investigated in Markellos and Mills (2001). Most econometric research on the CAPM is based on the 'excess market' regression

$$r_t - f_t = \alpha + \beta(m_t - f_t) + u_t$$

where r_t is the return on an asset at time t, f_t is the return on a proxy for the risk-free interest rate and m_t is the return on a proxy for the market portfolio returns, respectively. The variables $r_t - f_t$ and $m_t - f_t$ are typically called excess asset returns and excess market returns (or equity premia), respectively.

Estimation using standard techniques requires that the two excess returns are stationary so that the CAPM regressions are 'balanced' (Banerjee et al., 1993, pp. 164–8). While stationarity may be a stylized fact of asset and market returns, no such claim can be made for the risk-free rate. Markellos and Mills (2001) point out that, if r_t and m_t are assumed to be $I(0)$ processes, and f_t is $I(1)$, then $r_t - f_t$ and $m_t - f_t$ will asymptotically form $I(1)$ processes. Although the excess market regression will not be unbalanced, the slope, the so-called 'beta coefficient', will measure the relationship only between the dominant non-stationary parts on either side of the regression.

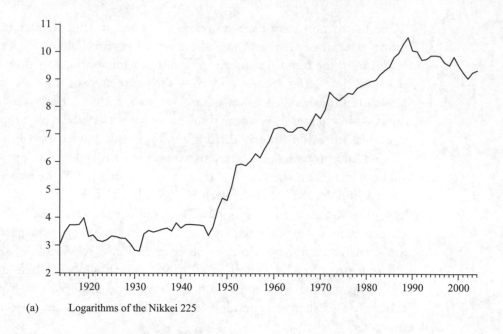

(a)   Logarithms of the Nikkei 225

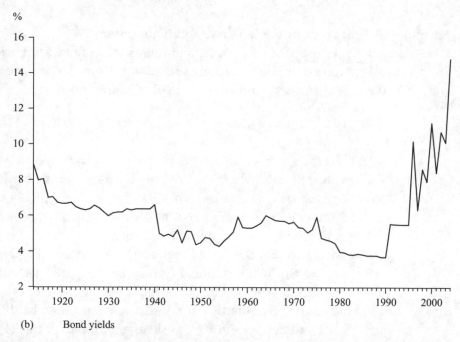

(b)   Bond yields

Figure 3.8   Nikkei 225 index prices and seven-year Japanese government bond yields (end of year 1914–2003)

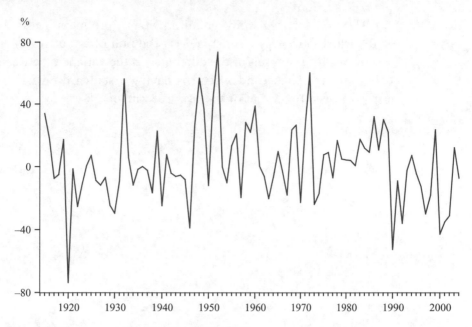

Figure 3.9   Japanese equity premium (end of year 1914–2003)

Since these variables have an identical basis – the $I(1)$ f_t process – it would be expected that the beta from such a regression would converge to unity. Markellos and Mills provide simulation evidence showing that the correct null of a unit root in excess returns may not be accepted by standard Dickey–Fuller tests and that it is also possible to produce upward biases in betas. The size of the unit root tests on excess returns was found to improve somewhat as the variance of the underlying risk-free rates increased compared to that of the market returns. Conversely, biases in beta estimates became more severe as this variance increased. Empirical results supporting these arguments using UK and US data have been provided by Markellos and Mills (2001) and Yoon (2005). Yoon finds that a stochastic unit root process offers a better description of the proxy he used for the risk-free rate. Simulation and empirical results show that the implications of the existence of a stochastic unit root are qualitatively similar to those of a standard unit root.

Figure 3.8 shows the logarithms of the Nikkei 225 index and seven-year Japanese government bond yields, respectively. Both series appear to contain a unit root, which was confirmed by a range of unit root tests. As shown in figure 3.9, however, the Japanese equity premium, the difference between the $I(0)$ Nikkei returns and the $I(1)$ risk-free rate, appears to be stationary.

(An ADF test for the equity premium $m_t - f_t$ produces a test statistic of -8.09, which obviously strongly rejects the null of a unit root.) As argued previously, this is a result of the difference in the variances between the two series, with the Nikkei index returns having a standard deviation of 24.4, nearly fourteen times that of the risk-free rate of 1.8.

4 Univariate linear stochastic models: further topics

4.1 Decomposing time series: unobserved component models and signal extraction

4.1.1 Unobserved component models

If a time series is difference stationary then it can be decomposed into a stochastic non-stationary, or trend, component and a stationary, or noise, component – i.e.

$$x_t = z_t + u_t \tag{4.1}$$

Such a decomposition can be performed in various ways. For instance, Muth's (1960) classic example assumes that the trend component z_t is a random walk

$$z_t = \mu + z_{t-1} + v_t$$

while u_t is white noise and independent of v_t, i.e. $u_t \sim WN(0, \sigma_u^2)$ and $v_t \sim WN(0, \sigma_v^2)$, with $E(u_t v_{t-i}) = 0$ for all i. It thus follows that Δx_t is a stationary process

$$\Delta x_t = \mu + v_t + u_t - u_{t-1} \tag{4.2}$$

and has an ACF that cuts off at lag one with coefficient

$$\rho_1 = -\frac{\sigma_u^2}{\sigma_u^2 + 2\sigma_v^2} \tag{4.3}$$

It is clear that $-0.5 \le \rho_1 \le 0$, the exact value depending on the relative sizes of the two variances, and that Δx_t is an MA(1) process:

$$\Delta x_t = \mu + e_t - \theta e_{t-1} \tag{4.4}$$

where $e_t \sim WN(0, \sigma_e^2)$. On defining $\kappa = \sigma_v^2 / \sigma_u^2$ to be the *signal-to-noise* variance ratio, the relationship between the parameters of (4.2) and (4.4) can be shown to be

$$\theta = \frac{1}{2}\left((\kappa + 2) - \left(\kappa^2 + 4\kappa\right)^{1/2}\right), \quad \kappa = (1-\theta)^2 / \theta, \quad \kappa \geq 0, \quad |\theta| < 1$$

and

$$\sigma_u^2 = \theta \sigma_e^2$$

Thus $\kappa = 0$ corresponds to $\theta = 1$, so that the unit roots in (4.4) 'cancel out' and the overdifferenced x_t is stationary, while $\kappa = \infty$ corresponds to $\theta = 0$, in which case x_t is a pure random walk. A test of the stationarity null of $\theta = 1$ has been set out in section 3.4. It can therefore also be regarded as a test of the null $\sigma_v^2 = 0$, for if this is the case then z_t is a deterministic linear trend.

Models of the form (4.1) are known as *unobserved component* (UC) models, a more general formulation for the components being

$$\Delta z_t = \mu + \gamma(B) v_t \tag{4.5}$$

and

$$u_t = \lambda(B) a_t$$

where v_t and a_t are independent white-noise sequences with finite variances σ_v^2 and σ_a^2 and where $\gamma(B)$ and $\lambda(B)$ are stationary polynomials having no common roots. It can be shown that x_t will then have the form

$$\Delta x_t = \mu + \theta(B) e_t \tag{4.6}$$

where $\theta(B)$ and σ_e^2 can be obtained from

$$\sigma_e^2 \frac{\theta(B)\theta(B^{-1})}{(1-B)(1-B^{-1})} = \sigma_v^2 \frac{\gamma(B)\gamma(B^{-1})}{(1-B)(1-B^{-1})} + \sigma_a^2 \lambda(B)\lambda(B^{-1}) \tag{4.7}$$

From this we see that it is not necessarily the case that the parameters of the components can be identified from knowledge of the parameters of (4.6) alone; indeed, in general the components will not be identified. If z_t is restricted to be a random walk ($\gamma(B) = 1$), however, the parameters of the UC model will be identified. This is clearly the case for Muth's (1960) model, since σ_u^2 can be estimated by the lag one autocovariance of Δx_t

(the numerator of (4.3)) and σ_v^2 can be estimated from the variance of Δx_t (the denominator of (4.3)) and the estimated value of σ_u^2.

This example illustrates that, even though the variances are identified, such a decomposition may not always be feasible, however, for it is unable to account for positive first-order autocorrelation in Δx_t. To do so requires relaxing either the assumption that z_t is a random walk, so that the trend component contains both permanent and transitory movements, or the assumption that v_t and a_t are independent. If either of these assumptions is relaxed, the parameters of the Muth model will not be identified.

As a second example, consider Poterba and Summers' (1988) model for measuring mean reversion in stock prices. Rather than assuming the noise component to be purely random, they allow it to follow an AR(1) process

$$u_t = \lambda u_{t-1} + a_t$$

so that

$$\Delta x_t = \mu + v_t + (1 - \lambda B)^{-1}(1 - B)a_t$$

or

$$\Delta x_t^* = (1 - \lambda)\mu + (1 - \lambda B)v_t + (1 - B)a_t$$

where $x_t^* = (1 - \lambda B)x_t$. Δx_t thus follows the ARMA(1,1) process

$$(1 - \lambda B)\Delta x_t = \theta_0 + (1 - \theta_1 B)e_t$$

where $e_t \sim WN(0, \sigma_e^2)$ and $\theta_0 = \mu(1 - \lambda)$. The formula (4.7) can be used to obtain

$$\theta_1 = \left\{2 + (1 + \lambda)^2\kappa - (1 - \lambda)\left((1 + \lambda)^2\kappa^2 + 4\kappa\right)^{1/2}\right\}\Big/2(1 + \lambda\kappa)$$

and

$$\sigma_e^2 = \left(\lambda\sigma_v^2 + \sigma_a^2\right)\big/\theta_1$$

which, of course, reduce to the Muth formulae when $\lambda = 0$.

The assumption that the trend component, z_t, follows a random walk is not as restrictive as it may first seem. Consider the Wold decomposition for Δx_t

$$\Delta x_t = \mu + \psi(B)e_t = \mu + \sum_{j=0}^{\infty} \psi_j e_{t-j} \tag{4.8}$$

Since $\psi(1) = \sum \psi_j$ is a constant, we may write

$$\psi(B) = \psi(1) + C(B)$$

so that

$$
\begin{aligned}
C(B) &= \psi(B) - \psi(1) \\
&= 1 + \psi_1 B + \psi_2 B^2 + \psi_3 B^3 + \cdots - (1 + \psi_1 + \psi_2 + \psi_3 + \cdots) \\
&= -\psi_1(1 - B) - \psi_2(1 - B^2) - \psi_3(1 - B^3) - \cdots \\
&= (1 - B)\left(-\psi_1 - \psi_2(1 + B) - \psi_3(1 + B + B^2) - \cdots\right)
\end{aligned}
$$

i.e.

$$
\begin{aligned}
C(B) &= (1 - B)\left(-\left(\sum_{j=1}^{\infty} \psi_j\right) - \left(\sum_{j=2}^{\infty} \psi_j\right)B - \left(\sum_{j=3}^{\infty} \psi_j\right)B^2 - \cdots\right) \\
&= \Delta \tilde{\psi}(B)
\end{aligned}
$$

Thus

$$\psi(B) = \psi(1) + \Delta \tilde{\psi}(B)$$

implying that

$$\Delta x_t = \mu + \psi(1)e_t + \Delta \tilde{\psi}(B)e_t$$

This gives the decomposition due to Beveridge and Nelson (1981), with components

$$\Delta z_t = \mu + \left(\sum_{j=0}^{\infty} \psi_j\right)e_t = \mu + \psi(1)e_t \qquad (4.9)$$

and

$$u_t = -\left(\sum_{j=1}^{\infty} \psi_j\right)e_t - \left(\sum_{j=2}^{\infty} \psi_j\right)e_{t-1} - \left(\sum_{j=3}^{\infty} \psi_j\right)e_{t-2} - \cdots = \tilde{\psi}(B)e_t$$

Since e_t is white noise, the trend component is therefore a random walk with a rate of drift equal to μ and an innovation equal to $\psi(1)e_t$, which is thus proportional to that of the original series. The noise component is clearly stationary, but, since it is driven by the same innovation as the trend component, z_t and u_t must be *perfectly correlated*, in direct contrast to the Muth decomposition, which assumes that they are independent. For example, the

Beveridge–Nelson decomposition of the IMA(1,1) (integrated moving average) process (4.4) is

$$\Delta z_t = \mu + (1 - \theta)e_t \tag{4.10}$$

$$u_t = \theta e_t \tag{4.11}$$

The relationship between the Beveridge–Nelson and Muth decompositions is exact. Rather than assuming that u_t and v_t are independent, suppose that $v_t = \alpha u_t$. Equating (4.2) and (4.4) then yields

$$\Delta x_t = \mu + (1 + \alpha)u_t - u_{t-1} = \mu + e_t - \theta e_{t-1}$$

so that $e_t = (1 + \alpha)u_t$ and $\theta e_t = u_t$, thus recovering (4.11) and implying that $\theta = 1/(1 + \alpha)$. The trend (4.10) then becomes

$$\Delta z_t = \mu + (1 - \theta)e_t = \mu + \frac{(1 - \theta)}{\theta} u_t = \mu + \alpha u_t = \mu + v_t$$

which recovers the Muth trend.

Following Cuddington and Winters (1987), Miller (1988) and Newbold (1990), a simple way of estimating the Beveridge–Nelson components is to approximate the Wold decomposition (4.8) by an ARIMA $(p,1,q)$ process

$$\Delta x_t = \mu + \frac{\left(1 - \theta_1 B - \cdots - \theta_q B^q\right)}{\left(1 - \phi_1 B - \cdots - \phi_p B^p\right)} e_t = \mu + \frac{\theta(B)}{\phi(B)} e_t \tag{4.12}$$

so that

$$\Delta z_t = \mu + \psi(1)e_t = \mu + \frac{\theta(1)}{\phi(1)} e_t = \mu + \frac{\left(1 - \theta_1 - \cdots - \theta_q\right)}{\left(1 - \phi_1 - \cdots - \phi_p\right)} e_t \tag{4.13}$$

where $\psi(1) = \theta(1)/\phi(1)$. Equation (4.12) can also be written as

$$\frac{\phi(B)}{\theta(B)} \psi(1) \Delta x_t - \mu + \psi(1)e_t \tag{4.14}$$

and comparing (4.13) and (4.14) shows that

$$z_t = \frac{\phi(B)}{\theta(B)} \psi(1) x_t = \omega(B)x_t$$

The trend is therefore a weighted average of current and past values of the observed series, with the weights summing to unity since $\omega(1) = 1$. The noise component is then given by

$$u_t = x_t - \omega(B)x_t = (1 - \omega(B))x_t = \tilde{\omega}(B)x_t = \frac{\phi(1)\theta(B) - \theta(1)\phi(B)}{\phi(1)\theta(B)}x_t$$

Since $\tilde{\omega}(1) = 1 - \omega(1) = 0$, the weights for the noise component sum to zero. Using (4.12), this component can also be expressed as

$$u_t = \frac{\phi(1)\theta(B) - \theta(1)\phi(B)}{\phi(1)\phi(B)\Delta}e_t \tag{4.15}$$

Since u_t is stationary, the numerator of (4.15) can be written as $\phi(1)\theta(B) - \theta(1)\phi(B) = \Delta\varphi(B)$, since it must contain a unit root to cancel out the one in the denominator. As the order of the numerator is $\max(p,q)$, $\varphi(B)$ must be of order $r = \max(p,q) - 1$, implying that the noise has the ARMA (p,r) representation

$$\phi(B)u_t = (\varphi(B)/\phi(1))e_t$$

For example, for the IMA(1,1) process (4.4), the components are

$$z_t = (1 - \theta B)^{-1}(1 - \theta)x_t = \left(1 + \theta B + \theta^2 B^2 + \cdots\right)(1 - \theta)x_t$$
$$= (1 - \theta)\sum_{j=0}^{\infty}\theta^j x_{t-j}$$

and

$$u_t = \frac{(1 - \theta B) - (1 - \theta)}{(1 - \theta B)}x_t = \frac{\theta(1 - B)}{(1 - \theta B)}x_t = \theta(1 - \theta B)^{-1}\Delta x_t$$
$$= \theta\sum_{j=0}^{\infty}\theta^j x_{t-j}$$

Thus, the trend can be recursively estimated as

$$\hat{z}_t = \theta\hat{z}_{t-1} + (1 - \theta)x_t, \quad \hat{u}_t = x_t - \hat{z}_t$$

with starting values $\hat{z}_1 = x_1$ and $\hat{u}_1 = 0$.

In a more general context, it is possible for an x_t with Wold decomposition (4.8) to be written as (4.1), with z_t being a random walk and u_t being stationary and where the innovations of the two components are correlated to an arbitrary degree. Only the Beveridge–Nelson decomposition is *guaranteed* to exist, however.

Example 4.1 Beveridge–Nelson decomposition of UK equities

In example 2.6 the following ARIMA $(2,1,2)$ model was fitted to the UK FTA All Share index

$$\left(1 + 0.953B + 0.756B^2\right)\Delta x_t = 1.81 + \left(1 + 1.062B + 0.760B^2\right)e_t$$

Thus,

$$\psi(1) = \frac{(1 + 1.062 + 0.760)}{(1 + 0.953 + 0.756)} = 1.041$$

and the Beveridge–Nelson trend is therefore

$$\Delta z_t = 1.81 + 1.041e_t$$

or, equivalently,

$$z_t = -1.062z_{t-1} - 0.760z_{t-2} + 1.041x_t + 0.993x_{t-1} + 0.787x_{t-2}$$

Since

$$\phi(1)\theta(B) - \theta(1)\phi(B) = -0.114 + 0.188B - 0.074B^2$$
$$= \Delta(-0.114 - 0.074B)$$

the noise component is thus the ARMA $(2,1)$ process

$$u_t = -0.953u_{t-1} - 0.756u_{t-2} - 0.042e_t - 0.027e_{t-1}$$

4.1.2 Signal extraction

Given a UC model of the form (4.1) and models for z_t and u_t, it is often useful to provide estimates of these two unobserved components: this is known as *signal extraction*. An MMSE estimate of z_t is an estimate $\hat{z}_t$ that minimises $E(\zeta_t^2)$, where ζ_t is the estimation error $z_t - \hat{z}_t$. From, for example, Pierce (1979), given the *infinite sample* $\{x_t\}_{-\infty}^{\infty}$, such an estimator is

$$\hat{z}_t = v_z(B)x_t = \sum_{j=-\infty}^{\infty} v_{zj}x_{t-j}$$

where the filter $v_z(B)$ is defined as

$$v_z(B) = \frac{\sigma_v^2 \gamma(B)\gamma(B^{-1})}{\sigma_e^2 \theta(B)\theta(B^{-1})}$$

in which case the noise component can be estimated as

$$\hat{u}_t = x_t - \hat{z}_t = [1 - v_z(B)]x_t = v_u(B)x_t$$

For example, for the Muth model of a random walk overlaid with stationary noise,

$$v_z(B) = \frac{\sigma_v^2}{\sigma_e^2}(1 - \theta B)^{-1}\left(1 - \theta B^{-1}\right)^{-1} = \frac{\sigma_v^2}{\sigma_e^2}\frac{1}{(1 - \theta^2)}\sum_{j=-\infty}^{\infty}\theta^{|j|}B^j$$

so that, using $\sigma_v^2 = (1 - \theta)^2\sigma_e^2$, obtained using (4.6), we have

$$\hat{z}_t = \frac{(1 - \theta)^2}{1 - \theta^2}\sum_{j=-\infty}^{\infty}\theta^{|j|}x_{t-j}$$

Thus, for values of θ close to unity, $\hat{z}_t$ will be given by a very long moving average of future and past values of x. If θ is close to zero, however, $\hat{z}_t$ will be almost equal to the most recently observed value of x. From (4.3) it is clear that large values of θ correspond to small values of the signal-to-noise ratio $\kappa = \sigma_v^2/\sigma_u^2$; when the noise component dominates, a long moving average of x values provides the best estimate of trend, while, if the noise component is only small, the trend is given by the current position of x.

The estimation error, $\zeta_t = z_t - \hat{z}_t$, can be written as

$$\zeta_t = v_z(B)z_t - v_u(B)u_t$$

and Pierce (1979) shows that ζ_t will be stationary if z_t and u_t are generated by processes of the form (4.4). In fact, ζ_t will follow the process

$$\zeta_t = \theta_\zeta(B)\xi_t$$

where

$$\theta_\zeta = \frac{\gamma(B)\lambda(B)}{\theta(B)} \qquad \sigma_\xi^2 = \frac{\sigma_a^2\sigma_v^2}{\sigma_e^2}$$

and $\xi_t \sim WN\left(0, \sigma_\xi^2\right)$.

For the Muth model we therefore have it that ζ_t follows the AR(1) process

$$(1 - \theta B)\zeta_t = \xi_t$$

and the mean square error (MSE) of the optimal signal extraction procedure is

$$E(\zeta_t^2) = \frac{\sigma_a^2 \sigma_v^2}{\sigma_e^2 (1 - \theta^2)}$$

As noted earlier, if we are given only $\{x_t\}$ and its model, i.e. (4.6), then models for z_t and u_t are in general unidentified. If x_t follows the IMA(1,1) process

$$(1 - B)x_t = (1 - \theta B)e_t \tag{4.16}$$

then the most general signal-plus-white-noise UC model has z_t given by

$$(1 - B)z_t = (1 - \Theta B)v_t \tag{4.17}$$

and for any Θ value in the interval $- \leq \Theta \leq \theta$ there exist values of σ_a^2 and σ_v^2 such that $z_t + u_t$ yields (4.16). It can be shown that setting $\Theta = -1$ minimises the variance of both z_t and u_t, and this is known as the *canonical decomposition* of x_t. Choosing this value implies that $\gamma(B) = 1 + B$, and we thus have

$$\hat{z}_t = \frac{\sigma_v^2 (1 + B)(1 + B^{-1})}{\sigma_e^2 (1 - \theta B)(1 - \theta B^{-1})}$$

and

$$(1 - \theta B)\zeta_t = (1 + B)\xi_t$$

In this development we have assumed that, in estimating z_t, the future of $\{x_t\}$ is available as well as its past. In many situations it is necessary to estimate z_t given only data on x_t up to $s = t - m$, for finite m. This includes the problems of signal extraction based either on current data ($m = 0$) or on recent data ($m < 0$), and the problem of forecasting the signal ($m > 0$). We therefore need to extend the analysis to consider signal extraction given only the *semi-infinite* sample $\{x_s, s \leq t - m\}$. Pierce (1979) shows that, in this case, an estimate of z_t is given by

$$\hat{z}_t^{(m)} = v_z^{(m)}(B)x_t$$

where

$$v_z^{(m)}(B) = \frac{(1 - B)}{\sigma_e^2 \theta(B)} \left[\frac{\sigma_v^2 \gamma(B)\gamma(B^{-1})}{(1 - B)\theta(B^{-1})} \right]_m$$

in which we use the notation

$$[h(B)]_m = \sum_{j=m}^{\infty} h_j B^j$$

Thus, for the Muth model we have

$$v_z^{(m)}(B) = \frac{\sigma_v^2(1-B)}{\sigma_e^2(1-\theta B)} \left[\frac{(1-B)^{-1}}{(1-\theta B^{-1})} \right]_m$$

and Pierce (1979) shows that this becomes, for $m \geq 0$,

$$v_z^{(m)}(B) = \frac{\sigma_v^2 B^m}{\sigma_e^2(1-\theta)} \sum_{j=0}^{\infty} (\theta B)^j = (1-\theta)B^m \sum_{j=0}^{\infty} (\theta B)^j$$

while, for $m < 0$,

$$v_z^{(m)}(B) = \theta^{-m}(1-\theta)B^m \sum_{j=0}^{\infty} (\theta B)^j + \frac{1}{(1-\theta B)} \sum_{j=0}^{-m-1} \theta^j B^{-j}$$

Therefore, when either estimating z_t for the current time period ($m = 0$) or forecasting z_t ($m > 0$), we apply an exponentially weighted moving average to the observed series, beginning with the most recent data available, but not otherwise depending on the value of m. For $m < 0$, when we are estimating z_t based on some, but not all, of the relevant future observations of x_t, the filter comprises two parts: the same filter as in the $m \geq 0$ case applied to the furthest forward observation but with a declining weight (θ^{-m}) placed upon it, and a second term capturing the additional influence of the observed future observations.

UC models can also be analysed within a *state space* framework, in which the Kalman filter plays a key role in providing both optimal forecasts and a method of estimating the unknown model parameters. In this framework, models such as the random-walk-plus-white-noise are known as *structural models*, and a thorough discussion of the methodological and technical ideas underlying such formulations is contained in Harvey (1989) and Harvey and Shephard (1992), while Koopman, Shephard and Doornik (1999) and Koopman *et al.* (2006) provide computer software.

The UC model (4.5) is also related to the *Hodrick–Prescott (H-P) trend filter* (Hodrick and Prescott, 1997), which is a very popular method of detrending economic time series. This filter is derived by minimising the variation in the noise component, $u_t = x_t - z_t$, subject to a condition on the 'smoothness' of the trend component z_t. This smoothness condition penalises acceleration in the trend, so the minimisation problem becomes that of minimising the function

$$\sum_{t=1}^{T} u_t^2 + \delta \sum_{t=1}^{T} \left((z_{t+1} - z_t) - (z_t - z_{t-1}) \right)^2$$

with respect to z_t, $t = 0,1 \ldots, T+1$, where δ is a Lagrangean multiplier that can be interpreted as a smoothness parameter. The higher the value of δ the smoother the trend, so that in the limit, as $\delta \to \infty$, z_t becomes a linear trend. The first-order conditions are

$$0 = -2(x_t - z_t) + 2\delta((z_t - z_{t-1}) - (z_{t-1} - z_{t-2}))$$
$$- 4\delta((z_{t+1} - z_t) - (z_t - z_{t-1})) + 2\delta((z_{t+2} - z_{t+1}) - (z_{t+1} - z_t))$$

which may be written as

$$x_t = z_t + \delta(1-B)^2(z_t - 2z_{t+1} + z_{t+2}) = \left(1 + \delta(1-B)^2\left(1-B^{-1}\right)^2\right)z_t$$

so that the H-P trend estimator is

$$\hat{z}_t(\delta) = \left(1 + \delta(1-B)^2\left(1-B^{-1}\right)^2\right)^{-1} x_t$$

The MMSE trend estimator can be written using (4.7) as

$$\hat{z}_t = \frac{\sigma_v^2 \gamma(B)\gamma(B^{-1})}{\sigma_e^2 \theta(B)\theta(B^{-1})} x_t = \frac{\gamma(B)\gamma(B^{-1})}{\gamma(B)\gamma(B^{-1}) + (\sigma_a^2/\sigma_v^2)\lambda(B)\lambda(B^{-1})} x_t$$

Comparing this with the H-P trend estimator shows that, for the latter to be optimal in the MMSE sense, we must set

$$\gamma(B) = (1-B)^{-1}, \quad \lambda(B) = 1, \quad \delta = \sigma_a^2/\sigma_v^2$$

In other words, the underlying UC model must have the trend component $\Lambda^2 z_t = v_t$ and u_t must be white noise. Related filters are the *band-pass* of Baxter and King (1999) and Christiano and Fitzgerald (2003), and the *Butterworth*, suggested by Pollock (2000): see, for example, Mills (2003, chap. 4) for details.

Example 4.2 Estimating expected real rates of interest

A long-standing example of the unobserved random walk buried in white noise is provided by the analysis of expected real rates of interest under the assumption of rational expectations, or, equivalently, financial market efficiency: see, for example, Fama (1975), Nelson and Schwert (1977) and Mills and Stephenson (1986). In this model, the unobservable expected real rate, z_t, is assumed to follow a driftless random walk, i.e. equation (4.10) with $\theta = 0$, and it differs from the observed real rate, x_t, by the amount of unexpected inflation, u_t, which, under the assumption of market efficiency, will be a white-noise process. The observed real rate will thus follow the ARIMA(0,1,1) process shown in (4.9).

Such a model fitted to the real UK Treasury bill rate over the period 1952Q1 to 2005Q3 yielded

$$\Delta x_t = (1 - 0.810B)e_t, \quad \hat{\sigma}_e^2 = 15.61$$

From the relationships linking σ_v^2 and σ_u^2 to θ and σ_e^2, it follows that the unobserved variances may be estimated as

$$\hat{\sigma}_v^2 = (1 - 0.810)^2 \hat{\sigma}_e^2 = 0.56$$

$$\hat{\sigma}_u^2 = 0.810 \hat{\sigma}_e^2 = 12.64$$

yielding a signal-to-noise variance ratio of $\kappa = \hat{\sigma}_v^2 / \hat{\sigma}_u^2 = 0.04$, so that variations in the expected real rate are small compared to variations in unexpected inflation. Expected real rates based on information up to and including time t, i.e. $m = 0$, can then be estimated using the exponentially weighted moving average

$$\hat{z}_t = v_z^{(0)}(B)x_t$$

where

$$v_z^{(0)}(B) = (1 - \theta) \sum_{j=0}^{\infty} (\theta B)^j = 0.19 \sum_{j=0}^{\infty} (0.81B)^j$$

i.e.

$$\hat{z}_1 = x_1$$
$$\hat{z}_t = 0.81\hat{z}_{t-1} + 0.19x_t \quad t = 2, 3, \ldots$$

Unexpected inflation can then be obtained as $\hat{u}_t = x_t - \hat{z}_t$. Figure 4.1 provides plots of x_t, $\hat{z}_t$ and $\hat{u}_t$, showing that the expected real rate is considerably smoother than the observed real rate, as was suggested by the small signal-to-noise ratio. In the early part of the 1950s expected real rates were

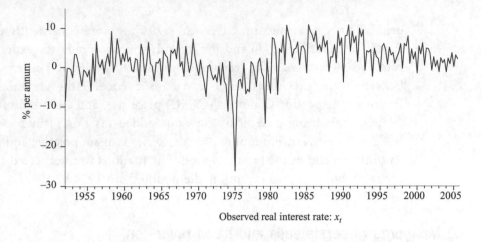

Observed real interest rate: x_t

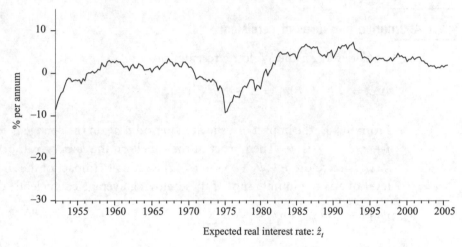

Expected real interest rate: $\hat{z}_t$

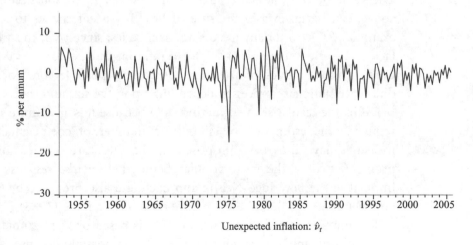

Unexpected inflation: $\hat{v}_t$

Figure 4.1   Real UK Treasury bill rate decomposition (quarterly January 1952–September 2005)

generally negative, but from 1956 to 1970 they were consistently positive. From the middle of 1970 and for the subsequent decade the expected real rate was always negative, reaching a minimum in 1975Q1 after inflation peaked in the previous quarter as a consequence of the Organization of Petroleum Exporting Countries (OPEC) price rise, and a local minimum in 1979Q2, this being a result of the value added tax (VAT) increase in the budget of that year. From mid-1980 the series is again positive and remains so until the end of the sample period. Fluctuations in unexpected inflation are fairly homogenous except for the period from 1974 to 1982.

4.2 Measures of persistence and trend reversion

4.2.1 Alternative measures of persistence

Consider again the Wold representation

$$\Delta x_t = \mu + \psi(B)a_t = \mu + \sum_{j=0}^{\infty} \psi_j a_{t-j} \tag{4.18}$$

From (4.18), the impact of a shock in period t, a_t, on the change in x in period $t+k$, Δx_{t+k}, is ψ_k. The impact of the shock on the *level* of x in period $t+k$, x_{t+k} is therefore $1 + \psi_1 + \cdots + \psi_k$. The ultimate impact of the shock on the level of x is the infinite sum of these moving average coefficients, defined as

$$\psi(1) = 1 + \psi_1 + \psi_2 + \cdots = \sum_{j=0}^{\infty} \psi_j$$

The value of $\psi(1)$, which is used in the Beveridge–Nelson decomposition above, can be taken as a measure of how persistent shocks to x are. For example, $\psi(1) = 0$ for any trend stationary series, since $\psi(B)$ must contain a factor $(1 - B)$, whereas $\psi(1) = 1$ for a random walk, since $\psi_j = 0$ for $j > 0$. Other positive values of $\psi(1)$ are, of course, possible for more general difference stationary processes, depending upon the size and signs of the ψ_j.

Difficulties can arise in estimating $\psi(1)$ because it is an infinite sum, thus requiring the estimation of an infinite number of coefficients. Various measures have thus been proposed in the literature to circumvent this problem, two of the most popular being the *impulse response function*, implicit in the Beveridge–Nelson approach and also proposed by Campbell and Mankiw (1987), and the *variance ratio* of Cochrane (1988).

The impulse response measure of $\psi(1)$ is based on approximating $\psi(B)$ by a ratio of finite-order polynomials. This is possible because, since it is assumed that Δx_t is a linear stationary process, it follows that it has an ARMA(p, q) representation

$$\phi(B)\Delta x_t = \theta_0 + \theta(B)a_t$$

Equation (4.18) is then interpreted as the moving average representation, or impulse response function, of Δx_t:

$$\Delta x_t = \phi(1)^{-1}\theta_0 + \phi(B)^{-1}\theta(B)a_t$$

From the equality $\psi(B) = \phi(B)^{-1}\theta(B)$, the measure $\psi(1)$ can then be calculated directly as $\psi(1) = \theta(1)/\phi(1)$.

Cochrane (1988), on the other hand, proposes a non-parametric measure of persistence known as the variance ratio, defined as $V_k = \sigma_k^2/\sigma_1^2$, where

$$\sigma_k^2 = k^{-1}V(x_t - x_{t-k}) = k^{-1}V(\Delta_k x_t)$$

$\Delta_k = 1 - B^k$ being the kth differencing operator. This measure is based on the following argument. If x_t is a pure random walk with drift, so that $\Delta x_t = \theta + a_t$, then the variance of its kth differences will grow linearly with k; using the fact that $\Delta_k = \Delta(1 + B + \cdots + B^{k-1})$,

$$V(\Delta_k x_t) = V((x_t - x_{t-1}) + (x_{t-1} - x_{t-2}) + \cdots + (x_{t-k+1} - x_{t-k}))$$
$$= \sum_{j=1}^{k} V(x_{t-j+1} - x_{t-j}) = \sum_{j=1}^{k} V(a_t) = k\sigma^2$$

If, on the other hand, x_t is trend stationary, the variance of its kth differences approaches a constant, this being twice the unconditional variance of the series: if $x_t = \beta_0 + \beta_1 t + a_t$, $V(\Delta_k x_t) = V(a_t) + V(a_{t-k}) = 2\sigma^2$.

Cochrane thus suggests plotting a sample estimate of σ_k^2 as a function of k. If x_t is a random walk the plot should be constant at σ^2, whereas if x_t is trend stationary the plot should decline towards zero. If fluctuations in x_t are partly permanent and partly temporary, so that the series can be modelled as a combination of random walk and stationary components, the plot of σ_k^2 versus k should settle down to the variance of the innovation to the random walk component.

In providing a sample estimate of σ_k^2, Cochrane corrects for two possible sources of small sample bias. First, the sample mean of Δx_t is used to estimate the drift term μ at all k, rather than a different trend term at each k being estimated from the mean of the k-differences. Second, a degrees of freedom correction $T/(T-k-1)$ is included, for, without this, σ_k^2 will decline towards zero as $k \to T$ because, in the limit, a variance cannot be taken with just one observation. These corrections produce an estimator of σ_k^2 that is unbiased when applied to a pure random walk with drift. The actual formula used to compute the estimator from the sample $\{x_t\}_0^T$ is (Cochrane, 1988, equation (A3), p. 917)

$$\hat{\sigma}_k^2 = \frac{T}{k(T-k)(T-k+1)} \sum_{j=k}^{T} \left(x_j - x_{j-k} - \frac{k}{T}(x_T - x_0) \right)^2 \qquad (4.19)$$

From Cochrane (1988), the asymptotic standard error of $\hat{\sigma}_k^2$ is $(4k/3T)^{0.5}\hat{\sigma}_k^2$. The variance ratio can then be estimated as $\hat{V}_k = \hat{\sigma}_k^2/\hat{\sigma}_1^2$. Cochrane shows that V_k can also be written as

$$V_k = 1 + 2 \sum_{j=1}^{k-1} \frac{k-j}{k} \rho_j$$

so that the *limiting variance ratio, V*, can be defined as

$$V \equiv \lim_{k \to \infty} V_k = 1 + 2 \sum_{j=1}^{\infty} \rho_j$$

Furthermore, since it can also be shown that

$$\lim_{k \to \infty} \sigma_k^2 = \frac{\left(\sum \psi_j\right)^2}{\sum \psi_j^2} \sigma_1^2 = \left(\sum \psi_j\right)^2 \sigma^2 = |\psi(1)|^2 \sigma^2$$

V can also be written as

$$V = \left(\sigma^2/\sigma_1^2\right)|\psi(1)|^2$$

which provides the link between the two persistence measures. By defining $R^2 = 1 - (\sigma^2/\sigma_1^2)$, the fraction of the variance that is predictable from knowledge of the past history of Δx_t, we have

$$\psi(1) = \sqrt{\frac{V}{1-R^2}}$$

so that $\psi(1) \geq \sqrt{V}$: the more predictable is Δx_t the greater the difference between the two measures.

4.2.2 Testing for trend reversion

Whether a random walk is present in a financial time series has been shown to be a question of some importance. The various unit root tests discussed in chapter 3 are, of course, one approach to testing whether a series contains a random walk component. As we have seen, however, such tests can have difficulties in detecting some important departures from a random walk, and the associated distributions of the test statistics tend to have awkward dependencies on nuisance parameters.

When the null hypothesis under examination is that the series is generated by a random walk with strict white-noise normal increments, a test based on the variance ratio may be preferred. Consider again the observed series $\{x_t\}_0^T$ and suppose that x_t is generated by the random walk

$$x_t = \theta + x_{t-1} + a_t$$

where $a_t \sim NID(0, \sigma^2)$. For this model, the variance ratio, V, is unity. Lo and MacKinlay (1988, 1989) consider the test statistic

$$M(k) = \hat{\sigma}_k^2 / \hat{\sigma}_1^2 - 1 = \hat{V}_k - 1$$

and show that

$$z_1(k) = M(k) \cdot \left(\frac{2(2k-1)(k-1)}{3Tk} \right)^{-1/2} \overset{a}{\sim} N(0,1)$$

They also derive a version of the variance ratio test that is robust to serial correlation and heteroskedasticity. If a_t takes the conditions (3.11), the test statistic becomes

$$z_2(k) = M(k) \cdot \Omega^{-1/2}(k)$$

where

$$\Omega(k) = \sum_{j=1}^{k-1} \left(\frac{2(k-j)}{k} \right)^2 \delta_j, \quad \delta_j = \frac{\sum_{t=j+1}^{T} \alpha_{0t}\alpha_{jt}}{\left(\sum_{t-1}^{T} \alpha_{0t} \right)^2},$$

$$\alpha_{jt} = \left(x_{t-j} - x_{t-j-1} - \frac{1}{T}(x_T - x_0) \right)^2$$

The δ_j are heteroskedastic-consistent estimators of the asymptotic variances of the estimated autocorrelations of Δx_t.

Lo and MacKinlay (1989) find that this large-sample normal approximation works well when k is small and T is large. They emphasise, however, that it can become unsatisfactory for large k because the empirical distribution of $M(k)$ is highly skewed in these circumstances. Although the empirical sizes of the test statistic are close to their nominal values, almost all the rejections occur in the upper tail of the distribution. It is therefore clear that the normal approximation to the distribution of $M(k)$ is likely to be of only limited practical use. As a consequence, the empirical distributions of the test statistics need to be evaluated by simulation.

In any case, the asymptotic normality of $M(k)$ relies on fixing k and allowing T to increase, so that $k/T \to 0$. Richardson and Stock (1989) consider a different perspective, however, in which k is allowed to tend asymptotically to a non-zero fraction (δ) of T, i.e. $k/T \to \delta$. Under this asymptotic theory, $M(k)$ has a limiting distribution that is not normal but has a representation in terms of functionals of Brownian motion, $W(r)$, which under the null does not depend on any unknown parameters:

$$M(k) \Rightarrow \frac{1}{\delta} \int_{\delta}^{1} [Y(r)]^2 \mathrm{d}r$$

where

$$Y(r) = W(r) - W(r - \delta) - \delta W(1)$$

Richardson and Stock (1989) argue that the $k/T \to \delta$ theory provides a much better approximation to the finite sample distribution of $M(k)$ than does the fixed k theory. Moreover, this limiting distribution is valid even under non-normality and certain forms of heteroskedasticity. Lo and MacKinlay (1989) find that the power of the variance ratio test is comparable in power to τ_τ when x_t is trend stationary. Deo and Richardson (2003), however, point out some difficulties with the asymptotic consistency and power of the test, which suggest that k should not be set too large when T is small.

A typical use of the variance ratio test is to calculate the statistic for various values of k and reject the null of a random walk if *any* of the statistics are significant at a pre-assigned significance level (see, for example, Liu and He, 1991). This gives rise to the problem of multiple comparisons among test statistics, as it is inappropriate to focus on the significance of individual test statistics without controlling for the size of the implicit joint test. Chow and Denning (1993) and Fong, Koh and Ouliaris (1997) thus propose *joint* variance ratio tests. Chow and Denning propose a joint test based on the maximum absolute value of the variance ratio statistics, which is compared to the studentised maximum modulus distribution, for which tables of critical values are available. Unfortunately, this test assumes that the vector of variance ratio test statistics is multivariate normal, but, as we have seen, this is unlikely to be the case when k/T is large. In this situation, there will also be a high degree of 'overlap' in the data induced by taking k-differences, which will in turn induce dependencies between the individual statistics.

Fong, Koh and Ouliaris (1997) use the results of Richardson and Smith (1991) and Richardson (1993) on modelling serial correlation induced by overlapping data to derive the following Wald statistic to examine the joint hypothesis that an $m \times 1$ vector of variance ratio test statistics

$$M_m = (M(m_1), M(m_2), \ldots, M(m_m))^\top$$

is equal to zero:

$$T \cdot M_m^\top \Phi^{-1} M_m \sim \chi^2(m)$$

where Φ is the covariance matrix of M_m. For any pair of lags $m_j = r$ and $m_k = s$, $1 \leq j, k \leq m$, Φ has the elements

$$\Phi_{jj} = \frac{2(2r-1)(r-1)}{3r} \qquad \Phi_{kk} = \frac{2(2s-1)(s-1)}{3s}$$

$$\Phi_{jk} = \Phi_{kj} = \frac{2((3s-r-1)(r-1))}{3s}$$

Simulation results presented by Fong, Koh and Ouliaris suggest that the size and power of this statistic is satisfactory.

Example 4.3 Persistence and mean reversion in UK stock prices

In example 2.6 we fitted an ARIMA(2, 1, 2) process to the logarithms of the FTA All Share index, with $\phi(B) = (1 + 0.953B + 0.756B^2)$ and $\theta(B) = (1 + 1.062B + 0.760B^2)$. Thus, $A(1) = 2.822/2.709 = 1.041$, which provides some evidence in favour of *mean aversion*, whereby a series will continue to diverge from its previously forecast value following a shock. Since the null hypothesis $A(1) = 1$ can be parameterised as $\phi_1 + \phi_2 - \theta_1 - \theta_2 = 0$, however, a Wald test of this linear restriction has a marginal significance level of 0.07, suggesting that such evidence is quite weak. Cochrane (1988) has criticised the use of fitted ARIMA models for constructing the long-run measure $A(1)$ because they are designed to capture *short-run* dynamics (recall their

Table 4.1 Variance ratio test statistics for UK stock prices (monthly 1965–2002)

k	M	$p(z_1)$	5%	50%	95%
12	0.13	0.23	−0.29	−0.04	0.30
24	0.01	0.48	−0.41	−0.08	0.41
36	−0.06	0.57	−0.49	−0.11	0.46
48	−0.15	0.67	−0.55	−0.14	0.58
60	−0.11	0.61	−0.60	−0.18	0.61
72	−0.11	0.60	−0.65	−0.20	0.64
84	−0.18	0.65	−0.70	−0.25	0.64
96	−0.21	0.66	−0.72	−0.30	0.64

Note: $p(z_1)$ denotes the probability under the null hypothesis of observing a larger variance ratio than that observed using the asymptotic $N(0,1)$ distribution. 5%, 50%, 95% are percentiles of the empirical distributions of $M(k)$ computed under the $k/T \to \delta$ asymptotic theory using $NID\,(0,1)$ returns with 5000 replications for each k.

development for short-term forecasting by Box and Jenkins, 1976), rather than the *long-run* correlations that are of interest here.

Table 4.1 presents $M(k)$ statistics for a sequence of k values associated with 'long-differences' of prices of between one and eight years. Also provided are the p-values using the normal approximation and simulated upper tail percentiles using the Richardson and Stock (1989) $k/T \to \delta$ asymptotic theory. Using either distribution, there is no evidence to reject the random walk null, although for $k \geq 36$ the $\hat{V}_k$ statistics are all less than unity, unlike the estimate of the variance ratio given by $A(1)$. In support of this conclusion, the joint test statistic has a value of 13.32. As it is distributed as χ_8^2, this also cannot reject the random walk null, having a marginal significance level of 0.101.

4.2.3 Mean reverting models in continuous time

Several continuous processes have been developed for modelling mean reversion in interest rates (for a recent review, see Bali and Wu, 2006). Chan *et al.* (1992) show that many of the single-factor term structure models for the short-term interest rate r can be nested in the differential equation

$$dr = (a + br)dt + \sigma r^\gamma dZ$$

where Z is a Weiner process. These dynamics imply that the conditional mean and the variance of the process depend on the level of r through the parameters b and γ, with mean reversion being captured by $b < 0$. This stochastic differential equation nests a broad class of interest rate processes, with eight of the most popular specifications being obtained by placing appropriate parameter restrictions (for references and detailed descriptions of these models, see Chan *et al.*, 1992).

Model 1 (Merton's model) is obtained if we assume that $b = \gamma = 0$ and corresponds to a simple Brownian motion with drift. By setting just $\gamma = 0$ we get model 2 (Vasicek's model), which is a mean-reverting process known as the Ornstein–Uhlenbeck. Obviously, the conditional volatility is constant in these first two specifications since γ is equal to zero. Model 3 (Cox, Ingersoll and Ross' 'square root process'), which sets $\gamma = 0.5$, implies that conditional volatility is proportional to r. By letting $a = 0$ and $\gamma = 1$, model 5 is obtained, which corresponds to the geometric Brownian motion process, while the additional restriction $b = 0$ allows the simpler driftless specification in model 4 (Dothan's model). Model 6 (Brennan and Schwartz's model) encompasses the two previous specifications and is obtained by just setting $\gamma = 1$. In these last three models the conditional volatility is proportional to r^2. Finally, model 7 (Cox, Ingersoll and Ross' variable rate process) and Model 8 (constant elasticity of variance) are obtained by restricting $a = b = 0$ and $\gamma = 1.5$, and $a = 0$, respectively.

Model 1:	$dr = adt + \sigma dZ$	Merton	$b = \gamma = 0$
Model 2:	$dr = (a + br)dt + \sigma dZ$	Vasicek	$\gamma = 0$
Model 3:	$dr = (a + br)dt + \sigma\sqrt{r}dZ$	Cox, Ingersoll and Ross (CIR)	$\gamma = 0.5$
Model 4:	$dr = \sigma r dZ$	Dothan	$a = b = 0, \gamma = 1$
Model 5:	$dr = brdt + \sigma r dZ$	Geometric Brownian motion	$a = 0, \gamma = 1$
Model 6:	$dr = (a + br)dt + \sigma r dZ$	Brennan and Schwartz	$\gamma = 1$
Model 7:	$dr = \sigma r^{1.5} dZ$	CIR variable rate	$a = b = 0, \gamma = 1.5$
Model 8:	$dr = brdt + \sigma r^{\gamma} dZ$	Constant elasticity of variance	$a = 0$

Chan *et al.* (1992) base estimation of these models on the following discrete-time approximation of the continuous-time differential equations:

$$\Delta r_t = a + br_{t-1} + \varepsilon_t$$

where ε_t is a disturbance term with moments $E(\varepsilon_t) = 0$ and $E(\varepsilon_t^2) = \sigma^2 r_{t-1}^{2\gamma}$. If interest rates are measured over a short time span then the approximation error in this model will be of second-order importance. Generalised method of moments (GMM) estimation is appropriate since it requires only that the distribution of interest rate changes is stationary and ergodic and that the relevant expectations exist. This is particularly useful here since the various models imply different distributions. For example, the first two imply that the distribution of interest rate changes is normal, while model 3 assumes that these changes are distributed as a random variable proportional to a non-central χ^2. Finally, the GMM estimators have the additional advantage of being consistent even if the disturbances are conditionally heteroskedastic.

Estimation begins by determining the moment conditions. Let θ be the parameter vector with elements a, b, σ^2 and γ. Four moment conditions are sufficient to identify the system exactly. Two conditions follow from the mean and variance of the error term. Given that $\varepsilon_t = r_t - r_{t-1} - a - b r_{t-1}$, the other two reflect orthogonality conditions:

$$
f_t(\theta) = \begin{bmatrix} \varepsilon_t \\ \varepsilon_t r_{t-1} \\ \varepsilon_t^2 - \sigma^2 r_{t-1}^{2\gamma} \\ \left(\varepsilon_t^2 - \sigma^2 r_{t-1}^{2\gamma} \right) r_{t-1} \end{bmatrix}
$$

Under the null hypothesis that the restrictions implied by the model are satisfied, $E(f_t(\theta)) = 0$. The GMM estimation procedure uses the T observations to replace $E(f_t(\theta)) = 0$ with its sample counterpart $g_T(\theta)$, given by

$$
g_T(\theta) = \frac{1}{T} \sum_{t=1}^{T} f_t(\theta)
$$

and then chooses parameter estimates that minimise the quadratic form

$$
J_T(\theta) = g_T^\top(\theta) W_T(\theta) g_T(\theta)
$$

where $W_T(\theta)$ is a positive-definite symmetric weighting matrix. The minimised value of $J_T(\theta)$ is distributed under the null hypothesis that the model is true as χ^2 with degrees of freedom equal to the number of orthogonality conditions minus the number of estimated parameters: see Newey (1985) for further details on the use and asymptotic properties of this statistic for testing general model misspecification.

Hansen (1982) shows that choosing $W_T(\theta) = S^{-1}(\theta)$, where $S(\theta) = E\left[f_t(\theta) f_t^\top(\theta) \right]$, produces the estimator of θ with the smallest asymptotic covariance matrix, given by $T^{-1}(D_0^\top(\theta) S_0^{-1}(\theta) D_0(\theta))^{-1}$, where $D_0(\theta)$ is the Jacobian of $g_T(\theta)$ evaluated at the estimated parameters. This can be used to test the significance of individual parameter estimates. (Further discussion of GMM estimation within a regression framework may be found in chapter 8, section 1.4.)

A number of other mean-reverting continuous-time processes have been developed for describing the dynamics of interest rates. For example,

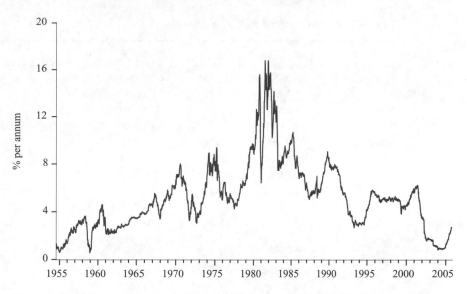

Figure 4.2   Three-month US Treasury bills, secondary market rates (monthly April 1954–February 2005)

Aït-Sahalia (1996a) places restrictions on the drift coefficient of a diffusion process and proposes a non-parametric estimator for its diffusion coefficient. Empirical results in Aït-Sahalia (1996b) suggest that the linearity of the drift appears to be the main source of misspecification in several one-factor diffusion models of interest rates. He thus favours a non-linear mean reversion process, which is globally stationary despite local random walk behaviour, and uses non-parametric methods for estimating the drift and volatility.

Example 4.4 Approximating mean reversion in continuous time for US interest rates

We estimate the various models discussed above by the GMM method using monthly data on the US three-month Treasury bill rate, shown in figure 4.2. The data span the period from April 1954 to February 2005, a total of 623 observations. The estimated parameters and J-statistics for each of the models are shown in table 4.2. In terms of these statistics, models 2 and 3 are likely to be misspecified, as the J-statistics have p-values of less than 5 per cent. Inspection of the parameter estimates and standard errors suggests that this is a consequence of insignificant mean reversion parameter estimates. On this criterion, models 4 and 7 offer the best fit to the data. The unrestricted model estimates suggest that, although mean reversion appears to be insignificant, conditional volatility is sensitive to the level of the process through the statistically significant estimate of $\gamma = 1.54$.

Table 4.2 Interest rate model parameter estimates

Specification	a	b	σ^2	γ	J
Unrestricted	0.0079	− 0.1365	0.7818	1.5422	
	(0.0060)	(0.1236)	(0.8898)	(0.2093)	
Model 1	0.0008		0.0001		4.6943
	(0.0019)		(0.0000)		[0.0957]
Model 2	0.0039	− 0.0664	0.0001		4.8159
	(0.0056)	(0.1174)	(0.0000)		[0.0282]
Model 3	0.0034	− 0.0582	0.0021	0.5	4.6168
	(0.0056)	(0.1164)	(0.0004)		[0.0317]
Model 4			0.0384	1	3.3644
			(0.0057)		[0.3388]
Model 5		0.0151	0.0381	1	3.3142
		(0.0402)	(0.0058)		[0.1907]
Model 6	0.0039	− 0.0651	0.0379	1	3.0430
	(0.0055)	(0.1157)	(0.0058)		[0.0811]
Model 7			0.6095	1.5	1.8888
			(0.0788)		[0.5958]
Model 8		0.0178	0.4577	1.4475	1.6531
		(0.0403)	0.5778)	(0.2304)	[0.1986]

Note: Figures in parentheses denote asymptotic standard errors. In square brackets we give the p-values associated with each J-statistic, which is distributed under the null that the model is true as χ_k^2. The degrees of freedom k are equal to the number of orthogonality conditions minus the number of estimated parameters.

These results are comparable to those of Chan *et al.* (1992) and others, who also find no evidence of mean reversion and a comparable value for γ of around 1.5. Insignificant mean reversion implies that interest rates are non-stationary. Recent research by Faff and Gray (2006) suggests that this insignificant mean reversion, which has been reported by several researchers, may be due to the poor finite sample properties of the GMM estimator. Moreover, as shown by Aït-Sahalia (1999), among others, non-linear specifications of the drift component may produce different results.

4.3 Fractional integration and long memory processes

4.3.1 A broader definition of stationarity

A great deal of theoretical and empirical research has been produced in recent years on long memory processes, which generalise the conventional unit root model of non-stationarity and allow a wide range of short- and long-run dynamic behaviour. Research in this area has brought into the open several concerns about the correct definition of stationarity and long-run behaviour. Although most researchers agree that 'smoothness' can be related to the long-run properties of a time series, there are no conclusive empirical results on what the best models to use are. The issue of comparing alternative models of long-run time series behaviour becomes even more elusive once non-linearities are considered. As noted by Granger (1997), it is possible that some of these controversies originate from the fact that the term 'trend' has not received satisfactory mathematical attention. Moreover, the treatment of trends within the standard unit root and trend stationary framework is not sufficiently general to model all the situations that may arise, although Phillips (2001, 2003, 2005b) has made important advances in this area in recent years.

Motivated by these concerns, Granger and Hallman (1991) and Granger (1995), among others, have discussed a framework based on the notion of *extended memory*. Although the general concept of stationarity is, as we have consistently emphasised, central to the theory of modern time series analysis, it is almost impossible to test for directly and can be defined only in terms of individual properties, such as constancy of moments and extent of memory. Consider the conditional probability density function of x_{t+h} given the information set $I_t : x_{t-j}, \mathbf{q}_{t-j}, j \geq 0$, where $\mathbf{q}_t$ is a vector of other explanatory variables. The series x_t is said to be *short memory in distribution* (SMD) with respect to I_t if

$$|P(x_{t+h} \text{ in } A | I_t \text{ in } B) - P(x_{t+h} \text{ in } A)| \to 0$$

as $h \to \infty$ for all appropriate sets A and B such that $P(I_t \text{ in } B) > 0$, where $P(\Im)$ denotes the probability of the event $\Im$ occurring. The complement of an SMD process is *long memory in distribution* (LMD).

A more narrow definition of memory can be made with respect to the mean of a process. The conditional mean may be defined as

$$E(x_{t+h} | I_t) = \xi_{t, h}$$

so that $\xi_{t, h}$ is the optimum least squares forecast of x_{t+h} using I_t. Then x_t is said to be *short memory in mean* (SMM) if

$$\lim_{h \to \infty} \xi_{t, h} = \Xi_t$$

where Ξ_t is a random variable with a distribution that does not depend on I_t. The most interesting case is when this distribution is singular, so that Ξ_t takes just the single value μ, which is the unconditional mean of x_t, assumed to be finite. If $\xi_{t,h}$ depends on I_t for all h, then x_t is said to be *extended memory in mean* (EMM).

Using the above definition, a process is characterised as SMM if a conditional h-step forecast of the mean tends to a constant as h increases. This implies that any historical information that is available at time t should become progressively less relevant as the forecast horizon increases. SMMs are complemented by EMM processes, in which present information is generally useful in forecasting the mean irrespective of the forecast horizon. Essentially, SMM and EMM correspond to the conventional properties of mixing and non-mixing in the mean, respectively. The notion of extended memory can be used in defining non-linear forms of persistence: for example, an EMM process can be defined as 'extended $I(1)$' if it has increments that are SMM. Granger (1995) emphasises that only monotonic, non-decreasing functions of an EMM will remain EMM (e.g. a logarithmic, polynomial or logistic transformation of a random walk): for example, the cosine of a random walk will be SMM, while non-linear transformations of homoskedastic SMM processes will also be SMM.

Park and Phillips (1999) have developed some asymptotic theory for non-linear transformations of integrated stochastic processes. They demonstrate that this theory differs from that of integrated and stationary time series and that the convergence rates of sample functions depend on the type of non-linear transformation. Granger (1995) discusses the use of the attractor concept in generalising the notion of mean reversion and the definition of $I(0)$ processes. More specifically, he uses the attractor to characterise non-linear processes that have a tendency to return to some set of values, rather than to a single value (e.g. the mean). This set could be a limit cycle or, in the case of a so-called 'chaotic process', a fractal set (or strange attractor).

The following section reviews ARFIMA models, which constitute the most widely researched class of long memory models, although a variety of alternative models have been proposed in the literature that are not covered here (see, for example, Ding, Granger and Engle, 1993, and Granger and Ding, 1996).

4.3.2 ARFIMA models

Much of the analysis of financial time series considers the case when the order of differencing, d, is either zero or one. If the latter, x_t is $I(1)$, an EMM process, and its ACF declines linearly. If the former, x_t is $I(0)$ and its ACF exhibits an exponential decay; observations separated by a long time span may, therefore, be assumed to be independent, or at least nearly so. As we have seen, $I(1)$ behaviour in the levels of financial time series is an implication of many models of efficient markets, and the previous sections of this chapter have discussed the analysis of such behaviour in considerable detail. Nevertheless, many empirically observed time series, although appearing to satisfy the assumption of stationarity (perhaps after some differencing transformation), seem to exhibit a dependence between distant observations that, although small, is by no means negligible.

Such series are particularly found in hydrology, where the 'persistence' of river flows is known as the Hurst effect (see, for example, Mandlebrot and Wallis, 1969, and Hosking, 1984), but many financial time series also exhibit similar characteristics of extremely long persistence. This may be characterised as a tendency for large values to be followed by further large values of the same sign in such a way that the series seem to go through a succession of 'cycles', including long cycles whose length is comparable to the total sample size.

This viewpoint has been persuasively argued by Mandelbrot (1969, 1972) in extending his work on non-Gaussian (marginal) distributions in economics, particularly financial prices (see Mandelbrot, 1963b: this is discussed in chapter 7) to an exploration of the structure of serial dependence in economic time series. While Mandelbrot considered processes that were in the form of discrete-time 'fractional Brownian motion', attention has focused more recently on an extension of the ARIMA class to model long-term persistence.

We have so far considered only integer values of d. If d is non-integer, x_t is said to be *fractionally integrated*, and models for such values of d are referred to as ARFIMA (autoregressive fractionally integrated moving average). This notion of fractional integration seems to have been proposed independently by Hosking (1981) and Granger and Joyeux (1980), and Beran (1992), Baillie (1996), Robinson (2003) and Velasco (2006) provide detailed surveys of such models. To make the concept operational, we may use the binomial series expansion for any real $d > -1$:

$$
\begin{aligned}
\Delta^d = (1 - B)^d &= \sum_{k=0}^{\infty} \begin{bmatrix} d \\ k \end{bmatrix} (-B)^k \\
&= 1 - dB + \frac{d(d-1)}{2!} B^2 - \frac{d(d-1)(d-2)}{3!} B^3 + \cdots
\end{aligned}
\tag{4.20}
$$

How does the ARFIMA model incorporate 'long memory' behaviour? Let us first consider the ARFIMA$(0, d, 0)$ process

$$(1 - B)^d x_t = (1 - \pi_1 B - \pi_2 B^2 - \cdots) x_t = a_t$$

where, using the gamma function $\Gamma(n) = (n - 1)!$, the coefficients are given by

$$\pi_j = -\frac{\Gamma(j - d)}{\Gamma(-d)\Gamma(j + 1)}$$

This process can thus be interpreted as an infinite autoregression. It is often referred to as *fractional white noise*, and is the discrete-time analogue of fractional Brownian motion, just as the random walk is the discrete-time analogue of Brownian motion.

The ARFIMA model nests the ARIMA model and is able to represent both short- and long-term time series behaviour as functions of a single innovation. By inverting the fractional difference operator, we obtain an MA representation

$$x_t = (1 - B)^{-d} a_t = (1 - \psi_1 B - \psi_2 B^2 - \cdots) a_t$$

with

$$\psi_j = \frac{\Gamma(j + d)}{\Gamma(d)\Gamma(j + 1)}$$

For $d = 0$, x_t is simply white noise and its ACF declines immediately to zero, whereas, for $d = 1$, x_t is a random walk and hence has an ACF that remains (approximately) at unity. For non-integer values of d, it can be shown that the ACF of x_t declines *hyperbolically* to zero (see figure 4.3). To be precise, the autocorrelations are given by

$$\rho_k = \frac{\Gamma(1 - d)}{\Gamma(d)} \cdot \frac{\Gamma(k + d)}{\Gamma(k + 1 - d)} \approx \frac{\Gamma(1 - d)}{\Gamma(d)} k^{2d - 1}$$

for large k, so that the autocorrelations exhibit a hyperbolic decay, the speed of which depends upon d, and this property is also seen for the π- and ψ-weights.

The process is SMM for $0 < d < 1$, weakly stationary for $d < 0.5$ and invertible for $d > -0.5$. For $d \geq 0.5$ the variance of x_t is infinite, and so the process is non-stationary, but Robinson (1994) refers to it as being 'less

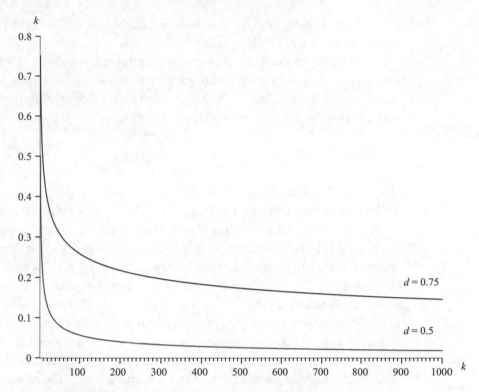

Figure 4.3   ACFs of ARFIMA(0,d,0) processes with $d=0.5$ and $d=0.75$

non-stationary' than a unit root process, so smoothly bridging the gulf between $I(0)$ and $I(1)$ processes. The autocorrelation properties of fractional white noise are conveniently set out in Baillie (1996, table 4.2). Smooth persistent trending behaviour and positive dependencies are obtained only when d is positive. Processes with negative orders of d are characterised by a non-smooth form of persistence, or antipersistence, which is associated with negative short- and long-range dependencies.

These same properties are displayed by the more general ARFIMA(p,d,q) process,

$$\phi(B)(1 - B)^d x_t = \theta(B)a_t$$

although parametric expressions for the π- and ψ-weights are particularly complicated: again, see Baillie (1996). The impulse response function is defined from

$$\Delta x_t = (1 - B)^{1-d}\phi(B)^{-1}\theta(B)a_t = A(B)a_t$$

From Baillie (1996), $(1 - B)^{1-d} = 0$ for $d < 1$, so that any ARFIMA process is trend-reverting since $A(1) = 0$.

The intuition behind the concept of long memory and the limitation of the integer-d restriction emerge more clearly in the frequency domain. The series x_t will display long memory if its spectral density, $f_x(\omega)$, increases without limit as the frequency ω tends to zero,

$$\lim_{\omega \to 0} f_x(\omega) = \infty$$

If x_t is ARFIMA then $f_x(\omega)$ behaves like ω^{-2d} as $\omega \to 0$, so that d parameterises its low-frequency behaviour. When $d = 1$, $f_x(\omega)$ thus behaves like ω^{-2} as $\omega \to 0$, whereas when the integer-d restriction is relaxed a much richer range of spectral behaviour near the origin becomes possible. Indeed, the 'typical spectral shape' of economic time series (Granger, 1966), which exhibits monotonically declining power as frequency increases (except at seasonals), is well captured by an $I(d)$ process with $0 < d < 1$. Moreover, although the levels of many series have spectra that appear to be infinite at the origin, and so might seem to warrant first differencing, after such differencing they often have no power at the origin. This suggests that first differencing takes out 'too much' and that using a fractional d is therefore a more appropriate form of detrending. This difficulty is compounded by the finding that unit root tests have even lower power than usual against fractional alternatives. Although such tests are consistent when the alternative is a fractionally cointegrated process, $d = 1$ will often be chosen rather than a correct d that is less than unity: see Sowell (1990), Diebold and Rudebusch (1991), Hassler and Wolters (1994) and Lee and Schmidt (1996). A variety of testing procedures have been developed to overcome this lack of power, and some of these are discussed in the following section.

Fractionally integrated processes have the significant drawback of not being able to be modelled by finite-order difference equations. This is counter-intuitive in most situations in finance, where we would expect agent behaviour, as reflected in observed time series, to depend on the near past and to affect only the near future. Long-memory models, such as ARFIMA processes, involve an infinite memory and thus present a real challenge for theorists. Where ARFIMA models seem to make much sense is in terms of approximating aggregate agent or time series behaviour. For example, Granger (1980) notes that the summation of low-order ARMA processes will yield ARMA processes of increasing, and eventually infinite, order that can be well approximated using an ARFIMA model.

4.3.2 Testing for fractional differencing

A 'classic' approach to detecting the presence of long-term memory in a time series – or long-range dependence, as it is also known – is to use the 'range over standard deviation' or 'rescaled range' statistic. This was originally developed by Hurst (1951) when studying river discharges and was proposed in an economic context by Mandelbrot (1972). This 'R/S' statistic is the range of partial sums of deviations of a time series from its mean, rescaled by its standard deviation – i.e.

$$R_0 = \hat{\sigma}_0^{-1} \left[\max_{1 \le i \le T} \sum_{t=1}^{i} (x_t - \bar{x}) - \min_{1 \le i \le T} \sum_{t=1}^{i} (x_t - \bar{x}) \right] \tag{4.21}$$

where

$$\hat{\sigma}_0^2 = T^{-1} \sum_{t=1}^{T} (x_t - \bar{x})^2$$

The first term in brackets is the maximum of the partial sums of the first i deviations of x_t from the sample mean. Since the sum of all T deviations of the x_ts from their mean is zero, this maximum is always non-negative. The second term is the minimum of the same sequence of partial sums, and hence is always non-positive. The difference between the two quantities, called the 'range', for obvious reasons, is therefore always non-negative: hence $R_0 \ge 0$.

Although it has long been established that the R/S statistic has the ability to detect long-range dependence, it is sensitive to short-range influences. Consequently, any incompatibility between the data and the predicted behaviour of the R/S statistic under the null hypothesis of no long-run dependence need not come from long-term memory, but may merely be a symptom of short-run autocorrelation.

Lo (1991) therefore considers a modified R/S statistic in which short-run dependence is incorporated into its denominator, which becomes (the square root of) a consistent estimator of the variance of the partial sum in (4.21),

$$R_q = \hat{\sigma}_q^{-1} \left[\max_{1 \le i \le T} \sum_{t=1}^{i} (x_t - \bar{x}) - \min_{1 \le i \le T} \sum_{t=1}^{i} (x_t - \bar{x}) \right]$$

where $\hat{\sigma}_q^2$ is of the form (3.12) and may be written as

$$\hat{\sigma}_q^2 = \hat{\sigma}_0^2 \left(1 + \frac{2}{T} \sum_{j=1}^{q} w_{qj} r_j \right), \quad w_{qj} = 1 - \frac{j}{q+1}, \quad q < T$$

the r_j, $j = 1, \ldots, q$, being the sample autocorrelations of x_t as defined in chapter 2, section 5.1. Lo provides the assumptions and technical details to allow the asymptotic distribution of R_q to be obtained. $T^{-1/2} R_q$ converges in distribution to a well-defined random variable (the range of a Brownian bridge on the unit interval), whose distribution and density functions are plotted and significance levels reported in Lo (1991, fig. I, table II, respectively). The statistics are consistent against a class of long-range dependent alternatives that include all ARFIMA(p, d, q) models with $-0.5 \le d \le 0.5$.

The appropriate choice of q (i.e. how to distinguish between short- and long-range dependencies) remains an unresolved issue, however (see, for example, Pagan, 1996). Moreover, there is evidence that, if the distribution of x_t is 'fat-tailed' (a phenomenon that is discussed in detail in chapter 7), then the sampling distribution of R_q is shifted to the left relative to the asymptotic distribution. This would imply that rejection rates on the left tail (rejections in favour of $d < 0$: antipersistence) are above the nominal sizes given by the asymptotic distribution, whereas rejection rates on the right tail (rejections in favour of $d > 0$: persistent long memory) are below the nominal size (see Hiemstra and Jones, 1997). Lo thus argues that the R/S approach may perhaps be best regarded as a kind of portmanteau test that may complement, and come prior to, a more comprehensive analysis of long-range dependence.

An obvious approach to testing for fractional differencing is to construct tests against the null of either $d = 1$ or $d = 0$. The ADF and non-parametric tests of $d = 1$ discussed in chapter 3, section 1, are consistent against fractional d alternatives (see Diebold and Rudebusch, 1991, and Hassler and Wolters, 1994), although the power of the tests grows more slowly as d diverges from unity than with the divergence of the AR parameter ϕ from unity. Similarly, Lee and Schmidt (1996) show that the η statistics of Kwiatkowski *et al.* (1992) for testing the null of $d = 0$ are consistent against fractional d alternatives in the range $-0.5 < d < 0.5$, and their power compares favourably to Lo's modified R/S statistic.

Alternatively, we may be able to construct tests based on the residuals from fitting an ARIMA$(p, 0, q)$ model to x_t. Suppose the fitted model is $\hat{\phi}(B) x_t = \hat{\theta}(B) \hat{a}_t$. Agiakloglou and Newbold (1994) derive an LM test of $d = 0$ as the t-ratio on δ in the regression

$$\hat{a}_t = \sum\nolimits_{i=1}^{p} \beta_i W_{t-i} + \sum\nolimits_{j=1}^{q} \gamma_j Z_{t-j} + \delta K_t(m) + u_t \qquad (4.22)$$

where

$$\hat{\theta}(B)W_t = x_t, \quad \hat{\theta}(B)Z_t = \hat{a}_t$$

and

$$K_t(m) = \sum_{j=1}^{m} j^{-1}\hat{a}_{t-j}$$

Agiakloglou and Newbold also derive a test based on the residual auto-correlations, $\hat{r}_1, \hat{r}_2, \ldots, \hat{r}_m$, but this requires a rather greater computational effort. They find that, although both tests have empirical size close to nominal size, low power is a particular problem when p and q are positive rather than zero and when a non-zero mean of x_t has to be estimated.

Mean estimation for long-memory processes is a general problem, as the sample mean is a poor estimate of the true mean in these models (see Samarov and Taqqu, 1988). Indeed, Newbold and Agiakloglou (1993) also find that the SACF of fractional white noise (when $d > 0$) is a severely biased estimator of the true ACF, so that it will be very difficult to detect long-memory behaviour from the SACFs of moderate length series.

Dolado, Gonzalo and Moayoral (2002) proposed a simple Wald-type test for fractionally integrated processes that extends the Dickey–Fuller approach to the more general case of testing $d > d_0$ against $d = d_1$ with $d_1 < d_0$. When d_1 is not known a priori, they show that the choice of any $T^{1/2}$ consistent estimator of $d_1 \in \lfloor 0,1)$ is sufficient to implement the test while retaining asymptotic normality. The test, coined *FD-F*, has acceptable power and provides an estimate of d under the alternative hypothesis. The test has the advantage of not assuming any known density for the errors and retains the simplicity of the standard DF test, where an $I(1)$ null hypothesis can be evaluated against some composite alternative.

The test evaluates the null hypothesis that a series is $I(d_0)$ against the alternative that it is $I(d_1)$, where d_0 and d_1 are real numbers. By analogy to the DF procedure, the testing regression is

$$\Delta^{d_0} x_t = \phi \Delta^{d_1} x_{t-1} + a_t$$

where a_t is an $I(0)$ process. The procedure is based upon testing the statistical significance of the coefficient ϕ. As with the DF test, $\Delta^{d_0} x_t$ and $\Delta^{d_1} x_{t-1}$ have been differenced according to their order of integration under the null and alternative hypotheses, respectively. When $\phi = 0$ the series is fractional white noise, implying that x_t is $I(d_0)$ under the null. When $\phi < 0$, x_t can be expressed as

$$(\Delta^{d_0 - d_1} - \phi B) \Delta^{d_1} x_t = a_t$$

The polynomial $\pi(B) = (1 - B)^{d_0 - d_1} - \phi B$ has absolutely summable coefficients with $\pi(0) = 1$ and $\pi(1) = -\phi \neq 0$. The non-explosivity condition of the polynomial is $-2^{1-d_1} < \phi < 0$. When $\phi < 0$, $\Delta^{d_1} x_{t-1}$ is $I(0)$, implying that x_t is $I(d_0)$ under the alternative, whereas if $\phi = 0$ then x_t is $I(d_0)$ under the null. As with the conventional DF test, the statistic can either be formulated as the normalised estimate of ϕ or its t-statistic.

When $d_0 = 1$ and $d_1 = 1$, we have the conventional unit root testing framework of chapter 3 and the asymptotic distributions of the test statistics correspond to those derived there. In general, the asymptotic distribution of the test statistics depends on the distance between the null and the alternative hypothesis and on the nature of the process under the null hypothesis. More specifically, the *FD-F* test statistics will be standard (Gaussian) either if the processes under both hypotheses are (asymptotically) stationary or when the process is non-stationary under the null, $(d_0 > 0.5)$, and $(d_0 - d_1 < 0.5)$. The test statistics will be non-standard otherwise. Dolado, Gonzalo and Moayoral (2002) provide critical values for three sample sizes $(T = 100, 400, 1000)$ for the range of values of d for which the test does not have a non-standard distribution under the null, for the case of a random walk with or without a constant and linear trend. Finally, the authors augment the *FD-F* test, by analogy to the ADF test, and find that the asymptotic distribution of the t-statistic remains valid under serial correlation, as long as a sufficient number of lags of $\Delta^{d_0} x_t$ are included in the testing regression.

A wide variety of other Wald-type and LM long-memory testing procedures have been developed in the literature. Wald-type tests (Geweke and Porter-Hudak, 1983; Fox and Taqqu, 1986; Sowell, 1992a; Robinson, 1992) work under the alternative hypothesis and are based on point estimates and confidence intervals of d. The parametric and semi-parametric methods of estimating d, both in the frequency and the time domains, have been found to possess low power when used for testing purposes. The LM approaches, such as those proposed by Robinson (1994) and Tanaka (1999), in the frequency and time domains, respectively, evaluate the statistics under the null hypothesis. They have the advantage, unlike unit root tests, of having standard asymptotic distributions, but do not provide estimates about d when the null hypothesis is rejected.

Tieslau, Schmidt and Baillie (1996) and Chong (2000) have suggested estimating d and testing for fractional integration by minimising the difference between the sample and population autocorrelations and partial autocorrelations, respectively. Delgado and Velasco (2005) propose sign-based tests for simple and composite hypotheses on d. Giraitis *et al.* (2003) develop a rescaled variance test which has a simpler asymptotic distribution and a better balance of size and power than Lo's modified R/S test and the KPSS test of Kwiatkowski *et al.* (1992).

It is important to note that, as shown by several authors (Diebold and Inoue, 2001; Engle and Smith, 1999; Granger and Hyung, 2004; Dittmann and Granger, 2002), long-memory tests are sensitive to a variety of factors, such as structural breaks, outliers, regime switching and non-linear transformations.

4.3.3 Estimation of ARFIMA models

The fractional differencing parameter d can be estimated by a variety of methods. The earliest approach was to use the result in R/S analysis that $\operatorname{plim}_{T \to \infty} T^{-d-0.5} R_0$ is a constant (Lo, 1991) and estimate d as

$$d = \frac{\ln(R_0)}{\ln(T)} - \frac{1}{2}$$

Another early and popular approach was the log-periodogram regression proposed by Geweke and Porter-Hudak, 1983 (GPH). The spectral density of x_t is given by

$$f_x(\omega) = |1 - \exp(-i\omega)|^{-2d} f_w(\omega) = \left(4\sin^2(\omega/2)\right)^{-d} f_w(\omega)$$

where $f_w(\omega)$ is the spectral density of $w_t = (1 - B)^d x_t$. It then follows that

$$\ln(f_x(\omega)) = \ln(f_w(\omega)) - d\ln\left(4\sin^2(\omega/2)\right)$$

and, given the sample $\{x_t\}_1^T$, this leads GPH to propose estimating d as (minus) the slope estimator of the least squares regression of the periodogram

$$I_T(\omega_j) = 2\hat{\sigma}_0^2 \left(1 + 2 \sum_{s=1}^{T-1} r_s \cos(s\omega_j)\right)$$

on a constant and $\ln\left(4\sin^2(\omega_j/2)\right)$, at frequencies $\omega_j = 2\pi j/T, j = 1, \ldots, K$, where typically $K = [T^{4/5}]$ (other choices for K are discussed in Baillie, 1996).

A critical assumption of the GPH estimator is that the spectrum of the ARFIMA(p, d, q) process is the same as that of an ARFIMA(0, d, 0) process.

Robinson (1995a), Hurvich, Deo and Brodsky (1998), Tanaka (1999), Velasco (1999) and Lieberman (2001) have analysed the GPH estimator $\hat{d}$ in great detail. Under the assumption of normality for x_t, it has now been proved that the estimator is consistent for $-0.5 < d < 1$ and asymptotically normal, so that the estimated standard error attached to $\hat{d}$ can be used for inference. Alternatively, the asymptotic result that $\sqrt{K}\left(\hat{d} - d\right) \overset{a}{\sim} N(0, \pi^2/24)$ may be used.

An alternative semi-parametric estimator has been proposed by Robinson (1995b). This is defined as $\bar{d} = \arg\min_d R(d)$, where

$$R(d) = \log\left(K^{-1} \sum\nolimits_{j=1}^{K} \omega_j^{2d} I_T(\omega_j)\right) - (2d/K) \sum\nolimits_{j=1}^{K} \omega_j$$

Inference on $\bar{d}$ uses the result that $\sqrt{K}(\bar{d} - d) \overset{a}{\sim} N(0, 1/4)$. Once an estimate of d has been obtained, the series $\Delta^d x_t$ may be constructed by using (4.20) and truncating appropriately, and the ARMA part of the model can then be identified and estimated using the techniques outlined in chapter 2. Hurvich and Ray (1995) have extended the GPH estimator to the case of a non-stationary, non-invertible process. More recently, Andrews and Sun (2004) have proposed an alternative semi-parametric spectral approach, based on a generalisation of the local polynomial Whittle estimator of Künsch (1987), which achieves the optimal rate of convergence. Sun and Phillips (2003) propose a non-linear log-periodogram regression approach to accommodate fractional processes that are perturbed by weakly dependent series and allow different sources of variation in the short- and long-run dynamics.

The standard approach following the estimation of d is to fit an ARMA model to the fractionally differenced data. The filtered data are often assumed to be normally distributed in order to employ standard estimation and inference when analysing the final ARFIMA model. Not surprisingly, semi-parametric estimators of d can often perform poorly in terms of bias and MSE when the orders p and q are known.

An alternative estimator of d is the approximate ML estimator of Beran (1995). The test assumes an ARFIMA(p,d,q) process with $d = m + \delta$, $-0.5 < \delta < 0.5$, where m is a known integer denoting the number of times the series must be differenced in order to attain stationarity. The estimator is formed by fitting an ARFIMA model for various values of δ and selecting the parameter $d = m + \delta$ that minimises the sum of squared residuals.

Obviously, the choice of m is crucial, since the method yields asymptotically normal estimates of the ARFIMA parameters if $-0.5 < \delta < 0.5$.

Significant attention has also been given to joint ML estimation of all the parameters in the ARFIMA(p, d, q) model, as developed by Sowell (1992a, 1992b) and surveyed by Baillie (1996). These methods do have the drawback, however, that specialised software is required, and they entail particularly cumbersome computations for higher-order ARMA specifications and for even moderate sample sizes. Moreover, it can be difficult to identify the correct values of p and q at the same time as determining the value of d. Nonetheless, ML routines for ARFIMA models are provided in PcGive 11 (Hendry and Doornik, 2006), for example, along with NLS and other estimation techniques.

Evidence of long memory has been found in a variety of financial time series, including stock returns, exchange rates and interest rates (see Baillie, 1996). Little has been said about the relative usefulness of the ARFIMA model for forecasting purposes, however. Bhardwaj and Swanson (2006) have recently analysed the predictive ability of ARFIMA models using three previously analysed financial and macroeconomic data sets. They employ a variety of long-memory testing and estimation procedures and evaluate the *ex ante* forecasting ability of ARFIMA models against standard short-memory models.

Their results show that ARFIMA models are able to approximate the true data-generating process and sometimes to perform significantly better in out-of-sample forecasting than simple short-memory models. Samples exceeding 5000 observations are sufficient to provide very stable rolling and recursive estimates of d, although samples of fewer than 2500 observations substantially increase estimation error. Moreover, it appears that ARFIMA models may be particularly useful at longer forecasting horizons. Finally, they observe, against conventional wisdom, that ARFIMA models were often superior in terms of forecasting ability even though they are less parsimonious than ARMA models, in terms of the additional parameter d and the ad hoc application of the truncation filter.

Example 4.5 Long-memory and fractional differencing in exchange rates and stock returns

In example 3.1 we confirmed that the dollar/sterling exchange rate contains a unit root, while in example 3.2 we confirmed that this was also the case for the FTA All Share index. We now consider whether the differences of the two series, the returns, are really stationary or whether they exhibit long memory.

We first compute the modified R/S statistic, $T^{-1/2}R_q$ for the exchange rate differences. Lo (1991) recommends choosing q as $[T^{0.25}] = 8$, as with the non-parametric unit root statistic. Using this setting we obtain $T^{-1/2}R_8 = 1.092$, and, since a 95 per cent confidence interval for this statistic is (0.809, 1.862) (see Lo, 1991, table II), we cannot reject the hypothesis that exchange rate returns are short memory. This finding is confirmed by both LM tests and the semi-parametric estimates of d. Since the levels are effectively a driftless random walk (see example 2.5), LM tests were constructed using Δx_t; (4.22) therefore reduces to a regression of Δx_t on $K_t(m) = \sum_{j=1}^{m} \Delta x_{t-j}$. The calculated t-ratios for δ are around -1 for m set equal to 25, 50, 75 and 100, respectively. The GPH estimate computed using $K = [T^{4/5}] = 667$ is $\hat{d} = 0.005$ with a standard error of 0.03, while $\bar{d} = 0.01$.

For the FTA All Share returns, we obtain $T^{-1/2}R_5 = 1.504$, which is again insignificant. The GPH estimate is $\hat{d} = 0.05$ with a standard error of 0.06, computed using $K = 142$, while $\bar{d}$ is only 0.01, with a standard error of 0.04. The LM t-ratios were never remotely significant for a wide range of m values. This is, in fact, consistent with the simulation results of Agiakloglou and Newbold (1994), who find that the power of this test to reject $d = 0$ is very weak when the sample mean (the drift in the index here) has to be estimated.

As a further example, we investigate the daily returns for the S&P 500 index from January 1928 to August 1991, a total of $T = 17,054$ observations, a series that was originally analysed in Ding, Granger and Engle (1993). The GPH estimate for the returns is $\hat{d} = 0.11$, with a standard error of 0.06, so there is little evidence that the series is long memory. For the *squared returns* series we obtain $\hat{d} = 0.56$, however, while for the *absolute returns* we obtain $\hat{d} = 0.73$. Thus, simple non-linear transformations of returns do appear to be long memory, and this is also found to be the case for a wide variety of other financial series: see the results in Ding and Granger (1996), Granger and Ding (1996), and Mills (1996a, 1997a). These types of models are analysed in greater detail in the next chapter.

Example 4.6 An ARFIMA process for US Treasury bills
As has been seen in figure 4.2, weekly observations on the US Treasury bill rate demonstrate locally trending behaviour, reaching a peak during December 1980 of 16.76 per cent. Both ADF and Phillips–Perron tests (including a constant but no trend) cannot reject the null hypothesis of a unit root in the data, the test statistics being -1.91 and -2.13, respectively. The notion of non-stationary interest rates contradicts financial theory and the restriction that they are bounded by zero, however.

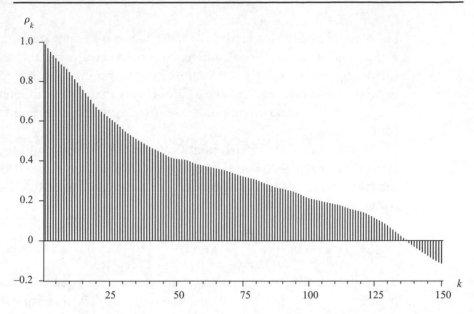

Figure 4.4   SACF of three-month US Treasury bills

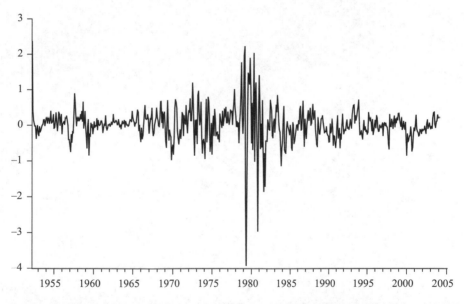

Figure 4.5   Fractionally differenced ($d = 0.88$) three-month US Treasury bills (monthly April 1954–Februray 2005)

The autocorrelation function of the series, shown in figure 4.4, suggests some type of long-memory process. The KPSS test strongly rejects the null hypothesis of $I(0)$ with a statistic of 0.651, much larger than the 5 per cent critical value of 0.463. Further evidence of a long-memory process is provided by Lo's modified R/S test statistic of 4.709, which is a highly significant value. Estimation of the fractional differencing parameter using the semi-parametric approaches of GPH and Robinson (1994) produces estimated d values of 0.905 and 0.487, respectively. These suggest that simple differencing, as suggested by the standard unit root tests, may remove too much information from the data.

On the basis of these tests, joint Gaussian ML estimation of the parameters of an ARFIMA model was attempted. The best fit was finally offered by the following ARFIMA$(0, d, 1)$ model with d estimated to be 0.88 (t-ratios in parentheses):

$$\Delta^d x_t = \underset{(30.89)}{2.279} + \hat{a}_t - \underset{(4.90)}{0.593}\, \hat{a}_{t-1}$$

The fractional differencing parameter is found to be close to the GPH estimate and is highly significant with a t-ratio of 9.47. It is interesting to observe the now clearly stationary fractionally differenced Treasury bill series in figure 4.5.

5 Univariate non-linear stochastic models: martingales, random walks and modelling volatility

As we have seen in previous chapters, financial time series often appear to be well approximated by random walks. The relationship between random walks and the theory of efficient capital markets was briefly discussed in chapter 1, where it was argued that the random walk assumption that asset price changes are independent is usually too restrictive to be consistent with a reasonably broad class of optimising models; what is in fact required is that a variable related to the asset price be a martingale (see, for example, Andreou, Pittis and Spanos, 2001).

Martingales and random walks are discussed formally in section 5.1, with tests of the random walk hypothesis being the subject of section 5.2. The relaxation of the assumption that changes in a time series must be independent and identically distributed allows the possibility of examining non-linear stochastic processes, and the remainder of the chapter therefore introduces various non-linear models that are now used regularly in analysing the volatility of financial time series – a fundamental concern of financial modellers. Ways of measuring volatility itself are introduced in section 5.3, before formal stochastic models are considered. Stochastic volatility (SV) models are discussed in section 5.4, ARCH processes in section 5.5, further models related to ARCH in section 5.6, and section 5.7 briefly looks at the forecasting performance of alternative volatility models.

5.1 Martingales, random walks and non-linearity

A *martingale* is a stochastic process that is a mathematical model of 'fair play'. The term 'martingale', which also denotes part of a horse's harness or a ship's rigging, refers in addition to a gambling system in which every losing bet is doubled – a usage that may be felt to be rather apposite when considering the behaviour of financial data!

A martingale may be formally defined as a stochastic process $\{x_t\}$ having the following properties:

(a) $E(|x_t|)<\infty$ for each t;

(b) $E(x_t|\Im_s) = x_s$, whenever $s\leq t$, where $\Im_s$ is the σ-algebra comprising events determined by observations over the interval $[0, t]$, so that $\Im_s \subseteq \Im_t$ when $s\leq t$. This is known as the 'martingale property'.

While the 'history' $\{\Im_t\}_0^t$ can, in general, include observations on any number of variables, it is often restricted to be just the past history of $\{x_t\}_0^t$ itself – i.e. $\Im_t = \sigma(x_s; s \leq t)$. Written as

$$E(x_t - x_s|\Im_s) = 0, \quad s \leq t \tag{5.1}$$

the martingale property implies that the MMSE forecast of a future increment of a martingale is zero. This property can be generalised to situations, quite common in finance, where

$$E(x_t - x_s|\Im_s) \geq 0, \quad s \leq t$$

in which case we have a *submartingale*, and to the case where the above inequality is reversed, giving us a *supermartingale*.

The martingale given by (5.1) can be written equivalently as

$$x_t = x_{t-1} + a_t$$

where a_t is the martingale increment or *martingale difference*. When written in this form, the sequence $\{x_t\}_0^t$ looks superficially identical to the random walk, a model that was first introduced formally in chapter 2. There a_t was defined to be a stationary and uncorrelated sequence drawn from a fixed distribution, i.e. to be white noise. As was discussed in chapter 2, section 4, however, alternative definitions are possible: a_t could be defined to be strict white noise, so that it is both a stationary and an independent sequence, rather than just being uncorrelated. Moreover, it is possible for a_t to be uncorrelated but not necessarily stationary. While the white-noise assumptions rule this out, such behaviour is allowed for martingale differences; this implies that there could be dependence between higher-conditional moments, most notably conditional variances.

The possibility of this form of dependence in financial time series, which often go through protracted quiet periods interspersed with bursts of turbulence, leads naturally to the consideration of *non-linear* stochastic processes capable of modelling such volatility. Non-linearity can be introduced in many other ways, however, some of which may violate the martingale model. As an illustration, suppose that x_t is generated by the process $\Delta x_t = \eta_t$, with η_t being defined as

$$\eta_t = a_t + \beta a_{t-1} a_{t-2}$$

where a_t is strict white noise. It follows immediately that η_t has zero mean, constant variance and ACF given by

$$E(\eta_t \eta_{t-k}) = E\big(a_t a_{t-k} + \beta a_{t-1} a_{t-2} a_{t-k} + \beta a_t a_{t-k-1} a_{t-k-2} \\ + \beta^2 a_{t-1} a_{t-2} a_{t-k-1} a_{t-k-2}\big)$$

For all $k \neq 0$, each of the terms in the ACF has zero expectation, so that, as far as its second-order properties are concerned, η_t behaves just like an independent process. The MMSE forecast of a future observation, η_{t+1}, is not zero (the unconditional expectation), however, but is the conditional expectation

$$\hat{\eta}_{t+1} = E(\eta_{t+1} | \eta_t, \eta_{t-1}, \ldots) = \beta a_t a_{t-1}$$

It then follows that x_t is not a martingale, because

$$E(x_{t+1} - x_t | \eta_t, \eta_{t-1}, \ldots) = \hat{\eta}_{t+1} \neq 0$$

and the non-linear structure of the η_t process could be used to improve the forecasts of x_t over the simple 'no change' forecast associated with the martingale model.

5.2 Testing the random walk hypothesis

Notwithstanding the above discussion, the random walk model has played a major role in the empirical analysis of financial time series: see, for example, the seminal research of Fama (1965) and Granger and Morgenstern (1970). In chapter 3 we examined various tests of an observed time series being a random walk. In the main these were developed by assuming that there was a specific alternative to the random walk null, such as the stationary AR(1) process used for expository purposes in chapter 3, section 1.2, but also advanced by Shiller (1981a) as a model of stock market fads, and the Poterba and Summers (1988) UC model in which this AR(1) process is added to a pure random walk. There have also been numerous other tests developed against a variety of different alternatives, some of which we now discuss.

5.2.1 Autocorrelation tests

Using the results stated in chapter 2, section 5.1, if $w_t = \Delta x_t$ is strict white noise then the asymptotic distribution of the sample autocorrelations (standardised by $\sqrt{T}$) calculated from the realisation $\{w_t\}_1^T$ will be $N(0, 1)$, so that the random walk null would be rejected at the 5 per cent significance level if, for example, $\sqrt{T}|r_1| > 1.96$.

If a set of sample autocorrelations are considered, say $r_1, \ldots, r_K$, then some will probably be significant even if the null is true: on average one out of twenty will be significant at the 5 per cent level. As noted in example 2.1, the portmanteau statistics $Q^*(K)$ and $Q(K)$ may be used in these circumstances. On the random walk null, both statistics are distributed as χ_K^2, so that the null would be rejected for sufficiently high values. Note that these tests do not require a specific alternative hypothesis; they may thus be regarded as 'diagnostic' tests with, hopefully, some power against the null for a wide range of alternatives.

The tests do, however, require that the innovations to the random walk be strict white noise. If the innovations are merely uncorrelated, rather than independent, then the above testing procedure will be unreliable. To show this, relax the strict white-noise assumption on w_t to that of just satisfying the weak dependence conditions (3.11). In this case, $\sqrt{T} r_1 \overset{a}{\sim} N(0, \tau^2)$, where

$$\tau^2 = \sigma_w^{-4}\left(V(w_1 w_2) + 2\sum_{i=1}^{\infty} Cov(w_1 w_2, w_{i+1} w_{i+2})\right)$$

(Romano and Thombs, 1996, theorem 2.1). An example of such a process is $w_t = z_t z_{t-1}$, where z_t is itself zero-mean strict white noise with $E(z_t^2) = \sigma_z^2$ and $E(z_t^4) < \infty$. It is therefore clear that, for all $i > 0$,

$$Cov(w_1 w_2, w_{i+1} w_{i+2}) = 0$$

$$V(w_1 w_2) = E(w_1^2 w_2^2) = \left(E(z_0^2)\right)^2 \cdot E(z_1^4) = \sigma_z^4 \cdot E(z_1^4)$$

and

$$\sigma_w^2 = E(w_t^2) = E(z_t^2 z_{t-1}^2) = \sigma_z^4$$

Thus,

$$\tau^2 = E(z_1^4)/\sigma_z^4 > 1$$

For example, if the z_t are standard normal, $\tau^2 = 3$, and, in general, τ_2 can be made arbitrarily large. Hence, a test of zero correlation based on, say, $\sqrt{T}|r_1| > 1.96$ will lead to a high probability of incorrectly rejecting the hypothesis of zero correlation.

It is straightforward to construct examples for which $\tau^2 < 1$. Suppose that $E|z_t^{-2}| < \infty$. Then $w_t = z_t/z_{t+1}$ will again be uncorrelated, but now

$$V(w_1 w_2) = V(z_1/z_3) = E(z_1^2)E(1/z_1^2) = V(w_1)$$

Thus,

$$\tau^2 = \frac{V(w_1 w_2)}{(V(w_t))^2} = (V(w_1))^{-1} = \left(E(z_1^2)E(1/z_1^2)\right)^{-1} < 1$$

Romano and Thombs (1996, example 3.5) show that, if w_t is no longer strict white noise, then $Q^*(K)$ is no longer asymptotically distributed as χ_K^2. For example, if $w_t = z_t z_{t-1}$, then $Q^*(K)$ is distributed as a weighted sum of independent χ_1^2 variates, leading to a rejection probability greater than the nominal significance level using the χ_K^2 distribution.

Three approaches have been developed in response to this problem. The first is to modify the test statistic. Lobato, Nankervis and Savin (2001, 2002) propose modifying the portmanteau statistic to

$$\tilde{Q}^*(K) = T \sum_{i=1}^{K} \left(r_i^2/v_i\right) \overset{a}{\sim} \chi_K^2$$

where

$$v_i = T^{-1} \sum_{t=i+1}^{T} (w_t - \bar{w})^2 (w_{t-i} - \bar{w})^2 / \hat{\sigma}_w^4$$

They also propose further extensions based on considering the covariance matrix of the set of sample autocorrelations $r_1, r_2, \ldots, r_K$: see the above references for details. The second approach is to continue to use $Q^*(K)$ but to estimate its distribution using bootstrap simulation techniques: see Horowitz *et al.* (2006). Kim, Nelson and Startz (1998) propose a similar approach for the variance ratio statistic, in which w_t is first standardised by a simulated set of conditional variances.

The third approach is to construct non-parametric versions of the tests. Wright (2000), for example, develops variance ratio tests based on the ranks and signs of w_t. Thus, if $r(w_t)$ is the rank of w_t in the sample $\{w_t\}_1^T$, then the standardisation

$$r_t = \left(r(w_t) - \frac{T+1}{2} \right) \Big/ \sqrt{\frac{(T-1)(T+1)}{12}}$$

ensures a series with zero mean and unit variance. The rank-based variance ratio test is then defined as

$$R(k) = \left(\frac{\sum_{t=k+1}^{T} \left(\sum_{i=0}^{k} r_{t-i} \right)^2}{k \sum_{t=1}^{T} r_t^2} - 1 \right) \cdot \left(\frac{2(2k-1)(k-1)}{3kT} \right)^{-1/2} \tag{5.2}$$

Wright provides critical values for the distribution of this statistic under the random walk null for a variety of choices of k and T and also proposes a second statistic based on an alternative transformation of $r(w_t)$.

For a test based on signs, let

$$s_t = \begin{cases} 1 & \text{if } w_t > 0 \\ -1 & \text{if } w_t \leq 0 \end{cases}$$

A test statistic S can then be defined analogously to R in (5.2). This statistic assumes that w_t has zero mean. If not, Wright provides a related test statistic, and the statistics have been further generalised by Luger (2003).

5.2.2 Calendar effects

As remarked above, autocorrelation tests are generally diagnostic checks aimed at detecting general departures from white noise and do not consider autocorrelations associated with specific timing patterns – i.e. patterns associated with 'calendar effects'. There has been a great deal of research carried out in recent years on detecting such effects. To date, researchers have found evidence of a January effect, in which stock returns in this month are exceptionally large when compared to the returns observed for other months; a weekend effect, in which Monday mean returns are negative rather than positive, as for all other weekdays; a holiday effect, showing a much larger mean return for the day before holidays; a turn-of-the-month effect, in which the four-day return around the turn of a month is *greater* than the average total monthly return; an intramonth effect, in which the return over the first half of a month is significantly larger than the return over the second half; and a variety of intraday effects.

Early reviews of these 'anomalies' are Thaler (1987a, 1987b) and Mills and Coutts (1995), while Schwert (2003) provides a more recent survey and additional evidence. A wide range of statistical techniques have been employed to detect such anomalies, and discussion of them here would take us too far afield from our development of formal time series models. Taylor (1986, pp. 41–4) discusses some of the techniques, and the interested reader is recommended to examine both this and further papers cited in the above references.

5.3 Measures of volatility

Since the seminal work of Markowitz on portfolio theory, volatility has become an extremely important variable in finance, appearing regularly in models of asset pricing, portfolio theory, risk management, etc. Much of the interest in volatility has to do with its not being directly observable, and several alternative measures have been developed to approximate it empirically, the most common being the unconditional standard deviation of historical returns. Despite being convenient and simple, this measure is severely limited by the fact that returns are typically non-*iid* (independent and identically distributed), with distributions that are leptokurtic and skewed (see chapter 7). Moreover, the standard deviation may not be an appropriate representation of financial risk, so that some other measure should be used, such as the semi-variance (see the review by Nawrocki, 1999) or the absolute deviation (see Granger and Ding, 1995).

In practice, the standard deviation is typically calculated from a sample of daily close-to-close logarithmic returns using the ML estimator of the variance

$$\hat{\sigma}^2_{ML} = n^{-1} \sum\nolimits_{t=1}^{n} r_t^2$$

where $r_t = p_t - p_{t-1}$ is the logarithmic return, p_t being the logarithm of price, and $n \geq 1$ is the sample size. Standard results show that $\hat{\sigma}^2_{ML}$ has the following asymptotic distribution:

$$\sqrt{n}(\hat{\sigma}^2_{ML} - \sigma^2) \stackrel{a}{\sim} N(0, 2\sigma^4)$$

where σ^2 is the true return variance. A mean adjusted estimator is easily obtained as

$$\hat{\sigma}^2 = \frac{1}{n-1} \left(\sum\nolimits_{t=1}^{n} r_t^2 - \frac{\log(p_n/p_0)^2}{n} \right)$$

where p_0 and p_n are the first and last price observations in the sample.

The term 'volatility' in finance typically corresponds to the annualised historical standard deviation of returns. Assuming that the underlying logarithmic price process is a random walk, this can be calculated by multiplying the standard deviation by the square root of time. This implies that uncertainty, or risk, as measured by volatility, increases with the square root of the time horizon. For example, if the standard deviation for a stock is estimated from historical daily returns to be 0.002, and assuming that a calendar year corresponds to a business year of 250 trading days, volatility will be $0.002\sqrt{250} = 31.62$ per cent. A word of caution is put forward by Diebold *et al.* (1998), who demonstrate that volatility estimates may depend significantly on the sampling frequency of the returns used to estimate the standard deviation, caused by returns not necessarily being *iid*.

In addition to the historical standard deviation, several *extreme value estimators* have also been proposed. These try to improve efficiency by exploiting the information contained in the opening, closing, high and low prices during the trading day. For example, assuming a driftless and continuous price process, Garman and Klass (1980) propose the following minimum-variance unbiased extreme-value estimator:

$$\hat{\sigma}_{GK} = n^{-1}\left(\sum_{i=1}^{n}\left(\begin{array}{l} 0.511\log(H_t/L_t)^2 - 0.383\log(C_t/O_t)^2 \\ -0.019\left(\log(C_t/O_t)\log\left(H_tL_t/O_t^2\right) - 2\log(H_t/O_t)\log(L_t/O_t)\right)\end{array}\right)\right)$$

where H_t, L_t, O_t and C_t are the highest, lowest, opening and closing price for each trading day. It can be shown that this estimator has a sampling variance that is almost 7.5 times smaller than that of the historical standard deviation. Several alternative extreme-value estimators have been developed that extend the information set and relax the assumptions of this estimator (see Bali and Weinbaum, 2005). The empirical literature has shown that, although extreme-value estimators generally perform well in terms of efficiency, they often suffer from bias when compared to the simple historical standard deviation approach.

An interesting development in volatility measurement has been the emergence of the *integrated* or *realised variance* non-parametric estimator. This has become extremely popular over the past decade after a series of papers by Andersen, Bollerslev, Diebold and co-authors, and Barndorff-Nielsen and Shephard. For reviews of this growing literature, see Barndorff-Nielsen, Gravesen and Shephard (2004) and Andersen, Bollerslev and Diebold (2007). Realised variance, often termed *realised volatility* (RV), measures the quadratic variation of the underlying diffusion process in continuous time. In discrete time, it can be conveniently estimated by taking the sum of M squared returns within a fixed time interval:

$$\hat{\sigma}_R^2 = \sum_{i=1}^{M} r_i^2$$

Realised volatility can be then calculated as $\hat{\sigma}_R$. Assuming that the underlying process is a *semi-martingale* and that arbitrage is not possible, it can be proved that, as $M \to \infty$, RV is a uniformly consistent estimator of the unobserved, true variability of the process and that, under certain additional conditions, it provides unbiased estimates. Barndorff-Nielsen and Shephard (2005) use log-based limit theory to show that volatility based on the RV estimator has the following asymptotic distribution:

$$\frac{\log\left(\sum_{i=1}^{M} r_i^2\right) - \log \sigma^2}{\sqrt{\frac{2}{3}\sum_{i=1}^{M} r_i^4 \Big/ \left(\sum_{i=1}^{M} r_i^2\right)^2}} \overset{a}{\sim} N(0, 1)$$

RV measures total variation without requiring that the underlying process is free of discontinuous jump behaviour. Empirical research on jumps has shown that they may play a significant role and may account for a non-trivial part of the total variability. Jumps are particularly important in finance, since they play a critical role in risk management and option pricing (see Psychoyios, Dotsis and Markellos, 2006, and Huang and Tauchen, 2005). In the context of realised variance, it is possible to disentangle the effect of jumps on the total variation of the process. This can easily be accomplished in a non-parametric manner by employing the realised *bipower variation* (*BPV*) proposed by Barndorff-Nielsen and Shephard (2004):

$$BPV = \frac{\pi}{2} \sum_{i=2}^{M} |r_i||r_{i-1}|$$

Simulations by Huang and Tauchen (2005) show that an empirically robust measure of the relative contribution of jumps to the total price variation is given by the relative jump statistic $RJ = \left(\hat{\sigma}_R^2 - BPV\right)/\hat{\sigma}_R^2$, or the corresponding logarithmic ratio $J = \log(\hat{\sigma}_R^2) - \log(BPV)$.

Realised variance allows us, in the continuous time limit, to approximate the *ex post, instantaneous* variance over any time interval, and to any desired degree of accuracy, by just sampling at sufficiently high frequencies. At first glance, this is a particularly powerful estimator, since it appears to be model- and error-free. In practice, however, only finite samples of discrete data are available. Sampling at very high frequencies may be possible but, unfortunately, may introduce several well-known microstructure biases related to, for example, bid–ask bounce, screen fighting, price discreteness, irregular spacing of quotes, illiquidity, seasonalities, etc. Empirical research has shown that a sampling interval of thirty minutes typically offers a good balance between increasing sampling frequency and reducing microstructure effects. RV is now widely used as a proxy for unobservable volatility to evaluate the performance of volatility estimators. For example, Bali and Weinbaum (2005) evaluate the performance of several extreme-value estimators against historical volatility using daily, weekly and monthly data on equities and exchange rates. Using RV as a proxy for unobserved volatility, they find that the extreme-value estimators were less biased and more efficient than the historical standard deviation, especially at the daily level. Moreover, the Garman and Klass estimator has been found to have one of the best performances amongst competing extreme-value estimators.

Another class of estimator is based on the volatility obtained by inverting financial option pricing formulae using observed option prices. Let us assume that the price x_t for an option contract can be calculated from the following pricing model:

$$x_t = f(S_t, T - t, r_t, \sigma)$$

where S_t is the spot price of the asset underlying the option, $T - t$ is the life or time to maturity of the option, r_t is the risk-free rate and σ is the volatility of the asset. All the variables in the model, except for volatility, are observable and can be approximated using market data, so that a proxy for volatility can also be estimated by inverting f. Although these *implied volatility estimators* are widely used, especially in the financial industry, they depend on the pricing model chosen. Moreover, they do not always provide a single volatility estimate across various option prices for the same asset.

A related development has been the treatment of volatility as a distinct asset that can be packaged in an index and traded using volatility swaps, futures and options. Traditionally, derivatives have allowed investors and firms to hedge against factors such as market, interest rate and foreign exchange volatility. Volatility derivatives provide protection against volatility risk – i.e. unexpected changes in the level of volatility itself. The first volatility index, the VIX (currently termed VXO), was introduced in 1993 by the Chicago Board Options Exchange (CBOE). Since 2003 the VIX has been calculated as the average implied volatility of out-of-money option prices across all available strikes on the S&P 500 index. Several other implied volatility indices, in the United States and elsewhere, have since been developed, with the financial press regularly quoting the VIX as an 'investor fear gauge'. A number of recent empirical studies have examined the properties of implied volatility indices. For example, Psychoyios, Dotsis and Markellos (2006) analyse daily data on the VIX index over a period of ten years and find evidence of mean reversion, heteroskedasticity and jumps. Although the VIX is found to be stationary, the possibility of long memory cannot be excluded.

Empirical research has shown that any measure of volatility exhibits persistent variations through time, and this has motivated the development of reduced-form forecasting models. These models are sometimes called *autonomous*, since they model volatility alone without reference to models for the conditional mean return. A naïve, yet common, practice is to estimate volatility as a simple or exponential moving average of a rolling window of past squared returns or shocks.

A more sophisticated approach is to model the observable volatility proxies using standard time series methods. For example, Taylor (1986) estimates ARMA models for absolute and squared returns (see also Granger and Ding, 1995). Andersen *et al.* (2003) introduce formal links between realised volatility and the conditional covariance matrix of returns and estimate various AR and ARFIMA models directly on the *RV*, while Engle and Gallo (2006) model volatility by jointly considering measures such as absolute daily returns, the daily high–low range and realised volatility. Since all these measures correspond to non-negative series, Engle and Gallo develop a multiplicative error model that is consistent and asymptotically normal under a wide range of error specifications. Finally, an alternative approach is to use continuous-time models to describe the dynamics of implied volatility indices. Psychoyios, Dotsis and Markellos (2006) estimate a variety of such models with data on the VIX and find that the widely used mean-reverting square root process can be significantly improved by the addition of jumps. Model performance is found to be further enhanced if jumps are conditioned on the level of the index.

It should be emphasised that all the volatility proxies described above are calculated from a finite set of data and are obviously subject to sampling error. The use of noisy volatility estimates in financial models gives rise to an interesting econometric problem involving estimation risk, whereby the model is valid but the input parameters are uncertain (see, for example,

Gibson *et al.*, 1999). For example, within option pricing, the use of estimates in place of the true, but unknown, volatility in the Black–Scholes formula involves estimation risk as the estimate of the variance affects the estimate of the corresponding option price. An additional complication arises from the fact that even an unbiased estimate of volatility will not necessarily produce an unbiased estimate of the option price, since option pricing models are highly non-linear with respect to volatility (for a description of this literature, see Dotsis and Markellos, 2007, and the references therein).

Example 5.1 Measuring the volatility of the DJI

In this example we compare the volatility estimates obtained using some of the approaches discussed above. We use daily opening, closing, high and low prices for the Dow-Jones Industrial Average index (DJI) for 1996, a total of 254 observations. We also utilise intradaily data, provided by the Olsen and Associates database, on the DJI. This data set corresponds to the average between the bid and ask price sampled at thirty-minute intervals. Since the market is open between 10 a.m. and 5 p.m., we have fifteen prices per trading day, or a total of 3810 observations. The SACF and Q-statistics indicate no autocorrelation in the returns. Significant autocorrelation is found in both the absolute and squared returns, however, suggesting that volatility may be predictable.

Using the standard deviation of daily logarithmic returns calculated from closing prices we obtain a volatility estimate of 12.01 per cent. If opening prices are used instead, we obtain a somewhat lower volatility estimate of around 11.7 per cent. Such differences can be caused by well-known microstructure effects that are present in the opening and closing of the market (see, for example, Stoll and Whaley, 1990). Based on the standard deviation of the intraday returns we obtain a volatility estimate of 11.97 per cent. The difference between the volatility estimated using the daily and intradaily intervals is very small here, since the effect of microstructures is not so pronounced at the thirty-minute sampling frequency. The Garman and Klass (1980) extreme-value volatility estimator gives a much higher average volatility over the complete period of 21.06 per cent. We treat this estimate with some caution, as we know that, although the sampling error of this estimator may be small, extreme-value estimators can demonstrate bias.

We have also estimated realised volatility for each day of the sample using the intradaily data. The time series of annualised realised volatilities is shown in figure 5.1. Although the unconditional distribution of returns is non-normal, daily returns standardised by *RV* estimates are almost normally distributed. As discussed by Barndorff-Nielsen and Shephard (2004),

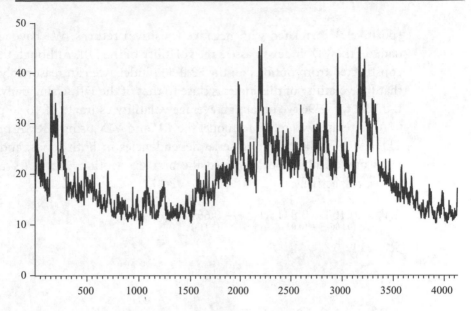

Figure 5.1   Annualised realised volatility estimator for the DJI

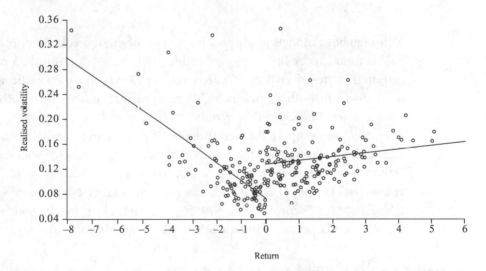

Figure 5.2   Annualised realised volatility estimator versus return for the DJI

non-normality of RV-standardised returns is an indication of the importance of incorporating jumps and innovation volatility interactions into volatility forecasting models. Another interesting point to examine is whether, as predicted by standard financial theory, returns and volatility have an inverse linear relationship. As shown in figure 5.2, and in line with empirical research, we find an asymmetry in this relationship: RV is negatively (positively) correlated with negative (positive) returns. We have also used data on the VIX index to assess the volatility of the DJI. Although the VIX is constructed from options on the S&P 500 index, we can reasonably assume that the volatility of this index is close to that of the DJI. Using daily data on the VIX for 1996 we obtain an average volatility estimate of 16.46 per cent.

An attempt was made to model the RV and VIX using ARMA processes. The SACFs indicate strong serial dependencies in both series, and ARMA (1,1) and AR(1) models offered the best description of the RV and VIX series, respectively:

$$RV_t = \underset{(0.006)}{0.108} + \underset{(0.080)}{0.841}\,RV_{t-1} - \underset{(0.113)}{0.651}\,\varepsilon_{t-1} + \varepsilon_t$$
$$R^2 = 11.10\%$$

and

$$VIX_t = \underset{(0.004)}{0.167} + \underset{(0.031)}{0.868}\,VIX_{t-1} + \varepsilon_t$$
$$R^2 = 75.21\%$$

Although both models imply positive persistence in the volatility process, the VIX is found to be far more predictable, with an R^2 of around 75 per cent. Although autocorrelation is effectively removed, the distribution of the residuals from both models is highly non-normal, mostly due to the existence of a few large, positive errors.

Finally, we compare the performance of the Garman and Klass and VIX estimators in terms of their proximity to daily realised volatility. The extreme-value estimator has a much stronger correlation with realised volatility than the VIX. The VIX has a much smaller error, however, since $RMSE_{VIX} = 0.072$ compared to $RMSE_{GK} = 0.104$. Thus, we can conclude that the VIX is a superior estimator of volatility for this particular sample.

Example 5.2 A jump diffusion model for the VIX implied volatility index

Using VIX daily prices from January 1990 to September 2005 we estimate the parameters of the mean-reverting square root process augmented by upward jumps (SRJ). This continuous-time model has been used to model the autonomous dynamics of implied volatility indices, and assumes that volatility follows the process

$$dVIX_t = \alpha(\mu - VIX_t)dt + \sigma_{VIX}\sqrt{VIX_t}\,dB_t + y\,dq_t$$

where dB_t is a standard Brownian motion, dq_t is a compound Poisson process and y is the jump amplitude. In the SRJ process, dq_t has constant arrival parameter h with $P(dq_t = 1) = hdt$, and dB_t and dq_t are assumed to be independent processes. We further assume that the jump amplitude y follows an exponential distribution and is restricted to be positive: $f(y) = \eta e^{-\eta y} 1_{\{y \geq 0\}}$, where $1/\eta$ is the mean of the jump.

This exponential distribution allows us to capture upward jumps in implied volatility and to derive the characteristic function in closed form. The mean and the variance of the process are given by

$$E(VIX_{t+\tau}) = VIX_t e^{-\alpha\tau} + \mu(1 - e^{-\alpha\tau}) + \frac{h}{\alpha\eta}(1 - e^{-\alpha\tau})$$

$$V(VIX_{t+\tau}) = \frac{VIX_t \sigma_{VIX}^2}{\alpha} e^{-\alpha\tau}(1 - e^{-\alpha\tau}) + \frac{\sigma_{VIX}^2 \mu}{2\alpha}(1 - e^{-\alpha\tau})^2$$
$$+ \frac{h\sigma_{VIX}^2}{2\eta\alpha^2}(1 - e^{-\alpha\tau})^2 + \frac{h}{\alpha\eta^2}(1 - e^{-2\alpha\tau})$$

where τ is a discrete time interval. The density functions of these models can now be obtained via Fourier inversion of the characteristic function. Maximising the likelihood function, though computationally intensive, provides asymptotically efficient estimates of the unknown parameters (see Singleton, 2001). Fourier inversion, using a Gauss–Legendre quadrature, of the characteristic function provides the necessary transition density function and the log-likelihood function. Using the VIX sample, the following parameters are obtained:

$$dVIX_t = \underset{(9.51)}{7.38}\left(\underset{(21.76)}{0.15} - VIX_t\right)dt + \underset{(61.32)}{0.35}\sqrt{VIX_t}dB_t + ydq_t$$
$$h = 19.41(4.50) \qquad 1/\eta = 0.017(8.22)$$

Figures in brackets denote asymptotic t-statistics and suggest that all parameter estimates are highly significant.

This supports the argument that the VIX exhibits significant jumps. The model implies an average jump frequency (h) of around twenty per year with an average jump magnitude ($1/\eta$) equal to 1.7 per cent. Implied volatility is strongly mean-reverting. Since the average half-life of volatility can be defined for this process as $\log(2)/\alpha$, the intuitive interpretation of the speed of mean reversion is that, if volatility unexpectedly jumps upwards, it will take $1/\alpha = 0.094$ years, or 1.13 months, to get (halfway) back to its long-run mean. We can also see that the addition of jumps decreases the estimated long-run mean (μ) in comparison with the unconditional mean of the data, which is 0.196.

5.4 Stochastic volatility

An alternative approach to measuring volatility is to embed it within a formal stochastic model for the time series itself. A simple way to do this is to allow the variance (or conditional variance) of the process generating the time series to change either at certain discrete points in time or continuously. Although a stationary process must have a constant variance, certain conditional variances can change. For a non-linear stationary process x_t, the variance, $V(x_t)$, is a constant for all t, but the conditional variance $V(x_t|x_{t-1}, x_{t-2}, \ldots)$ depends on the observations and thus can change from period to period.

5.4.1 Stochastic volatility models

Suppose that the sequence $\{x_t\}_1^t$ is generated by the *product process*

$$x_t = \mu + \sigma_t U_t \tag{5.3}$$

where U_t is a standardised process, so that $E(U_t) = 0$ and $V(U_t) = 1$ for all t, and σ_t is a sequence of positive random variables usually such that $V(x_t|\sigma_t) = \sigma_t^2$; σ_t is thus the conditional standard deviation of x_t. The term μ gives the expected return of x_t.

Typically $U_t = (x_t - \mu)/\sigma_t$ is assumed to be normal and independent of σ_t; we will further assume that it is strict white noise. Equation (5.3) can then be shown to be obtained as the discrete-time approximation to the stochastic differential equation

$$\frac{\mathrm{d}P}{P} = \mathrm{d}(\log P) = \mu \mathrm{d}t + \sigma \mathrm{d}W$$

where $x_t = \Delta \log P_t$ and $W(t)$ is standard Brownian motion. This is the usual *diffusion process* used to price financial assets in theoretical models of finance (see, for example, Hull, 2005).

The above assumptions together imply that x_t has mean μ, variance

$$E(x_t - \mu)^2 = E\left(\sigma_t^2 U_t^2\right) = E\left(\sigma_t^2\right) E\left(U_t^2\right) = E\left(\sigma_t^2\right)$$

and autocovariances

$$E(x_t - \mu)(x_{t-k} - \mu) = E(\sigma_t \sigma_{t-k} U_t U_{t-k}) = E(\sigma_t \sigma_{t-k} U_t) E(U_{t-k}) = 0$$

i.e. it is white noise. Note that both the squared and absolute deviations, $S_t = (x_t - \mu)^2$ and $M_t = |x_t - \mu|$, can be autocorrelated, however. For example,

$$
\begin{aligned}
Cov(S_t, S_{t-k}) &= E(S_t - E(S_t))(S_{t-k} - E(S_t)) = E(S_t S_{t-k}) - (E(S_t))^2 \\
&= E(\sigma_t^2 \sigma_{t-k}^2) E(U_t^2 U_{t-k}^2) - (E(\sigma_t^2))^2 \\
&= E(\sigma_t^2 \sigma_{t-k}^2) - (E(\sigma_t^2))^2
\end{aligned}
$$

in which case we have

$$\rho_{k,S} = \frac{E(\sigma_t^2 \sigma_{t-k}^2) - (E(\sigma_t^2))^2}{E(\sigma_t^4) - (E(\sigma_t^2))^2}$$

where $\rho_{k,S}$ is the kth autocorrelation of S_t.

What models are plausible for the conditional standard deviation σ_t? Since it is a sequence of positive random variables a normal distribution is inappropriate, but, as it is likely that σ_t will be skewed to the right, a log-normal distribution would seem to be a plausible choice. We can define the basic log-normal autoregressive stochastic volatility (ARSV) model of order one as

$$h_t = \log(\sigma_t^2) = \gamma_0 + \gamma_1 h_{t-1} + \eta_t \tag{5.4}$$

where $\eta_t \sim NID(0, \sigma_\eta^2)$ and is independent of U_t, i.e. $E(\eta_t U_t) = 0$. A common interpretation of h_t is that it represents the random and uneven flow of new information into financial markets: see Clark (1973) and Tauchen and Pitts (1983). The parameter γ_1 captures the persistence in volatility; when it approaches one and σ_η^2 is close to zero, volatility evolves smoothly. Returns are homoskedastic in the limit when $\gamma_1 = 1$ and $\sigma_\eta^2 = 0$. We then have

$$x_t = \mu + U_t \exp(h_t/2)$$

It can easily be shown that x_t is a martingale difference process. Also, since U_t is always stationary, x_t will be (weakly) stationary if and only if h_t is, which will be the case if $|\gamma_1| < 1$. Assuming this, then using the properties of the log-normal distribution shows that all even moments of x_t and S_t will exist, being given by

$$E(x_t - \mu)^r = E(S_t)^{r/2} = E(U_t^r)E\left(\exp\left(\frac{r}{2}h_t\right)\right)$$

$$= \left(r!/\left(2^{r/2}(r/2!)\right)\right)\exp\left(\frac{r}{2}\mu_h + \left(\frac{r}{2}\right)\left(\frac{\sigma_h^2}{2}\right)\right)$$

where $\mu_h = E(h_t) = \gamma_0/(1 - \gamma_1)$ and $\sigma_h^2 = V(h_t) = \sigma_\eta^2\big/(1 - \gamma_1^2)$. All odd moments are zero. The moment measure of kurtosis is then given by

$$\frac{E(S_t^2)}{(E(S_t))^2} = \frac{E(x_t - \mu)^4}{\left(E(x_t - \mu)^2\right)^2} = 3\exp(\sigma_h^2) > 3$$

so that the process has fatter tails than a normal distribution. The auto-correlation function of S_t follows from the fact that

$$E(S_t S_{t-k}) = E(\sigma_t^2 \sigma_{t-k}^2) = E(\exp(h_t)\exp(h_{t-k})) = E(\exp(h_t + h_{t-k}))$$

$$= \exp\left((\mu_h + \sigma_h^2) + (\mu_h + \gamma_1^k\sigma_h^2)\right) = \exp\left(2\mu_h + \sigma_h^2(1 + \gamma_1^k)\right)$$

Hence

$$Cov(S_t, S_{t-k}) = \exp\left(2\mu_h + \sigma_h^2(1 + \gamma_1^k)\right) - \exp\left(2\mu_h + \sigma_h^2\right)$$

$$= \exp\left(2\mu_h + \sigma_h^2\right)\left(\exp(\sigma_h^2\gamma_1^k) - 1\right)$$

and

$$\rho_{k,S} = \frac{\left(\exp(\sigma_h^2\gamma_1^k) - 1\right)}{3\left(\exp(\sigma_h^2) - 1\right)}$$

Taking logarithms of (5.3) yields

$$\log(S_t) = h_t + \log(U_t^2) = \mu_h + \frac{\eta_t}{(1 - \gamma_1 B)} + \log(U_t^2)$$

which shows that $\log(S_t) \sim \text{ARMA}(1,1)$, but with non-normal innovations: if U_t is normal then $\log(U_t^2)$ has mean -1.27 and variance 4.93 and a very long left-hand tail, caused by taking logarithms of very small numbers. The autocorrelation function of $\log(S_t)$ is

$$\rho_{k,\log(S)} = \frac{\gamma_1^k}{(1 + 4.93/\sigma_h^2)}$$

Note that it is possible that some values of S_t may be zero, in which case their logarithms cannot be taken. One way of overcoming this difficulty is to employ the modified log-squared transformation (see Broto and Ruiz, 2004)

$$S_t^* = \log\left(S_t + cs_S^2\right) - cs_S^2 \big/ \left(S_t + cs_S^2\right)$$

where s_S^2 is the sample variance of S_t and c is a small number, often set to be 0.02.

Several extensions have been made to the basic ARSV model described above (for a review, see Ghysels, Harvey and Renault, 1996). A variety of heavy-tailed distributions have been proposed for the error process η_t, and when the errors follow a t-distribution the model can be interpreted as having two independent volatility processes (see Liesenfeld and Richard, 2003). Harvey and Shephard (1996) and Jacquier, Polson and Rossi (2004) have developed two different models that allow for correlation between the shocks in the mean and variance processes. These models are able to capture the 'leverage' effect, in which negative (positive) shocks to returns are associated with increases (decreases) in volatility. This effect stems from the observation that bad news about a firm, which decreases the price of the firm's stock and hence increases the debt-to-equity ratio (i.e. its financial leverage), makes the firm riskier and tends to increase future expected volatility. In the Harvey and Shephard (1996) model the errors in the mean and variance equations have correlation ρ, i.e. $E(\eta_t U_t) = \rho\sigma_\eta$. The ARSV with leverage can then be written

$$h_t = \gamma_0 + \gamma_1 h_{t-1} + \rho\sigma_\eta\sigma_{t-1} U_{t-1} \exp(-0.5 h_{t-1}) + \eta_{t-1}^*$$

where η_t^* is distributed as $N(0, \sigma_\eta^2(1 - \rho^2))$ with $E(U_t\eta_t^*) = 0$.

Yu (2005) shows that the specification proposed by Harvey and Shephard (1996) is superior to the Jacquier, Polson and Rossi (2004) model in terms of both its interpretability of the leverage effect and its empirical validity. Moreover, it has the advantage of retaining the martingale difference property for the underlying process. Ding, Granger and Engle (1993), among others, have argued that volatility may be better modelled using a persistent, long-memory process. This is motivated by empirical findings demonstrating that the autocorrelations of squared returns decay at a much slower rate than the expected exponential decline. As with the aggregation of ARMA processes (Granger, 1980), Zaffaroni (2007) shows that long memory in variance can result from aggregating certain stochastic volatility processes. Breidt, Crato and de Lima (1998) and Harvey (1998) have developed long-memory specifications of stochastic volatility models where the logarithmic variance follows an ARFIMA(p, d, q) process. Liu (2000) proposes a regime-switching

ARSV process that also exhibits long memory. Finally, various multivariate extensions of stochastic volatility models have also been developed (see, for example, Harvey, Ruiz and Shephard, 1994, and Chib, Nardarib and Shephard, 2006).

Stochastic volatility models have the significant advantage of having representations in both continuous and discrete time. This is very important for option pricing and theoretical finance, since most of the models in this literature are expressed in continuous time. Using the results of Meddahi and Renault (2004), a general class of autoregressive stochastic volatility models that are closed under temporal aggregation may be defined that allow for a precise relation to be derived between continuous- and discrete-time parameterisations. For example, it can easily be shown that the ARSV(1) is a discrete-time approximation to the continuous-time Ornstein–Uhlenbeck diffusion process that is widely used in the option pricing and interest rate literature (see Davidson, 2006b).

One of the most popular of these models is the one-factor, square root volatility model, or scalar affine diffusion, of Heston (1993). The equations for the conditional mean and conditional variance are

$$dp_t = (\mu - 0.5\sigma_t)dt + \sqrt{V_t}dB_{1t}$$

and

$$dV_t = (\alpha - \beta\sigma_t)dt + \sigma_V\sqrt{V_t}dB_{2t}$$

Here p_t is the logarithm of the asset price and V_t is the instantaneous (latent) stochastic volatility, which is assumed to follow a square root process. The dB_{it}, $i = 1, 2$, are Brownian motions with instantaneous correlation ρdt, implying that the stochastic volatility premium is linear. When the correlation is unity, we obtain a single-factor model such as the autonomous volatility model discussed in the previous section. The parameters σ_V, β and ρ are of great importance for option pricing, since they express the manner by which p_t deviates from the standard log-normal assumption. Heston (1993) uses Fourier inversion to derive convenient analytical formulae for option pricing under stochastic volatility, and these have become very popular. The parameter α expresses the unconditional mean of volatility, β is the speed of mean reversion and σ_V is the volatility of volatility parameter. The presence of kurtosis and fat tails is dependent upon the size of σ_V relative to β. For the process to be well defined, the following inequalities must hold: $\alpha, \beta > 0$ and $\sigma_V^2 \leq 2\alpha\beta$. Empirical studies typically find a negative correlation ρ, which is sometimes referred to as a 'continuous-time' leverage effect.

Although the Heston model has not been found to offer a realistic representation of index returns, primarily due to insufficient kurtosis, the addition of a jump component improves performance considerably (see, for example, Eraker, Johannes and Polson, 2003). Eraker (2004) proposes a model with discontinuous correlated jumps in stock prices and volatility with a state-dependent arrival intensity. A simple generalisation of the Heston model is the constant elasticity of variance (CEV) model, which can be derived by replacing the square root in the variance diffusion term by an exponent of undetermined magnitude (see, for example, Jones, 2003). Bollerslev and Zhou (2006) have recently used the Heston model to study various volatility puzzles concerning the leverage effect and the difference between realised and option-market-implied volatilities. They also try to explain the empirical controversies with respect to the relationships between contemporaneous returns and realised volatility, and returns and implied volatility, respectively.

5.4.2 Estimation of stochastic volatility models

Until a few years ago, stochastic volatility models were rarely used in empirical applications because they were particularly difficult to estimate. Despite the fact that their statistical properties are easy to derive using established results on log-normal distributions, the likelihood for the transition density functions and parameters are rarely available in closed form. Moreover, volatility is a latent factor that cannot be observed directly from historical data, and therefore it must either be approximated, typically by inverting an option pricing formula, or it must be 'backed out' via integration from the stochastic volatility model.

Fortunately, powerful estimation schemes have been proposed in recent years (for reviews, see Shephard, 1996, and Broto and Ruiz, 2004), and these have led to the development of several empirical methods, including simulated methods of moments, efficient methods of moments, analytic approximations to the likelihood function and spectral methods. Much interest has centred on the Markov chain Monte Carlo (MCMC) approach (see the review by Johannes and Polson, 2007). This is a computationally intensive technique that is well suited to continuous-time stochastic volatility models, as it directly computes the distribution of the latent variables and parameters given the observed data. Due to the Bayesian nature of the estimation it can also quantify estimation and model risk. Although all these approaches can deliver consistent and often asymptotically efficient estimates, they are still computationally demanding and rather difficult to implement.

A special case of the MCMC algorithm that is based on Gibbs sampling can be applied using the freely available software BUGS (for a description, see Meyer and Yu, 2000). A convenient and popular estimation method is still, however, quasi-maximum likelihood (QML), as outlined in Koopman *et al.* (2006, chap. 7.5) and available in their STAMP software package. This technique, which uses the Kalman filter, also provides an estimate of the volatility σ_t^2. Although it has been shown that this estimator is consistent and asymptotically normal, it is inefficient since it does not rely on the exact likelihood function. Another practical approach has been proposed by Bollerslev and Zhou (2002), who exploit the distributional information contained in realised volatility to construct a simple conditional moment estimator for stochastic volatility diffusions using GMM. Although this approach has the shortcoming of requiring high-frequency data, Bollerslev and Zhou demonstrate using simulation that it provides highly reliable and accurate estimators in finite samples.

Example 5.3 A stochastic volatility model for the dollar/sterling exchange rate
In this example we fit the SV model

$$x_t = \mu + U_t \exp(h_t/2)$$

$$h_t = \log(\sigma_t^2) = \gamma_0 + \gamma_1 h_{t-1} + \eta_t$$

to the daily series of dollar/sterling first differences initially examined in example 2.5, where it was found to be close to zero-mean white noise. To use the QML technique of Koopman *et al.* (2006), the model is rewritten as

$$x_t = \sigma U_t \exp(h_t/2)$$

$$h_t = \gamma_1 h_{t-1} + \eta_t,$$

where $\sigma = \exp(\gamma_0/2)$, or as

$$\log(x_t^2) = \kappa + h_t + u_t$$

$$h_t = \gamma_1 h_{t-1} + \eta_t$$

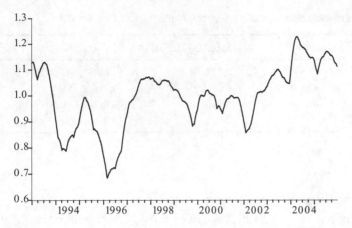

Figure 5.3   Dollar/sterling exchange rate 'volatility' (daily January 1993–December 2005)

where

$$u_t = \log(U_t^2) - E(\log(U_t^2))$$

and

$$\kappa = \log(\sigma^2) - E(\log(U_t^2))$$

QML estimation yields the following estimates: $\hat{\sigma}_\eta = 0.050$, $\hat{\sigma} = 1.906$, $\hat{\gamma}_0 = 1.312$ and $\hat{\gamma}_1 = 0.995$, and a plot of the exchange rate volatility, given by the 'smoothed' estimates (of the square root) of $\exp(h_t/2)$, is shown in figure 5.3. The conditional variance equation is close to a random walk and the time-varying nature of the volatility can clearly be seen.

Example 5.4 A leveraged logarithmic ARSV(1) model for the DJI

In this example we estimate the leveraged stochastic volatility model proposed by Harvey and Shephard (1996). The model is estimated by the MCMC methodology, using the all-purpose Bayesian software package BUGS. This software allows an easy and efficient implementation of the Gibbs sampler, a specific MCMC technique that constructs a Markov chain by sampling from all univariate full-conditional distributions in a cyclical way. The BUGS code necessary for estimating the model accompanies the paper by Yu (2005).

The model can be conveniently represented as

$$h_t \big| h_{t-1}, \gamma_0, \gamma_1, \sigma_\eta^2 \sim N\left(\gamma_0 + \gamma_1 h_{t-1}, \sigma_\eta^2\right)$$

$$x_t \big| h_{t+1}, h_t, \gamma_0, \gamma_1, \sigma_\eta^2, \rho \sim N\left((\rho/\sigma_\eta) \exp(h_t/2)(h_{t+1} - \gamma_0 - \gamma_1 h_t), \exp(h_t)(1 - \rho^2)\right)$$

Table 5.1 Empirical estimates of the leveraged ARSV(1) model for the DJI

	Average	Standard deviation	95% credible intervals
ω	−7.912	0.337	(−8.557, −7.241)
γ_1	0.998	0.001	(0.996, 1.000)
ρ	−0.758	0.090	(−0.911, −0.561)
σ_η	0.102	0.015	(0.078, 0.136)

The prior distributions are assumed to be independent using the specifications adopted by Yu (2005), following Kim, Nelson and Startz (1998). More specifically, σ_η^2 is distributed as inverse gamma with parameters 2.5 and 0.025, so that it has a mean of 0.167 and a standard deviation of 0.024, and $(\gamma_1 + 1)/2$ is beta distributed with parameters 20 and 1.5, so that it has a mean of 0.93 and a standard deviation of 0.055. We also assume that $\omega = \gamma_0/(1 - \gamma_1) \sim N(0, 25)$ and that ρ is uniformly distributed with support between −1 and 1. We perform 20,000 iterations and discard the first 10,000. The algorithm is initialised by setting $\omega = 0$, $\gamma_1 = 0.98$, $\sigma_\eta^2 = 0.025$, and $\rho = -0.4$. We use daily data for the DJI between 20 September 2002 and 8 September 2006, a total of 1000 observations.

The posterior means for the parameters of the estimated model are reported in table 5.1, which also gives the standard deviations and the 95 per cent Bayes credible intervals of the posterior distributions. It is evident that all parameter estimates are significant, while the significantly negative value found for ρ confirms the existence of a leverage effect.

5.5 ARCH processes

5.5.1 Development of generalised ARCH processes

In the previous section, the process determining the conditional standard deviations of x_t was assumed not to be a function of x_t. For example, for the AR(1) log-normal model of equation (5.4), σ_t was dependent upon the information set $\{\eta_t, \sigma_{t-1}, \sigma_{t-2}, \ldots\}$. We now consider the case where the conditional standard deviations are a function of past values of x_t, i.e.

$$\sigma_t = \Im(x_{t-1}, x_{t-2}, \ldots)$$

A simple example is

$$\sigma_t = \Im(x_{t-1}) = \left(\alpha_0 + \alpha_1(x_{t-1} - \mu)^2\right)^{1/2} \tag{5.5}$$

where α_0 and α_1 are both positive. With $U_t \sim NID(0,1)$ and independent of σ_t, $x_t = \mu + U_t\sigma_t$ is then white noise and conditionally normal – i.e.

$$x_t | x_{t-1}, x_{t-2}, \ldots \sim NID(\mu, \sigma_t^2)$$

so that

$$V(x_t | x_{t-1}) = \alpha_0 + \alpha_1(x_{t-1} - \mu)^2$$

If $\alpha_1 < 1$ the unconditional variance is $V(x_t) = \alpha_0/(1 - \alpha_1)$ and x_t is weakly stationary. The fourth moment of x_t is finite if $3\alpha_1^2 < 1$ and, if so, the kurtosis is given by $3(1 - \alpha_1^2)/(1 - 3\alpha_1^2)$. This exceeds three, so that the unconditional distribution of x_t is fatter-tailed than the normal. If this moment condition is not satisfied, then the variance of x_t^2 will not be finite and hence x_t^2 will not be weakly stationary.

This model was first introduced by Engle (1982) and is known as the *first-order autoregressive conditional heteroskedastic*, or ARCH(1), process. ARCH processes have proved to be an extremely popular class of non-linear models for financial time series, as can be seen from the various and many surveys of the literature that have been published: Engle and Bollerslev (1986), Bollerslev, Chou and Kroner (1992), Bera and Higgins (1993), Bollerslev, Engle and Nelson (1994), Engle (2002), Li, Ling and McAleer (2002), Giraitis, Leipus and Surgailis (2006) and Teräsvirta (2007) is a by no means exhaustive list. Instructive expositions of ARCH modelling from a practical perspective can be found in Engle (2001) and Engle and Patton (2001).

A more convenient notation is to define $\varepsilon_t = x_t - \mu = U_t \sigma_t$, so that the ARCH(1) model can be written as

$$\varepsilon_t | x_{t-1}, x_{t-2}, \ldots \sim NID(0, \sigma_t^2)$$

$$\sigma_t^2 = \alpha_0 + \alpha_1 \varepsilon_{t-1}^2$$

Defining $v_t = \varepsilon_t^2 - \sigma_t^2$, the model can also be written as

$$\varepsilon_t^2 = \alpha_0 + \alpha_1 \varepsilon_{t-1}^2 + v_t$$

Since $E(v_t|x_{t-1}, x_{t-2}, \ldots) = 0$, the model corresponds directly to an AR(1) model for the squared innovations ε_t^2. As $v_t = \sigma_t^2(U_t^2 - 1)$, however, the errors are obviously heteroskedastic.

The ARCH(1) model can be interpreted in various ways. For example, suppose the parameters in the ARCH equation are defined as $\alpha_0 = V(u_t)$ and $\alpha_1 = V(\phi_t)$, where u_t and ϕ_t are independent. Thus,

$$V(\varepsilon_t) = V(u_t) + V(\phi_t)\varepsilon_{t-1}^2$$

which is consistent with ε_t being generated by a *random coefficient* AR(1) process

$$\varepsilon_t = \phi_t \varepsilon_{t-1} + u_t$$
$$= \phi_t \sigma_{t-1} U_{t-1} + u_t$$

where $E(\phi_t) = \phi$ and u_t has mean zero (see Bera and Higgins, 1993, for more on this interpretation).

A natural extension is the ARCH(q) process, where (5.5) is replaced by

$$\Im(x_{t-1}, x_{t-2}, \ldots, x_{t-q}) = \left(\alpha_0 + \sum\nolimits_{i=1}^{q} \alpha_i(x_{t-i} - \mu)^2\right)^{1/2}$$

where $\alpha_0 = 0$ and $\alpha_i \geq 0$, $1 \leq i \leq q$. The process will be weakly stationary if all the roots of the characteristic equation associated with the ARCH parameters, $\alpha(B)$, lie outside the unit circle – i.e. if $\sum_{i=1}^{q} \alpha_i < 1$, in which case the unconditional variance is $V(x_t) = \alpha_0 / \left(1 - \sum_{i=1}^{q} \alpha_i\right)$. In terms of ε_t and σ_t^2, the conditional variance function is

$$\sigma_t^2 = \alpha_0 + \sum\nolimits_{i=1}^{q} \alpha_i \varepsilon_{t-i}$$

or, equivalently,

$$\varepsilon_t^2 = \alpha_0 + \alpha(B)\varepsilon_{t-1}^2 + v_t$$

Detailed discussion of the ARCH(q) model, setting out further technical conditions that need not concern us here, may be found in, for example, Engle (1982), Milhøj (1985) and Weiss (1986a).

A practical difficulty with ARCH models is that, with q large, unconstrained estimation (to be discussed later) will often lead to the violation of the non-negativity constraints on the α_i s that are needed to ensure that the conditional variance σ_t^2 is always positive. In many early applications of the model a rather arbitrary declining lag structure was thus imposed on the α_is to ensure that these constraints were met. To obtain more flexibility, a further extension, to the *generalised ARCH* (GARCH) process, was proposed (Bollerslev, 1986, 1988); the GARCH(p,q) process has the conditional variance function

$$\sigma_t^2 = \alpha_0 + \sum_{i=1}^{q} \alpha_i \varepsilon_{t-i}^2 + \sum_{i=1}^{p} \beta_i \sigma_{t-i}^2$$

$$= \alpha_0 + \alpha(B)\varepsilon_t^2 + \beta(B)\sigma_t^2$$

where $p>0$ and $\beta_i \geq 0$, $1 \leq i \leq p$.

For the conditional variance of the GARCH(p,q) model to be well defined, all the coefficients in the corresponding ARCH(∞) model $\sigma_t^2 = \theta_0 + \theta(B)\varepsilon_t^2$ must be positive. Provided that $\alpha(B)$ and $\beta(B)$ have no common roots and that the roots of $\beta(B)$ lie outside the unit circle, this positivity constraint is satisfied if and only if all the coefficients in $\theta(B) = \alpha(B)/(1 - \beta(B))$ are non-negative. Necessary and sufficient conditions for this are given in Nelson and Cao (1992). For the GARCH$(1,1)$ process,

$$\sigma_t^2 = \alpha_0 + \alpha_1 \varepsilon_{t-1}^2 + \beta_1 \sigma_{t-1}^2$$

a model that has proved extremely popular for modelling financial time series, these conditions require that all three parameters are non-negative.

The equivalent form of the GARCH(p,q) process is

$$\varepsilon_t^2 = \alpha_0 + (\alpha(B) + \beta(B))\varepsilon_{t-1}^2 + v_t - \beta(B)v_{t-1} \tag{5.6}$$

so that $\varepsilon_t^2 \sim \text{ARMA}(m, p)$, where $m = \max(p,q)$. This process will be weakly stationary if and only if the roots of $\alpha(B) + \beta(B)$ lie outside the unit circle – i.e. if $\alpha(1) + \beta(1) < 1$. This also ensures that ε_t is weakly stationary, but it is only a sufficient, rather than a necessary, condition for strict stationarity. Because ARCH processes are thick-tailed, the conditions for weak stationarity arc often more stringent than those for strict stationarity. For example, Nelson (1990a) shows that ε_t and σ_t^2 will be strictly stationary in the GARCH$(1,1)$ model if and only if

$$E\big(\log\big(\beta_1 + \alpha_1 U_t^2\big)\big) < 1$$

and this will be satisfied if, for example, $U_t \sim N(0,1)$, $\alpha_1 = 3$ and $\beta_1 = 0$, although the conditions for weak stationarity are clearly violated. Stationarity conditions for the general GARCH(p,q) process are derived in Bougerol and Picard (1992).

These complications with stationarity conditions carry over to the concept of 'volatility persistence' in GARCH models. If $\alpha(1) + \beta(1) = 1$ in (5.6) then $\alpha(B) + \beta(B)$ contains a unit root, and we say that the model is *integrated GARCH*, or IGARCH(p,q) (see Engle and Bollerslev, 1986). It is often the case that $\alpha(1) + \beta(1)$ is very close to unity for financial time series, and, if this condition holds, a shock to the conditional variance is persistent in the sense that it remains important for all future forecasts. As Bollerslev, Engle and Nelson (1994) argue, however, the concept of persistence in GARCH models is ambiguous. One reasonable definition is to say that shocks fail to persist when σ_t^2 is stationary, so that the conditional expectation $E\big(\sigma_{t+s}^2|\varepsilon_t, \varepsilon_{t-1}, \ldots\big)$ converges, as $s \to \infty$, to the unconditional variance $\alpha_0/(1 - \alpha(1) - \beta(1))$. An alternative definition concentrates on forecast moments and says that shocks fail to persist if and only if $E\big(\sigma_{t+s}^{2\eta}|\varepsilon_t, \varepsilon_{t-1}, \ldots\big)$, for some $\eta > 0$, converges to a finite limit independent of $\varepsilon_t, \varepsilon_{t-1}, \ldots$.

Unfortunately, whether or not shocks persist can depend on which definition is adopted. For example, consider the GARCH(1,1) model

$$\sigma_{t+1}^2 = \alpha_0 + \alpha_1\varepsilon_t^2 + \beta_1\sigma_t^2 = \alpha_0 + \alpha_1\sigma_t^2\big(U_t^2 + \beta_1\big)$$

from which we have

$$E\big(\sigma_{t+s}^2|\varepsilon_t, \varepsilon_{t-1}, \ldots\big) = \alpha_0\left(\sum_{k=0}^{s-1}(\alpha_1 + \beta_1)^k\right) + \sigma_t^2(\alpha_1 + \beta_1)^s$$

It is easy to see that the conditional expectation converges to the unconditional variance $\alpha_0/(1 - \alpha_1 - \beta_1)$ if and only if $\alpha_1 + \beta_1 < 1$, whereas in the IGARCH model with $\alpha_1 + \beta_1 = 1$ the conditional expectation will tend to infinity as s increases – i.e.

$$E\big(\sigma_{t+s}^2|\varepsilon_t, \varepsilon_{t-1}, \ldots\big) = s\alpha_0 + \sigma_t^2$$

Yet IGARCH models are strictly stationary and, in this case, $E\big(\sigma_{t+s}^{2\eta}|\varepsilon_t, \varepsilon_{t-1}, \ldots\big)$ converges to a finite limit whenever $0 < \eta < 1$ (see Nelson, 1990a). The implication of this is that any apparent persistence of shocks may be a consequence of thick-tailed distributions rather than of inherent non-stationarity.

Persistence may also be characterised by the impulse response coefficients. The GARCH(1,1) process can be written, with $\phi_1 = \alpha_1 + \beta_1$, as

$$(1 - \phi_1 B)\varepsilon_t^2 = \alpha_0 + (1 - \beta_1 B)v_t$$

or as

$$\Delta\varepsilon_t^2 = (1 - B)(1 - \phi_1 B)^{-1}(1 - \beta_1 B)v_t = \theta(B)v_t$$

The impulse response coefficients are found from the coefficients in the $\theta(B)$ lag polynomial

$$\theta_0 = 1, \quad \theta_1 = \phi_1 - \beta_1 - 1, \quad \theta_j = (\phi_1 - \beta_1)(\phi_1 - 1)\phi_1^{j-2}, \quad j \geq 2$$

The cumulative impulse response $\theta(1)$ is zero because $\theta(B)$ contains a unit root or, equivalently, because $\sum_j \theta_j = (\phi_1 - \beta_1)\phi_1^{j-1}$, which exponentially tends to zero in the limit as long as $\phi_1 = \alpha_1 + \beta_1 < 1$. When $\phi_1 = \alpha_1 + \beta_1 = 1$, however, so that we have an IGARCH(1,1) process

$$\Delta\varepsilon_t^2 = \alpha_0 + (1 - \beta_1 B)v_t$$

$\sum_j \theta_j = 1 - \beta_1 = \theta(1) \neq 0$, and hence shocks persist indefinitely.

5.5.2 Modifications of GARCH processes

Although we have assumed that the distribution of ε_t was conditionally normal, this is not essential. Bollerslev (1987), for example, considers the case where the distribution is standardised-t with unknown degrees of freedom v that may be estimated from the data: for $v > 2$ such a distribution is leptokurtic and hence has thicker tails than the normal. Other distributions that have been considered include the normal–Poisson mixture distribution (Jorion, 1988), the power exponential distribution (Baillie and Bollerslev, 1989), the normal–log-normal mixture (Hsieh, 1989a) and the generalised exponential distribution (Nelson, 1991). Estimation procedures have also been developed that either estimate semi-parametrically the density of ε_t (Engle and Gonzalez-Rivera, 1991) or adaptively estimate the parameters of ARCH models in the presence of non-normal ε_t (Linton, 1993).

Further modifications result from allowing the relationship between σ_t^2 and ε_t to be more flexible than the quadratic mapping that has so far been assumed. These modifications often lead to general classes of GARCH models that have been used to study asymptotic properties, the existence of moments and other time series characteristics. To simplify the exposition, we shall concentrate on variants of the GARCH(1,1) process

$$\sigma_t^2 = \alpha_0 + \alpha_1\varepsilon_{t-1}^2 + \beta_1\sigma_{t-1}^2 = \alpha_0 + \alpha_1\sigma_{t-1}^2 U_{t-1}^2 + \beta_1\sigma_{t-1}^2 \qquad (5.7)$$

An early alternative was to model conditional standard deviations rather than variances (Taylor, 1986, and Schwert, 1989):

$$\sigma_t = \alpha_0 + \alpha_1|\varepsilon_{t-1}| + \beta_1\sigma_{t-1} = \alpha_0 + \alpha_1\sigma_{t-1}|U_{t-1}| + \beta_1\sigma_{t-1} \qquad (5.8)$$

This makes the conditional variance the square of a weighted average of absolute shocks rather than the weighted average of squared shocks. Consequently, large shocks have a smaller effect on the conditional variance than in the standard GARCH model.

Rather than concentrating on the variance or standard deviation, Ding, Granger and Engle (1993) proposed a more flexible and general class of *power ARCH* (PARCH) models by estimating an additional parameter:

$$\sigma_t^\gamma = \alpha_0 + \alpha_1|\varepsilon_{t-1}|^\gamma + \beta_1\sigma_{t-1}^\gamma$$

A non-symmetric response to shocks is made explicit in Nelson's (1991) *exponential GARCH* (EGARCH) model

$$\log(\sigma_t^2) = \alpha_0 + \alpha_1 f(\varepsilon_{t-1}/\sigma_{t-1}) + \beta_1\log(\sigma_{t-1}^2) \qquad (5.9)$$

where

$$f(\varepsilon_{t-1}/\sigma_{t-1}) = \theta_1\varepsilon_{t-1}/\sigma_{t-1} + (|\varepsilon_{t-1}/\sigma_{t-1}| - E|\varepsilon_{t-1}/\sigma_{t-1}|)$$

The 'news impact curve', $f(.)$, relates revisions in conditional volatility, here given by $\log(\sigma_t^2)$, to 'news', ε_{t-1}. It embodies a non-symmetric response since $\partial f/\partial\varepsilon_{t-1} = \theta_1 + 1$ when $\varepsilon_{t-1} > 0$ and $\partial f/\partial\varepsilon_{t-1} = \theta_1 - 1$ when $\varepsilon_{t-1} < 0$. (Note that volatility will be at a minimum when there is no news: $\varepsilon_{t-1} = 0$).

This asymmetry is potentially useful, as it allows volatility to respond more rapidly to falls in a market than to corresponding rises, which is an important stylised fact for many financial assets and is known as the leverage effect. This model also has the advantage that no parameter restrictions are necessary in order to ensure that the variance is positive. It is easy to show that $f(\varepsilon_{t-1})$ is strict white noise with zero mean and constant variance, so that $\log(\sigma_t^2)$ is an ARMA(1,1) process and will be stationary if $\beta_1 < 1$.

A model that nests (5.7), (5.8) and (5.9) is the *non-linear ARCH* (NARCH) model (Higgins and Bera, 1992), a general form of which is

$$\sigma_t^\gamma = \alpha_0 + \alpha_1 f^\gamma(\varepsilon_{t-1}) + \beta_1\sigma_{t-1}^\gamma$$

while an alternative is the process

$$\sigma_t^\gamma = \alpha_0 + \alpha_1 g^{(\gamma)}(\varepsilon_{t-1}) + \beta_1 \sigma_{t-1}^\gamma$$

where

$$g^{(\gamma)}(\varepsilon_{t-1}) = \theta \mathbf{I}(\varepsilon_{t-1}>0) \cdot |\varepsilon_{t-1}|^\gamma + \theta \mathbf{I}(\varepsilon_{t-1} \leq 0) \cdot |\varepsilon_{t-1}|^\gamma$$

$\mathbf{I}(\cdot)$ being the indicator function. If $\gamma = 1$, we have the *threshold ARCH* (TARCH) model of Zakoian (1994), while for $\gamma = 2$ we have the GJR model of Glosten, Jagannathan and Runkle (1993), which allows a quadratic response of volatility to news but with different coefficients for good and bad news, although it maintains the assertion that the minimum volatility will result when there is no news. More general but less popular versions of threshold models that allow for richer behaviour include Rabemananjara and Zakoian (1993), Li and Li (1996) and Audrino and Bühlmann (2001).

Hentschel (1995) defines a very general class of model that nests all the above ARCH models. The model can be written using the Box and Cox (1964) transformation as

$$\frac{\sigma_t^\lambda - 1}{\lambda} = \alpha_0 + \alpha_1 \sigma_{t-1}^\lambda f^\gamma(U_{t-1}) + \beta_1 \frac{\sigma_{t-1}^\lambda - 1}{\lambda} \tag{5.10}$$

where

$$f(U_t) = |U_t - b| - c(U_t - b)$$

Several variants cannot be nested within (5.10). Engle's (1990) *asymmetric ARCH* (AARCH) and Sentana's (1995) *quadratic ARCH* (QARCH) are two such models. These can be written in the simple case being considered here as

$$\sigma_t^2 = \alpha_0 + \alpha_1 \varepsilon_{t-1}^2 + \delta \varepsilon_{t-1} + \beta_1 \sigma_{t-1}^2$$

where a negative value of δ means that good news increases volatility less than bad news. It is the presence of a quadratic form in ε_{t-1} that precludes them from being included as special cases of (5.10).

An alternative way of formalising the GARCH(1,1) model (5.7) is to define $\alpha_0 = \varpi(1 - \alpha_1 - \beta_1)$, where ϖ is the unconditional variance, or long-run volatility, to which the process reverts to:

$$\sigma_t^2 = \varpi + \alpha_1(\varepsilon_{t-1}^2 - \varpi) + \beta_1(\sigma_{t-1}^2 - \varpi)$$

Engle and Lee (1999) extend this formalisation to allow reversion to a varying level, defined by q_t:

$$\sigma_t^2 = q_t + \alpha_1\left(\varepsilon_{t-1}^2 - q_{t-1}\right) + \beta_1\left(\sigma_{t-1}^2 - q_{t-1}\right)$$

$$q_t = \varpi + \xi(q_{t-1} - \varpi) + \zeta\left(\varepsilon_{t-1}^2 - \sigma_{t-1}^2\right)$$

Here q_t is long-run volatility, which converges to ϖ through powers of ζ, while $\sigma_t^2 - q_t$ is the transitory component, converging to zero via powers of $\alpha_1 + \beta_1$. This *component* GARCH model can also be combined with the TARCH model to allow asymmetries in both the permanent and transitory parts: this *asymmetric component* GARCH model automatically introduces asymmetry into the transitory equation.

The stochastic variance and GARCH classes of models have some obvious similarities, and a comparison between them is provided in Taylor (1994). Finally, as in Robinson (1991), we can form the ARCH(∞) class:

$$\sigma_t^2 = b_0 + \sum_{j=1}^{\infty} b_j \varepsilon_{t-j}^2$$

This can be shown to include the finite-order ARCH and GARCH models as special cases. For example, the GARCH(p, q) can be expressed as

$$\sigma_t^2 = (1 - \beta(1))^{-1}\alpha_0 + (1 - \beta(B))^{-1}\alpha(B)\varepsilon_t^2$$

This allows an ARCH(∞) representation with $b_0 = (1 - \beta(1))^{-1}\alpha_0$ and with positive weights that decay exponentially according to $\alpha(z)/(1 - \beta(z)) = \sum_{i=1}^{\infty} b_i z^i$. In this manner the conditional variance can be represented as a moving average of past squared errors with exponentially decaying coefficients and an absolutely summable exponentially decaying autocovariance function. For a detailed discussion of ARCH (∞) models, see Giraitis, Leipus and Surgailis (2006).

5.5.3 Non-linear GARCH processes

Attempts have been made in the literature to develop 'non-linear' versions of GARCH models that allow for even more flexibility in the functional relationship between variance and lagged errors. Although non-linear specifications for the conditional mean process will be discussed in more detail in chapter 6, a brief introduction to the most popular of these non-linear conditional variance models will be made here.

The *smooth transition GARCH* (STRGARCH) model can be defined as

$$\sigma_t^2 = \alpha_{10} + \alpha_{11}\varepsilon_{t-1}^2 + (\alpha_{20} + \alpha_{21}\varepsilon_{t-1})f(\varepsilon_{t-1}; \delta, c) + \beta_1\sigma_{t-1}^2$$

where $f(\varepsilon_{t-1}; \delta, c)$ is a continuous bounded transition function. If a logistic transition function is used with $c = 0$, then the model is equivalent to the GJR-GARCH. The STRGARCH can be useful in situations where we do not want to limit the analysis by allowing only two distinct regimes for the conditional variance (for a discussion of these models, see Gonzalez-Rivera, 1998). Lanne and Saikkonen (2005) proposed a smooth transition GARCH process where the lagged conditional variance acts conveniently as the transition variable, thus enabling the persistence in the conditional variance to depend on its level:

$$\sigma_t^2 = \alpha_0 + \alpha_1\varepsilon_{t-1}^2 + \delta f\left(\sigma_{t-1}^2; \theta\right) + \beta_1\sigma_{t-1}^2$$

The transition function is modelled using the cumulative distribution function of the gamma distribution. The original motivation for using this model was to overcome the tendency of GARCH models to exaggerate the persistence in the conditional variance process – i.e. to estimate $\sum(\alpha_i + \beta_i)$ to be very close to unity.

It has been argued that GARCH parameters may not remain constant when dealing with data spanning a long time period. For example, Sensier and van Dijk (2004) report extensive evidence of changes in volatility for a wide set of US macroeconomic time series, while Andreou and Ghysels (2002) have evaluated the performance of various tests for detecting structural breaks in the conditional variance dynamics of asset returns. As shown by Mikosch and Starica (2004) and Hillebrand (2005), the alleged exaggeration of shock persistence implied by estimated GARCH models may be due to shifts in the unconditional variance. Various modelling approaches have been proposed to deal with such shifts. For example, Teräsvirta (2007) discusses a time-varying GARCH process where parameters may vary according to a smooth transition function of a normalised time index. Two additional classes of models have also been suggested, the *structural ARCH* (STARCH) model proposed by Harvey, Ruiz and Sentana (1992) and the *switching ARCH* (SWARCH) model proposed by both Cai (1994) and Hamilton and Susmel (1994). Both require estimation by the Kalman filter: the former decomposes ε_{t-1} into various unobserved components, each of which have ARCH forms; the latter postulates several different ARCH models between which the process switches via a Markov chain (see chapter 6 for models of this type).

Semi- and non-parametric methods have also been used in order to relax the assumptions concerning the distribution of residuals and the functional form in GARCH models. A comprehensive treatment of such approaches can be found in Linton (2007).

5.5.4 Long-memory volatility processes: the FIGARCH model

An apparent stylised fact of return series is that the absolute values or powers, particularly squares, of returns tend to have very slowly decaying auto-correlations. For example, Ding, Granger and Engle (1993) find that the first negative autocorrelation of the squared returns of the daily S&P 500 index over the period 1928 to 1991, analysed in example 4.3, occurred at lag 2598, and a similar finding has been provided by Mills (1996a) for the daily returns of the London FT30 for the period 1935 to 1994. Additional evidence of this feature for financial series is provided by, for example, Taylor (1986) and Dacorogna *et al.* (1993).

In the spirit of Granger (1980), it has been suggested that long memory in the volatility of stock indices may be due to the aggregation of covariance stationary processes that individually exhibit short-memory conditional heteroskedasticity. Although it has been found that this is not possible through a summation of the GARCH process, Zaffaroni (2007) discusses conditions and models that can lead to long memory under aggregation.

It is also interesting to note the effect of scaling, since it has very important applications in risk management and option pricing. As has been discussed earlier, a common practice is to derive an estimate of the annualised standard deviation, or volatility, by simply multiplying the daily standard deviation by the square root of the number of trading days in a year. This procedure assumes that returns are *iid*, however – something that is clearly violated for most financial time series. Assuming that the data follow a GARCH(1,1) process, Diebold *et al.* (1998) use the results of Drost and Nijman (1993) on the temporal aggregation of GARCH processes to show that simple scaling is inappropriate and potentially very misleading.

In response to these findings of long memory, Baillie, Bollerslev and Mikkelson (1996) consider the *fractionally integrated GARCH* (FIGARCH) process (a closely related process, the *long-memory GARCH* (LMGARCH) model, has been analysed by Karanasos, Psaradakis and Sola, 2004). The FIGARCH$(1, d, 1)$ process is most transparently defined as an extension of (5.6):

$$\Delta^d \varepsilon_t^2 = \alpha_0 + (\alpha_1 + \beta_1)\Delta^d \varepsilon_{t-1}^2 + v_t - \beta_1 v_{t-1} \tag{5.11}$$

Equivalently, but perhaps less transparently, it can be written as

$$\sigma_t^2 = \alpha_0 + \left(1 - \Delta^d\right)\varepsilon_t^2 - \left(\beta_1 - (\alpha_1 + \beta_1)\Delta^d\right)\varepsilon_{t-1}^2 + \beta_1\sigma_{t-1}^2 \tag{5.12}$$

(5.12) can be expressed as

$$\Delta\varepsilon_t^2 = \alpha_0^* + \Delta^{1-d}(1 - (\alpha_1 + \beta_1)B)^{-1}(1 - \beta_1 B)v_t = \alpha_0^* + \theta(B)v_t$$

and (5.11) as

$$\sigma_t^2 = \alpha_0/(1 - \beta_1) + \left(1 - (1 - (\alpha_1 + \beta_1)B)(1 - \beta_1 B)^{-1}\Delta^d\right)\varepsilon_t^2 = \alpha_0^{**} + \pi(B)\varepsilon_t^2$$

Baillie, Bollerslev and Mikkelson (1996) show that the FIGARCH(p, d, q) class of processes is strictly but not weakly stationary for $0 \leq d \leq 1$. FIGARCH processes with $0 < d < 1$ have $\theta(1) = 0$, so that shocks to the conditional variance ultimately die out. Unlike the $d = 0$ case, however, $\sum_j \theta_j$ decays eventually at a hyperbolic, rather than an exponential, rate, so that the fractional differencing parameter provides important information about the pattern and speed with which shocks to volatility are propagated. For $d > 1$, $\theta(1)$ is undefined and the conditional variance is explosive. The conditions that ensure a positive conditional variance for the FIGARCH$(1, d, 1)$ process are $\alpha_0 > 0$, $\alpha_1 + d \geq 0$ and $1 - 2(\alpha_1 + \beta_1) \geq d \geq 0$.

Baillie, Bollerslev and Mikkelson (1996) argue that the presence of FIGARCH processes may explain the common finding of IGARCH behaviour in high-frequency financial data. It is commonly argued (Nelson, 1990b; Nelson and Foster, 1994) that GARCH$(1,1)$ models provide consistent discrete-time approximations to continuous-time diffusion processes and, as the sampling interval goes to zero, the sum of the two GARCH parameters tends to one, indicating IGARCH behaviour. IGARCH implies that shocks to the conditional variance persist indefinitely, however, and this is difficult to reconcile with the persistence observed after large shocks such as the crash of October 1987, and also with the perceived behaviour of agents who do not appear to alter the composition of their portfolios frequently and radically, as would be implied by IGARCH. Temporal aggegation issues also cast doubt on the reasonableness of IGARCH models. Drost and Nijman (1993) show that an IGARCH generating process at high frequencies should carry over to low frequencies of observation, but this seems at odds with most reported empirical findings.

Given these anomalies, Baillie, Bollerslev and Mikkelson suggest that the widespread observation of IGARCH behaviour may be an artefact of a long-memory FIGARCH data-generating process, and they provide a simulation experiment that provides considerable support for this line of argument. It would thus seem that FIGARCH models should be seriously considered when modelling volatility.

5.5.5 Estimation of ARMA models with ARCH errors

The analysis has so far proceeded on the assumption that $\varepsilon_t = x_t - \mu$ is serially uncorrelated. A natural extension is to allow x_t to follow an ARMA (p,q) process, so that the combined ARMA-ARCH model becomes

$$\Phi(B)(x_t - \mu) = \Theta(B)\varepsilon_t \tag{5.13}$$

$$\sigma_t^2 = E\big(\varepsilon_t^2 | \varepsilon_{t-1}, \varepsilon_{t-2}, \ldots\big) = \alpha_0 + \sum_{i=1}^{p} \alpha_i \varepsilon_{t-i}^2 + \sum_{i=1}^{q} \beta_i \sigma_{t-i}^2 \tag{5.14}$$

This latter equation can be written as

$$\sigma_t^2 = z_t^\top \omega = z_{1t}^\top \omega_1 + z_{2t}^\top \omega_2$$

where

$$z_t^\top = \big(z_{1t}^\top : z_{2t}^\top\big) = \Big(1, \varepsilon_{t-1}^2, \ldots, \varepsilon_{t-p}^2 : \sigma_{t-1}^2, \ldots, \sigma_{t-q}^2\Big)$$

and

$$\omega^\top = \big(\omega_1^\top : \omega_2^\top\big) = \Big(\alpha_0, \alpha_1, \ldots, \alpha_p : \beta_1, \ldots, \beta_q\Big)$$

Using this notation, ML estimates of the model can be obtained in the following way. Define Ω as the vector of parameters in the model given by equations (5.13) and (5.14) and partition it as $\Omega = \big(\omega^\top : \psi^\top\big)$, $\psi^\top = (\Phi_1, \ldots, \Phi_P, \Theta_1, \ldots, \Theta_Q, \mu)$ being a vector containing the parameters in the ARMA equation. We may also define $\Omega_0 = \big(\omega_0^\top : \psi_0^\top\big)$ as the true parameter vector.

The log-likelihood function for a sample of T observations is, apart from some constants,

$$L_T(\Omega) = T^{-1} \sum_{t=1}^{T} l_t(\Omega)$$

where

$$l_t(\Omega) = \log\{f(\varepsilon_t/\sigma_t : \varsigma)\} - 0.5\log\sigma_t^2$$

is the log-likelihood for the tth observation and $f(\varepsilon_t/\sigma_t : \varsigma)$ denotes the conditional density function for the standardised innovations ε_t / σ_t, which has mean zero, variance one and nuisance parameters ς. Precise details of ML estimation may be found in, for example, Engle (1982), Weiss (1986a, 1986b) and Bollerslev (1988). The BHHH alogorithm of Berndt, Hall, Hall and Hausman (1974) is a convenient method of computation. If $\hat{\Omega}^{(i)}$ denotes the parameter estimates after the ith iteration, then $\hat{\Omega}^{(i+1)}$ is calculated by the algorithm as

$$\hat{\Omega}^{(i+1)} = \hat{\Omega}^{(i)} + \lambda_i \left(\sum_{t=1}^{T} \frac{\partial l_t}{\partial \Omega} \frac{\partial l_t}{\partial \Omega^\top} \right)^{-1} \sum_{t=1}^{T} \frac{\partial l_t}{\partial \Omega}$$

where $\partial l_t / \partial \Omega$ is evaluated at $\hat{\Omega}^{(i)}$ and λ_i is a variable step length chosen to maximise the likelihood function in the given direction. Because the information matrix, $I = -E(\partial^2 l_t / \partial \Omega \partial \Omega^\top)$, is block diagonal, ω can be estimated without loss of asymptotic efficiency based on a consistent estimate of ψ, and vice versa, so that the iterations for $\omega^{(i)}$ and $\psi^{(i)}$ can be carried out separately.

The ML estimate $\hat{\Omega}$ is strongly consistent for Ω_0 and asymptotically normal with mean Ω_0 and covariance matrix I^{-1}, consistently estimated by $T^{-1} \left(\sum_{t=1}^{T} (\partial l_t / \partial \Omega)(\partial l_t / \partial \Omega^\top) \right)^{-1}$, which may be obtained from the last BHHH iteration.

Of course, the actual implementation of the ML procedure requires an explicit assumption about the conditional density $f(\varepsilon_t / \sigma_t : \varsigma)$. The most commonly employed distribution is the normal, for which

$$\log f(\varepsilon_t / \sigma_t : \varsigma) = -\tfrac{1}{2} \log(2\pi) - \tfrac{1}{2} \log \sigma_t^2 - \tfrac{1}{2} \left(\varepsilon_t^2 / \sigma_t^2 \right)$$

From the discussion in section 5.5.1, the ARCH model with conditionally normal errors results in a leptokurtic unconditional distribution. Nonetheless, the degree of leptokurtosis so induced often does not capture all the fat tails present in financial data; this is discussed in detail in chapter 7. Consequently, various alternatives were discussed in section 5.2. Perhaps the two most popular are Bollerslev's (1987) standardised t-distribution, and Nelson's (1991) generalised exponential distribution (GED).

For the t-distribution,

$$\log f(\varepsilon_t / \sigma_t : \varsigma) = -\frac{1}{2} \log \left(\frac{\pi(v - 2)\Gamma(v/2)^2}{\Gamma((v+1)/2)^2} \right) - \frac{1}{2} \log \sigma_t^2$$
$$- \frac{(v+1)}{2} \log \left(1 + \frac{\varepsilon_t^2}{(v-2)\sigma_t^2} \right)$$

Here $\Gamma(\cdot)$ denotes the gamma function, and the degrees of freedom parameter $\upsilon > 2$, which controls the tail behaviour of the distribution, may also be estimated from the data. As is well known, the t-distribution is symmetric around zero and converges to the normal distribution as $\upsilon \to \infty$, but for $2 < \upsilon < \infty$ the conditional kurtosis equals $3(\upsilon - 1)/(\upsilon - 2)$, which exceeds the normal value of three, so the estimate of υ will provide an indication of the fatness of the tails.

For the GED,

$$\log f(\varepsilon_t/\sigma_t; \varsigma) = -\frac{1}{2}\log\left(\frac{\Gamma(1/\xi)^3}{\Gamma(3/\xi)(\xi/2)^2}\right) - \frac{1}{2}\log \sigma_t^2 - \left(\frac{\Gamma(3/\xi)\varepsilon_t^2}{\Gamma(1/\xi)\sigma_t^2}\right)$$

The tail parameter is $\xi > 0$. The normal distribution is obtained when $\xi = 2$ and for smaller values the distribution is fat-tailed. An alternative approach uses mixtures of normals to represent the conditional distribution (e.g. see Haas, Mittnik and Paoelella, 2004). This preserves the assumption of normality for the error process while capturing characteristics of the data such as asymmetry and fat tails. For a detailed discussion of the issues involved in estimation and inference in GARCH models, see Li, Ling and McAleer (2002), Bollerslev, Engle and Nelson (1994) and Straumann (2004).

What are the consequences of ignoring possible non-normality and continuing to use the normal density for $f(\varepsilon_t/\sigma_t : \varsigma)$? This is known as *quasi-ML* (QML) estimation and produces an estimated $\tilde{\Omega}$ that is consistent and asymptotically normal. Indeed, Jensen and Rahbek (2004) prove that, unlike the unit root case, these properties hold for the GARCH$(1,1)$ model over the entire parameter region, including both stationary and explosive behaviour. Although standard errors will be inconsistent, they can be corrected using robust alternatives (Bollerslev and Wooldridge, 1992).

For symmetric departures from conditional normality, the QML estimator $\tilde{\Omega}$ is generally close to the exact ML estimator $\hat{\Omega}$, but for non-symmetric conditional distributions both the asymptotic and the finite sample loss in efficiency may be quite large, and semi-parametric estimation may be preferred. For a comparison of the loss in asymptotic efficiency of QML and semi-parametric estimation compared to ML, see Gonzalez-Rivera and Drost (1999). While the asymptotic properties of the GARCH QML estimators are well understood, the limiting distribution of the ARMA-GARCH model has been established under the rather strict assumption of finite fourth moments. Recently, Ling (2007) has proposed a self-weighted QML approach for estimating ARMA-GARCH and IGARCH models and shows that it is consistent and asymptotically normal under only a fractional moment condition for errors.

In practice, different software packages, optimisation algorithms and initial value parameterisations may, unfortunately, lead to significant variations in estimates (e.g. see Brooks, Burke and Persand 2001). In an attempt to overcome these problems, Kristensen and Linton (2006) have recently developed a closed-form estimator for the parameters of the GARCH$(1,1)$ model that has the advantage of not requiring numerical optimisation and an arbitrary selection of initial values. Assuming that fourth moments exist, Kristensen and Linton show that the combination of the estimator with a finite-order Newton–Raphson procedure will yield asymptotically the same distribution as QML.

Finally, it should be noted that the application of ARCH estimation techniques depends on the variance process being observable and measurable. ARCH models have been widely used in a variety of applications in finance and economics as latent processes, however, in which case the log-likelihood function cannot be expressed analytically. To circumvent this problem, Fiorentini, Sentana and Shephard (2004) develop exact likelihood-based estimators of latent variable ARCH-type models using an MCMC algorithm.

5.5.6 Testing for the presence of ARCH errors

Let us suppose that an ARMA model for x_t has been estimated, from which the residuals e_t have been obtained. The presence of ARCH can lead to serious model misspecification if it is ignored; as with all forms of heteroskedasticity, analysis assuming its absence will result in inappropriate parameter standard errors, and these will typically be too small. For example, Weiss (1984) shows that ignoring ARCH will lead to the identification of ARMA models that are overparameterised, and Milhøj (1985) demonstrates that standard tests of serial correlation may over-reject the null.

Methods for testing whether ARCH is present are therefore essential, particularly as estimation incorporating it requires the complicated iterative techniques discussed above. Equation (5.6) has shown that if ε_t is GARCH (p,q) then ε_t^2 is ARMA(m,q), where $m = \max\ (p,q)$, and Bollerslev (1986) shows that standard ARMA theory follows through in this case. This implies that the squared residuals e_t^2 can then be used to identify m and q, and therefore p, in a fashion similar to the way the usual residuals are used in conventional ARMA modelling. McLeod and Li (1983), for example, show that the sample autocorrelations of e_t^2 have asymptotic variance T^{-1} and that portmanteau statistics calculated from them are asymptotically χ^2 if the ε_t^2 are independent.

Formal tests are also available. Engle (1982) shows that a test of the null hypothesis that ε_t has a constant conditional variance against the alternative that the conditional variance is given by an ARCH(q) process – i.e. a test of $\alpha_1 = \cdots = \alpha_q = 0$ in (5.13) conditional upon $\beta_1 = \cdots = \beta_p = 0$ – may be based on the Lagrange multiplier principle. The test procedure is to run a regression of e_t^2 on $e_{t-1}^2, \ldots, e_{t-q}^2$ and to test the statistic $T \cdot R^2$ as a χ_q^2 variate, where R^2 is the squared multiple correlation coefficient of the regression. An asymptotically equivalent form of the test, which may have better small sample properties, is to compute the standard F test from the regression. The intuition behind this test is clear. If the data are indeed homoskedastic, then the variance cannot be predicted and variations in e_t^2 will be purely random. If ARCH effects are present, however, such variations will be predicted by lagged values of the squared residuals. Of course, if the residuals themselves contain some remaining autocorrelation or, perhaps, some other form of non-linearity, then it is quite likely that this test for ARCH will reject, since these errors may induce autocorrelation in the squared residuals; we cannot simply assume that ARCH effects are necessarily present when the ARCH test rejects.

Strictly, since the parameters of an ARCH model must be positive, a test of ARCH should be formulated as a one-sided test, which should presumably be more powerful than the above $T \cdot R^2$ test. Engle, Hendry and Trumble (1985) thus suggest a one-sided test for ARCH(1) by using the square root of the LM test with an appropriate sign, but this approach cannot be extended to test higher-order ARCH(q) alternatives. In this situation, either the test proposed by Lee and King (1993), and extended by Hong (1997), or that of Demos and Sentana (1998) may be employed. These tests are necessarily more complicated to derive and compute, and we refer the reader to the above references for details.

When the alternative is a GARCH(p,q) process, some complications arise. In fact, a general test of $p > 0$, $q > 0$ against a white-noise null is not feasible, nor is a test of GARCH($p + r_1, q + r_2$) errors, where $r_1 > 0$ and $r_2 > 0$, when the null is GARCH(p,q). Furthermore, under this null, the LM test for GARCH(p,r) and ARCH($p + r$) alternatives coincide. What can be tested is the null of an ARCH(p) process against a GARCH(p,q) alternative – i.e. a test of $\omega_2 = 0$ using the notation of the previous section: Bollerslev (1988) provides details.

Lumsdaine and Ng (1999), among others, have studied the behaviour of LM tests for ARCH when the conditional mean equation is misspecified due to, for example, omitted lags, parameter instability and structural change. They show that misspecification will typically result in an over-rejection of the null hypothesis of no ARCH and propose a heuristic approach using recursive residuals to improve performance. Blake and Kapetanios (2007) demonstrate that the effect of misspecification in the conditional mean equation, due to neglected non-linearity in particular, will affect severely the size of LM tests for ARCH. They also propose new robust testing procedures that rely on testing for ARCH via standard approaches after removing possible non-linearity from the conditional mean process using a non-parametric approach. A general approach to testing for ARCH effects and misspecification has been proposed by Lundbergh and Teräsvirta (2002), who develop a number of LM-type procedures to test for the presence of ARCH and misspecification in GARCH models with respect to asymmetry and parameter constancy. Finally, Dufour *et al.* (2004) have proposed a Monte Carlo approach to derive finite-sample GARCH tests under possibly non-normal error distributions.

As with ARMA modelling, information criteria have also been used to identify the correct lag structure and type of GARCH model amongst competing specifications. As shown by Brooks and Burke (2002), however, information criteria may not be able to identify the true model but, rather, the best approximating model from those available. Brooks and Burke (2003) derive appropriate modifications of standard information criteria for selecting models from the AR family with GARCH errors. Hughes, King and Teng (2004) suggest using a modification of the AIC to account for the one-sided nature of ARCH parameters.

5.5.7 ARCH and theories of asset pricing

The importance of ARCH processes in modelling financial time series is seen most clearly in models of asset pricing that involve agents maximising expected utility over uncertain future events. To illustrate this, consider the following example, taken from Engle and Bollerslev (1986). Suppose a representative agent must allocate his or her wealth, W_t, between the shares of a risky asset q_t at a price p_t and those of a risk-free asset x_t, whose price is set equal to one. The shares of the risky asset will be worth y_{t+1} each at the end of the period (if there are no dividends, then $y_{t+1} = p_{t+1}$). The risk-free asset will be worth $r_t x_t$, where r_t denotes one plus the risk-free rate of interest.

If the agent has a mean-variance utility function in end-of-period wealth, $W_{t+1} = q_t y_{t+1} + r_t x_t$, then the allocation problem for the agent is to maximise this utility function with respect to holdings of the risky asset, q_t — i.e. to maximise

$$2E_t(q_t y_{t+1} + r_t x_t) - \gamma_t V_t(q_t y_{t+1})$$

subject to the start-of-period wealth constraint

$$W_t = x_t + p_t q_t$$

This has the solution

$$p_t = r_t^{-1} E_t(y_{t+1}) - \gamma_t q_t r_t^{-1} V_t(y_{t+1}) \tag{5.15}$$

If the outstanding stock of the risky asset is fixed at q, and γ_t and r_t are taken as constants (γ and r respectively), then (5.15) describes the asset pricing model.

If the risky asset is interpreted as a forward contract for delivery in s periods' time, the price that a pure speculator would be willing to pay is

$$p_t = r^{-s}(E_t(y_{t+s}) - \delta V_t(y_{t+s})) \tag{5.16}$$

where r^{-s} gives the present discounted value at the risk-free rate r and $\delta = \gamma q$. A simple redating of the model shows that the price of the forward contract at time $t+1$, for $s \geq 2$ periods remaining to maturity, can be expressed as

$$p_{t+1} = r^{1-s}(E_{t+1}(y_{t+s}) - \delta V_{t+1}(y_{t+s}))$$

Taking expectations at time t, multiplying by r^{-1} and subtracting from (5.16) gives

$$p_t = r^{-1} E_t(p_{t+1}) - \delta r^{-s}(V_t(y_{t+s}) - E_t(V_{t+1}(y_{t+s}))) \tag{5.17}$$

Now, suppose y_t can be represented by an infinite moving average process where the innovations are uncorrelated but have time-varying conditional variance σ_t^2:

$$y_t = \varepsilon_t + \sum_{i=1}^{\infty} \theta_i \varepsilon_{t-i} = \theta(B)\varepsilon_t \tag{5.18}$$

$$V_t(y_{t+1}) = V_t(\varepsilon_{t+1}) = \sigma_{t+1}^2$$

Thus,

$$V_t(y_{t+s}) = E_t\left(\sum_{i=1}^{s}\theta_{s-i}\varepsilon_{t+i}\right)^2 = \sum_{i=1}^{s}\theta_{s-i}^2 E_t\left(\sigma_{t+1}^2\right)$$

Consequently,

$$V_t(y_{t+s}) - E_t(V_{t+1}(y_{t+s})) = \theta_{s-1}^2\sigma_{t+1}^2$$

and (5.17) becomes

$$p_t = r^{-1}E_t(p_{t+1}) - \delta r^{-s}\theta_{s-1}^2\sigma_{t+1}^2$$

which is the familiar formula for a one-period holding yield with the explicit calculation of the effect of the changing variance of y_{t+s} for a risk-averse agent.

In this simple model the only source of uncertainty derives from the future spot price to which the contract relates. In many other situations, however, there is a flow of uncertain distributions that accrue to the owner of the asset: for example, the price of a share is determined by the present discounted value of the expected dividend stream. The precise form in which the variability of future pay-offs enters the asset pricing formulation will depend, amongst other things, on the utility function of the agents and the intertemporal substitutability of the payouts. A simple formulation might be

$$p_t = \sum_{s=1}^{\infty} r^{-s}(E_t(y_{t+s}) - \delta V_t(y_{t+s}))$$

where $\{y_t\}_{t+1}^{\infty}$ is the future income stream generated by the asset. If y_t again follows the process (5.18), this pricing equation can be converted to the holding yield expression

$$p_t = r^{-1}\left(E_t(p_{t+1}) + E_t(y_{t+1}) - \delta\lambda\sigma_{t+1}^2\right)$$

where λ depends upon $\theta(B)$ and r.

It is clear therefore that, if $\delta \neq 0$, the conditional variance of y_t in the future will affect the price of the asset today. If such variances can be forecast as in a GARCH process, then the current information on y_t and the current conditional variance will have an effect on the current price. The size of the effect, however, will depend upon the persistence of the variance – i.e. on how important current information is in predicting future variances.

A closed-form solution to the simple asset pricing formula (5.16) depends upon the process assumed to generate the 'forcing variable' y_t. Suppose y_t is a random walk with innovations that follow an IGARCH(1,1) process. Then $E_t(y_{t+s}) = y_t$ and

$$V_t(y_{t+s}) = E_t\left(\sum_{i=1}^{s} \varepsilon_{t+i}^2\right) = E_t\left(\sum_{i=1}^{s} \sigma_{t+i}^2\right) = s\sigma_{t+1}^2$$

so that

$$p_t = r^{-s}\left(y_t - \delta s \sigma_{t+1}^2\right)$$

For a future contract where no money changes hands until the terminal date $t+s$, the risk-free rate of return is zero so that $r=1$, i.e. the solution simplifies to

$$p_t = y_t - \delta s \sigma_{t+1}^2$$

If $\delta \neq 0$ there will be a time-varying risk premium in the future contract. For contracts far in the future, new information will have a substantial effect on asset prices as it changes agents' perceptions of the variance of the final pay-off as well as all the intermediate variances. This persistence gives time-varying risk premia even for contracts many periods into the future, and thus implies sizeable effects on asset prices.

Alternatively, suppose that the random walk innovations to y_t are serially independent with constant variance σ^2. In this case $V_t(y_{t+s}) = s\sigma^2$ and the solution to (5.16) is

$$p_t = y_t - \delta s \sigma^2$$

so that, although the variance of the spot price enters the pricing equation, it does not give rise to a time-varying risk premium since new information casts no light on future uncertainty.

Finally, consider an intermediate case where the innovations are GARCH (1,1) such that $\alpha_1 + \beta_1 < 1$. The unconditional variance will be $\sigma^2 = \alpha_0/(1 - \alpha_1 - \beta_1)$, and it is easy to show that

$$E_t\left(\sigma_{t+s}^2 - \sigma^2\right) = (\alpha_1 + \beta_1)^{s-1}\left(\sigma_{t+1}^2 - \sigma^2\right)$$

and

$$V_t(y_{t+s}) = \sum_{i=1}^{s} \left(\sigma^2 + E_t\left(\sigma_{t+i}^2 - \sigma^2\right)\right) = s\sigma^2 + \left(\sigma_{t+i}^2 - \sigma^2\right)\left(\frac{1 - (\alpha_1 + \beta_1)^s}{1 - \alpha_1 - \beta_1}\right)$$

Substituting into (5.16), the solution of the future contract is

$$p_t = y_t - \delta s \sigma^2 + \delta \left(\sigma_{t+1}^2 - \sigma^2 \right) \left(\frac{1 - (\alpha_1 + \beta_1)^s}{1 - \alpha_1 - \beta_1} \right)$$

Current information, embodied in the term $\sigma_{t+1}^2 - \sigma^2$, continues to be an important part of the time-varying risk premium even for large s, but, in contrast to the solution for the IGARCH(1,1) model, where $\alpha_1 + \beta_1 = 1$, its importance decreases with the length of the contract.

These examples thus establish that a solution to an asset pricing equation depends in a crucial way on the distribution of the forcing variable, y_t, in particular on its conditional variance, which is naturally modelled as an ARCH process.

We should also note that, in a manner analogous to stochastic variance models being discrete approximations to continuous-time option valuation models that use diffusion processes, ARCH models can also approximate a wide range of stochastic differential equations. This was first shown by Nelson (1990b), and further developments are contained in, for example, Nelson and Foster (1994), Drost and Nijman (1993) and Drost and Werker (1996). Further analysis of the predictive aspects of ARMA-ARCH models is developed in Baillie and Bollerslev (1992). The survey by Bollerslev, Chou and Kroner (1992) focuses on the application of ARCH models to stock return and interest rate data, emphasising the use of ARCH to model volatility persistence, and to foreign exchange rate data, where the characterisation of exchange rate movements has important implications for many issues in international finance.

Example 5.5 GARCH models for the dollar/sterling exchange rate

Here we fit various GARCH(p,q) models to the first differences of the dollar/sterling exchange rate, the level of which was found to be a driftless random walk (see examples 2.5 and 4.3). Thus, with $\Delta x_t = \varepsilon_t$, assuming homoskedasticity – i.e. GARCH(0,0) – produces an LM test statistic for twelfth-order ARCH of 72.2, which shows that there is strong evidence of conditional heteroskedasticity, and, as six of the twelve lag coefficients in the autoregression of the squared residuals are significant, a GARCH formulation is suggested. Not surprisingly, the residuals are highly non-normal, being fat-tailed and positively skewed.

GARCH(1,1) estimates under normality, t and GED distributional assumptions are reported in table 5.2. In all cases, both GARCH parameters

Table 5.2 GARCH(1,1) estimates for the dollar/sterling exchange rate

	Normal	t	GED
$\hat{\alpha}_0$	7.11 (1.36)	3.12 (1.50)	4.64 (1.86)
$\hat{\alpha}_1$	0.032 (0.004)	0.033 (0.006)	0.033 (0.006)
$\hat{\beta}$	0.957 (0.005)	0.963 (0.006)	0.961 (0.007)
ζ	–	5.45 (0.59)	1.21 (0.040)
$\hat{\alpha}_1 + \hat{\beta}$	0.989	0.997	0.993
ARCH(12)	10.0 [0.61]	8.7 [0.72]	9.4 [0.67]
L	11627.0	11710.7	11731.1

Figures in ( ) are standard errors; figures in [ ] are prob-values. ARCH(12) is the LM test for twelfth-order ARCH. L is the log-likelihood. Estimation was performed in *EVIEWS 5* using the BHHH algorithm. Estimates of α_0 are scaled by 10^{-7}.

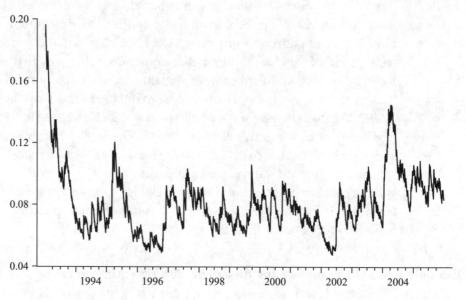

Figure 5.4 Conditional standard deviations of the dollar sterling exchange rate from the GARCH(1,1) model with GED errors

are significant and the LM test for any neglected ARCH is insignificant. Note that the GARCH parameters sum to just under unity, suggesting strong persistence in conditional variance. The distribution parameter estimates are what might be expected from a fat-tailed x_t distribution. In terms of log-likelihoods, the GED assumption produces the best fit, but little difference is found in the GARCH parameter estimates for all three models. The conditional standard deviations from this model are shown in figure 5.4.

A comparison with the volatility series from the SV model fitted in example 5.3, shown in figure 5.3, reveals a close similarity.

A variety of non-linear GARCH variants were also entertained. Noting that the EGARCH model (5.9) can be written as

$$\log(\sigma_t^2) = \alpha + \alpha_1|\varepsilon_{t-1}/\sigma_{t-1}| + \gamma\varepsilon_{t-1}/\sigma_{t-1} + \beta_1\log(\sigma_{t-1}^2)$$

where $\alpha = \alpha_0 - \alpha_1\sqrt{2/\pi}$ and $\gamma = \alpha_1\theta_1$, estimation of this model with GED errors obtained

$$\log(\sigma_t^2) = \underset{(0.034)}{-0.129} + \underset{(0.013)}{0.070}|\varepsilon_{t-1}/\sigma_{t-1}| + \underset{(0.008)}{0.018}\,\varepsilon_{t-1}/\sigma_{t-1} + \underset{(0.003)}{0.992}\log(\sigma_{t-1}^2)$$

$\tilde{\gamma}$ is significantly different from zero, so there does appear to be an asymmetric news effect. The estimate of the GED parameter is $\hat{\xi} = 1.21$, but, as $L = 11730.7$, this model is just inferior to the GARCH specification. Both TARCH and component GARCH models produced no improvement over the basic GARCH formulation, and the PARCH(1,1) model was estimated as

$$\sigma_t^{1.82} = \underset{(2.12\times10^{-7})}{1.01 \times 10^{-7}} + \underset{(0.008)}{0.033}|\varepsilon_{t-1}|^{1.82} + \underset{(0.007)}{0.963}\,\sigma_{t-1}^{1.82}$$

For this model $\hat{\xi} = 1.21$ and $L = 11731.9$. Since $\hat{\lambda} = 1.82$ is accompanied by a standard error of 0.41, the null that $\lambda = 2$ cannot be rejected, thus supporting the choice of the GARCH(1,1) specification (a comparison of the L values for the two models also confirms this).

Example 5.6 GARCH models for S&P 500 daily returns

In this example we again analyse the daily returns (logarithmic first differences) of the S&P 500 index from January 1928 to August 1991, first looked at in example 3.7. Ding, Granger and Engle (1993) initially fitted an MA(1)-GARCH(1,1) model with normal innovations to the returns, x_t. We find that an MA(1)-GARCH(1,2) model with standardised–t innovations provides a somewhat better fit:

$$x_t = \underset{(0.00006)}{0.00054} + \varepsilon_t + \underset{(0.008)}{0.137}\,\varepsilon_{t-1}$$

$$\sigma_t^2 = \underset{(1.28\times10^{-7})}{8.58\times10^{-7}} + \underset{(0.009)}{0.104}\,\varepsilon_{t-1}^2 + \underset{(0.108)}{0.586}\,\sigma_{t-1}^2 + \underset{(0.101)}{0.306}\,\sigma_{t-2}^2$$

$$\hat{\nu} = 5.86(0.24) \qquad L = 57425.8 \qquad ARCH(12) = 18.1[0.11]$$

The GARCH parameters sum to 0.992, indicating IGARCH behaviour.

The model can, nevertheless, be improved upon. The TARCH extension of this model is

$$x_t = \underset{(0.00006)}{0.00042} + \varepsilon_t + \underset{(0.008)}{0.140}\,\varepsilon_{t-1}$$

$$\sigma_t^2 = \underset{(1.26\times10^{-7})}{9.24\times10^{-7}} + \underset{(0.007)}{0.0047}\,\varepsilon_{t-1}^2 + \underset{(0.012)}{0.107}\,I(\varepsilon_{t-1}<0)\cdot\varepsilon_{t-1}^2 + \underset{(0.105)}{0.624}\,\sigma_{t-1}^2$$
$$+ \underset{(0.097)}{0.268}\,\sigma_{t-2}^2$$

$$\hat{\upsilon} = 6.23(0.26) \qquad L = 57505.9$$

while the EGARCH variant is

$$x_t = \underset{(0.00006)}{0.00039} + \varepsilon_t + \underset{(0.008)}{0.136}\,\varepsilon_{t-1}$$

$$\log(\sigma_t^2) = \underset{(0.020)}{-0.261} + \underset{(0.012)}{0.188}\,|\varepsilon_{t-1}/\sigma_{t-1}| - \underset{(0.007)}{0.088}\,\varepsilon_{t-1}/\sigma_{t-1}$$
$$+ \underset{(0.072)}{0.658}\,\log(\sigma_{t-1}^2) + \underset{(0.072)}{0.329}\,\log(\sigma_{t-2}^2)$$

$$\hat{\upsilon} = 6.25(0.26) \qquad L = 57553.3$$

Both models provide a significant leverage effect, with 'bad' news, $\varepsilon_{t-1}<0$, increasing volatility more than 'good' news.

The TARCH model can be extended by using the *asymmetric power ARCH* (APARCH) of Ding, Granger and Engle (1993). This model, now estimated with standardised-t innovations, is

$$x_t = \underset{(0.00006)}{0.00039} + \varepsilon_t + \underset{(0.008)}{0.137}\,\varepsilon_{t-1}$$

$$\sigma_t^{1.14} = \underset{(0.000021)}{0.000057} + \underset{(0.008)}{0.100}\left(|\varepsilon_{t-1}| - \underset{(0.039)}{0.464}\,\varepsilon_{t-1}\right)^{1.14} + \underset{(0.091)}{0.616}\,\sigma_{t-1}^{1.14}$$
$$+ \underset{(0.085)}{0.294}\,\sigma_{t-2}^{1.14}$$

$$\hat{\upsilon} = 6.24(0.26) \qquad L = 57554.2$$

The standard error attached to $\hat{\lambda} = 1.14$ is 0.07, so that the traditional conditional variance model having $\lambda = 2$ is certainly rejected, although the conditional standard deviation model with $\lambda = 1$ (see (5.8)) is marginally acceptable. Nevertheless, the leverage effect remains significant.

5.6 Some models related to ARCH

5.6.1 Simple and exponential moving averages

An ad hoc modelling approach that is popular amongst practitioners for predicting short-term variance is based on smoothing methods using moving averages of historical squared returns. Simple moving averages cannot easily capture volatility clustering and require the selection of an arbitrary window length. The exponential moving average is more popular, and has been shown by Boudoukh, Richardson and Whitelaw (1997) to perform well in empirical applications. A variance forecast can be derived by using the simple exponential recursive formula with smoothing parameter, or decay factor, λ:

$$\hat{\sigma}_t^2 = \lambda \varepsilon_{t-1}^2 + (1 - \lambda) \hat{\sigma}_{t-1}^2$$

The size of the decay factor determines the relative weight assigned to more recent observations. The larger (smaller) the factor is, the smaller (larger) the weight given to recent observations; recall the analysis of chapter 4, section 1.2. The exponential moving average is the preferred method of volatility forecasting within the RiskMetrics risk management approach (see Mina and Xiao, 2001, for a comprehensive description) and is, of course, a special case of an IGARCH model. The proponents of this approach suggest that values $\lambda = 0.94$ and 0.97 seem to work well for predicting volatility at a daily and monthly interval, respectively, reflecting the high persistence found in many volatility measures.

Adaptive exponential moving average models have also been proposed to allow for variation in the smoothing parameter. Taylor (2004) uses a logistic function of some user-defined variable(s) as an adaptive smoothing parameter. This smooth transition exponential smoothing (STES) variance estimator can be formulated as

$$\hat{\sigma}_t^2 = \lambda_1 \varepsilon_{t-1}^2 + (1 - \lambda_{t-1}) \hat{\sigma}_{t-1}^2$$

where

$$\lambda_{t-1} = (1 + \exp(\beta + \gamma V_{t-1}))^{-1}$$

The smoothing parameter changes between zero and one according to the variations in the transition variable V_{t-1}. By analogy to non-linear GARCH models, Taylor proposes using both actual and absolute values of the lagged residual as transition variables.

He also notes the analogy between STES and the smooth transition GARCH(1,1) model proposed by Anderson, Nam, and Vahid (1999):

$$\sigma_t^2 = (1 - f(\varepsilon_{t-1}))\left(\alpha_0 + \alpha_1 \varepsilon_{t-1}^2 + \beta_1 \sigma_{t-1}^2\right) + f(\varepsilon_{t-1})\left(\gamma_0 + \gamma_1 \varepsilon_{t-1}^2 + \delta_1 \sigma_{t-1}^2\right)$$

In this model the transition is governed by the logistic function

$$f(\varepsilon_{t-1}) = (1 + \exp(-\vartheta \varepsilon_{t-1}))^{-1}$$

The STES model is a constrained formulation with $\alpha_0 = \alpha_1 = 0$, $\beta_1 = 1$, $\gamma_0 = 0$, $\gamma_1 = 1$ and $\delta_1 = 0$. Taylor (2004) proposes estimating the parameters of the STES model by minimising the sum of squared deviations between realised and forecast volatility, and presents empirical evidence that it performs well in capturing the dynamics of the variance when compared to a variety of GARCH models and simple exponential moving averages.

5.6.2 Autoregressive conditional duration models

The rapid advances in information technology during the 1990s both enabled and motivated the collection of financial data at very high sampling frequencies. These developments opened up a new area in empirical finance, that of high-frequency or tick data analysis (see the review by Goodhart and O'Hara, 1997, and the contributions in Lequeux, 1999). From a broader point of view, as discussed by Granger (1998) and Engle (2000), the availability of huge high-frequency data sets is changing the science and practice of statistics, econometrics and decision making in many different ways. The time series properties of high-frequency data have been investigated with respect to a variety of features, including market microstructures, autocorrelations in mean and variance, intradaily seasonalities, long memory, interaction between market variables (volume, volatility, returns, trading frequency, spreads, etc.), dynamic and contemporaneous linkages between markets, forecastability and non-linearities.

An interesting direction concerns the development of econometric models to describe the behaviour of time series that are sampled at irregular intervals. In these, the time between sampling intervals is treated as a random variable rather than assumed to be fixed. A major application concerns modelling intertemporally correlated variations in price duration – i.e. in the time between successive quote changes or transactions. Let t_i be the ith transaction time with $0 = t_0 < t_1 < \cdots < t_T$. The duration between transactions can then be represented by $.X_i = t_i - t_{i-1}$. Let the expectation of the ith duration, conditional on all past durations and a parameter vector θ, be represented by

$$\psi_i = \psi_i(X_i|X_{i-1}, \ldots, X_1; \theta) = E(X_i|X_{i-1}, \ldots, X_1), \qquad X_i/\psi_i = u_i$$

where u_i is an *iid* non-negative process of disturbances with a given parametric density distribution $p(u, \phi)$. This distribution is related to the hazard function, or baseline hazard, which is given by the probability density of u_i divided by the survival function of u_i, the latter being one minus the cumulative distribution function.

Engle and Russell (1997, 1998) have proposed the *auto regressive conditional duration*, or ACD(p, q), process to model the dynamics of the conditional duration process and to predict how long it will be until prices change:

$$\psi_i = \alpha_0 + \sum_{m=1}^{p} \alpha_m X_{i-m} + \sum_{n=1}^{q} \beta_n \psi_{i-n}$$

Although Engle and Russell (1998) use exponential and Weibull distributions for the residuals, other distributions, such as the generalised gamma, the log-logistic and the log-normal, are also relevant. Since the distribution of u_i is fully specified, maximum likelihood is applicable for estimation and inference purposes. As shown by Engle and Russell, under certain conditions the conditional ML estimates will be asymptotically normally distributed. It is interesting to note that, although the ACD is formulated in transaction time, it models the frequency and distribution of the calendar time between events.

The ACD is closely related to the GARCH, since it models the conditional mean duration as a function of lagged durations and their conditional expectations. As with the variance process and GARCH models, the ACD attempts to exploit the fact that transactions are not homogeneously distributed through time but tend to cluster in a stochastic manner. Since the ACD can also be shown to have an ARMA representation, forecasts can be obtained using the standard ARMA approach. The ACD modelling framework can be combined with GARCH models to allow for dynamics in both the conditional duration and variance process, respectively (e.g. see Engle, 2000, and Grammig and Wellner, 2002). Note that standard GARCH software and routines can be applied to obtain consistent estimates of the ACD model parameters using QML. In this setting, the square root of the duration is the dependent variable while the conditional mean equation is zero.

A number of extensions to the ACD models have been proposed that are analogous to the various modifications of the GARCH model. For example, Bauwens and Giot (2003) consider a logarithmic transformation of the ACD model that enables the non-negativity restriction on ψ_i to be relaxed. This model avoids the overprediction of duration, originally noted by Engle and Russell (1998), by allowing for a concave shocks impact curve. Zhang, Russell and Tsay (2001) develop a non-linear *threshold ACD* (TACD) model with different regimes for the persistence, conditional means and error distributions, respectively. More flexible hazard rate function specifications have also been considered. Following Hentschel (1995), Fernandes and Grammig (2006) derive a general class of *augmented ACD* (AACD) models by using a Box–Cox transformation of the conditional duration. The AACD class is shown to include most of the ACD specifications that have been proposed as special cases.

Modelling via ACD processes is typically followed by simple diagnostic procedures to evaluate whether the residuals are *iid*. Fernandes and Grammig (2005) develop a testing procedure for the distribution of the error term in ACD models. In the first step, the ACD model is estimated and consistent estimates of the errors are obtained. In the second step, non-parametric and parametric estimates of the baseline density and hazard rate functions are compared. In addition to the fact that ACD models allow a more careful examination of microstructure theories and a more accurate estimation of conditional volatility, these models have found application in risk management (Giot, 2000) and option pricing (Prigent, Renault and Scaillet, 2001).

5.6.3 Modelling higher moments of the conditional distribution

ARMA-GARCH models are able to capture dependencies in the mean and variance and can produce non-Gaussian unconditional distributions that are asymmetric and fat-tailed. Although the first two moments are permitted to change through time, the shape of the underlying distributions remains constant. Since finance theory and empirical evidence both suggest that variations in higher moments are potentially important for portfolio optimisation and risk management, there has been some effort put into modelling time variation in skewness and kurtosis.

A direct approach involves using an autoregressive conditional moments (ARCM) model, which imposes dynamics directly on higher moments (see Harvey and Siddique, 2000, and Brooks *et al.*, 2005). The estimation of ARCM models can be extremely burdensome on computational resources, however, with the result that modelling both skewness and kurtosis is not straightforward. Gallant, Rossi and Tauchen (1992) employ a semi-non-parametric approach based on a series expansion of the Gaussian density. This allows the density to be expressed as a polynomial in the past history of the time series. This parameterisation is not parsimonious, however, and large data sets are necessary in order to achieve a reasonable level of accuracy. The implementation of the model is also computationally expensive and involves the arbitrary determination of the order of expansion.

To overcome these problems, Hansen (1994) has proposed using a GARCH model in which the shape parameters of a closed-form distribution vary according to conditioning variables. Under this autoregressive conditional density (ARCD) model, the standardised density of the residuals follows a generalised skewed t-distribution:

$$g(\varepsilon_t|\eta, \lambda) = \begin{cases} bc\left(1 + \frac{1}{\eta-2}\left(\frac{b\varepsilon_t+a}{1-\lambda}\right)^2\right)^{-(\eta+1)/2} & \varepsilon_t < -\frac{a}{b} \\ bc\left(1 + \frac{1}{\eta-2}\left(\frac{b\varepsilon_t+a}{1+\lambda}\right)^2\right)^{-(\eta+1)/2} & \varepsilon_t \geq -\frac{a}{b} \end{cases}$$

$$a = 4\lambda c\left(\frac{\eta-2}{\eta-1}\right) \quad b^2 = 1 + 3\lambda^2 - a^2 \quad c = \frac{\Gamma(\eta+1)}{\sqrt{\pi(\eta-2)}\Gamma(\eta/2)}$$

The skewness and kurtosis coefficients, $\lambda \in (-1, 1)$ and $\eta \in (2, \infty)$, respectively, are the degrees of freedom. Although the distribution is parsimonious, it can produce a rich variety of asymmetric and fat-tailed shapes. If λ is positive (negative) then the variable is skewed to the right (left). When $\lambda = 0$ the density collapses to a standard t while a normal distribution is obtained when $\eta = \infty$.

In the ARCD model, shape parameters are allowed to vary through time according to functions of lagged error terms. Hansen (1994) uses a logistic transformation to satisfy the boundary constraints on the conditional skewness and kurtosis coefficients. Although the shape parameters are stationary, they are allowed to assume extreme values, which is useful for capturing jump behaviour in empirical data. Jondeau and Rockinger (2003) derive analytical formulae for skewness and kurtosis under ARCD in terms of the parameters of the generalised t-distrubution. The third and fourth moments are shown to exist if η exceeds three and four, respectively. They also determine the largest possible domain of values for the shape parameters for which a density exists. Since a parametric density is assumed for the standard error, maximum likelihood estimation is possible and estimates will be asymptotically normal. Jondeau and Rockinger propose constrained optimisation via a sequential quadratic programming algorithm to avoid the instabilities that arise in parameter estimation.

5.7 The forecasting performance of alternative volatility models

It is evident from this chapter that substantial efforts have been put into the development, specification and estimation of volatility models. Naturally, the issue of forecasting is also important, since volatility figures prominently in a variety of applications in investment, portfolio management, asset pricing, risk management and monetary policy. A large literature has appeared over recent years on investigating which model is superior in terms of predictive power and why. Poon and Granger (2003) review some ninety-three papers that appeared over two decades on this subject, and conclude that implied volatility estimated from options data appears to provide the most reliable forecasts as a wider information set is used. GARCH models generally rank second, often having comparable performance to that of simple volatility forecasts based on smoothing filters, especially for series that are likely to contain nonstationarities.

Poon and Granger (2003) emphasise that the issue of evaluating volatility forecasts is complicated by a number of factors. First, the latent nature of volatility means that it is not clear what is to be predicted. Most of the early research concentrated on the ability of models to predict squared daily returns. As shown by Hansen and Lunde (2005, 2006a), if this approach is used in the evaluation of ARCH models then it is likely to result in an inconsistent ranking. More recent studies in forecast evaluation tend to adopt realised variance as a more accurate proxy of the volatility process. Even this is far from perfect, however, since, at very high frequencies, market microstructures may significantly influence the results (see Hansen and Lunde, 2006b).

Model performance appears to vary across different markets and forecast horizons. Extensive recent empirical evidence by Pong et al. (2004) suggests that forecasts of realised volatility produced by ARMA models estimated over intradaily data are more accurate than implied volatilities only at daily and weekly forecast horizons. The incremental value of information in high-frequency data over implied volatilities becomes increasingly less important as the forecasting horizon increases. Unlike Koopman, Jungbacker and

Hol (2005), Pong *et al.* (2004) find that ARFIMA models estimated with intradaily data do not outperform their ARMA counterparts. Ghysels, Santa-Clara and Valkanov (2006) have proposed a promising approach using mixed data sampling (MIDAS) regressions in order to assess the forecasting performance of volatility models, as such regressions are able to compare forecasting models that differ in terms of the measure of volatility, the sampling frequency and the lag structure.

Another significant problem facing empirical studies concerns the selection of an appropriate cost function and evaluation method. For a review of the alternative methods, see Diebold and Lopez (1996) and Poon and Granger (2003). Many studies are limited to a comparison between simple measures such as MSE and MAE (mean absolute error), and, as noted by Poon and Granger, even such simple comparisons are confounded by the typically very wide confidence intervals arising from the leptokurtic nature of the data. Moreover, results may vary depending on whether the variance or the standard deviation is used as a benchmark in the cost function.

Despite the large number of papers that have evaluated the predictive value of various models, Poon and Granger (2003) argue that research in this area is still in its infancy, pointing towards several interesting areas of investigation involving combinations of forecasts, exploiting additional regressors, modelling mean absolute deviations and dealing with structural breaks.

6 Univariate non-linear stochastic models: further models and testing procedures

As discussed in chapter 2, the Wold decomposition theorem allows us to write every weakly stationary, purely non-deterministic stochastic process as a linear combination of a sequence of uncorrelated random variables:

$$x_t - \mu = a_t + \psi_1 a_{t-1} + \psi_2 a_{t-2} + \cdots = \sum_{j=0}^{\infty} \psi_j a_{t-j}, \qquad \psi_0 = 1$$

A weakly stationary, purely non-deterministic stochastic process can be considered non-linear if it does not satisfy the assumptions underlying (2.1). In particular, a more general 'non-linear' representation can be obtained as

$$x_t - \mu = f(a_t, a_{t-1}, a_{t-2}, \ldots) \tag{6.1}$$

where $f(\cdot)$ is some arbitrary non-linear function. The 'curse of dimensionality' means that this representation is of little practical use however.

Allowing for regularity conditions, consider a Taylor expansion of (6.1) around zero:

$$
\begin{aligned}
x_t - \mu = {} & f(0, a_{t-1}, a_{t-2}) + a_t f'(0, a_{t-1}, a_{t-2}) \\
& + 0.5 a_t^2 f''(0, a_{t-1}, a_{t-2}) + \cdots
\end{aligned}
$$

where f' and f'' are the first and second derivatives of f with respect to a_t. By dropping higher-order terms, we can express x_t in terms of its conditional moments. For example, by keeping only the first two terms, x_t can be expressed as a function of the conditional mean and variance, respectively. Simple forms of non-linearity can be obtained by assuming some low-order polynomial function f; for example, the first-order non-linear moving average (see Robinson, 1977):

$$x_t = a_t + \psi_1 a_{t-1}^2$$

Polynomial functions of lagged x_t can also be used (Jones, 1978), while another simple way of introducing non-linearity is to allow x_t to respond in a different manner to innovations depending on their sign. For example, Wecker (1981) has introduced the asymmetric MA(1) process,

$$x_t = a_t + \theta^+ a_{t-1}^+ - \theta^- a_{t-1}^-$$

where θ^+ and θ^- are positive and negative innovations, respectively. A wide variety of non-linear models have been developed that allow for combinations of AR and MA terms and for deterministic or stochastic variations in their parameters through time. The most popular of these models are now described in subsequent sections.

6.1 Bilinear and related models

6.1.1 The bilinear process

An important class of non-linear model is the *bilinear*, which takes the general form

$$\phi(B)(x_t - \mu) = \theta(B)\varepsilon_t + \sum_{i=1}^{R}\sum_{j=1}^{S} \gamma_{ij} x_{t-i}\varepsilon_{t-j} \tag{6.2}$$

where $\varepsilon_t \sim SWN(0, \sigma_\varepsilon^2)$. The second term on the right-hand side of (6.2) is a bilinear form in ε_{t-j} and x_{t-j}, and this accounts for the non-linear character of the model: if all the γ_{ij} are zero, (6.2) reduces to the familiar ARMA model. The bilinear model can be thought of as a higher-order Taylor expansion of the unknown non-linear function $f(\cdot)$ underlying the time series dynamics than that provided by the Wold decomposition.

Little analysis has been carried out on this general bilinear form, but Granger and Andersen (1978) have analysed the properties of several simple bilinear forms, characterised as

$$x_t = \varepsilon_t + \gamma_{ij} x_{t-i}\varepsilon_{t-j}$$

If $i > j$ the model is called *superdiagonal*, if $i = j$ it is *diagonal* and if $i < j$ it is *subdiagonal*. If we define $\lambda = \gamma_{ij}\sigma$ then, for superdiagonal models, x_t has zero mean and variance $\sigma^2/(1 - \lambda^2)$, so that $|\lambda| < 1$ is a necessary condition for stability. Conventional identification techniques using the SACF of x_t would identify this series as white noise, but Granger and Andersen show that, in theory at least, the SACF of the squares of x_t would identify x_t^2 as an ARMA

(i, j) process, so that we could distinguish between white noise and this bilinear model by analysing x_t^2.

Diagonal models will also be stationary if $|\lambda| < 1$. If $i = j = 1$, x_t will be identified as MA(1), with $0 < \rho_1 < 0.1547$ (corresponding to $\lambda = \pm 0.605$), while x_t^2 will be identified as ARMA(1,1). If x_t actually is MA(1), however, then x_t^2 will also be MA(1), so that this result allows the bilinear model to be distinguished from the linear model. In general, the levels of a diagonal model will be identified as MA(i). Subdiagonal models are essentially similar to superdiagonal models in that they appear to be white noise but generally have x_t^2 following an ARMA (i, j) process.

Charemza, Lifshits and Makarova. (2005) discuss non-stationary generalisations of bilinear models that allow for unit roots. For example, they consider the following simple model:

$$x_t = (a + b\varepsilon_{t-1})x_{t-1} + \varepsilon_t \tag{6.3}$$

As shown by Granger and Andersen (1978), this process will be stationary if $a^2 + b^2\sigma_\varepsilon^2 < 1$. The process collapses to a random walk if $a = 1$ and $b = 0$. If we assume that b differs from zero, however, while a equals one, we can express the process in first differences as

$$\Delta x_t = bx_{t-1}\varepsilon_{t-1} + \varepsilon_t \tag{6.4}$$

Assuming $x_0 = \varepsilon_0 = 0$, it can be shown that $E(x_t) = b\sigma_\varepsilon^2(t-1)$ and $E(\Delta x_t) = b\sigma_\varepsilon^2$. This implies that we should expect a positive sign for b in empirical applications. The variance of the differenced process is (Charemza, Lifshits and Makarova, 2005, appendix A)

$$V(\Delta x_t) = \left(5\sigma_\varepsilon^2 + b^2 E(\varepsilon_t^4)\right)\left(1 + b^2\sigma_\varepsilon^2\right)^{t-2} - 4tb^2\sigma_\varepsilon^4 + 7b^2\sigma_\varepsilon^4 - 4\sigma_\varepsilon^2$$

Although the process is capable of producing mean-reverting behaviour, it is evident that it does not retain the desirable difference stationarity property of the random walk. The fact that the process allows predictability imposes a significant limitation with respect to its theoretical validity within standard financial theories.

When $a = 1$, (6.3) can be considered to be a special case of the more general process

$$x_t = \varphi_t x_{t-1} + \varepsilon_t$$

where φ_t is a random autoregressive coefficient with $E(\varphi_t) = 1$. This *unit root bilinear* (URB) model resembles the random coefficient autoregressive process (Leybourne, McCabe and Mills, 1996) and the stochastic unit root processes (Granger and Swanson, 1997) discussed in chapter 3, section 7. The non-stationary bilinear process explicitly relates the unit root dynamics to the lagged residuals, however. Charemza, Lifshits and Makarova (2005) develop a simple t-ratio-type test for detecting bilinearity in a unit root process.

For small values of $b < 1/\sqrt{T}$, we can reasonably assume that $\Delta x_t \approx \varepsilon_t$ and the test regression can be formulated as

$$\Delta x_t = \hat{b} x_{t-1} \Delta x_{t-1} + u_t$$

The test statistic is simply the t-statistic of $\hat{b}$ in this regression estimated via OLS. Under the null of no bilinearity – i.e. $a = 1$ and $b = 0$ – this test statistic is asymptotically normally distributed. The test regression can be augmented by a constant, drift or further autoregressive components in a straightforward manner by just adding the relevant terms. Charemza, Lifshits and Makarova suggest a two-step procedure: first test for a unit root and then test for bilinearity. This is consistent, in the sense that the size of the unit root test is not affected by the possible detection of bilinearity in the second step. Charemza, Lifshits and Makarova put forward theoretical arguments and empirical evidence that support the usefulness of URB processes in finance.

Detailed analysis of the properties of bilinear models can be found in Granger and Andersen (1978), Subba Rao (1981), Subba Rao and Gabr (1984), Guégan (1987) and Pham (1993). Most of the results are of considerable theoretical interest but are of little relevance in practice: for example, most of the conditions for stationarity and invertibility are too complicated to be used as constraints on the parameters in actual models.

6.1.2 A comparison of ARCH and bilinearity

Weiss (1986b) provides a detailed comparison of the ARMA-ARCH model, given by equations (5.13) and (5.14), and the bilinear model (6.2). At first sight, the models appear quite different: whereas the addition of the ARCH equation to the pure ARMA process (5.13) introduces non-linearity by affecting the conditional variance, the addition of the bilinear terms contained in (6.2) changes the *conditional mean* of x_t. Weiss argues that, despite these different influences, the two processes can have similar properties, and, for example, the bilinear process may be mistaken for an ARMA model with ARCH errors.

Why might this be? Suppose the true model for x_t is (6.2) but the ARMA model

$$\tilde{\phi}(B)(x_t - \tilde{\mu}) = \tilde{\theta}(B)\tilde{\varepsilon}_t$$

is fitted. The residual, $\tilde{\varepsilon}_t$, is given by

$$\tilde{\varepsilon}_t = \vartheta_1(B)\varepsilon_t + \vartheta_2(B)\sum_{i=1}^{R}\sum_{j=1}^{S}\gamma_{ij}x_{t-i}\varepsilon_{t-j}$$

where $\vartheta_1(B) = \phi^{-1}(B)\tilde{\theta}^{-1}(B)\tilde{\phi}(B)\theta(B)$ and $\vartheta_2(B) = \tilde{\phi}^{-1}(B)\tilde{\theta}^{-1}(B)\phi(B)$. On squaring this expression and taking conditional expectations, it is clear that $E(\tilde{\varepsilon}_t^2 \mid x_{t-1}, x_{t-2}, \ldots)$ is not constant but will be a function of lagged ε_t^2, and hence may be thought to have ARCH. For example, suppose the true model is

$$x_t = \varepsilon_t + \gamma_{21}x_{t-1}\varepsilon_{t-1} \tag{6.5}$$

As $E(x_t) = 0$ and $E(x_t x_{t+i}) = 0$, $i > 0$, the use of traditional modelling techniques may identify the trivial ARMA model $x_t = \tilde{\varepsilon}_t$, where

$$\tilde{\varepsilon}_t = \varepsilon_t + \gamma_{21}\varepsilon_{t-1}\tilde{\varepsilon}_{t-1}$$

Squaring this and taking expectations gives

$$E(\tilde{\varepsilon}_t^2 \mid x_{t-1}, x_{t-2}, \ldots) = \sigma_\varepsilon^2 + \gamma_{21}^2\sigma_\varepsilon^2\tilde{\varepsilon}_{t-1}^2$$

Now, the LM statistic for testing whether $\tilde{\varepsilon}_t$ is ARCH(1) is $T \cdot R^2$ from the regression of $\tilde{\varepsilon}_t^2$ on a constant and $\tilde{\varepsilon}_{t-1}^2$; given the above expectation, such a statistic may well be large even if the correct model is really the bilinear process (6.2).

The correct LM statistic for testing $x_t = \tilde{\varepsilon}_t$ against the bilinear alternative (6.5) is, in fact, $T \cdot R^2$ from the regression of $\tilde{\varepsilon}_t$ on a constant, $\tilde{\varepsilon}_{t-1}$ and $\tilde{\varepsilon}_{t-1}^2$. In general, if $\phi(B)$ and $\theta(B)$ in (6.5) are of orders P and Q respectively, then the LM statistic for testing (6.5) against the simple linear ARMA specification (5.13) is $T \cdot R^2$ from the regression of $\tilde{\varepsilon}_t$ on a constant, $x_{t-1}, \ldots, x_{t-P}, \tilde{\varepsilon}_{t-1}, \ldots, \tilde{\varepsilon}_{t-Q}$, and $x_{t-i}\tilde{\varepsilon}_{t-j}$, $i = 1, \ldots, R, j = 1, \ldots, S$; the statistic is distributed as χ^2_{RS}. Weiss shows, however, that such a test will not have the correct size if, in fact, ARCH is present as well; nor, indeed, will the LM test for ARCH have the correct size if bilinearity is present.

Weiss (1986b) shows that LS and ML estimates of the bilinear model (5.19) coincide. Although estimation of a bilinear model is straightforward, identification of that model can pose difficulties, particularly when, as we have seen, both bilinearity and ARCH are present and one can be confused with the other.

Weiss thus considers the combined bilinear model with ARCH errors – i.e. the bilinear process (6.2) with the ARCH specification (5.14). The identification of this model is based on the relative difficulties introduced by the different specification errors. First, ignoring bilinearity can lead to residuals appearing to have ARCH even though they may not be autocorrelated. On the other hand, misspecifying the ARCH will affect the variance of a process but not the specification of the mean equation. Given the greater complexity of bilinear models and the difficulties faced in their specification, this suggests that it is easier to mistake bilinearity for ARCH than vice versa. Weiss thus suggests that the bilinear model should be specified before ARCH is considered explicitly.

The suggested procedure is to use the SACFs of x_t^2, $\tilde{\varepsilon}_t$ and $\tilde{\varepsilon}_t^2$ and associated LM tests to specify the bilinear process after a pure ARMA model has been identified and fitted by conventional techniques. The SACFs, which do not allow for ARCH, will suggest possible bilinear specifications or extra bilinear terms, and the formal tests, which do allow for ARCH, can then be used to determine which specifications are appropriate. Because we wish to test bilinearity in the possible presence of ARCH, however, the LM test, although not requiring the actual form of ARCH, nevertheless does not have a $T \cdot R^2$ representation; the exact form, derived in Weiss (1986b), is

$$\left(\sum \tilde{\varepsilon}_t \frac{\partial \varepsilon_t}{\partial \Lambda} \right)^{\top} \left(\sum \tilde{\varepsilon}_t^2 \frac{\partial \varepsilon_t}{\partial \Lambda} \frac{\partial \varepsilon_t}{\partial \Lambda^{\top}} \right) \left(\sum \tilde{\varepsilon}_t \frac{\partial \varepsilon_t}{\partial \Lambda} \right)$$

where Λ contains both the ARMA and bilinear parameters.

Once the bilinearity has been determined, the ARCH equation can be specified using the ACF of the squared residuals obtained from the estimation of the bilinear model. Estimation of the combined model then follows, and overfitting and LM tests for extra ARCH or bilinear parameters can be undertaken.

Since the LM test for bilinearity in the presence of ARCH does not have the usual $T{\cdot}R^2$ form, and because the subsequent ARCH test requires first estimating a bilinear model, this procedure is rather burdensome if we just want a simple test for non-linearity that is sensitive to both ARCH and bilinear alternatives. Higgins and Bera (1988) thus propose an easily computed simultaneous test for a joint ARCH and bilinear alternative. This is an LM test whose construction exploits the result that the individual LM tests for ARCH and bilinearity are additive: the joint test statistic is thus the sum of the individual test statistics. Moreover, because the two forms of non-linearity are considered simultaneously, the LM test for bilinearity again has the standard $T{\cdot}R^2$ representation, being the test outlined above. Hence, the combined test statistic will be distributed as χ^2_{RS+p}.

Maravall (1983) considers an alternative form of bilinearity in which x_t is given by the ARMA process

$$\phi(B)(x_t - \mu) = \theta(B)a_t$$

but where the *uncorrelated* sequence $\{a_t\}$ is bilinear in a_t and the strict white-noise sequence $\{\varepsilon_t\}$:

$$a_t = \varepsilon_t + \sum_{i=1}^{R}\sum_{j=1}^{S} \gamma_{ij} a_{t-i}\varepsilon_{t-j}$$

This may be interpreted as a bilinear model 'forecasting white noise'.

Giraitis and Surgailis (2002) describe a general class of fractional bilinear models that exhibit long-run dependence in both conditional mean and variance. These models have the general form

$$x_t = \varepsilon_t \left(\gamma_0 + \sum_{i=1}^{\infty} \gamma_i x_{t-i} \right) + \alpha_0 + \sum_{i=1}^{\infty} \alpha_i x_{t-i}$$

The AR(∞) model is obtained when $\gamma_i = 0$ for $i > 0$ and the *linear ARCH* (LARCH) model when $\alpha_i = 0$ for $i > 0$. This bilinear model can be shown to be equivalent to an ARCH(∞) process when $\gamma_0 = 0$. Depending on the rate of decay of the autocorrelations for x_t and x_t^2, the process is dominated by long memory in the mean or variance, giving rise to either an ARFIMA or LARCH model, respectively.

Kristensen (2005) has recently established necessary and sufficient conditions for the stationarity of various ARCH models that can be written as subdiagonal bilinear models – e.g. GARCH, power GARCH, EGARCH, etc. The sufficient conditions employ the Lyapunov exponent of the model and are weaker than those established previously in the literature. For example, consider the following bilinear model:

$$x_t = (a + b\varepsilon_t)x_{t-1} = ax_{t-1} + b\varepsilon_t x_{t-1}$$

A sufficient condition for stationarity is that the Lyapunov exponent $E(\log(|a + b\varepsilon_t|))$ is less than zero. This becomes a necessary condition if we can further assume model irreducibility – something that is not true for the model given above (see Kristensen, 2005).

How useful are bilinear models in modelling financial time series? De Gooijer (1989), among others, presents evidence to suggest that such processes can provide useful models for certain daily stock return series, although the residual variance of the bilinear models are usually only marginally smaller than those obtained from alternative linear models.

Example 6.1 Is the dollar/sterling exchange rate bilinear?

Given the above discussion, is it possible that the GARCH model fitted to the dollar/sterling exchange rate in example 5.5 is a misspecification and the true process generating the series is of bilinear form? An obvious way to proceed is to consider the SACFs and PACFs of the differences and squared differences. Recall that in example 5.5 it was found that the SACF of $\tilde{\varepsilon}_t = \Delta x_t$ was consistent with a white-noise process. For $\tilde{\varepsilon}_t^2$, all the first twelve sample autocorrelations are significant, as are the first eleven partial autocorrelations, which suggests that an ARMA(1, 1) process could be appropriate. This pair of findings is consistent with a diagonal bilinear model with $R = S = 1$. The LM test for such bilinearity, obtained from regressing $\tilde{\varepsilon}_t$ on $\tilde{\varepsilon}_{t-1}$ and $\tilde{\varepsilon}_{t-1}^2$, produced a $T \cdot R^2$ of just 1.58, distributed as χ_1^2, thus indicating no evidence in favour of bilinearity. Of course, this statistic is strictly valid only in the absence of ARCH, which we know exists. Construction of the ARCH-adjusted statistic produced a value of only 0.48, however, confirming the absence of bilinearity.

Example 6.2 Modelling IBM stock prices as a combined bilinear and ARCH process

The daily closing price for IBM common stock for the 169 trading days starting 17 May 1961, presented as part of series B in Box and Jenkins (1976)

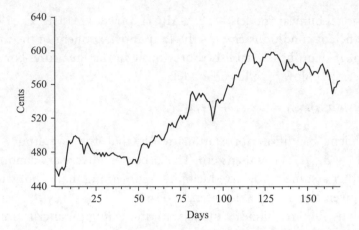

Figure 6.1   IBM common stock price (daily from 17 May 1961)

and plotted as figure 6.1, has been investigated by various researchers (see, in particular, Weiss, 1986b). Conventional (linear) identification procedures suggest that the differences of the series, denoted x_t, follow an MA(1) process, least squares (LS) estimation of which yields

$$x_t = \tilde{\varepsilon}_t - 0.26\tilde{\varepsilon}_{t-1}, \quad \sigma_{\tilde{\varepsilon}}^2 = 24.8, \quad r_{1,\tilde{\varepsilon}} = -0.02, \quad r_{1,\tilde{\varepsilon}^2} = 0.18$$

An LM test for ARCH(1) errors, ignoring the possibility of bilinearity, yields a $T \cdot R^2$ statistic of 15.1, which is clearly significant (note that this confirms the evidence of non-linearity provided by the lag one auto-correlation of $\tilde{\varepsilon}_t^2$). Tests for first-order diagonal bilinearity yield values of 7.9 and 8.1, the latter being corrected for first-order ARCH. Incorporating an ARCH(1) error specification yields, on ML estimation,

$$x_t = \varepsilon_t - 0.24\varepsilon_{t-1}, \quad \sigma_{\varepsilon}^2 = 24.8, \quad r_{1,\varepsilon} = 0.01, \quad r_{1,\varepsilon^2} = 0.02$$

$$\sigma^2 = \underset{(2.6)}{17.9} + \underset{(0.12)}{0.28}\,\varepsilon_{t-1}^2$$

and then including bilinear terms produces either

$$x_t = \varepsilon_t - \underset{(0.08)}{0.24}\,\varepsilon_{t-1} + \underset{(0.010)}{0.023}\,x_{t-1}\varepsilon_{t-1}, \quad \sigma_{\varepsilon}^2 = 23.7$$

$$\sigma^2 = \underset{(2.6)}{18.3} + \underset{(0.11)}{0.23}\,\varepsilon_{t-1}^2$$

or

$$x_t = a_t - \underset{(0.08)}{0.23} a_{t-1}, \qquad \sigma_a^2 = 23.7$$

$$a_t = \varepsilon_t + \underset{(0.010)}{0.023} a_{t-1}\varepsilon_{t-1}$$

$$\sigma^2 = \underset{(2.6)}{18.3} + \underset{(0.11)}{0.23}\, \varepsilon_{t-1}^2$$

The bilinear terms are significant and their introduction decreases the estimate of the ARCH parameter somewhat. Note that the mean equation for the second model can be written as

$$x_t = \varepsilon_t - 0.23\varepsilon_{t-1} + 0.023x_{t-1}\varepsilon_{t-1} - 0.005\big(a_{t-2}\varepsilon_{t-1} - a_{t-2}\varepsilon_{t-2}\big)$$

so it is no surprise that the fits of the two models are virtually identical. The same specification is also arrived at if a bilinear process is first fitted after tests for bilinearity on the original MA(1) model are performed.

6.1.3 State-dependent and related models

Using the concept of 'Volterra expansions', Priestley (1980, 1988) shows that a general relationship between x_t and ε_t can be represented as

$$x_t = f\big(x_{t-1}, \ldots, x_{t-p}, \varepsilon_{t-1}, \ldots, \varepsilon_{t-q}\big) \tag{6.6}$$

If $f(\cdot)$ is assumed analytic, the right-hand side of (6.6) can be expanded in a Taylor's series expansion about an arbitrary but fixed time point, allowing the relationship to be written as the state-dependent model (SDM) of order (p, q)

$$x_t - \sum_{i=1}^{p} \phi_i(\mathbf{x}_{t-1})x_{t-i} = \mu(\mathbf{x}_{t-1}) + \sum_{i=1}^{q} \theta_i(\mathbf{x}_{t-1})\varepsilon_{t-i} \tag{6.7}$$

where $\mathbf{x}_t$ denotes the state vector

$$\mathbf{x}_t = \big(x_t, \ldots, x_{t-p+1}, \varepsilon_t, \ldots, \varepsilon_{t-q+1}\big)$$

Priestley (1980, p. 54) remarks that this model has the interpretation of a locally linear ARMA model in which the evolution of the process at time $t-1$ is governed by a set of AR coefficients, $\{\phi_i(\cdot)\}$, a set of MA coefficients, $\{\theta_i(\cdot)\}$, and a local 'mean', $\{\mu_i(\cdot)\}$, all of which depend on the 'state' of the process at time $t-1$.

If $\mu(\cdot)$, $\{\phi_i(\cdot)\}$ and $\{\theta_i(\cdot)\}$ are all taken as constants, i.e. as independent of $\mathbf{x}_{t-1}$, (6.6) reduces to the usual ARMA(p, q) model. Moreover, if only $\mu(\cdot)$ and $\{\phi_i(\cdot)\}$ are taken as constants but we set

$$\theta_i(\mathbf{x}_{t-1}) = \theta_i + \sum_{j=1}^{p} \gamma_{ij} x_{t-j}, \quad i = 1, ..., q$$

then the SDM reduces to the bilinear model (6.2), with $R = p$ and $S = q$.

The SDM class of non-linear models can also be shown to include the *threshold AR* model (Tong and Lim, 1980), the *exponential AR* model (Haggan and Ozaki, 1981) and various other non-linear specifications that have been developed over recent years; for example, a non-linear AR(1) model could be

$$x_t = \phi_1 x_{t-1} + \exp\left(-\gamma x_{t-1}^2\right)\phi_2 x_{t-1} + \varepsilon_t$$

Haggan, Heravi and Priestley (1984) provide an extensive study of the application of SDMs to a wide variety of non-linear time series, although they use no financial, or even economic, data.

6.2 Regime-switching models: Markov chains and smooth transition autoregressions

An alternative way of introducing asymmetry is to consider 'regime-switching' models. We consider here two of the most popular of these: the two-state Markov model and the smooth transition autoregression. Hamilton (1989, 1990), Engle and Hamilton (1990) and Lam (1990) propose variants of a regime-switching Markov model, which can be regarded as a non-linear extension of an ARMA process that can accomodate complicated dynamics such as asymmetry and conditional heteroskedasticity. The set-up is that of the UC model developed in chapter 4, section 1 – i.e.

$$x_t = z_t + u_t \tag{6.8}$$

where, again, z_t is a non-stationary random walk component, but where its drift now evolves according to a two-state Markov process:

$$z_t = \mu(S_t) + z_{t-1} = \alpha_0 + \alpha_1 S_t + z_{t-1} \tag{6.9}$$

where

$$P(S_t = 1 \mid S_{t-1} = 1) = p$$
$$P(S_t = 0 \mid S_{t-1} = 1) = 1 - p$$
$$P(S_t = 1 \mid S_{t-1} = 0) = 1 - q$$
$$P(S_t = 0 \mid S_{t-1} = 0) = q$$

The component u_t is assumed to follow an AR(r) process

$$\phi(B)u_t = \varepsilon_t \tag{6.10}$$

where the innovation sequence $\{\varepsilon_t\}$ is strict white noise, but $\phi(B)$ is allowed to contain a unit root so that, unlike the conventional UC specification, u_t can be non-stationary. In fact, a special case of the conventional UC model results when $p = 1 - q$; the random walk component then has an innovation restricted to being a two-point random variable, taking the values zero and one with probabilities q and $1 - q$, respectively, rather than a zero-mean random variable drawn from a continuous distribution such as the normal.

The stochastic process for S_t is strictly stationary, having the AR(1) representation

$$S_t = (1 - q) + \lambda S_{t-1} + V_t$$

where $\lambda = p + q - 1$ and where the innovation V_t has the conditional probability distribution

$$P(V_t = (1 - p) \mid S_{t-1} = 1) = p$$
$$P(V_t = -p \mid S_{t-1} = 1) = 1 - p$$
$$P(V_t = -(1 - q) \mid S_{t-1} = 0) = q$$
$$P(V_t = q \mid S_{t-1} = 0) = 1 - q$$

This innovation is uncorrelated with lagged values of S_t, since

$$E(V_t \mid S_{t-j} = 1) = E(V_t \mid S_{t-j} = 0) = 0 \quad \text{for } j \geq 1$$

but it is not independent of such lagged values as, for example,

$$E(V_t^2 \mid S_{t-1} = 1) = p(1 - p)$$
$$E(V_t^2 \mid S_{t-1} = 0) = q(1 - q)$$

The variance of the Markov process can be shown to be

$$\alpha_1^2 \frac{(1-p)(1-q)}{(2-p-q)^2}$$

As this variance approaches zero – i.e. as p and q approach unity – so the random walk component (6.9) approaches a deterministic trend. If $\phi(B)$ contains no unit roots, x_t will thus approach a TS process, whereas, if $\phi(B)$ does contain a unit root, x_t approaches a DS process.

Given $\{x_t\}_0^T$, ML estimates of the model are obtained by first expressing (6.8) as

$$u_t = u_{t-1} - x_t - x_{t-1} - \alpha_0 - \alpha_1 S_t$$

and solving backwards in time to yield

$$u_t = x_t - x_0 - \alpha_0 t - \alpha_1 \sum_{i=1}^{t} S_t + u_0 \qquad (6.11)$$

Using (6.10) and (6.11), the innovations ε_t can be expressed as

$$\varepsilon_t = \phi(B)(x_t - x_0 - \alpha_0 t) + \phi(1)u_0$$
$$- \alpha_1 \phi(1) \sum_{i=1}^{t} S_i + \alpha_1 \sum_{j=1}^{r} \left(\sum_{k=j}^{r} \phi_k \right) S_{t-j+1}$$

Assuming that the innovations are normal, this expression can be utilised to calculate the log-likelihood function on noting that this can be decomposed as the sum of the conditional (on past observations) log-likelihoods. These conditional log-likelihoods depend on unobserved current and past realisations of the Markov states. A recursive relationship can be shown to hold between the conditional distribution of the states and the conditional likelihood of the observations, and this can be exploited to obtain an algorithm for evaluating the log-likelihood function. Inferences about the unobserved components and states are then obtained as by-products of this evaluation: details of the algorithm may be found in Hamilton (1989) and Lam (1990).

The Markov approach assumes that the process can shift randomly and abruptly from one regime to the other. An alternative is to consider a process in which the transition from one regime to the other occurs only once and in a smooth fashion. We have already encountered a model of this type in chapter 3, section 6, the logistic smooth transition regression, or LSTR, trend model, and this idea is easily extended to *smooth transition* AR models, termed STAR models by Teräsvirta (1994). The *logistic STAR*, or LSTAR(p), model is defined as

$$x_t = \pi_{10} + \sum_{i=1}^{p} \pi_{1i} x_{t-i} + \left(\pi_{20} + \sum_{i=1}^{p} \pi_{2i} x_{t-i} \right) \cdot S_{t,d}(\gamma, c) + u_t$$

where $S_{t,d}(\gamma, c) = (1 + \exp(-\gamma(x_{t-d} - c)))^{-1}$ is the smooth transition. An alternative model replaces $S_{t,d}(\gamma, c)$ with $S_{t,d}^*(\gamma^*, c^*) = (1 - \exp(-\gamma^* (x_{t-d} - c^*)^2))$, which is known as the *exponential STAR* (ESTAR) model. Either model can be estimated by NLS for a given value of the delay parameter d, although, as Teräsvirta (1994) and van Dijk, Teräsvirta and Franses (2002) discuss, obtaining convergence and accurately estimating the 'smoothing' parameter, γ or γ^*, is not always easy.

Example 6.3 Are there long swings in the dollar/sterling exchange rate?

In this example, inspired by Engel and Hamilton (1990), we fit a two-state Markov process to quarterly observations on the dollar/sterling exchange rate from 1972 to 1996 inclusive and, in the spirit of Engel and Hamilton, ask whether the series is characterised by 'long swings' – i.e. a sequence of stochastic segmented trends.

This exchange rate is close to being a driftless random walk, so that the differences are approximately white noise, but not strict white noise, as they are conditionally heteroskedastic. We therefore fitted the two-state Markov model, with $\phi(B) = (1 - B)$, to the series using Hamilton's (1990) expectation maximisation (EM) algorithm (see also Engle and Hamilton, 1990). The differences are thus given by

$$\Delta x_t = \alpha_0 + \alpha_1 S_t + \varepsilon_t$$

which can equivalently be interpreted as a model in which Δx_t is assumed to be drawn from a $N(\mu_0, \sigma_0^2)$ distribution when $S_t = 0$ and a $N(\mu_1, \sigma_1^2)$ distribution when $S_t = 1$, where $\mu_0 = \alpha_0$ and $\mu_1 = \alpha_0 + \alpha_1$.

This simple model allows a wide variety of exchange rate behaviour. For example, asymmetry in the persistence of the two regimes can be characterised by μ_0 being large and positive and p being small, so that upward moves are short and sharp, and μ_1 being negative and small and q being large, so that downward moves are drawn out and gradual. If the change in the exchange rate is completely independent of the previous state, then we have a random walk with $p = 1 - q$. The long swings hypothesis can be represented by μ_0 and μ_1 being opposite in sign and p and q both being large.

The following ML estimates were obtained, with standard errors shown in parentheses:

$$\hat{\mu}_0 = 2.605 \ (0.964), \quad \hat{\mu}_1 = -3.277 \ (1.582)$$
$$\hat{p} = 0.857 \ (0.084), \quad \hat{q} = 0.866 \ (0.097)$$
$$\hat{\sigma}_0^2 = 13.56 \ (3.34), \quad \hat{\sigma}_1^2 = 20.82 \ (4.79)$$

The estimates associate regime zero with a 2.61 per cent quarterly rise in sterling and regime one with a fall of 3.28 per cent. Figure 6.2 shows the levels of the exchange rate and a plot of the 'smoothed' probability that the process was in regime zero at each date in the sample. These smoothed probabilities are estimates of the probability that $S_t = 0$ conditional upon the full sample of observations and the ML estimates of the parameters (see Engel and Hamilton, 1990, for further discussion). The dates at which the exchange rate was in an 'upswing' – i.e. periods for which these smoothed probabilities are greater than 0.5 – are shown as shaded areas.

These estimates show that movements in the exchange rate are indeed characterised by long swings, since the point estimates of p and q are both greater than 0.85 and those of μ_0 and μ_1, as we have seen, are opposite in sign. Hence, once the exchange rate is in a particular regime, it is likely to stay there, although there is an indication that such swings are shorter in the 1990s. The expected length of stay in regime zero is given by $(1-p)^{-1} = 7.0$ quarters, while that for regime one is $(1-q)^{-1} = 7.5$ quarters. Two hypothesis tests are of interest. The first is the random walk (strictly, the martingale) hypothesis that $p = 1 - q$, for which a Wald test, distributed asymptotically as χ_1^2, yields the statistic 26.9, which clearly rejects the null. The second is the hypothesis that the mean appreciation and depreciation rates are the same, i.e. $\mu_0 = -\mu_1$. This produces a Wald statistic of only 0.09 and so clearly cannot be rejected.

Example 6.4 An LSTAR model for UK gilt yields

In this example we fit a smooth transition model to the twenty-year UK gilt series, $R20$, used to derive the spread analysed in examples 2.2, 2.4 and 3.1. As $R20$ is $I(1)$, we analyse the differences of the series, $\Delta R20$, whose plot is shown in figure 6.3. The plot shows a pattern of changing variability, so there is certainly the potential for successfully fitting a non-linear model. Within the class of linear ARMA models, an AR(2) provides an adequate fit:

$$\Delta R20_t = \underset{(0.039)}{0.313} \, \Delta R20_{t-1} - \underset{(0.039)}{0.122} \, \Delta R20_{t-2} + e_t$$

$$\hat{\sigma} = 0.297, \quad Q(12) = 9.1, \quad Q^2(12) = 301$$

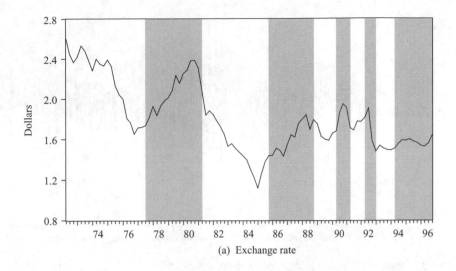

(a) Exchange rate

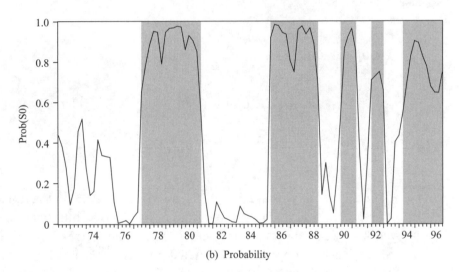

(b) Probability

Figure 6.2   Dollars/sterling exchange rate (quarterly 1973–1996) and probability of being in state 0

The Q^2 statistic, which is a portmanteau statistic using the *squared* residuals (see section 5.5.6), reveals considerable evidence of non-linearity. We thus initially fitted an LSTAR(2) model (with the delay set at $d=1$), but this did not eliminate the non-linearity and so we extended the model to a combined LSTAR(2)-GARCH(1,1) process, for which estimation yields

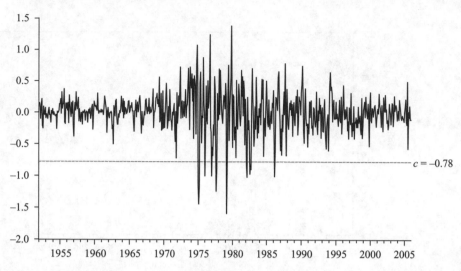

Figure 6.3   Twenty-year gilt yield differences (monthly 1952–2005)

$$\Delta R20_t = \underset{(0.040)}{0.178} \, \Delta R20_{t-1}$$

$$+ \left(\underset{(0.222)}{0.564} \, \Delta R20_{t-1} - \underset{(0.262)}{0.501} \, \Delta R20_{t-2} \right) \cdot S_{t,1} \left(130, -0.780 \right) + \varepsilon_t$$

$$\sigma_t^2 = \underset{(0.00016)}{0.00040} + \underset{(0.014)}{0.068} \, \varepsilon_{t-1}^2 + \underset{(0.012)}{0.929} \, \sigma_{t-1}^2$$

For this model we have $\hat{\sigma} = 0.294$, and $Q^2(12) = 8.3$, so that the GARCH error process successfuly removes the non-linearity, but, nevertheless, the smooth transition component enters significantly (the smoothness parameter γ is very imprecisely estimated but, as Teräsvirta (1994) discusses, this is not unusual for such models). The transition is abrupt at a value for $\Delta R20$ of -0.78, with $S_{t,1}(\cdot)$ switching from zero to one at this point. When $S = 0$, which we might refer to as the 'lower' regime, the mean process for $\Delta R20$ is an AR(1) with a root of 0.18. When $S = 1$, the 'upper' regime, the AR(2) process $\Delta R20_t = 0.742 \Delta R20_{t-1} - 0.501 \Delta R20_{t-2}$ has complex roots $0.37 \pm 0.63i$ with modulus 0.73 and period of five and a half months. By way of contrast, the linear AR(2) model has roots $0.16 \pm 0.31i$ with modulus 0.35 and period of six and a half months. As usual, the GARCH process for the errors is almost integrated, the sum of the coefficients being 0.999.

6.3 Non-parametric and neural network models

6.3.1 Non-parametric modelling

Recent advances in computer power have motivated the development of non-parametric or semi-parametric time series methods that make very few assumptions about the functional form of the underlying dynamic dependencies (see Fan and Yao, 2003). Most of these methods allow the reduction of observational error through the use of smoothing estimators. For expository purposes, we can assume the following non-linear autoregressive model:

$$Y_t = f(X_t) + \varepsilon_t = f\left(Y_{t-1}, Y_{t-2}, \ldots, Y_{t-p}\right) + \varepsilon_t$$

where $f(\cdot)$ is an arbitrary non-affine function that has to be estimated from the data, Y_t is a stationary stochastic process and ε_t is a white-noise process.

Consider first the general case of estimating $f(\cdot)$ at a particular point in time for which $X_t = x$ and $y_1, y_1, \ldots, y_N$ repeated observations are available for Y_t. A natural smoothing estimator of $f(x)$ is the average of the available data for Y_t:

$$\hat{f}(x) = N^{-1} \sum\nolimits_{i=1}^{N} y_i = N^{-1} \sum\nolimits_{i=1}^{N} \left(f(x) + \varepsilon_i\right) = f(x) + N^{-1} \sum\nolimits_{i=1}^{N} \varepsilon_i$$

Large-sample theory dictates that this is a consistent estimator, since, as N increases, the average of the white-noise term ε_t will converge to zero. Obviously, in a time series context repeated observations for Y_t are not available for each data point x. Nevertheless, assuming that $f(\cdot)$ is sufficiently smooth, for time series observations near x, $f(x)$ can be approximated by an average of the corresponding Y_ts. This is based on the reasonable assumption that, for X_ts close to x, Y_t will also be close to $f(x)$. In order to account for the potentially varying distances between the X_ts and x, a local weighted average of Y_t is appropriate:

$$\hat{f}(x) = T^{-1} \sum\nolimits_{t=1}^{T} w_t(x) y_t \tag{6.12}$$

where the weights $w_t(x)$ depend on the proximity of the X_ts to x.

The different ways of measuring the distance between adjacent points and of assigning weights to a given distance give rise to the variety of non-parametric methods and techniques that have been developed in the literature. These include kernel regression, neural networks (NNs), orthogonal series expansions, wavelets, projection pursuit, nearest-neighbour estimators, splines, non-linear state space models, regressogram approaches, convolution smoothing, delta function sequence estimators and median smoothing, among others.

Non-parametric time series methods have apparent advantages over parametric alternatives, particularly in cases where little is known or can be inferred about the functional form underlying the dynamic dependencies. Unfortunately, non-parametric approaches come with significant costs and shortcomings. They often require substantial computational resources and data. Statistical inference is problematic and often depends on non-standard statistical theory and computationally demanding resampling techniques. The inherent flexibility of non-parametric models means that, under certain circumstances, they are prone to overfitting, where a model performs well within the particular sample selected for estimation but has very poor out-of-sample forecasting performance.

A further limitation of non-parametric models is related to the curse of dimensionality, according to which the sample size requirement increases exponentially with the number of variables. This means that non-parametric estimates have consistency rates that are much slower than the typical square root convergence of parametric approaches. Also, outliers may cause serious problems, since non-parametric models tend to stretch the function space in order to include all available observations. Finally, the application of non-parametric models is complicated by the requirements for specialised software, the large number of tuning parameters and the variety of available model configurations and estimation procedures.

The remainder of this section discuss two of the most commonly used non-parametric approaches: kernel regression and neural networks.

6.3.2 Kernel regression

One of the most widely used non-parametric approaches determines the weights using a kernel function, defined to have the properties

$$K(u) \geq 0 \qquad \int K(u)du = 1$$

The kernel $K(u)$ is typically a probability density function. This is done for reasons of mathematical convenience and has no probabilistic implications.

The kernel is usually rescaled by the bandwidth, a positive variable h, such that

$$K_h(u) = h^{-1}K(u/h) \qquad \int K_h(u)\,du = 1$$

The weight function is then defined as

$$w_t(x) = \frac{K_h(x - x_t)}{T^{-1}\sum_{t=1}^{T} K_h(x - x_t)} \tag{6.13}$$

By substituting the weight function (6.13) into (6.12) we obtain the Nadaraya–Watson kernel estimator. A variety of alternative kernel functions have been proposed, with the most popular being the Epanechnikov and Gaussian kernels. The Nadaraya–Watson kernel estimator can be shown to be a local linear regression and, under regularity conditions, can be generalised to local polynomial and non-linear regressions. The choice of bandwidth may significantly affect the results obtained by kernel methods. If h is close to zero, only values of X_t close to x will be weighted highly in the averaging process. Conversely, if h assumes an excessive value, a large neighbourhood of points around each X_t will be averaged, and this may lead to oversmoothing. Although several different approaches have been developed for automatic bandwidth selection (see Härdle, 1990), one must also keep in mind the particular objective of the data analysis. For presentation and descriptive purposes an oversmoothed curve may be desirable, while for forecasting a slightly undersmoothed curve may be more appropriate.

By estimating the function $\hat{f}(x)$ as a weighted average of the response variables in a varying, rather than fixed, neighbourhood of points, we obtain the nearest-neighbour estimator. As with kernel regression, this approach also fits polynomial regressions locally around each data point. The neighbourhood is defined as those Xs that are the k-nearest neighbour of x in terms of a Euclidean distance. The smoothing parameter k of the nearest-neighbour approach has a similar role to that of the bandwidth in the kernel method. It assumes values between zero and one and denotes the number kT of observations nearest to a given point that should be included in the neighbourhood and the local polynomial fit.

A number of techniques have been developed to reduce the computational burden of non-parametric estimation. For example, kernel estimators are typically estimated using local polynomial regressions at a subset M of equidistant points of the whole sample. Similarly, for the nearest-neighbour estimator, rather than fitting local polynomials around each point in the sample, the Cleveland subsampling approach provides an adaptive algorithm that skips adjacent points in such a way that the subsample is representative of all the values of the regressor. For relatively large samples, well over 100, the computational savings can be drastic with often insignificant loss of information.

A complete treatment of computational shortcuts can be found in Härdle (1990). In time series models where several lags are considered, researchers sometimes assume an additive model and estimate separately via kernel or nearest-neighbour methods the relationship between the dependent variable and each of the right-hand variables. This assumption conveniently reduces the computational and data problems caused by the curse of dimensionality. Several techniques, such as the regression tree and projection pursuit regression, have been developed in order to accommodate multidimensional non-parametric estimation under model additivity in a time series and regression context (see Härdle, 1990).

To demonstrate the application of the above methods, we simulate 200 observations from a cubic deterministic trend process,

$$y_t = 5 + 10^{-6} t^3 + \varepsilon_t$$

where ε_t is a standard normal variate. Figure 6.4 depicts the results of applying kernel and nearest-neighbour smoothers in estimating the functional relationship between y_t and t. For the kernel method we used a Nadaraya–Watson estimator with an Epanechnikov kernel function. The kernel bandwidth was first set according to an arbitrary rule suggested by the estimation software (*EViews 5*) based on the range of the data: $h = 0.15$ $(y_{max} - y_{min})$. For the nearest-neighbour estimator, a value of $k = 0.3$ was originally selected with a local linear polynomial. In order to demonstrate the effects of undersmoothing, we also show the results for smaller values for h and k, respectively. It is evident that both estimators offer a reasonably good fit to the data, except for the area near the origin.

6.3.3 Neural networks

Artificial neural networks (ANNs), often just called neural networks, refer to a broad class of non-parametric models that have found much popularity in recent years across a wide spectrum of disciplines, including

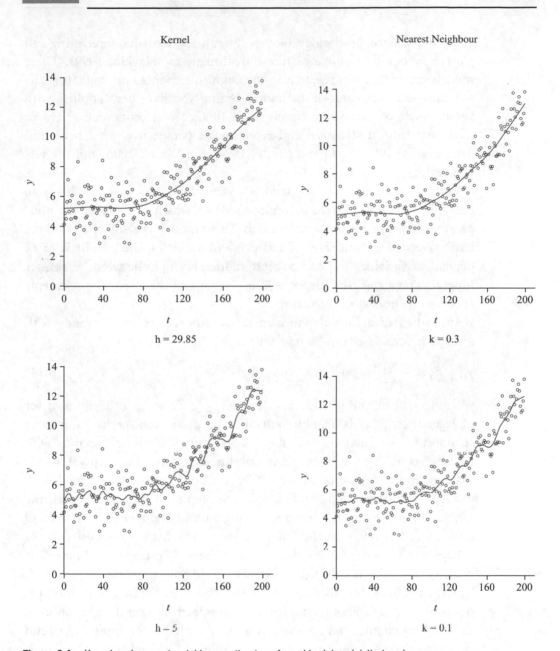

Figure 6.4   Kernel and nearest-neighbour estimates of a cubic deterministic trend process

computer science, psychology, biology, linguistics, statistics, forecasting and pattern recognition (for a textbook treatment, see Haykin, 1999). These models originate from research in the cognitive sciences on emulating the structure and behaviour of the human brain. NNs have been applied, with varied levels of success, to problems in finance and econometrics (for a treatment from a statistical and econometric perspective, see Cheng and Titterington, 1994, Kuan and White, 1994, and White, 2006, and the references therein).

One of the most commonly used NN variations is the feed-forward type, also called the multilayered perceptron (MLP), which can be used for non-parametric regression and classification. These models are organised in three basic layers: the input layer of independent variables, the output layer of dependent variables and one or more hidden layers in between. A transfer function regulates the dependencies (synapses) between the elements (neurons or nodes) of each layer.

In mathematical formulation, a univariate autoregressive MLP model with a single hidden layer can be represented as

$$y_t = \beta_0^\top \mathbf{z}_t + \sum_{i=1}^{p} \beta_i G(\gamma_i^\top \mathbf{z}_t) + \varepsilon_t \tag{6.14}$$

where y_t is the output variable, $\mathbf{z}_t = (1, y_{t-1}, y_{t-2}, \ldots, y_{t-p})$ is the input vector of lagged y_ts, $\beta_0^\top \mathbf{z}_t$ is a linear unit and the β_i are the model parameters (connection weights). $G(\cdot)$ is the transfer (or activation) function with parameters γ_i. This is a bounded non-linear function and operates in a manner similar to that of the transition functions used in STAR models. A number of different transfer functions are employed in practice, with the most common being the hyperbolic tangent and the logistic. The second term in (6.14) refers to the hidden layer in the MLP. Obviously, (6.14) collapses to a standard AR(p) model when the transfer function is linear. The residual term ε_t is usually assumed to be an *iid* random variable.

The basic MLP described above can easily be extended to include multiple output/input variables and hidden layers, respectively. An interpretation of the MLP mechanics can be given as follows: units in the input layer send signals to y_t over connections that are amplified by weights γ_i. The signals arriving at each hidden layer unit are summed and then the outcome signal of the hidden unit is produced using the transfer function. The weighted signals from the hidden layer(s) are transmitted to the output layer. The most celebrated property of MLPs, and, indeed, most NNs, lies in their universal approximation capability: they can approximate any function, under mild regularity conditions, to any desired degree of accuracy by increasing the number of units in the hidden layer (see Hornik, Stinchcombe, and White, 1989). In the context of non-parametric regression, White (1990) proves that NNs can be used for the consistent estimation of any unknown square integrable conditional expectation function.

The high flexibility, rich parameterisation and non-linear nature of NNs renders estimation particularly difficult (see White, 2006). One of the main problems is that NNs are very susceptible to overfitting. The estimation strategy of NNs is rather different from traditional linear econometric model estimation, in that it typically involves two steps: sample optimisation (training or learning) with recurrent out-of-sample testing (cross-validation), and out-of-sample testing. The in-sample optimisation is usually terminated, prior to reaching the maximum possible performance, when the performance of the model in the cross-validation sample starts to deteriorate. In this way overfitting is avoided and a good forecasting performance in the testing sample is more likely. The ability of an NN to perform well in out-of-sample forecasting refers to the generalisation capabilities of the model in neural network jargon. The estimation (training) algorithms used vary considerably and typically involve adjusting the direction of the negative gradient of some error criterion (e.g. mean squared or absolute error).

Several iterative methods have been proposed for solving this non-linear estimation problem, and usually these are combined with additional constraints in order to ensure the smoothness of the estimated function. In the case of MLPs, most of these methods are based on variants of the back-propagation algorithm, which works backwards from the output layer and uses a gradient rule to vary biases and weights iteratively. The algorithm is sensitive to local minima in the error space and is therefore applied several times with different starting values.

An additional pitfall in MLP estimation concerns the selection of the appropriate model architecture: the number of hidden layers and the number of neurons in each layer. One can either start with a small model and add hidden layers and neurons until performance is optimal, or start with an oversized model and prune small weights or reduce its size. Sometimes a preliminary optimisation is undertaken, using a genetic algorithm, simulated annealing or some other heuristic method, in order to select a good set of starting values and model architecture and to reduce the computational burden. Model performance is often evaluated according to parsimony metrics such as the BIC and AIC.

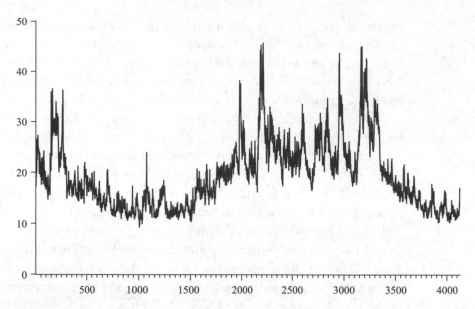

Figure 6.5   VIX implied volatility index (daily January 1990–September 2005)

A major problem with MLPs is their 'black box' property, since the parameters and structure of the model offer little intuition and conclusions can be drawn only implicitly via simulation or sensitivity analysis. Moreover, assessing the statistical significance of the parameters is problematic. Although MLPs have become a popular model for applied non-linear modeling in finance, theoretical and applied research on alternatives is also under way (see Al-Falou and Trummer, 2003).

Example 6.5 Modelling the non-linear structure of the VIX

Indices of the volatility implied by options are becoming increasingly popular as a measure of market uncertainty and as a vehicle for developing derivative instruments to hedge against unexpected changes in volatility. In example 5.2 we fitted a jump diffusion model to the VIX implied volatility index. The series, shown in figure 6.5, exhibits extreme variations and appears to be a good candidate for non-linear modelling. As shown by Psychoyios, Dotsis and Markellos (2006), the VIX is stationary, although the possibility of a fractional unit root cannot be excluded.

We proceed by modelling the logarithms of the VIX using a variety of univariate linear and non-linear models, the performance of which are summarised in table 6.1 Overall, the results suggest that regime-switching models offer the best approximation to the data-generating process, since the

Table 6.1 Linear and non-linear models for the VIX

	R^2	BIC	AIC	Skew	Kurtosis	JB	Q(12)
ARMA(1,61)	0.968	−5814.6	−5827.2	0.66	6.49	2298	78.5
ARMA(4, 3)	0.969	−5831.7	−5859.9	0.77	6.65	2584	27.4
ARFIMA(1, 0.76, 0)	0.969	−5863.6	−5876.2	0.75	6.70	2622	37.7
Bilinear − AR(1)	0.968	−5807.4	−5819.9	0.49	6.38	2045	91.0
Markov switching	0.974	−5920.9	−5942.9	−0.10	3.48	42.7	78.4
Hamilton	0.973	−5851.2	−5870.0	0.07	4.16	225.8	85.2
MLP(5:3:1)	0.969	−5778.7	−5825.8	0.78	6.55	2472	42.0

model with a Markov switching constant and a single autoregressive lag produces the highest R^2 and the smallest BIC and AIC values. This model leaves some serial dependencies in the residuals, as measured by a large Q statistic. It manages to remove most of the leptokurtosis from the original data, however, leaving almost normally distributed residuals. Hamilton's regime-switching mean process also performs reasonably well.

The ARFIMA $(1, d, 0)$ model has the second best performance in terms of the information criteria considered. It implies a long-memory process with a fractional root of $d = 0.76$ and a single autoregressive lag. An MLP with five autoregressive lags and three elements in a single hidden layer appears to have the worst performance in terms of the BIC and AIC. The MLP was estimated via cross-validation on a sample of 100 observations using the back-propagation algorithm and 5000 optimisation cycles. The fact that it has a performance very close to that of the linear ARIMA models suggests that the MLP may have been trapped in a local minimum or that further optimisation is necessary. It is interesting to note the small differences in performance between the linear and non-linear models considered.

The parameters of the estimated models, except for the MLP, are as follows:

ARMA(1, 1)

$$y_t = -1.687 + 0.987\, y_{t-1} + \varepsilon_t + 0.074\, \varepsilon_{t-1}$$
$$\underset{(0.061)}{} \quad \underset{(0.003)}{} \quad \underset{(0.002)}{}$$

ARMA(4, 3)

$$y_t = -1.715 + 0.118\, y_{t-1} + 1.209\, y_{t-2} + 0.443\, y_{t-3} - 0.774\, y_{t-4}$$
$$\underset{(0.103)}{} \quad \underset{(0.039)}{} \quad \underset{(0.034)}{} \quad \underset{(0.029)}{} \quad \underset{(0.040)}{}$$
$$+ \varepsilon_t - 0.770\, \varepsilon_{t-1} + 0.495\, \varepsilon_{t-2} + 0.863\, \varepsilon_{t-3}$$
$$\underset{(0.032)}{} \quad \underset{(0.051)}{} \quad \underset{(0.031)}{}$$

ARFIMA(1, 0.76, 0)

$$\Delta^{0.76} y_t = -\underset{(0.222)}{1.278} + \underset{(0.034)}{0.137}\, y_{t-1} + \varepsilon_t$$

Bilinear – AR(1)

$$y_t = -\underset{(0.728)}{1.385} + \underset{(0.018)}{0.994}\, y_{t-1} + \underset{(0.005)}{0.189}\, y_{t-1}\varepsilon_{t-1} + \varepsilon_t$$

Markov switching AR(1) and constant

$$y_t = \begin{cases} -\underset{(0.065)}{1.798} + \underset{(0.002)}{0.984}\, y_{t-1} + \varepsilon_t \\[2ex] \underset{(0.093)}{0.464} + \underset{(0.005)}{0.899}\, y_{t-1} + \varepsilon_t \end{cases}$$

Hamilton's regime-switching mean model

$$y_t = \begin{cases} -\underset{(0.041)}{0.913} + \underset{(0.002)}{0.982}\, y_{t-1} + \varepsilon_t \\[2ex] \underset{(0.304)}{6.098} + \underset{(0.002)}{0.982}\, y_{t-1} + \varepsilon_t \end{cases}$$

6.4 Non-linear dynamics and chaos

The processes introduced so far in this chapter all have in common the aim of modelling *stochastic* non-linearities in financial time series. This would seem a natural approach to take by those used to dealing with stochastic time series processes, but a literature has also developed that considers the question of whether such series could have been generated, at least in part, by non-linear *deterministic* laws of motion.

Research on non-linear dynamics is concerned with the behaviour of deterministic and stochastic non-linear systems that have an implicit discrete- or continuous-time dimension. The field originates in the pioneering work of the great mathematician Henri Poincaré, at the turn of the twentieth century, on the stability of the Solar System. Both applied and theoretical research has flourished over the past three decades across a variety of disciplines, including mathematics, statistics, physics, engineering, econometrics, economics and finance. An extensive overview of the research on non-linear dynamics, with a bias towards the natural sciences, is given by Hilborn (1997). The meaning of the term 'non-linear dynamics' seems to vary considerably across scientific disciplines and time periods. For example, a popular interpretation since the early 1980s associates non-linear dynamics with deterministic non-linear systems and a particular dynamic behaviour called *chaos*. The term 'chaos' itself has also received several different interpretations, to the extent of becoming a scientifically dangerous concept (see Griffeath, 1992).

This diversity of meanings with respect to chaos is mainly because no formal and complete mathematical definition of chaotic systems exists other than a somewhat loose symptomatology (see, for example, Berliner, 1992). Broadly speaking, chaos is the mathematical condition whereby a simple (low-dimensional) non-linear dynamical system produces highly complex (infinite-dimensional or random-like) behaviour. Even though these systems are deterministic (they have finite 'phase space' dimension), they are completely unpredictable in the long run, due to 'sensitive dependence on initial conditions' (or Lyapunov instability). Chaotic systems also invariably exhibit power-law behaviour (continuous, broadband and power-law declining spectral density) and have 'fractal' or 'self-similar' pictorial representations ('strange' or non-integer phase-space dimension attractors).

An example of a chaotic process is one that is generated by a deterministic difference equation

$$x_t = f(x_{t-1}, \ldots, x_{t-p})$$

such that x_t does not tend to a constant or a (limit) cycle and has estimated covariances that are very small or zero. A simple example is provided by Brock (1986), where a formal development of deterministic chaos models is provided. Consider the difference equation

$$x_t = f(x_{t-1}), \quad x_0 \in [0, 1]$$

where

$$f(x) = \begin{cases} x/\alpha & x \in [0, \alpha] \\ (1-x)/(1-\alpha) & x \in [\alpha, 1] \quad 0 < \alpha < 1 \end{cases}$$

Most realisations (or trajectories) of this difference equation generate the same SACFs as an AR(1) process for x_t with parameter $\phi = (2\alpha - 1)$. Hence, for $\alpha = 0.5$, the realisation will be indistinguishable from white noise, although it has been generated by a purely deterministic non-linear process. For further discussion of this particular function, called a *tent map* because the graph of x_t against x_{t-1} (known as the *phase diagram*) is shaped like a 'tent', see Hsieh (1991), who also considers other relevant examples of chaotic systems, such as the *logistic map*:

$$x_t = 4x_{t-1}(1 - x_{t-1}) = 4x_{t-1} - 4x_{t-1}^2, \qquad 0 < x_0 < 1$$

This also has the same autocorrelation properties as white noise, although x_t^2 has an SACF consistent with an MA(1) process.

Are such models useful in finance? One must keep in mind that systematic research on chaos was first undertaken in the natural sciences and, in accordance with tradition, the enthusiasm and mathematics associated with the new field were quickly carried over to economics. Many non-linear systems in the natural sciences are low-dimensional, either by experimental construction or from first principles, so chaos is a natural choice for explaining complex empirical behaviour. This is because, in deterministic systems, the standard types of dynamic behaviour are limited to fixed-point equilibria and limit cycles, and hence complexity can arise only in the presence of chaos or high-dimensionality. High-dimensional or 'stochastic' chaos is of little interest, since it is typically considered for all practical purposes to be equivalent to randomness. Unfortunately, a deduction analogous to the above is not possible in finance, since it is generally accepted that financial markets and agents are inherently highly stochastic and evolving and hence there is no practical need to resort to chaos in order to explain complex behaviour. Although chaos may have a prominent place in the study of deterministic low-dimensional dynamic behaviour, it seems to have a limited and rather exotic role to play in the context of stochastic linear and non-linear dynamics.

It is therefore not surprising that applications of chaos theory in finance and economics have been far less popular and successful than in the natural sciences. Nevertheless, the interest in chaos in finance is considerable and continues to persist. Much has been motivated by the ability of chaotic systems to produce complicated behaviour without resorting to exogenous stochastic factors and shocks. An underlying hope was that the apparently stochastic behaviour and long-run unpredictability of financial systems could be the product of a low-dimensional, and hence tractable, chaotic system.

Broadly speaking, research on chaos in finance has followed two distinct directions. The first starts with a non-linear deterministic theoretical model and demonstrates that specific configurations can produce chaotic behaviour (see the selective review by Fernández-Rodriguez, Sosvilla-Rivero and Andrada-Félix, 2005). For example, Brock (1988) considers some models of equilibrium asset pricing that might lead to chaos and complex dynamics. In these models, the idea that there should be no arbitrage profits in financial equilibrium is linked with the theory of economic growth to show how dynamics in the 'dividend' process are transmitted through the equilibrating mechanism to equilibrium asset prices. These dynamics can be linear, non-linear or chaotic depending on the constraints imposed on the models. Although several models of this type were found to be capable of producing such 'mathematical' chaos, especially in economics, empirical validation was never undertaken. Furthermore, the underlying strong assumptions regarding deterministic dynamic behaviour are highly questionable (see Granger, 1992).

The second approach is model-free and uses non-parametric procedures to test observed economic time series for signs of chaotic behaviour (e.g. see the recent studies by Fernández-Rodriguez, Sosvilla-Rivero and Andrada-Félix, 2005, Kyrtsou and Serletis, 2006, and Shintani and Linton, 2006, and the references contained therein). Although some studies claim to have found 'empirical' chaos, such evidence cannot be considered as conclusive since the testing procedures used are susceptible to problems with respect to autocorrelation, small sample size, noise, heteroskedasticity, non-stationarities, aggregation, microstructures and seasonalities. More importantly, all the evidence presented is merely circumstantial, since no formal testing procedure has been developed for stochastic time series where chaos enters as the null hypothesis. Even if chaos was present in the data, estimating the unknown parameters of the underlying model would be practically impossible (Geweke, 1993).

Finally, the literature has not provided convincing arguments about the practical implications of chaos in finance and the marginal benefits of assuming chaotic behaviour. In addition, there has been little empirical evidence of chaotic dynamics uncovered in financial time series, although much evidence of other types of stochastic non-linearities. This has been obtained from a variety of tests for non-linearity, to which we now turn.

6.5 Testing for non-linearity

As the previous sections have demonstrated, there has been a wide variety of non-linear models proposed for modelling financial time series. We have, in particular, compared and contrasted the ARCH and bilinear models, and in so doing have discussed LM tests for each. Nevertheless, given the range of alternative non-linear models, it is not surprising that a number of other tests for non-linearity have also been proposed. Since the form of the departure from linearity is often difficult to specify a priori, many tests are 'diagnostic' in nature – i.e. a clear alternative to the null hypothesis of linearity is not specified, and this, of course, leads to difficulties in discriminating between the possible causes of 'non-linear misspecification'.

The detection of non-linearity is further complicated by the fact that it has similar symptoms to other types of time series behaviour. For example, Andersson, Eklund and Lyhagen (1999) have shown that long-memory may lead to spurious rejection of the linearity hypothesis. As demonstrated by Granger and Teräsvirta (1999) and Diebold and Inoue (2001), the opposite may also be true, since some non-linear processes exhibit characteristics that justify modelling via a long-memory model. An interesting direction considers testing and modelling non-linearity within a long-memory process (see, for example, Baillie and Kapetanios, 2007). Koop and Potter (2001) have shown that unpredictable structural instability in a time series may also produce erroneous evidence of threshold-type non-linearity. An alarming finding by Ghysels, Granger and Siklos (1996) is that non-linear transformations, such as the X11 seasonal adjustment procedure, that are routinely applied prior to time series modelling may also induce non-linear behaviour. Equally, seasonal adjustments may smooth out structural shifts and switching between regimes (see Franses and Paap, 1999). Finally, as discussed by van Dijk, Franses and Lucas (1999) and de Lima (1997), neglecting outliers and non-normalities may also lead to spurious evidence of non-linearity. Despite the difficulties, testing for non-linearity is usually an effort well spent, since the burden associated with the specification and estimation of non-linear models is often substantial and complex.

Empirical applications and simulation studies (e.g. Lee, White and Granger, 1993, and Barnett et al., 1996, 1997) have shown that no non-linearity test dominates in all situations and that power varies with sample size and the characteristics of the underlying stochastic process. This means that, in practice, it is advisable to apply a variety of non-linearity tests to the data to guide the model specification process. Some of the most popular tests that have appeared in the financial literature are described in the remainder of this section.

On the basis of Volterra expansions, Ramsey (1969), Keenan (1985) and Tsay (1986) provide regression type tests of linearity against unspecified alternatives. These appear to have good power against the non-linear moving average (see Robinson, 1977) and bilinear alternatives, but possibly have low power against ARCH models. In developing these tests, we assume that an $AR(p)$ process has been fitted to the observed series x_t and that the residuals, e_t, and the fitted values, $\hat{x}_t = x_t - e_t$, have been calculated. Ramsey's original *regression error specification test* (RESET) is constructed from the auxiliary regression

$$e_t = \sum_{i=1}^{p} \varphi_i x_{t-i} + \sum_{j=2}^{h} \delta_j \hat{x}_t^h + v_t$$

and is the F-test of the hypothesis H_0: $\delta_j = 0$, $j = 2, \ldots, h$. If $h = 2$, this is equivalent to Keenan's test, while Tsay augments the auxiliary regression with second-order terms:

$$e_t = \sum_{i=1}^{p} \varphi_i x_{t-i} + \sum_{i=1}^{p} \sum_{j=i}^{p} \delta_{ij} \, x_{t-i} \, x_{t-j} + v_t$$

in which the linearity hypothesis is H_0: $\delta_{ij} = 0$, for all i and j. These tests have LM interpretations and Tsay's test has power against a greater variety of non-linear models than the RESET. A further extension is provided by Teräsvirta, Lin and Granger (1993), in which the auxiliary regression becomes

$$e_t = \sum_{i=1}^{p} \varphi_i x_{t-i} + \sum_{i=1}^{p} \sum_{j=i}^{p} \delta_{ij} x_{t-i} x_{t-j}$$
$$+ \sum_{i=1}^{p} \sum_{j=i}^{p} \sum_{k=j}^{p} \delta_{ijk} x_{t-i} x_{t-j} x_{t-k} + v_t$$

with the linearity hypothesis now being H_0: $\delta_{ij} = 0$, $\delta_{ijk} = 0$ for all i, j and k. This is related to the 'neural network' test discussed by Lee, White and Granger (1993) and appears to have better power.

A portmanteau test for nonlinearity developed by McLeod and Li (1983) is based on the Ljung–Box statistic calculated using the squared residuals obtained from a linear fit. The test exploits an idea by Granger and Andersen (1978) that, if the residuals from an $AR(p)$ fit are *iid*, then the cross-product of their squares should have a correlation structure that is the same as that of the square of their cross-products (see section 6.1). Under the null hypothesis of linearity, the first m autocorrelations among the squared residuals are zero and the Ljung–Box test statistic is distributed as χ^2_{m-p}. This test has good power against ARCH behaviour and is asymptotically equivalent to the LM test statistic developed by Engle (1982): see Granger and Teräsvirta (1993). As expected, the power of the test is sensitive to departures from normality.

When residuals from an ARMA-GARCH model are used the test no longer follows a χ^2 distribution and must be corrected along the lines suggested by Li and Mak (1994). Pena and Rodriguez (2005) have recently proposed a simple extension of this test that employs information criteria in the selection of the optimal lag structure for the autoregressive models fitted to the squared residuals. The checking procedure posits that, if the optimal lag structure is non-zero, then it can be inferred that there are non-linearities present in the data. Simulation evidence shows that, when the Bayesian information criterion (BIC) is used, this test performs favourably for a wide variety of non-linear processes and sample sizes. It was found, however, to have poor power against threshold non-linear processes and certain types of heteroskedastic behaviour.

Once evidence in favour of non-linearity has been found, Hsieh (1989b) has developed a test that can shed light on the type of non-linearity present. More specifically, the test attempts to discriminate between two types of non-linearity: 'additive' and 'multiplicative'. In the former, non-linearity enters solely through the conditional mean of the process

$$e_t = g(x_{t-1}\ldots, x_{t-k}, e_{t-1}, \ldots, e_{t-k}) + u_t$$

where $g(\cdot)$ is an arbitrary non-linear function. This suggests that a model from the bilinear or SDM family may be appropriate. Multiplicative non-linearity manifests itself through the conditional variance, thus pointing towards the direction of an ARCH-type model:

$$e_t = g(x_{t-1}, \ldots, x_{t-k}, e_{t-1}, \ldots, e_{t-k}) u_t$$

The test exploits the fact that, unlike additive dependence, multiplicative dependence implies that

$$E(e_t \,|\, x_{t-1}, \ldots, x_{t-k}, e_{t-1}, \ldots, e_{t-k}) = 0 \qquad (6.15)$$

Assuming that $g(\cdot)$ is at least twice continuously differentiable, it can be approximated via a Taylor expansion around zero. The test is based on the fact that the residuals, u_t, must be uncorrelated with the terms in this expansion under multiplicative dependence. The test is implemented by estimating the scaled third moment of the data:

$$r_{eee}(i, j) = \frac{T^{-1} \sum e_t e_{t-i} e_{t-j}}{\left(T^{-1} \sum e_t^2\right)^{1.5}}$$

Under the null hypothesis of multiplicative non-linearity, $T^{0.5}r_{eee}(i,j)$ is asymptotically normally distributed with a variance that can be consistently estimated by

$$\sigma^2 = \frac{T^{-1}\sum e_t^2 e_{t-i}^2 e_{t-j}^2}{\left(T^{-1}\sum e_t^2\right)^3}$$

As discussed by Hsieh (1989b), the approach is similar to that of Tsay (1986), who tests jointly $r_{eee}(i,j)$ for $0 < i, j < k$. The difference is that Tsay's test assumes that e_t is *iid* while Hsieh's test assumes only that the expectation in (6.15) is zero under sufficient moment conditions. The former test thus captures any departures from linearity while the later rejects the null only in the presence of additive, but not multiplicative, non-linearity.

Non-linearity tests have also been developed on the basis of the reversibility of a stochastic process. A stationary process is said to be *time-reversible* (TR) if all its finite dimensional distributions are invariant to the reversal of time indices. In other words, if the probabilistic structure of a time series is identical whether going forwards or backwards in time, the series is time-reversible; otherwise it is said to be irreversible. Sequences that are *iid* and stationary Gaussian, such as ARMA processes, will be time-reversible. A linear, non-Gaussian process will, in general, be *time-irreversible*, however. Ramsey and Rothman (1996) have proposed the *TR* test statistic, estimated for various lags k as

$$TR(k) = \hat{B}_{2,1}(k) - \hat{B}_{1,2}(k)$$

where $\hat{B}_{2,1}(k)$ and $\hat{B}_{1,2}(k)$ are the method of moments estimators of the *bicovariances* $E(x_t^2 x_{t-k})$ and $E(x_t x_{t-k}^2)$, respectively. These can be estimated using the residuals from a linear fit as

$$\hat{B}_{i,j}(k) = (T-k)^{-1}\sum_{t=k+1}^{T} e_t^i e_{t-k}^j \quad i,j = 1,2$$

Although ARCH processes are irreversible, the *TR* test has no power against them since their bicovariances are zero. Under the null hypothesis of time reversibility, *TR* has an expected value of zero for all lags. When the process is *iid*, *TR* is asymptotically normally distributed with variance

$$V(TR) = 2\frac{(\mu_4\,\mu_2 - \mu_3)}{T-k} - 2\frac{\mu_2^3(T-2k)}{(T-k)^2}, \quad \mu_i = E(e_t^i)$$

As shown by Rothman (1992), the convergence to asymptotic normality is adequately fast even when the process is non-*iid* and the test is applied to residuals from a linear fit with non-normal errors. Rothman shows that the test has reasonable power against simple bilinear and threshold autoregressive (TAR) models and that the distinct rejection pattern of the test can be utilised in the model identification process. A time reversibility test with milder moment restrictions than the *TR* has been proposed by Chen, Chou and Kuan (2000).

Non-parametric tests of serial independence have also attracted interest as a means of searching for non-linearity (see Dufour, 1982). These include a wide variety of procedures, including sign, permutation and rank tests for independence. Non-parametric approaches have also been developed to test against serial dependence of fixed order (see Pinske, 1998). Most of these non-parametric tests are based on the actual series, rather than on standardised residuals from some linear fit, and therefore the applicability of their limit distributions for, say, AR residuals is mostly unknown.

A non-parametric test that has created considerable interest is the BDS statistic, named after Brock, Dechert and Scheinkman, based on the concept of the *correlation integral*: see, for example, Brock (1986), Brock, Hsieh and LeBaron (1991), Brock and Dechert (1991) and Dechert (1996). The test is based on the idea that the evolution of the next values of any two blocks of observations that are close in some metric should also be close in the same metric. For an observed series $\{x_t\}_1^T$, the correlation integral $C_N(\ell, T)$ is defined as

$$C_N(\ell, T) = \frac{2}{T_N(T_N - 1)} \sum_{t < s} \mathbf{I}_t\left(x_t^N, x_s^N\right)$$

where

$$x_t^N = (x_t, x_{t+1}, \ldots, x_{t+N-1})$$

and

$$x_s^N = (x_s, x_{s+1}, \ldots, x_{s+N-1})$$

are called '*N*-histories', $\mathbf{I}_t\left(x_t^N, x_s^N\right)$ is an indicator function that equals one if $\left\|x_t^N - x_s^N\right\| < \ell$ and zero otherwise, $\|\cdot\|$ being the sup-norm, and $T_N = T - N + 1$.

The correlation integral is an estimate of the probability that any two *N*-histories, x_t^N and x_s^N, are within ℓ of each other. If the x_ts are strict white noise, then

$$C_N(\ell, T) \rightarrow C_1(\ell, T)^N$$

as $T \rightarrow \infty$, and

$$w_N(\ell, T) = \sqrt{T}\big(C_N(\ell, T) - C_1(\ell, T)^N\big)/\sigma_N(\ell, T)$$

has a standard normal limiting distribution, where the expression for the variance $\sigma_N^2(\ell, T)$ may be found in, for example, Hsieh (1989b, p. 343). Thus, the BDS statistic $w_N(\ell, T)$ tests the null hypothesis that a series is strict white noise; it is a diagnostic test, since a rejection of this null is consistent with some type of dependence in the data, which could result from a linear stochastic system, a non-linear stochastic system or a non-linear deterministic system. Additional diagnostic tests are therefore needed to determine the source of the rejection, but simulation experiments do suggest that the BDS test has power against simple linear deterministic systems as well as non-linear stochastic processes.

A number of non-linearity testing procedures have been developed in the frequency domain. These are based on the bispectrum $f(\omega_i, \omega_j)$ – i.e. the third-order moments, in the frequency domain, of a third-order stationary series. When appropriately normalised, the bispectrum is constant for a linear series, irrespective of frequency, and assumes the value of zero for a Gaussian process. More specifically, the normalised bispectrum is given by

$$b(\omega_i, \omega_j) = \frac{|f(\omega_i, \omega_j)|}{f(\omega_i)f(\omega_j)f(\omega_i + \omega_j)}$$

where $f(\omega)$ is the spectral density of the series. Subba Rao and Gabr (1980) and Hinich (1982) have developed tests of linearity and normality using the bispectrum that have the advantage of not requiring pre-filtering, but they have disadvantages in terms of implementation and sample requirements.

A related procedure has been developed by Hinich and Patterson (1985) that is based on the sample bicovariance of a series, and it can be thought of as a generalisation of the Box–Pierce portmanteau statistic. The test statistic is calculated as

$$x_3 = \sum_{s=2}^{\zeta} \sum_{r=1}^{s-1} (G(r, s))^2$$

where $G(r,s) = C_3(r,s)\sqrt{T-s}$. The sample bicovariances

$$C_3(r,s) = (T-s)^{-1}\sum\nolimits_{t=1}^{T-s} x_t x_{t+r} x_{t+s}$$

can be thought of as a generalisation of skewness and are all equal to zero for zero-mean iid data. Under the null hypothesis that the process is iid, Hinich and Patterson (1985) prove that x_3 is asymptotically distributed as χ^2 with $\zeta(\zeta-1)/2$ degrees of freedom for $\zeta < T^{0.5}$ and recommend using $\zeta = T^{0.4}$. Hong and Lee (2003) use a generalised spectral approach to develop a diagnostic testing procedure for non-linear and linear models. As with the BDS test, this has an appealing nuisance-parameter-free property, and it is shown to be asymptotically more efficient.

Tests are also available for specific non-linear alternatives. Tests against ARCH and bilinear alternatives have already been discussed in sections 6.1 and 6.2 and there is also a fully developed testing procedure against STAR models. From Teräsvirta (1994), an LM-type test statistic for the null of linearity against an LSTAR alternative can be constructed from the auxiliary regression

$$e_t = \sum\nolimits_{i=1}^{p} \varphi_i x_{t-i} + \sum\nolimits_{i=1}^{p} \delta_{1j} x_{t-i} x_{t-d} + \sum\nolimits_{i=1}^{p} \delta_{2j} x_{t-i} x_{t-d}^2 + \sum\nolimits_{i=1}^{p} \delta_{3j} x_{t-i} x_{t-d}^3 + v_t$$

with the linearity hypothesis being $H_0: \delta_{ij} = 0$, for all i and j. To test against an ESTAR alternative the same auxiliary regression is estimated, but without the fourth-order terms – i.e. we set $\delta_{3j} = 0$ a priori. This relationship between the two tests leads naturally to a method for discriminating between the two types of STAR models (see Teräsvirta, 1994, for details, and example 6.6 below). Of course, these tests assume that the delay parameter d is known. Typically its value will be unknown, and Teräsvirta suggests that it should be chosen on the basis of a sequence of LM tests for alternative values of d; we choose the value that minimises the p-value of the individual tests in the sequence. The auxiliary regression can also be estimated with x_t rather than e_t as the dependent variable, and this may be preferred as it provides a direct comparison with the AR(p) model under the null of linearity. Van Dijk, Teräsvirta and Franses (2002) discuss some extensions to this testing procedure.

Further tests are discussed, within a general econometric context, in Granger and Teräsvirta (1993, chap. 6) and in the survey by Teräsvirta, Tjostheim and Granger (1994). It should be emphasised, however, that all these tests are designed to distinguish between linear and non-linear *stochastic* dynamics. They are not, as yet, capable of distinguishing non-linear stochastic dynamics from deterministic chaotic dynamics, although the rejection of linearity may, of course, motivate the investigation of chaotic models, as discussed in section 6.4 A test that is claimed to be able to detect chaos in noisy data is the Lyaponuv exponent estimator of Nychka *et al.* (1992), which has been subject to rigourous scrutiny in Barnett *et al.* (1996, 1997).

Example 6.6 Non-linearity tests and an ANN model for UK gilt yields

The residuals from the linear AR(2) model fitted to $\Delta R20$ in example 6.4 were used to construct various tests of non-linearity. The LM test for twelfth-order ARCH produced the statistic $\chi^2_{12} = 114.5$, which is obviously significant, and LM tests for bilinearity with $R = S = 1$ and $R = S = 2$, respectively, obtained $\chi^2_1 = 6.19$ and $\chi^2_4 = 12.75$, both significant at the 5 per cent level. The RESET test with $h = 2$ (i.e. Keenan's test) has a p-value of 0.017, Tsay's test a p-value of 0.10, and Teräsvirta, Lin and Granger's test a p-value of 0.003. Thus, all bar Tsay's test indicate substantial non-linear dependence in the data, the non-rejection of linearity by this test occurring because the additional regressors over the RESET test, $x_{t-1}x_{t-2}$ and x^2_{t-2}, are individually insignificant.

Following, for example, Hsieh (1989b), the BDS tests were computed for a selection of ℓ and N values and are shown in table 6.2. All the statistics are highly significant, thus again indicating substantial non-linear dependence in the residuals.

Why was an LSTAR(2) model with delay parameter set at $d = 1$ fitted to $\Delta R20$ in example 6.3? Auxiliary regressions for $d = 1$ and $d = 2$ suggested

Table 6.2 BDS statistics for twenty-year gilts

	$\ell = 0.5$		$\ell = 1$		$\ell = 1.5$
N	w_N	N	w_N	N	w_N
2	7.62	2	7.87	2	7.60
3	11.63	3	11.09	3	9.97
4	15.21	4	13.86	4	12.11
5	20.20	5	16.49	5	13.67
6	26.51	6	19.00	6	14.94

Note: ℓ is set in terms of the standard deviation of the residuals from the AR(2) fit – i.e. $\ell = 1$ is one standard deviation.

that the former setting was appropriate; after deletion of insignificant regressors the auxiliary regression was

$$x_t = \underset{(0.053)}{0.233}\, x_{t-1} - \underset{(0.045)}{0.075}\, x_{t-2} + \underset{(0.063)}{0.197}\, x_{t-1}^3 - \underset{(0.131)}{0.372}\, x_{t-1}^2 x_{t-2} - \underset{(0.082)}{0.218}\, x_{t-1}^3 x_{t-2}$$

To choose between an LSTAR and an ESTAR model, Teräsvirta (1994) suggests the following procedure: (i) test whether all 'fourth-order' terms are insignificant; (ii) conditional on all fourth-order terms being zero, test the joint significance of all third-order terms; and (iii) conditional on all third- and fourth-order terms being zero, test the significance of the second-order terms. If the test in (ii) produces the smallest p-value, select an ESTAR model; if not, choose an LSTAR model. The p-values are found to be (i) 0.126, (ii) 0.159 and (iii) 0.042; thus, we chose to fit an LSTAR model.

Methods of testing the adequacy of fitted STAR models are discussed in Eitrhem and Teräsvirta (1996). To check whether such a model is adequate, we can use the approach discussed above for linear models – e.g., to test against general 'neglected' non-linearity, second- and third-order terms of the form $x_{t-i}x_{t-j}$ and $x_{t-i}x_{t-j}x_{t-k}$ may be added to the LSTAR model and tested for significance. Doing so for the fitted LSTAR(2) model leads to a statistic that is significant at less than the 0.01 level. Eitrhem and Teräsvirta remark, however, that this does not give us much of a clue as to what model we should fit next; given the nature of the residuals from the LSTAR(2) model, we decided to fit GARCH(1, 1) errors, leading to the model discussed in example 6.4.

Given the evidence of non-linearity, we also investigated the performance of ANNs. The *logarithmic* changes, $\Delta r20$, were used in this exercise, as this series is used in a sequence of examples in subsequent chapters. An AR(2), an LSTAR(2) with $d = 1$, and an ANN – an MLP with two inputs, $\Delta r20_{t-1}$ and $\Delta r20_{t-2}$, and five hidden neurons organised in one layer, denoted ANN(2:5) – were estimated over the sample January 1952 to December 2000. The MLP was estimated using 1500 training cycles and cross-validation. Table 6.3

Table 6.3 Within-sample and forecasting performance of three models for $\Delta r20$

	RMSE in-sample: 1952–2000	RMSE outside-sample: 1991–2005
AR(2)	0.0311	0.0289
LSTAR(2)	0.0309	0.0294
ANN(2:5)	0.0294	0.0298

presents the within-sample root mean squared errors (RMSEs) for the three models, where we see that both non-linear models have smaller RMSEs than the AR(2) process, the ANN quite considerably so. The three models were also used to forecast the remaining five years of data, these outside-sample RMSEs also being shown in the table. Now we see that goodness of fit is reversed: the linear AR(2) model has the smallest RMSE and the ANN the largest, leading to the suspicion that perhaps the ANN had been over-trained.

Example 6.7 The non-linear structure of the VIX

In this example we apply various non-linearity tests to the VIX series that was modelled in example 6.5. As we saw, the best approximation to this process was found to be given by a Markov switching AR(1) model. The AIC and BIC for various AR models suggest an optimal lag of twelve and five, respectively. Since we are interested more in removing linear dependencies than in out-of-sample forecasting, we adopt the less parsimonious AR(12) model. The SACF and PACF statistics of the AR(12) residuals confirm that all auto-correlations have been removed from the series, but the squared residuals show strong evidence of serial dependence, with a highly significant $Q^2(15)$ statistic of 175.0. The Pena and Rodriguez (2005) testing procedure also finds non-linearity, since the optimal lag suggested by the BIC for auto-regressive models for the squared residuals was clearly non-zero. Evidence of ARCH was provided by a highly significant LM test. Although Ramsey's RESET test was only marginally significant using lags h from one to five, Tsay's test was highly significant when implemented with additional second-order terms up to five lags.

Table 6.4 BDS statistics for the VIX residuals

	$\ell = 0.5$		$\ell = 1$		$\ell = 1.5$
N	w_N	N	w_N	N	w_N
2	17.72	2	17.54	2	16.31
3	23.97	3	22.69	3	20.43
4	30.09	4	23.31	4	23.67
5	37.19	5	31.68	5	26.30
6	46.17	6	36.35	6	28.53

Note: ℓ is set in terms of the standard deviation of the residuals from the AR(12)-GARCH $(1, 1)$ fit – i.e. $\ell = 1$ is one standard deviation.

Since evidence in favour of heteroskedasticity is present in the data, we augment the AR(12) filtering procedure by using a GARCH(1, 1) process for modelling the conditional variance of the VIX. Reapplication of the above testing procedures suggests that heteroskedasticity is successfully removed by this specification. We now turn to testing for serial independence in the ARMA(12)-ARCH(1) residuals using the BDS procedure, the results of which are shown in table 6.4. It is clear that there is significant dependence remaining in the series even after filtering out linear and GARCH effects. Finally, using the *Nonlinear Toolkit* software distributed freely by Ashley and Patterson, we applied the bicovariance and bispectrum tests, adopting the specifications suggested by them. The test statistics were both found to be significant at the 5 per cent level, thus indicating some kind of non-linear dependence in the data, consistent with the results of the BDS test.

Modelling return distributions

The choice of unconditional distribution is something that has always puzzled academics and practitioners in finance. The standard assumption since the 1960s has been that financial prices are geometric Brownian motions and, therefore, logarithmic returns follow a normal distribution. This assumption has profound implications for a variety of theoretical and practical problems in finance, as expected returns and risks in a multivariate normal financial world can be fully described probabilistically using just means, variances and covariances. Much of finance analysis, such as primary and derivative asset pricing, portfolio optimisation and risk management, is built upon the assumption of normally distributed returns. The normal distribution also has important implications for econometric and statistical analysis, since most of the underlying theory is parametric and has been developed on the basis of normality.

The popularity of the normal distribution is easily justifiable from a practical point of view because it offers tractability and computational simplicity. Furthermore, the normality assumption is supported theoretically by the central limit theorem (CLT), which states that the sum of *iid* random variables with finite mean and variance will asymptotically converge to a normal distribution. Under these assumptions, the normal distribution will offer the best approximation to empirical return distributions in samples of reasonable size. An important point to note is that independence of returns is not only one of the basic assumptions that leads to the CLT but is also consistent with intuitive and theoretical arguments (e.g. Samuelson, 1965, 1973) that exclude the possibility of 'free lunches' in finance. Given the advantages of assuming normality and the fact that independence was considered to hold reasonably well for a variety of financial return series (e.g. see Cootner, 1964, and Fama, 1970), it is not surprising that the normal distribution quickly became a standard assumption in finance. The assumption of independence, which is closely related to the normal distribution under the CLT, is not a necessary or sufficient condition for theoretically consistent financial prices, however (under, for example, rational expect-ations: LeRoy, 1973, and Lucas, 1978; noise trading: Frankel and Froot, 1988; or incomplete knowledge: Goldberg and Frydman, 1996).

In tandem with these theoretical developments, empirical research on returns distributions has also been ongoing since the early 1960s: see, for example, the surveys in Kon (1984), Badrinath and Chatterjee (1988) and Mittnik and Rachev (1993a), and the recent book by Rachev, Menn and Fabozzi (2005). These have almost universally found that such distributions are characterised not by normality but by the 'stylised facts' of fat tails, high peakedness (excess kurtosis) and skewness. Consequently, there have been several recent developments in statistics and econometrics that have led to considerable advances in the analysis of empirical returns distributions.

To set the scene for subsequent analysis, section 1 presents an initial descriptive analysis of the distributional properties of two typical return series, before section 2 reviews two of the most important theoretical models for examining return distributions: the stable process and, much more briefly since it was analysed in great detail in chapter 5, the ARCH process. Section 3 generalises the discussion to consider tail shapes of distributions and methods of estimating indices of these shapes, while section 4 reviews existing empirical research and offers new evidence from our own returns series. Section 5 considers the implications of fat-tailed distributions for testing the conventional maintained assumption of time series models of returns, that of weak, or covariance, stationarity. Section 6 switches attention to modelling the central part of returns distributions, and section 7 reviews data-analytic methods of modelling skewness and kurtosis. The distributional properties of absolute returns are the focus of section 8, and a summary and some further extensions are provided in section 9.

7.1 Descriptive analysis of returns series

The techniques discussed in this chapter are illustrated using two return series: (i) the daily returns of the London FT30 for a sixty-year period from 1935 to 1994, which has previously been analysed in terms of its long-memory properties and the profitability of technical trading rules in Mills (1996a, 1997b); and (ii) the daily returns of the S&P 500, which has been used in earlier examples. Unlike other chapters, however, because the use of these series is integral to the development of the techniques, separate,

Table 7.1 Descriptive statistics on returns distributions

	T	Mean	Median	Std.dev.	Max.	Min.	Range	Skew	Kurtosis
FT30	15,003	0.022	0.000	1.004	10.78	−12.40	23.2	−0.14	14.53
S&P 500	17,054	0.020	0.047	1.154	16.37	−22.80	38.2	−0.49	26.04

numbered, examples will not be presented; rather, the techniques will be illustrated within the main body of the text itself.

Descriptive distributional statistics are thus presented in table 7.1 and graphical representations of these distributions are shown in figure 7.1. The empirical densities shown are computed as a smoothed function of the histogram using a normal kernel (see Silverman, 1986, chap. 3). Superimposed on the empirical density is a normal distribution having the same variance as that estimated from the sample.

The empirical cumulative distributions are plotted against the cumulative reference normal distributions in the form of normal probability or Q-Q plots (see Mills, 1990, chap. 3). From this information it is clear that both returns distributions diverge substantially from the normal in the manner expected: they have fatter tails, are more highly peaked and are skewed.

7.2 Two models for returns distributions

The 'fat-tailed and highly peaked' stylised fact about financial return series was first emphasised by Mandelbrot (1963a, 1963b), who proposed using the stable (also known as the stable Paretian, Pareto–Lévy or Lévy flight) class of distributions, which includes the normal as a special case, to model the fat tailed nature of stock returns. Since then, many, but certainly by no means all, researchers have found that the stable distribution provides a good fit to a wide variety of returns series: see, for example, the references provided by Ghose and Kroner (1995). Alternative lines of modelling take the empirical returns distribution to be a mixture either of normals or of a normal and a stable, or use some other distribution capable of modelling fat tails, such as the student-t or the double Weibull distribution. These alternatives will not, however, be pursued here, although they have undoubtedly contributed to our knowledge of the distributional behaviour of asset returns: see, in particular, Mittnik and Rachev (1993a, 1993b), McDonald (1996), and Rachev, Menn and Fabozzi (2005) and the references contained therein.

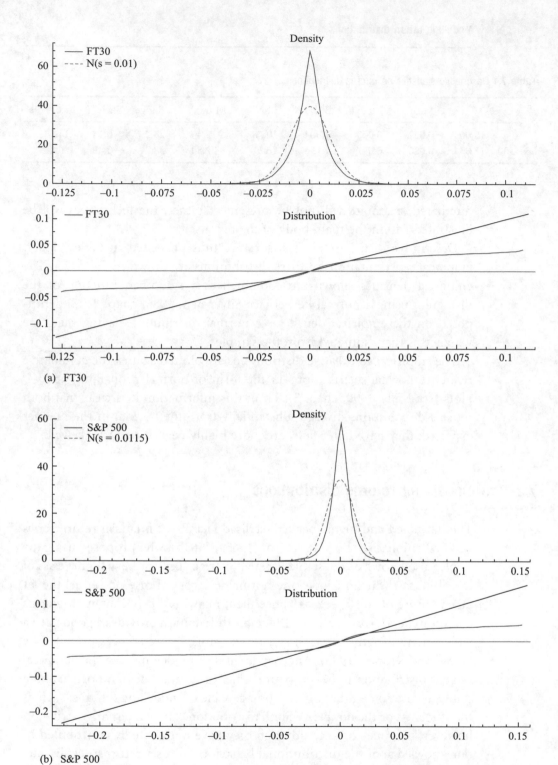

Figure 7.1 Distributional properties of two returns series

The symmetric about zero stable class of distributions is characterised by two parameters: a scale factor and the characteristic exponent, which indexes the distribution. (We restrict attention to symmetric about zero stable distributions so that we may more easily focus on the behaviour of the tails of the distributions; allowing asymmetry about a non-zero location measure introduces two further parameters that merely complicate matters for the purposes at hand.) Most attention is focused on the characteristic exponent because, since closed-form density functions do not exist for most stable distributions, they are usually defined by their characteristic functions, which always exist.

Suppose $\{X_t\}_1^T$ is a strict white-noise zero-mean process with probability distribution $F(X) = P(X < x)$. The characteristic function of X is defined as the Fourier–Stieltjes transform of $F(X)$

$$\varphi(\varsigma) = \int_{-\infty}^{+\infty} e^{i\varsigma x} dF(X)$$

where ς is real (see Feller, 1966, p. 473). The symmetric (about zero) stable characteristic function has the form

$$\varphi(\varsigma) = \exp(-\sigma^\alpha |\varsigma|^\alpha)$$

where $0 < \alpha \leq 2$ is the characteristic exponent and σ is a scale parameter. Samorodnitsky and Taqqu (1994) refer to X being $S\alpha S$ (symmetric α-stable). The $N(0,2)$ distribution is obtained when $\alpha = 2$ and the Cauchy distribution is obtained when $\alpha = 1$. Using the Fourier inversion formula provided by Feller (1966, p. 482), the stable probability distribution becomes

$$
\begin{aligned}
F(X) &= \frac{1}{2\pi} \int_{-\infty}^{+\infty} \exp(-\sigma^\alpha |\varsigma|^\alpha) \exp(-i\varsigma X) d\varsigma \\
&= \frac{1}{\pi} \int_0^{+\infty} \exp(-\sigma^\alpha |\varsigma|^\alpha) \cos(\varsigma X) d\varsigma
\end{aligned}
\tag{7.1}
$$

As remarked above, when $\alpha = 2$ the distribution is normal and all moments are finite, whereas if $\alpha < 2$ all moments greater than α are infinite. This property produces the fat-tailed (relative to the normal) behaviour of stable distributions. A necessary and sufficient condition for a distribution to be fat-tailed is that of regular variation at infinity (Feller, 1966, chap. 8.8). The stable $F(X)$ of equation (7.1) can be demonstrated to have the property

$$\lim_{s \to \infty} \frac{(1 - F(sX))}{(1 - F(s))} = X^{-\alpha}$$

which implies that the stable distribution displays a power-declining tail, $X^{-\alpha}$, rather than an exponential decline, as is the case with the normal. It is in this sense that α is also often referred to as the tail index.

Apart from its empirical usefulness, is there any theoretical justification as to why the stable distribution should be an appropriate generating process for financial data? Mandelbrot (1963b, sect. IID) argues that such a justification arises from a generalisation of the CLT. This establishes that if the limiting distribution of an appropriately scaled sum of *iid* random variables exists then it must be a member of the stable class, *even if* these random variables have infinite variance. It thus differs from the usual CLT, which says that if the second moments are finite then the limiting distribution is normal.

This result, for which a proof may be found in Feller (1966), generalises the moment requirements of the CLT and thus expands the set of limiting distributions. More importantly for our purposes, it also implies that if daily returns, say, follow a stable distribution then, since weekly, monthly and quarterly returns, for example, can be viewed as the sum of daily returns, they too will follow stable distributions having identical characteristic exponents. This is known as the stability or invariance under addition property of stable distributions. For more detailed technical discussion of stable distributions, see, for example, Mandelbrot (1963a, 1963b), Feller (1966), Brockwell and Davis (1996), Mittnik and Rachev (1993a, 1993b), Samorodnitsky and Taqqu (1994) and Rachev, Menn and Fabozzi (2005). These references also deal with the correlation of stable processes over time; moving averages of a stable random variable are also stable, as long as certain conditions on the coefficients are satisfied. We are therefore not restricted to analysing uncorrelated series, and correlated series can be filtered in the usual ways – e.g. by fitting autoregressions.

Correlated stable variables may thus be able to explain a second stylised fact of returns: the volatility clustering that is so prevalent in financial data. The GARCH class of models discussed in chapter 5, section 5, can also, of course, exhibit volatility clustering – i.e. serial correlation of *conditional* variances. For example, the simple 'ARCH(1) with normal innovations' process for X_t is

$$X_t = U_t \sigma_t \tag{7.2}$$

where $U_t \sim NID(0,1)$ and

$$\sigma_t^2 = \omega + \beta X_{t-1} \tag{7.3}$$

Equations (7.2) and (7.3) can be written as

$$X_t^2 = \omega U_t^2 + \beta U_t^2 X_{t-1}^2 = B_t + A_t X_{t-1}^2 \tag{7.4}$$

say, thus demonstrating the volatility clustering property (X_t is serially uncorrelated but is *not* independent). The ARCH(1) process may also exhibit fat tails. De Haan *et al.* (1989) show that the X_t of (7.4) regularly varies at infinity and has a tail index ζ defined implicitly by the equation

$$\Gamma\left(\frac{\zeta+1}{2}\right) = \pi^{1/2}(2\beta)^{-\zeta/2}$$

where $\Gamma(.)$ is the gamma function, as long as, amongst other things, $\beta < \bar{\beta} = 2e^{\upsilon} \approx 3.56856$, where υ is Euler's constant. From Groenendijk, Lucas and de Vries (1995, fig. 1) we have it that $\zeta = 2$ at $\beta = 1$, $\zeta = \infty$ at $\beta = 0$ and $\zeta = 0.00279$ at $\beta = \bar{\beta}$. It thus follows that, in terms of tail behaviour, the stable and ARCH models partially overlap. At $\beta = 0$ and 1 ($\zeta = \infty$ and 2) the two models have normal tails, while for $1 < \beta < \bar{\beta}$ the tail indices can be equal. For $0 < \beta < 1$, $\zeta > 2$, however, X_t is covariance stationary, has finite variance and there is no stable counterpart, whereas for $\zeta < 0.00279$ there is no ARCH counterpart. Tail behaviour can therefore discriminate between the two classes of models in the regions only where they do not overlap.

Although stable distributions have many desirable properties, results regarding their empirical appropriateness for describing financial returns have been conflicting (see Ghose and Kroner, 1995, and Baillie, 1996). Overall, it seems that any supporting evidence fades away as the sampling interval of returns increases. Another inconsistency is that estimates of variance appear to converge instead of being infinite. Nevertheless, the reluctance to replace the normal distribution by the stable family has not been based only on empirical or theoretical criteria but also, and perhaps most importantly, on the basis of practical convenience. This is because stable distributions bring about acute mathematical problems – e.g. they have no simple analytical representation, no theory exists for mixing stable distributions with different characteristics, distribution parameters are notoriously difficult to estimate, standard asymptotic theory is inapplicable, etc. Furthermore, the infinite variance property essentially prohibits direct applications within the framework of a standard finance theory that requires finite second and often higher moments.

7.3 Determining the tail shape of a returns distribution

If $\alpha < 2$ then, through the property of regular variation at infinity, the tails of a stable process are a function of α and display a power decline. In fact, they follow an asymptotic Pareto distribution, so that

$$P(X > x) = P(X < -x) = C^{\alpha} x^{-\alpha}, \qquad x > 0$$

where C is a finite and positive parameter measuring dispersion. As we have seen for the GARCH process, however, the tail index ζ may be defined for distributions other than the stable, and for these the index will not equal the characteristic exponent, although it will determine the maximal finite exponent – i.e. the tail index ζ is such that $E|X|^k < \infty$ for all $0 \le k < \zeta$. If $\zeta < 2$ then the variance of X is infinite and X may be characterised as being generated by a stable distribution for which $\alpha < \zeta$. If $\zeta \ge 2$ the variance of X is finite, but the distribution is not necessarily normal and may thus still have fat tails – for example, it may be student-t, in which case ζ defines the degrees of freedom. Distributions such as the normal and the power exponential possess all moments, and for these ζ is infinite, and they may be described as being thin-tailed.

For fat-tailed distributions other than the stable, and which also have the property of regular variation at infinity, tail behaviour will also be asymptotically Pareto (this will typically be the case for return distributions: see the arguments in Koedijk, Schafgans and de Vries, 1990, for example). Loretan and Phillips (1994) formalise this by defining the tail behaviour of the distribution of X_t to take the form

$$P(X > x) = C^{\zeta} x^{-\zeta}(1 + \zeta_R(x)), \qquad x > 0$$
$$P(X < -x) = C^{\zeta} x^{-\zeta}(1 + \zeta_L(x)), \qquad x > 0$$

where $\zeta_i \to 0$ as $x \to \infty$, $i = R, L$. The parameters C and ζ can be estimated using order statistics. If $X_{(1)} \le X_{(2)} \le \ldots \le X_{(T)}$ are the order statistics of $\{X_t\}_1^T$ in ascending order, then ζ can be estimated by

$$\hat{\zeta} = \left(s^{-1} \sum_{j=1}^{s} \log X_{(T-j+1)} - \log X_{(T-s)} \right)^{-1}$$

$$= \left(s^{-1} \sum_{j=1}^{s} \left(\log X_{(T-j+1)} - \log X_{(T-s)} \right) \right)^{-1}$$

$\hat{\zeta}$ is related to the simpler estimator proposed by de Haan and Resnick (1980) and modified by Groenendijk, Lucas and de Vries (1995), being approximately a weighted average of their estimator

$$\left(\frac{\log X_{(T-j+1)} - \log X_{(T-s)}}{\log(s/j)}\right)^{-1}$$

evaluated at different values of $j < s$. An estimate of the scale dispersion parameter is

$$\hat{C} = (s/T)X_{(T-s)}^{\hat{\zeta}}$$

Hill (1975) is the original reference for these estimators, which are conditional ML estimators, while Hall (1982) provides their asymptotic theory. To make these estimators operational, the order statistic truncation number $s = s(T)$ must be selected. Although we require that $s(T) \to \infty$ as $T \to \infty$, various approaches have been taken in empirical applications with a finite sample. Typically $\hat{\zeta}$ is computed for different values of s, selecting an s in the region over which $\hat{\zeta}$ is more or less constant. Koedijk, Schafgans and de Vries (1990) use Monte Carlo simulation to choose s such that the MSE of $\hat{\zeta}$ is minimised, while Loretan and Phillips (1994) suggest that s should not exceed $0.1T$.

Phillips, McFarland and McMahon (1996), following Hall and Welsh (1985), deduce an 'optimal' choice of $s(T)$ using the asymptotic theory of Hall (1982), from which the MSE of the limit distribution of $\hat{\zeta}$ is minimised by choosing $s(T) = [\lambda T^{2/3}]$, where [] signifies the integer part of its argument, and where λ is estimated adaptively by

$$\hat{\lambda} = \left|\hat{\xi}_1/2^{1/2}(T/s_2)(\hat{\xi}_1 - \hat{\xi}_2)\right|^{2/3}$$

Here $\hat{\xi}_1$ and $\hat{\xi}_2$ are preliminary estimates of ζ using data truncations $s_1 = [T^\sigma]$ and $s_2 = [T^\tau]$, respectively, where $0 < \sigma < 2/3 < \tau < 1$. Phillips, McFarland and McMahon (1996) recommend setting $\sigma = 0.6$ and $\tau = 0.9$. Note that, as defined, these estimates pertain to the right or upper tail of the distribution of X; to estimate the parameters of the left or lower tail, we simply multiply the order statistics by -1 and repeat the calculations. We can also estimate a single pair of ζ and C estimates by redoing the calculations with absolute values of the order statistics.

Confidence intervals and hypothesis tests for ζ and C can be calculated using the results, from Hall (1982), that asymptotically

$$s^{1/2}(\hat{\zeta} - \zeta) \sim N(0, \zeta^2)$$

and

$$s^{1/2}(\ln(T/s))^{-1}(\hat{C}_s - C) \sim N(0, C^2)$$

A hypothesis of particular interest is that of $H_0\!:\!\zeta < 2$ against the alternative $H_1\!:\!\zeta \geq 2$, since, from the parameter's definition, $\zeta = 2$ divides off finite variance distributions – e.g. the student-t and the ARCH process – from infinite variance distributions.

Constancy of the estimated tail indexes can be examined by using the following useful result. Suppose that we obtain estimates $\hat{\zeta}^{(1)}$ and $\hat{\zeta}^{(2)}$ from two independent samples. The statistic

$$Q = \left(\frac{\zeta^{(1)}}{\hat{\zeta}^{(1)}} - 1\right)^2 s_1 + \left(\frac{\zeta^{(2)}}{\hat{\zeta}^{(2)}} - 1\right)^2 s_2$$

where $\zeta^{(1)}$ and $\zeta^{(2)}$ are hypothesised values of the tail index in the two samples, is then asymptotically distributed as χ_2^2. Thus, constancy of the tail index can be assessed in the following way. Suppose the null hypothesis is $H_{0,\alpha}\!:\!\zeta^{(1)} = \zeta^{(2)} = \zeta$ and we wish to test at the 5 per cent significance level. Solving the quadratic equation

$$\left(\frac{\zeta}{\hat{\zeta}^{(1)}} - 1\right)^2 s_1 + \left(\frac{\zeta}{\hat{\zeta}^{(2)}} - 1\right)^2 s_2 - \chi_{2,.05}^2 = 0$$

will then provide the upper and lower bounds for the tail indices that are consistent with the null.

An alternative parameter constancy test is proposed by Loretan and Phillips (1994). If $\hat{\tau}_\zeta = \hat{\zeta}^{(1)} - \hat{\zeta}^{(2)}$ then the statistic

$$V_\zeta = \frac{\hat{\tau}_\zeta^2}{\left(\frac{\hat{\zeta}^{(1)2}}{s_1} + \frac{\hat{\zeta}^{(2)2}}{s_2}\right)}$$

is asymptotically distributed as χ_1^2. A similar statistic is available to test $H_{0,c}\!:$ $C^{(1)} = C^{(2)} = C$ using $\hat{\tau}_C = \hat{C}^{(1)} - \hat{C}^{(2)}$, and these can be used to assess whether the parameters are equal across the right and left tails of the distribution as well as across time periods.

There is some evidence, however, provided by McCulloch (1997), that $\hat{\zeta}$ is an upwardly biased estimate of the true value ζ when the distribution really is stable, so these testing procedures should be used with considerable care.

Given an estimate of the tail index ζ, extreme return levels that are only rarely exceeded can be established by extrapolating the empirical distribution function outside the sample domain, and this can be useful for analysing 'safety first' portfolio selection strategies (see Jansen and de Vries, 1991, and de Haan *et al.*, 1994). A consistent estimate of the 'excess level' $\hat{x}_p$, for which

$$P\left(X_1 \leq \hat{x}_p, X_2 \leq \hat{x}_p, \ldots, X_k \leq \hat{x}_p\right) = 1 - p$$

for small p and given k, is given by

$$\hat{x}_p = \frac{(kr/pT)^{\hat{\gamma}}}{1 - 2^{-\hat{\gamma}}} \left(X_{(T-r)} - X_{(T-2r)}\right) + X_{(T-r)} \tag{7.5}$$

where $\hat{\gamma} = \hat{\zeta}^{-1}$, $r = s/2$, k is the time period considered and p is the 'probability of excess' (see Dekkers and de Haan, 1989). This equation can be 'inverted' to obtain the probability $\hat{p}$ of sustaining a loss of x_p.

7.4 Empirical evidence on tail indices

A number of papers have investigated the tail behaviour of the empirical distribution of foreign exchange rate returns, and, as well as assessing how fat-tailed returns are, they also investigate the stability of the distributions across different regimes (see Koedijk, Schafgans and de Vries, 1990, Hols and de Vries, 1991, Koedijk and Kool, 1992, Koedijk, Stork and de Vries, 1992, and Loretan and Phillips, 1994). The general finding from these papers is that exchange rate returns are fat-tailed but with $\zeta < 4$ and, during a variety of fixed exchange rate regimes, have tail indices that are in the region $1 \leq \zeta \leq 2$. For floating rate regimes, however, ζ tends to exceed two, which is interpreted as suggesting that a float lets exchange rates adjust more smoothly than regimes that involve some amount of fixity. It would also appear that ζ is stable across tails.

Jansen and de Vries (1991), Loretan and Phillips (1994) and de Haan *et al.* (1994) estimate tail indices for US stock and bond market returns, finding that estimates lie in the region $2 < \zeta < 4$, so that, although the distributions

Table 7.2 Point estimates of tail indices

	FT30		
s	Left tail	Right tail	Both tails
25	3.167 (0.633)	3.598 (0.720)	4.377 (0.875)
50	3.138 (0.444)	2.847 (0.403)	3.253 (0.460)
75	3.135 (0.362)	3.028 (0.350)	3.357 (0.385)
100	3.305 (0.330)	3.113 (0.311)	3.082 (0.308)
320	2.937 (0.164)	2.922 (0.163)	3.111 (0.174)
$\hat{s}$	2.887[298] (0.345)	2.918[317] (0.277)	3.024[405] (0.150)

	S&P 500		
s	Left tail	Right tail	Both tails
25	3.192 (0.638)	4.272 (0.854)	4.445 (0.889)
50	3.983 (0.563)	3.062 (0.433)	3.917 (0.554)
75	3.269 (0.373)	3.246 (0.375)	3.672 (0.424)
100	2.966 (0.297)	3.040 (0.304)	3.554 (0.355)
320	2.809 (0.157)	2.625 (0.147)	2.925 (0.163)
$\hat{s}$	2.749[335] (0.150)	2.574[365] (0.135)	2.783[474] (0.128)

Note: $\hat{s}$ optimal estimate of s using $\sigma = 0.6$ and $\tau = 0.9$. Actual value of $\hat{s}$ reported in [] in each column. Standard errors are shown in parentheses.

are fat-tailed, they appear to be characterised by finite variances. Again, estimates of ζ for stock returns are stable across tails and across subperiods. As McCulloch (1997) points out, though, even $\hat{\zeta}$ values well in excess of two could still be consistent with true values of ζ less than two, so these results, while confirming the fat-tailed nature of the returns distributions, cannot be interpreted as conclusively ruling out infinite variances.

Estimates of tail indices for our series are shown in table 7.2. Both return distributions have estimated tail indices (for the 'optimal' setting of the truncation lag) lying in the region $2 < \zeta < 4$, with the left tail indices usually being a little smaller than the right, although not significantly so on the basis of the V_ζ test for constancy across tails (not reported).

Figure 7.2 plots the left tail shapes of the empirical distribution functions of the returns in double-logarithmic coordinates – i.e. it plots $\log_{10} (P(X < -x))$ against $\log_{10} x$ for $x > 0$. In these coordinates the Pareto distribution, for which $P(X < -x) = Dx^{-\zeta}$, where $D = C^\zeta$, appears as a straight line with a slope of $-\zeta$. Straight lines of slopes -2 and -4 are plotted against the empirical tails to facilitate comparison, the former line because it divides off

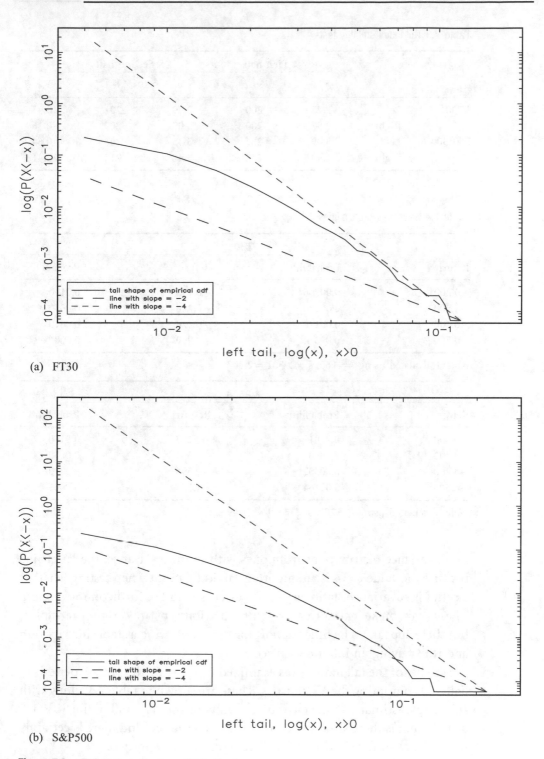

(a) FT30

(b) S&P500

Figure 7.2   Tail shapes of return distributions

Table 7.3 Tail index stability tests

		First half		Second half		
		$\hat{\zeta}$	$\hat{s}$	$\hat{\zeta}$	$\hat{s}$	V_ζ
FT30	Left	2.78	200	2.99	201	0.53
	Right	2.97	200	3.09	203	0.16
S&P 500	Left	3.09	207	3.35	208	0.64
	Right	2.48	236	3.48	219	12.41

Table 7.4 Lower tail probabilities

FT30			
Return	Probability	Return	Probability
−0.200	0.00906	−0.193	0.0100
−0.300	0.00280	−0.246	0.0050
−0.400	0.00122	−0.428	0.0010
−0.500	0.00064	−0.950	0.0001

Note: Calculated using $k = 260$, $\hat{s} = 298$, $\hat{\zeta} = 2.887$.

S&P 500			
Return	Probability	Return	Probability
−0.200	0.02019	−0.258	0.0100
−0.300	0.00665	−0.333	0.0050
−0.400	0.00302	−0.598	0.0010
−0.500	0.00164	−1.383	0.0001

Note: Calculated using $k = 260$, $\hat{s} = 335$, $\hat{\zeta} = 2.749$.

finite variance distributions from ones with infinite variance, the latter line because the value $\zeta = 4$ is an important dividing point when testing whether a series is covariance stationary – as is discussed in the forthcoming section. These again make it clear that the return distributions are certainly fat-tailed, but there appears to be little support for them following a stable distribution and thus having an infinite variance.

Stability of the tail indices was examined by splitting the sample periods in half and computing the V_ζ statistics. These are shown in table 7.3, along with subsample estimates of the tail indices. Only for the right tail of the S&P 500 distribution is there strong evidence of non-constancy, and there is certainly no evidence of the subperiod estimates coming close to two.

Estimates of extreme levels can also be calculated using the formula (7.5), and some calculations are shown in table 7.4. For example, the probability that *within a given year* the FT30 will experience a one-*day* fall of more than 20 per cent is 0.009 – i.e. about once in every 110 years – but for the S&P 500 this probability is 0.02, about once every fifty years.

7.5 Testing for covariance stationarity

As we have seen, the assumption of covariance stationarity, that the unconditional variance and covariances do not depend on time, is central to much of time series econometrics. This assumed constancy of second moments is, however, rarely implied by models of optimising behaviour, which are typically formulated in terms of restrictions on the *conditional* moments, as in the efficient markets hypothesis, or in terms of relationships between conditional moments, as in the CAPM. In financial markets we might reasonably expect that unconditional second moments would not remain constant over long periods of time; for example, information and technology are subject to temporal evolution and can be hypothesised to affect the unconditional variance of assets.

Nonetheless, the assumption of covariance stationarity is a convenient one to make and is frequently employed. For example, a GARCH X_t will be covariance stationary as long as certain conditions are met on the specification of the *conditional* variance. As we demonstrated in chapter 5, for the ARCH(1) process, $\beta < 1$ is required, while general conditions for a GARCH process are given in Bougerol and Picard (1992). Notwithstanding the wide popularity of GARCH models, however, considerable empirical evidence has been accumulated to suggest that *unconditional* second moments of returns data tend not to be constant, thus throwing into doubt the assumption of covariance stationarity.

Mandelbrot (1963a), in arguing that returns have infinite unconditional variance, proposes examining the recursive estimates

$$\hat{\mu}_{2,t} = t^{-1} \sum\nolimits_{j=1}^{t} X_j^2 \qquad t = 1, 2, \ldots, T$$

If $\hat{\mu}_{2,t}$ converges to a constant as T increases, covariance stationarity would seem to be a reasonable assumption, whereas if it wanders around then an infinite variance might be suggested (see also Granger and Orr, 1972). Pagan and Schwert (1990) remark that this idea is equivalent to the cumulative sum of squares test of Brown, Durbin and Evans (1975), but they point out that it assumes that the maintained distribution is normal, which is obviously inappropriate when dealing with series of returns. Pagan and Schwert thus propose using

$$\psi(r) = (T\hat{v})^{-1/2} \sum_{j=1}^{[Tr]} \left(X_j^2 - \hat{\mu}_{2,T} \right)$$

where $0 < r < 1$, $[Tr]$ is the integer part of Tr and

$$\hat{v}^2 = \hat{\gamma}_0 + 2 \sum_{j=1}^{l} (1 - j/(l+1))\hat{\gamma}_j$$

is a kernel-based estimate of the 'long-run' variance of X_t^2, using the covariances $\hat{\gamma}_0, \dots, \hat{\gamma}_l$ of the series.

This statistic is a studentised version of the cumulative sum of squares statistic, since it standardises the partial sums by a sample-based estimate of v^2 rather than its expected value under normality. Inference about $\psi(r)$ depends crucially on the value taken by the tail index ζ of the distribution of X. For $\zeta < 4$ and $T \to \infty$, Loretan and Phillips (1994) show that $\psi(r)$ converges weakly to a Brownian bridge (a tied-down Brownian motion: see chapter 3, section 4), making the probability that $\psi(r) < c$ equal to the probability that a $N(0, r(1-r))$ random variable is less than c.

For $\zeta < 4$, however, $\psi(r)$ converges to a standardised, tied-down stable process. Critical values thus depend in a complicated fashion on ζ, and are tabulated in Loretan and Phillips (1994, table 2). For example, for $\zeta > 4$, the 5 per cent critical value of $\psi(0.9)$ is 0.49, whereas for $\zeta = 2.1$ it is 0.27; nevertheless, while the $\zeta > 4$ 5 per cent critical value of $\psi(0.1)$ is also 0.49, because of the symmetry of the limit distribution, for $\zeta = 2.1$ it is 0.66. Moreover, the test has decreasing power as ζ tends to two from above, since its rate of divergence from the null becomes much slower because of the presence of increasing amounts of outliers. For $\zeta \leq 2$ the test is inconsistent, which is hardly surprising, as in this case variances are infinite anyway.

The entire sequence of $\psi(r)$ values may also be investigated by considering scalar-valued test statistics, for example $\sup_r(\psi(r))$, $\inf_r(\psi(r))$ and $R = \sup_r(\psi(r)) - \inf_r(\psi(r))$, the latter in fact being identical to Lo's (1991) modified rescaled range statistic discussed in chapter 4, section 3. Again, critical values for these statistics are provided in Loretan and Phillips (1994). While we have assumed throughout this section that X_t is strict white noise or, more generally, that it may be generated as the *iid* innovations from an autoregression of an observed series, the above propositions do not depend

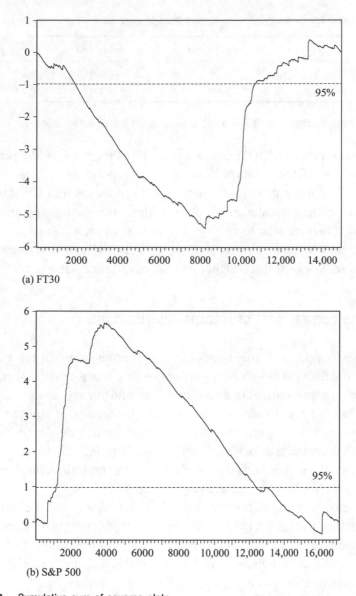

(a) FT30

(b) S&P 500

Figure 7.3   Cumulative sum of squares plots

crucially on this assumption, which may be relaxed considerably. What matters for the purposes of testing for constancy of the unconditional variance is the value taken by the maximal finite moment of X_t, ζ, and in particular whether it exceeds four or not.

Figure 7.3 provides plots of the $\psi(r)$ sequences for the return series. As has been found, both series have tail indices in the range $2 < \zeta < 4$. 95 per cent

Table 7.5 Cumulative sum of squares tests of covariance stationarity

	$\sup_r(\psi(r))$	$\inf_r(\psi(r))$	R
FT30	0.39	-6.44^*	6.83^*
S&P 500	6.60^*	-0.35	6.95^*

Note: * denotes significance at 1 per cent level for all values of $\zeta > 2$.

critical values for $\sup_r(\psi(r))$ decrease from 1.224 for $\zeta > 4$ to 0.98 for $\zeta = 2.1$, the negatives of these values being the corresponding critical values for $\inf_r(\psi(r))$. Appropriate critical values are superimposed on each of the plots. Before computing the statistics, however, the return series were pre-filtered using an autoregression to remove a non-zero mean and any serial correlation. Table 7.5 shows values of $\sup_r(\psi(r))$, $\inf_r(\psi(r))$, and the range statistic R, and these confirm the evidence against covariance stationarity.

7.6 Modelling the central part of returns distributions

We have concentrated attention so far on the tail shape of returns distributions because tail observations are more important from both statistical (e.g. for assessing normality and dispersion, and for regression and Monte Carlo analysis) and financial (e.g. for risk, probability of ruin and option pricing) viewpoints. Until recently, there had been little discussion of the shape of the central part of such distributions. This lack of attention is a little surprising, given that returns distributions are typically characterised by being highly 'peaked' as well as being too fat-tailed.

To overcome some of the problems that accompany stable distributions, Mantegna and Stanley (1994, 1995) have introduced the *truncated* stable distribution, or truncated Lévy flight (TLF). TLFs have central parts of their density function that behave according to a stable distribution, while the tails decline exponentially, as in a normal distribution, rather than according to a power law. In this simple yet appealing way, TLFs maintain all the advantages of the stable distribution in the central part of the density while avoiding the problems of infinite variance and infinite higher moments. TLF processes have the very interesting property of converging to a normal distribution after some scaling interval. Mantegna and Stanley (1995) and Gavridis, Markellos and Mills (1999) have found evidence of TLF processes in high-frequency financial data and that the point where the distribution converges to a normal is around one month. This is consistent with previous studies, which find that returns at intervals longer than one month have distributions that are very close to normal.

The good mathematical properties of truncated Lévy flights allow the application of standard finance theory and the development of analytical solutions (e.g. the option pricing models of Matacz, 2000). If, as suggested by the literature, we accept the point of convergence at around one month, this implies that investors with horizons of one month and longer face Gaussian risks and that conventional risk management and asset pricing is applicable. On the other hand, investors at shorter horizons will face non-Gaussian fat-tailed distributions and must therefore use high-frequency data and non-Gaussian probability tools (e.g. fat-tail estimators and rare event analysis) to quantify their risks.

Mantegna and Stanley (1995) employ a straightforward method to estimate the characteristic exponent, α, of the TLF, which is based on the idea that the scaling behaviour of the probability of a return to the origin scales as Δt^{α}. More specifically, this methodology can be performed using the following three steps.

(i) Calculate logarithmic returns at different sampling frequencies Δt. The lowest frequency of data must be well below the point after which it is suspected that the distribution of returns becomes normal. Since this point is around a month, only data from tick to, say, intervals of a few days should be considered.

(ii) Estimate the probability that returns for each of the intervals Δt equals the mean (origin) – i.e. $P(X = \mu(\Delta t))$, where $\mu(\Delta t)$ is the mean value of X at interval Δt. In practice, X 'equals' the mean if it is within a range of values close to the origin, say within ± 5 per cent.

(iii) Regress the logarithms of the probabilities $P(X = \mu(\Delta t))$ on the logarithms of Δt; (minus) the inverse of the slope estimate from this regression provides an estimate of the characteristic exponent α.

The results from applying this regression procedure to our two returns series are shown in table 7.6, and both series have characteristic exponents that are below two. Of particular interest is the estimate of α for the S&P 500. Mantegna and Stanley (1995) use transactions data on this index for the six-year period from 1984 to 1989 and obtain an estimate of 1.40. With daily data over sixty-four years, we obtain $\hat{\alpha} = 1.42$: a remarkable confirmation of the invariance property of stable distributions.

Recently, the basic TLF model has been extended to develop a number of very flexible stable processes for continuous-time modelling with applications in option pricing. This research exploits the ability of stable distributions to

Table 7.6 Estimates of characteristic exponents from the central part of distributions

	Slope	$\hat{\alpha}$	R^2
FT30	− 0.636	1.573	0.993
S&P 500	− 0.703	1.423	0.980

produce discontinuous variations or jumps, behaviour that is consistent with the crashes and fat tails observed empirically in financial markets. Merton (1976) was the first to propose a jump diffusion model, which augments Brownian motion for returns with a compound Poisson process with jump sizes that are normally distributed. In this manner, the distribution becomes a mixture of normals weighted by Poisson probabilities. The Merton model has since been extended in a variety of ways to allow for alternative jump specifications and finite moments (for a review of this rapidly expanding literature, see Wu, 2006).

7.7 Data-analytic modelling of skewness and kurtosis

So far in this chapter we have concentrated on the fat-tailed and highly peaked characteristics of return distributions and ignored, both theoretically and empirically, the possibility that the distributions may exhibit some degree of skewness. Skewness is important both because of its impact on portfolio choice and because kurtosis is not independent of skewness; the latter may 'induce' the former.

Skewness measures for our series were reported in table 7.1; all are negative and significantly different from zero on using the fact that $\sqrt{(T/6)} \cdot skew \sim N(0, 1)$. We investigate skewness further by constructing plots using the order statistics introduced earlier. The median can be defined as $X_{med} = X_{([T/2])}$. For a symmetric distribution, the order statistics $X_{(p)}$, $X_{(T-p)}$, $p < [T/2]$ are equidistant from the median – i.e.

$$X_{(T-p)} - X_{med} = X_{med} - X_{(T)}$$

so that a plot of the upper-order statistics $X_{(T-p)}$ against the lower statistics $X_{(p)}$ should be linear with a slope of −1 if the distribution is symmetric.

Figure 7.4 shows these 'upper–lower' plots, which suggest that the distributions are symmetric over a wide range of values, with asymmetry appearing only in the tails of the distributions. Interestingly, the asymmetry is characterised by negative skewness, so there is a greater probability of large falls in price than large increases. This is what we would expect from our knowledge of the episodic nature of market 'crashes', but is not what would be expected from three-moment portfolio analysis, in which investors should have a preference for positive skewness, for they should prefer portfolios with a larger probability of very large pay-offs.

Badrinath and Chatterjee (1988, 1991) and Mills (1995) analyse skewness and kurtosis in returns distributions by fitting g, h and $g \times h$ distributions (see Tukey, 1977, and Hoaglin, 1985). These distributions are non-linear transformations of the normal. A g-distributed random variable Y_g is defined as

$$Y_g = A + Bg^{-1}(\exp(gZ) - 1)$$

where $Z \sim N(0,1)$, and is thus a shifted log-normal random variable bounded by $-g^{-1}$. An h-distributed random variable is defined as

$$Y_h = A + BZ \exp(hZ^2/2)$$

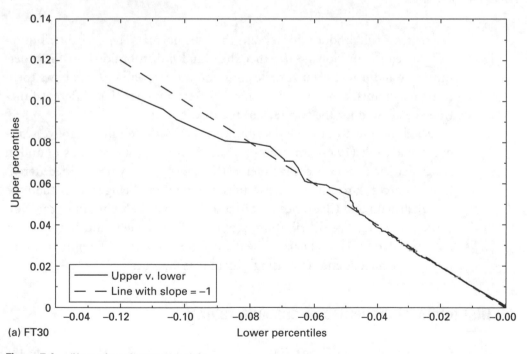

(a) FT30

Figure 7.4   'Upper–lower' symmetry plots

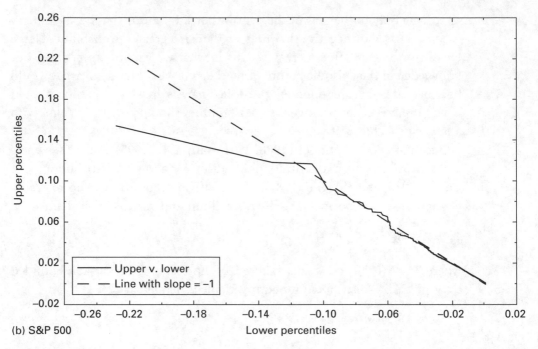

(b) S&P 500

Figure 7.4   (continued)

A positive h will produce thicker tails than the normal. The $g \times h$ distribution is obtained by multiplying together the g and h distributions. In these definitions g and h are assumed to be constant, but Hoaglin (1985) allows them to be polynomial functions of Z^2 and also recommends that different functions be allowed for the two tails of the distribution.

Details of how to fit these distributions may be found in the above references, and Mills (1995), for example, finds that the post-1987 crash London stock market indices are characterised by positive skewness and different levels of excess kurtosis in the two tails, the right tail being thicker than the left. Badrinath and Chatterjee (1988) also find that the right tail of the New York market returns distribution is thicker than the left, and both studies conclude that the central part of the distribution behaves differently from the tails, as we have found here using different techniques.

7.8 Distributional properties of absolute returns

Granger, Spear and Ding (2000) and Mills (1996a, 1997a) investigate the distributional properties of absolute daily returns, the usefulness of such a transformation for measuring risk being discussed in Granger and Ding (1995). The use of absolute returns is suggested by the decomposition

$$X_t = |X_t| \cdot \text{sign } X_t \tag{7.6}$$

where

$$X_t = \begin{cases} 1 & \text{if} & X_t > 0 \\ 0 & \text{if} & X_t = 0 \\ -1 & \text{if} & X_t < 0 \end{cases}$$

Granger, Spear and Ding suggest three distributional properties related to the decomposition (7.6): (i) $|X_t|$ and sign X_t are independent, which will be the case if the conditional distributions $|X_t| | (\text{sign } X_t = 1)$ and $|X_t| | (\text{sign } X_t = -1)$ are the same; (ii) the mean and variance of $|X_t|$ are equal; and (iii) the marginal distribution of $|X_t|$ is exponential after outlier reduction. This will be the case if both conditional distributions are exponential. Note that an exponential distribution with parameter ε has both mean and variance equal to ε, a skewness of two and a kurtosis of nine.

Granger, Spear and Ding (2000) show that all three properties hold for the S&P 500 series, which we confirm here in table 7.7, which reports conditional means and standard deviations of the absolute returns of the FT30 and the S&P 500. We use both the original observations and 'outlier adjusted' data: this was produced by replacing any observation greater than four times the standard deviation (S.D.) by the 4S.D. value having the same sign. We also report the ratio of these statistics plus skewness and kurtosis measures. For each series, these quantities are shown conditionally for $X_t > 0$ and $X_t < 0$ (denoted as $+$ and $-$), together with the frequencies (given in the row labelled 'Probability') of those signs occurring. The number of outliers reduced in each subsample are also reported.

For both returns series there is evidence of asymmetry, in that Prob $(X_t > 0)$ exceeds $\text{Prob}(X_t < 0)$, which obviously reflects their underlying secular drift. The estimated conditional means and standard deviations of the 'outlier adjusted' series are approximately equal, and the skewness and kurtosis measures are close to two and nine, respectively. This suggests that the marginal distributions of the outlier adjusted series are fairly well approximated by an exponential distribution. While formal testing of this hypothesis is inappropriate, as the series are not independent and identically distributed, it is interesting to note that very similar findings have been observed for the post-1987 crash data on the London FTSE 100 and Mid 250

Table 7.7 Properties of marginal return distributions

| | FT30 | | | |
| | Observed | | 'Outlier adjusted' | |
	+	−	+	−
Probability	0.50	0.44	−	−
Mean × 100	0.69	0.73	0.68	0.71
S.D. × 100	0.74	0.78	0.66	0.70
Mean/S.D.	0.93	0.93	1.02	1.01
Skewness	3.55	3.55	2.10	2.01
Kurtosis	26.87	28.76	8.77	8.13
Outliers	−	−	95	50

| | S&P 500 | | | |
| | Observed | | 'Outlier adjusted' | |
	+	−	+	−
Probability	0.52	0.46	−	−
Mean × 100	0.72	0.73	0.71	0.76
S.D. × 100	0.85	0.94	0.74	0.81
Mean/S.D.	0.86	0.82	0.96	0.93
Skewness	4.30	4.82	2.49	2.30
Kurtosis	37.97	59.13	11.13	9.45
Outliers	−	−	138	74

indices (Mills, 1997a). For both series the first property, that $|X_t|$ and sign X_t are independent, is confirmed using a Kolmogorov–Smirnov test. It would thus appear that the properties of absolute returns suggested by Granger and Ding (1995) do indeed hold for this further selection of speculative price series (but see Rydén, Teräsvirta and Åsbrink, 1998, for further research in this area).

Granger, Spear and Ding (2000) argue that, if $|X_t|$ is exponential, then it is reasonable to expect that the pair $|X_t|$, $|X_{t-k}|$, will be jointly exponential. This joint distribution has the properties that the marginal distributions are each exponential and that the conditional mean $E(|X_t|\,||X_{t-k}|)$ is a linear function of $|X_{t-k}|$. This suggests that linear regressions of absolute returns on lagged absolute returns may have some predictive power, although the results presented by Granger, Spear and Ding (2000) and Mills (1996a, 1997a) show that any predictability is quite weak.

7.9 Summary and further extensions

We have surveyed a wide range of techniques for modelling the distribution of financial returns. The 'stylised facts' that come out of both our own empirical analysis and of the others surveyed here may be summarised thus. Returns are certainly not normally distributed but are characterised by fat tails and peakedness, both of which are unsurprising, and negative skewness, which is rather more surprising. It is only in the tails that skewness appears, however, with much of the distribution being symmetric. Although symmetric, this central part of the distribution is not normal but tends to approximate a stable distribution. The tails are not stable, however, but are exponentially declining, being consistent with a finite variance. While having a finite variance, returns do not generally appear to have a constant (unconditional) variance, or, indeed, covariances – covariance stationarity is rejected for all series. Absolute returns, when adjusted for outliers, approximate to an exponential distribution.

These stylised facts suggest two broad areas of further research. The breakdown of covariance stationarity over all but the shortest of sample periods casts doubt on the validity and empirical accuracy of models that assume that the unconditional variance is constant – e.g. ARCH models. This suggests that extensions to time series models that explicitly incorporate error distributions that can effectively model outlier activity and time-varying unconditional variances would be very useful.

The possibility that time series may have infinite variance has been taken into account for certain procedures discussed in earlier chapters. Phillips (1990) considers unit root tests under the assumption of infinite variance errors and shows that the non-parametric tests of chapter 3, section 1.4, continue to operate without any modification. Runde (1997) shows that the asymptotic distribution of the Box–Pierce Q^* statistic, introduced in example 2.1, is no longer χ^2 under an infinite variance assumption. Rather than using Q^*, he proposes scaling it by the factor $T^{(2-\alpha)/\alpha}/(\log T)^{2\alpha}$, and provides simulated critical values for the new statistic. Scaling by this factor will reduce the size of the statistic for typical situations – e.g. $T \leq 10,000$ and $\alpha > 1.5$. Some advances have been made in combining infinite variances with both short- and long-memory ARMA processes (Cioczek-Georges and Taqqu, 1995, and Kokoszka and Taqqu, 1994, 1996), but further research is clearly required.

It is also important that theoretical models of rational economic behaviour continue to be developed that can explain the outlier activity that leads to these common and distinctive distributional properties of financial returns. Some extensions of this type are discussed in McCulloch (1996), for example. Related to this, it is clear that evaluations of models should not rely on tests that are based on normal approximations. For example, trading rules should not be evaluated using tests that assume normal, stationary, and time-independent distributions. The use of bootstrap methodology (see Efron and Tibshirani, 1993) is one possibility, and two examples are Brock, Lakonishok and LeBaron (1992) and Mills (1997b).

Another interesting approach that is receiving increasing attention is the use of non-parametric or data-driven distributions (for a general description, see Silverman, 1986) for approximating the empirical distribution of financial returns. Non-parametric distribution estimation has made use of powerful new technologies, such as bootstrap simulation (Efron and Tibshirani, 1993) and neural networks (Modha and Fainman, 1994). Although most approaches estimate non-parametric distributions on the basis of independence, recent extensions relax this assumption (e.g. the 'moving-blocks' bootstrap). Applications of non-parametric distributions in finance are growing rapidly, and most studies are concerned with problems in econometric analysis and estimation (see Horowitz, 2001).

The overall conclusion from empirical studies of the unconditional distribution of financial returns is that no single parametric model dominates all situations (e.g. for exchange rates, see Boothe and Glassman, 1987; for stock market data, see Kon, 1984). Theoretically, non-normality could be due to a combination of reasons that include non-stationarity, mis-specification and pre-asymptotic behaviour. In finite samples, however, unconditional distributions will always have fatter tails than conditional distributions when the data have some type of conditional dependence, especially if this is non-linear. It must be emphasised that uncorrelatedness of returns is not sufficient to prove independence, especially in view of the unconditional non-normality, since it is possible that non-linear predictabilities exist. Although it may be the case that the normal distribution and the underlying CLT assumptions do not hold for actual returns data and that other distributions offer better fits, one must be wary of atheoretical solutions of convenience. Moreover, if the deviations from normality are highly irregular (e.g. due to outliers, structural breaks, regime switching, etc.) or cannot be isolated from the data, then the normal distribution may provide a relatively good approximation, especially from an out-of-sample perspective.

In many cases the normal distribution will provide a good approximation if returns are independent but not identically distributed. In general, even if the underlying distribution is non-normal, the standard deviation can still be used, provided that there are only small probabilities of extremely high and low returns (see Levy and Markowitz, 1979). Even if second moments are non-constant, these can be measured accurately if the conditional distribution of returns is not too fat-tailed and volatility changes are smooth (Nelson, 1990b). Covariances can be used not only for studying multivariate normal distributions but also for the more general class of joint elliptic distributions. Although statistical inference will be problematic, correlations are also applicable when assessing relationships between stable distributions.

8 Regression techniques for non-integrated financial time series

The analysis of the general linear regression model forms the basis of every standard econometrics text and we see no need to repeat such a development here. Models relating to financial time series, however, often cannot be analysed within the basic framework of ordinary least squares regression, or even its extensions incorporating generalised least squares or instrumental variables techniques. This chapter therefore develops a general theory of regression, based on the original work of Hansen (1982), White (1984) and White and Domowitz (1984), that builds upon the univariate time series techniques of the previous chapters and is applicable to many, but by no means all, of the regression problems that arise in the analysis of the relationships between financial time series.

Section 8.1 thus sets out the basic dynamic linear regression model, while section 8.1 incorporates ARCH error effects into the framework. Misspecification testing is the topic of section 8.3, and section 8.4 discusses robust estimation techniques and generalised method of moments (GMM) estimation, which may be used when the standard assumptions of regression are found to be invalid. The multivariate linear regression model is briefly introduced in section 8.5. This paves the way for more general multivariate regression techniques, and the remaining sections of the chapter deal with vector autoregressions and its various extensions, including a discussion of the concepts of exogeneity and causality.

8.1 Regression models

8.1.1 Regression with non-integrated time series

We now extend our modelling techniques to consider relationships between a group of time series $\{z_t\}$. We begin by analysing the simplest case in which a *single* variable y_t is postulated to be a (linear) function of past values of itself and present and past values of a vector of other variables $\mathbf{x}_t^\top = (x_{1t}, \ldots, x_{kt})$. Here $\mathbf{z}_t = (y_t, \mathbf{x}_t^\top)^\top$ and, for the observed realisation $\{\mathbf{z}_t\}_1^T$, the model can be written as

$$y_t = \alpha_0 + \sum_{i=1}^m \alpha_i y_{t-i} + \sum_{i=0}^m \boldsymbol{\beta}_i \mathbf{x}_{t-i} + u_t, \quad m+1 \le t \le T \tag{8.1}$$

or

$$y_t = \mathbf{X}_t \boldsymbol{\beta} + u_t$$

In matrix form, we have

$$\mathbf{y} = \mathbf{X}\boldsymbol{\beta} + \mathbf{u} \tag{8.2}$$

where

$$\mathbf{y} = (y_{m+1}, \ldots, y_T)^\top$$

$$\mathbf{X} = (\mathbf{X}_{m+1}, \ldots, \mathbf{X}_T)^\top$$

$$\mathbf{X}_t = (1, y_{t-1}, \ldots, y_{t-m}, \mathbf{x}_t^\top, \ldots, \mathbf{x}_{t-m}^\top)$$

$$\mathbf{u} = (u_{m+1}, \ldots, u_T)^\top$$

$$\boldsymbol{\beta} = (\alpha_0, \alpha_1, \ldots, \alpha_m, \boldsymbol{\beta}_0, \ldots, \boldsymbol{\beta}_m)^\top$$

$$\boldsymbol{\beta}_i = (\boldsymbol{\beta}_{i1}, \ldots, \boldsymbol{\beta}_{ik}), \quad i = 0, \ldots, m$$

To estimate the parameters of interest contained in the vector $\boldsymbol{\beta}$, certain assumptions are needed about $\{\mathbf{z}_t\}_1^T$ and the error process $\{u_t\}_1^T$. We begin by assuming that $\{\mathbf{z}_t\}_1^T$ is a normally distributed (weakly) stationary stochastic process. Noting that $\mathbf{z}_t$ is of dimension $k+1$, extending the stationarity requirements for a univariate series given in chapter 2, section 1, to this multivariate setting yields

$$E(\mathbf{z}_t) = \boldsymbol{\mu} = (\mu_y, \mu_1, \ldots, \mu_k)$$

and

$$Cov(\mathbf{z}_t, \mathbf{z}_s) = E(\mathbf{z}_t - \boldsymbol{\mu})(\mathbf{z}_{t-|t-s|} - \boldsymbol{\mu}) = \Gamma(|t - s|), \quad 1 \leq t, s \leq T$$

so that the $\mathbf{z}_t$s have identical means and variances and their temporal covariances depend only on the absolute value of the time difference between them.

Note, however, that the assumption of stationarity alone is not sufficient to obtain an operational model of the form (8.1). This is because the non-zero covariances allow dependence between, for example, $\mathbf{z}_1$ and $\mathbf{z}_T$, implying that the lag length m in (8.1) should strictly be set at $t - 1$, so that the number of unknown parameters in the model increases with T. We thus need to restrict the form of the dependence in $\{\mathbf{z}_t\}_1^T$, and, to this end, the following concepts are important (see White, 1984, and Spanos, 1986, for detailed formal discussion): $\mathbf{z}_t$ is said to be *asymptotically independent* if

$$\Gamma(\tau) \to 0 \quad \text{as} \quad \tau = |t - s| \to \infty$$

and *ergodic* if

$$\lim_{T \to \infty} \left(\frac{1}{T} \sum_{\tau=1}^{T} \Gamma(\tau) \right) = 0$$

It is conventional to make either the assumption of asymptotic independence or the somewhat weaker assumption of ergodicity (cf. the univariate development in chapter 2), and this allows us to restrict the *memory* of the process $\{\mathbf{z}_t\}_1^T$ and hence to fix the maximum lag at an appropriate value – m, say – in (8.1). The error $\{u_t\}_1^T$ is defined formally as

$$u_t = y_t - E\big(y_t | \mathbf{y}_{t-1}^0, \mathbf{x}_t^0\big)$$

where

$$\mathbf{y}_{t-1}^0 = (y_{t-1}, y_{t-2}, \ldots, y_1)$$

and

$$\mathbf{x}_t^0 = (\mathbf{x}_t, \mathbf{x}_{t-1}, \ldots, \mathbf{x}_1)$$

We assume that it satisfies the following properties:

$$E(u_t) = E\big(u_t | \mathbf{y}_{t-1}^0, \mathbf{x}_t^0\big) = 0$$

$$E(u_t u_s) = E\{E(u_t u_s | \mathbf{y}_{t-1}^0, \mathbf{x}_t^0)\} = \begin{cases} \sigma^2 & t = s \\ 0 & t > s \end{cases}$$

These two properties define u_t to be a martingale difference relative to the 'history' $\left(\mathbf{y}_{t-1}^0, \mathbf{x}_t^0\right)$ and to have a finite variance – i.e. it is an *innovation* process. Note that the assumption of asymptotic independence implies that the roots of the polynomial $z^m - \sum_{i=1}^m \alpha_i z^{m-i} = 0$ are all less than unity in absolute value.

Assuming $\mathbf{X}$ to be of full rank $K = (m+1)(k+1)$, so that $\mathbf{X}^\top\mathbf{X}$ is non-singular, and u_t to be $NID(0, \sigma^2)$, the LS (and approximate ML) estimator of $\boldsymbol{\beta}$ obtained using the sample $\{\mathbf{z}_t\}_1^T$ is

$$\hat{\boldsymbol{\beta}}_T = \left(\mathbf{X}^\top\mathbf{X}\right)^{-1}\mathbf{X}^\top\mathbf{y}$$

while the LS and approximate ML estimators of σ^2 are

$$\hat{\sigma}_T^2 = (T - m)^{-1}\hat{\mathbf{u}}^\top\hat{\mathbf{u}}$$

and

$$\tilde{\sigma}_T^2 = T^{-1}\hat{\mathbf{u}}^\top\hat{\mathbf{u}}$$

respectively, where $\hat{\mathbf{u}} = \mathbf{y} - \mathbf{X}\hat{\boldsymbol{\beta}}_T$ is the regression residual vector. (The ML estimators are said to be approximate because the initial conditions involving the observations $y_1, \ldots, y_m$ are ignored.) Since u_t is not independent of future y_ts, $E\left(\mathbf{X}^\top\mathbf{u}\right) \neq \mathbf{0}$, and so $\hat{\boldsymbol{\beta}}_T$ is a biased estimator of $\boldsymbol{\beta}$:

$$E\left(\hat{\boldsymbol{\beta}}_T - \boldsymbol{\beta}\right) = E\left(\left(\mathbf{X}^\top\mathbf{X}\right)^{-1}\mathbf{X}^\top\mathbf{u}\right) \neq \mathbf{0}$$

Nevertheless, assuming $\mathbf{G}_T = E(\mathbf{X}^\top\mathbf{X}/T)$ to be uniformly positive definite and since $E\left(\mathbf{X}_t^\top u_t\right) = \mathbf{0}$, then, under certain conditions concerning the magnitude of $E(\mathbf{X}^\top\mathbf{X})$, $\hat{\boldsymbol{\beta}}_T$ can be shown to be a *strongly consistent* estimator of $\boldsymbol{\beta}$, as indeed is $\hat{\sigma}_T^2$ of σ^2. The estimators are also *asymptotically normal*:

$$\mathbf{G}_T^{-\frac{1}{2}}T^{\frac{1}{2}}\left(\hat{\boldsymbol{\beta}}_T - \boldsymbol{\beta}\right) \overset{a}{\sim} N(\mathbf{0}, \mathbf{I})$$

$$T^{\frac{1}{2}}\left(\hat{\sigma}_T^2 - \sigma^2\right) \overset{a}{\sim} N\left(\mathbf{0}, 2\sigma^4\right)$$

(for formal derivations of these results, see, for example, White, 1984, and Spanos, 1986). $\mathbf{G}_T$ can be consistently estimated in this case as $\hat{\sigma}_T^2\left(\mathbf{X}^\top\mathbf{X}\right)^{-1}$, this being the conventional formula in LS regression.

These results can be extended to allow both $\mathbf{z}_t$ and u_t to exhibit time dependence and heterogeneity simultaneously. Specifically, the memory requirement can be relaxed from that of stationarity and asymptotic independence (or ergodicity) to one of *strong mixing*, as discussed in chapter 3, section 2.3 (see conditions (3.10)). White (1984, exercise 3.51, theorem 4.25) provides a formal statement of the required conditions and shows that, in these circumstances, $\hat{\boldsymbol{\beta}}_T$ is still consistent and asymptotically normal, although we now have

$$\mathbf{D}_T^{-\frac{1}{2}} T^{\frac{1}{2}} \left(\hat{\boldsymbol{\beta}}_T - \boldsymbol{\beta} \right) \overset{a}{\sim} N(\mathbf{0}, \mathbf{I})$$

where

$$\mathbf{D}_T = \left(\mathbf{X}^\top \mathbf{X}/T \right)^{-1} \hat{\mathbf{V}}_T \left(\mathbf{X}^\top \mathbf{X}/T \right)^{-1}$$

$\hat{\mathbf{V}}_T$ is an estimate of $\mathbf{V}_T = E(\mathbf{X}^\top \mathbf{u}\mathbf{u}^\top \mathbf{X}/T)$, which can be expressed in terms of individual observations as

$$\mathbf{V}_T = E\left(T^{-1} \sum_{t=1}^{T} \mathbf{X}_t^\top u_t u_t^\top \mathbf{X}_t \right) = T^{-1} \sum_{t=1}^{T} E\left(\mathbf{X}_t^\top u_t u_t^\top \mathbf{X}_t \right)$$

$$+ T^{-1} \sum_{\tau=1}^{T-1} \sum_{t=\tau+1}^{T} E\left(\mathbf{X}_t^\top u_t u_{t-\tau}^\top \mathbf{X}_{t-\tau} + \mathbf{X}_{t-\tau}^\top u_{t-\tau} u_t^\top \mathbf{X}_t \right)$$

$$= T^{-1} \sum_{t=1}^{T} V\left(\mathbf{X}_t^\top u_t \right)$$

$$+ T^{-1} \sum_{\tau=1}^{T-1} \sum_{t=\tau+1}^{T} \left(Cov\left(\mathbf{X}_t^\top u_t, \mathbf{X}_{t-\tau}^\top u_{t-\tau} \right) + Cov\left(\mathbf{X}_{t-\tau}^\top u_{t-\tau}, \mathbf{X}_t^\top u_t \right) \right)$$

thus revealing that $\mathbf{V}_T$ is the average of the variances of $\mathbf{X}_t^\top u_t$ plus a term that takes account of the covariance between $\mathbf{X}_t^\top u_t$ and $\mathbf{X}_{t-\tau}^\top u_{t-\tau}$ for all t and τ.

With our mixing assumptions, the covariance between $\mathbf{X}_t^\top u_t$ and $\mathbf{X}_{t-\tau}^\top u_{t-\tau}$ goes to zero as $\tau \to \infty$, and hence $\mathbf{V}_T$ can be approximated by

$$\tilde{\mathbf{V}}_T = T^{-1} \sum_{t=1}^{T} E\left(\mathbf{X}_t^\top u_t u_t^\top \mathbf{X}_t \right)$$

$$+ T^{-1} \sum_{\tau=1}^{n} \sum_{t=\tau+1}^{T} E\left(\mathbf{X}_t^\top u_t u_{t-\tau}^\top \mathbf{X}_{t-\tau} + \mathbf{X}_{t-\tau}^\top u_{t-\tau} u_t^\top \mathbf{X}_t \right) \qquad (8.3)$$

for some value n, because the neglected terms (those for which $n < \tau \leq T$) will be small in absolute value if n is sufficiently large.

Note, however, that, if n is simply kept fixed as T grows, the number of neglected terms grows, and may grow in such a way that the sum of these terms does not remain negligible. The estimator $\hat{\mathbf{V}}_T$, obtained by replacing u_t by $\hat{u}_t$ in (8.3), will then be a consistent estimator of $\tilde{\mathbf{V}}_T$ (and hence of $\mathbf{V}_T$) if n does not grow too rapidly as T grows; specifically, we must ensure that n grows more slowly than $T^{\frac{1}{3}}$. Unfortunately, although it is consistent, $\hat{\mathbf{V}}_T$ need not be positive semi-definite in small samples. For this reason, we may use the Newey and West (1987) modified estimator, first introduced in chapter 3, section 2.3, and defined here as

$$
\hat{\mathbf{V}}_T = T^{-1} \sum_{t=1}^{T} \left(\mathbf{X}_t^\top \hat{u}_t \hat{u}_t^\top \mathbf{X}_t \right) + T^{-1} \sum_{\tau=1}^{n} \left(1 - (\tau/(n+1)) \right)
$$
$$
\times \sum_{t=\tau+1}^{T} \left(\mathbf{X}_t^\top \hat{u}_t \hat{u}_{t-\tau}^\top \mathbf{X}_{t-\tau} + \mathbf{X}_{t-\tau}^\top \hat{u}_{t-\tau} \hat{u}_t^\top \mathbf{X}_t \right)
$$

(8.4)

8.1.2 Hypothesis testing

As is traditional, we consider hypotheses that can be expressed as linear combinations of the parameters in $\boldsymbol{\beta}$:

$$\mathbf{R}\boldsymbol{\beta} = \mathbf{r}$$

where $\mathbf{R}$ and $\mathbf{r}$ are a matrix and a vector of known elements, both of row dimension q, that specify the q hypotheses of interest.

Several different approaches can be taken in computing a statistic to test the null hypothesis $\mathbf{R}\boldsymbol{\beta} = \mathbf{r}$ against the alternative $\mathbf{R}\boldsymbol{\beta} \neq \mathbf{r}$; we consider here the use of Wald, Lagrange multiplier and (quasi-)likelihood ratio statistics. Although the approaches to forming the test statistics differ, in each case an underlying asymptotic normality property is exploited to obtain a statistic that is asymptotically distributed as χ^2. Detailed development of the theory of hypothesis testing using these approaches may be found in Godfrey (1988).

The Wald statistic allows the simplest analysis, although it may not be the easiest to compute. Its motivation is the observation that, when the null hypothesis is correct, $\mathbf{R}\hat{\boldsymbol{\beta}}_T$ should be close to $\mathbf{R}\boldsymbol{\beta} = \mathbf{r}$, so that a value of

$\mathbf{R}\hat{\boldsymbol{\beta}}_T - \mathbf{r}$ far from zero should be viewed as evidence against the null hypothesis. To tell how far from zero $\mathbf{R}\hat{\boldsymbol{\beta}}_T - \mathbf{r}$ must be before we reject the null hypothesis, we need to determine its asymptotic distribution. White (1984) shows that, if the rank of $\mathbf{R}$ is $q \leq K$, then the Wald statistic is

$$W_T = T\left(\mathbf{R}\hat{\boldsymbol{\beta}}_T - \mathbf{r}\right)^{\top}\hat{\boldsymbol{\Omega}}_T^{-1}\left(\mathbf{R}\hat{\boldsymbol{\beta}}_T - \mathbf{r}\right) \overset{a}{\sim} \chi_q^2 \qquad (8.5)$$

where

$$\hat{\boldsymbol{\Omega}}_T = \mathbf{R}\mathbf{D}_T\mathbf{R}^{\top} = \mathbf{R}\left(\mathbf{X}^{\top}\mathbf{X}/T\right)^{-1}\hat{\mathbf{V}}_T\left(\mathbf{X}^{\top}\mathbf{X}/T\right)^{-1}\mathbf{R}^{\top}$$

This version of the Wald statistic is useful regardless of the presence of heteroskedasticity or serial correlation in the error $\mathbf{u}$ because a consistent estimator $\hat{\mathbf{V}}_T$ is used to construct $\hat{\boldsymbol{\Omega}}_T$. In the special case where $\mathbf{u}$ is white noise, $\hat{\mathbf{V}}_T$ can be consistently estimated by $\hat{\sigma}_T^2\left(\mathbf{X}^{\top}\mathbf{X}/T\right)$, and the Wald statistic then has the form

$$W_T = T\left(\mathbf{R}\hat{\boldsymbol{\beta}}_T - \mathbf{r}\right)^{\top}\left(\mathbf{R}\left((\mathbf{X}^{\top}\mathbf{X})/T\right)^{-1}\mathbf{R}^{\top}\right)^{-1}\left(\mathbf{R}\hat{\boldsymbol{\beta}}_T - \mathbf{r}\right)\Big/\hat{\sigma}_T^2$$

which is simply q times the standard F-statistic for testing the hypothesis $\mathbf{R}\boldsymbol{\beta} = \mathbf{r}$. The validity of the asymptotic χ_q^2 distribution for this statistic, however, depends crucially on the consistency of the estimator $\hat{\sigma}_T^2\left(\mathbf{X}^{\top}\mathbf{X}/T\right)$ for $\mathbf{V}_T$; if this $\hat{\mathbf{V}}_T$ is not consistent for $\mathbf{V}_T$, the asymptotic distribution of this form for W_T is not χ_q^2, and hence failure to take account of serial correlation and heterogeneity in the errors will lead to inferences being made using an incorrect distribution.

The Wald statistic is the most convenient test to use when the restrictions $\mathbf{R}\boldsymbol{\beta} = \mathbf{r}$ are not easy to impose in estimating $\boldsymbol{\beta}$. When these restrictions can be imposed easily, the Lagrange multiplier statistic is more convenient to compute. The motivation for the LM statistic is that a constrained LS estimator can be obtained by solving the first-order condition of the Lagrangian expression

$$L = (\mathbf{y} - \mathbf{X}\boldsymbol{\beta})^{\top}(\mathbf{y} - \mathbf{X}\boldsymbol{\beta})/T + (\mathbf{R}\boldsymbol{\beta} - \mathbf{r})^{\top}\boldsymbol{\lambda}$$

The Lagrange multipliers $\boldsymbol{\lambda}$ give the shadow price of the constraint, and should therefore be small when the constraint is valid and large otherwise.

The LM test can thus be thought of as testing the hypothesis that $\lambda = 0$. Solving the first-order conditions for λ yields

$$\ddot{\lambda}_T = 2\left(\mathbf{R}(\mathbf{X}^{\top}\mathbf{X}/T)^{-1}\mathbf{R}^{\top}\right)^{-1}\left(\mathbf{R}\hat{\boldsymbol{\beta}}_T - \mathbf{r}\right)$$

so that $\ddot{\lambda}_T$ is simply a non-singular transformation of $\mathbf{R}\hat{\boldsymbol{\beta}}_T - \mathbf{r}$.

Also provided by solving the first-order conditions is the constrained LS estimator $\ddot{\boldsymbol{\beta}}_T$, given by

$$\ddot{\boldsymbol{\beta}}_T = \hat{\boldsymbol{\beta}}_T - (\mathbf{X}^{\top}\mathbf{X}/T)^{-1}\mathbf{R}^{\top}\ddot{\lambda}_T/2$$

from which can be calculated the constrained estimator of σ^2,

$$\ddot{\sigma}_T^2 = (T - m)\ddot{\mathbf{u}}^{\top}\ddot{\mathbf{u}}$$

where $\ddot{\mathbf{u}} = \mathbf{y} - \mathbf{X}\ddot{\boldsymbol{\beta}}_T$ are the residuals from the constrained regression. The LM test statistic is then defined as

$$LM_T = T\ddot{\lambda}_T^{\top}\boldsymbol{\Lambda}_T\ddot{\lambda}_T \overset{a}{\sim} \chi_q^2 \tag{8.6}$$

where

$$\boldsymbol{\Lambda}_T = 4\left(\mathbf{R}(\mathbf{X}^{\top}\mathbf{X}/T)^{-1}\mathbf{R}^{\top}\right)^{-1}\mathbf{R}(\mathbf{X}^{\top}\mathbf{X}/T)^{-1}\ddot{\mathbf{V}}_T(\mathbf{X}^{\top}\mathbf{X}/T)^{-1}\mathbf{R}^{\top}\left(\mathbf{R}(\mathbf{X}^{\top}\mathbf{X}/T)^{-1}\mathbf{R}^{\top}\right)^{-1}$$

$\ddot{\mathbf{V}}_T$ being computed from the constrained regression. Note that the Wald and LM statistics (8.5) and (8.6) would be identical if $\hat{\mathbf{V}}_T$ were used in place of $\ddot{\mathbf{V}}_T$ and, indeed, the two statistics are asymptotically equivalent.

As we have seen, when the errors u_t are $NID(0, \sigma^2)$ the LS estimator $\hat{\boldsymbol{\beta}}_T$ is also the ML estimator. When this is not the case, $\hat{\boldsymbol{\beta}}_T$ is said to be a QML estimator. When $\hat{\boldsymbol{\beta}}_T$ is the ML estimator, hypothesis tests can be based on the *log-likelihood ratio* (here *LR*)

$$LR_T = \log\left(L(\ddot{\boldsymbol{\beta}}_T, \ddot{\sigma}_T)/L(\hat{\boldsymbol{\beta}}_T, \hat{\sigma}_T)\right)$$

where

$$L(\boldsymbol{\beta}, \sigma) = \exp\left(-T\log\sqrt{2\pi} - T\log\sigma - \tfrac{1}{2}\sum_{t=m+1}^{T}(y_t - \mathbf{X}_t\boldsymbol{\beta})^2/\sigma^2\right)$$

is the sample likelihood based on the normality assumption. Simple algebra yields the following alternative form of the statistic,

$$LR_T = (T/2)\ln(\hat{\sigma}_T^2/\ddot{\sigma}_T^2)$$

and it can be shown that $-2LR_T$ is asymptotically equivalent to the Wald statistic (8.5) and thus has a χ_q^2 distribution asymptotically, *provided* that $\hat{\sigma}_T^2(\mathbf{X}^\top\mathbf{X}/T)$ is a consistent estimator of $\mathbf{V}_T$. If this is not true, then $-2LR_T$ is not asymptotically χ_q^2.

So far we have considered linear hypotheses of the form $\mathbf{R}\boldsymbol{\beta} = \mathbf{r}$. In general, non-linear hypotheses can be conveniently represented as

$$H_0: \mathbf{s}(\boldsymbol{\beta}) = \mathbf{0}$$

where $\mathbf{s}$ is a continuously differentiable function of $\boldsymbol{\beta}$. Just as with linear restrictions, we can construct a Wald test based on the asymptotic distribution of $\mathbf{s}(\hat{\boldsymbol{\beta}}_T)$, we can construct an LM test or we can form a log-likelihood ratio. Assuming that the rank of $\Delta\mathbf{s}(\boldsymbol{\beta}) = q \le K$, where $\Delta\mathbf{s}$ is the gradient (derivative) of $\mathbf{s}$, then under $H_0: \mathbf{s}(\boldsymbol{\beta}) = \mathbf{0}$, the Wald and LM test statistics are given by equations (8.5) and (8.6) with $\mathbf{s}(\hat{\boldsymbol{\beta}}_T)$ and $\Delta\mathbf{s}(\hat{\boldsymbol{\beta}}_T)$ replacing $\mathbf{R}\hat{\boldsymbol{\beta}}_T - \mathbf{r}$ and $\mathbf{R}$, respectively, in (8.5) and $\mathbf{s}(\ddot{\boldsymbol{\beta}}_T)$ and $\Delta\mathbf{s}(\ddot{\boldsymbol{\beta}}_T)$ similarly replacing these terms in (8.6).

8.1.3 Instrumental variable estimation

We have so far considered only (ordinary) LS estimation of the model (8.1). If the assumption $E(\mathbf{X}_t^\top u_t) = \mathbf{0}$ does not hold, but a set of l instrumental variables (IVs), say $\mathbf{W}_t = (w_{1t}, \ldots, w_{lt})$, are available such that $E(\mathbf{W}_t^\top u_t) = \mathbf{0}$ and $E(\mathbf{W}^\top\mathbf{X}/T)$ has uniformly full column rank, then we can form the IV estimator

$$\tilde{\boldsymbol{\beta}}_T = (\mathbf{X}^\top\mathbf{W}\hat{\mathbf{P}}_T\mathbf{W}^\top\mathbf{X})^{-1}\mathbf{X}^\top\mathbf{W}\hat{\mathbf{P}}_T\mathbf{W}^\top\mathbf{y}$$

where $\mathbf{W} = (\mathbf{W}_{m+1}, \ldots, \mathbf{W}_T)$ and $\hat{\mathbf{P}}_T$ is a symmetric $l \times l$ positive definite norming matrix. For example, with $\mathbf{W} = \mathbf{X}$ and $\hat{\mathbf{P}}_T = (\mathbf{W}^\top\mathbf{W}/T)^{-1}$, $\tilde{\boldsymbol{\beta}}_T = \hat{\boldsymbol{\beta}}_T$, while, for any $\mathbf{W}$, choosing $\hat{\mathbf{P}}_T = (\mathbf{W}^\top\mathbf{W}/T)^{-1}$ yields the *two-stage least squares* estimator. Analogous to the results for the LS estimator, if $\mathbf{W}_t$ is also mixing, then $\tilde{\boldsymbol{\beta}}_T$ is strongly consistent and

$$\mathbf{D}_T^{-\frac{1}{2}}T^{\frac{1}{2}}(\tilde{\boldsymbol{\beta}}_T - \boldsymbol{\beta}) \overset{a}{\sim} N(\mathbf{0}, \mathbf{I})$$

where now

$$\mathbf{D}_T = \left(\mathbf{X}^\top\mathbf{W}\hat{\mathbf{P}}_T\mathbf{W}^\top\mathbf{X}/T^2\right)^{-1}\left(\mathbf{X}^\top\mathbf{W}/T\right)\hat{\mathbf{P}}_T\hat{\mathbf{V}}_T\hat{\mathbf{P}}_T\left(\mathbf{W}^\top\mathbf{X}/T\right)\left(\mathbf{X}^\top\mathbf{W}\hat{\mathbf{P}}_T\mathbf{W}^\top\mathbf{X}/T^2\right)^{-1}$$

So far we have let $\hat{\mathbf{P}}_T$ be any positive definite matrix. By choosing $\hat{\mathbf{P}}_T = \hat{\mathbf{V}}_T^{-1}$, however, an *asymptotically efficient* estimator is obtained for the class of IV estimators with given instrumental variables $\mathbf{W}$ – i.e.

$$\boldsymbol{\beta}_T^* = \left(\mathbf{X}^\top\mathbf{W}\,\hat{\mathbf{V}}_T^{-1}\mathbf{W}^\top\mathbf{X}\right)^{-1}\mathbf{X}^\top\mathbf{W}\,\hat{\mathbf{V}}_T^{-1}\mathbf{W}^\top\mathbf{y}$$

is asymptotically efficient within the class of IV estimators $\tilde{\boldsymbol{\beta}}_T$.

How should we choose the set of instruments $\mathbf{W}_t$? It can be shown that the asymptotic precision of the IV estimator cannot be worsened by including additional instruments. There are situations, however, when nothing is gained by adding an additional instrument: this is when the additional instrument is uncorrelated with the residuals of the regression of $\mathbf{X}$ on the already included instruments.

When serial correlation or heteroskedasticity of unknown form is present in (8.1), there may, in fact, be no limit to the number of instrumental variables available for improving the efficiency of the IV estimator; functions of $\mathbf{X}$ and $\mathbf{W}$ are possible instruments. In the absence of serial correlation or heteroskedastcity, however, it is possible to specify precisely a finite set of instruments that yield the greatest possible efficiency: they will be those functions of $\mathbf{W}_t$ that appear in the conditional expectation of $\mathbf{X}_t$ given $\mathbf{W}_t$.

8.1.4 Generalised methods of moments estimation

Suppose we have a general, possibly non-linear, model that we can write as $u_t = f(y_t, \mathbf{X}_t, \boldsymbol{\theta})$, where $\boldsymbol{\theta}$ is an $s \times 1$ vector of parameters and u_t can be both serially correlated and heteroskedastic. Our model tells us only that there is some true set of parameters $\boldsymbol{\theta}_0$ for which u_t is orthogonal to a set of instruments $\mathbf{W}_t$, so that

$$E(\mathbf{W}_t u_t) = E(\mathbf{W}_t\, f(y_t, \mathbf{X}_t, \boldsymbol{\theta}_0)) = E(\mathbf{m}(y_t, \mathbf{X}_t, \mathbf{W}_t, \boldsymbol{\theta}_0)) = \mathbf{0}$$

The estimation technique known as generalised methods of moments (Hansen, 1982) focuses on these orthogonality conditions: see Hamilton (1994, chap. 14) and Campbell, Lo and MacKinlay (1997, appendix) for detailed treatments and Johnston and DiNardo (1997, chap. 10) for a textbook discussion.

If we define a vector $\mathbf{m}_T(\boldsymbol{\theta})$ containing the sample averages of the elements of $\mathbf{m}(\ )$,

$$\mathbf{m}_T(\boldsymbol{\theta}) = T^{-1} \sum\nolimits_{t=1}^{T} \mathbf{m}(y_t, \mathbf{X}_t, \mathbf{W}_t, \boldsymbol{\theta})$$

GMM minimises the quadratic form $\mathbf{m}_T(\boldsymbol{\theta})^{\top} \mathbf{A}_T \mathbf{m}_T(\boldsymbol{\theta})$, where $\mathbf{A}_T$ is a weighting matrix, leading to the first-order condition

$$\mathbf{M}_T\left(\hat{\boldsymbol{\theta}}_T\right)^{\top} \mathbf{A}_T \mathbf{M}_T\left(\hat{\boldsymbol{\theta}}_T\right) = \mathbf{0}$$

where

$$\mathbf{M}_T(\boldsymbol{\theta}) = \partial \mathbf{m}_T(\boldsymbol{\theta})/\partial \boldsymbol{\theta}$$

The asymptotic distribution of $\hat{\boldsymbol{\theta}}_T$ is

$$\mathbf{D}_{\mathbf{M},T}^{-\frac{1}{2}} T^{\frac{1}{2}}\left(\hat{\boldsymbol{\theta}}_T - \boldsymbol{\theta}_0\right) \overset{a}{\sim} N(\mathbf{0}, \mathbf{I})$$

where

$$\mathbf{D}_{\mathbf{M},T} = \left(\mathbf{M}_T^{\top} \mathbf{A}_T \mathbf{M}_T\right)^{-1} \mathbf{M}_T^{\top} \mathbf{W} \hat{\mathbf{V}}_{\mathbf{M},T} \mathbf{W}^{\top} \mathbf{M} \left(\mathbf{M}_T^{\top} \mathbf{A}_T \mathbf{M}_T\right)^{-1}$$

with $\hat{\mathbf{V}}_{\mathbf{M},T}$ being defined analogously to $\hat{\mathbf{V}}_T$ in (8.4). As in the IV case discussed in section 8.1.3, an asymptotically efficient estimator of $\hat{\boldsymbol{\theta}}_T$ is obtained by choosing the weighting matrix as $\mathbf{A}_T = \hat{\mathbf{V}}_{\mathbf{M},T}^{-1}$. When $f(y_t, \mathbf{X}_t, \boldsymbol{\theta})$ is linear then it is straightforward to show that the GMM estimator is the IV estimator and, if $\mathbf{W} = \mathbf{X}$, it is the LS estimator.

Example 8.1 Forward exchange rates as optimal predictors of future spot rates.

An important illustration of these estimation techniques is found in the analysis of foreign exchange markets, where the efficient markets hypothesis becomes the proposition that the expected rate of return to speculation in the forward market, conditioned on available information, is zero. Hansen and Hodrick (1980) test this 'simple' efficiency hypothesis in the following way. Let s_t and $f_{t,k}$ be the logarithms of the spot exchange rate and the k-period forward rate determined at time t, respectively. Since $s_{t+k} - f_{t,k}$ is an approximate measure of the rate of return to speculation, the simple efficient markets hypothesis is that

$$f_{t,k} = E(s_{t+k}|\Phi_t)$$

where Φ_t is the information set available at time t. This implies that the speculative rate of return, $y_{t+k} = S_{t+k} - f_{t,k}$, should be uncorrelated with information available at time t; for example, in the regression of the return on a constant and two lagged returns

$$y_{t+k} = \alpha_0 + \alpha_1 y_t + \alpha_2 y_{t-1} + u_{t+k}$$

the α_is, $i = 0, 1, 2$, should all be zero. Assuming that s_t and $f_{t,k}$, and hence y_t, are mixing and that $E(y_{t-j}u_{t+k}) = 0$ for $j \geq 0$, which is easily verified, LS estimation provides consistent estimates of the α_is.

In the present circumstances, however, the forecast error $u_{t+k} = y_{t+k} - E(y_{t+k}|\Phi_t)$ will be serially correlated, so the usual estimated covariance matrix will be inconsistent.

This serial correlation arises from the fact that the realised values of the spot exchange rate $s_{t+1}, s_{t+2}, \ldots, s_{t+k}$ are not known when the forward rate $f_{t,k}$ is set at time t, so that the corresponding k-period ahead forecast errors $u_{t+k-j} = s_{t+k-j} - f_{t-j,k}$, $j = 1, 2, \ldots, k-1$, are not observable. Since u_{t+1}, $u_{t+2}, \ldots, u_{t+k-1}$ are not part of the available information set, we cannot rule out the possibility that $E(u_{t+k}|u_{t+k-j}) \neq 0$, $1 \leq j \leq k-1$ or that

$$Cov(u_{t+k}, u_{t+k-j}) \neq 0, \quad j = 1, 2, \ldots, k-1$$

On the other hand, the preceding k-period forecast errors u_{t+k-j} for $j \geq k$ *are* observable. Efficiency thus requires $E(u_{t+k}|u_{t+k-j}) = 0$, $j \geq k$, and hence

$$Cov(u_{t+k}, u_{t+k-j}) = 0, \quad j \geq k$$

With our mixing assumptions concerning s_t and $f_{t,k}$, $u_{t+k} = s_{t+k} - f_{t,k}$ will also be mixing, and combining the above covariances shows that the forecast errors can be thought of as being generated by an MA($k-1$) process.

Can we use generalised least squares procedures to make inferences about the α_is? The answer is 'no', because such techniques require the regressors to be *strictly exogenous*, which means that $E(u_{t+k}|\ldots, y_{t-1}, y_t, y_{t+1}, \ldots) = 0$, i.e. that future y values would be useless in determining the optimal forecast for y_{t+k} (strict, and other forms of, exogeneity are formally discussed in section 8.5). This is clearly inappropriate, as such values would provide useful information for forecasting future rates of return. The use of regressors that are not strictly exogenous renders GLS techniques inconsistent, because the transformation used to eliminate the serial correlation in the residuals makes the transformed residuals for some particular period linear combinations of the original residuals and their lagged values. These, in turn, are likely to be correlated with the transformed data for the same period, since these include current values of the variables in the information set.

One way of avoiding these difficulties is to choose the sampling interval to equal the forecast interval, i.e. to set $k = 1$, in which case the forecast errors will be serially uncorrelated. This procedure of using *non-overlapping* data clearly does not make use of all the available information: $T(1 - k^{-1})$ observations are sacrificed. In the present application weekly observations are typically used with k set at thirteen (three-month forward exchange rates being readily available). Using non-overlapping data – i.e. sampling only every thirteen weeks – would thus throw away over 90 per cent of the available observations.

The complete data set can be used if we adjust the covariance matrix of $\hat{\beta} = (\hat{\alpha}_0, \hat{\alpha}_1, \hat{\alpha}_2)^\top$ in the appropriate fashion. As we have shown, a consistent covariance matrix is

$$\mathbf{D}_T = \left(\mathbf{X}^\top\mathbf{X}/T\right)^{-1}\hat{\mathbf{V}}_T\left(\mathbf{X}^\top\mathbf{X}/T\right)^{-1}$$

where now the columns making up the $\mathbf{X}$ matrix contain a constant and the two lagged values of y_{t+k}. In this application we have available an explicit expression for $\hat{\mathbf{V}}_T$, namely $\hat{\mathbf{V}}_T = T^{-1}\mathbf{X}^\top\hat{\mathbf{\Theta}}\mathbf{X}$, where, from the fact that the residuals $\hat{u}_{t+k}$ follow an MA($k - 1$) process, the elements of the $T \times T$ symmetric matrix $\hat{\mathbf{\Theta}}$ have the form

$$\hat{\Theta}_{i,i+j} = R(j), \quad i = 1, 2, \ldots, T - k + 1, \quad j = 0, 1, \ldots, k - 1$$

$$\hat{\Theta}_{i+j,i} = \hat{\Theta}_{i,i+j}$$

where

$$R(j) = T^{-1}\sum_{t=j+1}^{T}\hat{u}_{t+k}\hat{u}_{t+k-j}$$

and $\hat{\Theta}_{i,j} = 0$ otherwise – i.e. $\hat{\mathbf{\Theta}}$ is 'band diagonal', the bandwidth being $2k - 1$.

The hypothesis of market efficiency is $\boldsymbol{\beta} = 0$ and, in the framework of section 8.1.2, $\mathbf{R} = \mathbf{I}_3$, $\mathbf{r} = 0$ and $\hat{\boldsymbol{\Omega}}_T = \mathbf{D}_T$. The Wald statistic, for example, for testing this hypothesis takes the form

$$W_T = T\hat{\boldsymbol{\beta}}_T^\top \mathbf{D}_T^{-1} \hat{\boldsymbol{\beta}}_T \overset{a}{\sim} \chi_3^2$$

Hansen and Hodrick (1980) estimate regressions of this type for weekly data on spot and three-month ($k = 13$) forward exchange rates for seven currencies (expressed in US cents per unit of foreign currency) from March 1973 to January 1979, and for three currencies relative to the pound sterling for certain episodes after the First World War, in this case using one-month ($k = 4$) forward rates. Their findings indicate that the simple efficiency hypothesis is 'suspect' in both periods, but they offer a variety of reasons why this may be so, emphasising that rejection of the hypothesis $\boldsymbol{\beta} = 0$ cannot necessarily be identified with inefficiency in the foreign exchange market, as certain intertemporal asset allocation and risk considerations are ignored in this formulation of the efficient markets hypothesis.

8.2 ARCH-in-mean regression models

8.2.1 The GARCH-M model

The estimation techniques developed above are applicable when little is known about the structure of the serial correlation and heteroskedasticity present in the errors in model (8.1). On certain occasions, however, it may be possible to specify the form of these departures from white noise, and a specification that has proved to be particularly useful in financial applications is the *(G)ARCH-in-mean*, or GARCH-M, model proposed by Engle, Lilien and Robbins (1987), and employed initially by Domowitz and Hakkio (1985) for examining risk premia in the foreign exchange market and by French, Schwert and Stambaugh (1987) to model stock return volatility.

Bollerslev, Chou and Kroner (1992) provide many further references to early GARCH-M applications in finance, these often being attempts to model the linear relationship that emerges as a consequence of the intertemporal CAPM of Merton (1973, 1980). Unfortunately, although most asset pricing models imply that conditional excess market returns should be proportional to the market conditional variance, empirical evidence using various formulations of the GARCH-M model has been far from conclusive (see, for example, the studies cited by Li *et al.*, 2005).

The GARCH-M model extends the GARCH family developed in chapter 5, section 5, to the regression framework of equation (8.1):

$$y_t = \alpha_0 + \sum_{i=1}^{m} \alpha_i y_{t-i} + \sum_{i=0}^{m} \beta_i \mathbf{x}_{t-i} + \delta \sigma_t^\lambda + u_t \qquad (8.7)$$

$$u_t = \varepsilon_t - \sum_{i=1}^{n} \theta_i \varepsilon_{t-i} \qquad (8.8)$$

$$E\left(\varepsilon_t^2 | \Phi_{t-1}\right) = \sigma_t^2 = \gamma_0 + \sum_{i=1}^{p} \gamma_i \varepsilon_{t-i}^2 + \sum_{i=1}^{q} \phi_i h_{t-i} + \vartheta \xi_t \qquad (8.9)$$

Here we allow the serially correlated errors u_t to be modelled as an MA(n) process (equation (8.8)), and the conditional variance σ_t^2 (conditional upon the information set at time $t-1$, Φ_{t-1}) enters the 'mean' equation (8.7) and depends itself (equation (8.9) upon a vector of explanatory variables ξ_t. Typically, λ is set at one or two, so that either the conditional standard deviation or variance is included in the mean equation. Under the assumption that the ε_t are $NID(0, \sigma^2)$, QML estimates of the GARCH-M model given by equations (8.7) to (8.9) can be obtained by maximising the likelihood function using, for example, the BHHH algorithm analogous to that discussed in chapter 5, section 5.5.

There are some complications, however. For example, the information matrix is no longer block diagonal, so that all parameters must be estimated simultaneously, unlike the GARCH set-up, where the block diagonality of the information matrix allows estimates of the parameters of the mean and conditional variance equations to be obtained from separate iterations. Simulation evidence provided by Dotsis and Markellos (2007) on the finite sample properties of ML estimates of GARCH-M parameters suggests that biases are likely to occur even for sample sizes as large as 3000 observations. Moreover, the parameters that reflect the strength of association between returns and conditional variances are subject to the most severe biases.

If it is preferred, the alternative assumption that the ε_t follow a stand-ardised t-distribution may be employed to allow more adequate modelling of the fat tails often found in the observed unconditional distributions of financial time series. Baillie and Bollerslev (1989), for example, provide the relevant expression for the log-likelihood function.

The standard theory used to justify a relationship between returns and the conditional variance implies a linear functional form. It has been sug-gested, however, that this relationship could take any shape (see Backus and Gregory, 1993). Motivated by this, attempts have been made to derive semi-parametric GARCH-M models, in which the conditional variance is modelled using a GARCH process while the conditional mean is estimated non-parametrically using a flexible specification (see, for example, Linton and Perron, 2003). Li *et al.* (2005) derive a test for the existence of GARCH-M effects that allows for a flexible semi-parametric specification of the conditional variance process.

Example 8.2 Stock returns and volatility

Recalling the GARCH models fitted to the daily returns of the S&P 500 index in example 5.6, we now fit a GARCH-M model of the form (with the return series now denoted y_t)

$$y_t = \alpha_0 + \delta\sigma_t + u_t$$

$$u_t = \varepsilon_t - \theta_1\varepsilon_{t-1}$$

$$E\big(\varepsilon_t^2|\Phi_{t-1}\big) = \sigma_t^2 = \gamma_0 + \gamma_1\varepsilon_{t-1}^2 + \phi_1 h_{t-1} + \phi_2 h_{t-2}$$

i.e. the conditional standard deviation is included as a regressor in the mean equation of the previously fitted MA(1)-GARCH(1,2) model. QML estimation produces the following model, with robust *t*-statistics in parentheses:

$$y_t = \underset{(8.71)}{0.0729}\,\sigma_t + \varepsilon_t + \underset{(17.5)}{0.137}\,\varepsilon_{t-1}$$

$$\sigma_t^2 = \underset{(6.76)}{0.89{\times}10^{-6}} + \underset{(11.13)}{0.104}\,\varepsilon_{t-1} + \underset{(5.42)}{0.598}\,\sigma_{t-1}^2 + \underset{(2.87)}{0.294}\,\sigma_{t-2}^2$$

$$\hat{\upsilon} = 5.89(24.04)$$

The inclusion of σ_t in the returns equation is an attempt to incorporate a measure of risk into the returns-generating process and is an implication of the 'mean-variance hypothesis' underlying many theoretical asset pricing models, such as the intertemporal CAPM discussed above. Under this hypothesis, δ should be positive, and this is found to be the case, so that large values for the conditional variance are expected to be associated with large returns. The MA(1) error may capture the effect of non-synchronous trading and is highly significant. As before, the GARCH parameters sum to almost unity, indicating IGARCH behaviour and high persistence in the conditional variance. Similar models have been estimated by French, Schwert and Stambaugh (1987) for daily *excess* returns, defined to be the market return minus the risk-free interest rate.

Example 8.3 Conditional variance and the risk premium in the foreign exchange market

The evidence provided by Hansen and Hodrick (1980) for the rejection of the 'simple' efficiency hypothesis in foreign exchange markets, which was discussed in example 8.1, finds that rejection was often due to the intercept α_0 being non-zero. This finding could be regarded as evidence of a risk premium, the presence of which would allow the forward rate to be a biased predictor of the future spot rate without sacrificing the notion of market efficiency. Of course, for this to be plausible, we must have an empirically tractable theory of a risk premium, for without such a theory there is no way of empirically distinguishing between an inefficient market and a, perhaps time-varying, risk premium.

Although several theoretical models have been proposed that generate a risk premium in the foreign exchange market, it has been found to be extremely difficult to translate them into testable econometric models, and, consequently, their empirical performance provides only weak support for a time-varying risk premium. Domowitz and Hakkio (1985) therefore present a GARCH-M generalisation of the model used in example 8.1 to investigate the possible presence of a risk premium that depends on the conditional variance of the forecast errors. From example 8.1, the efficiency hypothesis states that the forward rate at time t, $f_{t,1}$, is an unbiased predictor of the future spot rate, s_{t+1}, where, as before, logarithms are used, but where we now set the forecast period at $k = 1$ for convenience. Thus,

$$s_{t+1} - f_{t,1} = u_{t+1}$$

where u_{t+1} is the one-period forecast error, which should be zero-mean white noise under the efficiency hypothesis.

This can equivalently be written as

$$\Delta s_{t+1} = \left(f_{t,1} - s_t \right) + u_{t+1}$$

which is then regarded as a restricted case of the GARCH-M model of equations (8.7) to (8.9) with $y_t = \Delta s_t$ and $\mathbf{x}_t = \left(f_{t-1,1} - s_{t-1} \right)$. The restrictions are $m = r = 0$, so that no lagged y's or $\mathbf{x}$'s appear in the equation for y_t and that the forecast error is serially uncorrelated, and $\beta_0 = 1$, so that forecasts are unbiased. Maintaining $\beta_0 = 1$ and u_t to be white noise, then $\alpha_0 \neq 0$ and $\delta = 0$ implies a non-zero but constant risk premium, while $\alpha_0 \neq 0$ and $\delta \neq 0$ implies a time-varying risk premium.

The risk premium is given by $\alpha_0 + \delta \sigma_t^2$ (assuming $\lambda = 2$ for convenience), and thus any change in it is due solely to changes in the conditional variance σ_t^2; it can, nevertheless, be positive or negative and can switch signs, depending on the values of α_0 and δ. For example, if $\alpha_0 \neq 0$ and $\delta \neq 0$, then for small forecast errors the risk premium will be negative (long positions in foreign currency require an expected loss), while for large forecast errors the risk premium may turn positive (long positions in forward foreign currency require an expected profit).

The model was fitted, with σ_t^2 assumed to follow an ARCH(4) process, to non-overlapping monthly data from June 1973 to August 1982 for five exchange rates vis-à-vis the US dollar: those of the United Kingdom, France, Germany, Japan and Switzerland. The null hypothesis of no risk premium ($\alpha_0 = 0$, $\beta_0 = 1$, and $\delta = 0$) could be rejected for the United Kingdom and Japan, but not for France, Germany or Switzerland, although for this last currency it is only because the standard error of $\hat{\beta}_0$ is so large that the null cannot be rejected, for the point estimate of β_0 is -1.092!

8.2.2 GARCH option pricing models

Stochastic volatility and GARCH models have begun to be used in option pricing. Stochastic volatility has not been very popular in practice since the models are difficult to implement and test. GARCH models, as we have shown, have a well-defined theoretical framework and the significant advantage that options can be priced solely on the basis of historical spot asset returns, without necessarily resorting to option market data. Moreover, the diffusion limits of GARCH models encompass many of the well-known stochastic volatility models: see, for example, Nelson (1990b) and, for a review of this literature, Christoffersen and Jacobs (2004). In most of the approaches that have been proposed, once the GARCH model is estimated, option pricing involves tedious numerical approximations through simulation or series expansions. A practical approach has been developed by Heston and Nandi (2000), who propose a closed-form option pricing model where spot asset returns follow a GARCH-M process.

For the GARCH(1,1)-M case, the conditional mean equation for the logarithmic returns is given by

$$y_t = r_f + \kappa_t - 0.5\sigma_t + \sqrt{\sigma_t}u_t$$

where r_f is the risk-free rate, $\kappa_t = (\lambda + 0.5)\sigma_t$ is a predictable risk premium and u_t is a standard normal disturbance. The conditional variance of the returns is governed by the following equation:

$$\sigma_t^2 = \gamma_0 + \gamma_1(\varepsilon_{t-1} - \delta\sigma_t)^2 + \phi\sigma_{t-1}^2$$

The specification is very similar to that of the non-linear asymmetric GARCH model of Engle and Ng (1993). The variance process remains stationary with finite mean and variance as long as $\phi + \gamma_1\delta^2 < 1$. The kurtosis of the returns distribution is determined by γ_1, and when this is zero we obtain a deterministic time-varying variance. The parameter δ controls the asymmetric effect of the disturbances, but the model is not fully consistent with the leverage effect as the quadratic specification of the GARCH process cannot generate a negative relationship between 'good news' and volatility (see Yu, 2005). By making appropriate transformations, Heston and Nandi (2000) use the characteristic function of the logarithm of the spot price to derive their option pricing formula.

Duan, Gauthier and Simonato (1999) employ Edgeworth expansions to derive an analytical approximation for European option pricing that assumes a similar process to that above for the conditional variance:

$$\sigma_t^2 = \gamma_0 + \gamma_1\sigma_{t-1}(\varepsilon_{t-1} - \delta)^2 + \phi\sigma_{t-1}^2$$

In this case, the risk premium in the conditional mean equation is assumed to be $\kappa_t = \lambda\sigma^2$. The non-negative parameter δ is likely to capture the negative relationship between returns and volatility. The remaining parameters must remain positive to ensure the positivity of the conditional variance. The stationarity condition for the variance is $\gamma_1(1 + \delta^2) + \phi < 1$, while the unconditional variance is given by $\gamma_1/(1 - \gamma_1(1 + \delta^2) - \phi)$. Note that, when the conditional variance follows a simple GARCH(1, 1) process, it can be shown that this model converges at higher sampling frequencies to the CIR continuous-time process, and the corresponding option pricing model to that of Heston (1993).

The use of GARCH parameter estimates in place of the true but unknown parameters in option pricing formulae gives rise to an 'estimation risk' problem, since the estimates of the parameters will also affect the estimate of the corresponding option price. An additional complication arises from the fact that even an unbiased estimate of the variance will not necessarily produce an unbiased estimate of the option price, since option pricing models are highly non-linear with respect to the variance. Dotsis and Markellos (2007) study the behavior of the Heston and Nandi (2000) option pricing model when the GARCH parameters are estimated via ML in finite samples. Although they find that the GARCH estimates contain significant biases even with samples of three years of daily data, the unconditional variance estimates are found to be relatively unbiased. In terms of option pricing, large over-pricing appears only for short-term, out-of-the-money option configurations, and Dotsis and Markellos show that jackknife resampling is an effective method for reducing bias. Reviews of the rapidly expanding literature on the econometric and empirical issues involved in option pricing are given by Garcia, Ghysels and Renault (2007) and Bates (2003).

8.3 Misspecification testing

The regression techniques developed in section 8.1 are based on the assumption that the model (8.1) is correctly specified – i.e. that the assumptions underlying the model are valid. If they are not, then some of the techniques can be invalidated. It is important therefore to be able to test these assumptions: such tests are known as *misspecification tests*, and we begin their development by rewriting (8.1) as

$$
\begin{aligned}
y_t &= \alpha_0 + \boldsymbol{\beta}_0 \mathbf{x}_t + \sum_{i=1}^{m} \left(\alpha_i y_{t-i} + \boldsymbol{\beta}_i \mathbf{x}_{t-i} \right) + u_t \\
&= \alpha_0 + \boldsymbol{\beta}_0 \mathbf{x}_t + \sum_{i=1}^{m} \boldsymbol{\beta}_i^* \mathbf{z}_{t-i} + u_t
\end{aligned}
\tag{8.10}
$$

where $\boldsymbol{\beta}_i^* = (\alpha_i, \boldsymbol{\beta}_i)$, so that $\boldsymbol{\beta} = (\boldsymbol{\beta}_0^*, \boldsymbol{\beta}_1^*, \dots, \boldsymbol{\beta}_m^*)$.

8.3.1 Choosing the maximum lag, m

The estimation theory developed in section 8.1 is based on the assumption that the maximum lag, m, is known. If this is so, then the assumption of mixing, which lets the errors u_t exhibit both serial correlation and heterogeneity, still allows the LS estimate $\hat{\boldsymbol{\beta}}_T$ to be consistent and asymptotically normal, although the associated covariance matrix is $\mathbf{D}_T = \left(\mathbf{X}^\top \mathbf{X} / T \right)^{-1} \hat{\mathbf{V}}_T \left(\mathbf{X}^\top \mathbf{X} / T \right)^{-1}$, where the expression for $\hat{\mathbf{V}}_T$ is given by equation (8.4). If m is chosen to be larger than its optimum but unknown value m^*, $\hat{\boldsymbol{\beta}}_T$ will still be consistent and asymptotically normal, but multicollinearity problems will often arise. This is because, as m increases, the same observed data $\{\mathbf{z}_t\}_1^T$ are required to provide more and more information about an increasing number of unknown parameters.

If, on the other hand, m is chosen to be 'too small', then the omitted lagged $\mathbf{z}_t$s will form part of the error term. If we assume that for the correct lag length m^*, u_t is a martingale difference, then the error term in the misspecified model will no longer be non-systematic relative to $\left(\mathbf{y}_{t-1}^0, \mathbf{x}_t^0\right)$ and hence will not be a martingale difference. This has the implication that $\hat{\boldsymbol{\beta}}_T$ and $\hat{\sigma}_T$ are no longer consistent or asymptotically normal, and, because of this, it is important to be able to test for $m < m^*$. Given that the 'true' model is

$$y_t = \alpha_0 + \boldsymbol{\beta}_0 \mathbf{x}_t + \sum_{i=1}^{m^*} \boldsymbol{\beta}_i^* \mathbf{z}_{t-i} + u_t$$

the error term in the misspecified model can be written as

$$u_t^* = u_t + \sum_{i=m+1}^{m^*} \boldsymbol{\beta}_i^* \mathbf{z}_{t-i}$$

This implies that $m < m^*$ can be tested using the null hypothesis $H_0 : \boldsymbol{\beta}_{m+1}^* = \ldots = \boldsymbol{\beta}_{m^*}^* = \mathbf{0}$. The Wald statistic for testing this null against the alternative that at least one of the vectors $\boldsymbol{\beta}_i^*$, $m+1 \leq i \leq m^*$, is non-zero is $q = (m^* - m)(k+1)$ times the standard F-statistic based on a comparison of the residual sums of squares from the regressions with the maximum lag length set at m and m^* respectively. The asymptotically equivalent LM statistic can be computed as $T \cdot R^2$ from the auxiliary regression of $\hat{u}_t^*$ on $\mathbf{x}_t, \mathbf{z}_{t-1}, \ldots, \mathbf{z}_{t-m^*}$, where the $\hat{u}_t^*$ are the residuals from the estimation of (8.10). Both the Wald and LM tests will be asymptotically χ_q^2.

The above analysis has assumed that, for the correct lag length m^*, u_t is a martingale difference. One consequence of incorrectly setting m to be less than m^* is that the residuals from the regression (8.10) will be serially correlated. An alternative LM test is $T \cdot R^2$ from the regression of $\hat{u}_t^*$ on $\mathbf{x}_t, \mathbf{z}_{t-1}, \ldots, \mathbf{z}_{t-m^*}$ and $\hat{u}_{t-1}^*, \ldots, \hat{u}_{t-m+m^*}^*$, which will be asymptotically $\chi_{m^*-m}^2$. This is strictly a test of residual serial correlation, and only an indirect test of lag length specification, but it points to the difficulty of distinguishing whether residual serial correlation is a consequence of an incorrect (too small) setting of the lag length m

or whether m is correct but, nevertheless, the error term is serially correlated. As we have seen, in the former case $\hat{\beta}_T$ will be inconsistent, whereas in the latter it will be consistent and asymptotically normal. For detailed discussion of this important distinction, see Spanos (1986).

8.3.2 Testing for normality, linearity and homoskedasticity

Although the assumption that the errors in (8.10) are normally distributed is not a crucial one in the context of the asymptotic theory developed in 8.1, its invalidity can have an important affect on LS estimates in finite samples; since chapter 7 has shown that many financial time series are observed to be non-normal, it is important to examine this normality assumption in regression applications. A popular test proposed by Jarque and Bera (1980) measures departures from normality in terms of the third and fourth moments – i.e. the skewness and kurtosis – of the residuals $\hat{u}_t$ from estimation of (8.10). Letting μ_3 and μ_4 be the third and fourth (central) moments of u_t, and defining $m_3 = (\mu_3/\sigma^3)$ and $m_4 = (\mu_4/\sigma^4)$ to be the moment measures of skewness and kurtosis, respectively, estimators of these measures are given by

$$\hat{m}_i = \left(T^{-1} \sum \hat{u}_t^i\right) \Big/ \left(T^{-1} \sum \hat{u}_t^2\right)^{1/2}, \quad i = 3, 4$$

The asymptotic distributions of these estimators under the null hypothesis of normality are

$$T^{\frac{1}{2}}\hat{m}_3 \overset{a}{\sim} N(0, 6)$$
$$T^{\frac{1}{2}}(\hat{m}_4 - 3) \overset{a}{\sim} N(0, 24)$$

and, since they are also asymptotically independent, the squares of their standardised forms can be added to obtain

$$\frac{T}{6}\hat{m}_3^2 + \frac{T}{24}(\hat{m}_4 - 3)^2 \overset{a}{\sim} \chi_2^2$$

so that large values of this statistic would flag significant departures from normality.

The model (8.10) assumes that the conditional mean $E\left(y_t | \mathbf{y}_{t-1}^0, \mathbf{x}_t^0\right)$ is linear in $\mathbf{X}_t$. To test this assumption we may consider the null hypothesis

$$H_0 : \mu_{yt} = E\left(y_t | \mathbf{y}_{t-1}^0, \mathbf{x}_t^0\right) = \mathbf{X}_t\boldsymbol{\beta}$$

which needs to be tested against the non-linear alternative

$$H_1 : \mu_{yt} = h(\mathbf{X}_t)$$

If $h(\cdot)$ is assumed to take the form

$$h(\mathbf{X}_t) = \mathbf{X}_t \Xi + c_2 \mu_{yt}^2 + c_3 \mu_{yt}^3 + \ldots + c_n \mu_{yt}^n$$

then Ramsey's (1969) RESET test for linearity is based on testing $H_0 : c_2 = c_3 = \ldots = c_n = 0$ against $H_1 : c_i \neq 0$, $i = 2, \ldots, n$. Its LM version is based on the auxiliary regression of $\hat{u}_t$ on $\mathbf{x}_t$, $\mathbf{z}_{t-1}, \ldots, \mathbf{z}_{t-m}$ and $\hat{\mu}_{yt}^2, \ldots, \hat{\mu}_{yt}^n$, where $\hat{\mu}_{yt} = \hat{y}_t = \mathbf{X}_t \hat{\boldsymbol{\beta}}_T$, so that $T \cdot R^2$ is asymptotically distributed as χ_n^2. If non-linearities are encountered then non-linear regression techniques will be required; these are developed in White and Domowitz (1984) and analysed in detail in Gallant and White (1988).

To test for departures from homoskedasticity (assuming no serial correlation), we may consider constructing a test based on the difference

$$\left(\mathbf{X}^\top \boldsymbol{\Omega} \mathbf{X}\right) - \sigma^2 \left(\mathbf{X}^\top \mathbf{X}\right)$$

where $\boldsymbol{\Omega} = \mathrm{diag}\left(\sigma_{m+1}^2, \sigma_{m+2}^2, \ldots, \sigma_T^2\right)$. This can be expressed in the form

$$\sum_{t=m+1}^{T} \left(E\left(u_t^2\right) - \sigma^2\right) \mathbf{X}_t \mathbf{X}_t^\top$$

and a test for heteroskedasticity could be based on the statistic

$$T^{-1} \sum_{t=m+1}^{T} \left(\hat{u}_t^2 - \hat{\sigma}_T^2\right) \mathbf{X}_t \mathbf{X}_t^\top$$

Given that this is symmetric, we can express the $\frac{1}{2}K(K-1)$, where again $K = (m+1)(k+1)$, different elements in the form

$$T^{-1} \sum_{t=m+1}^{T} \left(\hat{u}_t^2 - \hat{\sigma}_T^2\right) \boldsymbol{\Psi}_t \qquad (8.11)$$

where

$$\boldsymbol{\Psi}_t = \left(\psi_{1t}, \psi_{2t}, \ldots, \psi_{Jt}\right)^\top, \qquad \psi_{lt} = x_{it} x_{jt},$$
$$i \geq j, \; i, j = 2, \ldots, k, \quad l = 1, 2, \ldots, J, \quad J = \tfrac{1}{2}K(K-1)$$

the x_{it} being columns of $\mathbf{X}_t$. Although a test statistic can be based on (8.11), an asymptotically equivalent LM test (White, 1980) is the $T \cdot R^2$ statistic computed from the auxiliary regression of $\hat{u}_t^2$ on a constant and $\psi_{1t}, \ldots, \psi_{Jt}$, which is asymptotically distributed as χ_J^2. Note, however, that the constant in the original regression (8.10) should not be involved in defining the ψ_{lt}s in the auxiliary regression, since the inclusion of such regressors would lead to perfect multicollinearity.

This test, of course, does not propose any alternative form of heteroskedasticity. If such information is available – for example, that the errors follow an ARCH process – then tests specifically tailored to the alternative can be constructed. In the ARCH case the appropriate LM test is $T \cdot R^2$ from the regression of $\hat{u}_t^2$ on a constant and lags of $\hat{u}_t^2$ (cf. the testing of ARCH in chapter 5, section 5.6).

8.3.3 Parameter stability

Throughout this analysis we have assumed that the parameter vector $\boldsymbol{\beta}$ is *time-invariant*. Evidence has accumulated that this may be a rather heroic assumption in many regression applications in finance: see, for example, the references and results in Coutts, Roberts and Mills (1997). Parameter instability may occur in many different forms, and testing for departures from parameter time invariance is not straightforward. One approach is to use *recursive* and *rolling* estimates of the parameters to assess stability. A recursive least squares procedure estimates the parameters over an increasing sequence of samples $m+1, \ldots, t, \tau + m + k + 1 < t \leq T$, yielding the recursive estimates $\hat{\boldsymbol{\beta}}^{(t)}$ for $t = \tau + m + k + 1, \ldots, T$, where τ is chosen to provide an adequate number of degrees of freedom when starting the recursion. Note that, by definition, $\hat{\boldsymbol{\beta}}^{(T)} = \hat{\boldsymbol{\beta}}_T$. The *recursive residuals* are defined as $v_t = u_{t|t-1}/f_t$, where the *prediction error* $u_{t|t-1}$ is defined as

$$u_{t|t-1} = y_t - \mathbf{X}_{t-1} \boldsymbol{\beta}^{(t-1)}$$

and

$$f_t^2 = 1 + \mathbf{X}_t^\top \left(\mathbf{X}_{(t-1)}^\top \mathbf{X}_{(t-1)} \right)^{-1} \mathbf{X}_t$$

where $\mathbf{X}_{(t)} = (\mathbf{X}_{m+1}, \ldots, \mathbf{X}_t)$.

Subsample estimates may also be constructed; these may be denoted as $\hat{\beta}^{(t_1, t_2)}$ when the estimation period is from t_1 to t_2. When the estimation period is sequentially incremented by one observation, then sequences of rolling regressions with estimation window $t_1 - t_2 + 1$ are obtained.

All these estimates may be used to examine whether the parameters of (8.10) are stable. Plots of the recursive and rolling regression coefficients are simple to construct and are often very informative, but there are also a range of formal test statistics available. For example, the cumulative sum of squares (CUSUMSQ) statistic, originally proposed by Brown, Durbin and Evans (1975) and defined as

$$S_t = \sum_{i=\tau_1}^{t} v_i^2 \bigg/ \sum_{i=\tau_1}^{T} v_i^2, \quad \tau_1 = \tau + m + k + 2$$

provides a simple test of parameter stability. If S_t lies outside the range $c_0 \pm t/(T-2)$, where c_0 depends on the chosen level of significance, then there is evidence of some form of parameter instability. Edgerton and Wells (1994) have provided a range of critical values for the statistic, as well as an algorithm for calculating probability values. Although Krämer and Ploberger (1990) highlight the poor power properties of the CUSUMSQ test against structural change, it does have good properties against heteroskedasticity. This is important here, because if the parameters of (8.10) are time-varying but are estimated as being constant, as is implied by LS, then the residuals will be heteroskedastic. Thus, a test for heteroskedasticity may also be interpreted as a test for parameter constancy. Similarly, parameter instability may also lead to serial correlation in the recursive residuals, so that portmanteau statistics may be calculated using the v_t.

Ploberger, Krämer and Kontrus (1989) consider a test based on recursive coefficients rather than on recursive residuals. Their *fluctuation* test is defined as

$$max\left(\frac{t}{\hat{\sigma}T} \left\| (\mathbf{X}^\top \mathbf{X})^{\frac{1}{2}} (\hat{\beta}^{(t)} - \hat{\beta}_T) \right\| \right)$$

and critical values are provided in their table 8.1.

Following Dufour (1982), the recursive residuals can also be used to explore parameter instability within an auxiliary regression framework. For example, regressing v_t on $\mathbf{x}_t$ provides a general exploratory test, whereas regressing v_t on sets of dummy variables defined to represent periods of possible instability provides more specific tests of parameter constancy. If specific break points are hypothesised, then versions of the traditional Chow (1960) test may be computed: for details, see, for example, Hendry and Doornik (2006). A test that may be used without selecting explicit break points is that proposed by Hansen (1992), which is discussed in Johnston and DiNardo (1997, chap. 4). We emphasise that the tests discussed here are by no means exhaustive, having been chosen primarily because of their popularity and ease of computation (which are certainly not independent choices, of course). Many other tests have been proposed over the years: Chu, Hornik and Kuan (1995), for example, have provided further tests and Perron (2006) gives a recent and detailed survey.

Example 8.4 Testing the CAPM

The CAPM is an important asset pricing theory in financial economics and has been the subject of considerable econometric research. An excellent exposition of the derivation of the model, which, as we have noted earlier, postulates a linear relationship between the expected risk and return of holding a portfolio of financial assets, can be found in Berndt (1991, chap. 2), who also considers many of the econometric issues involved in the empirical implementation of the model.

The simple linear relationship between a small portfolio's return, r_p, and its associated risk, measured by the standard deviation of returns, σ_p, can be written as

$$r_p - r_f = (\sigma_p/\sigma_m) \cdot (r_m - r_f) \tag{8.12}$$

where r_m and σ_m are the returns on the overall market portfolio and the standard deviation of such returns, respectively, and r_f is the return on a risk-free asset. The term $r_p - r_f$ is thus the risk premium for portfolio p, while $r_m - r_f$ is the overall market's risk premium. Denoting these risk premia as y and x, respectively, letting $\beta = \sigma_p/\sigma_m$, and adding an intercept term α and a stochastic error term u, the latter reflecting the effects of specific (unsystematic) and diversifiable risk, the CAPM becomes the simple linear regression

$$y = \alpha + \beta x + u \tag{8.13}$$

The LS estimate of the slope coefficient β is $\hat{\beta} = Cov(x, y)/V(x)$, which is equivalent to σ_{pm}/σ_m^2, where σ_{pm} is the covariance between portfolio p and the market portfolio; this is known as the 'investment beta' for portfolio p, and measures the sensitivity of the return on the portfolio to variation in the returns on the market portfolio. Portfolios having $\hat{\beta}$s in excess of unity are thus relatively risky, while those with $\hat{\beta}$s less than unity are much less sensitive to market movements.

LS estimation of the CAPM regression from observed time series $\{y_t, x_t\}_1^T$ is, of course, trivial. In this time series context, however, the underlying CAPM theory requires certain assumptions to hold. Specifically, we must assume that the risk premia are stationary, normally distributed and serially uncorrelated, in which case the error process $\{u_t\}_1^T$ will be normally and independently distributed (NID). Note also that the intercept α has been included without any justification, for it does not appear in the original CAPM expression (8.12). The CAPM theory thus provides the testable hypothesis $\alpha = 0$, along with the following implications: the residuals of the regression (8.13) should be serially uncorrelated, homoskedastic and normal, the systematic relationship between y and x should be linear, and the estimate of β should be time-invariant.

The empirical performance of the CAPM was investigated using the data set provided by Berndt (1991, chap. 2), which contains monthly returns from January 1978 to December 1987 on seventeen US companies plus a monthly risk-free return. Treating each company's risk premia, calculated as the difference between the company return and the risk-free return, as a separate portfolio enabled seventeen CAPM regressions of the form (8.13) to be estimated, and these are reported in table 8.1.

Only three of the estimated regressions survive the battery of misspecification tests unscathed: those for CONED, DELTA and MOTOR (see Berndt, 1991, for the actual companies associated with these variable names). Little evidence of serial correlation or non-linearity is found in the residuals but, rather, more evidence of heteroskedasticity, non-normality and parameter non-constancy is encountered. Standard errors calculated using (8.3) have a tendency to be larger than their OLS counterparts for betas, but smaller for intercepts, although the differences are usually quite small. Those regressions that exhibited significant ARCH were estimated with GARCH errors, but little change was found in the coefficients of the mean equation. GARCH-M extensions were found to be unnecessary in all cases.

Example 8.5 Further modelling of the FTA All Share index
In example 2.6 we fitted an ARMA(2,2) process to the logarithmic changes of the FTA All Share index, which we now denote as Δp_t. Mills

Table 8.1 Estimates of the CAPM regression (7.13)

Company	$\hat{\alpha}$	$\hat{\beta}$	R^2	dw	Non-lin	Norm	Het	ARCH	Chow
BOISE	0.0031	0.94	0.43	2.17	2.95	4.72	9.57*	8.69*	2.69
	(0.0068)	(0.10)							
	[0.0053]	[0.13]							
CITCRP	0.0025	0.67	0.32	1.84	0.40	1.20	10.33*	2.50	6.44*
	(0.0062)	(0.09)							
	[0.0058]	[0.14]							
CONED	0.0110	0.09	0.02	2.15	0.74	1.12	0.20	5.04	0.05
	(0.0046)	(0.07)							
	[0.0036]	[0.06]							
CONTIL	-0.0132	0.73	0.11	2.07	0.45	2245*	0.37	0.06	2.56
	(0.0131)	(0.19)							
	[0.0128]	[0.24]							
DATGEN	-0.0067	1.03	0.31	2.08	7.20*	5.03	3.21	0.15	1.89
	(0.0098)	(0.14)							
	[0.0094]	[0.19]							
DEC	0.0068	0.85	0.34	2.14	0.72	9.23*	0.66	16.03*	5.67
	(0.0074)	(0.11)							
	[0.0066]	[0.13]							
DELTA	0.0014	0.49	0.12	1.99	0.01	2.55	0.43	2.46	3.67
	(0.0083)	(0.12)							
	[0.0082]	[0.15]							
GENMIL	0.0078	0.27	0.08	2.08	0.14	2.64	0.94	2.16	14.90*
	(0.0058)	(0.08)							
	[0.0050]	[0.10]							
GERBER	0.0051	0.63	0.24	2.25	8.38*	7.14*	0.27	1.72	6.62*
	(0.0071)	(0.10)							
	[0.0065]	[0.11]							
IBM	-0.0005	0.46	0.28	1.88	0.06	1.14	0.17	3.06	6.68*
	(0.0046)	(0.07)							
	[0.0054]	[0.07]							

MOBIL	0.0042	0.72	0.37	2.09	0.55	34.6*	6.93*	1.68	0.29
	(0.0059)	(0.09)							
	[0.0051]	[0.09]							
MOTOR	0.0069	0.10	0.01	1.86	0.90	2.23	0.97	0.73	2.05
	(0.0083)	(0.12)							
	[0.0077]	[0.10]							
PANAM	-0.0086	0.74	0.15	2.21	0.51	10.9*	2.52	4.46	0.14
	(0.0112)	(0.16)							
	[0.0103]	[0.15]							
PSNH	-0.0126	0.21	0.02	1.88	0.25	92.5*	1.64	10.46*	0.03
	(0.0100)	(0.15)							
	[0.0105]	[0.10]							
TANDY	0.0107	1.05	0.32	1.89	3.27	6.13*	2.76	0.66	0.13
	(0.0097)	(0.14)							
	[0.0100]	[0.14]							
TEXACO	0.0007	0.61	0.28	2.02	0.00	127.5*	2.59	3.10	0.14
	(0.0062)	(0.09)							
	[0.0049]	[0.10]							
WEYER	-0.0031	0.82	0.43	2.29*	1.76	1.44	15.07*	9.97*	9.88*
	(0.0059)	(0.09)							
	[0.0046]	[0.10]							
Asymptotic distribution					χ^2_1	χ^2_2	χ^2_2	χ^2_3	χ^2_2
Critical 0.05 value				1.72	3.84	5.99	5.99	7.81	5.99
				2.28					

Notes:
* = significant at 0.05 level.

(. . .) = conventional standard error; [. . .] = Newey–West (1987) standard error from (8.4).

dw = Durbin–Watson statistic.

Non-lin = Ramsey's (1969) RESET test for functional form, calculated from the regression of $\hat{u}_t$ on x_t and $\hat{y}_t^2$.

$Norm$ = Jarque–Bera (1980) test for normality.

Het = test for heteroskedasticity, calculated from the regression of $\hat{u}_t^2$ on a constant, $\hat{y}_t$ and $\hat{y}_t^2$.

$Chow$ = Chow's (1960) test for coefficient stability; break point taken to be December 1984.

Table 8.2 Estimates of the FTA All Share index regression (8.14)

1	Δp_{-1}	Δp_{-2}	Δp_{-3}	$\Delta r20$	$\Delta r20_{-1}$	$\Delta r20_{-2}$	$\Delta r20_{-3}$
−0.0035	0.515	0.114	0.072	−0.409	0.180	0.005	0.009
(0.0013)	(0.048)	(0.053)	(0.047)	(0.076)	(0.038)	(0.039)	(0.039)
[0.0016]	[0.067]	[0.075]	[0.051]	[0.106]	[0.046]	[0.042]	[0.039]

Δd	Δd_{-1}	Δd_{-2}	Δd_{-3}	R^2	$\hat{\sigma}$	W_{487}
0.820	0.172	0.070	−0.012	0.787	0.0273	3.55
(0.021)	(0.043)	(0.043)	(0.022)			
[0.043]	[0.058]	[0.052]	[0.019]			

Notes:
$(\dots)$ = conventional standard error; $[\dots]$ = Newey–West standard error.
W_{487} = Wald statistic (8.5) computed using $T = 487$ observations; there are $q = 6$ restrictions, and hence it is asymptotically distributed as χ_6^2, the 5 per cent critical value being 12.59.

(1991a) finds evidence that Δp_t is related to the logarithmic changes in long interest rates and dividends, and we therefore investigate the extended regression model

$$\Delta p_t = \alpha_0 + \sum_{i=1}^{3} \alpha_i \Delta p_{t-i} + \sum_{i=0}^{3} \beta_{1i} \Delta r20_{t-i} + \sum_{i=0}^{3} \beta_{2i} \Delta d_{t-i} + u_t \qquad (8.14)$$

Here $r20_t$ and d_t are the logarithms of twenty-year gilts and the dividend index, respectively, so that $k = 2$, and the lag length is set at $m = 3$, although this could be selected using an information criterion, by an obvious extension to the discussion in example 2.3. Unit root tests confirm that both series are $I(1)$, hence their appearance in first-differenced form.

Estimates of this model are presented in table 8.2, where it is seen that many of the coefficients are insignificant, particularly when measured against the Newey–West (1987) standard errors, computed using (8.4) with $n = 5$. The following set of hypotheses was therefore tested:

$$\alpha_{13} = 0$$
$$\beta_{11} = \beta_{12} = \beta_{13} = 0$$
$$\beta_{22} = \beta_{23} = 0$$

The Wald statistic reported in table 8.2 shows that this joint hypothesis cannot be rejected, the associated marginal significance level being 0.74, and estimation of the restricted equation yields

$$\Delta p_t = -\underset{[0.0014]}{0.0035} + \underset{[0.063]}{0.534}\,\Delta p_{t-1} + \underset{[0.055]}{0.166}\,\Delta p_{t-2}$$

$$-\underset{[0.044]}{0.181}\,\Delta r20_t + \underset{[0.042]}{0.817}\,\Delta d_t + \underset{[0.054]}{0.156}\,\Delta d_{t-2}$$

$$R^2 = 0.786, \quad \hat{\sigma} = 0.0271$$

The current change in the gilt yield enters negatively, reflecting the well known trade-off between the equity and gilt markets in the United Kingdom, while the current and lagged changes in the dividend yield enter positively.

The additional regressors reduce the residual standard error over the univariate model (see example 2.6, but note the rescaling of the standard error), but, as both contain contemporaneous terms, they are of little use in forecasting and, of course, beg the question of whether they can be regarded as exogenous – a question we return to later.

8.4 Robust estimation

As we have seen from the above examples, and from the variety of results presented in, for example, Coutts, Mills and Roberts (1994) and Mills and Coutts (1996), the non-normality of residuals may be a common occurence, being typically caused by the presence of some abnormally large outliers. Non-normality, per se, may not have important consequences theoretically, since, although LS estimators are no longer asymptotically efficient, they nevertheless remain unbiased and consistent, and standard hypothesis tests are still asymptotically χ^2. The power of such tests can be extremely sensitive to departures from normality and can lack robustness, however, in the sense that the finite sample distribution can be altered dramatically when the distribution of the error is altered only slightly (see Koenker, 1982).

Moreover, if the error variance is infinite, LS estimators lose their minimum variance property, and, since it is then impossible to obtain a meaningful estimate of the variance, conventional hypothesis tests can be very misleading. The strong likelihood of non-normal, and possibly infinite variance, errors has therefore led to the development of alternative estimation procedures that, relative to LS, place less weight on outliers, and these are generally known as *robust* estimators.

A wide variety of robust estimators have been proposed, and we will concentrate here on methods based on regression *quantiles*: for financial applications, see, for example, Tomczyk and Chatterjee (1984), Chan and Lakonishok (1992) and Mills and Coutts (1996), and, for a general textbook treatment, see Rousseeuw and Leroy (2003). The regression quantile family of estimators is based on minimising the criterion function

$$\sum_t \rho_\theta(u_t)$$

where, for $0 < \theta < 1$,

$$\rho_\theta(u_t) = \begin{cases} \theta|u_t| & \text{if } u_t \geq 0 \\ (1-\theta)|u_t| & \text{if } u_t < 0 \end{cases}$$

Since $r_\theta(u_t)$ is a weighted sum of the absolute values of the residuals, outliers are given less importance than under a squared residual criterion. When $\theta = 0.5$ the least absolute errors (LAE) estimator is obtained, whereas, more generally, large (small) values of θ attach a heavy penalty to observations with large positive (negative) residuals. For example, for a given value of θ, a bivariate regression line passes through at least two observations, with at most $T\theta$ observations lying below the line and at least $(T-2)\theta$ observations lying above it.

Varying θ between zero and one yields a set of 'regression quantile' estimators $\hat{\beta}(\theta)$ – for example, the LAE estimator is $\hat{\beta}(0.5)$. The effect of large outlying observations will tend to be concentrated in the regression quantiles corresponding to extreme values of θ, while the behaviour of the sample observations will determine how the regression quantiles change as θ varies. Consequently, a variety of estimators have been proposed that combine several regression quantiles – for example, the trimean (TRM):

$$\hat{\beta}_{\text{TRM}} = 0.25\hat{\beta}(0.25) + 0.5\hat{\beta}(0.5) + 0.25\hat{\beta}(0.75)$$

The regression quantiles can also be combined in the form of a *trimmed* regression quantile (TRQ) estimator,

$$\hat{\beta}_\phi = (1 - 2\phi)^{-1} \int_\phi^{1-\phi} \hat{\beta}(\theta)\,d\theta$$

where $0 < \phi < 0.5$. This estimator is obtained by computing $\hat{\beta}(\phi)$ and $\hat{\beta}(1 - \phi)$, excluding all observations lying on or below the ϕth regression quantile line and all those lying above the $(1 - \phi)$th quantile line, and applying OLS to the remaining observations. It can thus be interpreted as a 'trimmed least squares' estimator (Ruppert and Carroll, 1980). All these estimators can be shown to produce asymptotically normal estimators of β,

Table 8.3 Robust estimates of the CAPM regression

	CONTIL		DEC	
	$\hat{\alpha}$	$\hat{\beta}$	$\hat{\alpha}$	$\hat{\beta}$
OLS	−0.013 (0.013)	0.73 (0.19)	0.007 (0.007)	0.85 (0.11)
LAE	−0.013 (0.008)	0.67 (0.11)	0.007 (0.009)	0.74 (0.13)
TRM	−0.017 (0.004)	0.66 (0.05)	0.005 (0.004)	0.77 (0.06)
TRQ($\phi = 0.1$)	−0.018 (0.007)	0.62 (0.11)	0.005 (0.007)	0.71 (0.10)
TRQ($\phi = 0.2$)	−0.017 (0.008)	0.63 (0.11)	0.004 (0.008)	0.78 (0.11)

	GERBER		MOBIL	
	$\hat{\alpha}$	$\hat{\beta}$	$\hat{\alpha}$	$\hat{\beta}$
OLS	0.005 (0.007)	0.63 (0.10)	0.004 (0.006)	0.72 (0.09)
LAE	−0.008 (0.009)	0.57 (0.14)	0.004 (0.007)	0.59 (0.10)
TRM	−0.001 (0.004)	0.57 (0.06)	0.003 (0.003)	0.63 (0.04)
TRQ($\phi = 0.1$)	−0.001 (0.007)	0.58 (0.10)	0.002 (0.006)	0.64 (0.08)
TRQ($\phi = 0.2$)	−0.002 (0.007)	0.58 (0.10)	0.002 (0.006)	0.60 (0.09)

	PANAM		PSNH	
	$\hat{\alpha}$	$\hat{\beta}$	$\hat{\alpha}$	$\hat{\beta}$
OLS	−0.009 (0.011)	0.74 (0.16)	−0.013 (0.010)	0.21 (0.15)
LAE	−0.019 (0.009)	0.60 (0.13)	−0.007 (0.006)	0.21 (0.09)
TRM	−0.013 (0.006)	0.68 (0.08)	−0.009 (0.005)	0.24 (0.07)
TRQ($\phi = 0.1$)	−0.010 (0.011)	0.65 (0.16)	−0.008 (0.008)	0.19 (0.11)
TRQ($\phi = 0.2$)	−0.012 (0.010)	0.65 (0.14)	−0.008 (0.006)	0.24 (0.09)

	TANDY		TEXACO	
	$\hat{\alpha}$	$\hat{\beta}$	$\hat{\alpha}$	$\hat{\beta}$
OLS	0.011 (0.010)	1.05 (0.14)	0.001 (0.006)	0.61 (0.09)
LAE	0.004 (0.013)	0.96 (0.18)	−0.002 (0.006)	0.54 (0.09)
TRM	0.008 (0.005)	0.94 (0.08)	−0.002 (0.003)	0.58 (0.05)
TRQ($\phi = 0.1$)	0.007 (0.010)	0.99 (0.14)	−0.002 (0.005)	0.55 (0.08)
TRQ($\phi = 0.2$)	0.008 (0.010)	0.95 (0.15)	−0.002 (0.005)	0.57 (0.07)

with appropriate covariance matrices given in, for example, Judge *et al.* (1985, chap. 20), where a detailed treatment of robust estimators in econometrics in general can be found.

Example 8.6 Robust estimation of the CAPM

The eight CAPM regressions found to have significant non-normality in example 8.4 were re-estimated using four robust techniques: LAE, TRM, and

TRQ with the trimming parameter set at $\phi = 0.1$ and 0.2. These estimates, along with the OLS estimates for comparison, are reported in table 8.3. In seven of the regressions the robust beta estimators are consistently smaller than the OLS, while for the eighth, that of PSNH, the standard errors are sufficiently smaller to render the estimates significant. A similar pattern occurs for the estimates of α: for all except PSNH the robust estimates are smaller than the OLS. Moreover, some of the estimates even become significantly different from zero. Interestingly, only for PSNH are the OLS residuals negatively skewed. These findings are consistent with, for example, Mills and Coutts (1996), who also found that robust beta estimates for the industry baskets of the London Stock Exchange's 350 index were smaller than their OLS counterparts.

8.5 The multivariate linear regression model

An immediate extension of the regression model (8.1) is to replace the 'dependent' variable y_t by a vector, say $\mathbf{y}_t = (y_{1t}, \ldots, y_{nt})^\top$, so that we now have the *multivariate (dynamic) regression model*

$$\mathbf{y}_t = \mathbf{C} + \sum_{i=1}^{m} \mathbf{A}_i^\top \mathbf{y}_{t-i} + \sum_{i=0}^{m} \mathbf{B}_i^\top \mathbf{x}_{t-i} + \mathbf{u}_t, \quad m+1 \leq t \leq T \qquad (8.15)$$

where $\mathbf{C}$ is an $n \times 1$ vector of constants, $\mathbf{A}_1, \ldots, A_m$ are $n \times n$ matrices of lag coefficients, $\mathbf{B}_0, \mathbf{B}_1, \ldots, \mathbf{B}_m$ are $k \times n$ coefficient matrices and $\mathbf{u}_t$ is an $n \times 1$ vector of errors having the properties

$$E(\mathbf{u}_t) = E(\mathbf{u}_t | \mathbf{Y}_{t-1}^0, \mathbf{x}_t^0) = \mathbf{0}$$

and

$$E(\mathbf{u}_t \mathbf{u}_s^\top) = E(\mathbf{u}_t \mathbf{u}_s^\top | \mathbf{Y}_{t-1}^0, \mathbf{x}_t^0) = \begin{cases} \mathbf{\Omega} & t = s \\ \mathbf{0} & t \neq s \end{cases}$$

where

$$\mathbf{Y}_{t-1}^0 = (\mathbf{y}_{t-1}, \mathbf{y}_{t-2}, \ldots, \mathbf{y}_1)$$

In matrix form, we have

$$\mathbf{Y} = \mathbf{X}^* \mathbf{B} + \mathbf{U}$$

where

$$\mathbf{Y} = \left(\mathbf{y}_{m+1}, \ldots, \mathbf{y}_T\right)^\top$$
$$\mathbf{X}^* = \left(\mathbf{X}^*_{m+1}, \ldots, \mathbf{X}^*_T\right)^\top$$
$$\mathbf{X}^*_t = \left(1, \mathbf{y}_{t-1}, \ldots, \mathbf{y}_{t-m}, \mathbf{x}_t^\top, \ldots, \mathbf{x}_{t-m}^\top\right)$$
$$\mathbf{U} = \left(\mathbf{u}_{m+1}, \ldots, \mathbf{u}_T\right)^\top$$

and

$$\mathbf{B} = \left(\mathbf{C}^\top, \mathbf{A}_1^\top, \ldots, \mathbf{A}_m^\top, \mathbf{B}_0^\top, \ldots, \mathbf{B}_m^\top\right)$$

The estimation theory for this model is basically a multivariate extension of that developed for the univariate case ($n = 1$) above. For example, the LS and (approximate) ML estimator of $\mathbf{B}$ is

$$\hat{\mathbf{B}} = \left(\mathbf{X}^{*\top}\mathbf{X}^*\right)^{-1}\mathbf{X}^{*\top}\mathbf{Y}$$

while the ML estimator of Ω is

$$\hat{\Omega} = T^{-1}\hat{\mathbf{U}}^\top\hat{\mathbf{U}}, \qquad \hat{\mathbf{U}} = \mathbf{Y} - \mathbf{X}^{*\top}\hat{\mathbf{B}}$$

Spanos (1986, chap. 24) considers this model in some detail, presenting misspecification tests that are essentially multivariate extensions of those outlined in section 8.3.

Example 8.7 Multivariate tests of the CAPM

Since the publication of Gibbons (1982), multivariate tests of the CAPM have been the subject of considerable research: for a detailed treatment, see Campbell, Lo and MacKinlay (1997, chap. 5). The multivariate CAPM can be analysed empirically within the framework of the multivariate regression model. By letting y_t be the vector of n excess asset returns at time t and $\mathbf{x}_t$ be the excess market return at time t, the model can be written as

$$\mathbf{y}_t = \mathbf{C} + \mathbf{B}x_t + \mathbf{u}_t$$

where $\mathbf{C}$ and $\mathbf{B}$ are $n \times 1$ vectors of parameters and the error $\mathbf{u}_t$ is assumed to have the properties of the error in equation (8.15). The CAPM imposes the n restrictions that the intercepts in each asset return equation are zero – i.e. $\mathbf{C} = \mathbf{0}$. MacKinlay (1987; see also Gibbons, Ross and Shanken, 1989) shows that this hypothesis can be tested using the statistic

$$J = \frac{(T - n - 1)T}{(T - 2)n}\left(1 + \frac{\bar{x}^2}{s_x^2}\right)^{-1}\mathbf{C}^\top\hat{\boldsymbol{\Omega}}^{-1}\mathbf{C}$$

Under $H_0 : \mathbf{C} = \mathbf{0}$, J is distributed as F with n and $T - n - 1$ degrees of freedom.

The seventeen assets considered separately in example 8.4 were re-examined in this multivariate framework. Of course, since the same (single) regressor appears in each equation, the slope and intercept estimates are the same as the single-equation OLS estimates. A test of $\mathbf{C} = \mathbf{0}$ produces a J value of 0.71, with an associated marginal significance level of 0.79. Not surprisingly, given the intercept estimates reported in table 8.2, we cannot reject the null that all the intercepts are zero, in accordance with the predictions of the CAPM, although we should emphasise that none of the misspecifications uncovered in the individual asset models in example 8.4 have been tackled here.

8.6 Vector autoregressions

8.6.1 Concepts of exogeneity and causality

Throughout the various forms of regression models encountered so far in this chapter we have made the assumption that $\mathbf{y}_t$ is a function of past values of itself and present and past values of $\mathbf{x}_t$. More precisely, we have been assuming that $\mathbf{x}_t$ is *weakly exogenous*: the stochastic structure of $\mathbf{x}_t$ contains no information that is relevant for the estimation of the parameters of interest, $\mathbf{B}$ and $\boldsymbol{\Omega}$. Formally, $\mathbf{x}_t$ will be weakly exogenous if, when the joint distribution of $\mathbf{z}_t = \left(\mathbf{y}_t^\top, \mathbf{x}_t^\top\right)^\top$, conditional on the past, is factorised as the conditional distribution of $\mathbf{y}_t$ given $\mathbf{x}_t$ times the marginal distribution of $\mathbf{x}_t$; (a) the parameters of these conditional and marginal distributions are not subject to cross-restrictions, and (b) the parameters of interest can be uniquely determined from the parameters of the conditional model alone. Under these conditions $\mathbf{x}_t$ may be treated 'as if' it were determined outside the conditional model for $\mathbf{y}_t$.

For more details on weak exogeneity, see Engle, Hendry and Richard (1983), Engle and Hendry (1993) and Hendry (1995). Engle and Hendry (1993) extend weak exogeneity to that of *superexogeneity*: $\mathbf{x}_t$ will be superexogenous if it is weakly exogenous for $\mathbf{B}$ and $\boldsymbol{\Omega}$ and if the parameters of the conditional distribution of $\mathbf{y}_t$ are *invariant* to interventions that affect the marginal distribution of $\mathbf{x}_t$.

While the weak exogeneity of $\mathbf{x}_t$ allows efficient estimation of $\mathbf{B}$ and $\boldsymbol{\Omega}$ without any reference to the stochastic structure of $\mathbf{x}_t$, the marginal distribution of $\mathbf{x}_t$, while not containing $\mathbf{y}_t$, will contain $\mathbf{Y}_{t-1}^0$, and the possible presence of lagged $\mathbf{y}$s can lead to problems when attempting to forecast $\mathbf{y}_t$. In order to be able to treat $\mathbf{x}_t$ as given when forecasting $\mathbf{y}_t$, we need to ensure that no *feedback* exists from $\mathbf{Y}_{t-1}^0$ to $\mathbf{x}_t$; the absence of such feedback is equivalent to the statement that $\mathbf{y}_t$ *does not Granger-cause* $\mathbf{x}_t$. Weak exogeneity supplemented with Granger non-causality is called *strong exogeneity*.

Unlike weak exogeneity, Granger non-causality is directly testable (the original reference to this concept of causality is Granger, 1969). To investigate such tests, and to relate Granger non-causality to yet another concept of exogeneity, we need to introduce the *dynamic structural equation model* (DSEM) and the *vector autoregressive* (VAR) process. The DSEM extends the multivariate regression model in two directions: first, by allowing 'simultaneity' between the 'endogenous' variables in $\mathbf{y}_t$, and, second, by explicitly considering the process generating the 'exogenous' variables $\mathbf{x}_t$. We thus have (in this and the subsequent subsection constant terms are omitted for simplicity of notation)

$$\mathbf{A}_0\mathbf{y}_t = \sum_{i=1}^{m} \mathbf{A}_i\mathbf{y}_{t-i} + \sum_{i=0}^{m} \mathbf{B}_i\mathbf{x}_{t-i} + \mathbf{u}_{1t} \tag{8.16}$$

and

$$\mathbf{x}_t = \sum_{i=1}^{m} \mathbf{C}_i\mathbf{x}_{t-i} + \mathbf{u}_{2t} \tag{8.17}$$

The simultaneity of the model is a consequence of $\mathbf{A}_0 \neq \mathbf{I}_n$. The errors $\mathbf{u}_{1t}$ and $\mathbf{u}_{2t}$ are assumed to be jointly dependent processes, which could be serially correlated but will be assumed here to be white noise, and intercept vectors are omitted for simplicity: see Mills (1990, chap. 14) and, in particular, Lütkepohl (1991) for a more general development. The identification conditions for the set of *structural* equations (8.16) are summarised in Hendry, Pagan and Sargan (1984), while (8.17) shows that $\mathbf{x}_t$ is generated by an mth-order VAR process, in which current values of $\mathbf{x}$ are functions of m past values of $\mathbf{x}$ *only*.

If, in the DSEM (8.17), $E(\mathbf{u}_{1t}\mathbf{x}_{t-s}) = 0$ for *all* s, $\mathbf{x}_t$ is said to be *strictly exogenous*. Strict exogeneity is useful because no information is lost by limiting attention to distributions conditional on $\mathbf{x}_t$, which will usually result in considerable simplifications in statistical inference – for example, IV techniques may be used in the presence of serially correlated disturbances. A related concept is that of a variable being *predetermined*: a variable is predetermined if all its current and past values are independent of the current error $\mathbf{u}_{1t}$. If $\mathbf{x}_t$ is strictly exogenous then it will also be predetermined, while if $E(\mathbf{u}_{1t}\mathbf{y}_{t-s}) = 0$ for $s > 0$ then $\mathbf{y}_{t-s}$ will be predetermined as well.

In many cases, strictly exogenous variables will also be weakly exogenous in DSEMs, although one important class of exceptions is provided by rational expectations variables, in which behavioural parameters are generally linked to the distributions of exogenous variables. Similarly, predetermined variables will usually be weakly exogenous, except again in the case where there are cross-restrictions between behavioural parameters and the parameters of the distribution of the predetermined variables.

Strict exogeneity can be tested in DSEMs by using the *final form*, in which each endogenous variable is expresssed as an infinite distributed lag of the exogenous variables

$$\mathbf{y}_t = \sum_{i=0}^{\infty} \mathbf{J}_i \mathbf{x}_{t-i} + \mathbf{e}_t$$

where the $\mathbf{J}_i$ matrices are functions of the $\mathbf{A}_i$s and $\mathbf{B}_i$s and where $\mathbf{e}_t$ is a stochastic process possessing a VAR representation and having the property that $E(\mathbf{e}_t\mathbf{x}_{t-s}) = 0$ for all s. Geweke (1978) proves that, in the regression of $\mathbf{y}_t$ on *all* current, lagged and future values of $\mathbf{x}_t$,

$$\mathbf{y}_t = \sum_{i=-\infty}^{\infty} \mathbf{K}_i \mathbf{x}_{t-i} + \mathbf{e}_t \tag{8.18}$$

there will exist a DSEM relating $\mathbf{x}_t$ and $\mathbf{y}_t$ in which $\mathbf{x}_t$ is strictly exogenous if, and only if, the coefficients on *future* values of $\mathbf{x}_t$ (i.e. $\mathbf{x}_{t-s}$, $s < 0$) are all equal to zero. An equivalent test is based on the regression

$$\mathbf{x}_t = \sum_{i=1}^{\infty} \mathbf{E}_{2i}\mathbf{x}_{t-i} + \sum_{i=1}^{\infty} \mathbf{F}_{2i}\mathbf{y}_{t-i} + \mathbf{w}_t \tag{8.19}$$

in which $E\left(\mathbf{y}_{t-i}\mathbf{w}_t^\top\right) = 0$ for all t and $s > 0$. Geweke proves that $\mathbf{x}_t$ will be strictly exogenous in a DSEM relating $\mathbf{x}_t$ and $\mathbf{y}_t$ if, and only if, the coefficient matrices $\mathbf{F}_{2i}$, $i = 1, 2, \ldots$ are all zero.

Strict exogeneity is intimately related to Granger non-causality. Indeed, the two tests for strict exogeneity of $\mathbf{x}_t$ above can also be regarded as tests for $\mathbf{y}_t$ not Granger-causing $\mathbf{x}_t$. The two concepts are *not* equivalent, however. As Geweke (1984) points out, if $\mathbf{x}_t$ is strictly exogenous in the DSEM (8.16) then

$\mathbf{y}_t$ does not Granger-cause $\mathbf{x}_t$, where $\mathbf{y}_t$ is endogenous in that model. If $\mathbf{y}_t$ does not Granger-cause $\mathbf{x}_t$, however, then there exists *a* DSEM with $\mathbf{y}_t$ endogenous and $\mathbf{x}_t$ strictly exogenous, in the sense that there will exist systems of equations formally similar to (8.16), *but* none of these systems necessarily satisfy the overidentifying restrictions of the specific model. This implies that tests for the absence of a causal ordering can be used to refute the strict exogeneity specification in a given DSEM, but such tests cannot be used to establish it.

Furthermore, as we have already discussed, statistical inference may be carried out conditionally on a subset of variables that are not strictly exogenous; all that we require is that they be weakly exogenous. Thus, unidirectional Granger causality is neither necessary nor sufficient for inference to proceed conditional on a subset of variables.

8.6.2 Tests of Granger causality

To develop operational tests of Granger causality, we now consider the $g = n + k + r$ dimensional vector $\mathbf{z}_t = \left(\mathbf{y}_t^\top, \mathbf{x}_t^\top, \mathbf{r}_t^\top\right)^\top$, which we assume has the following mth-order VAR representation (see, for example, Sims, 1980):

$$\mathbf{z}_t = \sum_{i=1}^{m} \mathbf{\Pi}_i \mathbf{z}_{t-i} + \mathbf{v}_t \tag{8.20}$$

where

$$E(\mathbf{v}_t) = E\left(\mathbf{v}_t \big| \mathbf{Z}_{t-1}^0\right) = \mathbf{0}$$

$$E\left(\mathbf{v}_t \mathbf{v}_s^\top\right) = E\left(\mathbf{v}_t \mathbf{v}_s^\top \big| \mathbf{Z}_{t-1}^0\right) = \begin{cases} \mathbf{\Sigma}_\mathbf{v} & t = s \\ \mathbf{0} & t \neq s \end{cases}$$

and

$$\mathbf{Z}_{t-1}^0 = (\mathbf{z}_{t-1}, \mathbf{z}_{t-2}, \ldots, \mathbf{z}_1)$$

The VAR of equation (8.20) can be partitioned as (the r equations modelling $\mathbf{r}_t$ may be ignored here)

$$\mathbf{y}_t = \sum_{i=1}^{m} \mathbf{C}_{2i} \mathbf{x}_{t-i} + \sum_{i=1}^{m} \mathbf{D}_{2i} \mathbf{y}_{t-i} + \sum_{i=1}^{m} \mathbf{G}_{1i} \mathbf{r}_{t-i} + \mathbf{v}_{1t} \tag{8.21}$$

$$\mathbf{x}_t = \sum_{i=1}^{m} \mathbf{E}_{2i} \mathbf{x}_{t-i} + \sum_{i=1}^{m} \mathbf{F}_{2i} \mathbf{y}_{t-i} + \sum_{i=1}^{m} \mathbf{G}_{2i} \mathbf{r}_{t-i} + \mathbf{v}_{2t} \tag{8.22}$$

where $\mathbf{v}_t^\top = (\mathbf{v}_{1t}^\top, \mathbf{v}_{2t}^\top)$ and where $\mathbf{\Sigma}_\mathbf{v}$ is correspondingly partitioned as

$$\mathbf{\Sigma}_\mathbf{v} = \begin{pmatrix} \mathbf{\Sigma}_{11} & \mathbf{\Sigma}_{12} \\ \mathbf{\Sigma}_{12}^\top & \mathbf{\Sigma}_{22} \end{pmatrix}$$

Here $\mathbf{\Sigma}_{ij} = E\left(\mathbf{v}_{it}\mathbf{v}_{jt}^\top\right)$, $i, j = 1, 2$, so that, although the vectors $\mathbf{v}_{1t}$ and $\mathbf{v}_{2t}$ are both serially uncorrelated, they can be correlated with each other contemporaneously, although at no other lag. Given equations (8.21) and (8.22), $\mathbf{x}$ *does not Granger-cause* $\mathbf{y}$ if, and only if, $\mathbf{C}_{2i} \equiv 0$, for all i. An equivalent statement of this proposition is that $|\mathbf{\Sigma}_{11}| = |\mathbf{\Sigma}_1|$, where $\mathbf{\Sigma}_1 = E\left(\mathbf{w}_{1t}\mathbf{w}_{1t}^\top\right)$, obtained from the 'restricted' regression

$$\mathbf{y}_t = \sum\nolimits_{i=1}^m \mathbf{C}_{1i}\mathbf{y}_{t-i} + \sum\nolimits_{i=1}^m \mathbf{G}_{3i}\mathbf{r}_{t-i} + \mathbf{w}_{1t} \tag{8.23}$$

Similarly, $\mathbf{y}$ *does not Granger-cause* $\mathbf{x}$ if, and only if, $\mathbf{F}_{2i} \equiv 0$, for all i – or, equivalently, that $|\mathbf{\Sigma}_{22}| = |\mathbf{\Sigma}_2|$, where $\mathbf{\Sigma}_2 = E\left(\mathbf{w}_{2t}\mathbf{w}_{2t}^\top\right)$, obtained from the regression

$$\mathbf{x}_t = \sum\nolimits_{i=1}^m \mathbf{E}_{1i}\mathbf{x}_{t-i} + \sum\nolimits_{i=1}^m \mathbf{G}_{4i}\mathbf{r}_{t-i} + \mathbf{w}_{2t} \tag{8.24}$$

If the system (8.21)–(8.22) is pre-multiplied by the matrix

$$\begin{bmatrix} \mathbf{I}_n & -\mathbf{\Sigma}_{12}\mathbf{\Sigma}_{22}^{-1} \\ -\mathbf{\Sigma}_{12}^\top\mathbf{\Sigma}_{11}^{-1} & \mathbf{I}_k \end{bmatrix}$$

then the first n equations of the new system can be written as

$$\mathbf{y}_t = \sum\nolimits_{i=0}^m \mathbf{C}_{3i}\mathbf{x}_{t-i} + \sum\nolimits_{i=1}^m \mathbf{D}_{3i}\mathbf{y}_{t-i} + \sum\nolimits_{i=1}^m \mathbf{G}_{5i}\mathbf{r}_{t-i} + \boldsymbol{\omega}_{1t} \tag{8.25}$$

where the error $\boldsymbol{\omega}_{1t} = \mathbf{v}_{1t} - \mathbf{\Sigma}_{12}\mathbf{\Sigma}_{22}^{-1}\mathbf{v}_{2t}$, since it is also uncorrelated with $\mathbf{v}_{2t}$, is also uncorrelated with $\mathbf{x}_t$. Similarly, the last k equations can be written as

$$\mathbf{x}_t = \sum\nolimits_{i=1}^m \mathbf{E}_{3i}\mathbf{x}_{t-i} + \sum\nolimits_{i=0}^m \mathbf{F}_{3i}\mathbf{y}_{t-i} + \sum\nolimits_{i=1}^m \mathbf{G}_{6i}\mathbf{r}_{t-i} + \boldsymbol{\omega}_{2t} \tag{8.26}$$

Denoting $\mathbf{\Sigma}_{\omega i} = E\left(\boldsymbol{\omega}_{it}\boldsymbol{\omega}_{it}^\top\right)$, $i = 1, 2$, there is *instantaneous causality* between $\mathbf{y}$ and $\mathbf{x}$ if, and only if, $\mathbf{C}_{30} \neq 0$ and $\mathbf{E}_{30} \neq 0$, or, equivalently, if $|\mathbf{\Sigma}_{11}| > |\mathbf{\Sigma}_{\omega 1}|$ and $|\mathbf{\Sigma}_{22}| > |\mathbf{\Sigma}_{\omega_2}|$.

Tests of Granger causality can be constructed once estimates of the various covariance matrices have been obtained. Consistent and efficient estimates of the parameters of the regressions (8.21) to (8.26) are given by LS, so that the following matrices can be formed:

$$\hat{\mathbf{\Sigma}}_i = (T-m)^{-1} \sum_{t=m+1}^{T} \hat{\mathbf{w}}_{it}\hat{\mathbf{w}}_{it}^{\top}$$

$$\hat{\mathbf{\Sigma}}_{ii} = (T-m)^{-1} \sum_{t=m+1}^{T} \hat{\mathbf{v}}_{it}\hat{\mathbf{v}}_{it}^{\top}$$

$$\hat{\mathbf{\Sigma}}_{\omega i} = (T-m)^{-1} \sum_{t=m+1}^{T} \hat{\omega}_{it}\hat{\omega}_{it}^{\top}$$

for $i = 1, 2$, where $\hat{\mathbf{w}}_{it}$ is the vector of LS residuals corresponding to the error vector $\mathbf{w}_{it}$, etc. The LR test statistic of the null hypothesis $H_{01} : \mathbf{C}_{2i} = 0$ for all i (**x** does not Granger-cause **y**) is

$$LR_1 = (T - m)\log(|\hat{\mathbf{\Sigma}}_1|/|\hat{\mathbf{\Sigma}}_{11}|) \sim \chi^2_{nkm}$$

Similarly, the null that **y** does not Granger-cause **x**, $H_{02} : \mathbf{F}_{2i} = 0$, is tested by

$$LR_2 = (T - m)\log(|\hat{\mathbf{\Sigma}}_2|/|\hat{\mathbf{\Sigma}}_{22}|) \sim \chi^2_{nkm}$$

while the null that there is no instantaneous causality between **y** and **x**, $H_{03} : \mathbf{C}_{30} = \mathbf{E}_{30} = 0$, is tested by

$$LR_3 = (T - m)\log(|\hat{\mathbf{\Sigma}}_1|/|\hat{\mathbf{\Sigma}}_{\omega 1}|) = (T - m)\log(|\hat{\mathbf{\Sigma}}_2|/|\hat{\mathbf{\Sigma}}_{\omega 2}|) \sim \chi^2_{nk}$$

Since these are tests of nested hypotheses, they are asymptotically independent. All three restrictions can be tested at once since

$$LR_1 + LR_2 + LR_3 \sim \chi^2_{nk(2m+1)}$$

Wald and LM statistics may be constructed in analogous fashion. Although various other tests of causality have been proposed, they tend to require considerably more computation, and, in any event, simulation studies carried out by a variety of authors reach a consensus that inference should be carried out using the procedures detailed above, these being found to combine the greatest reliability with computational ease.

8.6.3 Determining the order of a VAR

These tests of causality assume that the order m of the underlying VAR is known. In practice, of course, m will be unknown and must be determined empirically. A traditional tool for determining the order is to use a sequential testing procedure. If we have the g-dimensional VAR given by (8.20), from which the ML estimate of $\boldsymbol{\Sigma}_v$ is

$$\hat{\boldsymbol{\Sigma}}_{v,m} = T^{-1}\hat{\mathbf{V}}_m\hat{\mathbf{V}}_m^{\top}$$

where $\hat{\mathbf{V}}_m = (\hat{\mathbf{v}}_{m+1}, \ldots, \hat{\mathbf{v}}_T)$ is the matrix of residuals obtained by LS estimation of the mth-order VAR – VAR(m) – then, for example, the LR statistic for testing m against l, $l < m$, is

$$LR(m, l) = (T - gm)\log\left(|\hat{\boldsymbol{\Sigma}}_{v,l}|/|\hat{\boldsymbol{\Sigma}}_{v,m}|\right) \sim \chi_{g^2(m-l)}$$

This uses the scaling factor $T - gm$ rather than T to account for possible small-sample bias in the statistic.

Other procedures are based upon minimising some objective function and are essentially multivariate analogues of those discussed in example 2.3. The objective function that is most favoured is the multivariate BIC criterion, defined here as

$$BIC(m) = \log\left|\hat{\boldsymbol{\Sigma}}_{v,j}\right| + g^2 m T^{-1} \log T \quad m = 0, 1, \ldots, m^*$$

where m^* is the *maximum* order considered. This can be shown to provide a consistent estimate of the correct lag order, and Lütkepohl (1985) finds that it also chooses the correct order most often, and the resulting VAR models provide the best forecasts, in a Monte Carlo comparison of objective functions.

After a tentative model has been specified using one of these procedures, checks on its adequacy may be carried out. These are analogous to the diagnostic checks used for univariate models, and might involve overfitting and testing the significance of the extra parameters, plotting standardised residuals against time and analysing the estimated cross-correlation matrices of the residual series. Multivariate portmanteau and LM statistics are also available, but with vector time series there is probably no substitute for detailed inspection of the residual correlation structure for revealing subtle relation ships that may indicate important directions for model improvement.

8.7 Variance decompositions, innovation accounting and structural VARs

A concise representation of the VAR(m) model is obtained by using lag operator notation

$$\boldsymbol{\Pi}(B)\mathbf{z}_t = \mathbf{v}_t$$

where

$$\boldsymbol{\Pi}(B) = \mathbf{I} - \boldsymbol{\Pi}_1 B - \boldsymbol{\Pi}_2 B^2 - \cdots - \boldsymbol{\Pi}_m B^m$$

Analogous to the univariate case, the vector MA representation of $\mathbf{z}_t$ is

$$\mathbf{z}_t = \boldsymbol{\Pi}^{-1}(B)\mathbf{v}_t = \boldsymbol{\Psi}(B)\mathbf{v}_t = \mathbf{v}_t + \sum_{i=1}^{\infty} \boldsymbol{\Psi}_i \mathbf{v}_{t-i} \tag{8.27}$$

where

$$\boldsymbol{\Psi}_i = \sum_{j=1}^{i} \boldsymbol{\Pi}_j \boldsymbol{\Psi}_{i-j} \quad \boldsymbol{\Psi}_0 = \mathbf{I}_n \quad \boldsymbol{\Psi}_i = 0, \quad i < 0$$

In this set-up, no distinction is made between endogenous and (strictly) exogenous variables, so the $\boldsymbol{\Psi}_i$ matrices can be interpreted as the *dynamic multipliers* of the system, since they represent the model's response to a unit shock in each of the variables. The response of z_i to a unit shock in z_j (i.e. to v_{jt} taking the value unity, where v_{jt} is the jth element of $\mathbf{v}_t$) is therefore given by the sequence, known as the *impulse response function*,

$$\boldsymbol{\Psi}_{ij,1}, \boldsymbol{\Psi}_{ij,2}, \ldots,$$

where $\boldsymbol{\Psi}_{ij,k}$ is the ijth element of the matrix $\boldsymbol{\Psi}_k$. If a variable or block of variables are strictly exogenous, then the implied zero restrictions ensure that these variables do not react to a shock to any of the endogenous variables. Recall, however, that $E(\mathbf{v}_t\mathbf{v}_t^\top) = \boldsymbol{\Sigma}_{\mathbf{v}}$, so that the components of $\mathbf{v}_t$ are contemporaneously correlated. If these correlations are high, simulation of a shock to z_j, while all other components of $\mathbf{z}_t$ are held constant, could be misleading, as there is no way of separating out the response of z_i to z_j from its response to other shocks that are correlated with v_{jt}.

If we define the lower triangular matrix $\mathbf{S}$ such that $\mathbf{S}\mathbf{S}^\top = \boldsymbol{\Sigma}_{\mathbf{v}}$ and $\mathbf{n}_t = \mathbf{S}^{-1}\mathbf{v}_t$, however, then $E(\mathbf{n}_t\mathbf{n}_t^\top) = \mathbf{I}_g$, so that the transformed shocks $\mathbf{n}_t$ are orthogonal to each other. We can then renormalise the MA representation (8.27) into the *recursive* form

$$\mathbf{z}_t = \sum_{i=0}^{\infty} (\mathbf{\Psi}_i \mathbf{S})(\mathbf{S}^{-1}\mathbf{v}_{t-i}) = \sum_{i=0}^{\infty} \mathbf{\Psi}_i^O \mathbf{n}_{t-i}$$

where $\mathbf{\Psi}_i^O = \mathbf{\Psi}_i \mathbf{S}$ (so that $\mathbf{\Psi}_0^O = \mathbf{\Psi}_0 \mathbf{S}$ is lower triangular). The impulse response function of z_i to a unit shock in z_j is then given by the sequence

$$\mathbf{\Psi}_{ij,0}^O, \ \mathbf{\Psi}_{ij,1}^O, \ \mathbf{\Psi}_{ij,2}^O, \ldots$$

where each impulse response can be written compactly as

$$\mathbf{\Psi}_{ij,h}^O = \mathbf{e}_j^\top \mathbf{\Psi}_h \mathbf{S} \mathbf{e}_i \tag{8.28}$$

where $\mathbf{e}_i$ is the $n \times 1$ selection vector containing unity as the ith element and zeros elsewhere. This sequence is known as the *orthogonalised impulse response function.*

The uncorrelatedness of the $\mathbf{n}_t$s allows the error variance of the H-step ahead forecast of z_i to be decomposed into components accounted for by these shocks, or innovations: hence the phrase coined by Sims (1981) for this technique, that of *innovation accounting.* In particular, the proportion of the H-step ahead forecast error variance of variable i accounted for by the orthogonalised innovations to z_j is given by

$$V_{ij,h}^O = \frac{\sum_{h=0}^H \mathbf{\Psi}_{ij,h}^{O^2}}{\sum_{h=0}^H \mathbf{e}_i^\top \mathbf{\Psi}_h \mathbf{\Sigma}_\mathbf{v} \mathbf{\Psi}_h^\top \mathbf{e}_i} = \frac{\sum_{h=0}^H \left(\mathbf{e}_i^\top \mathbf{\Psi}_h \mathbf{S} \mathbf{e}_j\right)^2}{\sum_{h=0}^H \mathbf{e}_i^\top \mathbf{\Psi}_h \mathbf{\Sigma}_\mathbf{v} \mathbf{\Psi}_h^\top \mathbf{e}_i}$$

For large H, this *orthogonalised forecast error variance decomposition* allows the isolation of those relative contributions to variability that are, intuitively, 'persistent' (for further details of this technique, see, for example, Doan, Litterman and Sims, 1984). The technique does, however, have an important disadvantage: the choice of the $\mathbf{S}$ matrix is not unique, so that different choices (for example, different orderings of the variables) will alter the $\mathbf{\Psi}_{ij,k}^O$ coefficients, and hence the impulse response functions and variance decompositions. The extent of these changes will depend upon the size of the contemporaneous correlations between the components of the $\mathbf{v}_t$ vector.

This non-invariance property has generated much detailed analysis and criticism of the variance decomposition methodology, focusing on the inability of VARs to be regarded as 'structural' in the traditional econometric sense, so that shocks cannot be uniquely identified with a particular variable unless prior identifying assumptions are made, without which the computed impulse response functions and variance decompositions would be invalid.

To make this point more concrete, suppose we have a (first-order) DSEM but, in keeping with the general philosophy of VARs, no variables are considered to be exogenous, at least a priori – i.e.

$$\mathbf{A}_0 \mathbf{y}_t = \mathbf{A}_1 \mathbf{y}_{t-1} + \mathbf{B} \mathbf{u}_t \qquad (8.29)$$

We also assume that the structural errors $\mathbf{u}_t$ have zero cross-correlation: hence,

$$E\left(\mathbf{u}_t \mathbf{u}_s^{\top}\right) = \begin{cases} \boldsymbol{\Sigma}_{\mathbf{u}} & t = s \\ \mathbf{0} & t \neq s \end{cases}$$

and $\boldsymbol{\Sigma}_{\mathbf{u}}$ is diagonal. The diagonal elements of $\mathbf{A}_0$ and $\mathbf{B}$ are normalised to unity, thus associating each structural equation with a natural left-hand-side variable and with a particular structural error. Contemporaneous interactions are captured by non-zero off-diagonal elements in these matrices, $\mathbf{A}_0$ capturing interactions between the variables and $\mathbf{B}$ modelling the direct effects of disturbances on variables other than those appearing on the left-hand side of the structural equations.

Pre-multiplying (8.29) by $\mathbf{A}_0^{-1}$ obtains the VAR (8.20) with $m = 1$, $\boldsymbol{\Pi}_1 = \mathbf{A}_0^{-1} \mathbf{A}_1$ and $\mathbf{A}_0 \mathbf{v}_t = \mathbf{B} \mathbf{u}_t$. The VAR is thus seen to be the *reduced form* of the DSEM, and the VAR error $\mathbf{v_t}$ is a linear combination of the errors of the DSEM. It is this fact that makes the interpretation of impulse response functions and variance decompositions potentially ambiguous. Recall that $\boldsymbol{\Psi}_{ij,k}$ measures the response of z_i to a unit shock in z_j after k periods. But a shock to z_j, given by the jth element of $\mathbf{v_t}$, is now seen to be made up of all the *structural* innovations $\mathbf{u_t}$, and hence, in the absence of further information, could have been the consequence of a shock to *any* of the variables in the DSEM. The recursive triangularisation introduced above implies that $\mathbf{v}_t = \mathbf{S} \mathbf{n_t}$, so the recursive innovations and the structural innovations will coincide only if $\mathbf{S} = \mathbf{A}_0^{-1} \mathbf{B}$, which will be satisfied if the DSEM itself has the same lower triangular structure – i.e. if $\mathbf{B}$ is diagonal and $\mathbf{A}_0$ lower triangular.

Numerous authors have argued that these assumptions have no particular economic rationale – that they are *atheoretical*, using the term of Cooley and LeRoy (1985). This has led to the development of other sets of identifying restrictions that are based more explicitly on economic considerations.

Bernanke (1986) and Blanchard (1989), for example, impose alternative sets of restrictions on $\mathbf{A}_0$ and $\mathbf{B}$ that in effect constrain the short-run impact of shocks to $\mathbf{z}$, while Blanchard and Quah (1989) exploit a different set of restrictions that constrain the long-run effects of shocks to $\mathbf{z}$ and thus impose restrictions across $\mathbf{A}_0$, $\mathbf{A}_1$ and $\mathbf{B}$. Swanson and Granger (1997) present a method that combines both prior economic knowledge and statistical analysis of the VAR residuals.

An alternative approach has been proposed by Pesaran and Shin (1997), extending the work of Koop, Pesaran and Potter (1996). This proposes using *generalised impulse responses* as a means of circumventing the dependence of the orthogonalised responses to the ordering of the variables. The generalised impulse response is defined by replacing $\mathbf{S}$ in (8.28) with $\sigma_{ii}^{-1/2}\mathbf{\Sigma}_v$, where σ_{ii} is the ith diagonal element of $\mathbf{\Sigma}_v$:

$$\mathbf{\Psi}_{ij,h}^G = \sigma_{ii}^{-1/2}\mathbf{e}_j^\top \mathbf{\Psi}_h \mathbf{\Sigma}_v \mathbf{e}_i$$

thus leading to the *generalised forecast error variance decomposition*

$$V_{ij,h}^G = \frac{\sum_{h=0}^{H} \mathbf{\Psi}_{ij,h}^{G2}}{\sum_{h=0}^{H} \mathbf{e}_i^\top \mathbf{\Psi}_h \mathbf{\Sigma}_v \mathbf{\Psi}_h^\top \mathbf{e}_i} = \frac{\sigma_{ii}^{-1} \sum_{h=0}^{H} \left(\mathbf{e}_i^\top \mathbf{\Psi}_h \mathbf{\Sigma}_v \mathbf{e}_j\right)^2}{\sum_{h=0}^{H} \mathbf{e}_i^\top \mathbf{\Psi}_h \mathbf{\Sigma}_v \mathbf{\Psi}_h^\top \mathbf{e}_i}$$

The generalised impulse responses are invariant to the ordering of the variables, are unique and fully take into account the historical patterns of correlations observed amongst the different shocks. The orthogonalised and generalised impulse responses will coincide only if $\mathbf{\Sigma}_v$ is diagonal, and in general are only the same for $j = 1$ (Pesaran and Shin, 1997).

Methods of computing standard errors of the impulse response functions in the above situations are discussed in detail in Hamilton (1994, chap. 11.7).

8.8 Vector ARMA models

A natural extension of the VAR is the vector ARMA process

$$\mathbf{z}_t = \sum_{i=1}^{p} \mathbf{\Phi}_i \mathbf{z}_{t-i} + \mathbf{v}_t + \sum_{i=1}^{q} \mathbf{\Theta}_i \mathbf{v}_{t-i}$$

or

$$\mathbf{\Phi}(B)\mathbf{z}_t = \mathbf{\Theta}(B)\mathbf{v}_t$$

where

$$\mathbf{\Phi}(B) = \mathbf{I} - \mathbf{\Phi}_1 B - \cdots - \mathbf{\Phi}_p B^p$$

and

$$\mathbf{\Theta}(B) = \mathbf{I} - \mathbf{\Theta}_1 B - \cdots - \mathbf{\Theta}_q B^q$$

which, of course, admits a VAR(∞) representation with $\mathbf{\Pi}(B) = \mathbf{\Theta}^{-1}(B)\mathbf{\Phi}(B)$. Unfortunately, the presence of a vector MA component complicates analysis somewhat, and vector ARMA models are rarely used nowadays. Details of such models, including estimation methods and model-building techniques, may be found in, for example, Mills (1990, chap. 14) and Lütkepohl (1991).

Example 8.8 The interaction of equity and bond markets in the United Kingdom

The example that is used to illustrate VAR modelling brings together four series that have been used in previous examples. These are the FTA All Share index and associated dividend index, first introduced in example 2.6, and the series on twenty-year UK gilts and ninety-one-day Treasury bills, used to construct the spread in example 2.2. Previous examples have shown that the logarithms are all $I(1)$, so that the first-differences, Δp, Δd, Δrs and $\Delta r20$, are individually stationary and hence suitable for modelling in a VAR framework. The first three series were analysed within a single-equation framework modelling Δp in example 8.5. The sample period is January 1965 to December 2005, so that the sample size is $T = 492$. Thus, $g = 4$ and $\mathbf{z}_t = (\Delta p_t, \Delta d_t, \Delta rs_t, \Delta r20_t)$. Table 8.4 presents BIC values for lags $m = 0, 1, \ldots, 12$, along with LR statistics for testing m against $m - 1$, beginning at $m = 12$. The minimum BIC is found at $m = 1$, whereas the first significant LR statistic, using the 5 per cent level for each test, is at $m = 2$. Setting $m = 2$ revealed no residual autocorrelation, and this order of VAR was therefore selected. Summary statistics for the VAR(2) are shown in table 8.5, along with the estimated contemporaneous residual correlation matrix.

To illustrate Granger causality testing, we first consider the set of pairwise test statistics: for example, with $\mathbf{y}_t = \Delta p_t$, $\mathbf{x}_t = \Delta r20_t$ and $\mathbf{r}_t = (\Delta d_t, \Delta rs_t)$, Granger causality between equity prices and long interest rates may be examined. These are shown in table 8.6(a), and indicate strong causality running from $\Delta r20$ to the other three variables and modest evidence of feedback between Δp and Δd. The presence of a large positive

Table 8.4 BIC values and LR statistics for determining the order of the VAR in example 8.8

m	$BIC(m)$	$LR(m, m-1)$
0	−12.74	−
1	−13.99†	688.25
2	−13.87	42.46*
3	−13.69	13.68
4	−13.53	19.99
5	−13.36	18.87
6	−13.19	17.10
7	−13.00	7.56
8	−12.83	15.40
9	−12.65	12.10
10	−12.49	18.81
11	−12.32	15.11
12	−12.15	14.67

Notes:
$LR(m, m-1) \sim \chi^2_{16}$, $\chi^2_{16,0.05} = 26.30$.
† = minimum BIC.
* = first significant LR statistic.

Table 8.5 Summary statistics for the VAR(2) of example 8.8

	R^2	s.e.	$Q(12)$
Δp	0.04	0.058	9.6
Δd	0.38	0.060	14.6
Δrs	0.13	0.054	16.5
$\Delta r20$	0.06	0.034	6.3

Contemporaneous residual correlation matrix

	Δp	Δd	Δrs	$\Delta r20$
Δp	1			
Δd	0.88	1		
Δrs	−0.14	−0.08	1	
$\Delta r20$	−0.26	−0.18	0.41	1

contemporaneous correlation between the residuals of the $\Delta r20$ and Δrs and Δp and Δd equations shows that there is also instantaneous causality in the bond and equity markets. A reasonably large but negative contemporaneous correlation between Δp and $\Delta r20$ indicates that a rise in equity prices is accompanied by a fall in long interest rates, presumably as

Table 8.6 Granger causality tests

$y \rightarrow x$	$LR_{y \rightarrow x} \sim \chi^2(2)$	
(a) Pairwise causality statistics		
$\Delta d \rightarrow \Delta p$	5.36	[0.07]
$\Delta rs \rightarrow \Delta p$	0.32	[0.85]
$\Delta r20 \rightarrow \Delta p$	7.60	[0.02]
$\Delta p \rightarrow \Delta d$	90.60	[0.00]
$\Delta rs \rightarrow \Delta d$	0.59	[0.74]
$\Delta r20 \rightarrow \Delta d$	6.08	[0.05]
$\Delta p \rightarrow \Delta rs$	0.31	[0.86]
$\Delta d \rightarrow \Delta rs$	0.04	[0.98]
$\Delta r20 \rightarrow \Delta rs$	10.34	[0.00]
$\Delta p \rightarrow \Delta r20$	3.85	[0.15]
$\Delta d \rightarrow \Delta r20$	0.03	[0.98]
$\Delta rs \rightarrow \Delta r20$	0.10	[0.95]

(b) $\mathbf{y}_t = (\Delta p_t, \Delta d_t, \Delta rs_t)$, $\mathbf{x}_t = (\Delta r20_t)$

	$LR_{y \rightarrow x} \sim \chi^2(8)$	
$\mathbf{y} \rightarrow \mathbf{x}$	21.95	[0.00]
$\mathbf{x} \rightarrow \mathbf{y}$	10.28	[0.11]

investors switch out of gilts into higher-yielding equities. Thus, it would seem that the primary source of dynamic response is from long interest rates to stock prices and to short interest rates – i.e. a positive shock to the gilts market leads to a positive shock in the short-term money market and a negative shock to the equity market.

By defining $\mathbf{y}_t = (\Delta p_t, \Delta d_t, \Delta rs_t)$, $\mathbf{x}_t = (\Delta r20_t)$ and $\mathbf{r}_t$ null, so that $n = 3$, $k = 1$ and $r = 0$, we can test whether long interest rates jointly Granger-cause the other three variables – i.e. whether the gilts market jointly Granger-causes the bond and equity markets, and whether there is any evidence of any joint feedback from them to the gilts market. From the set of statistics shown in table 8.6(b), the gilts market is confirmed to Granger-cause the bond and equity markets, but there is no evidence of feedback.

Two variance decompositions are reported in table 8.7. The first (denoted I) uses the ordering defining $\mathbf{z}$, while the second (II) reverses this – i.e. $\Delta r20$, Δrs, Δd, Δp. Own innovations have the major weight in the decompositions,

Table 8.7 Variance decompositions

		Explained by							
		Δp		Δd		Δrs		$\Delta r20$	
	h	I	II	I	II	I	II	I	II
	1	100	22.3	0	71.0	0	0.2	0	6.6
Δp	3	98.1	21.4	0.3	69.9	0.1	0.2	1.5	8.5
	6	98.1	21.4	0.3	69.9	0.1	0.2	1.5	8.5
	1	76.6	0	23.4	96.7	0	0	0	3.3
Δd	3	82.9	4.8	15.7	91.1	0	0.3	1.4	3.8
	6	83.0	4.8	15.5	91.1	0	0.3	1.5	3.8
	1	2.0	0	0.7	0	97.3	83.2	0	16.8
Δrs	3	2.7	0	0.8	0.1	94.4	77.9	1.9	22.0
	6	2.7	0	0.8	0.1	94.4	77.9	2.1	22.0
	1	6.6	0	0.8	0	13.7	0	78.8	100
$\Delta r20\$\$$	3	9.7	0.4	0.8	1.5	13.3	0	76.2	98.0
	6	9.7	0.4	0.8	1.6	13.3	0	76.2	98.0

but many of the other weights are reasonably large, although all the decompositions are, basically, settled after six months. Due to the large contemporaneous correlations, major shifts in weights are found when the ordering is changed. In the absence of any structural model suggesting a theoretical ordering, there is no way of establishing which of the variance decompositions is appropriate.

Figure 8.1 shows the accumulated generalised impulse responses, and these confirm the conclusions drawn from the Granger causality tests and the variance decomposition calculations.

8.9 Multivariate GARCH models

Increasingly, attention is being focused on building multivariate GARCH (MGARCH) models to account for the observation that asset and market volatilities appear to be correlated over time. This has also been motivated by the fact that, in most asset pricing theories, returns depend on the covariance with some benchmark portfolio. In addition to capturing the univariate temporal dependencies in conditional variances, MGARCH models also specify how covariances vary through time. Comprehensive reviews of this expanding literature can be found in Bauwens, Laurent and Rombouts (2006), Brooks (2006) and Silvennoinen and Teräsvirta (2007).

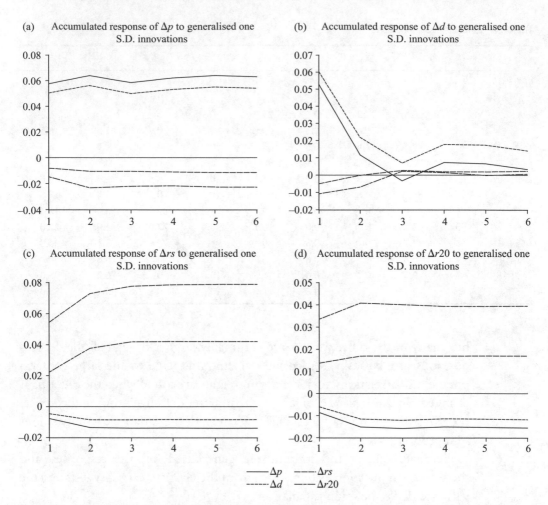

(a) Accumulated response of Δp to generalised one S.D. innovations

(b) Accumulated response of Δd to generalised one S.D. innovations

(c) Accumulated response of Δrs to generalised one S.D. innovations

(d) Accumulated response of $\Delta r20$ to generalised one S.D. innovations

——— Δp – – – Δrs
----- Δd —–— $\Delta r20$

Figure 8.1 Accumulated generalised impulse response functions

The basic framework for MGARCH modelling was first introduced by Bollerslev, Engle and Wooldridge (1988), who extended the univariate GARCH model to include a vectorised conditional covariance matrix. Although the unrestricted model, known as the VECH-GARCH, is very general, it is practically infeasible to estimate for more than two variables because of the large number of parameters contained within it. Consequently, Bollerslev, Engle and Wooldridge, and others, have proposed a number of restrictions and specifications to reduce the number of parameters needed to be estimated.

A popular modification is that of Bollerslev (1990), who assumes that the conditional correlation between the observed variables (or disturbances)

is constant through time. To ease exposition, we shall assume that the observed return series have zero means and that the conditional variance structure is limited to a single lag. Thus, if we have the vector of k returns $\mathbf{x}_t$, then we allow the conditional variance of $\mathbf{x}_t$ to vary through time according to

$$V(\mathbf{x}_t | I_{t-1}) = \Omega_t$$

where I_{t-1} is the information set available at time $t-1$. In the constant correlation MGARCH(1, 1) model, the conditional variances, $\sigma_{i,t}^2$, and the covariances, $\sigma_{ij,t}$, of Ω_t are given by

$$\sigma_{i,t}^2 = \omega_i + \alpha_i x_{i,t-1}^2 + \beta_i \sigma_{i,t-1}^2 \quad i = 1, 2, \dots, k$$

$$\sigma_{ij,t} = \rho_{ij} \sigma_{it} \sigma_{jt} \quad 1 \le i, j \le k$$

where the ρ_{ij} are the constant correlations. It must also be assumed that $\omega_i, \alpha_i, \beta_i > 0$, that $\alpha_i + \beta_i < 1$ for all $i = 1, 2, \dots, k$, and that the matrix of correlations is positive definite. Although the conditional correlation is constant, the model allows for time variation in the conditional covariances. Estimation is somewhat simpler than the more general MGARCH specifications since the sample correlation matrix of standardised residuals, which is by default positive definite, is the ML estimator of the correlation matrix. A convenient reduction in the number of parameters required to be estimated results from the fact that the correlation matrix can be concentrated out of the log-likelihood function.

In a more general setting, Ling and McAleer (2003) study the asymptotic theory of vector ARMA-GARCH processes, which include the Bollerslev (1990) model as a special case. They establish conditions for strict stationarity, ergodicity and higher-order moments for such models and prove the consistency and asymptotic normality of the QML estimator under certain conditions. Issues related to estimation and software packages that can be used for estimation are reviewed by Brooks, Persand and Burke (2003). To test the adequacy of the constant correlation MGARCH model, Bollerslev (1990) suggests using a portmanteau statistic on the cross-products of the standardised residuals across different equations, and auxiliary regressions that include products of standardised residuals. To relax the somewhat restrictive assumption of time-invariant correlations a number of alternative models have been proposed, but, typically, these can only be used at great computational expense. For example, Tse (2000) proposes the following specification for the conditional correlations and covariances:

$$\rho_{ij,t} = \rho_{ij} + \gamma_{ij} x_{i,t-1} x_{j,t-1}$$
$$\sigma_{ij,t} = \rho_{ij,t} \sigma_{it} \sigma_{jt} \quad 1 \leq i < j \leq k$$

In this way the correlations are allowed to respond to the products of previous observations. Since the γ_{ij} must also be estimated, however, the total number of parameters now becomes $k^2 + 2k$. Moreover, computationally cumbersome restrictions must be imposed on the γ_{ij} to ensure that the conditional variance matrices remain positive definite. Since this extended model contains the previous one as a special case, Tse (2000) develops an LM test for the null hypothesis of constant correlation, which requires that $\gamma_{ij} = 0$, $1 \leq i < j \leq k$.

MGARCH models have found significant applications in both industry and academia. For example, they have been used to study possible co-movements and spillovers between volatilities in different assets and markets, to obtain time-varying asset pricing models and hedge ratios, and to model more effectively the risk in portfolios of assets. Bauwens, Laurent and Rombouts (2006) provides references to key applications in this literature.

Example 8.9 MGARCH estimation of FTSE optimal hedge ratios

There has been a good deal of interest on the use of futures contracts as a hedging instrument against possible adverse movements in financial markets. The number of futures contracts needed to hedge a cash market position is calculated using the hedge ratio. Despite almost three decades of research, the formulation and implementation of an optimal hedge strategy – or, more precisely, the appropriate way to calculate the optimal hedge ratio – remains a controversial issue in finance and econometrics (see, for example, Brooks and Chong, 2001). The earliest and probably simplest approach estimates a static hedge ratio from the slope coefficient obtained by an OLS regression of spot returns, s_t, on futures returns, f_t. This static optimal hedge ratio can be calculated simply as $\beta = \sigma_{sf}/\sigma_f^2$, where σ_{sf} is the covariance between spot and futures price returns and σ_f^2 is the variance of futures price returns.

Since returns are known to exhibit time-varying covariances and variances, several alternative estimation methods have been developed to model *dynamic* hedge ratios. In this case, at time $t-1$, the expected return and variance of a portfolio consisting of one unit of the asset and β units of the futures contract will be $E(s_t - \beta_{t-1}E(f_t))$ and $\sigma_{s,t}^2 + \beta_{t-1}^2\sigma_{f,t}^2 - 2\beta_{t-1}\sigma_{sf,t}$, respectively. The conditional (and hence time-varying) variances of spot and futures returns are denoted here by $\sigma_{s,t}^2$ and $\sigma_{f,t}^2$, while the conditional covariance is $\sigma_{sf,t}^2$. The dynamic optimal hedge ratio that minimises the variance of the spot and futures portfolio returns will then be $\beta_{t-1} = -\sigma_{sf,t}/\sigma_{f,t}^2$.

To demonstrate the estimation of the optimal hedge ratio, we employ daily spot prices and respective futures contracts prices for the FTSE for the period 2 January 2003 to 31 December 2003. After removing non-trading days and matching trading dates between spot and futures prices, 253 observations were available. There are four delivery months for the FTSE futures contract: March, June, September and December. Due to the size of the market, at least two contracts were traded at any time, which facilitates contract rollover.

Using OLS, the static optimal hedge ratio regression was estimated between logarithmic returns of spot and futures prices to be

$$s_t = \underset{(0.011)}{0.987}\, f_t$$

with the Newey–West standard error being shown in parentheses. The constant was omitted since it was found to be statistically insignificant. As expected, tests for heteroskedasticity in the residuals suggest that the regression is misspecified. For example, an LM test for ARCH(1) produced an F-statistic of 24.1, which is highly significant.

Using the relevant program provided in EViews version 5.0, we implemented the restricted version of the bivariate BEKK-MGARCH model proposed by Engle and Kroner (1995) and named after an unpublished paper by Baba, Engle, Kraft and Kroner. This modelling approach resolves the problem of ensuring the positive definiteness of the covariance matrix by using a quadratic form for the conditional covariance equations. The estimated models for the conditional variances of spot and futures returns and the conditional covariance are

$$\sigma_{s,t}^2 = \underset{(0.0006)}{0.0021^2} + \underset{(0.020)}{0.922^2}\, \sigma_{s,t-1}^2 + \underset{(0.043)}{0.331^2}\, \varepsilon_{s,t-1}^2$$

$$\sigma_{f,t}^2 = \underset{(0.0001)}{0.0005^2} + \underset{(0.022)}{0.916^2}\, \sigma_{f,t-1}^2 + \underset{(0.047)}{0.343^2}\, \varepsilon_{f,t-1}^2$$

$$\sigma_{sf,t} = \underset{(0.0006)}{0.0021^2} \cdot \underset{(0.0001)}{0.0005^2} + \underset{(0.020)}{0.922^2} \cdot \underset{(0.022)}{0.916^2}\, \sigma_{sf,t-1} + \underset{(0.043)}{0.331^2} \cdot \underset{(0.047)}{0.343^2}\, \varepsilon_{s,t-1}^2\varepsilon_{f,t-1}^2$$

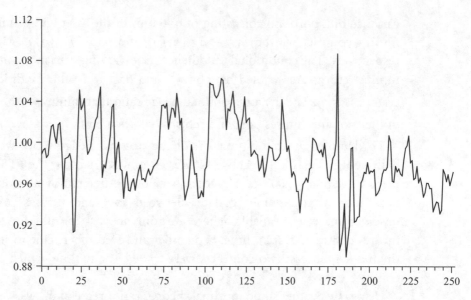

Figure 8.2   Estimated dynamic hedge ratio for FTSE futures contracts during 2003

where $\varepsilon_{s,t}$ and $\varepsilon_{f,t}$ are the residuals from the conditional mean equation for the spot and futures returns, respectively. An LR test clearly supports the MGARCH specification, as can also be seen from the highly significant parameter estimates in the condition variance and covariance equations.

The dynamic hedge ratio obtained by this approach is shown in figure 8.2. Although it has an average value of 0.985, very close to the static hedge ratio estimated via OLS, it varies throughout the sample between 0.889 and 1.087. In accordance with many empirical studies, however, we find that, despite OLS being misspecified, it nevertheless produces a smaller variance of portfolio returns. More specifically, we find that the static approach produces a variance of portfolio returns (4.70×10^{-6}) that is slightly smaller than that of the dynamic (5.07×10^{-6}). Moreover, even a naïve static hedging approach of purchasing one futures contract ($\beta = 1$) produces a smaller variance for the hedged position returns (4.72×10^{-6}). The usefulness of hedging is clearly demonstrated, however, by the unhedged position ($\beta = 0$) having a much larger variance of 1.50×10^{-4}.

9 Regression techniques for integrated financial time series

Chapter 8 has developed regression techniques for modelling relationships between *non-integrated* time series. As we have seen in earlier chapters, however, many financial time series are integrated, often able to be characterised as $I(1)$ processes, and the question thus arises as to whether the presence of integrated variables affects our standard regression results and conventional procedures of inference. This question is long-standing, since it has been known since Yule (1897) that an unremoved deterministic time trend could produce erroneous regression results by acting as a common but non-causal influence behind otherwise independent time series. Later, Yule (1926) was the first to explore directly the problem of 'nonsense correlations', arguing that these resulted from violations of the assumptions behind linear correlation, in particular that of serial independence. Through analytical examples, Yule showed that estimated correlations can be significantly biased if the underlying variables are polynomials of time. He also performed a set of impressive hand-calculated Monte Carlo experiments that demonstrated that nonsense correlations could also arise when analysing the relationships between pairs of $I(1)$ or $I(2)$ variables. Soon afterwards, Slutsky (1937) and Working (1934) were able to argue that random walk processes could produce conspicuous, yet erroneous, cyclical behaviour. Indeed, Working (1934, p. 11) expressed a view that, unfortunately, was ignored for many years: 'Economic theory has fallen far short of recognising the full implications of the resemblance of many economic time series to random-difference series; and methods of statistical analysis in general use have given these implications virtually no recognition.' Only much later, beginning in the early 1970s, were these concerns addressed seriously by modern time series econometricians.

The (re)starting point of this research programme can be traced to the paper by Granger and Newbold (1974) on the possibility of 'spurious regressions', which then led naturally to the concept of cointegration (Engle and Granger, 1987). This attempts to capture stochastically the idea of long-run equilibrium between a set of non-stationary variables. The intuition underlying cointegration was certainly not new, being related to the error correction mechanisms introduced by Phillips (1957) and given empirical content by Sargan (1964). Theoretical arguments for the existence of cointegrating relationships include market segmentation, non-instantaneous market clearing and the behaviour of steady-state solutions to intertemporal optimisation problems (see Pesaran, 1997). As noted by Markellos and Mills (1998), financial practitioners have long been aware, since at least the early 1900s, that certain trending financial time series have some form of long-run relationship, although they also realised that scaling transformations were required to be able to express these regularities as interpretable financial ratios that deviate around some average (equilibrium) value. Broadly speaking, in this context cointegration analysis can be viewed as a way of formalising financial ratio analysis and forecasting.

Section 9.1 thus analyses spurious regressions between integrated time series. This leads naturally on to the concept of cointegration, which is introduced in section 9.2. Testing for cointegration in regression models is discussed in section 9.3, and the estimation of cointegrating regressions is the subject material of section 9.4. Section 9.5 considers VARs containing integrated and, possibly, cointegrated variables, which enables us to develop the vector error correction model (VECM) framework. Causality testing in VECMs is discussed in section 9.6, and impulse response functions are analysed within a VECM framework in section 9.7. Section 9.8 focuses on the case when there is just a single long-run (cointegrating) relationship, which enables a simpler analysis to take place, and, finally, section 9.9 sets out a framework for modelling common trends and cycles.

9.1 Spurious regression

We begin by considering the simulation example analysed by Granger and Newbold (1974) in an important article examining some of the likely empirical consequences of nonsense, or *spurious*, regressions in econometrics. They consider a situation in which y_t and x_t are generated by the *independent* random walks

$$y_t = y_{t-1} + v_t, \quad x_t = x_{t-1} + w_t, \quad t = 1, 2, \ldots,$$

where v_t and w_t are independent white noises. The regression of y_t on a constant and x_t is then fitted:

$$y_t = \hat{\alpha}_T + \hat{\beta}_T x_t + \hat{u}_t, \quad t = 1, 2, \ldots, T \tag{9.1}$$

With $T = 50$, $y_0 = x_0 = 100$ and v_t and w_t drawn from independent $N(0, 1)$ distributions, Granger and Newbold report a rejection rate of 76 per cent when testing the (correct) null hypothesis that $\beta = 0$ in the regression (9.1) using the conventional t-statistic for assessing the significance of $\hat{\beta}_T$. Moreover, when five independent random walks are included as regressors in a multiple regression, the rejection rate of a conventional F-statistic testing that the coefficient vector is zero rises to 96 per cent. For regressions involving independent ARIMA(0,1,1) series the corresponding rejection rates are 64 per cent and 90 per cent, respectively, and Granger and Newbold thus conclude that conventional significance tests are seriously biased towards rejection of the null hypothesis of no relationship, and hence towards acceptance of a *spurious* relationship, when the series are generated as statistically independent integrated processes.

Moreover, such regression results are frequently accompanied by large R^2 values and highly autocorrelated residuals, as indicated by very low Durbin–Watson (dw) statistics. These findings led Granger and Newbold (1974) to suggest that, in the joint circumstances of a high R^2 and a low dw statistic (a useful rule being $R^2 > dw$), regressions should be run on the first differences of the variables. Further empirical evidence in favour of first-differencing in regression models was provided by Granger and Newbold (1986, pp. 205–15) and Plosser and Schwert (1978).

These essentially empirical conclusions have since been given an analytical foundation by Phillips (1986), who makes much weaker assumptions about the innovations $\xi_t^\top = (v_t, w_t)^\top$ than those made above. In fact, Phillips assumes that ξ_t follows a multivariate version of the conditions (3.10) used to develop non-parametric unit root tests, and which were also employed in the (stationary) regression framework of chapter 8, section 1 – i.e.

- $E(\xi_t) = 0$ for all t $\tag{9.2}$

- $\sup_{i,t} E\left(|\xi_{it}|^\beta\right) < \infty$ for some $\beta > 2, i = 1, 2 (\xi_{1t} = v_t, \ \xi_{2t} = w_t)$

$$\tag{9.2b}$$

- $\Sigma_S = \lim_{T\to\infty} T^{-1}E(S_T S_T^{\top})$ exists and is positive definite,

  where $S_T = \sum_{t=1}^{T}\xi_t$

  (9.2c)

- ξ_t is strong mixing   (9.2d)

In the special case when v_t and w_t are independent, the 'long-run' covariance matrix Σ_S is

$$\Sigma_S = \begin{bmatrix} \sigma_v^2 & 0 \\ 0 & \sigma_w^2 \end{bmatrix}$$

where

$$\sigma_v^2 = \lim_{T\to\infty} T^{-1}E(P_T^2), \quad \sigma_w^2 = \lim_{T\to\infty} T^{-1}E(Q_T^2)$$

and

$$P_t = \sum_{j=1}^{t} v_j, \qquad Q_t = \sum_{j=1}^{t} w_j, \qquad P_0 = Q_0 = 0$$

Phillips (1986) shows that, under these conditions, suitably standardised sample moments of the sequences $\{y_t\}_1^{\infty}$ and $\{x_t\}_1^{\infty}$ weakly converge to appropriately defined functionals of Brownian motion, rather than to constants as in the non-integrated regressor case discussed in chapter 8, which assumes that y_t and x_t are, for example, ergodic. As a consequence, the standard distributional results of least squares regression break down, since they are based on the ratios of sample moments converging to constants. While not providing too great a level of rigour, a sketch of the derivation of this crucial result is nonetheless illuminating. We begin by noting that we may write $y_t = P_t + y_0$ and $x_t = Q_t + x_0$, where the initial conditions y_0 and x_0 can either be constants or can have certain specified distributions, from which we construct the standardised sums (recall the development in chapter 3, section 2.1)

$$Y_T(r) = T^{-1/2}\sigma_v^{-1}P_{[rT]} = T^{-1/2}\sigma_v^{-1}P_{j-1}$$
$$X_T(r) = T^{-1/2}\sigma_w^{-1}Q_{[rT]} = T^{-1/2}\sigma_w^{-1}Q_{j-1}$$
$$(j-1)/T \le r < j/T, \quad j = 1,\ldots,T$$

Using the more general partial-sum process S_t, we can also construct

$$Z_T(r) = T^{-1/2}\Sigma_s^{-1/2}S_{[rT]} = T^{-1/2}\Sigma_s^{-1/2}S_{j-1}$$

where $\Sigma_s^{1/2}$ is the positive definite square root of Σ_s. Phillips (1987c) proves that, as $T \to \infty$, $Z_T(r)$ converges weakly to the vector Brownian motion $Z(r)$ – i.e.

$$Z_T(r) \Rightarrow Z(r)$$

From the properties of Brownian motion, $Z(r)$ is *multivariate* normal, with independent increments (so that $Z(s)$ is independent of $Z(r) - Z(s)$ for $0 < s < r \leq 1$) and with independent elements (so that the ith element $Z_i(r)$ is independent of the jth element $Z_j(r)$, $i \neq j$).

When the sequences v_t and w_t are independent,

$$Z_T(r) = \begin{bmatrix} Y_T(r) \\ X_T(r) \end{bmatrix}, \quad Z(r) = \begin{bmatrix} V(r) \\ W(r) \end{bmatrix}$$

and hence

$$Y_T(r) \Rightarrow V(r), \quad X_T(r) \Rightarrow W(r)$$

as $T \to \infty$, where $V(r)$ and $W(r)$ are independent Brownian motions. Phillips (1986) then proves the following results:

(i)
$$\hat\beta_T \Rightarrow \frac{\sigma_v\sigma_w^{-1}\left(\int_0^1 V(r)W(r)dr - \int_0^1 V(r)dr \int_0^1 W(r)dr\right)}{\int_0^1 W(r)^2 dr - \left(\int_0^1 W(r)dr\right)^2}$$

$$= \sigma_v\sigma_w^{-1}\frac{\varsigma_{VW}}{\varsigma_{WW}}$$

(ii)
$$T^{-1/2}t_{\hat\beta_T} \Rightarrow \frac{\varsigma_{VW}}{(\varsigma_{VV}\varsigma_{WW} - \varsigma_{VW})^{1/2}}$$

(iii)
$$R^2 \Rightarrow \frac{\varsigma_{VW}^2}{\varsigma_{VV}\varsigma_{WW}}$$

(iv)
$$dw \underset{p}{\to} 0$$

where we use the notation $\varsigma_{ab} = \int_0^1 a(r)b(r)dr - \int_0^1 a(r)dr \int_0^1 b(r)dr$.

As Phillips (1986) remarks, these analytical results go a long way towards explaining the Monte Carlo findings reported by Granger and Newbold (1974). Result (i) shows that, in contrast to the usual results of regression theory, $\hat{\beta}_T$ and, similarly, $\hat{\alpha}_T$, do not converge in probability to constants as $T \to \infty$. $\hat{\beta}_T$ has a non-degenerate limiting distribution, so that different arbitrary large samples will yield randomly differing estimates of β. The distribution of $\hat{\alpha}_T$ (not shown) actually diverges, so that estimates are likely to get further and further away from the true value of zero as the sample size increases. Thus, the uncertainty about the regression (9.1) stemming from its spurious nature persists asymptotically in these limiting distributions, being a consequence of the sample moments of y_t and x_t (and their joint sample moments) not converging to constants but, upon appropriate standardisation, converging weakly to random variables.

Result (ii) shows that the conventional t-ratio on $\hat{\beta}_T$ (and similarly for $\hat{\alpha}_T$,) does not have a t-distribution, and indeed does not have any limiting distribution, diverging as $T \to \infty$ so that there are *no* asymptotically correct values for these tests. We should thus expect the rejection rate when these tests are based on a critical value delivered from conventional asymptotics (such as 1.96) to continue to increase with sample size, and this is consistent with the findings of Granger and Newbold.

Results (iii) and (iv) show that R^2 has a non-degenerate limiting distribution and that dw converges in probability to zero as $T \to \infty$. Low values for dw and moderate values of R^2 are therefore to be expected in spurious regressions such as (9.1) with data generated by integrated processes, again confirming the simulation findings reported by Granger and Newbold.

These results are easily extended to multiple regressions of the form

$$y_t = \hat{\alpha}_T + \boldsymbol{\beta}_T^\top \mathbf{x}_t + \hat{u}_t \qquad (9.3)$$

where $\mathbf{x}_t = (x_{1t}, \ldots, x_{kt})^\top$ is a vector of $I(1)$ processes. Phillips (1986) shows that analogous results to (i) to (iv) above hold for (9.3) and, in particular, that the distribution of the customary F-statistic for testing a set of linear restrictions on $\boldsymbol{\beta}$ diverges as $T \to \infty$, so that there are no asymptotically correct critical values for this statistic either. Moreover, the divergence rate for the F-statistic is greater than that for individual t-tests, so in a regression with many regressors, therefore, we might expect a noticeably greater rejection rate for a 'block' F-test than for individual t-tests or for a test with fewer regressors, and this is again consistent with the results reported by Granger and Newbold.

We should emphasise that, although the derivation of the asymptotic results has assumed the independence of y_t and $\mathbf{x}_t$, so that the true values of α and $\boldsymbol{\beta}$ are zero, this is not crucial to the major conclusions. Although the correlation properties of the time series do have quantitative effects on the limiting distributions, these being introduced via the parameters of the limiting covariance matrix Σ_S in the bivariate regression analysed in detail above, such effects do not interfere with the main qualitative results: that $\hat{\alpha}_T$ and $\hat{\boldsymbol{\beta}}_T$ do not converge in probability to constants, that the distributions of F- and t-statistics diverge as $T \to \infty$, and that dw converges in probability to zero whereas R^2 has a non-degenerate limiting distribution as $T \to \infty$. Hamilton (1994, chap. 19.3) provides a detailed treatment of the spurious multiple regression model.

A Monte Carlo simulation similar to that of Granger and Newbold (1974) enables us to interpret these results in a perhaps more transparent fashion. The independent random walks y_t and x_t were generated for a sample now of size $T = 1000$, v_t and w_t were again drawn from independent $N(0,1)$ populations and $y_0 = x_0 = 0$, using 10,000 iterations. Figures 9.1 to 9.4 present the density functions of $\hat{\beta}_{1000}$, its associated t-ratio, and the R^2 and dw statistics. The distribution of $\hat{\beta}_{1000}$ is almost normally distributed (a central limit theorem does, in fact, hold as the simulations use independent replications).

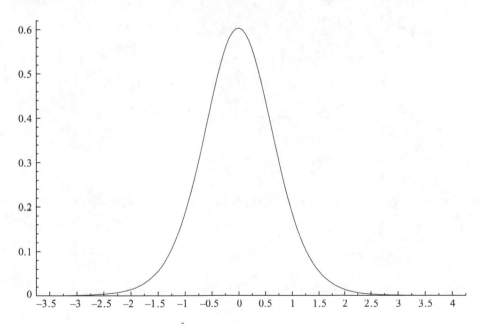

Figure 9.1   Simulated frequency distribution of $\hat{\beta}_{1000}$

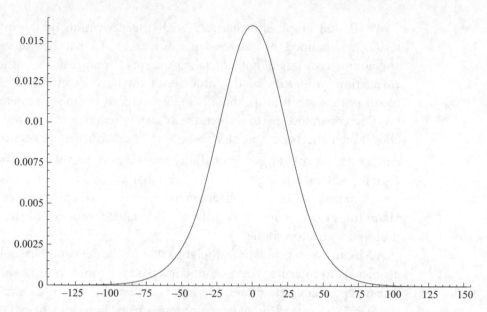

Figure 9.2   Simulated frequency distribution of the t-ratio of $\hat{\beta}_{1000}$

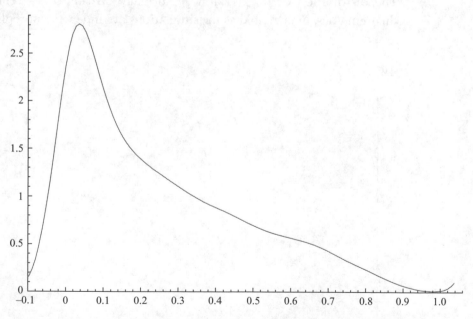

Figure 9.3   Simulated frequency distribution of the spurious regression R^2

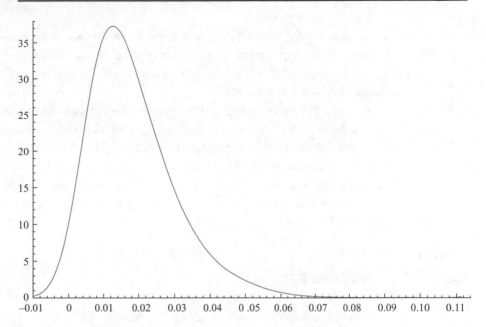

Figure 9.4   Simulated frequency distribution of the spurious regression *dw*

Although the sample mean is −0.0052, the sample standard deviation is 0.635, confirming that, for large *T*, the distribution does not converge to a constant and different samples produce very different estimates of β, the range of estimates being approximately ±3.0.

The distribution of the *t*-ratio, shown in figure 9.2, is again normal but with a standard deviation of 23.62. The 5 per cent critical values from this distribution are ±48.30, while using ±1.96 would entail a rejection rate of 93.4 per cent. The distribution of the R^2 statistic has a mean of 0.24, a standard deviation of 0.23 and a maximum value of 0.94, while that for the *dw* statistic has a mean of 0.018, a standard deviation of 0.011 and a maximum value of only 0.10. (Note that the smoothing involved in constructing the density functions leads to negative values in the left-hand tails of these two distributions; the actual minimum sample values of R^2 and *dw* are, of course, positive, although extremely small, being 0.0008 for *dw* and of the order of 10^{-10} for R^2.) Both sampling distributions thus illustrate the theoretical predictions of Phillips' (1986) analysis.

It should be emphasised that, in the general set-up discussed here, where both y_t and $\mathbf{x}_t$ are $I(1)$ processes, the error, u_t, since it is by definition a linear combination of $I(1)$ processes, will also be integrated, unless a special restriction (to be discussed subsequently) holds. Moreover, the usual respecification of the model to include y_{t-1} as an additional regressor on the finding of a very low *dw* value will have pronounced consequences: the estimated coefficient on y_{t-1} will converge to unity, while that on the integrated regressor(s) will converge to zero, thus highlighting the spurious nature of the static regression.

Indeed, the spurious nature of the regression is, in fact, a consequence of the error being $I(1)$. Achieving a stationary, or $I(0)$, error is usually a minimum criterion to meet in econometric modelling, for much of the focus of recent developments in the construction of dynamic regression models has been to ensure that the error is not only $I(0)$ but white noise. Whether the error in a regression between integrated variables is stationary is therefore a matter of considerable importance.

9.2 Cointegrated processes

As just noted, a linear combination of $I(1)$ processes will usually also be $I(1)$. In general, if y_t and x_t are both $I(d)$, then the linear combination

$$u_t = y_t - ax_t \tag{9.4}$$

will usually be $I(d)$. It is possible, however, that w_t may be integrated of a lower order, say $I(d-b)$, where $b > 0$, in which case a special constraint operates on the long-run components of the two series. If $d = b = 1$, so that y_t and x_t are both $I(1)$ and dominated by 'long-wave' components, u_t will be $I(0)$, and hence will not have such components; y_t and ax_t must therefore have long-run components that cancel out to produce u_t. In such circumstances, y_t and x_t are said to be *cointegrated*; we emphasise that it will *not* generally be true that there will exist such an *a* that makes $u_t \sim I(0)$, or, in general, $I(d-b)$.

The idea of cointegration can be related to the concept of *long-run equilibrium*, which can be illustrated by the bivariate relationship

$$y_t = ax_t$$

or

$$y_t - ax_t = 0$$

Thus, u_t given by (9.4) measures the extent to which the 'system' is out of equilibrium, and it can therefore be termed the 'equilibrium error'. Assuming that $d = b = 1$, so that y_t and x_t are both $I(1)$, the equilibrium error will then be $I(0)$ and u_t will rarely drift far from zero, and will often cross the zero line. In other words, equilibrium will occasionally occur, at least to a close approximation, whereas if y_t and x_t are not cointegrated, so that $u_t \sim I(1)$, the equilibrium error will wander widely and zero crossings would be very rare, suggesting that under these circumstances the concept of equilibrium has no practical implications.

How is the concept of cointegration linked to the analysis of spurious regressions? Condition (9.2c) on the innovation sequence ξ_t requires that the limiting covariance matrix Σ_S be non-singular. If we allow Σ_S to be singular, the asymptotic theory yielding the results (i) to (iv) no longer holds. In general, we have

$$\Sigma_S = \begin{bmatrix} \sigma_v^2 & \sigma_{vw} \\ \sigma_{vw} & \sigma_w^2 \end{bmatrix}$$

so that, for Σ_S to be singular, we require $|\Sigma_S| = \sigma_v^2 \sigma_w^2 - \sigma_{vw}^2 = 0$. This implies that $\Sigma_S \gamma = 0$, where $\gamma^\top = (1, -a)$ and $a = \sigma_{vw}/\sigma_w^2$. Singularity of Σ_S is a necessary condition for y_t and x_t to be cointegrated (Phillips, 1986; Phillips and Ouliaris, 1990), since in this case $|\Sigma_S| = 0$ implies that the 'long-run' correlation between the innovations v_t and w_t, given by $\rho_{vw} = \sigma_{vw}/\sigma_v \sigma_w$, is unity. For values of ρ_{vw} less than unity, y_t and x_t are not cointegrated, and when $\rho_{vw} = 0$, so that v_t and w_t are independent, we have Granger and Newbold's (1974) spurious regression.

What differences to the asymptotic regression theory for integrated regressors result when y_t is cointegrated with x_t? Since the equilibrium error u_t can be regarded as the error term in the regression of y_t on x_t, we may consider first the model

$$y_t = \beta x_t + u_t \tag{9.5a}$$

where

$$x_t = \pi + x_{t-1} + w_t \tag{9.5b}$$

and where u_t and w_t are contemporaneously correlated white noise – i.e. $E(u_t w_t) = \sigma_{uw}$.

The OLS estimator of β is

$$\hat{\beta}_T = \left(\sum_{t=1}^{T} x_t y_t \right) \left(\sum_{t=1}^{T} x_t^2 \right)^{-1} = \beta + \left(\sum_{t=1}^{T} x_t u_t \right) \left(\sum_{t=1}^{T} x_t^2 \right)^{-1}$$

Now, if $\pi = 0$, then, since $x_t \sim I(1)$, $\sum_{t=1}^{T} x_t^2$ needs to be scaled by T^{-2} for it to converge to a finite value, whereas $\sum_{t=1}^{T} x_t u_t$ just requires scaling by T^{-1} for it to converge to a finite value (see chapter 3, section 2.1). Thus,

$$T(\hat{\beta}_T - \beta) = \left(T^{-1} \sum_{t=1}^{T} x_t u_t\right)\left(T^{-2} \sum_{t=1}^{T} x_t^2\right)^{-1}$$

converges to zero – i.e. $\hat{\beta}_T$ converges to β at the rate T. Contrast this with the standard regression case, when $x_t \sim I(0)$; now $\sum_{t=1}^{T} x_t^2$ only needs scaling by T^{-1} and we have

$$T^{1/2}(\hat{\beta}_T - \beta) = \left(T^{-1/2} \sum_{t=1}^{T} x_t u_t\right)\left(T^{-1} \sum_{t=1}^{T} x_t^2\right)^{-1}$$

i.e. $\hat{\beta}_T$ converges to β at the rate $T^{-1/2}$. The faster rate of convergence under cointegration is known as the *super-consistency* property (Stock, 1987) and implies that, even though $E(x_t u_t)$ may be non-zero through σ_{uw} being non-zero, there is no asymptotic endogeneity bias.

Although $\hat{\beta}_T$ is super-consistent, however, it is not necessarily asymptotically unbiased or normally distributed. To obtain the limiting distribution of $\hat{\beta}_T$ and its t-ratio, we condition u_t on w_t through

$$u_t = \gamma w_t + v_t, \qquad \gamma = \sigma_{uw}/\sigma_w^2, \qquad \sigma_v^2 = \sigma_u^2 - \sigma_{uw}^2/\sigma_w^2 \qquad (9.6)$$

so that a non-zero contemporaneous correlation between the innovations u_t and w_t, and hence endogeneity between y_t and x_t, may be incorporated. The limiting distribution of $\hat{\beta}_T - \beta$ can then be written

$$T(\hat{\beta}_T - \beta) \Rightarrow (\gamma/2)\left(W(1)^2+1\right)\left(\int_0^1 W(r)^2 dr\right)^{-1} + \left((\sigma_u/\sigma_w)^2 - \gamma^2\right)N(0,1)$$

while that of the t-ratio is

$$t_{\hat{\beta}_T} \Rightarrow (\rho_{uw}/2)\left(W(1)^2+1\right)\left(\int_0^1 W(r)^2 dr\right)^{-1/2} + \left(1 - \rho_{uw}^2\right)^{1/2}N(0,1)$$

where $\rho_{uw} = \sigma_{uw}/\sigma_u \sigma_w$. In general, therefore, these limiting distributions will not have standard normal distributions unless $\gamma = \rho_{uw} = 0$, which is the condition for strong exogeneity of x_t. When this condition does not hold, the first terms in the limiting distributions give rise to 'second-order' endogeneity bias (Phillips and Hansen, 1990), which, although asymptotically negligible in estimating β because of super-consistency, can be important in finite samples.

These theoretical results can also be demonstrated via Monte Carlo simulation. The model given by (9.5) was used with $\beta = \pi = 0$ and with the settings $\sigma_w^2 = \sigma_v^2 = 1$ and $\sigma_{uw} = 0.75$, so that $\gamma = 0.75$ and $\rho_{uw} = 0.57$. With, once again, $T = 1000$ and 10,000 iterations, figure 9.5 shows the simulated frequency distribution of $\hat{\beta}_{1000}$. The sample mean is 0.0028, and 95 per cent of the estimates lie in the interval $(-0.0016, 0.0093)$, reflecting the super-consistency property. This interval also shows the skewness of the distribution, however – i.e. the presence of second-order endogeneity bias caused by the lack of strong exogeneity of x_t. Figure 9.6 shows the simulated t-ratio. Since γ is non-zero, the distribution will not be standard normal: although normal in shape, it is centred on 0.994 with a standard deviation of 0.884.

Figures 9.7 to 9.9 show the results of three related simulations. Figure 9.7 shows the simulated frequency distribution of the slope coefficient of the regression of y_t on x_t when x_t is generated by the stationary AR(1) process $x_t = 0.5x_{t-1} + w_t$, rather than the random walk of (9.5b), but when all other settings remain the same. The endogeneity bias is now readily apparent, with the distribution, although normal, having a mean of 0.565 and a standard deviation of 0.035. Figure 9.8 shows the simulated frequency distribution of

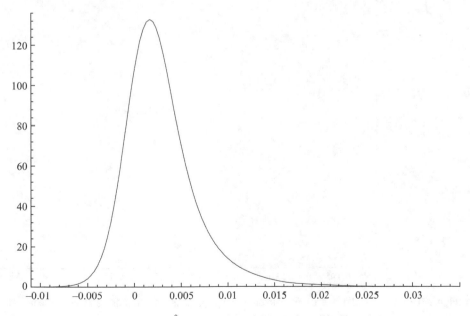

Figure 9.5   Simulated frequency distribution of $\hat{\beta}_{1000}$ from the cointegrated model with endogenous regressor

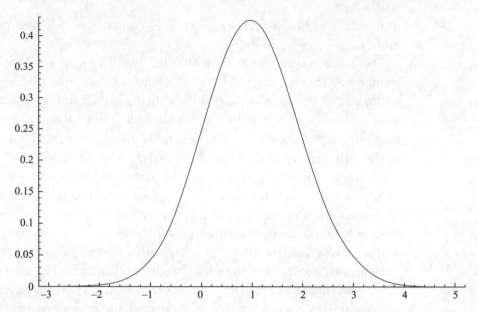

Figure 9.6   Simulated frequency distribution of the *t*-ratio on $\hat{\beta}_{1000}$ from the cointegrated model with endogenous regressor

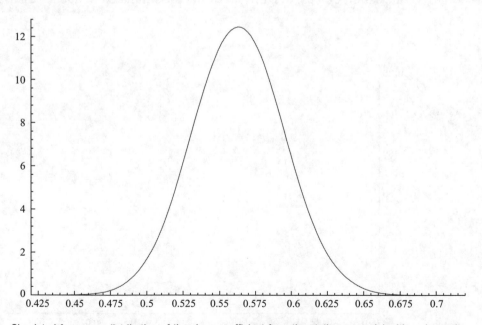

Figure 9.7   Simulated frequency distribution of the slope coefficient from the stationary model with endogeneity

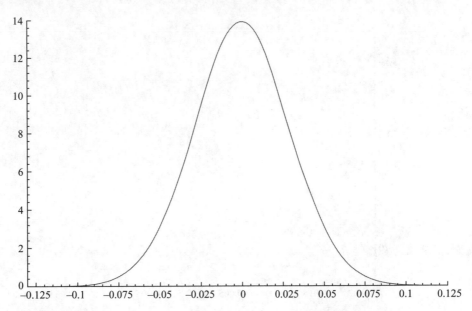

Figure 9.8 Simulated frequency distribution of the slope coefficient from the stationary model without endogeneity

the slope coefficient in the same stationary regression but where now $\sigma_{uw} = 0$, so that there is no endogeneity; consequently, the distribution is centred on zero. Finally, figure 9.9 shows the frequency distribution of $\hat{\beta}_{1000}$ from the cointegrated model but with $\sigma_{uw} = 0$. With no endogeneity, the distribution is normal, as compared to figure 9.5, but has a standard error of 0.0035, thus reflecting the super-consistency property of cointegrated regressions when compared to its stationary counterpart in figure 9.8.

The assumption made in all these simulations, that x_t is without drift ($\pi = 0$), is not innocuous, however, for when x_t contains a drift

$$x_t = t\pi + \sum_{j=1}^{t} w_j = t\pi + Q_t$$

and we need to consider

$$T^{-3/2} \sum_{t=1}^{T} x_t u_t = \pi T^{-3/2} \sum_{t-1}^{T} t u_t + T^{-3/2} \sum_{t-1}^{T} u_t Q_t$$

and

$$T^{-3/2} \left(\hat{\beta}_T - \beta \right) = \left(T^{-3/2} \sum_{t=1}^{T} x_t u_t \right) \left(T^{-3} \sum_{t=1}^{T} x_t^2 \right)^{-1}$$

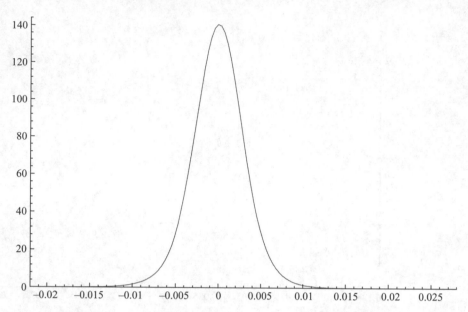

Figure 9.9   Simulated frequency distribution of the t-ratio on $\hat{\beta}_{1000}$ from the cointegrated model with exogenous regressor

West (1988) shows that the probability limits of $T^{-3/2}\sum_{t=1}^{T}u_t Q_t$ and $T^{-3}\sum_{t=1}^{T}x_t^2$ are zero and $\pi^2/3$, respectively, and that $\pi T^{-3/2}\sum_{t=1}^{T}tu_t$ is normally distributed with mean zero and variance $\pi^2\sigma_u^2/3$. Hence,

$$T^{3/2}\left(\hat{\beta}_T - \beta\right) \Rightarrow N\left(0, 3\sigma_u^2/\pi^2\right)$$

so that in these circumstances asymptotic normality does hold, irrespective of whether there is endogeneity or not. Thus, consider the model (9.5) with $\pi = 1$ and, again, $\sigma_w^2 = \sigma_v^2 = 1$ and $\sigma_{uw} = 0.75$. Since $\hat{\beta}_{1000}$ and $\beta = 0$, $\hat{\beta}_{1000}$ should be normally distributed with mean zero and standard deviation 0.000072. Figure 9.10 shows the simulated frequency distribution of $\hat{\beta}_{1000}$, which is indeed approximately normally distributed with a sample mean of zero and a standard deviation of 0.00069, and should be compared with the skewed distribution for $\hat{\beta}_{1000}$ that results from the absence of drift, shown in figure 9.5.

In general, we may consider regressions of the form (9.5) but with a vector of $I(1)$, rather than random walk, regressors $\mathbf{x}_t$ that may contain drifts, and with $u_t \sim I(0)$ rather than white noise, so that the sequence $e_t^{\top} = (u_t, w_t)$ of joint innovations may be assumed to satisfy the conditions (9.2). When the

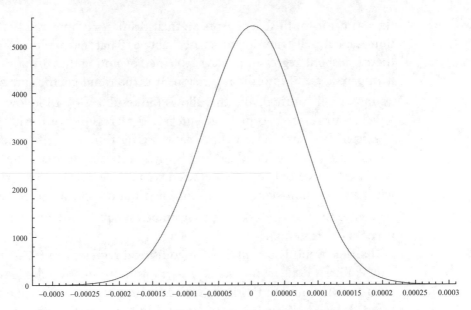

Figure 9.10 Simulated frequency distribution of $\hat{\beta}_{1000}$ from the cointegrated model with endogenous regressor and drift

regressor vector $\mathbf{x}_t$ is without drift, Phillips and Durlauf (1986) show that super-consistency again holds for the OLS estimator $\hat{\boldsymbol{\beta}}_T$ of the coefficient vector $\boldsymbol{\beta}$. They then go on to consider testing general linear hypotheses of the type considered in chapter 8, section 1.2. The limiting distribution of the Wald statistic (8.5), which is chi-square for non-integrated regressors, now contains nuisance parameters even if u_t is white noise, and is non-normal and asymmetric.

When some of the regressors have drifts, Park and Phillips (1988) show that super-consistency of $\hat{\boldsymbol{\beta}}_T$ again results. Unlike when there is just a single regressor, however, the limiting distribution of $T(\hat{\boldsymbol{\beta}}_T - \boldsymbol{\beta})$ is both non-normal and singular, since the regressors will be perfectly correlated asymptotically. This is because an $I(1)$ variable with drift can always be expressed as the sum of a time trend and an $I(1)$ variable without drift – e.g.

$$\Delta x_t = \pi + w_t = x_0 + \pi t + \Delta \ddot{x}_t, \quad \Delta x_t = w_t$$

so that the correlation between two such variables will be dominated by their trends rather than by the driftless $I(1)$ components. This suggests that these variables should be detrended and a time trend added to (9.5a). The estimator of the coefficient of the trend will be asymptotically normal, while the estimators of the coefficients on their driftless components will have the non-standard distribution discussed above. That normality occurs when there is just one regressor may be explained by noting that the non-zero drift π imparts a trend into the regression. It is the trend coefficient, $\pi\beta$, that is asymptotically normal, and this allows the result on $\hat{\beta}_T$ to follow.

When there are two or more integrated regressors with drift, the trend coefficient becomes a linear combination of the different drifts, and only this combination can be identified and is asymptotically normal. The vector $\hat{\boldsymbol{\beta}}_T$ can be estimated only by the coefficients on driftless $I(1)$ regressors, and this will have the non-standard limiting distribution. If all the regressors are strongly exogeneous, $\hat{\boldsymbol{\beta}}_T$ will once again be asymptotically normal on appropriate standardisation.

If a time trend is included as an additional regressor in (9.5a) then Park and Phillips (1988) show that the asymptotic results for the least squares estimators remain valid, although the estimator of the coefficient on the time trend depends on π. Furthermore, if additional stationary regressors are included in (9.5a) then their coefficients will be asymptotically normal.

9.3 Testing for cointegration in regression

Given the crucial role that cointegration plays in regression models with integrated variables, it is important to test for its presence. A number of tests have been proposed that are based on the residuals from the *cointegrating regression*

$$\hat{u}_t = y_t - \hat{\alpha}_T - \hat{\boldsymbol{\beta}}_T^\top \mathbf{x}_t \tag{9.7}$$

Such residual-based procedures seek to test a null hypothesis of *no* cointegration by using unit root tests applied to $\hat{u}_t$. Perhaps the simplest test to use is the usual Durbin–Watson dw statistic, but, since the null is that $\hat{u}_t$ is $I(1)$, the value of the test statistic under the null is $dw = 0$, with rejection in favour of the $I(0)$ alternative occurring for values of dw *greater* than zero (Sargan and Bhargava, 1983; Bhargava, 1986).

As is well known, the conventional critical values of the dw statistic depend upon the underlying processes generating the observed data, and Engle and Granger (1987) and Phillips and Ouliaris (1988) provide critical values, for various sample sizes and generating processes, in the 'non-standard' case considered here. Unfortunately, there are several difficulties associated with this simple test: under the no cointegration null the asymptotic distribution of dw depends on nuisance parameters such as the correlations among $\Delta \mathbf{x}_t$; the critical value bounds diverge as the number of regressors increases, becoming so wide as to have no practical value for inference; and the statistic assumes that under the null u_t is a random walk, and under the alternative u_t is a stationary AR(1) process. If this actually is the case, then Bhargava (1986) shows that dw has excellent power properties, but the critical bounds will not be correct if there is higher-order residual autocorrelation.

Engle and Granger (1987) therefore prefer to use the t-ratio on $\hat{u}_{t-1}$ from the regression of $\Delta \hat{u}_t$ on $\hat{u}_{t-1}$ and lagged values of $\Delta \hat{u}_t$, in a manner analogous to the unit root testing approach for an observed series discussed in chapter 3 (see, for example, equation (3.8)). The problem here is that, since $\hat{u}_t$ is derived as a residual from a regression in which the cointegrating vector is estimated, and since if the null of non-cointegration was true such a vector would not be identified, using the τ_μ critical values would reject the null too often, because least squares will seek the cointegrating vector that minimises the residual variance and hence is most likely to result in a stationary residual series. Moreover, an additional factor that influences the distribution of the t-ratio is the number of regressors contained in $\mathbf{x}_t$. Critical values are again available from many sources (see, for example, Hamilton, 1994, table B.9, and Banerjee *et al.*, 1993, table 9.1). For example, the large T 5 per cent, 2.5 per cent and 1 per cent critical values when $\mathbf{x}_t = x_t$ are -3.37, -3.64 and -3.97, respectively.

As with conventional unit roots tests, more extensive critical values than those given in standard tables are available in most econometric packages, again obtained using the response surfaces computed by MacKinnon (1991). For example, when $\mathbf{x}_t = x_t$, so that there are $n = 2$ variables in $(y_t, \mathbf{x}_t)$, the 1 per cent critical values, denoted $C_{.01}(T)$, are calculated using

$$C_{.01}(T) = -3.900 - 10.534T^{-1} - 30.03T^{-2}$$

MacKinnon (1996) can be consulted for details of how to obtain p-values for a wide range of sample sizes. As with the conventional unit root tests, different sets of critical values are to be used either if there is no constant in the cointegrating regression or if there is a constant and trend (corresponding to the τ and τ_τ variants). Non-parametric variants may also be constructed (see Phillips and Ouliaris, 1990).

Tests may also be derived using the *error correction model* (ECM) *representation* of a cointegrated system. Consider again the model given by

(9.5) and (9.6) with $\pi = 0$ and where u_t is now generated by a stationary AR (1) process:

$$
\begin{aligned}
y_t - \beta x_t &= u_t \\
u_t &= \rho u_{t-1} + \varepsilon_{1t}, \quad |\rho| < 1 \\
\Delta x_t &= w_t \\
u_t &= \gamma w_t + v_t
\end{aligned}
\tag{9.8}
$$

This can be written as

$$
\begin{aligned}
\Delta y_t - \beta \Delta x_t &= (\rho - 1)y_{t-1} - \beta(\rho - 1)x_{t-1} + \varepsilon_{1t} \\
\Delta y_t - \gamma \Delta x_t &= \varepsilon_{2t}
\end{aligned}
$$

where $\varepsilon_{2t} = v_t + \beta w_t - x_{t-1}$. Thus,

$$
\begin{bmatrix} \Delta y_t \\ \Delta x_t \end{bmatrix} = \begin{bmatrix} 1 & -\beta \\ 1 & -\gamma \end{bmatrix}^{-1} \begin{bmatrix} (\rho - 1)y_{t-1} - \beta(\rho - 1)x_{t-1} + \varepsilon_{1t} \\ \varepsilon_{2t} \end{bmatrix}
$$

or

$$
\begin{bmatrix} \Delta y_t \\ \Delta x_t \end{bmatrix} = (\beta - \gamma)^{-1} \begin{bmatrix} \gamma(1 - \rho)y_{t-1} - \gamma\beta(1 - \rho)x_{t-1} \\ (1 - \rho)y_{t-1} - \beta(1 - \rho)x_{t-1} \end{bmatrix} + \begin{bmatrix} \zeta_{1t} \\ \zeta_{2t} \end{bmatrix}
$$

where

$$
\begin{bmatrix} \zeta_{1t} \\ \zeta_{2t} \end{bmatrix} = (\beta - \gamma)^{-1} \begin{bmatrix} \beta\varepsilon_{2t} - \gamma\varepsilon_{1t} \\ \varepsilon_{2t} - \varepsilon_{1t} \end{bmatrix}
$$

This leads to the ECM representation

$$
\begin{aligned}
\Delta y_t &= \delta\gamma(y_{t-1} - \beta x_{t-1}) + \zeta_{1t} = \delta\gamma u_{t-1} + \zeta_{1t} = \theta_1 u_{t-1} + \zeta_{1t} \\
\Delta x_t &= \delta(y_{t-1} - \beta x_{t-1}) + \zeta_{2t} = \delta u_{t-1} + \zeta_{2t} = \theta_2 u_{t-1} + \zeta_{2t}
\end{aligned}
\tag{9.9}
$$

where we let $\delta = (\beta - \gamma)^{-1}(1 - \rho)$. From the ECM representation (9.9), δ is non-zero if and only if ρ is not equal to one, but $\rho = 1$ is the condition that ensures that *both* u_t and w_t are random walks, in which case y_t and x_t *cannot* be cointegrated – i.e. if $\rho = 1$ there does not exist a β that makes the linear combination of y_t and x_t stationary.

The tests discussed above investigate the null hypothesis $\rho = 1$ using the residuals from the cointegrating regression (9.7), but an alternative is to test either of the nulls $\theta_1 = 0$ and $\theta_2 = 0$, or the joint null $\theta_1 = \theta_2 = 0$, which would be more efficient given that the cross-equation restriction in (9.7) implies that the *error correction* u_{t-1} enters both equations of the ECM. There is a problem, however: since β is unknown, it must be estimated from the data. If $\rho = 1$ is valid, however, β is unidentified and the ECM (9.9) is invalid. Only if y_t and x_t are cointegrated can β be estimated from the cointegrated regression, but a test must be based upon the distribution of the statistic assuming that the null is true.

A solution to this problem may be found by rewriting the error correction equation for y_t, say, as

$$\Delta y_t = \theta_1(y_{t-1} - x_{t-1}) + dx_{t-1} + \zeta_{1t}$$

where $d = \theta_1(1 - \beta)$, so that a test of $\theta_1 = 0$ can be based on its associated *t*-ratio and tests of $\theta_2 = 0$ and $\theta_1 = \theta_2 = 0$ can be constructed analogously. This statistic will not be asymptotically normal, however, and Banerjee *et al.* (1993, table 9.6) provide fractiles for the simulated distribution for various sample sizes; they are slightly closer to zero than those of the corresponding residual unit root test.

How powerful are these tests of cointegration? Banerjee *et al.* (1993) investigate power by conducting a Monte Carlo experiment using two alternative data-generating processes for y_t and x_t. The first is the model (9.8), where we rewrite the equation for y_t as

$$y_t = \rho y_{t-1} + \beta x_t - \beta\rho x_{t-1} + \varepsilon_{1t}$$

The second is the general dynamic model

$$y_t = \alpha_1 y_{t-1} + \alpha_2 x_t + \alpha_3 x_{t-1} + u_t$$

from which the first model is obtained by imposing the 'common factor' restriction $\alpha_1\alpha_2 + \alpha_3 = 0$. Banerjee *et al.* find that the *t*-ratio test performs better than the unit root test in the absence of a common factor. For further analysis of these tests, see Ericsson and MacKinnon (2002).

Example 9.1 Cointegration and the market model: an example of testing for cointegration

The market model is typically defined as

$$r_{p,t} = \alpha + \beta_0 r_{m,t} + u_t$$

using the notation introduced in example 8.4 (in contrast to the CAPM analysed there, the actual returns on a stock or small portfolio in period t, $r_{p,t}$,

Table 9.1 Market model cointegration test statistics

	dw	C	t
CTLD	0.05	−1.38	−2.40
PRU	0.24*	−2.92	−3.03
LGEN	0.14*	−3.47*	−3.71*

Notes: dw is the Durbin–Watson statistic from the cointegrating regression. C is the unit root test on the cointegrating residuals. t is the t-ratio from the error correction model. * denotes significance at the 5 per cent level: critical values are, approximately, 0.14 for dw and −3.42 for C and t.

and on the corresponding market return, $r_{m,t}$, are used rather than excess returns). If we assume that either dividends are reinvested or that they are ignored completely, then the returns will typically be calculated as

$$r_{p,t} = \Delta y_t \quad r_{m,t} = \Delta x_t$$

where y_t and x_t are the logarithms of the stock price and market index respectively. If y_t and x_t are $I(1)$ then such a specification would be appropriate if the two series were *not* cointegrated; if they were cointegrated then the market model would be misspecified, in that an error correction term, $y_{t-1} - \beta x_{t-1}$, would be required as an additional regressor.

We illustrate the possibility of cointegration within the market model by using several examples taken from a data set that has been extensively analysed by Mills (1996b), Coutts, Roberts and Mills (1997) and Markellos and Mills (2003). This data set contains weekly observations on the London Stock Exchange FTSE 100 index and on the prices of the fifty-six companies that remained constituents of the index throughout the first ten years of its existence, January 1984 to December 1993, so that $T = 521$. The relationships between the (logarithmic) prices of three of these companies, Courtaulds (CTLD), Prudential (PRU) and Legal and General (LGEN), and the FTSE 100 are analysed in a sequence of examples. (Unit root tests confirm that all are $I(1)$, although the FTSE 100 is only marginally so; the possibility that it is $I(0)$ – more precisely, trend stationary – will be taken into account in a later example.)

Table 9.1 presents the three cointegration test statistics discussed above for each of the three series. There is no evidence of cointegration between CTLD and the FTSE 100 and little evidence of cointegration for PRU, but it appears that LGEN is cointegrated with the FTSE 100. Figure 9.11 plots each of the three series against the FTSE 100 and the lack of cointegration between CTLD and the market index is readily apparent. There is much more

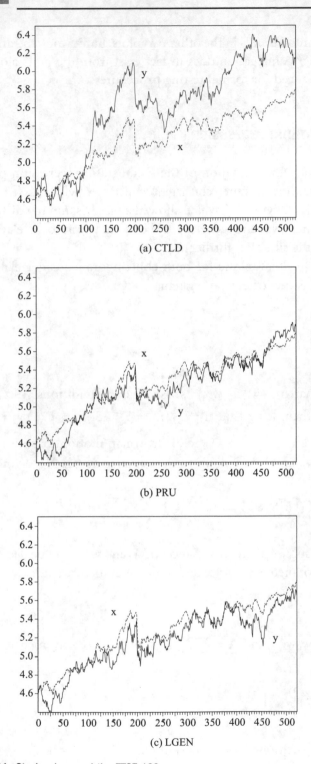

(a) CTLD

(b) PRU

(c) LGEN

Figure 9.11 Stock prices and the FTSE 100

evidence of common trends in the other two plots, but it would be difficult to ascertain whether cointegation does in fact exist from the plots alone, thus emphasising the need for formal testing procedures.

9.4 Estimating cointegrating regressions

As we have seen, OLS estimation of the cointegrating regression produces estimates that, although super-consistent, are nevertheless biased even in large samples (recall figure 9.5, which showed a biased sampling distribution for $\hat{\beta}_{1000}$ when there was endogeneity between y_t and x_t; autocorrelation in u_t will exacerbate the situation further).

A general set-up that allows for both contemporaneous correlation and autocorrelation is the 'triangular' system

$$y_t = \beta^\top \mathbf{x}_t + u_t \tag{9.10}$$

$$\Delta \mathbf{x}_t = \mathbf{w}_t$$

We assume that $\mathbf{u}_t^\top = \left(u_t, \mathbf{w}_t^\top\right)$ satisfies the conditions (9.2). With $\mathbf{S}_T = \sum_{t=1}^T \mathbf{u}_t$, then, for $r \in [0, 1]$, $\mathbf{U}_T(r) = T^{-\frac{1}{2}}\mathbf{S}_{[Tr]} \Rightarrow \mathbf{U}(r) = \left(U_1(r)^\top, U_2(r)^\top\right)^\top$, where $\mathbf{U}(r)$ is $(1+k)$ vector Brownian motion, partitioned conformably with $\mathbf{u}_t$, and having long-run covariance matrix $\mathbf{\Sigma_S}$, defined as

$$\mathbf{\Sigma_S} = \lim_{T \to \infty} T^{-1}E\left(\mathbf{S}_T\mathbf{S}_T^\top\right) = \lim_{T \to \infty} T^{-1} \sum_{t=1}^T \sum_{s=1}^T E\left(\mathbf{u}_t\mathbf{u}_s^\top\right)$$

Since this is the sum of all the covariances of $\mathbf{w}_t$ and $\mathbf{w}_s$, it can be decomposed into a contemporaneous variance and sums of autocovariances,

$$\mathbf{\Sigma_S} = \mathbf{\Lambda}_0 + \mathbf{\Lambda} + \mathbf{\Lambda}^\top$$

where $\mathbf{\Lambda}_0 = E\left(\mathbf{w}_0\mathbf{w}_0^\top\right)$ and $\mathbf{\Lambda} = \sum_{t=1}^\infty E\left(\mathbf{w}_0\mathbf{w}_t^\top\right)$. For convenience, we partition $\mathbf{\Sigma_S}$ as

$$\mathbf{\Sigma_S} = \begin{bmatrix} \Sigma_{11} & \Sigma_{21}^\top \\ \Sigma_{21} & \Sigma_{22} \end{bmatrix}$$

with $\mathbf{\Lambda}_0$ and $\mathbf{\Lambda}$ partitioned similarly (note that Σ_{11} is a scalar).

Park and Phillips (1988) show that the limiting distribution of $\hat{\boldsymbol{\beta}}_T$ is

$$T(\hat{\boldsymbol{\beta}}_T - \boldsymbol{\beta}) \Rightarrow \left(\int_0^1 U_2(r) U_2(r)^\top dr \right)^{-1} \left(\int_0^1 U_2(r) dU_1(r)^\top + \boldsymbol{\Delta}_{21} \right)$$

where $\boldsymbol{\Delta}_{21} = \boldsymbol{\Sigma}_{21} + \boldsymbol{\Lambda}_{21}$. It is this term that introduces the second-order bias, and, of course, it arises because of the contemporaneous and serial dependence of the regressors. Phillips and Hansen (1990) have proposed a modification to OLS that eliminates this bias. Define

$$y_t^+ = y_t - \hat{\boldsymbol{\Sigma}}_{12} \hat{\boldsymbol{\Sigma}}_{22}^{-1} \Delta \mathbf{x}_t$$

which uses any consistent estimator $\hat{\boldsymbol{\Sigma}}_S$ of $\boldsymbol{\Sigma}_S$. The *fully modified OLS* (FM-OLS) estimator is defined as

$$\hat{\boldsymbol{\beta}}_T^+ = \left(\sum_{t=1}^T y_t^+ \mathbf{x}_t^\top - T \hat{\boldsymbol{\delta}}^+ \right) \left(\sum_{t=1}^T \mathbf{x}_t \mathbf{x}_t^\top \right)^{-1}$$

where

$$\hat{\boldsymbol{\delta}}^+ = \left(\mathbf{I} - \hat{\boldsymbol{\Sigma}}_{12} \hat{\boldsymbol{\Sigma}}_{22}^{-1} \right) \hat{\boldsymbol{\Lambda}}_2$$

$\hat{\boldsymbol{\Lambda}}_2$ being a consistent estimator of $\boldsymbol{\Lambda}_2 = \sum_{t=0}^{\infty} E(\mathbf{w}_0 \mathbf{u}_t^\top)$.

The limiting distribution of the FM-OLS estimator is

$$T(\hat{\boldsymbol{\beta}}_T^+ - \boldsymbol{\beta}) \Rightarrow \left(\int_0^1 U_2(r) U_2(r)^\top dr \right)^{-1} \left(\int_0^1 U_2(r) dU_{1.2}(r)^\top \right)$$

where $U_{1.2}(r)$ is independent of $U(r)$. The use of y_t^+ corrects for long-run simultaneity, whilst incorporating $\hat{\boldsymbol{\delta}}^+$ accounts for any residual autocorrelation. This allows conventional chi-square asymptotics to be used for inference. For example, the null $\mathbf{R}\boldsymbol{\beta} = \mathbf{r}$ may be tested by constructing the *modified* Wald statistic (cf. equation (9.5))

$$W_T^! = T(\mathbf{R}\hat{\boldsymbol{\beta}}_T^+ - \mathbf{r})^\top \left[\mathbf{R}(\mathbf{X}^\top \mathbf{X}/T)^{-1} \hat{\mathbf{V}}_T^+ (\mathbf{X}^\top \mathbf{X}/T)^{-1} \mathbf{R}^\top \right] (\mathbf{R}\hat{\boldsymbol{\beta}}_T^+ - \mathbf{r})$$

where $\hat{\mathbf{V}}_T^+ = \hat{\boldsymbol{\Sigma}}_{11} - \hat{\boldsymbol{\Sigma}}_{12} \hat{\boldsymbol{\Sigma}}_{22}^{-1} \hat{\boldsymbol{\Sigma}}_{12}$ and $\mathbf{X}$ is as defined in (9.2). For $\hat{\boldsymbol{\Sigma}}_S$ we may use the Newey–West estimator (9.4).

Several other estimators have been proposed that correct for both correlation between u_t and $\mathbf{w}_t$ and autocorrelation in u_t. The approaches of Saikkonen (1991), Phillips and Loretan (1991), Stock and Watson (1993) and

Banerjee, Dolado and Mestre (1998) all suggest augmenting (9.10) with leads and lags of $\Delta\mathbf{x}_t$ when there is correlation between u_t and $\mathbf{w}_t$ – i.e. estimating

$$y_t = \boldsymbol{\beta}^\top \mathbf{x}_t + \sum\nolimits_{s=-p}^{p} \boldsymbol{\gamma}_s^\top \Delta\mathbf{x}_{t-s} + u_t \qquad (9.11)$$

where p is chosen such that the correlation between u_t and $\mathbf{w}_t$ is zero for $|s| > p$. If $\mathbf{x}_t$ is strongly exogeneous, so that u_t does not Granger-cause $\mathbf{w}_t$, then the leads of $\Delta\mathbf{x}_t$ will not be required ($\gamma_s = 0$, $s < 0$). Autocorrelation in u_t may be captured by assuming that u_t follows an AR(p) process and estimating (9.11) by generalised least squares, by including lags of Δy_t as additional regressors,

$$y_t = \boldsymbol{\beta}\mathbf{x}_t + \sum\nolimits_{s=-p}^{p} \gamma_s \Delta\mathbf{x}_{t-s} + \sum\nolimits_{s=1}^{p} \delta_s \Delta y_{t-s} + u_t \qquad (9.12)$$

or by including lagged values of the equilibrium error $y_t - \boldsymbol{\beta}^\top \mathbf{x}_t$,

$$y_t = \boldsymbol{\beta}^\top \mathbf{x}_t + \sum\nolimits_{s=-p}^{p} \boldsymbol{\gamma}_s^\top \Delta\mathbf{x}_{t-s} + \sum\nolimits_{s=1}^{p} \theta_s (y_{t-s} - \boldsymbol{\beta}\mathbf{x}_{t-s}) + u_t, \qquad (9.13)$$

in which case NLS estimation will be required.

Note that an equivalent form of (9.13) is the ECM

$$\Delta y_t = \sum\nolimits_{s=-p}^{p} \boldsymbol{\gamma}_s^{*\top} \Delta\mathbf{x}_{t-s} + \sum\nolimits_{s=1}^{p} \theta_s^* (y_{t-s} - \boldsymbol{\beta}\mathbf{x}_{t-s}) + u_t \qquad (9.14)$$

where $\gamma_0^* = \gamma_0 + \boldsymbol{\beta}$, $\theta_0^* = \theta_0 - 1$ and $\gamma_s^* = \gamma_s$ and $\theta_s^* = \theta_s$ for $s \neq 0$. While all these estimators can be shown to be asymptotically efficient, Phillips and Loretan (1991) point out that the NLS estimator of (9.13) – or, equivalently, (9.14) – has an important advantage over OLS estimation of (9.12). This is because, since both y_t and $\mathbf{x}_t$ are $I(1)$,

$$y_{t-s} = \sum\nolimits_{i=s}^{t-1} \Delta y_{t-i}, \qquad \mathbf{x}_{t-s} = \sum\nolimits_{i=s}^{t-1} \Delta\mathbf{x}_{t-i}$$

if we set initial conditions $y_0 = \mathbf{x}_0 = 0$. Substituting these partial sums into (9.13) will produce (9.12) but with the lag length p set equal to $t - 1$. Moreover, the lag coefficients will not, in general, decay as the lag increases, because the partial sums imply unit weights for individual innovations. Thus, in order to model short-run dynamics using the variables Δy_{t-s} and $\Delta\mathbf{x}_{t-s}$, it is necessary to include all lags because of this shock persistence, which is quite impractical in empirical applications and cannot be justified in theory, where lag truncation arguments are needed to develop the asymptotics.

Example 9.2 Estimating a cointegrated market model

Example 9.1 found strong evidence in favour of cointegration between LGEN and the FTSE 100 index, and this example considers the various estimators of the cointegration parameters that result from taking different approaches to dynamic modelling. Estimation of the static cointegrating regression by OLS obtains

$$y_t = -\underset{(0.063)}{0.036} + \underset{(0.012)}{0.988}\, x_t + \hat{u}_t$$

Of course, the standard errors shown in parentheses cannot be used for inference, but estimation by FM-OLS, using $n = [521]^{1/3} = 8$ lags in the Newey–West estimator of Σ_S, produces almost identical parameter estimates but considerably larger standard errors:

$$y_t = -\underset{(0.358)}{0.044} + \underset{(0.067)}{0.988}\, x_t + \hat{u}_t$$

In investigating the alternative dynamic estimators, we first ascertain whether x is strongly exogenous. Using four lags, the hypothesis that y does not Granger-cause x has a p-value of 0.58, and the inclusion of four leads of Δx_t in (9.11), after estimation by GLS, is only jointly significant at the 0.34 level. A parsimonious GLS-estimated model is

$$y_t = -\underset{(0.284)}{0.165} + \underset{(0.053)}{1.011}\, x_t + \underset{(0.051)}{0.103}\, \Delta x_t + \hat{u}_t$$

$$\hat{u}_t = \underset{(0.034)}{0.819}\, \hat{u}_{t-1} + \underset{(0.034)}{0.123}\, \hat{u}_{t-3} + \hat{a}_t$$

which has an equation standard error of 3.18 per cent. Attempts to fit a model of the form (9.12) were unsuccessful, for the reasons discussed above: the lag coefficients failed to die out, remaining significant at high lags, and the error term could not be reduced to white noise – exactly the problems that should be produced by the shock persistence caused by the unit roots in the system.

Fitting models of the form (9.13)/(9.14) was successful, however, yielding

$$y_t = -\underset{(0.023)}{0.005} + \underset{(0.075)}{0.997}\, x_t + \underset{(0.093)}{0.110}\, \Delta x_t$$

$$+ \underset{(0.034)}{0.815}(y_{t-1} - 0.997 x_{t-1}) + \underset{(0.034)}{0.128}(y_{t-3} - 0.997 x_{t-3}) + \hat{u}_t$$

which has an equation standard error of 3.03 per cent. All the models suggest that $\beta = 1$, and imposing this restriction leads to

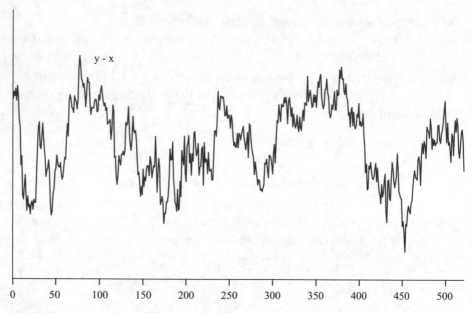

Figure 9.12 LGEN relative to the FTSE 100

$$y_t - x_t = -\underset{(0.002)}{0.006} + \underset{(0.056)}{0.107}\,\Delta x_t + \underset{(0.034)}{0.815}(y_{t-1} - x_{t-1})$$

$$+ \underset{(0.034)}{0.128}(y_{t-3} - x_{t-3}) + \hat{u}_t$$

Thus, the *price relative*, $y_t - x_t$, plotted in figure 9.12, is stationary, following an autoregressive process with one large root (0.943) and a pair of complex roots, and it is positively related to the current change in the market index.

9.5 VARs with integrated variables

9.5.1 VARs with *I*(1) variables

Consider again the VAR(m) process introduced in chapter 8, section 6,

$$\mathbf{\Pi}(B)\mathbf{z}_t = \boldsymbol{\mu} + \mathbf{v}_t \tag{9.15}$$

where $\mathbf{z}_t$, assumed to be $I(1)$, and $\mathbf{v}_t$ are both $n \times 1$ vectors, conditions (8.20) hold,

$$\mathbf{\Pi}(B) = \mathbf{I}_n - \sum\nolimits_{i=1}^{m} \mathbf{\Pi}_i B^i \tag{9.16}$$

and where we have introduced an $n \times 1$ vector of constants, $\boldsymbol{\mu}$. Assuming $m > 1$, the matrix polynomial $\boldsymbol{\Pi}(B)$ can always be written as

$$\boldsymbol{\Pi}(B) = (\mathbf{I}_n - \boldsymbol{\Pi}B) - \boldsymbol{\Phi}(B)B(1 - B)$$

where

$$\boldsymbol{\Pi} = \sum\nolimits_{i=1}^{m} \boldsymbol{\Pi}_i$$

and

$$\boldsymbol{\Phi}(B) = \sum\nolimits_{i=1}^{m-1} \boldsymbol{\Phi}_i B^{i-1}, \qquad \boldsymbol{\Phi}_i = -\sum\nolimits_{j=i+1}^{m} \boldsymbol{\Pi}_j$$

The $\boldsymbol{\Phi}_i$ can be obtained recursively from $\boldsymbol{\Phi}_1 = -\boldsymbol{\Pi} + \boldsymbol{\Pi}_1$ as $\boldsymbol{\Phi}_i = \boldsymbol{\Phi}_{i-1} + \boldsymbol{\Pi}_i$, $i = 2, \ldots , m - 1$. With this decomposition of $\boldsymbol{\Pi}(B)$, (9.15) can always be written as

$$\mathbf{z}_t = \boldsymbol{\Phi}(B)\Delta\mathbf{z}_{t-1} + \boldsymbol{\mu} + \boldsymbol{\Pi}\mathbf{z}_{t-1} + \mathbf{v}_t \tag{9.17}$$

or

$$\Delta\mathbf{z}_t = \boldsymbol{\Phi}(B)\Delta\mathbf{z}_{t-1} + \boldsymbol{\mu} + \mathbf{A}\mathbf{z}_{t-1} + \mathbf{v}_t \tag{9.18}$$

where

$$\mathbf{A} = \boldsymbol{\Pi} - \mathbf{I}_n = -\boldsymbol{\Pi}(1)$$

We consider first the case where

$$\boldsymbol{\Pi} = \mathbf{I}_n \tag{9.19}$$

so that $\mathbf{A} = \mathbf{0}$ and $\Delta\mathbf{z}_t$ follows the VAR($m-1$) process

$$\Delta\mathbf{z}_t = \boldsymbol{\Phi}(B)\Delta\mathbf{z}_{t-1} + \boldsymbol{\mu} + \mathbf{v}_t \tag{9.20}$$

The condition $\boldsymbol{\Pi} = \mathbf{I}_n$ implies that

$$|\mathbf{A}| = |\boldsymbol{\Pi}_1 + \cdots + \boldsymbol{\Pi}_m - \mathbf{I}_n| = \mathbf{0} \tag{9.21}$$

in which case the VAR (9.15) is said to contain *at least one* unit root. Note, however, that (9.21) does not necessarily imply (9.19), and it is this fact that leads to cointegrated or reduced-rank VARs, as we shall see later.

Consider OLS estimation of the levels VAR (9.15) and the differenced VARs (9.17) and (9.18) under the assumption that none of the variables making up $\mathbf{z}_t$ contain drifts, so that $\boldsymbol{\mu} = \mathbf{0}$, although constants are included in the estimated regressions. The fitted values from (9.15) and (9.17) will be the same, because the $\hat{\boldsymbol{\Pi}}_i$ are linked to the $\hat{\boldsymbol{\Phi}}_i$ by

$$\hat{\boldsymbol{\Pi}}_1 = \hat{\boldsymbol{\Pi}} + \hat{\boldsymbol{\Phi}}_1$$

$$\hat{\boldsymbol{\Pi}}_i = \hat{\boldsymbol{\Phi}}_i - \hat{\boldsymbol{\Phi}}_{i-1}, \quad i = 2, 3, \ldots, m-1$$

$$\hat{\boldsymbol{\Pi}}_m = -\hat{\boldsymbol{\Phi}}_{m-1}$$

Now, from Hamilton (1994, chap. 19.2), the $\hat{\boldsymbol{\Phi}}_i$ converge to $\boldsymbol{\Phi}_i$ at rate $T^{1/2}$, and $T^{1/2}(\hat{\boldsymbol{\Phi}}_i - \boldsymbol{\Phi}_i)$ is asymptotically normal. Since the $\hat{\boldsymbol{\Pi}}_i$, $i > 2$, are linear combinations of the $\hat{\boldsymbol{\Phi}}_i$, $T^{1/2}(\hat{\boldsymbol{\Pi}}_i - \boldsymbol{\Pi}_i)$, $i > 2$, is also asymptotically normal. $\hat{\boldsymbol{\Pi}}$, on the other hand, converges to $\boldsymbol{\Pi}$ at rate T, and, although its asymptotic distribution is non-normal, this faster rate of convergence ensures that $\hat{\boldsymbol{\Pi}}_1 = \hat{\boldsymbol{\Pi}} + \hat{\boldsymbol{\Phi}}_1$ also converges at rate $T^{1/2}$ to an asymptotic normal, as the speed of convergence is determined by the coefficients with the slower rate. Hence, if the VAR is estimated in levels, then, even though it contains a unit root, conventional t and F-tests involving a linear combination other than $\boldsymbol{\Pi} = \boldsymbol{\Pi}_1 + \cdots + \boldsymbol{\Pi}_m$ have usual asymptotic distributions. For example, tests for determining the order of the VAR, since they will not involve $\boldsymbol{\Pi} = \boldsymbol{\Pi}_1 + \cdots + \boldsymbol{\Pi}_m$, will have usual χ^2 distributions. On the other hand, Granger causality tests will involve coefficients of $\boldsymbol{\Pi}$ and will typically not have limiting χ^2 distributions.

If there is a drift in $\mathbf{z}_t$ then the above results still hold, unlike the univariate case, where a single regressor with drift makes *all* coefficients asymptotically normal and *all* F-tests asymptotically χ^2.

9.5.2 VARs with cointegrated variables

Let us now reconsider the case when (9.21) holds, so that $\mathbf{A}$ is singular, $|\mathbf{A}| = 0$, but $\mathbf{A} \neq \mathbf{0}$ and $\boldsymbol{\Pi} \neq \mathbf{I}_n$. Being singular, $\mathbf{A}$ will thus have reduced rank $- r$, say $-$ where $0 < r < n$. In such circumstances, $\mathbf{A}$ can be expressed as the product of two $n \times r$ matrices $\boldsymbol{\beta}$ and $\boldsymbol{\alpha}$, both of full-column rank r – i.e. $\mathbf{A} = \boldsymbol{\beta}\boldsymbol{\alpha}^\top$. To see this, note that $\boldsymbol{\alpha}^\top$ is the matrix containing the r linearly independent rows of $\mathbf{A}$, so that $\mathbf{A}$ must be able to be written as a linear combination of $\boldsymbol{\alpha}^\top$; $\boldsymbol{\beta}$ must then be the matrix of coefficients that are needed to do this. These r linearly independent rows of $\mathbf{A}$, contained as the rows of $\boldsymbol{\alpha}^\top = (\boldsymbol{\alpha}_1, \ldots, \boldsymbol{\alpha}_r)^\top$, are known as the *cointegrating vectors*, and $\mathbf{A}$ will contain only $n - r$ unit roots, rather than the n unit roots that it will contain if $\mathbf{A} = \mathbf{0}$, which will be the case if $r = 0$.

Why are the rows of $a^\top$ known as cointegrating vectors? Substituting $\mathbf{A} = \boldsymbol{\beta}a^\top$ into equation (9.18) yields

$$\Delta z_t = \boldsymbol{\Phi}(B)\Delta z_{t-1} + \boldsymbol{\mu} + \boldsymbol{\beta}a^\top z_{t-1} + \mathbf{v}_t$$

The assumption that z_t is $I(1)$ implies that, since Δz_t must then be $I(0)$, $a^\top z_t$ must also be $I(0)$ for both sides of the equation to 'balance'. In other words, $a^\top$ is a matrix whose rows, when post-multiplied by z_t, produce *stationary* linear combinations of z_t – i.e. the r linear combinations $a_1 z_t, \ldots, a_r z_t$ are all stationary.

Thus, if z_t is cointegrated with cointegrated rank r, then it can be represented as the vector error correction model

$$\Delta z_t = \boldsymbol{\Phi}(B)\Delta z_{t-1} + \boldsymbol{\mu} + \boldsymbol{\beta}\mathbf{e}_{t-1} + \mathbf{v}_t \tag{9.22}$$

where $\mathbf{e}_t = a^\top z_t$ are the r stationary *error corrections*. This is known as Granger's representation theorem (Engle and Granger, 1987), and a detailed proof can be found in, for example, Banerjee *et al.* (1993, chap. 5.3), where various additional technical conditions are discussed.

Several additional points are worth mentioning. The parameters a and $\boldsymbol{\beta}$ are not uniquely identified, since, for any non-singular $r \times r$ matrix $\boldsymbol{\xi}$, the products $\boldsymbol{\beta}a^\top$ and $\boldsymbol{\beta}\boldsymbol{\xi}(\boldsymbol{\xi}^{-1}a^\top)$ will both equal $\mathbf{A}$. If $r = 0$ then we have already seen that the model becomes a VAR$(m-1)$ in the first differences Δz_t. If $r = n$, on the other hand, $\mathbf{A}$ is of full rank, is non-singular, and z_t will contain *no* unit roots – i.e. z_t is in fact $I(0)$ and a VAR(m) in the levels is appropriate from the outset; we are then in the framework of chapter 8, section 6. The error corrections $\mathbf{e}_t$, although stationary, are not restricted to having zero means, so that, as (9.22) stands, growth in z_t can come about via both the error correction $\mathbf{e}_t$ and the autonomous drift component $\boldsymbol{\mu}$.

Note, however, that, without loss of generality, $\boldsymbol{\mu}$ can be written as $\boldsymbol{\mu} = \boldsymbol{\beta}\boldsymbol{\gamma} + \boldsymbol{\beta}_\perp \boldsymbol{\gamma}^*$, where $\boldsymbol{\beta}_\perp$ is an $n \times (n-r)$ matrix known as the *orthogonal complement* of $\boldsymbol{\beta}$, defined such that $\boldsymbol{\beta}_\perp^\top \boldsymbol{\beta} = \mathbf{0}$. Since $\boldsymbol{\beta}^\top \boldsymbol{\mu} = \boldsymbol{\beta}^\top \boldsymbol{\beta}\boldsymbol{\gamma} + \boldsymbol{\beta}^\top \boldsymbol{\beta}_\perp \boldsymbol{\gamma}^* = \boldsymbol{\beta}^\top \boldsymbol{\beta}\boldsymbol{\gamma}$, we have $\boldsymbol{\gamma} = (\boldsymbol{\beta}^\top \boldsymbol{\beta})^{-1}\boldsymbol{\beta}^\top \boldsymbol{\mu}$ and $\boldsymbol{\gamma}^* = (\boldsymbol{\beta}_\perp^\top \boldsymbol{\beta}_\perp)^{-1}\boldsymbol{\beta}_\perp^\top \boldsymbol{\mu}$, so that, geometrically, $\boldsymbol{\mu}$ has been decomposed in the directions of $\boldsymbol{\gamma}$ and $\boldsymbol{\gamma}^*$. The VECM (9.22) can then be written as

$$\Delta z_t = \boldsymbol{\Phi}(B)\Delta z_{t-1} + \boldsymbol{\beta}_\perp \boldsymbol{\gamma}^* + \boldsymbol{\beta}(\boldsymbol{\gamma} + \mathbf{e}_{t-1}) + \mathbf{v}_t \tag{9.23}$$

so that if the condition $\boldsymbol{\beta}_\perp \boldsymbol{\gamma}^* = 0$ holds – i.e. that $\boldsymbol{\mu} = \boldsymbol{\beta}\boldsymbol{\gamma}$ – then the constant enters the system only via the error correction term.

How the constant is treated is important in determining the appropriate estimation procedure and the set of critical values used for inference. An important extension is when a linear trend is included in the VAR:

$$\boldsymbol{\Pi}(B)\mathbf{z}_t = \boldsymbol{\mu}_0 + \boldsymbol{\mu}_1 t + \mathbf{v}_t \tag{9.24}$$

Here we can write $\boldsymbol{\mu}_i = \boldsymbol{\beta}\boldsymbol{\gamma}_i + \boldsymbol{\beta}_\perp \boldsymbol{\gamma}_i^*$, $i = 0, 1$, and the counterpart to (9.23) becomes

$$\Delta\mathbf{z}_t = \boldsymbol{\Phi}(B)\Delta\mathbf{z}_{t-1} + \boldsymbol{\beta}_\perp\left(\boldsymbol{\gamma}_0^* + \boldsymbol{\gamma}_1^* t\right) + \boldsymbol{\beta}(\boldsymbol{\gamma}_0 + \boldsymbol{\gamma}_1(t-1) + \mathbf{e}_{t-1}) + \mathbf{v}_t \tag{9.25}$$

In this case the constant and trend will be restricted to the error correction if $\boldsymbol{\mu}_i = \boldsymbol{\beta}\boldsymbol{\gamma}_i$, $i = 0,1$ – i.e. we define the 'trend-included' error correction as $\mathbf{e}_t^* = \mathbf{e}_t + \boldsymbol{\gamma}_0 + \boldsymbol{\gamma}_1 t$.

Further implications of the presence of a linear trend are best analysed by introducing the infinite-order vector polynomial $\mathbf{C}(B)$, defined such that $\mathbf{C}(B)\boldsymbol{\Pi}(B) = (1 - B)\mathbf{I}_n$, and which can be written, analogously to $\boldsymbol{\Pi}(B)$, as

$$\begin{aligned}
\mathbf{C}(B) &= \mathbf{I}_n + \mathbf{C}B + \left(\mathbf{C}_1^* B + \mathbf{C}_2^* B^2 + \ldots\right)(1 - B) \\
&= \mathbf{I}_n + \mathbf{C} + \left(\mathbf{C}_0^* + \mathbf{C}_1^* B + \mathbf{C}_2^* B^2 + \ldots\right)(1 - B) \\
&= \mathbf{I}_n + \mathbf{C} + \mathbf{C}^*(B)(1 - B) \\
&= \mathbf{C}(1) + \mathbf{C}^*(B)(1 - B)
\end{aligned}$$

The matrices of $\mathbf{C}(B)$, $\mathbf{C}_0, \mathbf{C}_1, \ldots$, are given by the recursions

$$\mathbf{C}_i = \sum\nolimits_{j=1}^{m} \mathbf{C}_{i-j}\boldsymbol{\Pi}_j, \quad i > 0, \quad \mathbf{C}_0 = \mathbf{I}_n$$

so that

$$\begin{aligned}
\mathbf{C} &= \sum\nolimits_{i=1}^{\infty} \mathbf{C}_i = \mathbf{C}(1) - \mathbf{I}_n \\
\mathbf{C}_0^* &= -\mathbf{C}
\end{aligned}$$

and

$$\mathbf{C}_i^* = \mathbf{C}_{i-1}^* + \mathbf{C}_i, \quad i > 0$$

Equation (9.24) can then be written as

$$\begin{aligned}
\Delta\mathbf{z}_t &= \mathbf{C}(B)(\boldsymbol{\mu}_0 + \boldsymbol{\mu}_1 t + \mathbf{v}_t) \\
&= (\mathbf{C}(1) + \mathbf{C}^*(1 - B))(\boldsymbol{\mu}_0 + \boldsymbol{\mu}_1 t) + \mathbf{C}(B)\mathbf{v}_t \\
&= \mathbf{C}(1)\boldsymbol{\mu}_0 + \mathbf{C}^*(1)\boldsymbol{\mu}_1 + \mathbf{C}(1)\boldsymbol{\mu}_1 t + \mathbf{C}(B)\mathbf{v}_t \\
&= \mathbf{b}_0 + \mathbf{b}_1 t + \mathbf{C}(B)\mathbf{v}_t
\end{aligned}$$

where

$$\mathbf{b}_0 = \mathbf{C}(1)\boldsymbol{\mu}_0 + \mathbf{C}^*(1)\boldsymbol{\mu}_1$$

and

$$\mathbf{b}_1 = \mathbf{C}(1)\boldsymbol{\mu}_1$$

In levels, this becomes

$$
\begin{aligned}
\mathbf{z}_t &= \mathbf{z}_0 + \mathbf{b}_0 t + \mathbf{b}_1 \frac{t(t+1)}{2} + \mathbf{C}(B) \sum\nolimits_{s=1}^{t} \mathbf{v}_t \\
&= \mathbf{z}_0 + \mathbf{b}_0 t + \mathbf{b}_1 \frac{t(t+1)}{2} + (\mathbf{C}(1) + \mathbf{C}^*(1-B)) \sum\nolimits_{s=1}^{t} \mathbf{v}_t \\
&= \mathbf{z}_0 + \mathbf{b}_0 t + \mathbf{b}_1 \frac{t(t+1)}{2} + \mathbf{C}(1)\mathbf{s}_t + \mathbf{C}^*(B)(\mathbf{v}_t - \mathbf{v}_0) \\
&= \mathbf{z}_0^* + \mathbf{b}_0 t + \mathbf{b}_1 \frac{t(t+1)}{2} + \mathbf{C}(1)\mathbf{s}_t + \mathbf{C}^*(B)\mathbf{v}_t
\end{aligned}
\tag{9.26}
$$

where

$$\mathbf{z}_0^* = \mathbf{z}_0 - \mathbf{C}^*(B)\mathbf{v}_0, \quad \mathbf{s}_t = \sum\nolimits_{s=1}^{t} \mathbf{v}_s$$

The inclusion of a linear trend in the VAR (9.24) implies a *quadratic* trend in the levels equation (9.26). Furthermore, since $\mathbf{b}_1 = \mathbf{C}(1)\boldsymbol{\mu}_1$, this quadratic trend will disappear only if $\mathbf{C}(1) = \mathbf{0}$. Recall that $\mathbf{C}(1)\boldsymbol{\Pi}(1) = \mathbf{0}$, so that $\mathbf{C}(1) = \mathbf{0}$ requires that $\boldsymbol{\Pi}(1) = -\mathbf{A} \neq \mathbf{0}$. This will be the case only if $\boldsymbol{\Pi}(B)$ does not contain the factor $(1 - B)$, i.e. that $\mathbf{z}_t$ is $I(0)$, which has been ruled out by assumption and implies that $\mathbf{A}$ is of full rank n. If $\boldsymbol{\Pi}(1) = \mathbf{0}$, so that $\mathbf{A} = \mathbf{0}$, is of rank zero and contains n unit roots, then there is no cointegration and $\mathbf{C}(1)$, and hence $\mathbf{b}_1$, are unconstrained. In the general case, where the rank of $\mathbf{A}$ is r, it then follows that the rank of $\mathbf{C}(1)$ is $n - r$ (see Banerjee *et al.*, 1993, chap. 5.3.1). The rank of $\mathbf{b}_1$, and hence the number of independent quadratic deterministic trends, is thus also equal to $n - r$, and will therefore decrease as the cointegrating rank r increases. Without the restriction on the trend coefficient $\mathbf{b}_1$, the solution (9.26) will have the property that the nature of the trend in $\mathbf{z}_t$ will vary with the number of cointegrating vectors.

To avoid this unsatisfactory outcome, the restriction $\mathbf{b}_1 = \mathbf{C}(1)\boldsymbol{\mu}_1 = \mathbf{0}$ may be imposed, in which case the solution for $\mathbf{z}_t$ will contain only linear trends, irrespective of the value of r. The choice of r then determines the split between the number of independent linear deterministic trends, r, and the number of stochastic trends, $n - r$, in the model.

$\mathbf{C}(1)$ can be shown (see, for example, Banerjee *et al.*, 1993, chap. 5.3.1) to have the representation

$$\mathbf{C}(1) = \boldsymbol{a}_\perp \left(\boldsymbol{\beta}_\perp^\top (\mathbf{I}_n - \Phi(1))\boldsymbol{a}_\perp\right)^{-1}\boldsymbol{\beta}_\perp^\top$$

so that the cointegrating vectors $\boldsymbol{a}^\top \mathbf{z}_t$ have a linear but not a quadratic trend: since $\boldsymbol{a}^\top \boldsymbol{a}_\perp = \mathbf{0}$, $\boldsymbol{a}^\top \mathbf{C}(1) = \mathbf{0}$ and

$$\boldsymbol{a}^\top \mathbf{z}_t = \boldsymbol{a}^\top \mathbf{z}_0^* + \boldsymbol{a}^\top \mathbf{C}^*(1)\boldsymbol{\mu}_1 t + \boldsymbol{a}^\top \mathbf{C}^*(B)\mathbf{v}_t \tag{9.27}$$

Note also that

$$\mathbf{C}(1)\boldsymbol{\mu}_1 = \boldsymbol{a}_\perp \left(\boldsymbol{\beta}_\perp^\top (\mathbf{I}_n - \Phi(1))\boldsymbol{a}_\perp\right)^{-1}\boldsymbol{\beta}_\perp^\top \boldsymbol{\mu}_1$$
$$= \boldsymbol{a}_\perp \left(\boldsymbol{\beta}_\perp^\top (\mathbf{I}_n - \Phi(1))\boldsymbol{a}_\perp\right)^{-1}\boldsymbol{\beta}_\perp^\top \boldsymbol{\beta}\boldsymbol{\gamma}_1 = \mathbf{0}$$

so that $\mathbf{b}_1 = \mathbf{0}$ in (9.26) and $\boldsymbol{\mu}_1 = \boldsymbol{\beta}\boldsymbol{\gamma}_1$ in (9.24) are equivalent restrictions. This restriction may be imposed by setting $\boldsymbol{\mu}_1 = \mathbf{A}\mathbf{c}$, where $\mathbf{c}$ is an $n \times 1$ vector of unknown coefficients. In this case $\mathbf{b}_1 = \mathbf{C}_1\mathbf{A}\mathbf{c} = -\mathbf{C}_1\Pi(1)\mathbf{c} = \mathbf{0}$ in (9.26). Furthermore, since $\mathbf{C}^*(1)\mathbf{A} = \mathbf{I}_n$ (see Pesaran and Shin, 2002), $\boldsymbol{a}^\top \mathbf{C}^* (1)\boldsymbol{\mu}_1 = \boldsymbol{a}^\top \mathbf{C}^*(1)\mathbf{A}\mathbf{c} = \boldsymbol{a}^\top \mathbf{c}$, so that (9.27) becomes

$$\boldsymbol{a}^\top \mathbf{z}_t = \boldsymbol{a}^\top \mathbf{z}_0^* + \boldsymbol{a}^\top \mathbf{c}t + \boldsymbol{a}^\top \mathbf{C}^*(B)\mathbf{v}_t$$

The cointegrating vectors will not contain linear trends if $\boldsymbol{a}^\top \mathbf{c} = \mathbf{0}$, and these are known as the 'co-trending' restrictions.

9.5.3 Estimation of VECMs and tests of the cointegrating rank

ML estimation of the VECM (9.22) is discussed in many texts: see, for example, Banerjee *et al.* (1993, chap. 8.2), Hamilton (1994, chap. 20.2) and Johansen (1995, chap. 6), and routines are available in most econometrics packages. Without going into unnecessary details, ML estimates are obtained in the following way. Consider (9.22) written as

$$\Delta \mathbf{z}_t = \boldsymbol{\mu} + \sum_{i=1}^{m-1} \Phi_i \Delta \mathbf{z}_{t-i} + \boldsymbol{\beta}\boldsymbol{a}^\top \mathbf{z}_{t-1} + \mathbf{v}_t \tag{9.28}$$

The first step is to estimate (9.28) under the restriction $\boldsymbol{\beta}\boldsymbol{a}^\top = \mathbf{0}$. As this is simply a VAR($m-1$) in $\Delta \mathbf{z}_t$, OLS estimation will yield the set of residuals $\hat{\mathbf{v}}_t$, from which is calculated the sample covariance matrix

$$\mathbf{S}_{00} = T^{-1} \sum_{t=1}^{T} \hat{\mathbf{v}}_t \hat{\mathbf{v}}_t^\top$$

The second step is to estimate the multivariate regression

$$\mathbf{z}_{t-1} = \boldsymbol{\kappa} + \sum_{i=1}^{m-1} \Xi_i \Delta \mathbf{z}_{t-i} + \mathbf{u}_t$$

and use the OLS residuals $\hat{\mathbf{u}}_t$ to calculate the covariance matrices

$$\mathbf{S}_{11} = T^{-1} \sum_{t=1}^{T} \hat{\mathbf{u}}_t \hat{\mathbf{u}}_t^\top$$

and

$$\mathbf{S}_{10} = T^{-1} \sum_{t=1}^{T} \hat{\mathbf{u}}_t \hat{\mathbf{v}}_t^\top = \mathbf{S}_{01}^\top$$

In effect, these two regressions partial out the effects of $(\Delta \mathbf{z}_{t-1}, \dots, \Delta \mathbf{z}_{t-m+1})$ from $\Delta \mathbf{z}_t$ and $\mathbf{z}_{t-1}$, leaving us to concentrate on the relationship between $\Delta \mathbf{z}_t$ and $\mathbf{z}_{t-1}$, which is parameterised by $\boldsymbol{\beta}\boldsymbol{a}^\top$. $\boldsymbol{a}$ is then estimated by the r linear combinations of $\mathbf{z}_{t-1}$ that have the largest squared partial correlations with $\Delta \mathbf{z}_t$; this is known as a *reduced-rank* regression. More precisely, this procedure maximises the likelihood of (9.28) by solving a set of equations of the form

$$\left(\lambda_i \mathbf{S}_{11} - \mathbf{S}_{10} \mathbf{S}_{00}^{-1} \mathbf{S}_{01} \right) v_i = \mathbf{0} \tag{9.29}$$

where $\hat{\lambda}_1 > \hat{\lambda}_2 > \cdots > \hat{\lambda}_n$ are the set of eigenvalues and $\mathbf{V} = (v_1, v_2, \dots, v_n)$ is the set of associated eigenvectors, subject to the normalisation

$$\mathbf{V}^\top \mathbf{S}_{11} \mathbf{V} = \mathbf{I}_n$$

The ML estimate of $\boldsymbol{a}$ is then given by the eigenvectors corresponding to the r largest eigenvalues,

$$\hat{\boldsymbol{a}} = (v_1, v_2, \dots, v_r)$$

and the ML estimate of $\boldsymbol{\beta}$ is then given by

$$\hat{\boldsymbol{\beta}} = \mathbf{S}_{01} \hat{\boldsymbol{a}}$$

which is equivalent to the estimate of $\boldsymbol{\beta}$ that would be obtained by substituting $\hat{\boldsymbol{a}}$ into (9.28) and estimating by OLS, which also provides ML estimates of the remaining parameters in the model.

This procedure can be straightforwardly adapted when a linear trend is included in (9.28) and when the various restrictions are placed upon the intercept and trend coefficients. This involves adjusting the first- and second-step regressions to accommodate the alterations (Pesaran and Pesaran, 1997, chap. 19.7, conveniently list the alternative set-ups).

Of course, ML estimation is based upon a known value of the cointegrating rank, r, and in practice this value will be unknown. Fortunately, the set of equations (9.29) also provides a method of determining the value of r. If $r = n$ and $\mathbf{A}$ is unrestricted, the maximised log-likelihood is given by Banerjee *et al.* (1993, chap. 9.3):

$$L(n) = K - (T/2)\sum_{i=1}^{n} \log(1 - \lambda_i)$$

where $K = -(T/2)(n(1 + \log 2\pi) + \log|\mathbf{S}_{00}|)$. For a given value of $r < n$, only the first r eigenvalues should be positive, and the restricted log-likelihood is

$$L(r) = K - (T/2)\sum_{i=1}^{r} \log(1 - \lambda_i)$$

A likelihood ratio test of the hypothesis that there are r cointegration vectors against the alternative that there are n is thus given by

$$\eta_r = 2(L(n) - L(r)) = -T\sum_{i=r+1}^{n} \log(1 - \lambda_i)$$

This is known as the *trace* statistic, and testing proceeds in the sequence η_0, $\eta_1, \ldots, \eta_{n-1}$. A cointegrating rank of r is selected if the *last* significant statistic is η_{r-1}, which thereby rejects the hypothesis of $n - r + 1$ unit roots in $\mathbf{A}$. The trace statistic measures the 'importance' of the adjustment coefficients $\boldsymbol{\beta}$ on the eigenvectors to be potentially omitted.

An alternative test of the significance of the largest eigenvalue is

$$\zeta_r = -T\log(1 - \lambda_{r+1}), \qquad r = 0, 1, \ldots, n-1$$

which is known as the *maximal-eigenvalue* or λ-*max* statistic. Both η_r and ζ_r have non-standard limiting distributions that are functionals of multivariate Brownian motions, and are generalisations of the Dickey–Fuller distributions discussed in chapter 3. Although there are no analytical forms for the distributions, critical values can be obtained by Monte Carlo simulation. The limiting distributions depend on n and on the restrictions imposed on the behaviour of the trends appearing in the VECM. For example, if $\boldsymbol{\mu}$ in (9.28) is replaced by $\boldsymbol{\mu}_0 + \boldsymbol{\mu}_1 t$, then the ML estimation and testing procedures outlined above need to be amended to take into account both the presence of a linear trend and the various possible restrictions that could be placed on μ_0 and μ_1 (see, for example, Johansen, 1995, chaps. 6 and 15, for extended discussion).

For this modelling framework to become operational, we have to determine the lag order m, the trend order l and the reduced (cointegrating) rank r. By 'trend order' we mean that if $l = 1$ then the linear trend model is appropriate, if $l = 0$ then only a constant is included, while if not even a constant is required we set $l = -1$ by convention. Typically, m and l are first determined using either an information criterion or a sequence of likelihood ratio or Wald tests, and, conditional on these settings, r is then determined by the sequence of trace or λ-max tests. In empirical applications, however, the choice of r is frequently sensitive to the choice of m and l and the trend restrictions.

A further problem is that the trace and λ-max tests rely on critical values drawn from limiting distributions, and these have been shown to have rather unreliable finite sample performance: see, inter alia, Reimers (1992), Haug (1996), Ho and Sørensen (1996) and Toda (1994, 1995). Small-sample corrections to the rank tests have been proposed by Johansen (2002a, 2002b), while Johansen (2006) summarises recent developments in the analysis of cointegrated systems.

Given these complications, it is appealing to consider whether we can select jointly the cointegrating rank, the lag length and the appropriate restriction on the trend component. One possibility for doing this is to use information criteria to select between all possible models, as suggested by Lütkepohl (1991, chap. 11.4); see also Mills (1998). For example, if we denote the set of models to be considered as VECM(m, l, r), we could select that model that minimises BIC(m, l, r) as defined in chapter 8, section 7.

Example 9.3 Cointegration in the UK financial markets

In example 8.8 we analysed the vector $(\Delta p_t, \Delta d_t, \Delta rs_t, \Delta r20_t)$ by implicitly assuming that there was no cointegration between the series. We now investigate whether the appropriate relationship between these four series is, in fact, a VECM in $\mathbf{z}_t = (p_t, d_t, rs_t, r20_t)$, although we do this using a shorter sample period, January 1969 to December 2000. With T thus equal to 384, we follow Saikkonen and Lütkepohl (1996) and set the maximum order of m to be considered as the integer part of $T^{1/3}$ – i.e. we set $m = 7$.

For all choices of l in the range $-1 < l < 1$, the BIC (and, indeed, various other information criteria) selected $m = 2$. Since the BIC values for this lag order and alternative settings of l were very close, we decided to work with the most general trend setting and therefore set $l = 1$, so that a linear trend was included in the VAR.

Table 9.2 Cointegrating rank test statistics

r	η_r	λ_r	$\eta_{r,0.05}$
(a) Trend and constant in cointegrating vector: $\mu_1 = \beta\gamma_1$			
$=0$	63.17	0.0852	47.21
≤ 1	29.68	0.0350	29.98
≤ 2	15.31	0.0294	15.41
≤ 3	3.84	0.0100	3.76
(b) Constant only in cointegrating vector: $\mu_1 = 0$, $\mu_0 = \beta\gamma_0$			
$=0$	69.98	0.0962	62.99
≤ 1	31.12	0.0356	42.44
≤ 2	19.19	0.0321	25.32
≤ 3	4.68	0.0121	12.25

Table 9.2 presents the sequence of trace statistics and associated eigen-values conditional upon $m = 2$ and $l = 1$. Employing a 5 per cent significance level, this suggests that $r = 1$, irrespective of whether the cointegrating vector contains both a trend and a constant or just a constant. We should note, however, that the statistic testing the null $r = 1$ for the former case is very close to its 5 per cent critical value, and, since Banerjee *et al.* (1993, chap. 9.5.3) warn against omitting cointegrating vectors in these circumstances, this perhaps points in favour of setting $r = 2$. Nevertheless, in either case there is clear evidence of cointegration, implying that using a VAR in the first differences to model z_t constitutes a misspecification.

With $r = 2$ and a trend included in the cointegrating vector, the ML estimation procedure produces

$$\hat{a}^\top = \begin{bmatrix} 7.878 & -7.750 & 0.620 & -6.789 \\ 2.442 & -2.381 & -2.577 & 1.633 \end{bmatrix}$$

but, as noted earlier, these estimates are not unique, so that the question of how they can be interpreted arises. This is now discussed within the context of identification of VECMs.

9.5.4 Identification of VECMs

The assumption that the rank of $\mathbf{A}$ is r implicitly imposes $(n - r)^2$ restrictions on its n^2 coefficients, leaving $n^2 - (n - r)^2 = 2nr - r^2$ free parameters. The two $n \times r$ matrices $\boldsymbol{\alpha}$ and $\boldsymbol{\beta}$ involve $2nr$ parameters, so that identifying

$\mathbf{A} = \boldsymbol{\beta}\boldsymbol{a}^\top$ requires a total of r^2 restrictions. If the identifying restrictions are imposed only on $\boldsymbol{a}$, if they are linear and if there are no cross-cointegrating vector restrictions, then the restrictions can be written for the ith cointegrating vector as

$$\mathbf{R}_i\boldsymbol{a}_i = \mathbf{a}_i \qquad (9.30)$$

where $\mathbf{R}_i$ and $\mathbf{a}_i$ are an $r \times n$ matrix and an $r \times 1$ vector, respectively. A necessary and sufficient condition for $\boldsymbol{a}$ to be uniquely identified is that the rank of each $\mathbf{R}_i\boldsymbol{a}_i$ is r, while the necessary condition is that there must be r restrictions placed on each of the r cointegrating vectors. The more general case of non-linear and cross-vector restrictions is discussed in Pesaran and Shin (2002). Note that identification of $\boldsymbol{a}$, and hence $\mathbf{A}$, is achieved solely through restrictions on $\boldsymbol{a}$ itself: long-run relationships cannot be identified through restrictions on the short-run dynamics – i.e. the Φ_i coefficients in (9.28) can be estimated freely.

If the number of restrictions that are imposed on $\boldsymbol{a}$ is k, then $k = r^2$ constitutes *exact identification*. The imposition of r restrictions on each of the r cointegrating vectors does not alter the likelihood $L(r)$, so that, while their imposition enables a unique estimate of α to be obtained, the validity of the restrictions cannot be tested. Typically r restrictions are obtained by normalisation, and if $r = 1$ then this is all that is required. For $r > 1$, a further $r^2 - r$ restrictions are required ($r - 1$ on each equation), and this forms the basis for Phillips' (1991) *triangular representation*. This writes α as

$$\boldsymbol{a}^\top = [\,\mathbf{I}_r \quad -\boldsymbol{\Gamma}\,]$$

where $\boldsymbol{\Gamma}$ is an $r \times (n - r)$ matrix. The r^2 just-identifying restrictions are thus made up of r normalisations and $r^2 - r$ zero restrictions, corresponding to solving $\boldsymbol{a}^\top \mathbf{z}_t$ for the first r components of $\mathbf{z}_t$.

When $k > r^2$, there are $k - r^2$ *overidentifying* restrictions. ML estimation subject to the restrictions (9.30) is discussed in, for example, Pesaran and Pesaran (1997). If $L(r:p)$ denotes the log-likelihood after the imposition of the $p = k - r^2$ overidentifying restrictions, then the validity of these restrictions can be tested using the likelihood ratio statistic

$$2(L(r) - L(r{:}p)) \overset{a}{\sim} \chi^2_p$$

Restrictions can also be imposed on $\boldsymbol{\beta}$, and may link both $\boldsymbol{a}$ and $\boldsymbol{\beta}$. The identification, estimation and testing of very general sets of restrictions is discussed in Hendry and Doornik (2006) and programmed in their PcFiml 11.0.

9.5.5 Exogeneity in VECMs

In the previous subsection we considered hypotheses about the cointegrating matrix $\boldsymbol{a}$. We now consider hypotheses concerning the adjustment factors $\boldsymbol{\beta}$. Suppose, as in chapter 8, section 6, we again make the partition $\mathbf{z}_t = \left(\mathbf{y}_t^\top, \mathbf{x}_t^\top\right)^\top$ and now write the VECM as

$$\Delta \mathbf{y}_t = \sum_{i=1}^{m-1} \Phi_{1i} \Delta \mathbf{z}_{t-i} + \boldsymbol{\beta}_1 \boldsymbol{a}^\top \mathbf{z}_{t-1} + \mathbf{T}_1 + \mathbf{v}_{1t} \tag{9.31}$$

$$\Delta \mathbf{x}_t = \sum_{i=1}^{m-1} \Phi_{2i} \Delta \mathbf{z}_{t-i} + \boldsymbol{\beta}_2 \boldsymbol{a}^\top \mathbf{z}_{t-1} + \mathbf{T}_2 + \mathbf{v}_{2t} \tag{9.32}$$

where

$$\Phi_i = \begin{bmatrix} \Phi_{1i} \\ \Phi_{2i} \end{bmatrix}, i = 1, \ldots, m-1, \quad \boldsymbol{\beta} = \begin{bmatrix} \boldsymbol{\beta}_1 \\ \boldsymbol{\beta}_2 \end{bmatrix}, \quad \mathbf{T}_j = \boldsymbol{\mu}_{0j} + \boldsymbol{\mu}_{1j}t \quad j = 1, 2$$

and where $\mathbf{v}_t$ and its covariance matrix $\boldsymbol{\Sigma}_v$ are partitioned as in chapter 8, section 7.2. Pre-multiplying (9.32) by $\boldsymbol{\omega} = \boldsymbol{\Sigma}_{12}\boldsymbol{\Sigma}_{22}^{-1}$ and subtracting the result from (9.31) yields the conditional model for Δy_t

$$\Delta \mathbf{y}_t = \boldsymbol{\omega}\Delta \mathbf{x}_t + \sum_{i=1}^{m-1} \tilde{\Phi}_{1i}\Delta \mathbf{z}_{t-i} + (\boldsymbol{\beta}_1 - \boldsymbol{\omega}\boldsymbol{\beta}_2)\boldsymbol{a}^\top \mathbf{z}_{t-1} + \tilde{\mathbf{T}}_1 + \tilde{\mathbf{v}}_{1t} \tag{9.33}$$

where $\tilde{\Phi}_{1i} = \Phi_{1i} - \boldsymbol{\omega}\Phi_{2i}$, $\tilde{\mathbf{T}}_1 = \mathbf{T}_1 - \boldsymbol{\omega}\mathbf{T}_2$ and $\tilde{\mathbf{v}}_{1t} = \mathbf{v}_{1t} - \boldsymbol{\omega}\mathbf{v}_{2t}$ with covariance matrix $\boldsymbol{\Sigma}_{11.2} = \boldsymbol{\Sigma}_{11} - \boldsymbol{\Sigma}_{12}\boldsymbol{\Sigma}_{22}^{-1}\boldsymbol{\Sigma}_{12}^\top$. $\boldsymbol{a}$ enters both the conditional model (9.33) and the marginal model (9.32) unless $\boldsymbol{\beta}_2 = \mathbf{0}$. This is the condition for $\mathbf{x}_t$ to be weakly exogenous for $(\boldsymbol{a}, \boldsymbol{\beta}_1)$, in which case the ML estimates of these parameters can be calculated from the conditional model alone (Johansen, 1995, theorem 9.1).

Example 9.4 Identifying the cointegrating vectors and testing for weak exogeneity

Given that we have found two cointegrating vectors in example 9.3, we now wish to identify them uniquely and, in so doing, see if we can provide them with an economic/financial interpretation. The estimates contained in the first row of $\hat{\boldsymbol{a}}^\top$ suggest that the just-identifying restrictions α_{11} and $\alpha_{13} = 0$ should be imposed, while the second row of $\hat{\boldsymbol{a}}^\top$ suggests the restrictions $\alpha_{21} = \alpha_{24} = -1$ and $\alpha_{22} = \alpha_{23} = 1$, i.e. on estimation

$$e_{1t}^* = p_t - d_t + r20_t - 5.548 + 0.0004t$$
$$e_{2t}^* = -p_t - d_t + rs_t - r20_t + 3.491 - 0.0006t$$

A likelihood ratio test of the set of overidentifying restrictions produces the statistic $\chi_4^2 = 4.71$, with a p-value of 0.32, so that the set of restrictions are accepted.

Mills (1991a) discusses the equilibrium relationship often thought to hold between the equity and gilt markets: that the gilt and dividend yields should be in constant proportion to each other. This is exactly the form taken by e_{1t}^*, which, in terms of the levels, P_t, D_t and $R20_t$, implies that the ratio

$$R20_t/(D_t/P_t)$$

is stationary. Since D_t/P_t is the dividend yield, in equilibrium the gilt yield and the dividend yield are in constant proportion to each other. Since deviations from this equilibrium are stationary, divergences from this ratio can only be temporary. This ratio was, in fact, exactly the decomposition used by investment analysts of the 1950s and early 1960s to analyse movements in equity prices, and it was termed by them the 'confidence factor' (see Mills, 1991a).

The second error correction implies that the interest rate 'spread' $R20_t/RS_t$ is directly proportional to the dividend yield D_t/P_t. Figure 9.13 plots the two error corrections, and both are seen to be stationary. Note that extreme values of the confidence factor are observed in 1975 and 1987, both periods of great upheaval in the UK equity market, but even here there is a marked tendency to move back towards equilibrium.

The estimated 'loading factor' or 'adjustment' matrix is, with standard errors shown in parentheses,

$$\hat{\beta} = \begin{bmatrix} -0.080 & 0.011 \\ (0.024) & (0.009) \\ 0.027 & 0.005 \\ (0.006) & (0.002) \\ 0.014 & -0.025 \\ (0.023) & (0.008) \\ -0.003 & -0.002 \\ (0.014) & (0.005) \end{bmatrix}$$

The coefficients in the fourth row are individually insignificant, while at least one of the coefficients in the each of the first three rows is significant, so it is possible that β can be partitioned as $\beta = [\beta_1 \ \mathbf{0}]^\top$ and the VECM can be partitioned as (9.31)/(9.32). Indeed, a test of $\beta_{41} = \beta_{42} = 0$ cannot reject this joint null hypothesis (the statistic is $\chi_2^2 = 0.19$), so $r20$ appears to be weakly exogenous with respect to α and $\beta_1, \beta_2, \beta_3$.

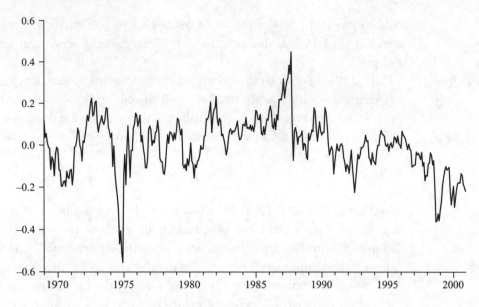

(a) Error correction e_1*: the 'confidence factor'

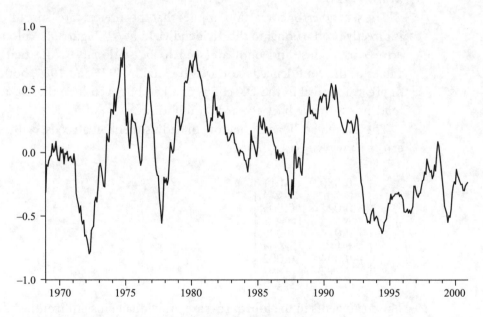

(b) Error correction e_2*: the 'corrected' interest rate spread

Figure 9.13 Estimated error corrections

9.5.6 Structural VECMs

Following Johansen and Juselius (1994), a 'structural VECM' may be written as (abstracting from deterministic components)

$$\Gamma_0 \Delta \mathbf{z}_t = \sum_{i=1}^{m-1} \Gamma_i \Delta \mathbf{z}_{t-i} + \mathbf{\Omega} \mathbf{a}^\top \mathbf{z}_{t-1} + \mathbf{v}_t \tag{9.34}$$

which is related to the 'reduced-form' VECM

$$\Delta \mathbf{z}_t = \sum_{i=1}^{m-1} \Phi_i \Delta \mathbf{z}_{t-i} + \boldsymbol{\beta} \mathbf{a}^\top \mathbf{z}_{t-1} + \mathbf{v}_t \tag{9.35}$$

through

$$\Gamma_i = \Gamma_0 \Phi_i \quad \Gamma_0 \boldsymbol{\beta} = \mathbf{\Omega} \quad \mathbf{v}_t = \Gamma_0 \mathbf{v}_t$$

so that

$$E\left(\mathbf{v}_t \mathbf{v}_t^\top\right) = \Sigma_v = \Gamma_0 \Sigma_{\mathbf{v}} \Gamma_0^\top$$

Note that in this framework we are assuming that the cointegrating vectors have already been identified, so that identification of the 'short-run' structure, the parameters $\Gamma_0, \Gamma_1, \ldots, \Gamma_{m-1}, \mathbf{\Omega}$, is carried out conditionally upon the form of $\mathbf{a}$. This can be done using conventional methods and will typically proceed in an exploratory fashion, as little is usually known a priori about the short-run structure (see Johansen and Juselius, 1994).

Identification in the traditional econometric simultaneous-equations framework requires an a priori partitioning of the variables into endogenous and exogenous categories – i.e. as $\mathbf{z}_t = \left(\mathbf{y}_t^\top, \mathbf{x}_t^\top\right)^\top$. Wickens (1996) and Hsiao (1997) analyse the identification of such cointegrated simultaneous-equation systems. Their analysis highlights the difference between the two approaches. In the structural approach, the presence or absence of cointegration is presumed in the structure of the model, along with the endogenous/exogenous classification of the variables. In the 'time series' approach, hypotheses about cointegration and exogeneity are determined by the data, so that, although less prior information is needed than in the structural approach, the data are required to be more informative so as to allow reliable inferences to be made.

Example 9.5 An estimated structural VECM

Table 9.3 presents the unrestricted ML estimates of the VECM(2,1,2) model selected in example 9.3, although the model is estimated conditionally upon the identified cointegrating vectors of example 9.4. The correlation matrix R suggests that there are contemporaneous relationships holding between Δp_t

Table 9.3 Unrestricted estimates of VECM(2,1,2) model

	Φ_1				β			
	Δp_{t-1}	Δd_{t-1}	Δrs_{t-1}	$\Delta r20_{t-1}$	$e^*_{1,t-1}$	$e^*_{2,t-1}$	$\beta_\perp \gamma^*_0$	$\hat{\sigma}$
Δp_t	0.149	0.150	0.073	−0.154	−0.080	0.011	0.0049	5.76%
	[2.74]	[0.80]	[1.33]	[1.58]	[3.37]	[1.26]	[1.52]	
Δd_t	−0.028	−0.013	0.007	0.009	0.027	0.005	0.0071	1.53%
	[1.95]	[0.26]	[0.46]	[0.35]	[4.38]	[1.96]	[9.34]	
Δrs_t	−0.111	0.222	0.275	0.222	0.014	−0.025	−0.0007	5.58%
	[2.11]	[1.21]	[5.16]	[2.35]	[0.62]	[2.91]	[0.22]	
$\Delta r20_t$	−0.136	0.058	−0.028	0.209	−0.003	−0.002	−0.0007	3.36%
	[4.28]	[0.52]	[0.89]	[3.68]	[0.25]	[0.49]	[0.35]	

$$R = \begin{bmatrix} 1 & & & \\ 0.09 & 1 & & \\ -0.17 & -0.02 & 1 & \\ -0.27 & -0.02 & 0.44 & 1 \end{bmatrix} \qquad |\hat{\Sigma}_{\varepsilon\varepsilon}| = 2.00 \times 10^{-12}$$

Note: R is the matrix of contemporaneous residual correlations.

and $\Delta r20_t$ and between $\Delta r20_t$ and Δrs_t. By embodying these relationships, the following estimated structural form was obtained by imposing various data-acceptable coefficient restrictions (a likelihood ratio test of the eighteen imposed restrictions yields a χ^2 statistic of 12.19):

$$\Delta p_t = \underset{[1.99]}{0.0059} + \underset{[3.10]}{0.158}\,\Delta p_{t-1} - \underset{[3.60]}{0.083}\,e^*_{1,t-1}, \qquad \hat{\sigma} = 5.78\%$$

$$\Delta d_t = \underset{[9.04]}{0.007} - \underset{[2.33]}{0.031}\,\Delta p_{t-1} + \underset{[4.61]}{0.028}\,e^*_{1,t-1} + \underset{[1.99]}{0.005}\,e^*_{2,t-1}, \qquad \hat{\sigma} = 1.52\%$$

$$\Delta rs_t = \underset{[10.30]}{0.747}\,\Delta r20_t + \underset{[7.58]}{0.320}\,\Delta rs_{t-1} - \underset{[3.01]}{0.022}\,e^*_{2,t-1}, \qquad \hat{\sigma} = 5.68\%$$

$$\Delta r20_t = - \underset{[5.46]}{0.153}\,\Delta p_t - \underset{[4.05]}{0.118}\,\Delta p_{t-1} + \underset{[3.31]}{0.162}\,\Delta r20_{t-1}, \qquad \hat{\sigma} = 3.22\%$$

The figures in [ ] are t-statistics. The error corrections appear in all but the $\Delta r20$ equation, but, as this contains Δp_{t-1} as a regressor, no variable is weakly exogenous for the parameters in any of the four equations. Indeed, Δp_{t-1} appearing in this and the Δd_t equation are the only cases when a lagged variable, other than a dependent variable, appears in an equation, thus demonstrating the importance of the cointegration framework in establishing the presence of the error corrections: without the information contained in the cointegration properties of the data, only a small part of the variation of the data would have been explained, and few interesting regularities would have been uncovered.

9.6 Causality testing in VECMs

Tests of hypotheses about $\boldsymbol{\alpha}$ and $\boldsymbol{\beta}$ also appear when questions of causality arise in VECMs. Consider again the partition used in chapter 8, section 8.2, $\mathbf{z}_t = \left(\mathbf{y}_t^\top, \mathbf{x}_t^\top, \mathbf{r}_t^\top \right)^\top$, where the dimensions of the three vectors are n_1, n_2 and $n_3 = n - n_1 - n_2$, and Φ_i and $\mathbf{A} = \boldsymbol{\beta}\boldsymbol{\alpha}^\top$ are partitioned conformably. The null hypothesis that $\mathbf{x}$ does not Granger-cause $\mathbf{y}$ can then be formulated as

$$H_0 : \Phi_{1,12} = \cdots = \Phi_{m-1,12} = \mathbf{0}, \quad \mathbf{A}_{12} = \mathbf{0}$$

where $\Phi_{i,12}$ and $\mathbf{A}_{12}$ are appropriate $n_1 \times n_2$ submatrices of Φ_i and $\mathbf{A}$, respectively.

Causality tests are often constructed from the OLS estimates of the VAR, however, which implicitly use an unrestricted estimate of Π. Toda and Phillips (1993, 1994), by extending the analysis of Sims, Stock and Watson (1990), conclude that, when cointegration is present (i.e. when $\mathbf{A}_{12} = \boldsymbol{\beta}_1 \boldsymbol{\alpha}_2^\top$, where $\boldsymbol{\beta}_1$ and $\boldsymbol{\alpha}_2$ are conformable partitions of $\boldsymbol{\beta}$ and $\boldsymbol{\alpha}$), standard Wald tests of causality constructed using an unrestricted estimate of $\mathbf{A}$ are distributed asymptotically as χ^2 only if $\boldsymbol{\alpha}_2$ is of rank n_2. If this rank condition fails, the limit distribution involves a mixture of a χ^2 and a non-standard distribution that involves nuisance parameters. Unfortunately, since we require knowledge of the cointegration properties of the system, which are not available simply from estimation of the 'levels' VAR, there is no valid statistical basis for ascertaining whether this rank condition actually holds.

If there is no cointegration, then the Wald statistic for causality again has a non-standard limit distribution, although in this case it is free of nuisance parameters, so that critical values can be tabulated conveniently. If it is known that the system is $I(1)$ with no cointegration, so that $\mathbf{A} = \mathbf{0}$, however, then of course we have a VAR in the differences $\Delta \mathbf{z}_t$, and causality tests in such models do have χ^2 distributions, for we are back in the framework of chapter 8, section 7. Toda and Phillips (1993) argue that such tests are likely to have higher power than tests from the levels VAR as they take account of the unit root constraint $\mathbf{A} = \mathbf{0}$, while the latter tests contain redundant parameter restrictions.

When we have cointegration, causality tests should optimally be constructed from the VECM, in which we know the value of the cointegrating rank r. In such models, it is often natural to refer to the first half of the hypothesis H_0 as 'short-run non-causality' and the second half as 'long-run non-causality'. It is testing for long-run non-causality in VECMs that gives rise to difficulties. Toda and Phillips (1993, theorem 3) show that the standard Wald statistic for testing H_0 will have an asymptotically valid χ^2 distribution only if either the rank of $\boldsymbol{\alpha}_2$ is n_2 or the rank of $\boldsymbol{\beta}_1$ is n_1, in which case the statistic will be asymptotically distributed as $\chi^2_{n_1 n_2 m}$.

Before we can apply these conventional χ^2 asymptotics, we need to test whether either of the two rank conditions actually holds. This can be done using the ML estimates of these matrices, after which causality tests can then be carried out. The Wald statistics required are extremely difficult to construct and the testing sequence is complicated, however, as the papers by Toda and Phillips show. Because of the complexity of this procedure, and because it requires prior knowledge of r (which typically can be obtained only by pre-tests), it would be useful if alternative, simpler, strategies were available.

A more straightforward procedure has been proposed by Toda and Yamamoto (1995) (see also Saikkonen and Lütkepohl, 1996). Suppose we consider the levels VAR(m) model again but now augment the order by one – i.e. we fit a VAR($m+1$). The non-causality hypothesis can now be tested by a conventional Wald statistic, because the additional lag, for which $\Phi_{m,12} = \mathbf{0}$ by assumption, allows standard asymptotic inference to be used once again. Under the assumption here that the elements of z_t are at most $I(1)$, the inclusion of one additional lag in the estimated model suffices. For general orders of integration, a VAR($m+d_{max}$) should be fitted, where d_{max} is the maximum order of integration of the components. It is thus not necessary to know precisely the orders of integration or the cointegration rank.

It is not surprising, then, that this approach is less powerful than the Toda and Phillips approach, and it is also inefficient, as the order of the VAR is intentionally set too large (see the discussion in Stock, 1997). If the number of variables in the VAR is relatively small and the lag order is quite large, however, adding an additional lag might lead to only minor inefficiencies, while the pre-test biases associated with cointegration tests may be more serious. Given the ease with which the tests can be constructed, this 'lag augmentation' VAR (LA-VAR) approach should be seriously considered, particularly as Monte Carlo evidence presented by Yamada and Toda (1998) shows that it has excellent performance in terms of size stability when testing for Granger causality.

Example 9.6 Causality tests using the LA-VAR approach

Causality tests using a VAR(2) model were constructed using the LA-VAR procedure. Since each series making up the VAR appears to be $I(1)$, a VAR(3)

Table 9.4 Granger causality tests using LA-VAR estimation

$\downarrow i \quad j \rightarrow$	p	d	rs	$r20$
p	–	7.85^*	4.79	9.22^*
d	13.58^*	–	2.00	14.18^*
rs	5.32	5.36	–	9.40^*
$r20$	21.53^*	9.42^*	1.23	–

was actually fitted, leading to the causality test statistics shown in table 9.4. There is strong evidence of causal patterns, except for those involving rs, which does not cause any other variable and is caused only by $r20$. These statistics therefore do not pick up the evidence of 'long-run' causality running from the other variables to rs found in the structural VECM formulation of example 9.5.

9.7 Impulse response asymptotics in non-stationary VARs

As shown in chapter 8, section 7, the various impulse responses of the VAR are computed from the sequence of matrices

$$\mathbf{\Psi}_i = \sum\nolimits_{j=1}^{m} \mathbf{\Pi}_j \mathbf{\Psi}_{i-j}, \quad \mathbf{\Psi}_0 = \mathbf{I}_n \quad \mathbf{\Psi}_i = \mathbf{0}, \quad i < 0$$

Their computation remains exactly the same in non-stationary VARs but, if $\mathbf{A} = -\sum_{j=1}^{m} \mathbf{\Pi}_j$ is of reduced rank, the elements of $\mathbf{\Psi}_i$ will not die out as i increases, and this leads to some analytical complications. Following Phillips (1998), we consider the behaviour of these impulse responses as the lead time $i \rightarrow \infty$, and the asymptotic behaviour of estimates of these quantities as $T \rightarrow \infty$.

In stationary VARs, where all the roots of the long-run multiplier matrix $\mathbf{A}$ lie outside the unit circle, the system's estimated impulse responses are $T^{1/2}$-consistent and, upon appropriate centring and scaling, have asymptotic normal distributions (see Lütkepohl, 1991, chap. 3.7): as $i \rightarrow \infty$, both the $\mathbf{\Psi}_i$ and their estimates $\hat{\mathbf{\Psi}}_i$ tend to zero. For non-stationary VARs, where the $\mathbf{\Psi}_i$ do not necessarily die out as $i \rightarrow \infty$, Phillips (1998) shows that a very different limit theory holds for the impulse response estimates, which may be summarised thus (see also Stock, 1996).

(i) When there are unit roots in the system, the long-horizon impulse responses estimated from a levels VAR by OLS are inconsistent, the limiting values of the estimated responses being random variables rather than the true impulse responses. The reason for this is that, because these true impulse responses do not die out as the lead time increases, they carry the effects of the unit roots with them indefinitely. Since the unit roots are estimated with error, the effects of the estimation error persist in the limit as $T \to \infty$. The limiting distributions of $\hat{\Psi}_i$ as $i \to \infty$ are asymmetric, so that confidence intervals for impulse responses will be as well.

(ii) The limiting impulse responses in a cointegrated VAR model are non-zero only in those directions where the model is non-stationary and has unit roots – i.e. $\boldsymbol{a}_\perp$. They are estimated consistently as long as the cointegrating rank is either known or is itself consistently estimated, either by an order selection method or by using classical likelihood ratio tests that are suitably modified to ensure that the size of the test goes to zero as the sample size goes to infinity. This is because, in a reduced-rank regression, the matrix product $\boldsymbol{\beta} \boldsymbol{a}^\top$ is estimated rather than $\mathbf{A}$, so that no unit roots are estimated (either explicitly or implicitly). Simulations reported by Phillips (1998) show that impulse responses are estimated accurately by such procedures. Nonetheless, these consistent selection procedures will tend to mistakenly take roots that are close to unity as actually being unity, so that, rather than dying out, they will converge to non-zero constants. Furthermore, as Stock (1996) shows, in these circumstances prediction intervals will be undesirably wide.

It is clear from these results that impulse responses for non-stationary VARs should not be computed from an unrestricted levels VAR. Knowledge of the number of unit roots in the system is very important for obtaining accurate estimates, so it is important that the cointegrating rank is selected by a consistent method that works well in practice.

Example 9.7 Impulse responses from the VECM

The VECM(2, 1, 2) model arrived at in example 9.5 has an implied long-run matrix, given by $\hat{\boldsymbol{\beta}} \hat{\boldsymbol{a}}^\top + \mathbf{I}_4$, that has two unit roots (given by the two cointegrating vectors) and two real roots of 0.974 and 0.889. Consequently, impulse responses converge to non-zero constants (rs to effectively zero), as shown in figure 9.14(a). Of particular interest is the long-run effect of d on p, which steadily accumulates over three years. This result has been remarked upon in Mills (1991a) as being consistent with the views of market professionals who believe that financial factors have only a short-run impact on equity prices, with dividends being the long-run driving force.

OLS estimation of the unrestricted VAR model provides the roots 1.004, 0.965, 0.934 and 0.880, and the impulse responses are shown in figure 9.14b.

The presence of even a very marginal explosive root has a dramatic effect on the impulse responses as the horizon increases, with all responses tending to get larger, particularly those associated with d. Thus, even though the long-run matrices are almost identical, estimating the two unit roots as 1.004 and 0.965 produces major differences to the impulse responses.

9.8 Testing for a single long-run relationship

Consider again the levels VAR of (9.24), now written as

$$\mathbf{z}_t = \boldsymbol{\mu}_0 + \boldsymbol{\mu}_1 t + \sum_{i=1}^{m} \boldsymbol{\Pi}_i \mathbf{z}_{t-i} + \mathbf{v}_t \tag{9.36}$$

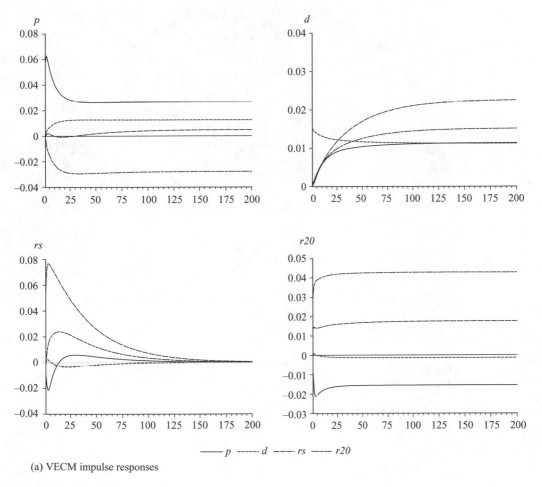

(a) VECM impulse responses

Figure 9.14 Estimated impulse response functions

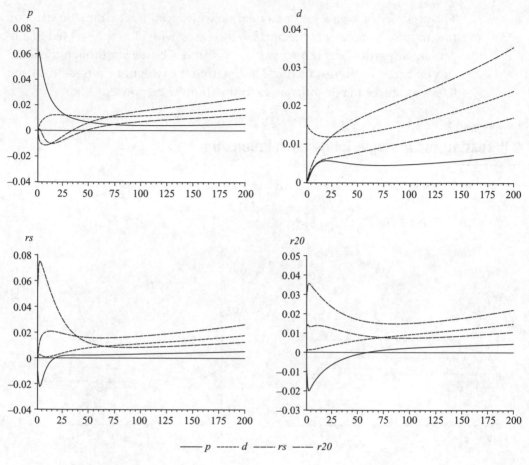

(b) OLS impulse responses

Figure 9.14   (continued)

where the elements of $\mathbf{z}_t$ are permitted to be either $I(0)$, $I(1)$ or cointegrated, along with the *unrestricted* VECM

$$\Delta \mathbf{z}_t = \boldsymbol{\mu}_0 + \boldsymbol{\mu}_1 t + \mathbf{A}\mathbf{z}_{t-1} + \sum_{i=1}^{m-1} \boldsymbol{\Phi}_i \Delta \mathbf{z}_{t-i} + \mathbf{v}_t, \qquad (9.37)$$

where

$$\mathbf{A} = \sum_{i=1}^{m} \boldsymbol{\Pi}_i - \mathbf{I}_n$$

and

$$\boldsymbol{\Phi}_i = -\sum_{j=i+1}^{m} \boldsymbol{\Pi}_j, \quad i = 1, \ldots, m-1$$

are now referred to as the matrices of the long-run multipliers and the short-run dynamic coefficients, respectively.

Consider now the partition $\mathbf{z}_t = \left(y_t, \mathbf{x}_t^\top \right)^\top$, where y_t is scalar, and define the conformable partitions $\mathbf{v}_t = \left(v_{it}, \mathbf{v}_{2t}^\top \right)^\top$ and

$$\boldsymbol{\mu}_j = \begin{bmatrix} \mu_{j1} \\ \boldsymbol{\mu}_{j2} \end{bmatrix} j = 0,1, \quad \mathbf{A} = \begin{bmatrix} A_{11} & \mathbf{A}_{12} \\ \mathbf{A}_{21} & \mathbf{A}_{22} \end{bmatrix}, \quad \boldsymbol{\Phi}_i = \begin{bmatrix} \phi_{11,i} & \boldsymbol{\phi}_{12,i} \\ \boldsymbol{\phi}_{21,i} & \boldsymbol{\Phi}_{22,i} \end{bmatrix}$$

$$\boldsymbol{\Sigma}^{\mathbf{v}} = \begin{bmatrix} \sigma_{11} & \boldsymbol{\sigma}_{12} \\ \boldsymbol{\sigma}_{21} & \boldsymbol{\Sigma}_{22} \end{bmatrix}$$

This is similar to the partitioning used in section 9.5.5 to investigate weak exogeneity in VECMs, although here we do not assume that $\mathbf{A}$ is necessarily of reduced rank. We do, though, assume that $\mathbf{A}_{21} = \mathbf{0}$, which ensures that there exists *at most* one (non-degenerate) long-run relationship between y_t and $\mathbf{x}_t$, irrespective of the order of integration of the $\mathbf{x}_t$ process. Equation (9.37) can then be written in terms of the *dependent* variable y_t and the *forcing* variables $\mathbf{x}_t$ as

$$\Delta y_t = \mu_{01} + \mu_{11}t + A_{11}y_{t-1} + \mathbf{A}_{12}\mathbf{x}_{t-1}$$
$$+ \sum_{i=1}^{m-1} \phi_{11,i}\Delta y_{t-i} + \sum_{i=1}^{m-1} \boldsymbol{\phi}_{12,i}\Delta\mathbf{x}_{t-i} + v_{1t} \tag{9.38}$$

$$\Delta\mathbf{x}_t = \boldsymbol{\mu}_{02} + \boldsymbol{\mu}_{12}t + \mathbf{A}_{22}\mathbf{x}_{t-1}$$
$$+ \sum_{i=1}^{m-1} \boldsymbol{\phi}_{21,i}\Delta y_{t-i} + \sum_{i=1}^{m-1} \boldsymbol{\Phi}_{22,i}\Delta\mathbf{x}_{t-i} + \mathbf{v}_{2t} \tag{9.39}$$

The contemporaneous correlation between v_{1t} and $\mathbf{v}_{2t}$ can be characterised by the regression

$$v_{1t} = \boldsymbol{\omega}^\top\mathbf{v}_{2t} + \xi_t \tag{9.40}$$

where $\boldsymbol{\omega} = \boldsymbol{\Sigma}_{22}^{-1}\boldsymbol{\sigma}_{21}$, $\{\xi_t\}$ is a $WN\left(0,\sigma_\xi^2\right)$ process with $\sigma_\xi^2 = \sigma_{11} - \boldsymbol{\sigma}_{12}\boldsymbol{\Sigma}_{22}^{-1}\boldsymbol{\sigma}_{21}$, and the $\{\mathbf{v}_{2t}\}$ and $\{\xi_t\}$ processes are uncorrelated by construction. Substituting (9.39) and (9.40) into (9.38) yields

$$\Delta y_t = a_0 + a_1 t + \phi y_{t-1} + \boldsymbol{\delta}^\top\mathbf{x}_{t-1}$$
$$+ \sum_{i=1}^{m-1} \psi_i\Delta y_{t-i} + \sum_{i=0}^{m-1} \boldsymbol{\varphi}_{12,i}\Delta\mathbf{x}_{t-i} + \xi_t \tag{9.41}$$

where

$$a_0 \equiv \mu_{01} - \boldsymbol{\omega}^\top\boldsymbol{\mu}_{02}, \qquad a_1 \equiv \mu_{11} - \boldsymbol{\omega}^\top\boldsymbol{\mu}_{12}, \qquad \phi \equiv A_{11}, \quad \boldsymbol{\delta} \equiv \mathbf{A}_{12}^\top - \boldsymbol{\Phi}_{22}^\top\boldsymbol{\omega}$$

$$\psi_i \equiv \phi_{11,i} - \boldsymbol{\omega}^\top\boldsymbol{\phi}_{21,i}, \qquad \boldsymbol{\varphi}_0 \equiv \boldsymbol{\omega}^\top, \qquad\qquad \boldsymbol{\varphi}_i \equiv \boldsymbol{\phi}_{12,i} - \boldsymbol{\omega}^\top\boldsymbol{\Phi}_{22,i}$$

It follows from (9.41) that, if $\phi \neq 0$ and $\boldsymbol{\delta} \neq \mathbf{0}$, then there exists a long-run relationship between the levels of y_t and $\mathbf{x}_t$ given by

$$y_t = \theta_0 + \theta_1 t + \boldsymbol{\theta}^\top \mathbf{x}_t + \upsilon_t \tag{9.42}$$

where $\theta_0 \equiv -a_0/\phi$, $\theta_1 \equiv -a_1/\phi$, $\boldsymbol{\theta} \equiv -\boldsymbol{\delta}/\phi$ is the vector of long-run response parameters and $\{\upsilon_t\}$ is a mean zero stationary process. If $\phi < 0$ then this long-run relationship is *stable* and (9.42) can be written in the ECM form

$$\Delta y_t = a_0 + a_1 t + \phi\left(y_{t-1} - \boldsymbol{\theta}^\top \mathbf{x}_{t-1}\right)$$
$$+ \sum_{i=1}^{m-1} \psi_i \Delta y_{t-i} + \sum_{i=0}^{m-1} \varphi_{12,i} \Delta \mathbf{x}_{t-i} + \xi_t \tag{9.43}$$

If $\phi < 0$ in (9.43) then no long-run relationship exists between y_t and $\mathbf{x}_t$. A test for $\phi < 0$ runs into the difficulty that the long-run parameter vector $\boldsymbol{\theta}$ is no longer identified under this null, being present only under the alternative hypothesis. Consequently, Pesaran, Shin and Smith (2001) test for the absence of a long-run relationship, and avoid the lack of identifiability of $\boldsymbol{\theta}$, by examining the joint null hypothesis $\phi = 0$ and $\boldsymbol{\delta} = \mathbf{0}$ in the unrestricted ECM (9.41). Note that it is then possible for the long-run relationship to be *degenerate*, in that $\phi \neq 0$ but $\boldsymbol{\delta} = \mathbf{0}$, in which case the long-run relationship involves only y_t and possibly a linear trend.

Pesaran, Shin and Smith (2001) consider the conventional Wald statistic of the null $\phi \neq 0$ and $\boldsymbol{\delta} = \mathbf{0}$ and show that its asymptotic distribution involves the non-standard unit root distribution and depends on both the dimension and cointegration rank $(0 \leq r \leq k)$ of the forcing variables $\mathbf{x}_t$. This cointegration rank is the rank of the matrix $\mathbf{A}_{22}$ appearing in (9.39). Pesaran, Shin and Smith obtain this asymptotic distribution in two polar cases: (i), when $\mathbf{A}_{22}$ is of full rank, in which case $\mathbf{x}_t$ is an $I(0)$ vector process; and (ii), when the $\mathbf{x}_t$ process is not mutually cointegrated ($\mathbf{r} = 0$ and $\mathbf{A}_{22} = \mathbf{0}$) and hence is an $I(1)$ process. They point out that the critical values obtained from stochastically simulating these two distributions must provide lower and upper critical value bounds for all possible classifications of the forcing variables into $I(0)$, $I(1)$ and cointegrated processes.

A *bounds procedure* to test for the existence of a long-run relationship within the unrestricted ECM (9.41) is therefore as follows. If the Wald (or related F-) statistic falls below the lower critical value bound, then the null $\phi = 0$ and $\boldsymbol{\delta} = \mathbf{0}$ is not rejected, irrespective of the order of integration or cointegration rank of the variables. Similarly, if the statistics are greater than their upper critical value bounds, the null is rejected and we conclude that there is a long-run relationship between y_t and $\mathbf{x}_t$. If the statistics fall within the bounds, inference is inconclusive and detailed information about the integration/cointegration properties of the variables is then necessary in order to proceed further. It is the fact that we may be able to make firm inferences without this information, and thus avoid the severe pre-testing problems usually involved in this type of analysis, that makes this procedure attractive in applied situations. Pesaran, Shin and Smith provide critical values for alternative values of k under two situations: case 1, when $a_0 \neq 0$, $a_1 = 0$ (with intercept but no trend in (9.41)), and case 2, when $a_0 \neq 0$, $a_1 \neq 0$ (with both intercept and trend in (9.41)).

Pesaran, Shin and Smith show that this testing procedure is consistent and that the approach is applicable in quite general situations. For example, equation (9.41) can be regarded as an autoregressive distributed lag (ARDL) model in y_t and $\mathbf{x}_t$ having all lag orders equal to m. Differential lag lengths can be used without affecting the asymptotic distribution of the test statistic.

Example 9.8 Is there a long-run market model?

In examples 9.1 and 9.2 we investigated whether there was cointegration between the LGEN stock price and the FTSE 100 index on the assumption that the logarithms of both series were $I(1)$. As was remarked in example 9.1, the latter series is only marginally $I(1)$: its ADF test statistic is -3.38, which is close to the 5 per cent critical value of -3.42. We thus investigate the existence of a long-run relationship between the two series (denoted once again as y_t and x_t) using the testing technique outlined above, which does not require a definite classification of the integration properties of x_t. Estimating equation (9.41) with $m = 3$ produced a Wald test statistic of 11.86 for both case 1 and case 2, as the trend was found to be completely insignificant. With $k = 1$ as here, the 5 per cent significance level bounds for the Wald statistic for case 1 are 9.87 and 11.53, so that the hypothesis of no long-run relationship is clearly rejected, irrespective of the order of integration of x_t.

Given this evidence in favour of a long-run relationship, we then fitted a parsimonious form of the ECM (9.43), obtaining

$$\Delta y_t = -\underset{(0.015)}{0.053}\left(y_{t-1} - \underset{(0.005)}{1.086}\, x_{t-1} \right) - \underset{(0.028)}{0.118}(\Delta y_{t-1} + \Delta y_{t-2})$$

$$+ \underset{(0.057)}{1.106}\,\Delta x_t + \underset{(0.063)}{0.151}\,\Delta x_{t-2}$$

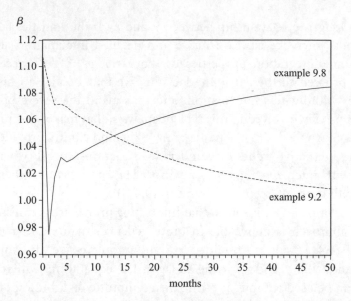

Figure 9.15 Impulse responses from the two market models

How does this model, which has an equation standard error of 3.02 per cent, compare with the model fitted in example 9.2? That model, written in ECM form, is

$$\Delta y_t = -\,0.006 - 0.057(y_{t-1} - x_{t-1}) - 0.128(\Delta y_{t-1} + \Delta y_{t-2})$$
$$+\ 1.107\Delta x_t + 0.128(\Delta x_{t-1} + \Delta x_{t-2})$$

There is thus a difference in the long-run response – 1.086 compared to 1 – and some differences in the short-run dynamics (as well as a constant being significant in the latter model). Written in levels, the two models are

$$y_t = 1.106x_t - 1.048x_{t-1} + 0.151x_{t-2} - 0.151x_{t-3} + 0.829y_{t-1} + 0.118y_{t-3}$$

and

$$y_t = 1.107x_t - 0.922x_{t-1} - 0.128x_{t-3} + 0.815y_{t-1} + 0.128y_{t-3} - 0.006$$

Figure 9.15 shows the impulse response functions calculated from the two models. It is seen that the impact effect is almost identical in the two models and that, after some initial fluctuations, both functions converge monotonically to long-run equilibrium, even though the shapes are very different. Nevertheless, the median lags are almost the same, being of the order of twelve months, so that convergence to equilibrium is rather slow.

9.9 Common trends and cycles

Consider again the VAR(m) process for the $I(1)$ vector $\mathbf{z}_t$,

$$\mathbf{\Pi}(B)\mathbf{z}_t = \mathbf{v}_t$$

where, for simplicity, we exclude the constant and linear trend and set initial values $\mathbf{z}_0 = \mathbf{v}_0 = \mathbf{0}$. Analogous to the 'levels solution' (9.26), we then have

$$\mathbf{z}_t = \mathbf{C}(1)\mathbf{s}_t + \mathbf{C}^*(B)\mathbf{v}_t$$

If there is cointegration then $\mathbf{C}(1)$ is of reduced rank $k = n - r$ and can be written as the product $\gamma\delta^\top$, both of which have rank k. Thus, on defining

$$\tau_t = \delta^\top \mathbf{s}_t \qquad \mathbf{c}_t = \mathbf{C}^*(B)\mathbf{v}_t$$

we have the Stock and Watson (1988) 'common trends' representation

$$\begin{aligned} \mathbf{z}_t &= \gamma\tau_t + \mathbf{c}_t \\ \tau_t &= \tau_{t-1} + \delta^\top \mathbf{v}_t \end{aligned} \tag{9.44}$$

which expresses $\mathbf{z}_t$ as a linear combination of $k = n - r$ random walks, being the common trends τ_t, plus some stationary 'transitory' components $\mathbf{c}_t$. Equation (9.44) may be regarded as a multivariate extension of the Beveridge and Nelson (1981) decomposition introduced in chapter 4, section 1.1. As Wickens (1996) shows, δ is not uniquely defined (cf. the argument concerning the cointegrating matrix $\mathbf{a}$), so these trends are also not uniquely defined without introducing additional identifying conditions.

In the same way that common trends appear in $\mathbf{z}_t$ when $\mathbf{C}(1)$ is of reduced rank, common cycles appear if $\mathbf{C}^*(B)$ is of reduced rank, since $\mathbf{c}_t = \mathbf{C}^*(B)\mathbf{v}_t$ is the cyclical component of $\mathbf{z}_t$. The presence of common cycles requires that there are linear combinations of the elements of $\mathbf{z}_t$ that do not contain these cyclical components – i.e. that there is a set of s linearly independent vectors, gathered together in the $n \times s$ matrix $\boldsymbol{\phi}$, such that

$$\boldsymbol{\phi}^\top \mathbf{c}_t = \boldsymbol{\phi}^\top \mathbf{C}^*(B)\mathbf{v}_t = \mathbf{0}$$

in which case

$$\boldsymbol{\phi}^\top \mathbf{z}_t = \boldsymbol{\phi}^\top \gamma\tau_t$$

Such a matrix will exist if all the $\mathbf{C}_i^*$ have less than full rank and if $\boldsymbol{\phi}^\top \mathbf{C}_i^* = \mathbf{0}$ for all i (see Vahid and Engle, 1993, and Engle and Issler, 1995).

Under these circumstances, we can write $\mathbf{C}_i^* = \mathbf{G}\tilde{\mathbf{C}}_i$ for all i, where $\mathbf{G}$ is an $n \times (n-s)$ matrix having full column rank and $\tilde{\mathbf{C}}_i$ may not have full rank. The cyclical component can then be written as

$$\mathbf{c}_t = \mathbf{G}\tilde{\mathbf{C}}(B)\mathbf{v}_t \equiv \mathbf{G}\tilde{\mathbf{c}}_t$$

so that the n-element cycle $\mathbf{c}_t$ can be written as linear combinations of an $n-s$-element cycle $\tilde{\mathbf{c}}_t$, thus leading to the common trend/common cycle representation

$$\mathbf{z}_t = \gamma\boldsymbol{\tau}_t + \mathbf{G}\tilde{\mathbf{c}}_t \qquad (9.45)$$

The number, s, of linearly independent 'cofeature' vectors making up $\boldsymbol{\phi}$ can be at most $k = n - r$, and these will be linearly independent of the cointegrating vectors making up $\boldsymbol{a}$ (Vahid and Engle, 1993, theorem 1). This is a consequence of the fact that $\boldsymbol{\phi}^\top \mathbf{z}_t$, being the vector of common trends, is $I(1)$, whereas $\boldsymbol{a}^\top \mathbf{z}_t$, being the vector of error corrections, is $I(0)$.

An interesting special case of the representation (9.45) occurs when $r + s = n$. In these circumstances, $\mathbf{z}_t$ has the unique trend/cycle decomposition $\mathbf{z}_t = \mathbf{z}_t^\tau + \mathbf{z}_t^c$, where

$$\mathbf{z}_t^\tau = \boldsymbol{\Theta}_1\boldsymbol{\phi}^\top \mathbf{z}_t = \boldsymbol{\Theta}_1\boldsymbol{\phi}^\top \gamma\boldsymbol{\tau}_t$$

contains the stochastic trends and

$$\mathbf{z}_t^c = \boldsymbol{\Theta}_1\boldsymbol{a}^\top \mathbf{z}_t = \boldsymbol{\Theta}_1\boldsymbol{a}^\top \mathbf{c}_t$$

contains the cyclical component. Here

$$\begin{bmatrix} \boldsymbol{\Theta}_1 & \boldsymbol{\Theta}_2 \end{bmatrix} = \begin{bmatrix} \boldsymbol{a}^\top \\ \boldsymbol{\phi}^\top \end{bmatrix}^{-1}$$

Note that $\mathbf{z}_t^c$ is a linear combination of the error correction terms $\mathbf{e}_t = \boldsymbol{a}^\top \mathbf{z}_t$. Since both $\mathbf{z}_t^\tau$ and $\mathbf{z}_t^c$ are functions of $\boldsymbol{a}$ and $\boldsymbol{\phi}$, they can easily be calculated as simple linear combinations of $\mathbf{z}_t$.

The common trend/common cycle representation (9.45) depends, of course, on the number of cointegrating and cofeature vectors, r and s, in the system. The number of cofeature vectors (i.e. common cycles) can be determined using the approach of Engle and Kozicki (1993), as extended by Vahid and Engle (1993) to the current context in which there may also be cointegration. The rank s of the cofeature matrix can be determined by calculating the test statistic

$$C(s) = -(T - m - 2) \sum_{i=1}^{s} \log\left(1 - \ell_i^2\right)$$

where $\ell_1, \ldots, \ell_s$ are the s smallest squared canonical correlations between $\Delta \mathbf{z}_t$ and the set $(\Delta \mathbf{z}_{t-1}, \ldots, \Delta \mathbf{z}_{t-m+1}, \mathbf{e}_{t-1})$. Under the null hypothesis that the rank of $\boldsymbol{\phi}$ is at least s, this statistic has a χ^2 distribution with $s^2 + sn(m-1) + sr - sn$ degrees of freedom (Vahid and Engle, 1993). The canonical correlations may be computed using the procedure outlined in Hamilton (1994, chap. 20.1).

An equivalent representation is obtained by incorporating the s cofeature vectors, as well as the r cointegrating vectors, into the VECM representation

$$\Delta \mathbf{z}_t = \boldsymbol{\Phi}(B) \Delta \mathbf{z}_{t-1} + \boldsymbol{\beta} \mathbf{e}_{t-1} + \mathbf{v}_t \tag{9.46}$$

directly. Vahid and Engle (1993) point out that the cofeature matrix $\boldsymbol{\phi}$ is identified only up to an invertible transformation, as any linear combination of the columns of $\boldsymbol{\phi}$ will also be a cofeature vector. The matrix can therefore be rotated to have an s-dimensional identity submatrix

$$\boldsymbol{\phi} = \begin{bmatrix} \mathbf{I}_s \\ \boldsymbol{\phi}^*_{(n-s) \times s} \end{bmatrix}$$

$\boldsymbol{\phi}^\top \Delta \mathbf{z}_t$ can then be considered as s 'pseudo-structural-form' equations for the first s elements of $\Delta \mathbf{z}_t$. The system can be completed by adding the unconstrained VECM equations for the remaining $n - s$ equations of $\Delta \mathbf{z}_t$ to obtain the system

$$\begin{bmatrix} \mathbf{I}_s & \boldsymbol{\phi}^{*\top} \\ \mathbf{0}_{(n-s) \times s} & \mathbf{I}_{n-s} \end{bmatrix} \Delta \mathbf{z}_t = \begin{bmatrix} \mathbf{0}_{s \times (n(m-1)+r)} \\ \boldsymbol{\Phi}_1^* \ldots \boldsymbol{\Phi}_{m-1}^* \; \boldsymbol{\beta}^* \end{bmatrix} \begin{bmatrix} \Delta \mathbf{z}_{t-1} \\ \vdots \\ \Delta \mathbf{z}_{t-m+1} \\ \mathbf{e}_{t-1} \end{bmatrix} + \mathbf{v}_t \tag{9.47}$$

where $\boldsymbol{\Phi}_1^*$ contains the last $n - s$ rows of $\boldsymbol{\Phi}_1$, etc. Writing the restricted model in this way makes it clear why there are $s^2 + sn(m-1) + sr - sn$ degrees of freedom for the common feature test statistic $C(s)$. The unrestricted VECM (9.46) has $n(n(m-1)+r)$ parameters, whereas the pseudo-structural model (9.47) has $sn - s^2$ parameters in the first s equations and $(n-s)(n(m-1) + r)$ parameters in the $n - s$ equations that complete the system, so imposing $s^2 + sn(m-1) + sr - sn$ restrictions.

The system (9.47) can be estimated by full-information maximum likelihood (FIML) or some other simultaneous equation estimation technique, and a likelihood ratio statistic of the restrictions imposed by the s cofeature vectors can then be constructed, which will be equivalent to $C(s)$. Equivalently, the common cycle restrictions can be imposed directly on the VECM to yield

$$\Delta \mathbf{z}_t = \begin{bmatrix} -\boldsymbol{\phi}^{*\top} \\ \mathbf{I}_{n-s} \end{bmatrix} \left[\boldsymbol{\Phi}_1^* \Delta \mathbf{z}_{t-1} + \cdots + \boldsymbol{\Phi}_m^* \Delta \mathbf{z}_{t-m+1} + \boldsymbol{\beta}^* \mathbf{e}_{t-1} \right] + \mathbf{v}_t \qquad (9.48)$$

which is a reduced-rank VECM. Note that, if $m=1$ and $r=n-s$, the system will be just-identified and no test for common cycles is needed, for the system will necessarily have r common cycles. As the lag order m increases, so the system will generally become overidentified and tests for common cycles become necessary.

From (9.48), it is clear that the presence of s common cycles implies that $\boldsymbol{\phi}^{\top} \Delta \mathbf{z}_t$ is independent of $\Delta \mathbf{z}_{t-1}, \ldots, \Delta \mathbf{z}_{t-m+1}$ and $\mathbf{e}_{t-1}$, and hence of all past values of $\mathbf{v}_t$. Vahid and Engle (1997) have subsequently generalised this approach to consider 'codependent' cycles. A codependent cycle of order q is the linear combination of $\Delta \mathbf{z}_t$ that is independent of $\mathbf{v}_{t-j}$, $j > q$, so that a common cycle is a codependent cycle of order 0. For a recent survey of common trends and cycles modelling, see Vahid (2006).

Example 9.9 Are there common cycles in the UK financial markets?
In example 9.3 we found that, in the VECM fitted to $\mathbf{z}_t = (p_t, d_t, rs_t, r20_t)$, there were $r=2$ cointegrating vectors and hence $k=2$ common trends. There can, then, be at most two common cycles. If s was two, then the structural model (9.47) with $m=2$ would take the form of two structural equations:

$$\Delta p_t = -\phi_{13}^* \Delta rs_t - \phi_{14}^* \Delta r20_t + v_{1t}$$
$$\Delta d_t = -\phi_{23}^* \Delta rs_t - \phi_{24}^* \Delta r20_t + v_{2t}$$

say, and two unrestricted reduced-form equations for the other two variables, Δrs_t and $\Delta r20_t$, which imposes a total of eight restrictions. The restricted reduced-form (9.48) replaces the above two structural equations with reduced-form equations in which the coefficients are linear combinations of $\boldsymbol{\Phi}_1^*$ and $\boldsymbol{\beta}^*$, the weights being given by (minus) the $\boldsymbol{\phi}^*$ coefficients.

Table 9.5 Common cycle tests

Null	$C(p, s)$	df	p-value
$s > 0$	6.15	3	.105
$s > 1$	35.47	8	.000

Table 9.5 provides the common-feature test statistics, from which we see that $s = 1$. The estimated common cycle in the pseudo-structural model (9.48) with $s = 1$ takes the form, after the deletion of insignificant coefficients,

$$\boldsymbol{\phi}_1 \Delta \mathbf{z}_t = \Delta p_t + 1.440 \Delta r20_t$$

so that, once again, we find that the equity and gilt markets are contemporaneously negatively correlated and their logarithmic changes share a common cycle.

10 Further topics in the analysis of integrated financial time series

In this chapter we investigate several further topics in the analysis of integrated time series. Section 1 looks at the links between present value models, excess volatility, rational bubbles and cointegration, while section 2 considers non-linear extensions of cointegration and error correction models, and briefly discusses some recent techniques for introducing structural breaks and infinite variance errors into the cointegrating framework.

10.1 Present value models, excess volatility and cointegration

10.1.1 Present value models and the 'simple' efficient markets hypothesis

As remarked in chapter 1, present value models are extremely popular in finance as they are often used to formulate models of efficient markets. Written generally, a present value model for two variables, y_t and x_t, states that y_t is a linear function of the present discounted value of the expected future values of x_t

$$y_t = \phi(1 - \delta) \sum_{i=0}^{\infty} \delta^{i+1} E(x_{t+i}|\Phi_t) + c \qquad (10.1)$$

where c, the constant, ϕ, the coefficient of proportionality, and δ, the constant discount factor, are parameters that may be known a priori or may need to be estimated. As usual, $E(x_{t+i}|\Phi_t)$ is the expectation of x_{t+i} conditional on the information set available at time t, Φ_t.

A simple example of how (10.1) might arise is to consider an implication of the efficient markets hypothesis, that stock returns, r_t, are unforecastable. This can be formalised as $E(r_{t+1}|\Phi_t) = r$, where r is a constant, sometimes referred to as the discount rate (see Shiller, 1981a, 1981b). If y_t is the beginning of period t stock price and x_t the dividend paid during the period, then

$$r_{t+1} = (y_{t+1} - y_t + x_t)/y_t$$

so that we can express y_t as the first-order rational expectations model of the form

$$y_t = \delta E(y_{t+1}|\Phi_t) + \delta E(x_t|\Phi_t) \tag{10.2}$$

where $\delta = 1/(1+r)$. This can be solved by recursive substitution to yield

$$y_t = \sum_{i=0}^{n} \delta^{i+1} E(x_{t+i}|\Phi_t) + \delta^n E(y_{t+n}|\Phi_t) \tag{10.3}$$

If we impose the terminal (or transversality) condition that the second term in (10.3) goes to zero as $n \to \infty$, the present value relation (10.1) is obtained with $c = 0$ and $\phi = 1/(1-\delta) = (1+r)/r$.

Typically, y_t and x_t will be $I(1)$ processes, so Campbell and Shiller (1987, 1988a) consider subtracting $(\delta/(1-\delta))x_t$ from both sides of (10.3). On defining $\theta = \delta/(1-\delta) = 1/r$ and rearranging, we obtain a new variable, S_t, which Campbell and Shiller (1987) term the 'spread':

$$S_t = y_t - \theta x_t = \phi \sum_{i=1}^{\infty} \delta^i E(\Delta x_{t+i}|\Phi_t) \tag{10.4}$$

If y_t and x_t are $I(1)$, then it follows from (10.4) that S_t must be $I(0)$, which in turn implies that y_t and x_t are cointegrated with cointegrating parameter θ. Consequently, S_t and Δx_t must together form a jointly covariance stationary process, which can be approximated in finite samples by a bivariate VAR(m) process:

$$\begin{aligned}
S_t &= \sum_{i=1}^{m} a_i S_{t-i} + \sum_{i=1}^{m} b_i \Delta x_{t-i} + v_{1t} \\
\Delta x_t &= \sum_{i=1}^{m} c_i S_{t-i} + \sum_{i=1}^{m} d_i \Delta x_{t-i} + v_{2t}
\end{aligned} \tag{10.5}$$

It is convenient to rewrite (10.5) in *companion form* – i.e. as

$$
\begin{bmatrix}
S_t \\
S_{t-1} \\
\vdots \\
S_{t-m+1} \\
\Delta x_t \\
\Delta x_{t-1} \\
\vdots \\
\Delta x_{t-m+1}
\end{bmatrix}
=
\begin{bmatrix}
a_1 & \cdots & a_{m-1} & a_m & b_1 & \cdots & b_{m-1} & b_m \\
1 & & & & & & & \\
& \ddots & & & & & & \\
& & 1 & 0 & & & & \\
c_1 & \cdots & c_{m-1} & c_m & d_1 & \cdots & d_{m-1} & d_m \\
& & & & 1 & & & \\
& & & & & \ddots & & \\
& & & & & & 1 & 0
\end{bmatrix}
\begin{bmatrix}
S_{t-1} \\
S_{t-2} \\
\vdots \\
S_{t-m} \\
\Delta x_{t-1} \\
\Delta x_{t-2} \\
\vdots \\
\Delta x_{t-m}
\end{bmatrix}
+
\begin{bmatrix}
v_{1t} \\
0 \\
\vdots \\
0 \\
v_{2t} \\
0 \\
\vdots \\
0
\end{bmatrix}
$$

where blank elements are zero. This can be written more compactly, in an obvious notation, as

$$\mathbf{z}_t = \Pi \mathbf{z}_{t-1} + \mathbf{v}_t \tag{10.6}$$

We can use the first-order formulation (10.6) to express the variant of the present value model presented as equation (10.4) in closed-form solution – i.e. as a function of variables known to agents at the time expectations are formed. If we restrict the information set to consist only of current and lagged S_t and Δx_t – i.e. $\Phi_t^* = \left(S_t^0, \Delta x_t^0\right)$, using the notation introduced in chapter 8 – then the conditional expectation of future values of $\mathbf{z}_t$, conditional on Φ_t^*, is

$$E\left(\mathbf{z}_{t+i}\middle|\Phi_t^*\right) = \Pi^i \mathbf{z}_t$$

Define $\mathbf{g}$ as a $(2m \times 1)$ selection vector with unity as the first element and zeros elsewhere, and $\mathbf{h}$ as another selection vector with unity as the $(m+1)$-th element and zeros elsewhere, so that $S_t = \mathbf{g}^\top \mathbf{z}_t$, $\Delta x_t = \mathbf{h}^\top \mathbf{z}_t$, and

$$E\left(\Delta x_{t+i}\middle|\Phi_t^*\right) = E\left(\mathbf{h}^\top \mathbf{z}_{t+i}\middle|\Phi_t^*\right) = \mathbf{h}^\top \Pi^i \mathbf{z}_t$$

Equation (10.4) can then be written as

$$\mathbf{g}^\top \mathbf{z}_t = \theta \mathbf{h}^\top \left(\sum_{i=1}^{\infty} \delta^i \Pi^i\right) \mathbf{z}_t = \theta \mathbf{h}^\top \delta \Pi (I - \delta \Pi)^{-1} \mathbf{z}_t \tag{10.7}$$

which is a closed-form variant of the present value model. The advantage of this formulation is that it imposes the model's restrictions on the coefficients of the VAR, since, if (10.7) is to hold non-trivially, the following $2m$ restrictions must hold:

$$\mathbf{g}^\top - \theta \mathbf{h}^\top \delta \Pi (I - \delta \Pi)^{-1} = \mathbf{0} \tag{10.8}$$

Although these restrictions appear complex and hard to interpret, for a given δ, and hence θ, they turn out to be equivalent to this set of linear restrictions:

$$
\begin{aligned}
1 - \delta a_1 - \theta \delta c_1 &= 0 \\
a_i + \theta c_i &= 0 \quad i = 2, \ldots, m \\
b_i + \theta d_i &= 0 \quad i = 2, \ldots, m
\end{aligned}
\tag{10.9}
$$

These restrictions can be interpreted as follows. The present value model implies that, from (10.2),

$$E\big(y_t - \delta^{-1}y_{t-1} + x_{t-1}\big|\Phi_t^*\big) = 0 \tag{10.10}$$

or, equivalently,

$$E\big(y_t\big|\Phi_t^*\big) = \delta^{-1}y_{t-1} - x_{t-1}$$

so that $\delta^{-1}y_{t-1} - x_{t-1}$ is an optimal predictor of y_t. Since

$$E\big(y_t\big|\Phi_t^*\big) = (1+r)y_{t-1} - x_{t-1}$$

we also have

$$E\big(((y_t - y_{t-1} + x_{t-1})/y_{t-1})\big|\Phi_t^*\big) - r = 0$$

i.e. that excess expected returns are zero. In terms of S_t and Δx_t, this can be written as

$$E\big(S_t - \delta^{-1}S_{t-1} + \theta\Delta x_t\big|\Phi_t^*\big) = 0$$

or

$$E\big(S_t\big|\Phi_t^*\big) = \delta^{-1}S_{t-1} - \theta\Delta x_t \tag{10.11}$$

Using the VAR formulation (10.5), we have

$$E\big(S_t - \delta^{-1}S_{t-1} + \theta\Delta x_{t-1}\big|\Phi_t\big) = \sum\nolimits_{i=1}^{m} (a_i + \theta c_i)S_{-i} + \sum\nolimits_{i=1}^{m} (b_i + \theta d_i)\Delta x_{t-i}$$

which is identically equal to zero under the restrictions (10.9).

A further implication of the present value model for the VAR (10.5) is that S_t must Granger-cause Δx_t unless S_t is itself an *exact* linear function of $\{x_t^0\}$. This is because S_t is an optimal forecast of a weighted sum of future values of Δx_t conditional on Φ_t (recall equation (10.4)). S_t will therefore have incremental explanatory power for future Δx_t if agents have information useful for forecasting Δx_t beyond $\{x_t^0\}$; if not, they form S_t as an exact linear function of $\{x_t^0\}$.

Following Campbell and Shiller (1987), we can also use these restrictions to construct 'volatility tests' of the model. If the 'theoretical spread', S_t^*, is defined as

$$S_t^* = \phi\sum\nolimits_{i=1}^{\infty} \delta^i E\big(\Delta x_{t+i}\big|\Phi_t^*\big) = \theta\mathbf{h}^\top \delta\Pi(I - \delta\Pi)^{-1}\mathbf{z_t}$$

then, if the present value model is correct, we have it from (10.4) that $S_t^* = S_t$ and hence $V(S_t^*) = V(S_t)$. This equality provides a way of assessing the model informally by examining the comovement of $V(S_t^*)$ and $V(S_t)$. In particular, if the model is correct, the ratio $V(S_t)/V(S_t^*)$ should differ from unity only because of sampling error in the estimated coefficients of the VAR.

Campbell and Shiller (1987) also suggest a second volatility test in addition to this 'levels variance ratio'. Denoting the innovation associated with (10.11) as

$$\xi_t = S_t - \delta^{-1} S_{t-1} + \theta \Delta x_t$$

the 'theoretical innovation' can be defined analogously as

$$\xi_t^* = S_t^* - \delta^{-1} S_{t-1}^* + \theta \Delta x_t$$

Under the present value model, $\xi_t^* = \xi_t$ as $S_t^* = S_t$, so the 'innovation variance ratio', $V(\xi_t)/V(\xi_t^*)$, should again be compared with unity.

The interpretation of (10.1) as the present value of a stock price given the future dividend stream relies on y_t and x_t being the *levels* of prices and dividends, respectively. If dividends grow at a constant rate $g < r$ then

$$E(x_{t+i}|\Phi_t) = (1+g)^i x_t$$

and

$$E(\Delta x_{t+i}|\Phi_t) = (1+g)^{i-1} g x_t$$

so that (10.4) becomes

$$S_t = \frac{(1+r)g}{r(r-g)} x_t \qquad (10.12)$$

which is clearly no longer $I(0)$. Since (10.12) implies, however, that

$$y_t = \frac{(1+g)}{(r-g)} x_t = \frac{1}{(r-g)} x_{t+1} \qquad (10.13)$$

the 'full spread',

$$Sf_t = y_t - \frac{(1+g)}{(r-g)} x_t = y_t - \frac{1}{(r-g)} x_{t+1}$$

will be $I(0)$. Equation (10.13) can be written as

$$\log(y_t) - \log(x_t) = \kappa$$

where $\kappa = (1 + g)/(r - g)$, so that, when expressed in logarithms, prices and dividends are cointegrated with a unit-cointegrating parameter. This representation leads to the 'dividend ratio' form of the model, to be developed in section 10.1.3.

10.1.2 Rational bubbles

These tests of the present value model have all been based on the assumption that the transversality condition in equation (10.3) holds – i.e. that

$$\lim_{n \to \infty} \delta^n E(y_{t+n}|\Phi_t) = 0$$

If this is the case then $y_t = y_t^f$, where y_t^f is the unique forward solution, often termed the 'market fundamentals' solution,

$$y_t^f = \sum_{i=0}^{\infty} \delta^{i+1} E(x_{t+i}|\Phi_t)$$

If this transversality condition fails to hold, however, there will be a family of solutions to (10.2): see, for example, Blanchard and Watson (1982), West (1987) and Diba and Grossman (1987, 1988). In such circumstances, any y_t that satisfies

$$y_t = y_t^f + B_t$$

where

$$E(B_{t+1}|\Phi_t) = \delta^{-1}B_t = (1 + r)B_t \qquad (10.14)$$

is also a solution. B_t is known as a *speculative*, or *rational*, *bubble*, an otherwise extraneous event that affects y_t because everyone expects it to do so – i.e. it is a self-fulfilling expectation.

An example of such a bubble is (see Blanchard and Watson, 1982, and West, 1987)

$$B_t = \begin{cases} (B_{t-1} - \overline{B})/\pi\delta & \text{with probability } \pi \\ \overline{B}/(1 - \pi)\delta & \text{with probability } 1 - \pi \end{cases} \qquad (10.15)$$

where $0 < \pi < 1$ and $\bar{B} > 0$ (other examples are provided by, for example, Hamilton, 1986). According to (10.15), strictly positive bubbles grow and burst, with the probability that the bubble bursts being $1 - \pi$. While the bubble floats it grows at the rate $(\delta\pi)^{-1} = (1 + r)/\pi > 1 + r$; investors in the asset thus receive an extraordinary return to compensate them for the capital loss that would have occurred had the bubble burst.

Equation (10.14) implies that the rational bubble has explosive conditional expectations, since

$$E(B_{t+i}|\Phi_t) = (1 + r)^i B_t$$

and $r > 0$. Thus, if y_t is the price of a freely disposable asset, say a stock, then a negative rational bubble ($B_t < 0$) cannot exist, because its existence would imply that y_t decreases without bound at the geometric rate $(1 + r)$, so that it becomes negative at some finite time $t + i$. Negative rational bubbles are, at least theoretically, possible if y_t is an exchange rate, for this characterises a continual currency appreciation.

While positive bubbles are theoretically possible, Diba and Grossman (1987, 1988) discuss a number of conditions that must be met for their existence. Positive bubbles imply that asset holders might expect such a bubble to come to dominate y_t, which would then bear little relation to market fundamentals. Bubbles would be empirically plausible only if, despite explosive conditional expectations, the probability is small that a rational bubble becomes arbitrarily large. Moreover, for exchange rates a positive bubble would imply a continual devaluation of the currency, and this can be ruled out by an argument symmetric to that used above for a negative rational bubble in stock prices.

Diba and Grossman also show that, if a rational bubble does not exist at time t, then it cannot get started at any later date $t + i$, $i > 0$, and that, if an existing rational bubble bursts, a new independent rational bubble cannot simultaneously start. Thus, if a rational bubble exists at time t, it must have started at time $t = 0$ (the first date of trading of the asset), it must not have burst, it will not restart if it bursts and, if it is a bubble in a stock price, the stock has been continuously overvalued relative to market fundamentals.

The presence of bubbles can be tested by examining their implications for cointegration between various series. When $y_t = y_t^f$, so that no bubbles are present, equation (10.13) implies that

$$U_{t+1} = y_t - \delta(y_{t+1} + x_t)$$

must be $I(0)$, and, as we have already shown, the spread $S_t = y_t - \theta x_t$ must also be $I(0)$, so that y_t must be cointegrated with both x_t and $y_{t+1} + x_t$ (it must also be the case that Δy_t is $I(0)$). If, on the other hand, a bubble is present, so that $y_t = y_t^f + B_t$, the bubble must appear in both U_t and S_t. Since, by definition, B_t is non-stationary, these variables cannot be $I(0)$ and the cointegration relationships cannot hold.

Hamilton and Whiteman (1985) discuss these implications in more detail, showing that, if $x_t \sim I(d)$, then rational bubbles can only exist if $y_t \sim I(d + b)$, where $b > 0$. The finding that y_t is of a higher order of integration than x_t is not necessarily evidence in favour of bubbles, however. As Hamilton and Whiteman point out, such a finding might be explained by numerous other factors: what appears to be a bubble could have arisen instead from rational agents responding solely to fundamentals not observed by the modeller.

One further important drawback with tests of stationarity and cointegration is the question of power. Diba (1990), for example, argues that, if $\bar{B}$ in (10.15) is sufficiently close to zero, the ensuing bubble would generate fluctuations in a finite sample that could not be distinguished from stationary behaviour. Meese (1986) provides both simulation and empirical evidence on exchange rate bubbles that is consistent with this.

Example 10.1 Testing stock market volatility

Campbell and Shiller (1987) employ the 'cointegration approach' to test the present value model for annual data on the real S&P Composite price index (y_t) and the associated dividend index (x_t) from 1871 to 1986. As a preliminary, unit root tests are needed to ensure that both y_t and x_t are $I(1)$; this was indeed found to be the case. Less conclusive evidence was presented that the spread was stationary, which would imply that y_t and x_t are cointegrated (in practice, Campbell and Shiller use $SL_t = y_t - \theta x_{t-1}$ rather than S_t to avoid timing problems caused by the use of beginning-of-year stock prices and dividends paid within the year).

Nonetheless, assuming cointegration and using the cointegrating regression estimate of θ (an implied discount rate of 3.2 per cent), a second-order VAR was constructed for the bivariate $(SL_t, \Delta x_t)$ process. The estimates suggested that dividend changes were highly predictable, and there was strong evidence that the spread Granger-caused dividend changes, one implication of the present value model. The restrictions (10.9) could not be rejected at conventional significance levels, and neither were the two variance ratios significantly larger than unity.

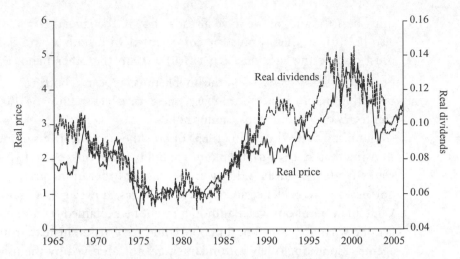

Figure 10.1   FTA All Share index: real prices and dividends (monthly 1965–2005)

Markedly different results were obtained, however, when the sample mean return was used to calculate a discount rate of 10.2 per cent. Now the restrictions (10.9) could be rejected at low significance levels and the two variance inequalities were sharply violated. Campbell and Shiller suggest that the implied discount rate of 3.2 per cent obtained from the cointegrating regression may be too low, which might be argued to be consistent with the proposition that the cointegration parameter is estimating the discount rate κ^{-1} rather than r. Nevertheless, although they prefer to use the higher discount rate of 10.2 per cent, which implies a 4.8 per cent growth in dividends and leads to excessive volatility, they do emphasise that the strength of the evidence depends sensitively on the assumed value of the discount rate.

Updating Mills (1993), we apply this technique to UK data on real stock prices and dividends, obtained by dividing the FTA All Share price and dividend series used in previous examples by the retail price index. The series are shown for the period January 1965 to December 2005 in figure 10.1. Following the Dickey and Pantula (1987) approach of chapter 3, section 5, to testing for more than one unit root, we confirm that both series are $I(1)$, thus ruling out the presence of rational bubbles.

Are the two series cointegrated? A unit root test on the residuals from the cointegrating regression of real prices on real dividends yields the statistic $C = -3.98$, which is significant at the 5 per cent level, although, on estimating a VECM, the trace statistic is only $\eta_0 = 11.9$, which is significant at the 16 per cent level. Given this, albeit somewhat weak, evidence in favour of cointegration, we proceed by assuming that the series are cointegrated. The estimates of the cointegration parameter θ from the two approaches are 37.55 and 38.89, respectively, implying respective discount rates of 2.7 per cent and 2.6 per cent. Since the two estimates are so close to each other, we continue the analysis using just the former.

Fitting a fourth-order VAR of the form (10.5) leads to a Wald test statistic of the restrictions (10.9) taking the value $\chi_5^2 = 17.4$, which is clearly significant, thus rejecting the present value restrictions. A test of S_t Granger-causing Δx_t, however, has a p-value of only 0.01, which supports the present value model implication. The variance ratio inequalities are also violated: $V(S_t)/V(S_t^*) = 3.6$ and $V(\xi_t)/V(\xi_t^*) = 0.3$.

Example 10.2 Testing the expectations hypothesis of the term structure of interest rates

Shiller (1979) shows that the expectations hypothesis of the term structure of interest rates – that the current long rate is the weighted average of current and expected future short rates – can be put into the form of the present value model (10.1). In this framework, y_t is the current interest rate (the yield to maturity) on a long bond (strictly, a perpetuity), x_t is the current one-period interest rate, θ is set to unity, δ is a parameter of linearisation, typically set equal to $(1 + \bar{y})^{-1}$, and c is a liquidity premium unrestricted by the model.

The expectations hypothesis thus asserts that, if y_t and x_t are both $I(1)$, then the spread, $S_t = y_t - x_t$ (noting that $\theta = 1$), must be $I(0)$ and hence that y_t and x_t must be cointegrated with cointegrating vector $(1, -1)$. S_t and Δx_t then have the VAR representation (10.5) and the expectations hypothesis implies the restrictions given by equation (10.9), although the first of these can now be written as $a_1 + c_1 = 1 + \bar{y}$. Equation (10.10) now has the implication that the excess return on holding a long bond for one period, rather than a one-period bond, should be unpredictable.

Although this form of the expectations hypothesis is strictly valid only when the long rate is a perpetuity, it can still be used for bonds of finite, but very long, life – e.g. twenty years. Campbell and Shiller (1987) thus test the model using monthly data on the yield on US Treasury twenty-year bonds and one-month Treasury bill rates for the period 1959 to 1983. Evidence is presented that the spread is stationary, but a test of the restrictions (10.9) rejects the expectations hypothesis very strongly. Nonetheless, the variance ratios are not significantly different from unity and the 'theoretical spread', S_t^*, is highly correlated with the actual spread, S_t. Campbell and Shiller interpret these conflicting findings as evidence that deviations from the present value model are only transitory and suggest that the model does, in fact, fit the data comparatively well.

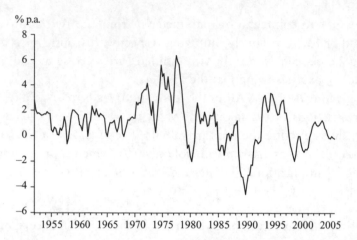

Figure 10.2   UK interest rate spread (quarterly 1952–2005)

Updating Mills (1991b), we consider here how the expectations hypothesis fits the UK interest rate data used in many previous examples. Because the short rate is the yield on ninety-one-day (three-month) Treasury bills, we use quarterly, rather than monthly, data for the period from the start of 1952 to the end of 2005, a total of $T = 216$ observations. The spread, shown in figure 10.2, is stationary, with an ADF test producing $\tau_\mu = -3.97$, which rejects a unit root at the 1 per cent level (note that we can carry out a unit root test directly on the spread, rather than test for cointegration between y_t and x_t, because the cointegration parameter is assumed to be $\theta = 1$ a priori).

A VAR(1) was then fitted to S_t and Δx_t, and imposing the single restriction $a_1 + c_1 = 1.072$ in (10.9) leads to the test statistic $\chi_1^2 = 3.70$, which is not quite significant at the 5 per cent level. S_t Granger-causes Δx_t at the 0.01 per cent level and the variance ratio $V(S_t)/V(S_t^*)$ is just 0.9. The theoretical spread S_t^* is very close to the actual spread, so that the evidence in favour of using the present value model to analyse the setting of interest rates is surprisingly strong.

10.1.3 The 'dividend ratio model': a log-linear approximation to the present value model

As has been remarked on above, the present value model (10.1) when applied to stock prices is specified in terms of the levels of prices and dividends, and this may present statistical problems if these series grow exponentially. To incorporate such non-stationarity, Campbell and Shiller (1988c) focus attention on the *logarithmic* return. Recall the definition of the one-period return as, in this case,

$$r_{t+1} = (P_{t+1} + D_t - P_t)/P_t = (P_{t+1} + D_t/P_t) - 1$$

Taking logarithms and using the approximation $r_{t+1} \cong \log(1 + r_{t+1}) = h_{1,t+1}$ yields

$$h_{1,t+1} = \log(P_{t+1} + D_t) - \log(P_t)$$

Campbell and Shiller examine the relationship between $h_{1,t+1}$ and the logarithms of dividends and prices, d_t and p_t. The relationship is non-linear, of course, but can be approximated as

$$h_{1,t+1} = k + \rho p_{t+1} + (1 - \rho)d_t - p_t = k + \zeta_t - \rho\zeta_{t-1} + \Delta d_t \qquad (10.16)$$

where $\zeta_t = d_{t-1} - p_t$ is the logarithmic 'dividend/price ratio' or dividend yield, ρ is the average of the ratio $P_t/(P_t + D_{t-1})$ and $k = -\log(\rho) - (1 - \rho)\log(1/\rho - 1)$: see Campbell and Shiller (1988b, 1988c) for details of the derivation of equation (10.16).

Equation (10.16) can be thought of as a difference equation relating ζ_t to ζ_{t-1}, Δd_t and $h_{1,t+1}$, and, on solving forwards and imposing the terminal condition that $\lim_{i\to\infty} \rho^i\zeta_{t+i} = 0$, we obtain

$$\zeta_t \cong \sum_{i=0}^{\infty} \rho^i\left(h_{1,t+i+1} - \Delta d_{t+i}\right) - \frac{k}{1 - \rho} \qquad (10.17)$$

As it stands, this equation has no economic content, since it simply says that ζ_t, the log dividend/price ratio, can be written as a discounted value of the differences between future returns and dividend growth rates discounted at the constant rate ρ, less a constant $k/(1 - \rho)$. Suppose, however, that, as before, expected one-period returns are constant: $E(h_{1,t+1}|\Phi_t) = r$. Then, on taking conditional expectations of (10.17), we obtain

$$\zeta_t \cong -\sum_{i=0}^{\infty} \rho^i E(\Delta d_{t+i}|\Phi_t) + \frac{r - k}{1 - \rho} \qquad (10.18)$$

which expresses the log dividend/price ratio as a linear function of expected real dividend growth into the infinite future.

The restrictions implicit in (10.18) can be tested using a framework analogous to that developed in section 10.1.2 above, noting that, in this context, ζ_t is the logarithmic counterpart of the spread $S_t = P_t - \theta D_t$. We therefore consider ζ_t and Δd_t to be generated by a VAR, which can be written in companion form as in equation (10.6) with $\mathbf{z}_t = (\zeta_t, \Delta d_t)^\top$. The implied solution to the present value model conditional on the restricted information set $\Phi_t^* = (\zeta_t^0, \Delta d_t^0)$ is then

$$\mathbf{g}^\top \mathbf{z}_t = -\mathbf{h}^\top \Pi (I - \rho \Pi)^{-1} \mathbf{z}_t$$

with the accompanying set of restrictions

$$\mathbf{g}^\top + \mathbf{h}^\top \Pi (I - \rho \Pi)^{-1} = \mathbf{0} \tag{10.19}$$

As with the analogous set (10.9), these restrictions imply that $E(h_{1,t+1}|\Phi_t^*) = 0$, so that returns are unpredictable. Moreover, as with the VAR of (10.6), a further implication of this model is that ζ_t should Granger-cause Δd_t.

Campbell and Shiller (1988c) argue that working with logarithms has certain advantages over the approach developed previously when testing the implications of the present value model for stock prices. One advantage is that it is easy to combine with individual log-linear models of prices and dividends, which, as stressed by Kleidon (1986b), for example, are both more appealing on theoretical grounds and do appear to fit the data better than linear ones. A second advantage is that using the variables ζ_t and Δd_t mitigates measurement error problems that may occur when deflating nominal stock prices and dividends by some price index to obtain real variables.

The model has been extended in various ways. Campbell and Shiller (1988c) allow expected log returns to be given by the model $E(h_{1,t+1}|\Phi_t) = r + R_t$, where R_t is the real return on, for example, Treasury bills. In this case $R_{t+i} - \Delta d_{t+i}$ replaces $-\Delta d_{t+i}$ in equation (10.18) and $\mathbf{z}_t = (\zeta_t, R_t - \Delta d_t)^\top$ becomes the vector modelled as a VAR. Campbell and Shiller (1988b) focus attention on the j-period discounted return

$$h_{j,t} = \sum_{i=0}^{j-1} \rho^i h_{1,t+i}$$

which leads to the following set of restrictions on the VAR:

$$\mathbf{g}^\top (I - \rho^j \Pi^j) + \mathbf{h}^\top \Pi (I - \rho \Pi)^{-1} (I - \rho^j \Pi^j) = 0$$

Although these restrictions are *algebraically* equivalent to those of (10.19) for all j, reflecting the fact that, if one-period returns are unpredictable, then j-period returns must also be, and vice versa, Wald tests may yield different results depending on which value of j is chosen. Nevertheless, the VAR framework confers yet another advantage in this set-up: it needs to be estimated only once, as tests can be conducted for any j without re-estimating the system.

Campbell and Shiller (1988b) also extend the VAR framework to incorporate a third variable, a long moving average of the earnings/price ratio, which is included as a potential predictor of stock returns. Campbell (1991), on the other hand, uses the model to analyse the unexpected component of returns, while Campbell and Shiller (1988a) concentrate on using the model to reinterpret the Marsh and Merton (1987) error correction model of dividend behaviour in the context of a 'near-rational expectations' model in which dividends are persistent and prices are disturbed by persistent random noise.

Campbell and Shiller (1988b, 1988c) apply the dividend ratio model to various data sets, including an updated Standard and Poor's. They find that the restrictions of the model tend to be rejected by the data and that the earnings variable is a powerful predictor of stock returns, particularly when returns are calculated over several years.

Example 10.3 The dividend ratio model for UK equity prices

This model was applied to the UK data analysed in example 10.1. As a prerequisite, we require that ζ_t and Δd_t are stationary. Example 3.1 has shown that the presence of a unit root in the levels of the dividend yield can be rejected, and a similar result occurs here for the logarithms: an ADF test rejects a unit root at the 5 per cent level. That Δd_t is stationary has been reported in example 6.5. On fitting a VAR(3) to $\mathbf{z}_t = (\zeta_t, \Delta d_t)^\top$, we find that ζ_t does Granger-cause Δd_t, the marginal significance level of the test being less than 0.001.

A Wald test of the restrictions (10.19) is equivalent to a test that the coefficients in the regression of $h_{1,t+1}$ on lags of ζ_t and Δd_t are all zero – i.e. that returns are unforecastable. Since the R^2 from this regression is around 0.9, it is clear that the dividend ratio model for UK equity prices is conclusively rejected.

10.2 Generalisations and extensions of cointegration and error correction models

10.2.1. Non-linear generalisations

Given the tendency for financial time series to contain important non-linearities, it comes as no surprise that several models have been developed that generalise cointegration and error correction models in non-linear directions. These have taken two general forms: a linear cointegrating vector has been allowed to enter as a non-linear error correction, and the cointegrating relationship itself has been allowed to be non-linear. For an overview of the issues involved in this context, see Granger and Teräsvirta (1993).

Granger and Swanson (1996) discuss instructive examples of non-linear cointegration and error correction. Suppose we are modelling the $I(1)$ process $\mathbf{z}_t = \left(y_t, \mathbf{x}_t^\top\right)^\top$ and there is the single cointegrating vector $e_t = \boldsymbol{a}^\top \mathbf{z}_t$. Granger and Swanson suggest the simple non-linear error correction model in which, rather than e_{t-1} appearing, it is replaced by e_{t-1}^+ and e_{t-1}^-, defined as

$$e_{t-1}^+ = \begin{cases} e_{t-1} \text{ if } e_{t-1} \geq 0 \\ 0 \quad \text{otherwise} \end{cases} \quad e_{t-1}^- = e_{t-1} - e_{t-1}^+$$

A rather less 'ad hoc' generalisation follows from the interpretation of $\boldsymbol{a}^\top \mathbf{z}_t = \mathbf{0}$ as an attractor or equilibrium, so that e_t is a measure of the extent to which the system is out of equilibrium. Thus, if the market 'prefers' e_t to be small, there must be costs associated with having non-zero values of e_t. The traditional approach is then to assume a quadratic cost function, in which case the linear error correction model is obtained (see Nickell, 1985). If the cost function is non-linear, perhaps because of transaction costs that prevent profitable arbitrage for small deviations from equilibrium, or because heterogeneity among arbitrageurs leads to differing transaction costs, then a non-linear error correction results, as, for example,

$$g(\delta e_{t-1}) = \left(1 + \exp(-\delta e_{t-1})\right)^{-1} - \tfrac{1}{2}$$

A variety of theoretical justifications have been suggested to explain why non-linear error correction mechanisms should emerge. These include arbitrage in the presence of transaction costs, heterogeneity among arbitrageurs, agents' maximising or minimising behaviour, constraints on central bank intervention, and intertemporal choice behaviour under asymmetric adjustment costs. In terms of modelling, non-linear error correction mechanisms can be accommodated rather straightforwardly, in that residuals from some linear cointegration relationship can be incorporated in a non-linear error correction model. A simple way of capturing non-linear error correction relationships is by including asymmetric or higher-order polynomial error correction terms.

Threshold-type models have also been used in modelling non-linear error correction models, in which only large errors from equilibrium, above some threshold, are corrected. For example, Balke and Fomby (1997) use a three-regime model of the cointegrating relationship with the process following a unit root in the middle regime. Granger and Teräsvirta (1993) extend the single threshold to include a smooth transition in the adjustment towards equilibrium, and this approach has become quite popular. Psaradakis, Sola and Spagnola (2004) employ a non-linear error correction model that follows a Markov switching process, where deviations from equilibrium are non-stationary in one state and mean-reverting in the other.

Error correction models can also be estimated using non-parametric approaches, such as neural networks (e.g. Haefke and Helmenstein, 1996). Rather than concentrating on the conditional mean, Lee (1994) uses a lagged error correction term to model the conditional variance of a series, terming this a GARCH-X process. This approach seems useful for situations where disequilibrium shocks to a cointegrated system are likely to cause increases in the variance – for example, the relationship between spot and futures prices.

Several procedures have been proposed for evaluating the null hypothesis of a unit root against a threshold autoregressive-type alternative. Michael, Nobay and Peel (1997) test the null hypothesis of a unit root in real exchange rates against a STAR error correction process when analysing the long-run purchasing power parity (PPP) relationship. Kapetanios, Shin and Snell (2006) have recently developed tests for the null of no cointegration that have power when the cointegrating error follows a stationary smooth transition process. One test is based on the cointegrating residuals, the other evaluates the null hypothesis by examining the significance of the parameter that controls the non-linearity in the speed of the error correction adjustment.

Non-linear cointegration and, in general, non-linear relationships between non-stationary variables bring about several econometric problems that appear to be different from those associated with non-linear error correction. At the theoretical level, some of the issues related to the asymptotic behaviour of non-linear transformations of non-linear time series are addressed in Park and Phillips (1999, 2001), where an asymptotic theory for non-linear regression with integrated processes is developed. For a broad family of bivariate non-linear regression functions, sufficient conditions for weak consistency, rates of convergence and limit distributions are obtained. When the regression functions are integrable and the errors are martingale differences, the estimators are shown to be mixed normal and standard non-linear inference is applicable.

At both the conceptual and modelling level, Granger and Hallman (1991) first consider the possibility of non-linear cointegration as a bivariate 'attractor' between variables that are individually EMM but have an SMM non-linear combination. They suggest that non-linear equilibrium relationships could emerge between prices of commodities traded at spatially separated markets due to the existence of varying marginal costs and profits. Granger and Hallman employ the alternating conditional expectations (ACE) algorithm to estimate bivariate non-parametric cointegrating regressions, and offer some simulation evidence regarding the behaviour of Engle and Granger's (1987) cointegration tests using ACE residuals. Creedy, Lye and Martin (1996) use a non-linear cointegration relationship to derive an error correction model in continuous time, the dynamics of which follow a generalised exponential stationary distribution. This was estimated via ML and allows a rich variety of distributional shapes, exhibiting properties such as leptokurtosis and multimodality. Creedy, Lye and Martin suggest that such models are useful in modelling switching behaviour between multiple equilibria, and discuss an empirical example using exchange rate data.

Hall, Psaradakis and Sola (1997) model non-linear cointegration between consumption and disposable income as a regime-switching process where shifts follow an unobserved Markov chain with unknown transition probabilities. Pfann, Schotman and Tschernig (1996) demonstrate that univariate non-linearities in the short-term interest rate can produce non-linear cointegration relationships between long and short interest rates, using self-exciting threshold autoregressive (SETAR) models to demonstrate the empirical validity of their case. Basu and Dua (1996) show that non-homogeneous utility functions for cash and credit goods imply non-linear cointegration between income velocity, nominal interest rates and real GDP. Finally, Bollerslev and Engle (1993), among others, have applied the cointegration concept to modelling common persistence between conditional variances.

Departures from the standard cointegration framework can also lead to time series behaviour that is consistent with non-linear cointegration. For example, non-linear equilibrium relationships may arise within the seasonal cointegration framework of Hylleberg et al. (1990) and the non-linear stochastic trend models of Granger, Inoue and Morin (1997). Siklos and Granger (1997) argue that cointegrating relationships may switch according to the monetary policy regime, and propose the concept of temporal cointegration to allow variables to be cointegrated in one regime and non-cointegrated in another, using this approach to test the hypothesis of uncovered interest rate parity. Granger and Yoon (2002) consider the case of 'hidden' cointegration, where cointegrated variables respond only to certain kinds of shocks, say positive or negative. They argue that this may be applicable, for example, when modelling the response of central banks, which may be more interested in rising than falling interest rates. A 'crouching' error correction model is proposed to model variables related through hidden cointegration.

An innovative regime-switching non-linear cointegration process has been developed by Granger and Hyung (2006) using 'm-m' models. In this context, two variables, x and y, vary according to a switching regime process that allows mixed integration and cointegration. In each step, a *max* or *min* operator is used to choose between integration (e.g. $x_{t+1} = x_t + \varepsilon_t$) or cointegration (e.g. $x_{t+1} = by_t + \varepsilon_t$) for each variable. Although in simple cases m-m processes imply linear cointegrating relationships, they always have threshold-type non-linear error correction representations.

Corradi, Swanson and White (2000) replace the concept of cointegration with the more general concept of linear stochastic comovement. This generalisation allows for non-linear cointegration, and is defined as the condition whereby linear combinations among the components of non-ergodic non-linear Markov processes produce ergodic non-linear Markov processes. Existing testing procedures for stationarity and cointegration are shown to be applicable in the linear stochastic comovement context. Moreover, Corradi, Swanson and White propose a consistent test for the null of a linear cointegration vector against general non-linear alternatives.

A more general definition of cointegration can be based on a set of non-stationary variables that do not necessarily have equal orders of integration but can be expressed in a 'more stationary' linear or non-linear combination. Such definitions allow for cointegration between fractionally integrated variables and between integrated variables of order greater than one. In practical terms, fractional cointegration can be used to model slow error correction adjustment towards long-run equilibria. Abadir and Taylor (1999) show that linearity of the cointegrating regression requires that the variables have identical orders of integration. This makes linear cointegration a nested and composite hypothesis, since it is not possible to specify the distribution theory for cointegration testing until a common order of integration has been established.

These problems can be avoided if the testing procedures allow for flexible functional forms and fractional unit roots. Cointegration between variables with unequal orders of integration requires that the cointegrating function is non-null and, possibly, non-linear. Motivated by the possibilities of fractional cointegration, a number of researchers have investigated if deviations from a cointegrating relationship follow a fractionally integrated process, and have devised relevant testing procedures. For example, Gil-Alana (2003) has proposed a simple two-step test of fractional cointegration in the spirit of Engle and Granger (1987). The procedure tests initially the order of integration of the series and then examines the degree of integration of the residuals from the cointegrating regression. In both steps the univariate fractional unit root test of Robinson (1994) is employed and relevant critical values are derived for finite samples. In an empirical application, Gil-Alana analyses the data used by Engle and Granger (1987) and Campbell and Shiller (1987) and presents evidence of fractional cointegration between consumption and income, nominal GNP and money, and stock prices and dividends.

Although standard linear cointegration tests will have some power against non-linear cointegration, a number of specialised testing procedures have been developed. Bierens (1997) suggests consistent cointegration tests that do not require strong assumptions about the data-generating process or the estimation of nuisance parameters. These tests can be considered as an extension of the Johansen (1995) testing procedure outlined in chapter 9, section 5.3, since they are also based on the ordered solutions of a generalised eigenvalue problem. Non-parametric testing procedures for non-linear cointegration have also been suggested by Breitung (2001), being based on the difference between the sequences of ranks. In an extension of the common features concept, Anderson and Vahid (1998) have proposed a generalised method of moments test for common non-linear components of specified or unspecified form between stationary time series. Bierens (2000) employs a generalised eigenvalue procedure to test non-parametrically for a special common features case concerning the existence of non-linear co-trending, where there are common non-linear deterministic time trends. Breitung (2002) proposes a generalisation of a variance ratio type statistic, similar to the KPSS test, to test the cointegration rank as in the Johansen approach.

Parametric tests of specific non-linear cointegrating relationships have also been considered. For example, Choi and Saikkonen (2004) discuss procedures for testing linearity in the cointegration relationship against alternatives from the smooth transition family of models. By employing a Taylor expansion of the transition function, the problem of unidentified nuisance parameters in the non-linear models under the null can be avoided. The derived tests are simple to implement, as they are based on OLS regression and χ^2 limit distributions.

Example 10.4 Non-linear cointegration in the S&P 500 dividend discount model

As we have seen in example 10.1, Campbell and Shiller (1987) provide less than conclusive evidence that the 'spread' between the real price and dividend indices for the S&P index was stationary. In this example we investigate the possibility of non-linear cointegration between the price and dividend indices over the period 1871 to 2002.

The dividend yield and the scatterplot of prices and dividends are shown in figure 10.3. Although the dividend yield appears to exhibit mean reversion, it is not obviously stationary, especially over the more recent years of the sample period. At the same time, the scatterplot of prices and dividends suggests that the relationship is weaker at higher data values. Although most of the non-linearity disappears on taking logarithms, evidence in favour of linear cointegration is still not clear-cut, with the trace and maximum eigenvalue test statistics confirming that the null hypothesis of non-cointegration cannot be rejected at the 5 per cent level for all test configurations.

Evidence provided by Gil-Alana (2003) suggests that the two series may be fractionally cointegrated between 1871 to 1986, which is the sample period analysed by Campbell and Shiller (1987). We find similar evidence by using the Robinson (1995b) semiparametric fractional unit root estimator (see chapter 4, section 3.3), finding estimates of d for the logarithmic price and dividend series equal to 0.476 and 0.484, respectively. Since these estimates may be biased by short-run dynamics, however, we also estimated d within an ARFIMA$(1,d,1)$ framework for both series. This approach produces estimates closer to unity with $\hat{d} = 1.046$ and 1.061, respectively. Nevertheless, using Robinson's estimator and an ARFIMA$(0,d,0)$ model, we find that the residuals from the linear cointegrating regression between the two series seem to be fractionally integrated with estimates of d equal to 0.414 and 0.925, respectively.

Since these results may be influenced by the assumption of a linear cointegration regression, we considered the non-linear cointegration tests of Bierens (1997, 2000) and Breitung (2002). These produced rather mixed evidence of non-linear cointegration, so we took a pragmatic approach and examined the actual predictive ability of various error correction specifications First, a linear error correction model for the logarithmic S&P 500

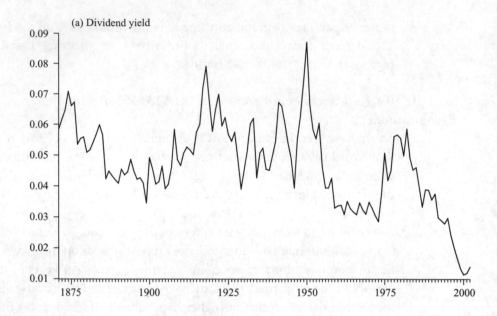

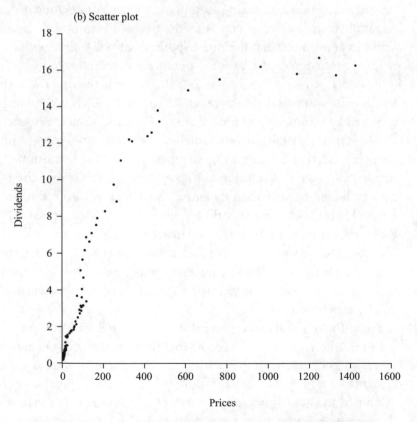

Figure 10.3   S&P dividend yield and scatterplot of prices and dividends (annual 1871–2002)

returns was estimated using OLS:

$$\Delta y_t = \underset{(0.016)}{0.041} - \underset{(0.052)}{0.116}\, z_{t-1} - \underset{(0.171)}{0.567}\, \Delta y_{t-1} + \varepsilon_t + \underset{(0.130)}{0.795}\, \varepsilon_{t-1}$$

$$R^2 = 0.0866$$

Here z_{t-1} is the lagged residual from the cointegrating regression between prices and dividends; standard errors are shown in parentheses. Incorporating positive and negative error correction terms separately shows that there is some asymmetry in the model since only negative residuals, z_{t-1}^-, turn out significant:

$$\Delta y_t = -\underset{(0.067)}{0.269}\, z_{t-1}^- - \underset{(0.164)}{0.558}\, \Delta y_{t-1} + \varepsilon_t + \underset{(0.134)}{0.786}\, \varepsilon_{t-1} \quad R^2 = 0.0834$$

By allowing for a fractional unit root in the error correction process, the following ARFIMA model was estimated via Gaussian ML:

$$\Delta^{-0.21} y_t = \underset{(0.009)}{0.039} - \underset{(0.043)}{0.107}\, z_{t-1} + \varepsilon_t - \underset{(0.149)}{0.436}\, \varepsilon_{t-1} \quad R^2 = 0.0791$$

The fractional differencing removes some of the negative persistence in the series, rendering the autoregressive coefficient insignificant. Finally, an LSTAR error correction model was also estimated via ML, assuming a skewed student's t distribution. The lagged cointegration errors were used as transition variables, while only the error correction term parameter and intercept were allowed to switch:

$$\Delta y_t = \underset{(0.023)}{0.033} - \underset{(0.077)}{0.165}\, z_{t-1} - \underset{(0.170)}{0.762}\, \Delta y_{t-1}$$

$$+ \left(\left(\underset{(0.365)}{1.289} - \underset{(0.384)}{1.541} \right) z_{t-1} \right) \left(1 + \exp\left(-\underset{(6.27)}{13.03}\left(z_{t-1} - \underset{(0.079)}{0.564} \right) \right) \right)^{-1}$$

$$+ \varepsilon_t - \underset{(0.079)}{0.916}\, \varepsilon_{t-1}$$

Although the LSTAR model appears to have a superior fit compared to the previous specifications, one must also consider that two additional parameters are needed for the transition function. Moreover, it is interesting to observe that the speed of adjustment to equilibrium does not differ significantly between the two regimes.

10.2.2 Testing for cointegration with infinite variance errors and structural breaks

In chapter 7 we presented considerable evidence that returns distributions were usually fat-tailed and may have infinite variance, and discussed briefly the impact of such an assumption on unit root tests for individual series. Caner (1998) considers the impact of infinite variance errors on both the residual-based tests of cointegration proposed by Phillips and Ouliaris (1990) and the VECM reduced-rank likelihood tests associated with Johansen (1995). Assuming that the errors are stable, rather than normal, results in statistics that are functionals of stable processes rather than functionals of Brownian motion, and that depend on the value taken by the tail index as well as the number of variables in the system. Critical values are larger (in absolute value) than the conventional critical values, so the size distortions induced by incorrectly assuming normality will lead to over-rejection of the null of no cointegration. Caner shows that these size distortions are only moderate for the residual-based tests, however, although they are more substantial for the trace and λ-max test statistics based on ML estimation of the VECM representation.

There have been several analyses looking at cointegration in the presence of structural shifts. Campos, Ericsson and Hendry (1996) consider the properties of several regression cointegration tests when one of the variables in the cointegrating relationship contains a structural break, finding that the break has little effect on the size of the tests but can affect their power when the data does not have a 'common factor', thus pointing towards the use of tests based on the ECM rather than on the cointegrating regression (recall chapter 9, section 3). Quintos and Phillips (1993) propose a recursive LM statistic to detect breaks in the cointegrating vector, while Quintos (1997) develops an extension of the fluctuation test, introduced in chapter 8, section 3.3, to examine both parameter and rank stability in VECMs. Other tests have been analysed by Gregory and Hansen (1996) and Gregory, Nason and Watt (1996), while Perron (2006) contains a recent survey of developments.

Siklos and Granger (1997) look at the problem of structural breaks in cointegrating relationships from an alternative perspective: their argument is that an empirical finding of non-cointegration could be a consequence of external shocks or structural breaks that interrupt the underlying equilibrium relationship, perhaps for an extended period of time. This leads them to define the concept of *temporary cointegration*, in which the cointegrating relationship can be switched on or off depending on the nature of the policy regime that is in place.

Data appendix

The following series can be obtained from http://lboro.ac.uk/departments/ec/cup.

RS: 91-day Treasury bill rate, monthly, March 1952 to December 2005 (648 observations).

R20: Yield on 20-year UK gilts, monthly, March 1952 to December 2005 (648 observations).

RSQ: 91-day Treasury bill rate, quarterly, 1952Q1 to 2005Q4 (216 observations).

R20Q: Yield on 20-year UK gilts, quarterly, 1952Q1 to 2005Q4 (216 observations).

RSQREAL: Real 91-day Treasury bill rate, quarterly, 1952Q1 to 2005Q (216 observations).

FTAPRICE: FTA All Share price index, monthly, January 1965 to December 2005 (492 observations).

FTADIV: FTA All Share dividend index, monthly, January 1965 to December 2005 (492 observations).

FTARET: FTA All Share nominal returns, monthly, January 1965 to December 2005 (492 observations).

RPI: U.K. Retail Price Index, monthly, January 1965 to December 2005 (492 observations).

USTB: U.S. 3-month Treasury bill rate, monthly, April 1953 to February 2005 (623 observations).

GIASE: Absolute returns on the General Index of the Athens Stock Exchange, daily, 1 June 1998 to 10 September 1998 (12,117 observations).

NORD: Nord Pool Exchange electricity prices, daily, 22 March 2002 to 3 December 2004 (988 observations)

VIX: VIX prices, daily, January 1990 to September 2005 (4130 observations)

EXCHD: Dollar/sterling exchange rate, daily, 1974 to 1994 (5192 observations).

EXCHQ: Dollar/sterling exchange rate, quarterly, 1972Q1 to 1996Q4 (100 observations).

S&P500: S&P 500 index, annual, 1871 to 2006 (136 observations).

S&P500R: S&P 500 real returns, annual 1872 to 2006 (135 observations)

S&P500D: S&P 500 index, daily, 1928 to 1991 (17,054 observations).

FT30: FT 30 index, daily, 1935 to 1994 (15,003 observations).

FTSE100: FTSE 100 index, weekly, 1984 to 1993 (521 observations).

CTLD: Courtaulds share price, weekly, 1984 to 1993 (521 observations).

LGEN: Legal and General share price, weekly, 1984 to 1993 (521 observations).

PRU: Prudential share price, weekly, 1984 to 1993 (521 observations).

References

Abadir, K. M., and Taylor, A. M. R. (1999), 'On the Definitions of (Co-)Integration', *Journal of Time Series Analysis*, 20, 129–37.

Agiakloglou, C., and Newbold, P. (1994), 'Lagrange Multiplier Tests for Fractional Difference', *Journal of Time Series Analysis*, 15, 253–62.

Aït-Sahalia, Y. (1996a), 'Nonparametric Pricing of Interest Rate Derivative Securities', *Econometrica*, 64, 527–60.

(1996b), 'Testing Continuous-time Models of the Spot Interest Rate', *Review of Financial Studies*, 9, 385–426.

(1999), 'Transition Densities for Interest Rates and Other Nonlinear Diffusions', *Journal of Finance*, 54, 499–547.

Akaike, H. (1974), 'A New Look at the Statistical Model Identification', *IEEE Transactions on Automatic Control*, AC–19, 716–23.

Al-Falou, A. A., and Trummer, D. (2003), 'Identifiability of Recurrent Neural Networks', *Econometric Theory*, 19, 812–28.

Andersen, T. G., Bollerslev, T., and Diebold, F. X. (2007), 'Parametric and Nonparametric Volatility Measurement', in Y. Aït-Sahalia and L. P. Hansen (eds.), *Handbook of Financial Econometrics*, New York: Elsevier.

Andersen, T. G., Bollerslev, T., Diebold, F. X., and Labys, P. (2003), 'Modeling and Forecasting Realized Volatility', *Econometrica*, 71, 529–626.

Anderson, H. M., Nam, K., and Vahid, F. (1999), 'Asymmetric nonlinear smooth transition GARCH models', in P. Rothman (ed.), *Nonlinear Time Series Analysis of Economic and Financial Data*, Boston: Kluwer, 191–207.

Anderson, H. M., and Vahid, F. (1998), 'Testing Multiple Equation Systems for Common Nonlinear Components', *Journal of Econometrics*, 84, 1–36.

Andersson, M. K., Eklund, B., and Lyhagen, J. (1999), 'A Simple Linear Time Series Model with Misleading Nonlinear Properties', *Economics Letters*, 65, 281–4.

Andreou, E., and Ghysels, E., (2002), 'Detecting Multiple Breaks in Financial Market Volatility Dynamics', *Journal of Applied Econometrics*, 17, 579–600.

Andreou, E., Pittis, N., and Spanos, A. (2001), 'On Modelling Speculative Prices: The Empirical Literature', *Journal of Economic Surveys*, 15, 187–220.

Andrews, D. W. K. (1991), 'Heteroskedasticity and Autocorrelation Consistent Covariance Matrix Estimation', *Econometrica*, 59, 817–58.

Andrews, D. W. K., and Sun, Y. (2004), 'Adaptive Local Polynomial Whittle Estimation of Long-range Dependence', *Econometrica*, 72, 569–614.

Audrino, F., and Bühlmann, P. (2001), 'Tree-structured Generalized Autoregressive Conditional Heteroscedastic Models', *Journal of the Royal Statistical Society*, Series B, 63, 727–44.

Bachelier, L. (1900), 'Théorie de la Spéculation', *Annales de l'Ecole Normale Superieure*, Series 3, 17, 21–86.

Backus, D. K., and Gregory, A. W. (1993), 'Theoretical Relations between Risk Premiums and Conditional Variances', *Journal of Business and Economic Statistics*, 11, 177–85.

Badrinath, S. G., and Chatterjee, S. (1988), 'On Measuring Skewness and Elongation in Common Stock Distributions: The Case of the Market Index', *Journal of Business*, 61, 451–72.

(1991), 'A Data-analytic Look at Skewness and Elongation in Common Stock Return Distributions', *Journal of Business and Economic Statistics*, 9, 223–33.

Bai, J. (1997), 'Estimating Multiple Breaks One at a Time', *Econometric Theory*, 13, 315–52.

Bai, J., and Perron, P. (1998), 'Estimating and Testing Linear Models with Multiple Structural Changes', *Econometrica*, 66, 47–78.

Baillie, R. T. (1996), 'Long Memory Processes and Fractional Integration in Econometrics', *Journal of Econometrics*, 73, 5–59.

Baillie, R. T., and Bollerslev, T. (1989), 'The Message in Daily Exchange Rates: A Conditional Variance Tale', *Journal of Business and Economic Statistics*, 7, 297–305.

(1992), 'Prediction in Dynamic Models with Time-dependent Conditional Variances', *Journal of Econometrics*, 52, 91–113.

Baillie, R. T., Bollerslev, T., and Mikkelson, H. O. (1996), 'Fractionally Integrated Generalized Autoregressive Conditional Heteroskedasticity', *Journal of Econometrics*, 74, 3–30.

Baillie, R. T., and Kapetanios, G. (2007), 'Testing for Neglected Nonlinearity in Long Memory Models', *Journal of Business and Economic Statistics*, 25, 447–61.

Bali, T. G., and Weinbaum, D. (2005), 'The Empirical Performance of Alternative Extreme-value Volatility Estimators', *Journal of Futures Markets*, 25, 873–92.

Bali, T. G., and Wu L. (2006), 'A Comprehensive Analysis of the Short-term Interest Rate Dynamics', *Journal of Banking and Finance*, 30, 1269–90.

Balke, N. S., and Fomby, T. B. (1997), 'Threshold Cointegration', *International Economic Review*, 38, 627–45.

Banerjee, A., Dolado, J. J., Galbraith, J. W., and Hendry, D. F. (1993), *Co-integration, Error Correction and the Econometric Analysis of Non-Stationary Data*, Oxford: Oxford University Press.

Banerjee, A., Dolado, J. J., and Mestre, R. (1998), 'Error-correction Mechanism Tests for Cointegration in a System Equation Framework', *Journal of Time Series Analysis*, 19, 267–83.

Barndorff-Nielsen, O. E., Graversen, S. E., and Shephard, N. (2004), 'Power Variation and Stochastic Volatility: a Review and some New Results', *Journal of Applied Probability*, 41, 133–43.

Barndorff-Nielsen, O. E., and Shephard, N. (2004), 'Power and Bipower Variation with Stochastic Volatility and Jumps', *Journal of Financial Econometrics*, 2, 1–37.

(2005), 'How Accurate is the Asymptotic Approximation to the Distribution of Realized Volatility?', in D. Andrews, J. Powell, P. Ruud and J. Stock (eds.), *Identification and Inference for Econometric Models: A Festschrift for Tom Rothenberg*, Cambridge: Cambridge University Press, 306–31.

Barnett, W. A., Gallant, A. R., Hinich, M. J., Jungeilges, J. A., Kaplan, D. T., and Jensen, M. J. (1996), 'An Experimental Design to Compare Tests of Nonlinearity and Chaos', in W. A. Barnett, A. P. Kirman and M. Salmon (eds.), *Nonlinear Dynamics and Economics*, Cambridge: Cambridge University Press, 163–90.

(1997), 'A Single-blind Controlled Competition among Tests of Nonlinearity and Chaos', *Journal of Econometrics*, 82, 157–92.

Basu, P., and Dua, P. (1996), 'The Behaviour of Velocity and Nominal Interest Rates in a Cash-in-advance Model', *Journal of Macroeconomics*, 18, 463–78.

Bates, D. S. (2003) 'Empirical Option Pricing: A Retrospection', *Journal of Econometrics*, 116, 387–404.

Bauwens, L., and Giot, P. (2003), 'Asymmetric ACD Models: Introducing Price Information in ACD Models with a Two State Transition Model', *Empirical Economics*, 28, 709–31.

Bauwens, L., Laurent, S., and Rombouts, J. V. K. (2006), 'Multivariate GARCH Models: A Survey', *Journal of Applied Econometrics*, 21, 79–109.

Baxter, M., and King, R. G. (1999), 'Measuring Business Cycles: Approximate Band-pass Filters for Economic Time Series', *Review of Economics and Statistics*, 81, 575–93.

Bera, A. K., and Higgins, M. L. (1993), 'On ARCH Models: Properties, Estimation and Testing', *Journal of Economic Surveys*, 7, 305–66.

Beran, J. A. (1992), 'Statistical Methods for Data with Long-range Dependence', *Statistical Science*, 7, 404–27.

(1995), 'Maximum Likelihood Estimation of the Differencing Parameter for Invertible Short and Long-memory Autoregressive Integrated Moving Average Models', *Journal of the Royal Statistical Society*, Series B, 57, 659–72.

Berliner, L. M. (1992), 'Statistics, Probability and Chaos', *Statistical Science*, 7, 69–90.

Bernanke, B. (1986), 'Alternative Explanations of the Money–Income Correlation', *Carnegie-Rochester Conference Series on Public Policy*, 25, 49–100.

Berndt, E. R. (1991), *The Practice of Econometrics: Classic and Contemporary*, Reading, MA: Addison-Wesley.

Berndt, E. R., Hall, B. H., Hall, R. E., and Hausman, J. A. (1974), 'Estimation and Inference in Nonlinear Structural Models', *Annals of Economic and Social Measurement*, 4, 653–65.

Beveridge, S., and Nelson, C. R. (1981), 'A New Approach to Decomposition of Economic Time Series into Permanent and Transitory Components with Particular Attention to Measurement of the "Business Cycle"', *Journal of Monetary Economics*, 7, 151–74.

Bhardwaj, G., and Swanson, N. R. (2006), 'An Empirical Investigation of the Usefulness of ARFIMA Models for Predicting Macroeconomic and Financial Time Series', *Journal of Econometrics*, 131, 539–78.

Bhargava, A. (1986), 'On the Theory of Testing for Unit Roots in Observed Time Series', *Review of Economic Studies*, 53, 369–84.

Bierens, H. J. (1997), 'Nonparametric Cointegration Analysis', *Journal of Econometrics*, 77, 379–404.

(2000), 'Nonparametric Nonlinear Co-trending Analysis, with an Application to Inflation and Interest Rates in the US', *Journal of Business and Economic Statistics*, 18, 323–37.

Blake, A. P., and Kapetanios, G. (2007), 'Testing for ARCH in the Presence of Nonlinearity of Unknown Form in the Conditional Mean', *Journal of Econometrics*, 137, 472–88.

Blanchard, O. J. (1989), 'A Traditional Interpretation of Macroeconomic Fluctuations', *American Economic Review*, 79, 1146–64.

Blanchard, O. J., and Quah, D. (1989), 'Dynamic Effects of Aggregate Demand and Aggregate Supply Disturbances', *American Economic Review*, 79, 655–73.

Blanchard, O. J., and Watson, M. W. (1982), 'Bubbles, Rational Expectations, and Financial Markets', in P. Wachtel (ed.), *Crises in the Economic and Financial Structure*, Lexington, MA: Lexington Books, 295–315.

Bollerslev, T. (1986), 'Generalised Autoregressive Conditional Heteroskedasticity', *Journal of Econometrics*, 31, 307–27.

(1987), 'A Conditionally Heteroskedastic Time Series Model for Speculative Prices and Rates of Return', *Review of Economics and Statistics*, 69, 542–6.

(1988), 'On the Correlation Structure for the Generalised Autoregressive Conditional Heteroskedastic Process', *Journal of Time Series Analysis*, 9, 121–32.

(1990), 'Modelling the Coherence in Short-run Nominal Exchange Rates: a Multivariate Generalized ARCH Model', *Review of Economics and Statistics*, 72, 498–505.

Bollerslev, T., Chou, R. Y., and Kroner, K. F. (1992), 'ARCH Modelling in Finance: A Review of the Theory and Empirical Evidence', *Journal of Econometrics*, 52, 5–59.

Bollerslev, T., and Engle, R. F. (1993), 'Common Persistence in Conditional Variances', *Econometrica*, 61, 166–87.

Bollerslev, T., Engle, R. F., and Nelson, D. B. (1994), 'ARCH Models', in R. F. Engle and D. L. McFadden (eds.), *Handbook of Econometrics*, Vol. IV, New York: North-Holland, 2959–3038.

Bollerslev, T., Engle, R. F., and Wooldridge, J. M. (1988), 'A Capital Asset Pricing Model with Time-varying Covariances', *Journal of Political Economy*, 96, 116–31.

Bollerslev, T., and Wooldridge, J. M. (1992), 'Quasi Maximum Likelihood Estimation and Inference in Dynamic Models with Time Varying Covariances', *Econometric Reviews*, 11, 143–72.

Bollerslev, T., and Zhou, H. (2002), 'Estimating Stochastic Volatility Diffusion Using Conditional Moments of Integrated Volatility', *Journal of Econometrics*, 109, 33–65

(2006), 'Volatility Puzzles: A Simple Framework for Gauging Return-volatility Regressions', *Journal of Econometrics*, 127, 123–50.

Boothe, P., and Glassman, D. (1987), 'The Statistical Distribution of Exchange Rates: Empirical Evidence and Economic Implications', *Journal of International Economics*, 22, 297–319.

Boudoukh, J., Richardson, M., and Whitelaw, R. F. (1997), 'Investigation of a Class of Volatility Estimators', *Journal of Derivatives*, 4, 63–71.

Bougerol, P., and Picard, N. (1992), 'Stationarity of GARCH Processes and of some Nonnegative Time Series', *Journal of Econometrics*, 52, 115–28.

Box, G. E. P., and Cox, D. R. (1964), 'An Analysis of Transformations', *Journal of the Royal Statistical Society*, Series B, 26, 211–43.

Box, G. E. P., and Jenkins, G. M. (1976), *Time Series Analysis: Forecasting and Control*, rev. edn., San Francisco: Holden Day.

Box, G. E. P., and Pierce, D. A. (1970), 'Distribution of Residual Autocorrelations in Autoregressive Moving Average Time Series Models', *Journal of the American Statistical Association*, 65, 1509–26.

Breidt, F. J., Crato, N., and de Lima, P. J. F. (1998), 'The Detection and Estimation of Long Memory in Stochastic Volatility', *Journal of Econometrics*, 83, 325–48.

Breitung, J. (2001), 'Rank Tests for Unit Roots and Cointegration', *Journal of Business and Economic Statistics*, 19, 331–40.

(2002), 'Nonparametric Tests for Unit Roots and Cointegration', *Journal of Econometrics*, 108, 343–64.

Brock, W. A. (1986), 'Distinguishing Random and Deterministic Systems: Abridged Version', *Journal of Economic Theory*, 40, 168–95.

(1988), 'Nonlinearity and Complex Dynamics in Economics and Finance', in P. Anderson, K. J. Arrow and D. Pines (eds.), *The Economy as an Evolving Complex System*, Reading, MA: Addison-Wesley, 77–97.

Brock, W. A., and Dechert, W. D. (1991), 'Non-linear Dynamical Systems: Instability and Chaos in Economics', in W. Hildenbrand and H. Sonnenschein (eds.), *Handbook of Mathematical Economics*, Amsterdam: North-Holland, 2209–35.

Brock, W. A., Hsieh, D., and LeBaron, B. (1991), *A Test for Nonlinear Dynamics, Chaos and Instability*, Cambridge, MA: MIT Press.

Brock, W. A., Lakonishok, J., and LeBaron, B. (1992), 'Simple Technical Trading Rules and the Stochastic Properties of Stock Returns', *Journal of Finance*, 47, 1731–64.

Brockwell, P. J., and Davis, R. A. (1996), *Time Series: Theory and Methods*, 2nd edn., New York: Springer-Verlag.

Brooks, C. (2006), 'Multivariate Volatility Models', in T. C. Mills and K. Patterson (eds.), *Palgrave Handbook of Econometrics*, Vol. I: *Econometric Theory*, Basingstoke: Palgrave Macmillan, 765–83.

Brooks, C., and Burke, S. P. (2002), 'Selecting from amongst Non-nested Conditional Variance Models: Information Criteria and Portfolio Determination', *Manchester School*, 70, 747–67.

(2003) 'Information Criteria for GARCH Model Selection', *European Journal of Finance*, 9, 557–80.

Brooks, C., Burke, S. P., Heravi, S., and Persand, G. (2005), 'Autoregressive Conditional Kurtosis', *Journal of Financial Econometrics*, 3, 399–421.

Brooks, C., Burke, S. P., and Persand, G. (2001) 'Benchmarks and the Accuracy of GARCH Model', *International Journal of Forecasting*, 17, 45–56.

Brooks, C., and Chong, J. (2001), 'The Cross-country Hedging Performance of Implied versus Statistical Forecasting Models', *Journal of Futures Markets*, 21, 1043–69.

Brooks, C., Persand, G., and Burke, S. (2003), 'Multivariate GARCH Models: Software Choice and Estimation Issues', *Journal of Applied Econometrics*, 18, 725–34.

Broto, C., and Ruiz, E. (2004), 'Estimation Methods for Stochastic Volatility Models: A Survey', *Journal of Economic Surveys*, 18, 613–49.

Brown, R. L., Durbin, J., and Evans, J. M. (1975), 'Techniques for Testing the Constancy of Regression Relationships over Time', *Journal of the Royal Statistical Society*, Series B, 39, 107–13.

Brown, S. J., Goetzmann, W. N., and Kumar, A. (1998), 'The Dow Theory: William Peter Hamilton's Track Record Reconsidered', *Journal of Finance*, 53, 1311–33.

Busetti, F., and Harvey, A. C. (2001), 'Testing for the Presence of a Random Walk in Series with Structural Breaks', *Journal of Time Series Analysis*, 22, 127–50.

(2003), 'Further Comments on Stationarity Tests in Series with Structural Breaks at Unknown Points', *Journal of Time Series Analysis*, 24, 137–40.

Cai, J. (1994), 'A Markov Model of Switching-regime ARCH', *Journal of Business and Economic Statistics*, 12, 309–16.

Campbell, J. Y. (1991), 'A Variance Decomposition for Stock Returns', *Economic Journal*, 101, 157–79.

Campbell, J. Y., Lo, A. W., and MacKinlay, A. C. (1997), *The Econometrics of Financial Markets*, Princeton, NJ: Princeton University Press.

Campbell, J. Y., and Mankiw, N. G. (1987), 'Permanent and Transitory Components in Macroeconomic Fluctuations', *American Economic Review, Papers and Proceedings*, 77, 111–17.

Campbell, J. Y., and Perron, P. (1991), 'Pitfalls and Opportunities: What Macroeconomists Should Know about Unit Roots', *NBER Macroeconomics Annual*, Cambridge, MA: MIT Press, 141–201.

Campbell, J. Y., and Shiller, R. J. (1987), 'Cointegration and Tests of Present Value Models', *Journal of Political Economy*, 95, 1062–88.

(1988a), 'Interpreting Cointegrated Models', *Journal of Economic Dynamics and Control*, 12, 503–22.

(1988b), 'Stock Prices, Earnings, and Expected Dividends', *Journal of Finance*, 43, 661–76.

(1988c), 'The Dividend–Price Ratio and Expectations of Future Dividends and Discount Factors', *Review of Financial Studies*, 1, 195–228.

Campos, J., Ericsson, N. R., and Hendry, D. F. (1996), 'Cointegration Tests in the Presence of Structural Breaks', *Journal of Econometrics*, 70, 187–220.

Caner, M. (1998), 'Tests for Cointegration with Infinite Variance Errors', *Journal of Econometrics*, 86, 155–75.

Chan, K. C., Karolyi, A., Longstaff, F., and Sanders, A. (1992), 'An Empirical Comparison of Alternative Models of the Short Term Interest Rate', *Journal of Finance*, 47, 1209–27.

Chan, L. K. C., and Lakonishok, J. (1992), 'Robust Measurement of Beta Risk', *Journal of Financial and Quantitative Analysis*, 27, 265–82.

Charemza, W. W., Lifshits, M., and Makarova, S. (2005), 'Conditional Testing for Unit-root Bilinearity in Financial Time Series: Some Theoretical and Empirical Results,' *Journal of Economic Dynamics and Control*, 29, 63–96.

Chen, Y.-T., Chou, R.-Y., and Kuan, C.-M. (2000), 'Testing Time Reversibility without Moment Restrictions', *Journal of Econometrics*, 95, 199–218.

Cheng, B., and Titterington, D. M. (1994), 'Neural Networks: A Review from a Statistical Perspective', *Statistical Science*, 9, 2–54.

Chib, S., Nardarib, F., and Shephard, N. (2006), 'Analysis of High Dimensional Multivariate Stochastic Volatility Models', *Journal of Econometrics*, 134, 341–71.

Choi, I., and Saikkonen, P. (2004), 'Testing Linearity in Cointegrating Smooth Transition Regressions', *Econometrics Journal*, 7, 341–65.

Chong, T. T. L. (2000), 'Estimating the Differencing Parameter via the Partial Autocorrelation Function', *Journal of Econometrics*, 97, 365–81.

Chow, G. C. (1960), 'Tests of Equality between Sets of Coefficients in Two Linear Regressions', *Econometrica*, 28, 591–605.

Chow, K. V., and Denning, K. C. (1993), 'A Simple Multiple Variance Ratio Test', *Journal of Econometrics*, 58, 385–401.

Christiano, L. J., and Fitzgerald, T. J. (2003), 'The Band Pass Filter', *International Economic Review*, 44, 435–65.

Christoffersen, P., and Jacobs, K. (2004), 'Which GARCH Model for Option Valuation?', *Management Science*, 50, 1204–21.

Chu, C.-S. J., Hornik, K., and Kuan, C.-M. (1995), 'The Moving-estimates Test for Parameter Stability', *Econometric Theory*, 11, 699–720.

Cioczek-Georges, R., and Taqqu, M. S. (1995), 'Form of the Conditional Variance for Symmetric Stable Random Variables', *Statistica Sinica*, 5, 351–61.

Clark, P. K. (1973), 'A Subordinated Stochastic Process Model with Finite Variances for Speculative Prices', *Econometrica*, 41, 135–55.

Cochrane, J. H. (1988), 'How Big is the Random Walk in GNP?', *Journal of Political Economy*, 96, 893–920.

  (1991), 'A Critique of the Application of Unit Root Tests', *Journal of Economic Dynamics and Control*, 15, 275–84.

Cooley, T. F., and LeRoy, S. F. (1985), 'Atheoretical Macroeconometrics: A Critique', *Journal of Monetary Economics*, 16, 283–308.

Cootner, P. A. (ed.) (1964), *The Random Character of Stock Market Prices*, Cambridge, MA: MIT Press.

Corradi, V., Swanson, N. R., and White, H. (2000), 'Testing for Stationarity–Ergodicity and for Comovements between Nonlinear Discrete Time Markov Processes', *Journal of Econometrics*, 96, 39–73.

Coutts, J. A., Mills, T. C., and Roberts, J. (1994), 'Misspecification of the Market Model: The Implications for Event Studies', *Applied Economic Letters*, 2, 143–5.

Coutts, J. A., Roberts, J., and Mills, T. C. (1997), 'Parameter Stability in the Market Model: Tests and Time Varying Parameter Estimation with UK Data', *The Statistician*, 46, 57–70.

Cowles, A. (1933), 'Can Stock Market Forecasters Forecast?', *Econometrica*, 1, 309–24.

  (1944), 'Stock Market Forecasting', *Econometrica*, 12, 206–14.

  (1960), 'A Revision of Previous Conclusions regarding Stock Price Behaviour', *Econometrica*, 28, 909–15.

Cowles, A., and Jones, H. E. (1937), 'Some A Posteriori Probabilities in Stock Market Action', *Econometrica*, 5, 280–94.

Cramer, H. (1961), 'On Some Classes of Non-stationary Processes', *Proceedings of the 4th Berkeley Symposium on Mathematical Statistics and Probability*, Berkeley: University of California Press, 57–78.

Creedy, J., Lye, J., and Martin, V. L. (1996), 'A Non-linear Model of the Real US/UK Exchange Rate', *Journal of Applied Econometrics*, 11, 669–86.

Cuddington, J. T., and Winters, L. A. (1987), 'The Beveridge–Nelson Decomposition of Economic Time Series: A Quick Computational Method', *Journal of Monetary Economics*, 19, 125–7.

Cuthbertson, K. (1996), *Quantitative Financial Economics: Stocks, Bonds, and Foreign Exchange*, New York: Wiley.

Dacarogna, M. M., Müller, U. A., Nagler, R. J., Olsen, R. B., and Pictet, O. V. (1993), 'A Geographical Model for the Daily and Weekly Seasonal Volatility in the Foreign Exchange Market', *Journal of International Money and Finance*, 12, 413–38.

Davidson, J. (2006a), *Time Series Modelling, Version 4.18*, Exeter: University of Exeter.

(2006b), 'Asymptotic Methods and Functional Central Limit Theorems', in T. C. Mills and K. Patterson (eds.), *Palgrave Handbook of Econometrics*, Vol. I: *Econometric Theory*, Basingstoke: Palgrave Macmillan, 159–211.

De Gooijer, J. G. (1989), 'Testing Non-linearities in World Stock Market Prices', *Economics Letters*, 31, 31–5.

De Haan, L., Jansen, D. W., Koedijk, K., and de Vries, C. G. (1994), 'Safety First Portfolio Selection, Extreme Value Theory and Long Run Asset Risks', in J. Galambos, J. A. Lechner, E. Simiu and C. Hagwood (eds.), *Extreme Value Theory and Applications*, Boston: Kluwer Academic, 471–87.

De Haan, L., and Resnick, S. I. (1980), 'A Simple Asymptotic Estimate for the Index of a Stable Distribution', *Journal of the Royal Statistical Society*, Series B, 42, 83–7.

De Haan L., Resnick, S. I., Rootzén, H., and de Vries, C. G. (1989), 'Extremal Behaviour of Solutions to a Stochastic Difference Equation with Applications to ARCH Processes', *Stochastic Processes and their Applications*, 32, 213–24.

De Lima, P. J. F. (1997), 'On the Robustness of Nonlinearity Tests to Moment Condition Failure', *Journal of Econometrics*, 76, 251–80.

Dechert, W. D. (1996), 'Testing Time Series for Nonlinearities: The BDS Approach', in W. A. Barnett, A. P. Kirman and M. Salmon (eds.), *Nonlinear Dynamics and Economics*, Cambridge: Cambridge University Press, 191–200.

DeJong, D. N., Nankervis, J. C., Savin, N. E., and Whiteman, C. H. (1992), 'The Power Problems of Unit Root Tests in Time Series with Autoregressive Errors', *Journal of Econometrics*, 53, 323–43.

DeJong, D. N., and Whiteman, C. H. (1991a), 'The Temporal Stability of Dividends and Stock Prices: Evidence from the Likelihood Function', *American Economic Review*, 81, 600–17.

(1991b), 'Trends and Random Walks in Macroeconomic Time Series: A Reconsideration Based on the Likelihood Principle', *Journal of Monetary Economics*, 28, 221–54.

Dekkers, A. L. M., and de Haan, L., (1989), 'On the Estimation of the Extreme-value Index and Large Quantile Estimation', *Annals of Statistics*, 17, 1795–832.

Delgado, M. A., and Velasco, C. (2005), 'Sign Tests for Long-memory Time Series', *Journal of Econometrics*, 128, 215–51.

Demos, A., and Sentana, E. (1998), 'Testing for GARCH Effects: A One-sided Approach', *Journal of Econometrics*, 86, 97–127.

Deo, R. S., and Richardson, M. (2003), 'On the Asymptotic Power of the Variance Ratio Test', *Econometric Theory*, 19, 231–9.

Diba, B. T. (1990), 'Bubbles and Stock-price Volatility', in G. P. Dwyer and R. W. Hafer (eds.), *The Stock Market: Bubbles, Volatility, and Chaos*, Boston: Kluwer Academic, 9–26.

Diba, B. T., and Grossman, H. I. (1987), 'On the Inception of Rational Bubbles', *Quarterly Journal of Economics*, 103, 697–700.

(1988), 'Explosive Rational Bubbles in Stock Prices?', *American Economic Review*, 81, 600–17.

Dickey, D. A., and Fuller, W. A. (1979), 'Distribution of the Estimators for Autoregressive Time Series with a Unit Root', *Journal of the American Statistical Association*, 74, 427–31.

(1981), 'Likelihood Ratio Statistics for Autoregressive Time Series with a Unit Root', *Econometrica*, 49, 1057–72.

Dickey, D. A., and Pantula, S. (1987), 'Determining the Order of Differencing in Autoregressive Processes', *Journal of Business and Economic Statistics*, 5, 455–61.

Diebold, F. X., Hickman, A., Inoue, A., and Schuermann, T. (1998), 'Scale Models', *Risk*, 11, 104–7.

Diebold, F. X., and Inoue, A. (2001), 'Long Memory and Regime Switching', *Journal of Econometrics*, 105, 131–59.

Diebold, F. X., and Lopez, J. (1996), 'Forecast Evaluation and Combination', in G. S. Maddala and C. R. Rao (eds.), *Handbook of Statistics*, Amsterdam: North-Holland, 241–68.

Diebold, F. X., and Nerlove, M. (1990), 'Unit Roots in Economic Time Series: A Selective Survey', in G. F. Rhodes and T. B. Fomby (eds.), *Advances in Econometrics*, Vol. VIII, Greenwich, CT: JAI Press, 3–69.

Diebold, F. X., and Rudebusch, G. D. (1991), 'On the Power of Dickey–Fuller Tests against Fractional Alternatives', *Economics Letters*, 35, 155–60.

Dimand, R. W. (1993), 'The Case of Brownian Motion: A Note on Bachelier's Contribution', *British Journal for the History of Science*, 26, 233–4.

Ding, Z., and Granger, C. W. J. (1996), 'Modeling Persistence of Speculative Returns: A New Approach', *Journal of Econometrics*, 73, 185–215.

Ding, Z., Granger, C. W. J., and Engle, R. F. (1993), 'A Long Memory Property of Stock Returns and a New Model', *Journal of Empirical Finance*, 1, 83–106.

Dittman, I., and Granger, C. W. J. (2002), 'Properties of Nonlinear Transformations of Fractionally Integrated Processes', *Journal of Econometrics*, 110, 113–33.

Doan, T. A., Litterman, R. B., and Sims, C. A. (1984), 'Forecasting and Conditional Projection Using Realistic Prior Distributions', *Econometric Reviews*, 3, 1–100.

Dolado, J. J., Gonzalo, J., and Moayoral, L. (2002), 'A Fractional Dickey–Fuller Test for Unit Roots', *Econometrica*, 70, 1963–2006.

Dolado, J. J., Jenkinson, T., and Sosvilla-Rivero, S. (1990), 'Cointegration and Unit Roots', *Journal of Economic Surveys*, 4, 249–73.

Domowitz, I., and El-Gamal, M. A. (2001), 'A Consistent Nonparametric Test of Ergodicity for Time Series with Applications', *Journal of Econometrics*, 102, 365–98.

Domowitz, I., and Hakkio, C. S. (1985), 'Conditional Variance and the Risk Premium in the Foreign Exchange Market', *Journal of International Economics*, 19, 47–66.

Dotsis, G., and Markellos, R. N. (2007), 'The Finite Sample Properties of the GARCH Option Pricing Model', *Journal of Futures Markets*, 27, 599–615.

Drost, F. C., and Nijman, T. E. (1993), 'Temporal Aggregation of GARCH Processes', *Econometrica*, 61, 909–27.

Drost, F. C., and Werker, B. J. M. (1996), 'Closing the GARCH Gap: Continuous Time GARCH Modeling', *Journal of Econometrics*, 74, 31–57.

Duan, J., Gauthier, G., and Simonato, J. (1999), 'An Analytical Approximation for the GARCH Option Pricing Model', *Journal of Computational Finance*, 2, 75–116.

Dufour, J.-M. (1982), 'Recursive Stability Analysis of Linear Regression Relationships: An Exploratory Analysis', *Journal of Econometrics*, 19, 31–75.

Dufour, J.-M., Khalaf, L., Bernard, J.-T., and Genest, I. (2004), 'Simulation-based Finite-sample Tests for Heteroskedasticity and ARCH Effects', *Journal of Econometrics*, 122, 317–47.

EViews (2003), *EViews User Guide Version 5.0*, Irvine, CA: Quantitative Micro Software.

Edgerton, D., and Wells, C. (1994), 'Critical Values for the CUSUMSQ Statistic in Medium and Large Sized Samples', *Oxford Bulletin of Economics and Statistics*, 56, 355–65.

Efron, B., and Tibshirani, R. J. (1993), *An Introduction to the Bootstrap*, London: Chapman and Hall.

Eitrhem, Ø., and Teräsvirta, T. (1996), 'Testing the Adequacy of Smooth Transition Autoregressive Models', *Journal of Econometrics*, 74, 59–75.

Elliott, G., Rothenberg, T. J., and Stock, J. H. (1996), 'Efficient Tests for an Autoregressive Unit Root', *Econometrica*, 64, 813–36.

Engle, C. R., and Hamilton, J. D. (1990), 'Long Swings in the Dollar; Are They in the Data and do Markets Know It?', *American Economic Review*, 80, 689–713.

Engle, R. F. (1982), 'Autoregressive Conditional Heteroskedasticity with Estimates of the Variance of UK Inflation', *Econometrica*, 50, 987–1008.

(1990), 'Discussion: Stock Market Volatility and the Crash of 1987', *Review of Financial Studies*, 3, 103–6.

(2000), 'The Econometrics of Ultra-high Frequency Data', *Econometrica*, 68, 1–22.

(2001), 'GARCH 101: An Introduction to the use of ARCH/GARCH Models in Applied Econometrics', *Journal of Economic Perspectives*, 15, 157–68.

(2002), 'New Frontiers for ARCH models', *Journal of Applied Econometrics*, 17, 425–46.

Engle, R. F., and Bollerslev, T. (1986), 'Modelling the Persistence of Conditional Variances', *Econometric Reviews*, 5, 1–50.

Engle, R. F., and Gallo, G. M., (2006), 'A Multiple Indicators Model for Volatility using Intra-daily Data', *Journal of Econometrics*, 127, 3–27.

Engle, R. F., and Gonzalez-Rivera, G. (1991), 'Semiparametric ARCH Models', *Journal of Business and Economic Statistics*, 9, 345–59.

Engle, R. F., and Granger, C. W. J. (1987), 'Cointegration and Error Correction: Representation, Estimation and Testing', *Econometrica*, 55, 251–76.

Engle, R. F., and Hendry, D. F. (1993), 'Testing Super Exogeneity and Invariance in Regression Models', *Journal of Econometrics*, 56, 119–39.

Engle, R. F., Hendry, D. F., and Richard, J.-F. (1983), 'Exogeneity', *Econometrica*, 51, 277–304.

Engle, R. F., Hendry, D. F., and Trumble, D. (1985), 'Small Sample Properties of ARCH Estimators and Tests', *Canadian Journal of Economics*, 43, 66–93.

Engle, R. F., and Issler, J. V. (1995), 'Estimating Common Sectoral Cycles', *Journal of Monetary Economics*, 35, 83–113.

Engle, R. F., and Kozicki, S. (1993), 'Testing for Common Features', *Journal of Business and Economic Statistics*, 11, 369–80.

Engle, R. F., and Kroner, K. F. (1995), 'Multivariate Simultaneous Generalized ARCH', *Econometric Theory*, 11, 122–50.

Engle, R. F., and Lee, G. J. (1999), 'A Permanent and Transitory Component Model of Stock Return Volatility', in R. F. Engle and H. White (eds.), *Cointegration, Causality, and Forecasting: A Festchrift in Honor of Clive W. J. Granger*, Oxford: Oxford University Press, 475–97.

Engle, R. F., Lilien, D. M., and Robbins, R. P. (1987), 'Estimating Time Varying Risk Premia in the Term Structure: The ARCH-M Model', *Econometrica*, 55, 391–408.

Engle, R. F., and Ng, V. (1993), 'Measuring and Testing the Impact of News on Volatility', *Journal of Finance*, 48, 1749–78.

Engle, R. F., and Patton, A. (2001), 'What Good is a Volatility Model?', *Quantitative Finance*, 1, 237–45.

Engle, R. F., and Russell, J. R. (1997), 'Forecasting the Frequency of Changes in Quoted Foreign Exchange Prices with the Autoregressive Conditional Duration Model', *Journal of Empirical Finance*, 4, 187–212.

(1998), 'Autoregressive Conditional Duration: A New Model for Irregularly-spaced Transaction Data', *Econometrica*, 66, 1127–62.

Engle, R. F., and Smith, A. D. (1999), 'Stochastic Permanent Breaks', *Review of Economics and Statistics*, 81, 553–74.

Eraker, B. (2004), 'Do Stock Prices and Volatility Jump? Reconciling Evidence from Spot and Option Prices', *Journal of Finance*, 59, 1367–403.

Eraker, B., Johannes, M., and Polson, N. (2003), 'The Impact of Jumps in Volatility and Returns', *Journal of Finance*, 59, 1269–300.

Ericsson, N. R., and MacKinnon, J. G. (2002), 'Distributions of Error Correction Tests for Cointegration', *Econometrics Journal*, 5, 285–318.

Faff, R., and Gray, P. (2006), 'On the Estimation and Comparison of Short-rate Models Using the Generalised Method of Moments', *Journal of Banking and Finance*, 30, 3131–46.

Fama, E. F. (1965), 'The Behaviour of Stock-Market Prices', *Journal of Business*, 38, 34–105.

(1970), 'Efficient Capital Markets: A Review of Theory and Empirical Work', *Journal of Finance*, 25, 383–417.

(1975), 'Short Term Interest Rates as Predictors of Inflation', *American Economic Review*, 65, 269–82.

(1991), 'Efficient Capital Markets II', *Journal of Finance*, 26, 1575–617.

(1998), 'Market Efficiency, Long-term Returns, and Behavioural Finance', *Journal of Financial Economics*, 49, 283–306.

Fama, E. F., and MacBeth, J. D. (1973), 'Risk, Return, and Equilibrium: Empirical Tests', *Journal of Political Economy*, 81, 607–36.

Fan, J., and Yao, Q. (2003), *Nonlinear Time Series: Nonparametric and Parametric Methods*, New York: Springer.

Feller, W. (1966), *An Introduction to Probability Theory and its Applications*, Vol. II, New York: Wiley.

Fernandes, M., and Grammig, J. (2005), 'Nonparametric Specification Tests for Conditional Duration Models', *Journal of Econometrics*, 27, 35–68.

(2006) 'A Family of Autoregressive Conditional Duration Models', *Journal of Econometrics*, 130, 1–23.

Fernández-Rodriguez, F., Sosvilla-Rivero, S., and Andrada-Félix, J. (2005), 'Testing Chaotic Dynamics via Lyapunov Exponents', *Journal of Applied Econometrics*, 20, 911–30.

Fiorentini, G., Sentana, E., and Shephard, N. (2004), 'Likelihood-based Estimation of Latent Generalized ARCH Structures', *Econometrica*, 72, 1481–517.

Fong, W. M., Koh, S. K., and Ouliaris, S. (1997), 'Joint Variance-ratio Tests of the Martingale Hypothesis for Exchange Rates', *Journal of Business and Economic Statistics*, 15, 51–9.

Fox, R., and Taqqu, M. S. (1986), 'Large-sample Properties of Parameter Estimates for Strongly Dependent Stationary Gaussian Time Series', *Annals of Statistics*, 14, 517–32.

Frankel, F. A., and Froot, K. A. (1988), 'Chartists, Fundamentalists and the Demand for Dollars', *Greek Economic Review*, 10, 49–102.

Franses, P. H., and Paap, R. (1999), 'Does Seasonal Adjustment Change Inference from Markov Switching Models?', *Journal of Macroeconomics*, 21, 79–92.

French, K. R., Schwert, G. W., and Stambaugh, R. F. (1987), 'Expected Stock Returns and Volatility', *Journal of Financial Economics*, 19, 3–29.

Fuller, W. A. (1976), *Introduction to Statistical Time Series*, New York: Wiley.

  (1996), *Introduction to Statistical Time Series*, 2nd edn., New York: Wiley.

Gallant, A. R., Rossi, P. E., and Tauchen, G. (1992), 'Stock Prices and Volume', *Review of Financial Studies*, 5, 199–242.

Gallant, A. R., and White, H. (1988), *A Unified Theory of Estimation and Inference for Nonlinear Dynamics*, Oxford: Blackwell.

Garcia, R., Ghysels, E., and Renault, E. (2007), 'The Econometrics of Option Pricing', in Y. Aït-Sahalia and L. P. Hansen (eds.), *Handbook of Financial Econometrics*, New York: Elsevier.

Garman, M. B., and Klass, M. J. (1980), 'On the Estimation of Security Price Volatilities from Historical Data', *Journal of Business*, 53, 67–78.

Gavridis, M., Markellos, R. N., and Mills, T. C. (1999), 'High-frequency Random Walks?', in P. Lequeux (ed.), *The Financial Markets Tick by Tick: Insights in Financial Markets Microstructure*, Chichester: Wiley, 227–54.

Geweke, J. (1978), 'Testing the Exogeneity Specification in the Complete Dynamic Simultaneous Equations Model', *Journal of Econometrics*, 7, 163–85.

  (1984), 'Inference and Causality in Economic Time Series Models', in Z. Griliches and M. D. Intriligator (eds.), *Handbook of Econometrics*, Vol. II, Amsterdam: North-Holland, 1101–44.

  (1993), 'Inference and Forecasting for Chaotic Nonlinear Time Series', in P. Chen and R. Day (eds.), *Nonlinear Dynamics and Evolutionary Economics*, Oxford: Oxford University Press, 459–512.

Geweke, J., and Porter-Hudak, S. (1983), 'The Estimation and Application of Long Memory Time Series Models', *Journal of Time Series Analysis*, 4, 221–38.

Ghose, D., and Kroner, K. F. (1995), 'The Relationship between GARCH and Symmetric Stable Processes: Finding the Source of Fat Tails in Financial Data', *Journal of Empirical Finance*, 2, 225–51.

Ghysels, E., Granger, C. W. J., and Siklos, P. L. (1996), 'Is Seasonal Adjustment a Linear or Nonlinear Data Filtering Process?', *Journal of Business and Economic Statistics*, 14, 374–86.

Ghysels, E., Harvey, A. C., and Renault, E. (1996), 'Stochastic Volatility', in G. S. Maddala (ed.), *Handbook of Statistics*, Vol. XIV: *Statistical Method in Finance*, Amsterdam: North-Holland, 119–91.

Ghysels, E., Santa-Clara P., and Valkanov, R. (2006), 'Predicting Volatility: Getting the Most out of Return Data Sampled at Different Frequencies', *Journal of Econometrics*, 131, 59–95.

Gibbons, M. R. (1982), 'Multivariate Tests of Financial Models', *Journal of Financial Economics*, 10, 3–27.

Gibbons, M. R., Ross, S. A., and Shanken, J. (1989), 'A Test of the Efficiency of a Given Portfolio', *Econometrica*, 57, 1121–52.

Gibson, R., Lhabitant, F. S., Pistre, N., and Talay, D. (1999), 'Interest Rate Model Risk: An Overview', *The Journal of Risk*, 1, 37–62.

Gil-Alana, L. A. (2003), 'Testing of Fractional Cointegration in Macroeconomic Time Series', *Oxford Bulletin of Economics and Statistics*, 65, 517–29.

Giot, P. (2000), 'Time Transformations, Intraday Data and Volatility Models', *Journal of Computational Finance*, 4, 31–62.

Giraitis, L., Kokoszka, P., Leipus, R., and Teyssière, G. (2003), 'Rescaled Variance and Related Tests for Long Memory in Volatility and Levels', *Journal of Econometrics*, 112, 265–94.

Giraitis, L., Leipus, R., and Surgailis, D. (2006), 'Recent Advances in ARCH Modelling', in A. Kirman and G. Teyssiere (eds.), *Long Memory in Economics*, Berlin: Springer, 3–38.

Giraitis, L., and Surgailis, D. (2002), 'ARCH-type Bilinear Models with Double Long Memory,' *Stochastic Proccesses and their Applications*, 100, 275–300.

Glosten, L. R., Jagannathan, R., and Runkle, D. (1993), 'Relationship between the Expected Value and the Volatility of the Nominal Excess Return on Stocks', *Journal of Finance*, 48, 1779–801.

Godfrey, L. G. (1979), 'Testing the Adequacy of a Time Series Model', *Biometrika*, 66, 67–72.
  (1988), *Misspecification Tests in Econometrics*, Cambridge: Cambridge University Press.

Goldberg, M. D., and Frydman, R. (1996), 'Imperfect Knowledge and Behaviour in the Foreign Exchange Market', *Economic Journal*, 106, 869–93.

Gonzalez-Rivera, G. (1998), 'Smooth Transition GARCH Models', *Studies in Nonlinear Dynamics and Econometrics*, 3, 161–78.

Gonzalez-Rivera, G., and Drost, F. C. (1999), 'Efficiency Comparisons of Maximum-likelihood Based Estimators in GARCH Models', *Journal of Econometrics*, 93, 93–111.

Goodhart, C. A. E., and O'Hara, M. (1997), 'High Frequency Data in Financial Markets: Issues and Applications', *Journal of Empirical Finance*, 4, 73–114.

Grammig, J., and Wellner, M. (2002), 'Modeling the Interdependence of Volatility and Inter-transaction Duration Processes', *Journal of Econometrics*, 106, 369–400.

Granger, C. W. J. (1966), 'The Typical Spectral Shape of an Economic Variable', *Econometrica*, 34, 150–61.
  (1969), 'Investigating Causal Relations by Econometric Models and Cross-spectral Methods', *Econometrica*, 37, 424–38.
  (1980), 'Long Memory Relationships and the Aggregation of Dynamic Models', *Journal of Econometrics*, 14, 227–38.
  (1992), 'Comment', *Statistical Science*, 7, 102–4.
  (1995), 'Modelling Nonlinear Relationships Between Extended-memory Variables', *Econometrica*, 63, 265–79.
  (1997), 'On Modelling the Long Run in Applied Economics', *Economic Journal*, 107, 169–77.

(1998), 'Extracting Information from Mega-panels and High-frequency Data', *Statistica Neerlandica*, 52, 258–72.

Granger, C. W. J., and Andersen, A. P. (1978), *An Introduction to Bilinear Time Series Models*, Göttingen: Vandenhoeck and Ruprecht.

Granger, C. W. J., and Ding, Z. (1995), 'Some Properties of Absolute Returns: An Alternative Measure of Risk', *Annales d'Economie et de Statistique*, 40, 67–91.

(1996), 'Varieties of Long Memory Models', *Journal of Econometrics*, 73, 61–78.

Granger, C. W. J., and Hallman, J. J. (1991), 'Long Memory Series with Attractors', *Oxford Bulletin of Economics and Statistics*, 53, 11–26.

Granger, C. W. J., and Hyung, N. (2004), 'Occasional Structural Breaks and Long Memory with an Application to the S&P 500 Absolute Stock Returns', *Journal of Empirical Finance*, 11, 399–421.

(2006), 'Introduction to M-M Processes', *Journal of Econometrics*, 130, 143–64.

Granger, C. W. J., Inoue, T., and Morin, N. (1997), 'Nonlinear Stochastic Trends', *Journal of Econometrics*, 81, 65–92.

Granger, C. W. J., and Joyeux, R. (1980), 'An Introduction to Long Memory Time Series Models and Fractional Differencing', *Journal of Time Series Analysis*, 1, 15–29.

Granger, C. W. J., and Morgenstern, O. (1970), *Predictability of Stock Market Prices*, Lexington, Heath MA: Lexington Books.

Granger, C. W. J., and Morris, M. J. (1976), 'Time Series Modelling and Interpretation', *Journal of the Royal Statistical Society*, Series A, 139, 246–57.

Granger, C. W. J., and Newbold, P. (1974), 'Spurious Regressions in Econometrics', *Journal of Econometrics*, 2, 111–20.

(1986), *Forecasting Economic Time Series*, 2nd edn., New York: Academic Press.

Granger, C. W. J., and Orr, D. (1972), ' "Infinite Variance" and Research Strategy in Time Series Analysis', *Journal of the American Statistical Association*, 67, 275–85.

Granger, C. W. J., Spear, S., and Ding, Z. (2000), 'Stylized Facts on the Temporal and Distributional Properties of Absolute Returns: An Update', in W.-S. Chan, W. K. Li and H. Tong (eds.), *Statistics and Finance: An Interface*, London: Imperial College Press, 97–120.

Granger, C. W. J., and Swanson, N. (1996), 'Future Developments in the Study of Cointegrated Variables', *Oxford Bulletin of Economics and Statistics*, 58, 537–53.

(1997), 'An Introduction to Stochastic Unit Root Processes', *Journal of Econometrics*, 80, 35–62.

Granger, C. W. J., and Teräsvirta, T. (1993), *Modeling Nonlinear Economic Relationships*, Oxford: Oxford University Press.

(1999), 'A Simple Nonlinear Time Series Model with Misleading Linear Properties', *Economics Letters*, 62, 161–5.

Granger, C. W. J., and Yoon, G. (2002), *Hidden Cointegration*, Economics Working Paper 2002–02, San Diego: University of California.

Gregory, A. W., and Hansen, B. E. (1996), 'Residual-based Tests for Cointegration in Models with Regime Shifts', *Journal of Econometrics*, 70, 99–126.

Gregory, A. W., Nason, J. M., and Watt, D. G. (1996), 'Testing for Structural Breaks in Cointegrating Relationships', *Journal of Econometrics*, 71, 321–41.

Griffeath, D. (1992), 'Comment: Randomness in Complex Systems', *Statistical Science*, 7, 108.

Groenendijk, P. A., Lucas, A., and de Vries, C. G. (1995), 'A Note on the Relationship between GARCH and Symmetric Stable Processes', *Journal of Empirical Finance*, 2, 253–64.

Guégan, D. (1987), 'Different Representations for Bilinear Models', *Journal of Time Series Analysis*, 8, 389–408.

Haas, M., Mittnik, S., and Paolella, M. S. (2004), 'A New Approach to Markov-switching GARCH Models', *Journal of Financial Econometrics*, 4, 493–530.

Haefke, C., and Helmenstein, C. (1996), 'Forecasting Austrian IPOs: An Application of Linear and Neural Network Error-correction Models', *Journal of Forecasting*, 15, 237–52.

Haggan, V., Heravi, S. M., and Priestley, M. B. (1984), 'A Study of the Application of State-dependent Models in Non-linear Time Series Analysis', *Journal of Time Series Analysis*, 5, 69–102.

Haggan, V., and Ozaki, T. (1981), 'Modelling Non-linear Vibrations Using an Amplitude Dependent Autoregressive Time Series Model', *Biometrika*, 68, 189–96.

Haldrup, N., and Jansson, M. (2006), 'Improving Size and Power in Unit Root Testing', in T. C. Mills and K. Patterson (eds.), *Palgrave Handbook of Econometrics*, Vol. I: *Econometric Theory*, Basingstoke: Palgrave Macmillan, 252–77.

Hall, P. (1982), 'On Some Simple Estimates of an Exponent of Regular Variation', *Journal of the Royal Statistical Society*, Series B, 44, 37–42.

Hall, P., and Welsh, A. H. (1985), 'Adaptive Estimates of Parameters of Regular Variation', *Annals of Statistics*, 13, 331–41.

Hall, S. G., Psaradakis, Z., and Sola, M. (1997), 'Cointegration and Changes in Regime: The Japanese Consumption Function', *Journal of Applied Econometrics*, 12, 151–68.

Hamilton, J. D. (1986), 'On Testing for Self-fulfilling Speculative Price Bubbles', *International Economic Review*, 27, 545–52.

(1989), 'A New Approach to the Economic Analysis of Nonstationary Time Series and the Business Cycle', *Econometrica*, 57, 357–84.

(1990), 'Analysis of Time Series Subject to Changes in Regime', *Journal of Econometrics*, 45, 39–70.

(1994), *Time Series Analysis*, Princeton, NJ: Princeton University Press.

Hamilton, J. D., and Susmel, R. (1994), 'Autoregressive Conditional Heteroskedasticity and Changes in Regime', *Journal of Econometrics*, 64, 307–33.

Hamilton, J. D., and Whiteman, C. H. (1985), 'The Observable Implications of Self-fulfilling Expectations', *Journal of Monetary Economics*, 16, 353–73.

Hamilton, W. P. (1922), *The Stock Market Barometer*, New York: Harper and Brothers.

Hansen, B. E. (1992), 'Testing for Parameter Instability in Linear Models', *Journal of Policy Modelling*, 14, 517–33.

(1994), 'Autoregressive Conditional Density Estimation', *International Economic Review*, 35, 705–30.

Hansen, L. P. (1982), 'Large Sample Properties of Generalized Method of Moments Estimators', *Econometrica*, 50, 1029–54.

Hansen, L. P., and Hodrick, R. J. (1980), 'Forward Exchange Rates as Optimal Predictors of Future Spot Rates', *Journal of Political Economy*, 88, 829–53.

Hansen, P. R., and Lunde, A. (2005), 'A Forecast Comparison of Volatility Models: Does Anything Beat a GARCH (1,1)?', *Journal of Applied Econometrics*, 20, 873–89.

(2006a), 'Consistent Ranking of Volatility Models', *Journal of Econometrics*, 131, 97–121.

(2006b), 'Realized Variance and Market Microstructure Noise', *Journal of Business and Economic Statistics*, 24, 127–61.

Härdle, W. (1990), *Applied Nonparametric Regression*, Oxford: Oxford University Press.

Harvey, A. C. (1989), *Forecasting Structural Time Series Models and the Kalman Filter*, Cambridge: Cambridge University Press.

(1998), 'Long Memory in Stochastic Volatility', in J. Knight and S. Satchell (eds.), *Forecasting Volatility in Financial Markets*, Oxford: Butterworth-Heinemann, 307–20.

Harvey, A. C., Ruiz, E., and Sentana, E. (1992), 'Unobserved Component Models with ARCH Disturbances', *Journal of Econometrics*, 52, 129–57.

Harvey, A. C., Ruiz, E., and Shephard, N. (1994), 'Multivariate Stochastic Variance Models', *Review of Economic Studies*, 61, 247–64.

Harvey, A. C., and Shephard, N. (1992), 'Structural Time Series Models', in G. S. Maddala, C. R. Rao and H. D. Vinod (eds.), *Handbook of Statistics*, Vol. XI: *Econometrics*, Amsterdam: North-Holland, 261–302.

(1996), 'Estimation of an Asymmetric Stochastic Volatility Model for Asset Returns', *Journal of Business and Economic Statistics*, 14, 429–34.

Harvey, C. R., and Siddique, A. (2000), 'Conditional skewness in asset pricing tests', *Journal of Finance*, 55, 1263–95.

Harvey, D. I., Leybourne, S. J., and Newbold, P. (2001), 'Innovational Outlier Unit Root Tests with an Endogenously Determined Break in Level', *Oxford Bulletin of Economics and Statistics*, 63, 559–75.

Harvey, D. I., and Mills, T. C. (2002), 'Unit Roots and Double Smooth Transitions', *Journal of Applied Statistics*, 29, 675–83.

(2003), 'A Note on Busetti–Harvey Tests for Stationarity in Series with Structural Breaks', *Journal of Time Series Analysis*, 24, 159–64.

(2004) 'Tests for Stationarity in Series with Endogenously Determined Structural Change', *Oxford Bulletin of Economics and Statistics*, 66, 863–94.

Hassler, U., and Wolters, J. (1994), 'On the Power of Unit Root Tests against Fractionally Integrated Alternatives', *Economics Letters*, 45, 1–5.

Haug, A. A. (1996), 'Tests for Cointegration: A Monte Carlo Comparison', *Journal of Econometrics*, 71, 89–115.

Haykin, S. (1999), *Neural Networks: A Comprehensive Foundation*, 2nd edn., Upper Saddle River, NJ: Prentice Hall.

Hendry, D. F. (1995), *Dynamic Econometrics*, Oxford: Oxford University Press.

Hendry, D. F., and Doornik, J. A. (2006), *PcGive 11*, London: Timberlake Consultants.

Hendry, D. F., Pagan, A. R., and Sargan, J. D. (1984), 'Dynamic Specification', in Z. Griliches and M. D. Intriligator (eds.), *Handbook of Econometrics*, Vol. II, Amsterdam: North-Holland, 1023–100.

Hentschel, L. (1995), 'All in the Family: Nesting Symmetric and Asymmetric GARCH Models', *Journal of Financial Economics*, 39, 71–104.

Heston, S. L. (1993), 'A Closed-form Solution for Options with Stochastic Volatility with Applications to Bond and Currency Options', *Review of Financial Studies*, 6, 327–43.

Heston, S. L., and Nandi, S. (2000), 'A Closed Form GARCH Option Pricing Model', *Review of Financial Studies*, 13, 585–625.

Hiemstra, C., and Jones, J. D. (1997), 'Another Look at Long Memory in Common Stock Returns', *Journal of Empirical Finance*, 4, 373–401.

Higgins, M. L., and Bera, A. K. (1988), 'A Joint Test for ARCH and Bilinearity in the Regression Model', *Econometric Reviews*, 7, 171–81.

(1992), 'A Class of Nonlinear ARCH Models', *International Economic Review*, 33, 137–58.

Hilborn, R. C. (1997), 'Resource Letter: Nonlinear Dynamics', *American Journal of Physics*, 65, 822–34.

Hill, B. M. (1975), 'A Simple General Approach to Inference about the Tail of a Distribution', *Annals of Statistics*, 3, 1163–74.

Hillebrand, E. (2005), 'Neglecting Parameter Changes in GARCH models', *Journal of Econometrics*, 129, 121–38.

Hinich, M. (1982), 'Testing for Gaussianity and Linearity of a Stationary Time Series' *Journal of Time Series Analysis*, 3, 169–76.

Hinich, M., and Patterson, D. M. (1985), 'Evidence of Nonlinearity in Daily Stock Returns', *Journal of Business and Economic Statistics*, 3, 69–77.

Ho, M. S., and Sørensen, B. E. (1996), 'Finding Cointegration Rank in High Dimensional Systems Using the Johansen Test: An Illustration Using Data Based Monte Carlo Simulations', *Review of Economics and Statistics*, 78, 726–32.

Hoaglin, D. C. (1985), 'Summarizing Shape Numerically: The *g*-and-*h* Distributions', in D. C. Hoaglin, F. Mosteller and J. W. Tukey (eds.), *Exploring Data Tables, Trends and Shapes*, New York: Wiley, 461–513.

Hodrick, R. J., and Prescott, E. C. (1997), 'Postwar US Business Cycles: An Empirical Investigation', *Journal of Money Credit and Banking*, 19, 1–16.

Hols, M. C. A. B., and de Vries, C. G. (1991), 'The Limiting Distribution of Extremal Exchange Rate Returns', *Journal of Applied Econometrics*, 6, 287–302.

Hong, Y. (1997), 'One-sided Testing for Conditional Heteroskedasticity in Time Series Models', *Journal of Time Series Analysis*, 18, 253–77.

Hong, Y., and Lee, T. H. (2003), 'Diagnostic Checking for the Adequacy of Nonlinear Time Series Models', *Econometric Theory*, 19, 1065–121.

Hornik, K., Stinchcombe, M., and White, H. (1989), 'Multilayer Feed-forward Networks Are Universal Approximators', *Neural Networks*, 2, 359–66.

Horowitz, J. L. (2001), 'The Bootstrap', in J. J. Heckman and E. E. Leamer (eds.), *Handbook of Econometrics*, Vol. V, Amsterdam: Elsevier Science, 3159–228.

Horowitz, J. L., Lobato, I. N., Nankervis, J. C., and Savin, N. E. (2006), 'Bootstrapping the Box–Pierce Q Test: A Robust Test of Uncorrelatedness', *Journal of Econometrics*, 133, 841–62.

Hosking, J. R. M. (1981), 'Fractional Differencing', *Biometrika*, 68, 165–76.

(1984), 'Modelling Persistence in Hydrological Time Series Using Fractional Differencing', *Water Resources Research*, 20, 1898–908.

Hsiao, C. (1997), 'Cointegration and Dynamic Simultaneous Equation Model', *Econometrica*, 65, 647–70.

Hsieh, D. A. (1989a), 'Modelling Heteroskedasticity in Daily Foreign Exchange Rates', *Journal of Business and Economic Statistics*, 7, 307–17.

(1989b), 'Testing for Nonlinear Dependence in Daily Foreign Exchange Rates', *Journal of Business*, 62, 339–68.

(1991), 'Chaos and Nonlinear Dynamics: Application to Financial Markets', *Journal of Finance*, 46, 1839–77.

Huang, X., and Tauchen, G. (2005), 'The Relative Contribution of Jumps to Total Price Variance', *Journal of Financial Econometrics*, 3, 456–99.

Hughes, A. W., King, M. L., and Teng, K. K. (2004), 'Selecting the Order of an ARCH Model', *Economic Letters*, 83, 269–75.

Hull, J. (2005), *Options, Futures and Other Derivatives*, 6th edn., London: Prentice Hall.

Hurst, H. (1951), 'Long Term Storage Capacity of Reservoirs', *Transactions of the American Society of Civil Engineers*, 116, 770–99.

Hurvich, C. M., Deo, R. S., and Brodsky, J. (1998), 'The Mean Square Error of Geweke and Porter-Hudak's Estimator of the Memory Parameter of a Long Memory Time Series', *Journal of Time Series Analysis*, 19, 19–46.

Hurvich, C. M., and Ray, B. K. (1995), 'Estimation of the Memory Parameter for Nonstationary or Noninvertible Fractionally Integrated Processes', *Journal of Time Series Analysis*, 16, 17–41.

Hylleberg, S., Engle, R. F., Granger, C. W. J., and Yoo, B. S. (1990), 'Seasonal Integration and Co-integration', *Journal of Econometrics*, 44, 215–28.

Hylleberg, S., and Mizon, G. E. (1989), 'A Note on the Distribution of the Least Squares Estimator of a Random Walk with Drift', *Economic Letters*, 29, 225–30.

Jacquier, E., Polson, N. G., and Rossi, P. E. (2004), 'Bayesian Analysis of Stochastic Volatility Models with Fat-tails and Correlated Errors', *Journal of Econometrics*, 122, 185–212.

Jansen, D. W., and de Vries, C. G. (1991), 'On the Frequency of Large Stock Returns: Putting Booms and Busts into Perspective', *Review of Economics and Statistics*, 73, 18–24.

Jarque, C. M., and Bera, A. K. (1980), 'Efficient Tests for Normality, Homoskedasticity and Serial Dependence of Regression Residuals', *Economics Letters*, 6, 255–9.

Jensen, S. T., and Rahbek, A. (2004), 'Asymptotic Inference for Nonstationary ARCH', *Econometric Theory*, 20, 1203–26.

Johannes, M., and Polson, N. G. (2007), 'MCMC Methods for Financial Econometrics', in Y. Aït-Sahalia and L. P. Hansen (eds.), *Handbook of Financial Econometrics*, New York: Elsevier.

Johansen, S. (1995), *Likelihood-based Inference in Cointegrated Vector Autoregressive Models*, Oxford: Oxford University Press.

(2002a), 'A Small Sample Correction of the Test for Cointegrating Rank in the Vector Autoregressive Model', *Econometrica*, 70, 1929–61.

(2002b), 'A Small Sample Correction for Tests of Hypotheses on the Cointegrating Vectors', *Journal of Econometrics*, 111, 195–221.

(2006), 'Cointegration: An Overview', in T. C. Mills and K. Patterson (eds.), *Palgrave Handbook of Econometrics*, Vol. I: *Econometric Theory*, Basingstoke: Palgrave Macmillan, 540–77.

Johansen, S., and Juselius, K. (1994), 'Identification of the Long-run and Short-run Structure: An Application to the ISLM Model', *Journal of Econometrics*, 63, 7–36.

Johnston, J., and DiNardo, J. (1997), *Econometric Methods*, 4th edn., New York: McGraw-Hill.

Jondeau, E., and Rockinger, M. (2003), 'Conditional Volatility, Skewness, and Kurtosis: Existence, Persistence, and Comovements', *Journal of Economic Dynamics and Control*, 27, 1699–737.

Jones, C. S. (2003), 'The Dynamics of Stochastic Volatility: Evidence from Underlying and Options Markets', *Journal of Econometrics*, 116, 181–224.

Jones, R. (1978), 'Nonlinear Autoregressive Processes', *Proceedings of the Royal Society of London*, A, 360, 71–95.

Jorion, P. (1988), 'On Jump Processes in the Foreign Exchange and Stock Markets', *Review of Financial Studies*, 1, 427–45.

Judge, G. G., Griffiths, W. E., Carter Hill, R., Lütkepohl, H., and Lee, T. C. (1985), *The Theory and Practice of Econometrics*, 2nd edn., New York: Wiley.

Kapetanios, G., Shin, Y., and Snell, A. (2006), 'Testing for Cointegration in Nonlinear Smooth Transition Error Correction Models', *Econometric Theory*, 22, 279–303.

Karanasos, M., Psaradakis, Z., and Sola, M. (2004), 'On the Autocorrelation Properties of Long-memory GARCH Processes', *Journal of Time Series Analysis*, 25, 265–81.

Keenan, D. M. (1985), 'A Tukey Nonadditivity-type Test for Time Series Nonlinearity', *Biometrika*, 72, 39–44.

Kendall, M. J. (1953), 'The Analysis of Economic Time Series, Part I: Prices', *Journal of the Royal Statistical Society*, Series A, 96, 11–25.

Kim, C. J., Nelson, C. R., and Startz, R. (1998), 'Testing for Mean Reversion in Heteroskedastic Data Based on Gibbs-sampling-augmented Randomization', *Journal of Empirical Finance*, 5, 131–54.

Kim, K., and Schmidt, P. (1990), 'Some Evidence on the Accuracy of Phillips–Perron Tests Using Alternative Estimates of Nuisance Parameters', *Economics Letters*, 34, 345–50.

Kleidon, A. W. (1986a), 'Variance Bounds Tests and Stock Price Valuation Models', *Journal of Political Economy*, 94, 953–1001.

    (1986b), 'Bias in Small Sample Tests of Stock Price Rationality', *Journal of Business*, 59, 237–61.

Koedijk, K. G., and Kool, C. J. M. (1992), 'Tail Estimates of East European Exchange Rates', *Journal of Business and Economic Statistics*, 10, 83–96.

Koedijk, K. G., Schafgans, M. M. A., and de Vries, C. G. (1990), 'The Tail Index of Exchange Rate Returns', *Journal of International Economics*, 29, 93–108.

Koedijk, K. G., Stork, P. A., and de Vries, C. G. (1992), 'Differences between Foreign Exchange Rate Regimes: The View from the Tails', *Journal of International Money and Finance*, 11, 462–73.

Koenker, R. (1982), 'Robust Methods in Econometrics', *Econometric Reviews*, 1, 213–55.

Kokoszka, P. S., and Taqqu, M. S. (1994), 'Infinite Variance Stable ARMA Processes', *Journal of Time Series Analysis*, 15, 203–20.

    (1996), 'Infinite Variance Stable Moving Averages with Long Memory', *Journal of Econometrics*, 73, 79–99.

Kon, S. (1984), 'Models of Stock Returns: A Comparison', *Journal of Finance*, 39, 147–65.

Koop, G. (1992), ' "Objective" Bayesian Unit Root Tests', *Journal of Applied Econometrics*, 7, 65–82.

Koop, G., Pesaran, M. H., and Potter, S. M. (1996), 'Impulse Response Analysis in Nonlinear Multivariate Models', *Journal of Econometrics*, 74, 119–47.

Koop, G., and Potter, S. M. (2001), 'Are Apparent Findings of Nonlinearity Due to Structural Instability in Economic Time Series?', *Econometrics Journal*, 4, 37–55.

Koopman, S. J., Harvey, A. C., Doornik, J. A., and Shephard, N. (2006), *Stamp 6: Structural Time Series Analyser, Modeller and Predictor*, London: Timberlake Consultants.

Koopman, S. J., Jungbacker, B., and Hol, E. (2005), 'Forecasting Daily Variability of the S&P 100 Stock Index Using Historical, Realised and Implied Volatility Measurements', *Journal of Empirical Finance*, 12, 445–75.

Koopman, S. J., Shephard, N., and Doornik, J. A. (1999), 'Statistical Algorithms for Models in State Space Using SsfPack 2.2', *Econometrics Journal*, 2, 113–66.

Krämer, W., and Ploberger, W. (1990), 'The Local Power of CUSUM and CUSUM of Squares Tests', *Econometric Theory*, 6, 335–47.

Kristensen, D. (2005), *On Stationarity and Ergodicity of the Bilinear Model with Applications to GARCH Models*, Working Paper, University of Wisconsin.

Kristensen, D., and Linton, O. (2006), 'A Closed-form Estimator for the GARCH(1,1)-Model', *Econometric Theory*, 22, 323–37.

Kuan, C.-M., and White, H. (1994), 'Artificial Neural Networks: An Econometric Perspective (with Discussion)', *Econometric Reviews*, 13, 1–143.

Künsch, H. R. (1987), 'Statistical Aspects of Self-similar Processes', in Yu. Prohorov and V. V. Sazanov (eds.), *Proceedings of the First World Congress of the Bernoulli Society*, Utrecht: VNU Science Press, 67–74.

Kwiatkowski, D., Phillips, P. C. B., Schmidt, P., and Shin, Y. (1992), 'Testing the Null Hypothesis of Stationarity against the Alternative of a Unit Root', *Journal of Econometrics*, 54, 159–78.

Kyrtsou, C., and Serletis, A. (2006), 'Univariate Tests for Nonlinear Structure', *Journal of Macroeconomics*, 28, 154–68.

Lam, P. S. (1990), 'The Hamilton Model with a General Autoregressive Component: Estimation and Comparison with Other Models of Economic Time Series', *Journal of Monetary Economics*, 20, 409–32.

Lanne, M., and Saikkonen, P. (2005), 'Nonlinear GARCH Models for Highly Persistent Volatility', *Econometrics Journal*, 8, 251–76.

Lee, D., and Schmidt, P. (1996), 'On the Power of the KPSS Test of Stationarity against Fractionally Integrated Alternatives', *Journal of Econometrics*, 73, 285–302.

Lee, J. H. H., and King, M. L. (1993), 'A Locally Most Mean Powerful Based Score Test for ARCH and GARCH Regression Disturbances', *Journal of Business and Economic Statistics*, 11, 17–27.

Lee, T.-H. (1994), 'Spread and Volatility in Spot and Forward Exchange Rates', *Journal of International Money and Finance*, 13, 375–83.

Lee, T.-H., White, H., and Granger, C. W. J. (1993), 'Testing for Neglected Nonlinearity in Time Series Models: A Comparison of Neural Network Methods and Alternative Tests', *Journal of Econometrics*, 56, 269–90.

Lequeux, P. (ed.) (1999), *The Financial Markets Tick by Tick: Insights in Financial Markets Microstructure*, Chichester: Wiley.

LeRoy, S. (1973), 'Risk Aversion and the Martingale Property of Stock Returns', *International Economic Review*, 14, 436–46.

(1982), 'Expectations Models of Asset Prices: A Survey of the Theory', *Journal of Finance*, 37, 185–217.

(1989) 'Efficient Capital Markets and Martingales', *Journal of Economic Literature*, 27, 1583–621.

Levy, H., and Markowitz, H. M. (1979), 'Approximating Expected Utility by a Function of Mean and Variance', *American Economic Review*, 69, 308–17.

Leybourne, S. J., and McCabe, B. P. M. (1994), 'A Consistent Test for a Unit Root', *Journal of Business and Economic Statistics*, 12, 157–66.

(1999) 'Modified Stationarity Tests with Data Dependent Model Selection Rules', *Journal of Business and Economic Statistics*, 17, 264–70.

Leybourne, S. J., McCabe, B. P. M., and Mills, T. C. (1996), 'Randomized Unit Root Processes for Modelling and Forecasting Financial Time Series: Theory and Applications', *Journal of Forecasting*, 15, 253–70.

Leybourne, S. J., McCabe, B. P. M., and Tremayne, A. R. (1996), 'Can Economic Time Series be Differenced to Stationarity?', *Journal of Business and Economic Statistics*, 14, 435–46.

Leybourne, S. J., Mills, T. C., and Newbold, P. (1998), 'Spurious Rejections by Dickey–Fuller Tests in the Presence of a Break under the Null', *Journal of Econometrics*, 87, 191–203.

Leybourne, S. J., Newbold, P., and Vougas, D. (1998), 'Unit Roots and Smooth Transitions', *Journal of Time Series Analysis*, 19, 83–97.

Li, C. W., and Li, W. K. (1996), 'On a Double Threshold Autoregressive Heteroskedasticity Time Series Model', *Journal of Applied Econometrics*, 11, 253–74.

Li, Q., Yang, J., Hsiao, C., and Chang, Y.-J. (2005), 'The Relationship between Stock Returns and Volatility in International Stock Markets', *Journal of Empirical Finance*, 12, 650–65.

Li, W. K., Ling, S., and McAleer, M. (2002), 'Recent Theoretical Results for Time Series Models with GARCH Errors', *Journal of Economic Surveys*, 16, 245–69.

Li, W. K., and Mak, T. K. (1994), 'On the Squared Residual Autocorrelations in Nonlinear Time Series with Conditional Heteroskedasticity', *Journal of Time Series Analysis*, 15, 627–36.

Lieberman, O. (2001), 'The Exact Bias of the Log-periodogram Regression Estimator', *Econometric Reviews*, 20, 369–83.

Liesenfeld, R., and Richard, J. F. (2003), 'Univariate and Multivariate Stochastic Volatility Models: Estimation and Diagnostics', *Journal of Empirical Finance*, 11, 1–27.

Ling, S. (2007), 'Self-weighted and Local Quasi-maximum Likelihood Estimators for ARMA-GARCH/IGARCH Models', *Journal of Econometrics*, 140, 849–73.

Ling, S., and McAleer, M. (2003), 'Asymptotic Theory for a Vector ARMA-GARCH Model', *Econometric Theory*, 19, 280–310.

Linton, O. (1993), 'Adaptive Estimation of ARCH Models', *Econometric Theory*, 9, 539–69.

(2007), 'Semi- and Nonparametric ARCH/GARCH Modelling', in T. G. Andersen, R. A. Davis, J. P. Kreiss and T. Mikosch (eds.), *Handbook of Financial Time Series*, New York: Springer.

Linton, O., and Perron, B. (2003), 'The Shape of the Risk Premium: Evidence from a Semiparametric Generalized Autoregressive Conditional Heteroscedasticity Model', *Journal of Business and Economic Statistics*, 21, 354–67.

Liu, C. Y., and He, J. (1991), 'A Variance Ratio Test of Random Walks in Foreign Exchange Rates', *Journal of Finance*, 46, 773–85.

Liu, M. (2000), 'Modeling Long Memory in Stock Market Volatility', *Journal of Econometrics*, 99, 139–71.

Ljung, G. M., and Box, G. E. P. (1978), 'On a Measure of Lack of Fit in Time Series Models', *Biometrika*, 65, 297–303.

Lo, A. W. (1991), 'Long-term Memory in Stock Market Prices', *Econometrica*, 59, 1279–313.

Lo, A. W., and MacKinlay, A. C. (1988), 'Stock Prices do not Follow Random Walks: Evidence from a Simple Specification Test', *Review of Financial Studies*, 1, 41–66.

(1989), 'The Size and Power of the Variance Ratio Test in Finite Samples: A Monte Carlo Investigation', *Journal of Econometrics*, 40, 203–38.

Lobato, I. N., Nankervis, J. C., and Savin, N. E. (2001), 'Testing for Autocorrelation Using a Modified Box–Pierce Q Test', *International Economic Review*, 42, 187–205.

(2002), 'Testing for Zero Autocorrelation in the Presence of Statistical Dependence', *Econometric Theory*, 18, 730–43.

Loretan, M., and Phillips, P. C. B. (1994), 'Testing the Covariance Stationarity of Heavy-tailed Time Series: An Overview of the Theory with Applications to Several Financial Datasets', *Journal of Empirical Finance*, 1, 211–48.

Lucas, R. E. (1978), 'Asset Prices in an Exchange Economy', *Econometrica*, 46, 1429–46.

Luger, R. (2003), 'Exact Non-parametric Tests for a Random Walk with Unknown Drift under Conditional Heteroskedasticity', *Journal of Econometrics*, 115, 259–76.

Lumsdaine, R. L., and Ng, S. (1999), 'Testing for ARCH in the Presence of a Possibly Mispecified Conditional Mean', *Journal of Econometrics*, 93, 257–79.

Lundbergh, S., and Teräsvirta, T. (2002), 'Evaluating GARCH Models', *Journal of Econometrics*, 110, 417–35.

Lütkepohl, H. (1985), 'Comparison of Criteria for Estimating the Order of a Vector Autoregresive Process', *Journal of Time Series Analysis*, 6, 35–52.

(1991), *Introduction to Multiple Time Series Analysis*, Berlin: Springer-Verlag.

MacKinlay, A. C. (1987), 'On Mulivariate Tests of the CAPM', *Journal of Financial Economics*, 18, 431–71.

MacKinnon, J. G. (1991), 'Critical Values for Cointegration Tests', in R. F. Engle and C. W. J. Granger (eds.), *Long-run Economic Relationships*, Oxford: Oxford University Press, 267–76.

(1996), 'Numerical Distribution Functions for Unit Root and Cointegration Tests', *Journal of Applied Econometrics*, 11, 601–18.

McCabe, B. P. M., and Tremayne, A. R. (1995), 'Testing a Time Series for Difference Stationarity', *Annals of Statistics*, 23, 1015–28.

McCulloch, J. H. (1996), 'Financial Applications of Stable Distributions', in G. S. Maddala and C. R. Rao (eds.), *Handbook of Statistics*, Vol. XIV: *Statistical Methods in Finance*, Amsterdam: Elsevier Science, 393–425.

(1997), 'Measuring Tail Thickness to Estimate the Stable Index α: A Critique', *Journal of Business and Economic Statistics*, 15, 74–81.

McDonald, J. B. (1996), 'Probability Distributions for Financial Models', in G. S. Maddala and C. R. Rao (eds.), *Handbook of Statistics*, Vol. XIV: *Statistical Methods in Finance*, Amsterdam: Elsevier Science, 427–61.

McKenzie, E. (1988), 'A Note on Using the Integrated Form of ARIMA Forecasts', *International Journal of Forecasting*, 4, 117–24.

McLeod, A. J., and Li, W. K. (1983), 'Diagnostic Checking ARMA Time Series Models using Squared-residual Correlations', *Journal of Time Series Analysis*, 4, 269–73.

Maddala, G. S., and Kim, I.-M. (1998), *Unit Roots, Cointegration, and Structural Change*, Cambridge: Cambridge University Press.

Malkiel, B. G. (2003). *A Random Walk down Wall Street*, New York: Norton.

Mandelbrot, B. B. (1963a), 'New Methods in Statistical Economics', *Journal of Political Economy*, 71, 421–40.

(1963b), 'The Variation of Certain Speculative Prices', *Journal of Business*, 36, 394–419.

(1966), 'Forecasts of Future Prices, Unbiased Markets and "Martingale" Models', *Journal of Business*, 39, 242–55.

(1969), 'Long-run Linearity, Locally Gaussian Process, *H*-Spectra, and Infinite Variances', *International Economic Review*, 10, 82–111.

(1972), 'Statistical Methodology for Nonperiodic Cycles: From the Covariance to *R/S* Analysis', *Annals of Economic and Social Measurement*, 1/3, 259–90.

(1989), 'Louis Bachelier', in J. Eatwell, M. Milgate and P. Newman (eds.), *The New Palgrave: Finance*, London: Macmillan, 86–8.

Mandelbrot, B. B., and Wallis, J. R. (1969), 'Some Long-run Properties of Geophysical Records', *Water Resources Research*, 5, 321–40.

Mantegna, R. N., and Stanley, H. E. (1994), 'Stochastic Process with Ultraslow Convergence to a Gaussian: The Truncated Lévy Flight', *Physical Review Letters*, 73, 2946–9.

(1995), 'Scaling Behaviour in the Dynamics of an Economic Index', *Nature*, 376, 46–9.

Maravall, A. (1983), 'An Application of Nonlinear Time Series Forecasting', *Journal of Business and Economic Statistics*, 3, 350–5.

Markellos, R. N., and Mills, T. C. (1998), 'Complexity Reduction for Co-trending Variables', *Journal of Computational Intelligence in Finance*, 6, 6–13.

(2001), 'Unit Roots in the CAPM?', *Applied Economics Letters*, 8, 499–502.

(2003), 'Asset Pricing Dynamics', *European Journal of Finance*, 9, 533–56.

Markellos, R. N., Mills, T. C., and Siriopoulos, C. (2003), 'Intradaily Behavior of Listed and Unlisted Security Basket Indices in the Emerging Greek Stock Market', *Managerial Finance*, 29, 29–54.

Marsh, T. A., and Merton, R. C. (1987), 'Dividend Behaviour for the Aggregate Stock Market', *Journal of Business*, 60, 1–40.

Matacz, A. (2000), 'Financial Modeling and Option Theory with the Truncated Lévy Process', *International Journal of Theoretical and Applied Finance*, 3, 143–60.

Meddahi, N., and Renault, E. (2004), 'Temporal Aggregation of Volatility Models', *Journal of Econometrics*, 119, 355–79.

Meese, R. A. (1986), 'Testing for Bubbles in Exchange Markets: A Case of Sparkling Rates?', *Journal of Political Economy*, 94, 345–73.

Meese, R. A., and Singleton, K. J. (1982), 'On Unit Roots and the Empirical Modelling of Exchange Rates', *Journal of Finance*, 37, 1029–35.

Merton, R. C. (1973), 'An Intertemporal Capital Asset Pricing Model', *Econometrica*, 41, 867–87.

(1976), 'Option Prices when the Underlying Stock Returns Are Discontinuous', *Journal of Financial Economics*, 3, 125–44.

(1980), 'On Estimating the Expected Return on the Market: An Exploratory Investigation', *Journal of Financial Economics*, 8, 323–61.

Meyer, R., and Yu, J. (2000), 'BUGS for a Bayesian Analysis of Stochastic Volatility Models', *Econometrics Journal*, 3, 198–215.

Michael, P., Nobay, A. R., and Peel, D. A. (1997), 'Transactions Costs and Nonlinear Adjustment in Real Exchange Rates: An Empirical Investigation', *Journal of Political Economy*, 105, 862–79.

Mikosch, T., and Starica, C. (2004), 'Changes of Structure in Financial Time Series and the GARCH Model', *Revstat Statistical Journal*, 2, 41–73.

Milhøj, A. (1985), 'The Moment Structure of ARCH Processes', *Scandinavian Journal of Statistics*, 12, 281–92.

Miller, S. M. (1988), 'The Beveridge–Nelson Decomposition of Economic Time Series: Another Economical Computational Method', *Journal of Monetary Economics*, 21, 141–2.

Mills, T. C. (1990), *Time Series Techniques for Economists*, Cambridge: Cambridge University Press.

(1991a), 'Equity Prices, Dividends and Gilt Yields in the UK: Cointegration, Error Correction and "Confidence"', *Scottish Journal of Political Economy*, 38, 242–55.

(1991b), 'The Term Structure of UK Interest Rates: Tests of the Expectations Hypothesis', *Applied Economics*, 23, 599–606.

(1993), 'Testing the Present Value Model of Equity Prices for the UK Stock Market', *Journal of Business Finance and Accounting*, 20, 803–13.

(1995), 'Modelling Skewness and Kurtosis in the London Stock Exchange FT-SE Index Return Distributions', *The Statistician*, 44, 323–32.

(1996a), 'Non-linear Forecasting of Financial Time Series: An Overview and Some New Models', *Journal of Forecasting*, 15, 127–35.

(1996b), 'The Econometrics of the "Market Model": Cointegration, Error Correction and Exogeneity', *International Journal of Finance and Economics*, 1, 275–86.

(1997a), 'Stylized Facts on the Temporal and Distributional Properties of Daily FT-SE Returns', *Applied Financial Economics*, 7, 599–604.

(1997b), 'Technical Analysis and the London Stock Exchange: Testing Trading Rules Using the FT30', *International Journal of Finance and Economics*, 2, 319–31.

(1998), 'Recent Developments in Modelling Nonstationary Vector Auto-regressions', *Journal of Economic Surveys*, 12, 279–312.

(2003), *Modelling Trends and Cycles in Economic Time Series*, Basingstoke: Palgrave Macmillan.

Mills, T. C., and Coutts, J. A. (1995), 'Anomalies and Calendar Effects in the New FT-SE Indices', *European Journal of Finance*, 1, 79–93.

(1996), 'Misspecification and Robust Estimation of the Market Model: Estimating Betas for the FT-SE Industry Baskets', *European Journal of Finance*, 2, 319–31.

Mills, T. C., and Stephenson, M. J. (1986), 'An Empirical Analysis of the UK Treasury Bill Market', *Applied Economics*, 17, 689–703.

Mina, J., and Xiao, J. Y. (2001), *Return to RiskMetrics: The Evolution of a Standard*, New York: RiskMetrics Group.

Mittnik, S., and Rachev, S. T. (1993a), 'Modeling Asset Returns with Alternative Stable Distributions', *Econometric Reviews*, 12, 261–330.

(1993b), 'Reply to Comments on "Modeling Asset Returns with Alternative Stable Distributions" and Some Extensions', *Econometric Reviews*, 12, 347–89.

Modha, D. S., and Fainman, Y. (1994), 'A Learning Law for Density Estimation', *IEEE Transactions on Neural Networks*, 5, 519–23.

Morgan, M. S. (1990), *The History of Econometric Ideas*, Cambridge: Cambridge University Press.

Muth, J. F. (1960), 'Optimal Properties of Exponentially Weighted Forecasts', *Journal of the American Statistical Association*, 55, 299–305.

Nawrocki, D. N. (1999), 'A Brief History of Downside Risk Measures', *Journal of Investing*, 8, 9–25.

Nelson, C. R., and Plosser, C. I. (1982), 'Trends and Random Walks in Macroeconomic Time Series', *Journal of Monetary Economics*, 10, 139–62.

Nelson, C. R., and Schwert, G. W. (1977), 'Short-term Interest Rates as Predictors of Inflation: On Testing the Hypothesis that the Real Rate of Interest is Constant', *American Economic Review*, 67, 478–86.

Nelson, D. B. (1990a), 'Stationarity and Persistence in the GARCH(1,1) Model', *Econometric Theory*, 6, 318–34.

(1990b), 'ARCH Models as Diffusion Approximations', *Journal of Econometrics*, 45, 7–38.

(1991), 'Conditional Heteroskedasticity in Asset Returns', *Econometrica*, 59, 347–70.

Nelson, D. B., and Cao, C. Q. (1992), 'Inequality Constraints in Univariate GARCH Models', *Journal of Business and Economic Statistics*, 10, 229–35.

Nelson, D. B., and Foster, D. P. (1994), 'Asymptotic Filtering for Univariate GARCH Models', *Econometrica*, 62, 1–41.

Nelson, S. A. (1902), *The ABC of Stock Speculation*, New York: S. A. Nelson.

Newbold, P. (1990), 'Precise and Efficient Computation of the Beveridge–Nelson Decomposition of Economic Time Series', *Journal of Monetary Economics*, 26, 453–7.

Newbold, P., and Agiakloglou, C. (1993), 'Bias in the Sample Autocorrelations of Fractional White Noise', *Biometrika*, 80, 698–702.

Newey, W. K. (1985), 'Generalized Method of Moment Specification Testing', *Journal of Econometrics*, 29, 229–56.

Newey, W. K., and West, K. D. (1987), 'A Simple Positive Semidefinite, Heteroskedasticity Consistent Covariance Matrix', *Econometrica*, 55, 703–8.

Ng, S., and Perron, P. (1995), 'Unit Root Tests in ARMA Models with Data Dependent Methods for Good Size and Power', *Journal of the American Statistical Association*, 90, 268–81.

(2001), 'Lag Length Selection and the Construction of Unit Root Tests with Good Size and Power', *Econometrica*, 69, 1519–54.

Nickell, S. (1985), 'Error Correction, Partial Adjustment and All That: An Expository Note', *Oxford Bulletin of Economics and Statistics*, 47, 119–29.

Nychka, D. W., Stephen, E., Gallant, A. R., and McCaffrey, D. F. (1992), 'Finding Chaos in Noisy Systems', *Journal of the Royal Statistical Society*, Series B, 54, 399–426.

Osborne, M. M. (1959), 'Brownian Motion in the Stock Market', *Operations Research*, 7, 145–73.

Pagan, A. R. (1996), 'The Econometrics of Financial Markets', *Journal of Empirical Finance*, 3, 15–102.

Pagan, A. R., and Schwert, G. W. (1990), 'Testing for Covariance Stationarity in Stock Market Data', *Economics Letters*, 33, 165–70.

Park, J. Y. (1990), 'Testing for Unit Roots and Cointegration by Variable Addition', in G. F. Rhodes and T. B. Fomby (eds.), *Advances in Econometrics*, Vol. VIII, Greenwich, CT: JAI Press, 107–33.

Park, J. Y., and Phillips, P. C. B. (1988), 'Statistical Inference in Regressions with Cointegrated Processes: Part I', *Econometric Theory*, 4, 468–97.

(1999) 'Asymptotics for Nonlinear Transformations of Integrated Time Series', *Econometric Theory*, 15, 269–98.

(2001), 'Nonlinear Regressions with Integrated Time Series', *Econometrica*, 69, 117–61.

Pearson, K., and Rayleigh, Lord (1905), 'The Problem of the Random Walk', *Nature*, 72, 294, 318, 342.

Pena, D., and Rodriguez, J. (2005), 'Detecting Nonlinearity in Time Series by Model Selection Criteria', *International Journal of Forecasting*, 21, 731–48.

Perron, P. (1988), 'Trends and Random Walks in Macroeconomic Time Series: Further Evidence from a New Approach', *Journal of Economic Dynamics and Control*, 12, 297–332.

(1989), 'The Great Crash, the Oil Price Shock, and the Unit Root Hypothesis', *Econometrica*, 57, 1361–401.

(1990), 'Testing for a Unit Root in a Time Series with a Changing Mean', *Journal of Business and Economic Statistics*, 8, 153–62.

(1991), 'Test Consistency with Varying Sampling Frequency', *Econometric Theory*, 7, 341–68.

(1997), 'Further Evidence on Breaking Trend Functions in Macroeconomic Variables', *Journal of Econometrics*, 80, 355–85.

(2006), 'Dealing with Structural Breaks', in T. C. Mills and K. Patterson (eds.), *Palgrave Handbook of Econometrics*, Vol. I: *Econometric Theory*, Basingstoke: Palgrave Macmillan, 278–352.

Perron, P., and Ng, S. (1996), 'Useful Modifications to Some Unit Root Tests with Dependent Errors and their Local Asymptotic Properties', *Review of Economic Studies*, 63, 435–63.

Perron, P., and Vogelsang, T. J. (1993), 'A Note on the Asymptotic Distributions in the Additive Outlier Model with Breaks', *Revista de Econometrica*, 8, 181–202.

Pesaran, M. H. (1997), 'The Role of Economic Theory in Modelling the Long Run', *Economic Journal*, 107, 178–91.

Pesaran, M. H., and Pesaran, B. (1997), *Working with Microfit 4.0: Interactive Econometric Analysis*, Oxford: Oxford University Press.

Pesaran, M. H., and Shin, Y. (1997), 'Generalized Impulse Response Analysis in Linear Multivariate Models', *Economics Letters*, 58, 17–29.

(2002), 'Long Run Structural Modelling', *Econometric Reviews*, 21, 49–87.

Pesaran, M. H., Shin, Y., and Smith, R. J. (2001), 'Bounds Testing Approaches to the Analysis of Levels Relationships', *Journal of Applied Econometrics*, 16, 289–326.

Pfann, G. A., Schotman, P. C., and Tschernig, R. (1996), 'Nonlinear Interest Rate Dynamics and Implications for the Term Structure', *Journal of Econometrics*, 74, 149–76.

Pham, D. T. (1993) 'Bilinear Times Series Models', in H. Tong, (ed.), *Dimension Estimation and Models*, Singapore: World Scientific Publishing, 191–223.

Phillips, A. W. (1957), 'Stabilisation Policy and the Time Form of Lagged Responses', *Economic Journal*, 67, 265–77.

Phillips, P. C. B. (1986), 'Understanding Spurious Regressions in Econometrics', *Journal of Econometrics*, 33, 311–40.

(1987a), 'Time Series Regression with a Unit Root', *Econometrica*, 55, 227–301.

(1987b), 'Towards a Unified Asymptotic Theory for Autoregression', *Biometrika*, 74, 535–47.

(1987c), 'Asymptotic Expansions in Nonstationary Vector Autoregressions', *Econometric Theory*, 3, 45–68.

(1990), 'Time Series Regression with a Unit Root and Infinite-variance Errors', *Econometric Theory*, 6, 44–62.

(1991), 'Optimal Inference in Co-integrated Systems', *Econometrica*, 59, 282–306.

(1998), 'Impulse Response and Forecast Error Asymptotics in Nonstationary VARs', *Journal of Econometrics*, 83, 21–56.

(2001), 'Trending Time Series and Macroeconomic Activity: Some Present and Future Challenges', *Journal of Econometrics*, 100, 21–7.

(2003), 'Laws and Limits of Econometrics', *Economic Journal*, 113, C26–C52.

(2005a), 'HAC Estimation by Automated Regression', *Econometric Theory*, 21, 116–42.

(2005b), 'Challenges of Trending Time Series Econometrics', *Mathematics and Computers in Simulation*, 68, 401–16.

Phillips, P. C. B., and Durlauf, S. N. (1986), 'Multiple Time Series Regression with Integrated Processes', *Review of Economic Studies*, 53, 99–125.

Phillips, P. C. B., and Hansen, B. E. (1990), 'Statistical Inference in Instrumental Variables Regression with $I(1)$ Processes', *Review of Economic Studies*, 57, 99–125.

Phillips, P. C. B., and Loretan, M. (1991), 'Estimating Long-run Economic Equilibria', *Review of Economic Studies*, 58, 407–36.

Phillips, P. C. B., McFarland, J. W., and McMahon, P. C. (1996), 'Robust Tests of Forward Exchange Market Efficiency with Empirical Evidence from the 1920s', *Journal of Applied Econometrics*, 11, 1–22.

Phillips, P. C. B., and Ouliaris, S. (1988), 'Testing for Cointegration Using Principal Components Methods', *Journal of Economic Dynamics and Control*, 12, 205–30.

(1990), 'Asymptotic Properties of Residual Based Tests for Cointegration', *Econometrica*, 58, 165–94.

Phillips, P. C. B., and Perron, P. (1988), 'Testing for Unit Roots in Time Series Regression', *Biometrika*, 75, 335–46.

Phillips, P. C. B., and Xiao, Z. (1998), 'A Primer on Unit Root Testing', *Journal of Economic Surveys*, 12, 423–69.

Pierce, D. A. (1979), 'Signal Extraction Error in Nonstationary Time Series', *Annals of Statistics*, 7, 1303–20.

Pierse, R. G., and Snell, A. J. (1995), 'Temporal Aggregation and the Power of Tests for a Unit Root', *Journal of Econometrics*, 65, 333–45.

Pinske, H. (1998), 'A Consistent Nonparametric Test for Serial Independence', *Journal of Econometrics*, 84, 205–31.

Ploberger, W., Krämer, W., and Kontrus, K. (1989), 'A New Test for Structural Stability in the Linear Regression Model', *Journal of Econometrics*, 40, 307–18.

Plosser, C. I., and Schwert, G. W. (1978), 'Money, Income, and Sunspots: Measuring Economic Relationships and the Effects of Differencing', *Journal of Monetary Economics*, 4, 637–60.

Pollock, D. S. G. (2000), 'Trend Estimation and De-trending via Rational Square Wave Filters', *Journal of Econometrics*, 99, 317–34.

Pong, E., Shackleton, M. B., Taylor, S. J., and Xu, X. (2004), 'Forecasting Currency Volatility: A Comparison of Implied Volatilities and AR(F)IMA Models', *Journal of Banking and Finance*, 28, 2541–63.

Poon, S.-H., and Granger, C. W. J. (2003) 'Forecasting Financial Market Volatility: A Review', *Journal of Economic Literature*, 41, 478–539.

Poskitt, D. S., and Tremayne, A. R. (1987), 'Determining a Portfolio of Linear Time Series Models', *Biometrika*, 74, 125–37.

Poterba, J. M., and Summers, L. H. (1988), 'Mean Reversion in Stock Prices: Evidence and Implications', *Journal of Financial Economics*, 22, 27–59.

Priestley, M. B. (1980), 'State-dependent Models: A General Approach to Nonlinear Time Series Analysis', *Journal of Time Series Analysis*, 1, 47–71.

(1988) *Non-linear and Non-stationary Time Series Analysis*, London: Academic Press.

Prigent, J.-L., Renault, O., and Scaillet, O. (2001), 'An Autoregressive Conditional Binomial Option Pricing Model', in H. Geman, D. Madan, S. Pliska and T. Vorst (eds.), *Selected Papers from the First World Congress of the Bachelier Finance Society*, Heidelberg: Springer, 353–73.

Psaradakis, Z., Sola, M., and Spagnolo, F. (2004), 'On Markov Error Correction Models with an Application to Stock Prices and Dividends', *Journal of Applied Econometrics*, 19, 69–88.

Psychoyios, D., Dotsis, G., and Markellos, R. N. (2006), *Does the VIX Jump? Implications for Pricing and Hedging Volatility Risk*, working paper, Athens University of Economics and Business.

Quintos, C. E. (1997), 'Stability Tests in Error Correction Models', *Journal of Econometrics*, 82, 289–315.

Quintos, C. E., and Phillips, P. C. B. (1993), 'Parameter Constancy in Cointegrating Regressions', *Empirical Economics*, 18, 675–706.

Rabemananjara, R., and Zakoian, J. M. (1993), 'Threshold ARCH Models and Asymmetries in Volatility', *Journal of Applied Econometrics*, 8, 31–49.

Rachev, S. T., Menn, C., and Fabozzi, F. J. (2005), *Fat Tailed and Skewed Asset Distributions*, New York: Wiley.

Ramsey, J. B. (1969), 'Tests for Specification Errors in Classical Linear Least Squares Regression Analysis', *Journal of the Royal Statistical Society*, Series B, 31, 350–71.

Ramsey, J. B., and Rothman, P. (1996), 'Time Irreversibility and Business Cycle Asymmetry', *Journal of Money, Credit, and Banking*, 28, 1–21.

Reimers, H.-E. (1992), 'Comparisons of Tests for Multivariate Cointegration', *Statistical Papers*, 33, 335–59.

Rhea, R. (1932), *The Dow Theory: An Explanation of its Development and Attempt to Define its Usefulness as an Aid in Speculation*, New York: Barron's.

Richardson, M. (1993), 'Temporary Components of Stock Prices: A Skeptic's View', *Journal of Business and Economic Statistics*, 11, 199–207.

Richardson, M., and Smith, T. (1991), 'Tests of Financial Models in the Presence of Overlapping Observations', *Review of Financial Studies*, 4, 27–54.

Richardson, M., and Stock, J. H. (1989), 'Drawing Inferences from Statistics Based on Multi-year Asset Returns', *Journal of Financial Economics*, 25, 323–48.

Roberts, H. V. (1959), 'Stock-Market "Patterns" and Financial Analysis: Methodo-logical Suggestions', *Journal of Finance*, 14, 1–10.

Robinson, P. M. (1977), 'The Estimation of a Non-linear Moving Average Model', *Stochastic Processes and their Applications*, 5, 81–90.

(1991), 'Testing for Strong Serial Correlation and Dynamic Conditional Heteroskedasticity in Multiple Regression', *Journal of Econometrics*, 47, 67–84.

(1992), 'Semiparametric Analysis of Long Memory Time Series', *Annals of Statistics*, 22, 515–39.

(1994), 'Time Series with Strong Dependence', in C. A. Sims (ed.), *Advances in Econometrics: Sixth World Congress*, Vol. I, Cambridge: Cambridge University Press, 47–95.

(1995a), 'Log-periodogram Regression for Time Series with Long Range Dependence', *Annals of Statistics*, 23, 1048–72.

(1995b), 'Gaussian Semiparametric Estimation of Long Run Dependence', *Annals of Statistics*, 23, 1630–61.

(2003), 'Long Memory Time Series', in P. M. Robinson (ed.) *Time Series with Long Memory*, Oxford: Oxford University Press, 4–32.

Rogers, L. C. G. (1997), 'Stochastic Calculus and Markov Methods', in M. A. H. Dempster and S. R. Pliska (eds.), *Mathematics of Derivative Securities*, Cambridge: Cambridge University Press, 15–40.

Romano, J. L., and Thombs, L. A. (1996), 'Inference for Autocorrelations under Weak Assumptions', *Journal of the American Statistical Association*, 89, 1303–131.

Rothman, P. (1992), 'The Comparative Power of the TR Test against Simple Threshold Models', *Journal of Applied Econometrics*, 7, S187–S195.

Rousseeuw, P. J., and LeRoy, A. M. (2003), *Robust Regression and Outlier Detection*, New York: Wiley.

Runde, R. (1997), 'The Asymptotic Null Distribution of the Box–Pierce Q-statistic for Random Variables with Infinite Variance: An Application to German Stock Returns', *Journal of Econometrics*, 78, 205–16.

Ruppert, D., and Carroll, R. J. (1980), 'Trimmed Least Squares Estimation in the Linear Model', *Journal of the American Statistical Association*, 75, 828–38.

Rydén, T., Teräsvirta, T., and Åsbrink, S. (1998), 'Stylized Facts of Daily Return Series and the Hidden Markov Model', *Journal of Applied Econometrics*, 13, 217–44.

Said, S. E., and Dickey, D. A. (1984), 'Testing for Unit Roots in Autoregressive Moving-average Models with Unknown Order', *Biometrika*, 71, 599–607.

(1985), 'Hypothesis Testing in ARIMA(p,1,q) Models', *Journal of the American Statistical Association*, 80, 369–74.

Saikkonen, P. (1991), 'Asymptotically Efficient Estimation of Cointegrating Regressions', *Econometric Theory*, 7, 1–21.

Saikkonen, P., and Lütkepohl, H. (1996), 'Infinite-order Cointegrated Vector Autoregressive Processes: Estimation and Inference', *Econometric Theory*, 12, 814–44.

Saikkonen, P., and Luukkonen R. (1993), 'Testing for a Moving Average Unit Root in Autoregressive Integrated Moving Average Models', *Journal of the American Statistical Association*, 88, 596–601.

Samarov, A., and Taqqu, M. S. (1988), 'On the Efficiency of the Sample Mean in Long Memory Noise', *Journal of Time Series Analysis*, 9, 191–200.

Samorodnitsky, G., and Taqqu, M. S. (1994), *Stable Non-Gaussian Random Processes*, New York: Chapman and Hall.

Samuelson, P. A. (1965), 'Proof that Properly Anticipated Prices Fluctuate Randomly', *Industrial Management Review*, 6, 41–9.

(1973), 'Proof that Properly Discounted Present Values of Assets Vibrate Randomly', *Bell Journal of Economics and Management Science*, 4, 369–74.

(1987), 'Paradise Lost and Refound: The Harvard ABC Barometers', *Journal of Portfolio Management*, 4, 4–9.

Sargan, J. D. (1964), 'Wages and Prices in the United Kingdom: A Study in Econometric Methodology', in P. E. Hart, G. Mills and J. K. Whitaker (eds.), *Econometric Analysis for National Economic Planning*, London: Butterworths, 25–63.

Sargan, J. D., and Bhargava, A. S. (1983), 'Testing Residuals from Least Squares Regression for being Generated by the Gaussian Random Walk', *Econometrica*, 51, 153–74.

Schmidt, P. (1990), 'Dickey–Fuller Tests with Drift', in G. F. Rhodes and T. B. Fomby (eds.), *Advances in Econometrics*, Vol. VIII, Greenwich, CT: JAI Press, 161–200.

Schwarz, G. (1978), 'Estimating the Dimension of a Model', *Annals of Statistics*, 6, 461–4.

Schwert, G. W. (1987), 'Effects of Model Specification on Tests for Unit Roots in Macroeconomic Data', *Journal of Monetary Economics*, 20, 73–105.

(1989), 'Why does Stock Market Volatility Change over Time?', *Journal of Finance*, 44, 1115–53.

(2003), 'Anomalies and Market Efficiency', in G. M. Constantinides, M. Harris and R. Stulz (eds.), *Handbook of the Economics of Finance*, Amsterdam: Elsevier, 935–71.

Sensier, M., and van Dijk, D. (2004), 'Testing for Volatility Changes in US Macroeconomic Time Series', *Review of Economics and Statistics*, 86, 833–9.

Sentana, E. (1995), 'Quadratic ARCH Models', *Review of Economic Studies*, 62, 639–61.

SHAZAM (1993), *SHAZAM User's Reference Manual Version 7.0*, New York: McGraw-Hill.

Shephard, N. (1996), 'Statistical Aspects of ARCH and Stochastic Volatility', in D. R. Cox, D. V. Hinkley and O. E. Barndorff-Nielsen (eds.), *Time Series Models in Econometrics, Finance and Other Fields*, London: Chapman and Hall, 1–67.

Shiller, R. J. (1979), 'The Volatility of Long Term Interest Rates and Expectations Models of the Term Structure', *Journal of Political Economy*, 87, 1190–209.

(1981a), 'Do Stock Prices Move Too Much to be Justified by Subsequent Changes in Dividends?', *American Economic Review*, 71, 421–36.

(1981b), 'The Use of Volatility Measures in Assessing Market Efficiency', *Journal of Finance*, 36, 291–304.

Shiller, R. J., and Perron, P. (1985), 'Testing the Random Walk Hypothesis: Power versus Frequency of Observation', *Economics Letters*, 18, 381–6.

Shintani, M., and Linton, O. (2006), 'Nonparametric Neural Network Estimation of Lyapunov Exponents and a Direct Test for Chaos', *Journal of Econometrics*, 120, 1–33.

Siklos, P. L., and Granger, C. W. J. (1997), 'Temporary Cointegration with an Application to Interest Rate Parity', *Macroeconomic Dynamics*, 1, 640–57.

Silvennoinen, A., and Teräsvirta, T. (2007), 'Multivariate GARCH Models', in T. G. Andersen, R. A. Davis, J.-P. Kreiss and T. Mikosch (eds.), *Handbook of Financial Time Series*, New York: Springer.

Silverman, B. W. (1986), *Density Estimation for Statistics and Data Analysis*, London: Chapman and Hall.

Sims, C. A. (1980), 'Macroeconomics and Reality', *Econometrica*, 48, 1–48.

(1981), 'An Autoregressive Index Model for the US 1948–1975', in J. Kmenta and J. B. Ramsey (eds.), *Large-scale Macroeconometric Models*, Amsterdam: North-Holland, 283–327.

(1988), 'Bayesian Skepticism of Unit Root Econometrics', *Journal of Economic Dynamics and Control*, 12, 463–75.

Sims, C. A., Stock, J. H., and Watson, M. W. (1990), 'Inference in Linear Time Series with Some Unit Roots', *Econometrica*, 58, 113–44.

Sims, C. A., and Uhlig, H. (1991), 'Understanding Unit Rooters: A Helicopter Tour', *Econometrica*, 59, 1591–9.

Singleton, K. (2001), 'Estimation of Affine Asset Pricing Models Using the Empirical Characteristic Function', *Journal of Econometrics*, 102, 111–41.

Slutsky, E. E. (1937), 'The Summation of Random Causes as the Source of Cyclic Processes, Problems of Economic Conditions', *Econometrica*, 5, 105–46.

Sollis, R., Leybourne, S. J., and Newbold, P. (1999), 'Unit Roots and Asymmetric Smooth Transitions', *Journal of Time Series Analysis*, 20, 671–7.

Sowell, F. B. (1990), 'The Fractional Unit Root Distribution', *Econometrica*, 58, 498–505.

(1992a), 'Maximum Likelihood Estimation of Stationary Univariate Fractionally Integrated Time Series Models', *Journal of Econometrics*, 53, 165–88.

(1992b), 'Modelling Long-run Behaviour with the Fractional ARIMA Model', *Journal of Monetary Economics*, 29, 277–302.

Spanos, A. (1986), *Statistical Foundations of Econometric Modelling*, Cambridge: Cambridge University Press.

Stock, J. H. (1987), 'Asymptotic Properties of Least Squares Estimators of Cointegrating Vectors', *Econometrica*, 55, 1035–56.

(1991), 'Confidence Intervals for the Largest Autoregressive Root in US Macroeconomic Time Series', *Journal of Monetary Economics*, 28, 435–69.

(1994), 'Unit Roots, Structural Breaks and Trends', in R. F. Engle and D. L. McFadden (eds.), *Handbook of Econometrics*, Vol. IV, New York: North-Holland, 2739–841.

(1996), 'VAR, Error Correction and Pretest Forecasts at Long Horizons', *Oxford Bulletin of Economics and Statistics*, 58, 685–701.

(1997), 'Cointegration, Long-run Movements, and Long-horizon Forecasting', in D. M. Kreps and K. F. Wallis (eds.), *Advances in Economics and Econometrics*, Vol. III: *Theory and Applications*, Cambridge: Cambridge University Press, 34–60.

Stock, J. H., and Watson, M. W. (1988), 'Testing for Common Trends', *Journal of the American Statistical Association*, 83, 1097–107.

(1993), 'A Simple Estimator of Cointegrating Vectors in Higher Order Integrated Systems', *Econometrica*, 61, 783–820.

Stoll. H. R., and Whaley, R. E. (1990), 'Stock Market Structure and Volatility', *Review of Financial Studies*, 3, 37–71.

Straumann, D. (2004), *Estimation in Conditionally Heteroskedastic Time Series Models*, New York: Springer.

Subba Rao, T. (1981), 'On the Theory of Bilinear Models', *Journal of the Royal Statistical Society*, Series B, 43, 244–55.

Subba Rao, T., and Gabr, M. (1980), 'A Test for Linearity of Stationary Time Series Analysis', *Journal of Time Series Analysis*, 1, 145–58.

(1984), *An Introduction to Bispectral Analysis and Bilinear Time Series Models*, Berlin: Springer-Verlag.

Sullivan, E. J., and Weithers, T. M. (1991), 'Louis Bachelier: The Father of Modern Option Pricing Theory', *Journal of Economic Education*, 22, 165–71.

Sun, Y., and Phillips, P. C. B. (2003), 'Nonlinear Log-periodogram Regression for Perturbed Fractional Processes', *Journal of Econometrics*, 115, 355–89.

Swanson, N. R., and Granger, C. W. J. (1997), 'Impulse Response Functions Based on a Causal Approach to Residual Orthogonalization in Vector Autoregressions', *Journal of the American Statistical Association*, 92, 357–67.

Tanaka, K. (1990), 'Testing for a Moving Average Unit Root', *Econometric Theory*, 6, 433–44.

(1999), 'The Nonstationary Fractional Unit Root', *Econometric Theory*, 15, 549–82.

Taniguchi, M., and Kakizawa, Y. (2000), *Asymptotic Theory of Statistical Inference for Time Series*, New York: Springer-Verlag.

Tauchen, G. E., and Pitts, M. (1983), 'The Price Variability–Volume Relationship on Speculative Markets', *Econometrica*, 51, 485–505.

Taylor, J. W. (2004), 'Volatility Forecasting with Smooth Transition Exponential Smoothing', *International Journal of Forecasting*, 20, 273–86.

Taylor, S. J. (1986), *Modelling Financial Time Series*, New York: Wiley.

(1994), 'Modelling Stochastic Volatility: A Review and Comparative Study', *Mathematical Finance*, 4, 183–204.

Teräsvirta, T. (1994), 'Specification, Estimation, and Evaluation of Smooth Transition Autoregressive Models', *Journal of the American Statistical Association*, 89, 208–18.

(2007), 'An Introduction to Univariate GARCH Models', in T. G. Andersen, R. A. Davis, J. P. Kreiss and T. Mikosch (eds.), *Handbook of Financial Time Series*, New York: Springer.

Teräsvirta, T., Lin, C.-F., and Granger, C. W. J. (1993), 'Power of the Neural Network Test', *Journal of Time Series Analysis*, 14, 209–20.

Teräsvirta, T., Tjostheim, D., and Granger, C. W. J. (1994), 'Aspects of Modelling Nonlinear Time Series', in R. F. Engle and D. L. McFadden (eds.), *Handbook of Econometrics*, Vol. IV, New York: North-Holland, 2919–57.

Thaler, R. (1987a), 'The January Effect', *Journal of Economic Perspectives*, 1, 197–201.

(1987b), 'Seasonal Movements in Security Prices II: Weekend, Holiday, Turn of the Month, and Intraday Effects', *Journal of Economic Perspectives*, 1, 169–77.

Tieslau, M. A., Schmidt, P., and Baillie, R. T. (1996), 'A Minimum Distance Estimator for Long-memory Processes', *Journal of Econometrics*, 71, 249–64.

Timmermann, A., and Granger, C. W. J. (2004), 'Efficient Market Hypothesis and Forecasting', *International Journal of Forecasting*, 20, 15–27.

Toda, H. Y. (1994), 'Finite Sample Properties of Likelihood Ratio Tests for Cointegrating Ranks when Linear Trends Are Present', *Review of Economics and Statistics*, 76, 66–79.

(1995), 'Finite Sample Performance of Likelihood Ratio Tests for Cointegrating Ranks in Vector Autorgressions', *Econometric Theory*, 11, 1015–32.

Toda, H. Y., and Phillips, P. C. B. (1993), 'Vector Autoregression and Causality', *Econometrica*, 61, 1367–93.

(1994), 'Vector Autoregression and Causality: A Theoretical Overview and Simulation Study', *Econometric Reviews*, 13, 259–85.

Toda, H. Y., and Yamamoto, T. (1995), 'Statistical Inference in Vector Autoregressions with Possibly Integrated Processes', *Journal of Econometrics*, 66, 225–50.

Tomczyck, S., and Chatterjee, S. (1984), 'Estimating the Market Model Robustly', *Journal of Business Finance and Accounting*, 11, 563–73.

Tong, H., and Lim, K. S. (1980), 'Threshold Autoregression, Limit Cycles, and Cyclical Data', *Journal of the Royal Statistical Society*, Series B, 42, 245–92.

Tremayne, A. R. (2006), 'Stationary Linear Univariate Time Series Models', in T. C. Mills and K. Patterson (eds.), *Palgrave Handbook of Econometrics*, Vol. I: *Econometric Theory*, Basingstoke: Palgrave Macmillan, 215–51.

Tsay, R. S. (1986), 'Nonlinearity Tests for Time Series', *Biometrika*, 73, 461–6.

Tse, Y. K. (2000), 'A Test for Constant Correlations in a Multivariate GARCH Model', *Journal of Econometrics*, 98, 107–27.

Tukey, J. W. (1977), *Exploratory Data Analysis*, Reading, MA: Addison-Wesley.

Vahid, F. (2006), 'Common Cycles', in T. C. Mills and K. Patterson (eds.), *Palgrave Handbook of Econometrics*, Vol. I: *Econometric Theory*, Basingstoke: Palgrave Macmillan, 610–30.

Vahid, F., and Engle, R. F. (1993), 'Common Trends and Common Cycles', *Journal of Applied Econometrics*, 8, 341–60.

(1997), 'Codependent Cycles', *Journal of Econometrics*, 80, 199–221.

Van Dijk, D. J. C., Franses, P. H., and Lucas, A. (1999), 'Testing for Smooth Transition Non-linearity in the Presence of Outliers', *Journal of Business and Economic Statistics*, 17, 217–35.

Van Dijk, D. J. C., Teräsvirta, T., and Franses, P. H. (2002), 'Smooth Transition Autoregressive Models: A Survey of Recent Developments', *Econometric Reviews*, 21, 1–47.

Velasco, C. (1999), 'Non-stationary Log-periodogram Regression', *Journal of Econometrics*, 91, 325–71.

(2006), 'Semiparametric Estimation of Long-memory Models', in T. C. Mills and K. Patterson (eds.), *Palgrave Handbook of Econometrics*, Vol. I: *Econometric Theory*, Basingstoke: Palgrave Macmillan, 353–95.

Vogelsang, T. J. (1997), 'Wald-type Tests for Detecting Breaks in the Trend Function of a Dynamic Time Series', *Econometric Theory*, 13, 818–49.

Vogelsang, T. J., and Perron, P. (1998), 'Additional Tests for a Unit Root Allowing for a Break in the Trend Function at an Unknown Point in Time', *International Economic Review*, 39, 1073–100.

Wecker, W. (1981), 'Asymmetric Time Series', *Journal of the American Statistical Association*, 76, 16–21.

Weiss, A. A. (1984), 'ARMA Models with ARCH Errors', *Journal of Time Series Analysis*, 5, 129–43.

(1986a), 'Asymptotic Theory for ARCH Models: Estimation and Testing', *Econometric Theory*, 2, 107–31.

(1986b), 'ARCH and Bilinear Time Series Models: Comparison and Combination', *Journal of Business and Economic Statistics*, 4, 59–70.

West, K. D. (1987), 'A Specification Test for Speculative Bubbles', *Quarterly Journal of Economics*, 102, 553–80.

(1988), 'Asymptotic Normality, When Regressors Have a Unit Root', *Econometrica*, 56, 1397–418.

White, H. (1980), 'A Heteroskedasticity Consistent Covariance Matrix Estimator and a Direct Test for Heteroskedasticity', *Econometrica*, 48, 817–38.

(1984), *Asymptotic Theory for Econometricians*, New York: Academic Press.

(1990), 'Connectionist Nonparametric Regression: Multilayer Feed-forward Networks can Learn Arbitrary Mappings', *Neural Networks*, 3, 535–50.

(2006), 'Approximate nonlinear forecasting methods', in G. Elliott, C. W. J. Granger and A. Timmermann (eds.), *Handbook of Economic Forecasting*, Amsterdam: Elsevier,

White, H., and Domowitz, I. (1984), 'Nonlinear Regression with Dependent Observations', *Econometrica*, 52, 643–61.

Wickens, M. (1996), 'Interpreting Cointegrating Vectors and Common Stochastic Trends', *Journal of Econometrics*, 74, 255–71.

Wold, H. (1938), *A Study in the Analysis of Stationary Time Series*, Stockholm: Almqvist and Wiksell.

Working, H. (1934), 'A Random-Difference Series for Use in the Analysis of Time Series', *Journal of the American Statistical Association*, 29, 11–24.

(1960), 'Note on the Correlation of First Differences of Averages in a Random Chain', *Econometrica*, 28, 916–18.

Wright, J. H. (2000), 'Alternative Variance-ratio Tests Using Ranks and Signs', *Journal of Business and Economic Statistics*, 18, 1–9.

Wu, L. (2006), 'Modeling Financial Security Returns Using Levy Processes', in J. R. Birge and V. Linetsky (eds.), *Handbook of Financial Engineering*, Amsterdam: Elsevier.

Yamada, H., and Toda, H. Y. (1998), 'Inference in Possibly Integrated Vector Autoregressive Models: Some Finite Sample Evidence', *Journal of Econometrics*, 86, 55–95.

Yoon, G. (2005), 'Stochastic Unit Roots in the Capital Asset Pricing Model?', *Bulletin of Economic Research*, 57, 369–89.

Yu, J. (2005), 'On Leverage in a Stochastic Volatility Model', *Journal of Econometrics*, 127, 165–78.

Yule, G. U. (1897), 'On the Theory of Correlation', *Journal of the Royal Statistical Society*, 60, 812–54.

(1926), 'Why do we Sometimes Get Nonsense-correlations between Time-series? A Study in Sampling and the Nature of Time Series', *Journal of the Royal Statistical Society*, 89, 1–65.

Zaffaroni, P. (2007), 'Aggregation and Memory of Models of Changing Volatility', *Journal of Econometrics*, 136, 237–49

Zakoian, J. M. (1994), 'Threshold Heteroskedastic Models', *Journal of Economic Dynamics and Control*, 18, 931–55.

Zhang, M. Y., Russell, J. R., and Tsay, R. S. (2001), 'A Nonlinear Autoregressive Conditional Duration Model with Applications to Financial Transaction Data', *Journal of Econometrics*, 104, 179–207.

Index